Second Edition

P9-DFG-039

Critical Perspectives in Food Studies

Edited by

Mustafa Koç
Jennifer Sumner
Anthony Winson

OXFORD
UNIVERSITY PRESS

OXFORD
UNIVERSITY PRESS

Oxford University Press is a department of the University of Oxford.
It furthers the University's objective of excellence in research, scholarship,
and education by publishing worldwide. Oxford is a registered trade mark of
Oxford University Press in the UK and in certain other countries.

Published in Canada by
Oxford University Press
8 Sampson Mews, Suite 204,
Don Mills, Ontario M3C 0H5 Canada

www.oupcanada.com

Library and Archives Canada Cataloguing in Publication

Critical perspectives in food studies / edited by Mustafa Koç, Jennifer
Sumner and Anthony Winson. — Second edition.

Includes bibliographical references and index.
ISBN 978-0-19-901961-8 (paperback)

1. Food. 2. Food—Canada. I. Koç, Mustafa, 1955–, editor II. Sumner,
Jennifer, 1949–, editor III. Winson, Anthony, 1952–, editor

TX353.C75 2016   641.3   C2016-901536-X

Cover image: Robert Daly/Getty Images

Oxford University Press is committed to our environment.
This book is printed on Forest Stewardship Council® certified paper
and comes from responsible sources.

Printed and bound in the United States of America

4 5 6 — 21 20 19

Contents

Part III   Crises and Challenges in the Food System   135

Part IV   Challenging Food Governance   237

Part V Food for the Future 305

Contributors

Robert Albritton was born in Los Angeles in 1941. He received a BA in political science from UC Berkeley in 1963. From 1963 to 1965 he taught political science in Ethiopia, and in 1969 began teaching political theory at York University. After receiving a PhD in political science from UCLA in 1973, he continued to teach political theory at York University until 2005, when he retired as professor emeritus, having published six single-authored books, six co-edited collections, and many articles.

Margaret Amos is a PhD student with the Department of Integrated Studies in Education at McGill University. She is a course lecturer for the First Nations and Inuit Education Department at McGill, project director for McGill's Initiative for Diversity and Global Education, and a certified wellness specialist. Her doctoral research links her experiences as an environmental researcher and a health educator to understand contemporary Indigenous youth perceptions of health and wellness in relation to healthy food security, academic attainment, and building healthy communities. Her research interests include youth leadership, community development, food justice, EcoHealth approaches to social change and policy, knowledge translation, and visual methodologies.

Lucy Aphramor is a UK dietitian with a PhD in critical dietetics and a passion for poetry. She is committed to finding ways to meaningfully link self-care and social justice so that our practice helps people make sense of their experiences and regain a sense of agency in their own lives and as empowered communities. Lucy is an honorary research fellow at Glyndwr University, and her work, often collaborative, appears in nutrition and social science journals plus books in critical weight studies and fat studies.

Yuka Asada is a doctoral candidate at the University of Illinois at Chicago (UIC) in the School of Public Health, Maternal and Child Health Division. She currently works at the Institute for Health Research and Policy at UIC. She is a registered dietitian and is passionate about school health and wellness, dietetic education, and the culinary world.

Margaret Bancerz is a PhD candidate in policy studies specializing in the social policy stream at Ryerson University. She holds a master of environmental studies (MES) from York University and a specialized honours bachelor of arts in international studies from Glendon College, York University. Her current research focuses on food policy and governance in Canada, specifically looking at industry engagement in food policy making and public policy making in general. Previous research has included topics relating to political economy in Latin America as well as Venezuela's food system created during the Chavez years. Additional interests include international political economy, consumerism, animal welfare, and environmental sustainability in the food system, as well as qualitative methodology.

Brenda L. Beagan is a sociologist and professor in the School of Occupational Therapy at Dalhousie University. Her research and teaching focus on everyday experiences of social inequalities, including sexism, heterosexism, gender binaries, racism, ethnocentrism, classism, and ableism.

Jennifer Brady is a PhD candidate in the School of Kinesiology and Health Studies at Queen's University, Kingston, Ontario. Her dissertation work seeks to understand the history and professionalization of dietetics to shed light on its contemporary reticence regarding pressing social justice issues. Her other research interests amalgamate health studies, food studies, and gender studies, as well as non-diet and critical approaches to health. Her work appears in *Journal of Critical Dietetics, Journal of Sport & Social Issues, Food and Foodways: Explorations in the History and Culture of Human Nourishment, Canadian Journal of Dietetic Practice and Research, Critical Public Health,* and *International Journal of Qualitative Methods.*

Sarah Cappeliez is a PhD candidate in sociology at the University of Toronto. Her past work for Slow Food and as a food writer form the foundation for her research interest in food and wine practices as a lens for examining cultural, identity, and consumption elements from a comparative perspective (Europe and North America). In her dissertation, she looks at the ways in which place and terroir are used in the wine sector in France and Canada, and examines questions of value and the dynamics between nature and culture.

Gwen E. Chapman is professor and dean in the College of Social and Applied Human Sciences at the University of Guelph, a recent move following a 25-year career at the University of British Columbia. Her research uses qualitative methods to study how people's everyday food practices and concerns are shaped by socially constructed notions about food, health, bodies, and social roles.

E. Ann Clark retired as an associate professor from the Department of Plant Agriculture, University of Guelph, in 2010. Her primary research interests were in pasture and grazing management, organic farming, and the critical assessment of GM agriculture. Recent journal articles and book chapters include "GM Crops Are Uncontainable: So What?" (2007), "Forages in Organic Crop-Livestock Systems" (2009), and "Ontario, Canada: Lessons in Sustainability from Organic Farmers" (2009, with Jennifer Sumner).

Nathalie Cooke is a professor of English at McGill University in Montreal. She is founding editor of the e-journal *CuiZine*, (2008) (see www.cuizine.mcgill.ca), editor of *What's to Eat? Entrées in Canadian Food History* (2009), and co-editor of *The Johnson Family Treasury, A Collection of Household Recipes and Remedies 1741–1848* (2015).

Naomi Dachner is the research manager of PROOF, an interdisciplinary program of research designed to identify effective policy interventions to reduce household food insecurity in Canada. Naomi has worked in the area of food insecurity for over 15 years, beginning with her MSc research on food access among homeless "squeegee kids" in Toronto. Currently, she works with Professor Tarasuk at the University of Toronto, helping to oversee research and communication activities. For more information on PROOF, see the website: http://nutritionalsciences.lamp.utoronto.ca.

Annette Aurélie Desmarais is Canada Research Chair in Human Rights, Social Justice and Food Sovereignty at the University of Manitoba. Prior to obtaining a PhD in geography she was a farmer in Saskatchewan, Canada, for 14 years and worked as technical support with La Vía Campesina for over a decade. She is the author of *La Vía Campesina: Globalization and the Power of Peasants* (Fernwood Publishing and Pluto Press, 2007), which has been published in French, Spanish, and Italian, and co-editor of *Food Sovereignty: Reconnecting Food, Nature and Community* (Fernwood Publishing, Food First Books, and Pambazuka Press, 2010) and *Food Sovereignty in Canada* (Fernwood Publishing, 2011). Her research

focuses on food sovereignty, agrarian change, and rural social movements.

Jessica Duncan is an assistant professor in rural sociology at Wageningen University (The Netherlands). She holds a PhD in food policy from City University London and is author of the book *Global Food Security Governance: Civil Society Engagement in the Reformed Committee on World Food Security* (Routledge, 2015). Her research areas include food policy, food security, global governance, environmental policy, and participation. She shares some of her research and thinking at www.foodgovernance.com.

Harriet Friedmann is a professor emeritus at the University of Toronto and visiting professor at Institute of Social Studies, The Hague (Erasmus University). She received the Canadian Association for Food Studies Lifetime Career Achievement Award in 2011. She developed the food regimes approach (with Philip McMichael) and has published in international and interdisciplinary journals on many dimensions of agriculture and food, including family farms; international corporate strategies in the food sector; food policies at municipal, regional, national, and international scales; changing patterns of diet and consumption; and social movements to change the food system. Friedmann is a member and former community chair of the Toronto Food Policy Council, a board member of USC Canada, and of the Toronto Seed Library, and a member of several editorial boards of journals related to food and agriculture.

Jacqui Gingras is an associate professor in the Department of Sociology at Ryerson University. Her current preoccupation is questioning the possibility for social justice in the health professions. Her work appears in *Critical Public Health*, the *Journal of Transformative Education*, and *Qualitative Inquiry*. She is the editor of the *Journal of Critical Dietetics*, an online, peer-reviewed, open-access journal for critical inquiry into the dietetic profession.

Josée Johnston is an associate professor of sociology at the University of Toronto. Her major substantive interest is the sociological study of food and how it relates to multiple forms of inequality. She is also interested in ethical consumption and how consumers seek social change within the constraints of contemporary markets. She is the co-author of *Foodies* (Routledge, 2015[2010]) with Shyon Baumann, and of *Food and Femininity* (Bloomsbury 2015) with Kate

Cairns. Dr. Johnston's research has been supported by SSHRC, CIHR, and the Province of Ontario's Early Research Award.

Irena Knezevic is an assistant professor of communication, culture and health in Carleton University's School of Journalism and Communication in Ottawa. She studies food systems, food labelling, health communication and advertising, health equity, informal economy in everyday practices, and the discourse of food and health regulations. Much of her research is interdisciplinary, collaborative, and community based. She is well versed in qualitative research methods, participatory methodologies, research ethics, and knowledge translation, all of which she actively brings into her teaching. Irena is a founding member of the Canadian Association of Food Studies and serves on the management board for the Laurier Centre for Sustainable Food Systems.

Mustafa Koç is a professor of sociology at Ryerson University. His research and teaching interests involve food studies, food security and food policy, globalization and sociology of migration. He was among the founders of the Ryerson Centre for Studies in Food Security, Food Secure Canada, and the Canadian Association for Food Studies. He has also been involved in various national and global debates on globalization, social change and development, food security, and peace. He publications include *For Hunger-proof Cities* (1999), *Working Together* (2001), *Interdisciplinary Perspectives in Food Studies* (2008), *Critical Perspectives in Food Studies*, and *Küresel Gıda Düzeni: Kriz Derinleşirken* (2013).

Shannon Kornelsen holds an MA in geography and environmental studies from Wilfrid Laurier University. Her thesis work focused on the role that food and agricultural literacy play in the building of sustainable food systems. Shannon has worked with several national animal protection organizations in various roles, including director, founding member, and consultant. Most notably, she coordinated a commissioned national report on factory farming in Canada—the first report of its kind.

Charles Z. Levkoe is the Canada Research Chair in Sustainable Food Systems and an assistant professor at Lakehead University. His interdisciplinary teaching, research, and publishing bridge the fields of agricultural, political and social geography, urban policy, and environmental sustainability. He is the principal investigator of a research project focusing on the role of non-wage labour on small-scale ecologically oriented farms. He is also an academic co-lead on the Community First: Impacts of Community Engagement (CFICE) project's Community Food Security Hub, a major cross-Canadian initiative exploring community campus engagement. His broader research focuses on the role of grassroots organizations in relation to sustainable food systems, their connection to place, and their ability to mobilize across sectors, scales, and places. He has published his research in multiple interdisciplinary academic journals and in public newsletters, reports, and magazines. Charles also sits on the executive board of directors of the Canadian Association for Food Studies.

Rod MacRae, PhD, is an associate professor in the Faculty of Environmental Studies at York University in Toronto. A political ecologist, his teaching and research focuses on the transition to sustainable and health-promoting food systems, with particular emphasis on Canadian food policy development. With many colleagues, he has written extensively on this subject in the popular and academic literature, with recent publications appearing in *Agriculture and Human Values*, the *Journal of Sustainable Agriculture*, *Renewable Agriculture and Food Systems*, *Sustainability*, and the *Journal of Health and Environmental Nutrition*. Prior to joining York University, he worked as a food policy analyst and consultant to all levels of government and numerous Canadian NGOs. He was the first coordinator of the Toronto Food Policy Council.

Matias E. Margulis is a lecturer in political economy at the University of Stirling. A former Canadian delegate to the WTO, OECD, and United Nations agencies, his research focuses on global governance, agriculture and food, and human rights. Recent publications include "Forum-Shopping for Global Food Security Governance? Canada's Approach at the G8 and UN Committee on World Food Security" (*Canadian Foreign Policy Journal*, 2015) and a co-edited book, *Land Grabbing and Global Governance* (Routledge 2014, with Nora McKeon and Saturnino Borras, Jr.).

Debbie Martin is a member of NunatuKavut, the territory of the South Inuit. Dr. Martin is currently an assistant professor, Faculty of Health Professions, and cross-appointed to Faculty of Dentistry at Dalhousie University. Her research interests include the social determinants of Indigenous peoples' health; chronic disease prevention; the relationships between

Aboriginal culture, health, and food; and Indigenous methodologies. Dr. Martin is a co-principal investigator of the Atlantic Aboriginal Health Research Program (AAHRP). Some of the literature used for this chapter is taken from Dr. Martin's PhD dissertation, which was defended in December 2009, called *Food Stories: A Labrador Inuit-Metis Community Speaks About Global Change.*

Ashley McInnes is a PhD candidate and Vanier Scholar in the Department of Geography at the University of Guelph. She has worked on research projects in Canada, Uganda, and Cambodia, and is a member of the Feeding 9 Billion research team at the University of Guelph. Her current research focuses on the role of food movements in developing a sustainable food system in Canada. She currently serves as co-chair of the Guelph-Wellington Food Round Table.

Dr. Wendy Mendes is an urban planner and academic with over 12 years' experience building healthy and sustainable communities. She holds a PhD in urban geography from Simon Fraser University. Her expertise focuses on healthy cities, sustainable food systems, local governance, and public policy. Dr. Mendes is currently adjunct professor at the School of Community and Regional Planning at the University of British Columbia, research associate and instructor with Ryerson University's Centre for Studies in Food Security, and urban planner (with a focus on sustainable food systems) for the City of Vancouver.

Phil Mount is a postdoctoral fellow at the Centre for Sustainable Food Systems and the Department of Geography and Environmental Studies at Wilfrid Laurier University. He is also the principal investigator of Project SOIL, a researcher with Nourishing Communities, associate editor at *Canadian Food Studies / La Revue canadienne des études sur l'alimentation*, and co-chair of the XIV World Congress of Rural Sociology (Toronto 2016). Phil's broader research program uses political economy as a lens to investigate the challenges of scale, growth, and governance in the transition to sustainable regional and alternative food systems. Much of this research takes place at the intersection of food, health, and agriculture, using the tools of community-based research, policy evaluation, and network and systems mapping. Publications include "Growing Local Food," "Visualising Community-Based Food Projects in Ontario," and "The Conventionalization of Local Food," while his latest research investigates the intersection of "Supply Management as Food Sovereignty."

Elaine Power is an associate professor in the School of Kinesiology and Health Studies at Queen's University, where she teaches social determinants of health, qualitative research methods, food studies, and fat studies. She is co-author of *Acquired Tastes: Why Families Eat the Way They Do* (UBC Press) and co-editor of the forthcoming volume, *Neoliberal Governance and Health: Duties, Risks and Vulnerabilities* (McGill-Queen's University Press).

Kelsey Speakman is pursuing a PhD in the Joint Graduate Program in Communication and Culture at York and Ryerson Universities. She holds an MA in Performance Studies from New York University, and an honours BA in English and drama from the University of Toronto. Currently, her research explores human–non-human interactions in relation to food practices, and she is particularly interested in contemporary American and Canadian supermarkets as sites of analysis.

Jennifer Sumner teaches in the Adult Education and Community Development Program of the Ontario Institute for Studies in Education at the University of Toronto. Her research interests include food studies, sustainable food systems, and the political economy of food, as well as globalization, sustainability, and organic agriculture. She is the author of the book *Sustainability and the Civil Commons: Rural Communities in the Age of Globalization* (University of Toronto Press, 2005/2007) and editor of the forthcoming book *Learning, Food and Sustainability: Sites for Resistance and Change* (Palgrave Macmillan).

Aparna Sundar has a PhD in political science from the University of Toronto. Currently she teaches political science at the School of Development, Azim Premji University, India. Her research and writing has been on issues facing small-scale fisheries, such as transformations in the nature of work, capital, labour relations, and collective action in this sector, as well as coastal zone governance. Her teaching and research interests focus on political economy, comparative politics, and development. She has also been active in social justice and equity work, including with the National Fishworkers Forum and the Toronto Social Forum.

Michelle Szabo is a professor of environmental studies and sociology in the Faculty of Humanities and Social Sciences at the Sheridan Institute of Technology and Advanced Learning. She received her PhD in environmental studies from York University and was subsequently a SSHRC postdoctoral fellow in sociology at the University of Toronto. She has published and taught on masculinities and cooking; consumer culture and sustainability; gender theory; the sociology of food; and issues of health, sustainability, and social justice in the food system. She is the head co-editor of the forthcoming book *Food, Masculinities and Home: Interdisciplinary Perspectives* (Bloomsbury, 2016), which brings together scholarly work from around the world.

Valerie Tarasuk is a professor in the Department of Nutritional Sciences at the University of Toronto. Much of her research is focused on food insecurity, elucidating the scope and nature of this problem in Canada and examining policy and programmatic responses. Paralleling this work is an ongoing research interest in Canadian food policy and population health. Professor Tarasuk currently leads a large, interdisciplinary program of research called PROOF designed to identify effective policy interventions to reduce household food insecurity in Canada, supported by the Canadian Institutes of Health Research.

Tony Weis is an associate professor in geography at Western University. He is the author of *The Ecological Hoofprint: The Global Burden of Industrial Livestock* (Zed Books, 2013) and *The Global Food Economy: The Battle for the Future of Farming* (Zed Books, 2007), and co-editor of *A Line in the Tar Sands: Struggles for Environmental Justice* (BTL/PM Press 2014), and *Critical Perspectives on Food Sovereignty* (Routledge 2014). His research is broadly located in the field of political ecology, with a focus on agriculture and food systems.

Nettie Wiebe farms near Delisle, Saskatchewan, growing organic grains and pulse crops as well as raising cattle. Nettie served in elected leadership positions of the National Farmers Union for 10 years and was the first woman to lead a national farm organization in Canada. She recently retired from teaching ethics at St. Andrews College, University of Saskatchewan. Dr. Wiebe is an active participant in public discourse on sustainable agriculture and rural communities; trade agreements; women's equality; human rights; peace; economic and environmental issues; and food sovereignty. Her recent publications include co-editing two volumes on food: *Food Sovereignty: Reconnecting Food, Nature and Community* (2010) and *Food Sovereignty in Canada: Creating Just and Sustainable Food Systems* (2011). She is a co-author of "Land Grabbing and Land Concentration: Mapping Changing Patterns of Farmland Ownership in Three Rural Municipalities in Saskatchewan, Canada" (*Canadian Journal of Food Studies*, 2015).

Anthony Winson is professor in the Department of Sociology and Anthropology, University of Guelph. He has written about agriculture, food, agrarian development, politics, and the state in the context of Canada, the United States, and the Third World, and more recently on the political economic determinants of diet and nutrition. His books include *Coffee and Democracy in Modern Costa Rica* (Macmillan, 1989); *The Intimate Commodity: Food and the Development of the Agro-Industrial Complex in Canada* (Garamond, 1993); *Contingent Work, Disrupted Lives: Labour and Community in the New Rural Economy* (University of Toronto, 2002 with Belinda Leach, which has won the John Porter book prize of the Canadian Sociology Association); and *The Industrial Diet: The Degradation of Food and the Struggle for Healthy Eating* (UBC Press and New York University Press, 2013).

Preface

This volume evolved out of our growing recognition that the emerging field of food studies needed a formal text to represent the depth and breadth of its diverse range of interests and to give it a critical orientation that would link the field to the larger problems humanity is facing. It began as an idea, germinated through a chance conversation, and blossomed through co-operation and love of learning.

Over recent years, the study of food has occupied increasing portions of our research, teaching, and writing. This preoccupation with food is in keeping with Marion Nestle's (2010) observation that within her academic lifetime, the use of food as a means to examine critical questions about the causes and consequences of production and consumption has grown dramatically. Her observation emphasizes what we have also realized—that food is not only a worthy object of study in itself, but also an entrée into larger issues that concern humankind: sustainability, development, globalization, governance, and power.

This volume addresses both emphases—the study of food itself and the exploration of larger issues surrounding food—from a critical perspective. In doing so, it aims to contribute to the development of the emerging field of food studies by presenting the work of leading Canadian scholars. Readers will learn about the changing meanings of food and food studies, the different theoretical lenses for looking at food, crises and challenges in the current food system, ways of challenging food governance, and visions of food for the future.

Reference:

Nestle, Marion. 2010. "Writing the Food Studies Movement." *Food, Culture and Society* 13(2):160–8.

Acknowledgements

More people than we can name contributed to the genesis of this volume. In particular, we would like to thank the Canadian Association for Food Studies (CAFS) for the stimulation provided by its annual meetings and Oxford University Press for its leadership in supporting this project. Special thanks to our editor Tanuja Weerasooriya, the anonymous reviewers, and all the contributors to this volume. And, we would also like to thank the many students in our respective classes who gave us feedback and suggestions for this second edition.

Introduction
The Significance of Food and Food Studies

Mustafa Koç, Jennifer Sumner, and Anthony Winson

To survive we need to eat. Yet food is more than a source of the energy and nutrients essential for human health and well-being. What we eat, if we eat, how we eat, when we eat, and with whom we eat reflect the complexity of our social, economic, political, cultural, and environmental relations with food. Eating is one of the most common human activities we engage in on a regular basis. Food is

> sustenance. . . . a symbol, a product, a ritual object, an identity badge, an object of guilt, a political tool, even a kind of money. Food determines how tall we are, how healthy, the extent of our civic peace, the sorts of jobs we hold, the amount of leisure we enjoy, the crowding of our cities and suburbs, what we look for in life, how long we look to live—all of that and much more. (Reardon 2000:1)

Most human interactions involve producing, preparing, and consuming **food**. The English word *companion* is derived from the Latin for "people sharing bread together." From birth to death, almost all human rituals involve food. It is an important element that unites family members around the table. It denotes ethnic, regional, and national identity. It helps us to develop friendships, offer hospitality, and provide gifts. It is an important part of holidays, celebrations, and special occasions. It plays an important role in many religious rituals and taboos. It is a marker of status. It can control the behaviour of others when used as a reward, punishment, or political tool. It is the subject of creative expression by cooks and artists. It can make people feel secure. For all these reasons, and many more, food is worthy of study.

And yet, despite our everyday encounters with eating, studying food seems to be a real challenge, given its multi-significant and complex nature. This tension between familiarity and complexity most likely explains why, until recent years, food studies did not emerge as a coherent field of inquiry. Instead, most disciplinary attempts have focused on a cross-section of activities, processes, and sectors dealing with food. In a sense, we have had many food studies fields as separate and only selectively interrelated areas of research and scholarship. For example, the study of nutrition has focused on the role of different nutrients in human health and the causes and consequences of malnutrition, but left the relationship between malnutrition and poverty, or between obesity and the food industry, to social scientists. Agricultural economics has focused on optimal approaches to increase food production but avoided the problem of simultaneous hunger and food surpluses or the role of the agri-food industry in the obesity epidemic or in the farm crisis. These examples can be multiplied. What is clear is that such a segmented focus leaves many questions unanswered and creates disciplinary silos, making difficult the cross-fertilization of ideas and insights from different disciplines.

For many years, various researchers in diverse areas of interest dealing with food practices, structures, institutions, and policies have recognized the need for a broader interdisciplinary perspective that would borrow analytical and methodological insights from various disciplines studying food. In response, New York

University offered the first graduate program in food studies in 1996.

As a relatively new field of research and scholarship, food studies focuses on the web of relations, processes, structures, and institutional arrangements that cover human interaction with nature and other humans involving the production, distribution, preparation, consumption, and disposal of food. For this reason, food studies can be considered to constitute a new movement, not only as an academic discipline but also as a means to change society (Berg et al. 2003).

Defining the boundaries of food studies is a challenging task because food is a topic of interest for diverse academic disciplines, such as food science and engineering, nutrition, chemistry, biology, agricultural sciences, environmental sciences, health sciences, business administration, the social sciences, and the humanities. Each body of scholarship has a unique, often discipline-focused approach to certain aspects of food. In contrast, food studies aims to create a space of critical scholarship for interdisciplinary inquiry. What distinguishes food studies from disciplinary or multidisciplinary studies of food is the awareness of a need for a synthetic approach that would use "every conceivable method for studying the historical, cultural, behavioral, biological, and socio-economic determinants and consequences of food production and consumption" (Berg et al. 2003).

Many influences over the years have contributed to the development of food studies. For example, anthropological approaches looking at continuity and change in different cultural traditions around the world have been one of the key influences. Among the anthropological contributions we can list French structuralists such as Claude Lévi-Strauss looking at the material aspects of culture and seeking universal behavioural codes; Roland Barthes and Mary Douglas's examination of different food conventions and the communicative properties of food; the American foodways school's folkloric focus on shared cuisines, eating styles, structures, and

behaviours; Arjun Appadurai's insights on the formation of national cuisines; Marvin Harris's cultural materialist approach looking at various taboos and cultural practices as forms of social adaptation to the material environment; and Sidney Mintz's examination of broader trends such as colonialism and industrialization in transforming tastes and cuisines.

A second major influence in food studies has been the political economy approach. Influenced by the Marxist critique of the transformative role of the capitalist economy in modern society, political economy became influential among a group of sociologists and geographers such as Larry Busch, Fred Buttel, William Friedland, Harriet Friedmann, Phillip McMichael, and Anthony Winson. The political economy approach has examined the role of economic institutions and inequalities of power and property in explaining the relationship between processes such as industrialization, urbanization, colonialism, imperialism, globalization, and many changes in the agri-food system, food regimes, and commodity chains. While the political economy approach has mostly focused on production, some scholars from this tradition, including Pierre Bourdieu, David Goodman, and Ben Fine, pointed to the role of consumption.

A third major source of influence behind food studies has been the emergence of interdisciplinary perspectives such as cultural studies, women's studies, and environmental studies—areas often neglected by earlier approaches. With the rise of cultural studies and especially **postmodern** and **poststructuralist** criticism, many researchers looked at knowledge and traditions of food and eating as social constructs and came to question, and even reject, the effectiveness of "objective" scientific or descriptive historical approaches to food. While the postmodern and poststructuralist approach is very diverse in itself, we can identify George Ritzer's study of "McDonaldization," Gyorgy Scrinis's critique of nutritionism, and Alan Warde, Jonathan Murdoch, and David Goodman's work on consumption as some of the major contributions reflecting this tradition.

Discourses of food, popular culture, analyses of identity and subjectivity, the role of the media, advertising, and institutional practices of industry and governments in constructing reality and patterns of consumption have been the focus of many studies sharing a postmodern viewpoint.

Like cultural studies, women's studies questioned the shortcomings of the mainstream disciplinary approaches. Women's studies brought feminist criticism—lacking in the major academic disciplines—to such subjects as the patterns of gender inequality and its consequences, the ignorance of the contributions of women's labour at home and in the workplace, and the relationship between food, the body, and eating disorders.

Another interdisciplinary influence in the development of food studies is environmental studies. Concern for the effects of factory farming and overfishing on the environment in general, and particularly issues such as sustainability, climate change, soil erosion, declining water quality, decreased biodiversity, and pollution from toxic chemicals have brought natural and social scientists together to offer a more critical perspective on the consequences of the modern industrial food system. The environmental perspective not only provided critique but also offered insights on alternative food systems that are sustainable and resilient. Notable pioneers in this area have been Lester Brown and Rachel Carson. Mathis Wackernagel and William Rees's concept of the ecological footprint and Stuart Hill's work on ecological agriculture also rank among early influences with environmental sensitivity. More recently, diverse contributions have emerged from scholars in a variety of disciplinary fields.

Influences on the development of food studies are not limited to academics. *The Land of Milk and Money*, reporting the findings of the People's Food Commission, presented a comprehensive profile of the agri-food system in Canada in the late 1970s. In addition, numerous public intellectuals and community-based researchers have contributed to the development of food studies from outside of academia, strengthening the links between communities and institutions of higher education. This cross-fertilization of insights between universities and community organizations—community–university partnerships—has provided fertile ground for research and policy contributions in food studies.

Finally, we should note the critical contributions of those coming from major academic disciplines who questioned some of the dominant professional practices and demanded change. These dissenting voices have been crucial in the development of critical inquiry and paradigm shifts not only within their own disciplinary frameworks but also in the development of food studies.

The common element in all these different influences is a critical perspective in perceiving existing problems as resulting from the normal operation of the food system and everyday practices. This critical inquiry examines how patterns of social inequalities, institutional arrangements, structures, and organizations such as the patriarchal family, corporations, governmental bodies, international treaties, and the media contribute to the farm crisis, hunger, the obesity epidemic, eating disorders, food insecurity, and environmental problems.

A critical perspective does not mean being negative, but rather developing a deeply inquiring attitude, analytical capacity, and research skills. Being critical also means understanding how our current food system works and envisioning an alternative food system that is more sustainable and just. Food studies in this sense offers both a critical and a constructive approach to issues pertaining to food.

In addition to a critical perspective, a few other commonalities can be identified within the wide-ranging field of food studies:

- interdisciplinarity
- linkages among the social sciences, the humanities, and the natural sciences
- holistic approach
- historical specificity

In spite of these commonalities, food studies utilizes diverse analytical and methodological approaches developed by various disciplines. In this sense, food studies has much in common with other interdisciplinary areas. By synthesizing insights from broad bodies of knowledge, perspectives, methodologies, skills, interconnections, theories, and epistemologies, food studies aims to contribute to research, scholarship, education, and change.

The emergence of food studies has been paralleled by a growing interest in food in the wider society. Television programming devoted to food and publications such as Michael Pollan's *The Omnivore's Dilemma* (2006) and Eric Schlosser's *Fast Food Nation* (2001) have raised the profile of food in the public mind. Food policy has emerged as a field of specialization required by government programs and international agencies. Community-based food projects, food policy councils, food security programs, anti-hunger and sustainable food systems initiatives, and international relief agencies require expertise in analytical and research skills that could respond to their special needs. These demands have created new career opportunities for people with a holistic understanding of how the food system operates.

This book aims to capture the excitement, vitality, and promise of food studies by presenting the work of leading Canadian scholars in this emerging area of inquiry. Our overall objective is to develop an accessible text responding to the needs of both students and faculty. Our task is to inform readers about the breadth and depth of this new "interdiscipline" and to introduce some of the key concepts and debates. We envision this volume as not only a book for those interested in food studies, but also an invitation for critical inquiry in this dynamic field of human endeavour.

References

Berg, J., M. Nestle, and A. Bentley. 2003. "Food Studies." Pp. 16–18 in *The Scribner Encyclopedia of Food and Culture*, Vol. 2, ed. S.H. Katz and W.W. Weaver. New York: Charles Scribner's Sons.

Pollan, Michael. 2006. *The Omnivore's Dilemma: A Natural History of Four Meals*. New York: Penguin.

Reardon, P.T. 2000. "We Are What We Ate." *Chicago Tribune*, 11 June. http://articles.chicagotribune.com/2000-05-11/entertainment/0006170192_1_hunger-food-french-revolution.

Schlosser, Eric. 2001. *Fast Food Nation: The Dark Side of the All-American Meal*. Boston: Houghton-Mifflin.

Part I

The Changing Meanings of Food and Food Studies

From source to stomach, food involves complex relations among people and between people and nature. While different aspects of these relations have been the focus of various academic disciplines, in recent years researchers have recognized the need for a critical approach that would integrate insights from diverse disciplinary perspectives and situate food at the centre of its focus. This recognition has led to the emergence of a new field of inquiry: food studies.

Part I looks at the changing meanings of food and food studies. What is common among these chapters is an awareness of the complexity of the field and the need for an interdisciplinary approach to respond to this complexity. In chapter 1, Koç, Bancerz, and

Speakman tell us why an interdisciplinary approach to food studies is needed and what is meant by critical perspectives in food studies. They offer a summary of key analytical perspectives useful for food studies researchers.

In chapter 2, Friedmann explores the larger socio-economic context in which food is traded as a commodity. Her chapter provides an introduction to food regimes as a way to understand changes in the global food system and concludes by introducing the concept of "communities of food practice," which support creative solutions to a food system in crisis. While food is essential for human survival, humans tend to be selective in choosing what they eat.

In chapter 3, Johnston and Cappeliez focus on the cultural aspects of food and eating, and the transformative power of food culture. They argue that by looking at culture as a tool kit, we can move beyond simplistic understandings of individual choice and willpower, and appreciate the complex and multi-dimensional ways individuals use culture in daily life. Their research provides insight on what makes an ethical foodscape.

While some researchers look at how the food system reflects and recreates patterns of socio-economic and political inequalities in society, others see these changes as reflections of multiple factors—cultural, economic, historical, and so on. By looking at the changes in cookbooks from a historical perspective in chapter 4, Cooke identifies the multi-faceted significance of food and the diverse factors that have influenced food choices in five periods of Canadian history, as seen through Canadian cookbooks.

In the final chapter of part I, Beagan and Chapman examine healthy eating as a "socially constructed, shifting discourse." They examine the variations in how healthy eating is currently understood, including mainstream discourses that reflect nutritional science approaches, discourses grounded in tradition and cultural histories, and alternative discourses that emphasize food system concerns. They show us how gender, age, ethnicity, and social class play a role in the social construction of what constitutes healthy eating.

1

The Interdisciplinary Field of Food Studies

Mustafa Koç, Margaret Bancerz, and Kelsey Speakman

Learning Objectives

Through this chapter, you can

1. Understand food studies as an interdisciplinary approach to studying food
2. Learn what is meant by "being critical" in food studies
3. Get an overview of the key analytical perspectives useful for food studies researchers

Introduction

In recent decades, food-related issues have received increasing public attention worldwide. While ongoing social problems such as hunger and poverty maintain their significance, the emergence of diet-related health issues and environmental problems further highlights the impact of the food system on human and environmental well-being. In the academic arena, these developments have been paralleled by increased scholarly interest in food beyond the traditional areas of agricultural sciences and nutrition, and within social and environmental sciences and humanities.

Food studies represents a new **interdisciplinary** approach in the social sciences and humanities, forming linkages and interconnections between food-related topics. These overlaps encourage a systems perspective, which involves looking at social reality as a sum of interrelated parts. Using rich methodological and analytical insights offered by various disciplines, researchers in this field study the "historically specific web of social relations, processes, structures, and institutional arrangements that cover human interactions with nature and with other humans involving production, distribution, preparation, and consumption of food" (Power and Koç 2008:2).[1] Applied to an emerging field of scholarship, however, the term *food studies* can be difficult to define. Academics have widely used it in recent years as an umbrella term to cover the study of food from a social sciences and humanities perspective. Despite this widespread usage and with a few exceptions, a rigorous analysis of food studies as a field or discipline has been lacking in the literature (Albala 2013; Koç et al. 2012).

From Disciplines to Interdisciplinarity

Many academic disciplines have their origins in the nineteenth and twentieth centuries when scientific inquiry into understanding natural and social phenomena through measurable evidence and principles of reasoning was applied to different fields of knowledge (Becher 1989). Clustering around certain subjects, emerging academic disciplines have developed particular sets of assumptions, epistemological and methodological approaches, professional associations, and journals. While disciplines play an important role in professionalization in that they offer coherence in the training of their members, they have also been criticized for their rigidity and lack of openness to insights from other disciplines (Krishnan 2009).

The rise of cultural studies and postmodernism offered one of the most consistent criticisms of the earlier prevailing structuralist and modernist approaches in social and natural sciences of the twentieth century (Nestle and McIntosh 2010). Area and regional studies (such as African studies, Indigenous studies, women's studies, and environmental studies) emerged and created new spaces for scholarship, borrowing analytical and methodological insights from diverse disciplinary traditions to develop their own perspectives. Food studies as an emerging field of focus can best be described as an interdisciplinary area of studies.

At first glance, interdisciplinarity emerges as one of the main defining characteristics of food studies. Belasco (2008), while discussing the "emerging" field of food studies, notes that "it may be premature to announce the birth of a new discipline." Instead, he highlights the need to use interdisciplinary approaches in the study of food, "which requires crossing of disciplinary boundaries" and "a careful integration of themes or models on which to hang all these disparate ideas and insights" (pp. 5, 7). Avakian and Haber (2005) also stress the interdisciplinary nature of food studies:

Like other interdisciplinary fields, food studies and women's studies cover a wide range of topics and use approaches and methodologies from more traditional disciplines or develop new interpretive modalities. (p. 7)

While interdisciplinarity is hailed by some (Wilk 2012) as a strength, a lack of clear analytical focus with which to connect diverse debates and perspectives is seen as a shortcoming by others (Jones 2009). Twenty years ago, Fine et al. (1996) identified the disparate and fragmented nature of food studies and questioned its adequacy to meet the emergent challenges:

Food studies has always been a disparate discipline or collection of disciplines. This proved more or less acceptable while each fragment could remain exclusively preoccupied with its own concerns in isolation from the concerns of the others. Developments over the past decade in the production of food, the composition of diet, the politics and content of policy-making, etc., have sorely revealed the inadequacies of food studies. (p. 2)

Early interdisciplinary food research focused on food for reasons related to other research agendas, such as looking at the food industry to demonstrate a theoretical perspective on the "new international division of labour," or the globalization of the economy (Bonanno et al. 1994). As Belasco and Scranton (2002) note, instead of being the end focus, food was "a novel means to illuminate already accepted disciplinary concerns" (p. 6). In this view, food studies as a new disciplinary approach would only emerge when researchers came to see various aspects of food from production to consumption as "important in themselves—and not just because they can illuminate some other dynamic or theory" (ibid).

Organizations such as the Association for the Study of Food and Society (ASFS—since 1985); the Agriculture, Food and Human Values Society (since 1987); the International Sociological Association's (ISA) Research Committee on Sociology of Agriculture and Food (since 1988); and the Canadian Association for Food Studies (CAFS—since 2005) were the academic homes of interdisciplinary researchers interested in a more holistic understanding of food. New journals emerged that would emphasize the importance of interdisciplinary/**multidisciplinary** collaboration (see a selected list at the end of this chapter). With various journals, lists of core readings, and compendiums of course syllabi (see ASFS and CAFS websites), a respectable body of literature now exists in food studies.

Food Studies in Canada

Founded in 2005, the Canadian Association for Food Studies (CAFS) has been the leading national organization aiming to advance interdisciplinary scholarship and research in food studies. The CAFS (2015) identifies its major objectives as the "promotion of critical, interdisciplinary scholarship in the broad area of food systems: food policy, production, distribution and consumption." Drawing a membership from a wide array of disciplinary backgrounds, the association recognizes the importance of coordinating interdisciplinary research efforts that respond to societal needs, inform policy makers and community organizations, and examine the social, economic, and environmental impacts of forces affecting food systems and food policies (CAFS 2015).

Despite its recent history in Canada, there has been impressive dynamism in food studies scholarship in the first two decades of the twenty-first century. A number of Canada Research Chairs in food-related fields as well as several projects funded by the Social Sciences and Humanities Research Council of Canada (SSHRC) and the Canadian Institutes of Health Research (CIHR) have brought together interdisciplinary research teams from academia and community organizations. Furthermore, a plethora of special journal issues, books, and articles (see the short list of relevant journals at the end of this chapter) have highlighted the work of Canadian scholars in social sciences and humanities who have focused on food.

While this book is the first extensive volume on Canadian food studies, other edited collections by Koç, MacRae, and Bronson (2007/2008) and Power and Koç (2008) present some of the early contributions of CAFS members. We should, however, recognize that this work follows in the footsteps of earlier interdisciplinary food systems thinking and research in Canada, dating back to the mid-1970s. A unique aspect of Canadian contributions to food studies is the inclusion of both academic and non-academic works. Among these earlier studies, we can list Mitchell's *Politics of Food* (1975); Warnock's *Profit Hungry: The Food Industry in Canada* (1978) and *The Politics of Hunger* (1987); the People's Food Commission report *The Land of Milk and Money* (1980); Bennett's *The Hunger Machine* (1987); Kneen's *From Land to Mouth: Understanding the Food System* (1989); and Winson's *The Intimate Commodity* (1993). These pioneering publications reflect an orientation toward social justice, democratic citizenship, and critical inquiry, and they were not confined to academia. Alongside this political engagement, a parallel line of inquiry emerged in folklore and culinary history. Though the authors never claimed to be food studies experts, Berton and Berton's writings, especially *The Centennial Food Guide* (1966); Visser's *Much Depends on Dinner* (1986) and *The Rituals of Dinner* (1991); Ferguson and Fraser's *A Century of Canadian Home Cooking: 1900 through the '90s* (1992); and Driver's monumental work *Culinary Landmarks: A Bibliography of Canadian Cookbooks, 1825–1949* (2008) are examples of a culinary, cultural, historical side of food studies that remains largely outside of the critical tradition.

What Does Being Critical Mean?

In everyday usage, being critical carries a negative connotation that is associated with a tendency to seek out the shortcomings and limitations of others. In social science research, however, being critical involves four components. First, it questions whether the arguments of a study are based on evidence rather than on biases. Critical perspectives therefore require reassessment and re-evaluation of analyses as new evidence, theories, and methods become available (King and Kitchener 1994). At the same time, being critical means questioning an empiricist orientation that only provides a description of what is happening but does not provide an analysis of why something is happening. In other words, while the empirical approach is necessary for a critical perspective, not all empirical research is critical. Some food-related disciplines, particularly agriculture and nutrition, have historically been tightly bound to traditional disciplinary paradigms relying on empiricism and have encouraged conformity to the dominant ways of thinking (Busch and Lacy 1983). Chapter 6 in this volume provides insights into why a critical perspective is a necessary part of moving beyond paradigms that prevail in certain academic disciplines and professions.

A second component of being critical involves questioning the basic values that lie behind the dominant ideologies and discourses that inform scholarly thinking. Institutions such as families, schools, and the media enforce particular processes of socialization and training that normalize everyday experiences. The routine nature of a morning cup of coffee, for instance, disguises the reasons behind the popularity of this legal stimulant, as well as the labour conditions of people who work on coffee plantations. Being critical in this instance involves a self-reflexive process of interrogating the key assumptions of society, its institutions, and everyday realities. Rather than assuming that the right answer can be found by appealing to authority or habit, critical thinking recognizes that "all knowledge is contextual and subjective" (Anderson 1996:28) and that multiple answers exist for every question.

That said, not every answer is equally valid. A third component of being critical involves questioning issues of power. Critical perspectives in food studies examine power dynamics that shape the food system by identifying connections between socio-political structures and daily food practices. A large volume of

critical food scholarship works to understand how the main tenets of the capitalist economy—growth-oriented economic models, consumerism, industrialization, urbanization, and corporate concentration—affect availability and accessibility of food, impact the environment, and limit food choices.

Beyond analyzing power in the capitalist system and its structures and institutions, the fourth component of being critical means considering possibilities for social change. Food studies exemplifies an activist orientation in its desire to explore solutions for transforming the food system and society at large. Productive partnerships have been formed between food studies researchers and community organizations outside of academia that share in the goal of creating a more just and sustainable food system (e.g. Sustain Ontario, Nourishing Ontario, Just Food). This collaborative approach to scholarship is called participatory action research (PAR), Community Based Research Canada, Food Action Research Centre (Food ARC). Rather than accepting the views of those in positions of authority as facts, PAR questions the validity of a top-down approach to knowledge dissemination and demands a research process *for the people with the people* (Chevalier and Buckles 2013).

Studies of food that incorporate some or all of these four components can be understood as critical food studies—they examine evidence, unearth values, question power, and encourage social change. The emergence of critical food studies indicates that the interdiscipline of food studies is not only maturing but also remaining relevant as it addresses real problems that people face every day.

Mapping the Critical Food Studies Landscape

Critical food studies scholars have approached the study of food with a variety of critical lenses. While an exhaustive examination is beyond the scope of this chapter, we will outline four major thematic approaches that have influenced critical food studies researchers. We should caution that this classification is somewhat arbitrary, developed in order to highlight general areas of focus, which are not mutually exclusive. In reality, both the nature of problems in the food system and the critical perspectives examining them tend to be complex and multi-faceted. Common to all these approaches, however, is an emphasis on critiquing systemic and internal structures rather than individual behaviours in order to locate the sources of problems in the food system.

Political Economy

Influenced by the Marxist critique of capitalism, political economy examines how historical processes or systems shape institutions in ways that reproduce patterns of social imbalance and conflict in society. Focusing primarily on class inequalities, political-economic analyses of food have provided insights on how the expansion of capitalist **relations of production** destroys rural livelihoods (chapter 8), creates poverty and hunger (chapter 14), and contributes to ill health and obesity (chapters 12, 13). Political-economic research considers how social change takes place over time rather than ascribing to the belief that universal laws can apply to all historical periods. Discussions around global and international policies and the governance of food have increased significantly in the last several decades due to the rise of international agreements and standards that has resulted from globalization. For example, Murphy (2008, 2009) takes a broad look at globalization and free-trade liberalization, exploring their impacts on food security and **sustainability** globally (chapter 18). Other scholars, like Akram-Lodhi (2013) examine the political-economic structures of the global food system and identify its effects on farmers and food. By taking a critical approach, he determines the reasons behind the contradictory increasing rates of both hunger and obesity in the world.

In examining the farm crisis (chapter 10), scholars consider how the increased average age of farmers and the **cost–price squeeze** contribute to a steadily shrinking number of farmers—a situation that calls into question the viability and continued existence of farms (Hanson 2007; Qualman and Tait 2004; White 2012). Similarly, rural **depeasantization**—or the movement of people, including smallholder producers, from rural areas to urban areas in the developing world—and the subsequent new and emerging peasantries, have also had a tremendous impact on the way food is produced in the **global South** (Borras 2009; Van der Ploeg 2010). Other scholars consider labour relations in the wake of a globalized food system. For instance, Preibisch (2007, 2010) discusses the reasons behind and impacts of **temporary migrant farm labour** originating from Mexico and Central America in countries like Canada, specifically focusing on the experiences of the migrant workers. Similarly, Barndt (2008) examines the "tangled routes" of labour across Mexico, the United States, and Canada that are involved in moving a commodity like the tomato across many state lines.

Post-colonial approaches in food studies look to the historical and politico-economic structures of countries that have previously experienced colonialism or **imperialism**. Scholars such as Gunder Frank (1978) and Wallerstein (2004) argue that these countries have had their economic systems, including their agricultural bases, restructured according to the commodity demands of the **global North**. For example, Bello (2009) and Bello and Baviera (2010) maintain that **structural adjustment programs** and trade liberalization supported by international institutions and corporate actors have shifted agricultural production in many developing countries. Countries like the Philippines that were previously net exporters of food have become net importers due to the increased demand of rice in the global commodity market. **Agrofuels** (Borras, McMichael, and Scoones 2010; White and Dasgupta 2010) and **land grabbing** (Borras and Franco 2012; Margulis,

McKeon, and Borras 2014) also play a large role in the continual restructuring of agricultural systems in the global South.

Governance is inseparably linked with the political-economic structures found in society. Many food studies scholars take a critical approach when looking at the governance of the food system (chapters 2, 15, 17, 18, 19, 23). One example is the development of a food policy that reflects the complex intricacies and connections of the food system (chapter 20) (Lang, Barling, and Caraher 2009; MacRae 2011). Some scholars focus on particular players in food governance. For instance, the participation of corporations in the governance of the food system has become a very salient topic, ranging from analyses of power (Clapp and Fuchs 2009), to the involvement of corporations in the creation of nutrition policies (Nestle 2013), to the development of private certification and standards by industry (Fagotto 2015; Fulponi 2006; Henson and Reardon 2005), to the authoritative involvement of corporations in governing global food supply chains (Konefal, Mascarenhas, and Hatanaka 2005; Moreira 2011) and food labelling (chapter 16). Other scholars study the involvement of non-governmental organizations (NGOs) and social movements in the food system and their struggle to create a different one (chapters 2, 23) (Desmarais 2010; Holt-Giménez 2011; Holt-Giménez and Shattuck 2011).

A growing critical idea in food studies bridging political economy and governance has been **food sovereignty** (chapter 24), an alternative mode of food governance. Food sovereignty exists in direct opposition to the current neo-liberal governance of the food system that centres on the market as the locus of control, placing governing power in the hands of big economic players (McMichael 2010). Food sovereignty, on the other hand, creates policies and governance structures based on local and democratic decision-making power (Andrée et al. 2014). It tends to be associated with the efforts of NGOs and social movements like La Vía Campesina (Desmarais 2010), which

look to reconstruct "small-scale, diverse agricultural systems" (McMichael 2010:171) aimed at remedying the social and environmental problems created by the modern global food system (McMichael 2010).

Social and Cultural Perspectives

A second thematic approach examines the intersections between food, society, and culture. Scholars who explore these connections draw on a variety of critical perspectives in their contributions to food studies (chapters 3, 4, 5, 6, 10, 14, 16). To begin, feminist perspectives (Abarca 2006; Avakian and Haber 2005; Barndt 2008; Bordo 1993; DeVault 1991; Inness 2006; Shapiro 1986) provide essential voices to the field (chapter 6), through analyses of food as "a source of both power and oppression for women" (Counihan 1999:9), while scholars who study masculinity (Julier and Lindenfeld 2005) and **queer theory** (Carrington 2013; Ehrhardt 2006) expand on and complicate feminist conceptions of the gendered nature of domestic food preparation (McLean 2013). Building from this scholarship on gendered experiences of feeding bodies (chapters 5, 6), the emerging fields of **fat studies** and disability studies challenge normative constructions of the body in terms of size and ability, offering possibilities for new depth into understanding the relationship between food and bodies (Gerber 2007; LeBesco 2004; Rothblum and Solovay 2009).

Anthropology houses a lineage of scholarship that recognizes food as a significant aspect of cultural formation (Bourdieu 1984; Douglas 1966; Harris 1974; Lévi-Strauss 1969; Mintz 1986). Scholars also identify food as a key vehicle through which ethnic identity is performed (Opie 2008; Pilcher 1998), and engagements with **critical race theory** illuminate the ways in which power relations are negotiated through food experiences (Narayan 1995; Williams-Forson 2006). Particularly in a globalized world, food practices are conceptualized as a significant way in which diasporic communities maintain a sense of "home" (Ray 2004), while influencing the cuisines and agricultural landscapes of the countries with which they come in contact (Friedmann 2011; Gabaccia 1998). Alongside the influence of immigrants who make permanent homes in low birth-rate countries like Canada and the United States, food studies scholars point to the key roles that migrant farm labourers play in shaping agricultural systems (Basok 2002; Griffith et al. 1995; Koç, Soo, and Liu 2015). Studies reveal that this frequently undocumented workforce is subject to a variety of injustices, even as they supply a large percentage of the farm labour in these countries (Perry 2012; Thompson and Wiggins 2009).

Working in concert with this diversity of scholarship on the intersections between food and race/ethnicity, the "race- and class-conscious analysis" (Alkon and Agyeman 2011:6) of the **food justice** movement considers social justice to be a priority in the creation of responsible food systems alongside an emphasis on ecological sustainability (Alkon and Agyeman 2011; Gottlieb and Joshi 2010; Holt-Giménez and Wang 2011). Employing the concept of **institutional racism**, which points to systemic inequality that disenfranchises people of colour in institutional contexts, food justice scholars and activists recognize ways in which the industrial food system works to disempower people based on their racial and/or ethnic identifications (Alkon and Agyeman 2011; Meals 2012). For example, researchers (Barker et al. 2012; Eisenhauer 2001) observe the ways in which racial and socio-economic discrimination operates in the creation of **food deserts**, areas in which residents have limited access to healthy, affordable food (Beaumont et al. 1995).

Indigenous studies researchers (chapter 14) also bring invaluable perspectives to the study of food and social justice (Elliott et al. 2012; Norgaard, Reed, and Van Horn 2011; Rudolph and McLachlan 2013; Walters 2012). Morrison's (2011) vision of Indigenous food sovereignty, for instance, presents the maintenance of traditional Indigenous food practices as a key part of transforming the industrial food system.

Animal studies theorists (chapter 11) expand considerations of justice beyond the human realm in numerous studies on the lives and representations of animals that are involved in food production (Adams 1990; Pachirat 2011; Singer 1975), and in posthumanist work (Derrida 2008; Haraway 2008; Wolfe 2012) that questions the anthropocentric (human-centred) frameworks that shape people's interactions with domestic animals.

Artists (Geyrhalter 2005; Knowles 1962; Simun 2011) and art scholars (Bower 2004; Kirshenblatt-Gimblett 2006) recognize the productive potential in pairing food and art in the service of social comprehension and critique. In addition to institutionally sanctioned art, community art projects (Burns, Viengener, and Young 2004; Jeremijenko 2011) have a part to play in the creation of diverse food systems through encouraging people to make their own culture alongside their own food (Barndt 2012). In contrast to these community-driven initiatives, practices of food advertising and marketing (chapter 16) inspire a variety of critiques from food researchers (Cochoy and Grandclément-Chaffy 2005; Elliott 2008; Parkin 2006). Ritzer (2001), for instance, uses the term **"eatertainment"** to indicate the ways in which food and entertainment experiences have become conflated in contemporary consumer culture. Along similar lines, work on food and popular culture (Parasecoli 2008; Naccarto and LeBesco 2012; Rousseau 2012a, 2012b) reveals the integration of food into a variety of media experiences (e.g. television, music, digital culture), and indicates that these spaces are ripe for critical interrogation.

Environmental Approaches

A third major source of critical thinking in food studies originates from rising concerns about the impacts that the food system has had on the environment in the last few centuries (chapters 8, 9, 21, 22, 24). Environmental issues such as pollution and climate change have become some of the defining concerns of the twenty-first century.

The food system is inseparable from such issues, especially since its very existence depends on the health of the environment. However, many of the environmental problems that we are facing today are being exacerbated by the food system itself (Horrigan et al. 2002). Examples of environmentally destructive practices include an increased use of fossil fuels, a strong reliance on synthetic pesticides and fertilizers, and high rates of water consumption (ibid).

A large portion of the environmental discussion in food studies is grounded in the concept of sustainability, although other topics not directly related to it are still popular in the literature, such as biodiversity, genetically modified organisms (chapter 17), food waste and fisheries (chapter 12), and natural resource management. Political ecology (chapter 9) is a common approach taken when looking at environmental issues and food because it connects environmental concerns with the broader political landscape of the way industrial food production is organized, showing that these matters are not apolitical (Friedmann 2002; Moore 2008). Many food studies scholars who look at environmental issues focus on sustainable agriculture and farming methods, some of which include **organic agriculture** (Lockeretz 2007), **biodynamic agriculture** (Steiner 2004), and **permaculture** (Mollison 1988). Other scholars consider sustainability and diets. For example, some researchers argue that the most destructive part of the current food system is the growing production of animal protein (Lappé 1971; Weis 2013). Weis (2013) contends that this impact has been intensified not only by the near doubling of human consumption of animal protein and animal derivatives, but also through the ways that these products are being produced. Eating more sustainably can also mean eating closer to where one lives, minimizing the distance between oneself and the distance food needs to travel to one's plate. Here the importance is placed on local food, produced as an alternative or even in opposition to the conventional industrial food system (Harris 2010).

Several scholars (Harris 2010; Goodman et al. 2011; Wiskerke 2009) study what are known as **alternative food networks** (AFNs) (chapter 23). These are small food systems that directly oppose the conventional industrial global food system and are argued to be more environmentally friendly and sustainable. Various initiatives fall under these networks such as " . . . farmers' markets, direct marketing schemes, community-supported agriculture, vegetable box delivery schemes, community gardens and food cooperatives" (Harris 2010:355). Urban agriculture (chapter 19) has been one of the most popular AFNs in the literature, with discussions centring on the sustainability of growing food in cities (Cockrall-King 2012; Gorgolewski, Komisar, and Nasr 2011).

Health Approaches

The last critical thematic approach to food studies centres on issues relating to health. While the connections may seem obvious, health leaders only recently began to draw linkages between health, food, and agricultural policy. Authors like Harvie, Mikkelsen, and Shak (2009) specifically consider the industrial food system and its implications for public health (chapter 13). They identify it as a system that uses chemical inputs and antibiotics, as well as one associated with a society that eats highly processed and packaged food. They argue that the ecological and nutritional consequences of such a food system have a tremendous impact on public health.

Another view of an ecological approach to health and food focuses on the structural factors of the environment that give rise to many non-communicable diseases, namely obesity, heart disease, and diabetes (Popkin 2009; Winson, MacRae, and Ostry 2012). Some scholars like Hawkes, Blouin, Henson, et al. (2010) look at how agricultural trade and global economic structures influence healthy food choices, while others examine schools (Winson 2008) and supermarkets (chapter 13) (Winson 2004,

2013). Some scholars identify food and health on a different level—healthy eating and diets. For example, Popkin (2003) is known to have coined the term *nutrition transition*. He observes dietary changes based on high consumption of saturated fats, sugar, and refined foods—often called the Western diet—moving into the developing world and subsequently increasing rates of non-communicable diseases.

In Canada, many scholars investigating healthy eating and diets concentrate on the efficacy and use of the Canadian Food Guide (Abramovitch et al. 2012; Anderson, Mah, and Sellen 2015; Bush, Martineau, Pronk, and Brulé 2007; Garcia and Piche 2001). Scrinis (2008) devised the term *nutritionism* to describe a dominant reductionist nutrition paradigm that has been co-opted by the food industry into a nutrition approach that sees food and diets reduced to their various nutrient components and their biological functionality addressed in terms of diseases. As such, an understanding of many complex cultural, ecological, and even health relationships are lost. Reacting to these tendencies, **critical dietetics** includes a body of work that seeks to consider the social, cultural, historical, and environmental contexts that inform nutrition (Aphramor et al. 2009).

Concerns around issues such as climate change, tainted food products, zoonotic diseases, food irradiation, and agrofuels have led to uncertainty about the future of the world's food supply in terms of safety and availability (Andrée et al. 2014). Scholars, activists, and policy makers use the concept of **food security** to discuss this situation (chapters 15, 18). While food security indicates a situation in which "all people, at all times, have physical, social and economic access to sufficient, safe and nutritious food that meets their dietary needs and food preferences for an active and healthy life," food insecurity occurs "when people do not have adequate physical, social or economic access to food" (FAO 2003:29).

On one hand, food studies scholars identify dominant responses to food insecurity as falling into neo-liberal paradigms of increased free trade and technological production (Clapp 2012). In their role as stopgaps, emergency food services such as food aid and food banks are criticized for exacerbating structural problems of hunger while preserving the positive images of donor countries and corporations (Poppendieck 1999; Riches and Silvasti 2014). The concept of food sovereignty, on the other hand, relocates power away from corporations and into the hands of people who are directly affected by food insecurity (Andrée et al. 2014). Building from research on **community food security** (Hamm and Bellows 2003) and the loss of food skills in industrialized cultures (Chenhall 2010), scholars also argue that in combining an understanding of personal health with knowledge of the broader food system, **food literacy** is a critical component in empowering people to make positive changes in the food system (Cullen et al. 2015).

Conclusion

Food studies is an interdisciplinary field of multi-level systems analysis that privileges applied work. Critical perspectives that question existing structures and institutional practices as well as disciplinary and analytical straightjackets allow food studies scholars to make valuable additions not only to this emerging field, but also to the debates in social sciences, humanities, and beyond. As represented by this volume, collective scholarly engagement with the diversity of issues surrounding food will continue to contribute to the development of shared analytical insights and methodological tools.

Discussion Questions

1. How does food studies differ from earlier discipline-based approaches to food?

2. What are the four components associated with being critical? How do they apply to food studies?

3. What are some of the advantages and challenges of an interdisciplinary approach to food research?

Further Reading

1. **Agriculture and Human Values.**
   An interdisciplinary journal published since 1983, it covers a wide range of issues that critically question the values that underlie and characterize conventional and alternative approaches to the agri-food system, encompassing production, processing, distribution, access, use, and waste management.

2. **Alternatives Journal.**
   Published since 1971, it is Canada's oldest environmental magazine. It focuses on issues of sustainability through a wide range of articles that examine the impacts of the food system on the environment.

3. **Appetite.**
   An international journal that focuses on eating and drinking, dietary attitudes and practices, and all aspects of human and animal behaviour toward food. Published since 1980, *Appetite* centres on behavioural nutrition, cultural, sensory, and physiological influences on choices and intakes of food and drinks.

4. **Canadian Food Studies / La Revue canadienne des études sur l'alimentation.**
   An online open-source journal published by the Canadian Association for Food Studies, it produced its first issue in 2014. The journal provides space for peer-reviewed articles and commentaries, as well as visuals and voices from the field, which collectively illuminate the multiple dimensions of the Canadian foodscape.

5. **Cuizine: The Journal of Canadian Food Cultures/ Revue des cultures culinaires au Canada.**
   Started in 2008, *Cuizine* is an interdisciplinary journal looking at Canada's diverse culinary traditions from a multicultural perspectives. It includes papers from a range of social science, humanities, and environmental studies viewpoints.

6. **Food, Culture and Society.**
   Published since 1997, this journal is dedicated to exploring the complex relationships between food, culture, and society from numerous disciplines in the humanities, social sciences, and natural sciences, as well as in the world of food beyond the academy. It is one of the few journals that specifically identifies food studies as its focus.

7. **Food and Foodways.**
   An interdisciplinary, international journal, *Food and Foodways* has published articles on the history and culture of human nourishment since 1985. It included work by anthropologists, biologists, economists, ethnobotanists, historians, literary critics, nutritionists, psychologists, sociologists, and others who use food as a lens of analysis.

8. **Food Policy.**
   Dating back to 1975, *Food Policy* is a multidisciplinary journal that publishes original research and critical reviews on issues about the formulation, implementation, and analysis of food sector policies that deal with diverse issues surrounding production, trade, food safety, food security, and food aid.

9. **Gastronomica.**
   Identifying itself as the journal of critical food studies, *Gastronomica* combines scholarship, humour, fiction, poetry, and visual imagery. Published since 2001, this journal views food as an

important source of knowledge about different cultures and societies, provoking discussion and encouraging reflection on the history, literature, representation, and cultural impacts of food.

10. *International Journal of Sociology of Agriculture and Food (IJSAF).*

An open-access journal published since 1991, *IJSAF* provides theoretical and empirical articles on the study of labour, production, market, policy, technology, and global and local change, mostly from a political economy perspective.

11. *Journal of Hunger and Environmental Nutrition (JHEN).*

Published since 2007, *JHEN* examines hunger and the interconnectedness among individual, political, and institutional factors that govern how people produce, procure, and consume food, and the implications for nutrition and health. It focuses on hunger and environmental nutrition issues—specifically, food access, food and water security, agriculture, food production, sustainable food systems, poverty, social justice, and human values.

Video Suggestions

1. **Colquhoun, James, and Carlo Ledesma. 2008.** *Food Matters.* http://foodmatters.tv/food -matters. **80 min.**
   This nutrition-based documentary makes the connection between diet and human health by looking at the industrial food system as well as the pharmaceutical industry.

2. **Jacobson, Kristi, and Lori Silverbush. 2012.** *A Place at the Table.* http://www.takepart.com/ place-at-the-table. **84 min.**
   This documentary examines hunger in the United States through the stories of three Americans who are dealing with food insecurity. Other people struggling to put healthy and affordable food on the table are also featured, sharing their stories of hardship.

3. **Joanes, Sofia Ana. 2009.** *Fresh.* www .freshthemovie.com. **72 min.**
   This documentary explores the idea of sustainable agriculture through the eyes of farmers, activists, and business owners.

4. **Kenner, Robert. 2008.** *Food Inc.* www.takepart .com/foodinc. **93 min.**
   This documentary looks at the industrial food system and its unsustainability in the production of various foods, including meat and grains. It also considers the concentration of corporate power and how this has structured the global food system.

Note

1. To explore the broad scope of food studies, see Barndt (2008), Desjardins et al. (2002), Hamelin et al. (2007), Friedmann (2000), Koç et al. (2007), Koç and Dahlberg (1999), McIntyre (2003), Ostry (2006), Riches and Silvasti (2014), and Tarasuk and Eakin (2005).

References

Abarca, Meredith. 2006. *Voices in the Kitchen: Views of Food and the World from Working-Class Mexican and Mexican American Women*. College Station: Texas A&M University Press.

Abramovitch, Sharona, Jacinta Reddigan, Mazen Hamadeh, Veronica Jamnik, Chip Rowan, and Jennifer Kuk. 2012. "Underestimating a Serving Size May Lead to Increased Food Consumption When Using Canada's Food Guide." *Applied Physiology, Nutrition, and Metabolism* 27(5):923–30.

Adams, Carol J. 1990. *The Sexual Politics of Meat: A Feminist-Vegetarian Critical Theory*. New York: Continuum.

Akram-Lodhi, A. Haroon. 2013. *Hungry for Change: Farmers, Food Justice and the Agrarian Question*. Halifax, NS: Fernwood.

Albala, Ken, ed. 2013. *Routledge International Handbook of Food Studies*. New York: Routledge.

Alkon, Alison Hope, and Julian Agyeman, eds. 2011. *Cultivating Food Justice: Race, Class, and Sustainability*. Cambridge, MA: MIT Press.

Anderson, L. Karen. 1996. *Sociology: A Critical Introduction*. Scarborough: Nelson Canada.

———, Catherine L. Mah, and Daniel W. Sellen. 2015. "Eating Well with Canada's Food Guide? Authoritative Knowledge about Food and Health among Newcomer Mothers." *Appetite* 91:357–65.

Andrée, Peter, Jeffrey Ayres, Michael J. Bosia, and Marie-Josée Massicotte. 2014. "Introduction: Crisis and Contention in the New Politics of Food." Pp. 3–19 in *Globalization and Food Sovereignty: Global and Local Change in the New Politics of Food*, ed. Peter Andrée, Jeffrey Ayres, Michael J. Bosia, and Marie-Josée Massicotte. Toronto: University of Toronto Press.

Aphramor, Lucy, Yuka Asada, Jennifer Atkins, Shawna Berenbaum, Jenna Brady, Shauna Clarke, and Kristen Yarker-Edgar. 2009. "Critical Dietetics: A Declaration." *Practice* 48(2):2.

Avakian, Arlene Voski, and Barbara Haber, eds. 2005. *From Betty Crocker to Feminist Food Studies: Critical Perspectives on Women and Food*. Boston: University of Massachusetts Press.

Barker, Charlene, Anderson Francois, Rachel Goodman, and Effat Hussain. 2012. *Unshared Bounty: How Structural Racism Contributes to the Creation and Persistence of Food Deserts*. http://www.racialjusticeproject.com/wp-content/uploads/sites/30/2012/06/NYLS-Food-Deserts-Report.pdf.

Barndt, Deborah. 2008. *Tangled Routes: Women, Work, and Globalization on the Tomato Trail*. 2nd edn. Lantham, MD: Rowman & Littlefield.

———. 2012. "Catalyzing Creativity: Education and Art Feed the Food Justice Movement." Pp. 65–84 in *Critical Perspectives in Food Studies*, 1st edn, ed. Mustafa Koç, Jennifer Sumner, and Anthony Winson. Don Mills, ON: Oxford University Press.

Basok, Tanya. 2002. *Tortillas and Tomatoes: Transmigrant Mexican Harvesters in Canada*. Montreal: McGill-Queen's University Press.

Beaumont, John, Tim Lang, Suzi Leather, and Carol Mucklow. 1995. *Report from the Policy Sub-group to the Nutrition Task Force Low Income Project Team*. Watford, UK: Institute of Grocery Distribution.

Becher, Tony. 1989. *Academic Tribes and Territories: Intellectual Enquiry and the Cultures of the Disciplines*. Bury St. Edmunds, UK: Society for Research into Higher Education, Open University Press.

Belasco, Warren. 2008. *Food: The Key Concepts*. Oxford: Berg.

——— and Philip Scranton. 2002. *Food Nations: Selling Taste in Consumer Societies*. London: Routledge.

Bello, Walden 2009. *The Food Wars*. Brooklyn, NY: Verso.

——— and Mara Baviera. 2010. "Capitalist Agriculture, the Food Price Crisis & Peasant Resistance." Pp. 62–75 in *Food Sovereignty: Reconnecting Food, Nature and Community*, ed. Hannah Wittman, Annette Aurélie Desmarais, and Nettie Wiebe. Winnipeg, MB: Fernwood.

Bennett, Jon. 1987. *The Hunger Machine: The Politics of Food*. Montreal: CBC Enterprises.

Berton, Pierre, and Janet Berton. 1966. *The Centennial Food Guides: A Century of Good Eating*. Toronto: McClelland & Stewart.

Bonanno, Alessandro, Lawrence Busch, William, H. Friedland, Lourdes Gouveia, and Enzo Mingione, eds. 1994. *From Columbus to Conagra: The Globalization of Agriculture and Food*. Lawrence, Kansas: University Press of Kansas.

Bordo, Susan. 1993. *Unbearable Weight: Feminism, Western Culture, and the Body*. Berkeley: University of California Press.

Borras, Saturnino. 2009. "Agrarian Change and Peasant Studies: Changes, Continuities and Challenges—An Introduction." *The Journal of Peasant Studies* 36(1):5–31.

——— and Jennifer Franco. 2012. "Global Land Grabbing and Trajectories of Agrarian Change: A Preliminary Analysis." *Journal of Agrarian Change* 12(1):34–59.

———, Philip McMichael, and Ian Scoones. 2010. "The Politics of Biofuels, Land and Agrarian Change: Editors' Introduction." *The Journal of Peasant Studies* 27(4):575–92.

Bourdieu, Pierre. 1984. *Distinction: A Social Critique of the Judgement of Taste*. Translated by Richard Nice. Cambridge: Routledge and Kegan Paul.

Bower, Anne L. 2004. *Reel Food: Essays on Food and Film*. New York: Routledge.

Burns, David, Matias Viengener, and Austin Young. 2004. *Fallen Fruit*. Public Art. Los Angeles.

Busch, Larry, and William B. Lacy. 1983. *Science, Agriculture and the Politics of Research*. Boulder, CO: Westview Press.

Bush, Mary, Chantal Martineau, Janet Pronk, and Janet Brulé. 2007. "Eating Well with Canada's Food Guide: 'A Tool for the Times.'" *Canadian Journal of Dietetic Practice and Research* 68(2):92–6.

CAFS. 2015. Canadian Association for Food Studies. Accessed 15 May 2015. http://cafs.landfood.ubc.ca/en/.

Carrington, Christopher. 2013. "Feeding Lesbigay Families." Pp. 187–210 in *Food and Culture: A Reader*, 3rd edn, ed. Carole Counihan and Penny Van Esterik. New York: Routledge.

Chenhall, Cathy. 2010. *Improving Cooking and Food Preparation Skills*. Ottawa: Public Health Agency of Canada.

Chevalier, Jacques M., and Daniel J. Buckles. 2013. *Participatory Action Research Theory and Methods for Engaged Inquiry*. London: Routledge.

Clapp, Jennifer. 2012. *Food*. Cambridge: Polity Press.

—— and Doris Fuchs. 2009. *Corporate Power in Global Agrifood Governance*. Cambridge, MA: MIT Press.

Cochoy, Franck, and Catherine Grandclément-Chaffy. 2005. "Publicizing Goldilocks' Choice at the Supermarket: The Political Work of Shopping Packs, Carts and Talk." Pp. 646–59 in *Making Things Public: Atmospheres of Democracy*, ed. Bruno Latour and Peter Weibel. Cambridge, MA: MIT Press.

Cockrall-King, Jennifer. 2012. *Food and the City: Urban Agriculture and the New Food Revolution*. Amherst, NY: Prometheus Books.

Counihan, Carole. 1999. *The Anthropology of Food and Body: Gender, Meaning, and Power*. New York: Routledge.

Cullen, Tracy, Janelle Hatch, Wanda Martin, Joan Wharf Higgins, and Rosanna Sheppard. 2015. "Food Literacy: Definition and Framework for Action." *Canadian Journal of Dietetic Practice and Research* 76(3):1–6.

Derrida, Jacques. 2008. *The Animal that Therefore I Am*. Edited by Marie-Louise Mallet. Translated by David Wills. New York: Fordham University Press.

Desjardins, Ellen, et al. 2002. *A Systemic Approach to Community Food Security: A Role for Public Health, a Position Paper of the Ontario Public Health Association Food Security Workgroup*. Accessed 15 November 2007. http://www.opha.on.ca/ppres/2002-01_pp.pdf.

Desmarais, Annette Aurélie. 2010. "Peasants Speak—The Vía Campesina: Consolidating an International Peasant and Farm Movement." *The Journal of Peasant Studies* 29(2):91–124.

DeVault, Marjorie. 1991. *Feeding the Family: The Social Organization of Caring Work*. Chicago: University of Chicago Press.

Douglas, Mary. 1966. *Purity and Danger: An Analysis of Concepts of Pollution and Taboo*. London: Routledge and Kegan Paul.

Driver, Elizabeth. 2008. *Culinary Landmarks: A Bibliography of Canadian Cookbooks, 1825–1949*. Toronto: University of Toronto Press.

Ehrhardt, Julia C. 2006. "Towards Queering Food Studies: Foodways, Heteronormativity, and Hungry Women in Chicana Lesbian Writing." *Food and Foodways* 14(2): 91–109.

Eisenhauer, Elizabeth. 2001. "In Poor Health: Supermarket Redlining and Urban Nutrition." *GeoJournal* 53:125–33.

Elliott, Bethany, Deepthi Jayatilaka, Contessa Brown, Leslie Varley, and Kitty K. Corbett. 2012. "'We Are Not Being Heard': Aboriginal Perspectives on Traditional Foods Access and Food Security." *Journal of Environmental and Public Health* 2012(6):1–9. doi:10.1155/2012/130945.

Elliott, Charlene. 2008. "Marketing Fun Foods: A Profile and Analysis of Supermarket Food Messages Targeted at Children." *Canadian Public Policy* 34(2): 259–73.

Fagotto, Elena. 2015. "Are We Being Served? The Relationship between Public and Private Food Safety Regulation." Pp. 201–22 in *The Changing Landscape of Food Governance*, ed. Tetty Havinga, Frans van Waarden and Donal Casey. Northampton, MA: Edward Elgar Publishing.

FAO. 2003. *Trade Reforms and Food Security: Conceptualizing the Linkages*. Accessed 3 May 2015. http://www.fao.org/docrep/005/y4671e/y4671e00.htm.

Ferguson, Carol, and Margaret Fraser. 1992. *A Century of Canadian Home Cooking: 1900 through the '90s*. Scarborough: Prentice-Hall Canada.

Fine, Ben, Michael Heasman, and Judith Wright. 1996. *Consumption in the Age of Affluence: The World of Food*. New York: Routledge.

Frank, Andre Gunder. 1978. *Dependent Accumulation and Underdevelopment*. London: Macmillan.

Friedmann, Harriet. 2000. "What on Earth is the Modern World-System? Food-Getting and Territory in the Modern Era and Beyond." *Journal of World-System Research* VI(2):480–515.

——. 2002. "From Colonialism to Green Capitalism: Social Movements and the Emergence of Food Regimes." Pp. 265–300 in *New Directions in the Sociology of Global Development*, Research in Rural Sociology, 11, ed. Frederick Buttel and Philip McMichael. Amsterdam: Elsevier.

——. 2011. "Food Sovereignty in the Golden Horseshoe Region of Ontario." Pp. 169–89 in *Food Sovereignty in Canada: Creating Just and Sustainable Food Systems*, ed. Hannah Wittman, Annette Aurélie Desmarais, and Nettie Wiebe. Winnipeg, MB: Fernwood.

Fulponi, Linda. 2006. "Private Voluntary Standards in the Food System: The Perspective of Major Food Retailers in OECD Countries." *Food Policy* 31:1–13.

Gabaccia, Donna R. 1998. *We Are What We Eat: Ethnic Food and the Making of the Americas*. Cambridge, MA: Harvard University Press.

Garcia, Alicia, and Leonard Piche. 2001. "Perceptions and Use of Canada's Food Guide to Healthy Eating." *Canadian Journal of Dietetic Practice and Research* 62(3):123–7.

Gerber, Elaine, ed. 2007. "Eat, Drink, & Inclusion: The Politics of Disability & Food." *Disability Studies Quarterly* Special Issue 27(3).

Geyrhalter, Nikolaus. 2005. *Our Daily Bread*. Film. New York: Icarus Films.

Goodman, David, E. Melanie DuPuis, and Michael K. Goodman. 2011. *Alternative Food Networks: Knowledge, Practice, and Politics*. New York: Routledge.

Gorgolewski, Mark, June Komisar, and Joe Nasr. 2011. *Carrot City: Creating Places for Urban Agriculture*. New York: Monacelli Press.

Gottlieb, Robert, and Anupama Joshi. 2010. *Food Justice*. Cambridge, MA: MIT Press.

Griffith, David Craig, Edward Kissam, and Jerónimo Camposeco. 1995. *Working Poor: Farmworkers in the United States*. Philadelphia: Temple University Press.

Hamelin, Anne-Marie, Céline Mercier, and Annie Bédard. 2007. "The Food Environment of Street Youth." *Journal of Hunger and Environmental Nutrition* 1(3):69–98.

Hamm, Michael W., and Anne C. Bellows. 2003. "Community Food Security and Nutrition Educators." *Journal of Nutrition Education and Behavior* 35(1):37–43.

Hanson, Lorelei. 2007. "Environmental Justice across the Rural Canadian Prairies: Agricultural Restructuring, Seed Production and the Farm Crisis." *Local Environment* 12(6):599–611.

Haraway, Donna. 2008. *When Species Meet*. Minneapolis: University of Minnesota Press.

Harris, Edmund. 2010. "Eat Local? Constructions of Place in Alternative Food Politics." *Geography Compass* 4(4): 355–69.

Harris, Marvin. 1974. *Cows, Pigs, Wars and Witches: The Riddles of Culture*. New York: Random House.

Harvie, Jamie, Leslie Mikkelsen, and Linda Shak. 2009. "A New Health Care Prevention Agenda: Sustainable Food Procurement and Agricultural Policy." *Journal of Hunger & Environmental Nutrition* 4:409–29.

Hawkes, Corinna, Chantal Blouin, Spencer Henson, et al., eds. 2010. *Trade, Food, Diet and Health: Perspectives and Policy Options*. Hoboken, NJ: Wiley-Blackwell.

Henson, Spencer, and Thomas Reardon. 2005. "Private Agri-food Standards: Implications for Food Policy and the Agri-food System." *Food Policy* 30:241–53.

Holt-Giménez, Eric. 2011. *Food Movements Unite! Strategies to Transform our Food System*. New York: Food First Books.

——— and Annie Shattuck. 2011. "Food Crises, Food Regimes and Food Movements: Rumblings of Reform or Tides of Transformation." *The Journal of Peasant Studies* 38(1): 109–44.

——— and Yi Wang. 2011. "Reform or Transformation?: The Pivotal Role of Food Justice in the US Food Movement." *Race/Ethnicity: Multidisciplinary Global Contexts* 5(1):83–102.

Horrigan, Lawrence, Robert S. Lawrence, and Polly Walker. 2002. "How Sustainable Agriculture Can Address the Environmental and Human Health Harms of Industrial Agriculture." *Environmental Health Perspectives* 110(5):445–56.

Inness, Sherrie A. 2006. *Secret Ingredients: Race, Gender, and Class at the Dinner Table*. New York: Palgrave Macmillan.

Jeremijenko, Natalie. 2011. *XClinic's Farmacy*. Public Art. New York.

Jones, Casey. 2009. "Interdisciplinary Approach—Advantages, Disadvantages and Future Benefits of Interdisciplinary Studies." *Essai* 7(article 26). Accessed 3 April 2015. http://dc.cod.edu/cgi/viewcontentcgi?article=1121&context=essai.

Julier, Alice, and Laura Lindenfeld. 2005. "Mapping Men onto the Menu: Masculinities and Food." *Food and Foodways* "Food and Masculinities" Special Issue 13(1–2):1–16.

King, Patricia, M., and Karen S. Kitchener. 1994. *Developing Reflective Judgement: Understanding and Promoting Intellectual Growth and Critical Thinking in Adolescents and Adults*. San Francisco: Jossey-Bass.

Kirshenblatt-Gimblett, Barbara. 2006. "Making Sense of Food in Performance: The Table and the Stage." Pp. 71–90 in *The Senses in Performance*, ed. Sally Banes and André Lepecki. New York: Routledge.

Kneen, Brewster. 1989. *From Land to Mouth: Understanding the Food System*. Toronto: NC Press.

Knowles, Alison. 1962. *Make a Salad*. Performance. London: Institute of Contemporary Art.

Koç, Mustafa, Kristin Soo, and Willa L. Liu. 2015. "Newcomer Food Security and Safety." Pp. 292–311 in *Immigrant Experiences in North America*, ed. H. Bauder and J. Shields. Toronto: Canadian Scholars' Press,.

———, Rod MacRae, and Kelly Bronson, eds. 2007/2008. *Interdisciplinary Perspectives in Food Studies*. Toronto: McGraw-Hill Ryerson.

———, ———, Andrea Noack, and Özlem Güçlü-Üstündağ. 2012. "What is Food Studies? Characterizing an Emerging Academic Field through the Eyes of Canadian Scholars." Pp. 4–15 in *Critical Perspectives in Food Studies*, 1st edn, ed. Mustafa Koç, Jennifer Sumner, and Anthony Winson. Don Mills, ON: Oxford University Press.

———, and Kenneth A. Dahlberg. 1999. "The Restructuring of Food Systems: Trends and Research and Policy Issues." *Agriculture and Human Values* 16(2):109–16.

Konefal, Jason, Michael Mascarenhas, and Maki Hatanaka. 2005. "Governance in the Global Agro-Food System: Backlighting the Role of Transnational Supermarket Chains." *Agriculture and Human Values* 22:291–302.

Krishnan, Armin. 2009. *What are Academic Disciplines? Some Observations on the Disciplinarity vs. Interdisciplinarity Debate*. ESRC National Centre for Research Methods NCRM Working Paper Series 03/09. Accessed 15 April 2015. http://eprints.ncrm.ac.uk/783/1/what_are_academic_disciplines.pdf.

Lang, Tim, David Barling, and Martin Caraher. 2009. *Food Policy: Integrating Health, Environment & Society*. Oxford: Oxford University Press.

Lappé, Frances Moore. 1971. *Diet for a Small Planet*. Toronto: Random House.

LeBesco, Kathleen. 2004. *Revolting Bodies? The Struggle to Redefine Fat Identity*. Amherst: University of Massachusetts Press.

Lévi-Strauss, Claude. 1969. *The Raw and the Cooked*. Translated by John and Doreen Weightman. New York: Harper & Row.

Lockeretz, William. 2007. *Organic Farming: An International History.* Cambridge, MA: CABI International.

MacRae, Rod. 2011. "A Joined-Up Food Policy for Canada." *Journal of Hunger & Environmental Nutrition* 6(4):424–57.

Margulis, Matias, E., Nora McKeon, and Saturnino M. Borras, Jr. 2014. *Land Grabbing and Global Governance.* New York: Routledge.

McIntyre, Lynn. 2003. "Food Security: More Than a Determinant of Health." *Policy Options* (March):46–51.

McLean, Alice. 2013. "The Intersection of Gender and Food Studies." Pp. 250–64 in *Routledge International Handbook of Food Studies,* ed. Ken Albala. New York: Routledge.

McMichael, Philip. 2010. "Food Sovereignty in Movement: Addressing the Triple Crisis." Pp. 168–85 in *Food Sovereignty: Reconnecting Food, Nature and Community,* ed. Hannah Wittman, Annette Aurélie Desmarais, and Nettie Wiebe. Halifax, NS: Fernwood.

Meals, Kate. 2012. "Nurturing the Seeds of Food Justice: Unearthing the Impact of Institutionalized Racism on Access to Healthy Food in Urban African-American Communities." *Scholar* 15:97–138.

Mintz, Sidney W. 1986. *Sweetness and Power: The Place of Sugar in Modern History.* New York: Penguin.

Mitchell, Don. 1975. *The Politics of Food.* Toronto: James Lorimer.

Mollison, Bill. 1988. *Permaculture: A Designer's Manual.* Tylagum, Australia: Tagari.

Moore, Jason. 2008. "Ecological Crises and the Agrarian Question in World-Historical Perspective." *Monthly Review* 60(6):54–63.

Moreira, Manuel B. 2011. "Changes in Food Chains in the Context of Globalization." *International Journal of Sociology of Agriculture and Food* 18(2):134–48.

Morrison, Dawn. 2011. "Indigenous Food Sovereignty: A Model for Social Learning." Pp. 97–113 in *Food Sovereignty in Canada: Creating Just and Sustainable Food Systems,* ed. Annette Aurélie Desmarais, Nettie Wiebe, and Hannah Wittman. Halifax, NS: Fernwood.

Murphy, Sophia. 2008. "Globalization and Corporate Concentration in the Food and Agricultural Sector." *Development* 51(4):527–33.

———. 2009. "Free Trade in Agriculture: A Bad Idea Whose Time is Done." *Monthly Review* 61(3):78–91.

Naccarto, Peter, and Kathleen LeBesco, eds. 2012. *Culinary Capital.* New York: Berg.

Narayan, Uma. 1995. "Eating Cultures: Incorporation, Identity and Indian Food." *Social Identities: Journal for the Study of Race, Nation and Culture* 1(1):63–86. doi: 10.1080/13504630.1995.9959426

———, 2013. *Food Politics: How the Food Industry Influences Nutrition and Health.* Los Angeles: University of California Press.

Nestle, Marion, and W. Alex McIntosh. 2010. "Writing the Food Studies Movement." *Food, Culture and Society* 13(2):159–79.

Norgaard, Kari Marie, Ron Reed, and Carolina Van Horn. 2011. "A Continuing Legacy: Institutional Racism, Hunger, and Nutritional Justice on the Klamath." Pp. 23–46 in *Cultivating Food Justice: Race, Class, and Sustainability,* ed. Alison Hope Alkon and Julian Agyeman. Cambridge, MA: MIT Press.

Opie, Frederick Douglass. 2008. *Hog and Hominy: Soul Food from Africa to America.* New York: Columbia University Press.

Ostry, Aleck. 2006. *Nutrition Policy in Canada, 1870–1939.* Vancouver: UBC Press.

Pachirat, Timothy. 2011. *Every Twelve Seconds: Industrialized Slaughter and the Politics of Sight.* New Haven, CT: Yale University Press.

Parasecoli, Fabio. 2008. *Bite Me: Food in Popular Culture.* New York: Berg.

Parkin, Katherine J. 2006. *Food is Love: Advertising and Gender Roles in Modern America.* Philadelphia: University of Pennsylvania Press.

People's Food Commission. 1980. *The Land of Milk and Money.* Kitchener, ON: Between the Lines.

Perry, J. Adam. 2012. "Barely Legal: Racism and Migrant Farm Labour in the Context of Canadian Multiculturalism." *Citizenship Studies* 16(2):189–201.

Pilcher, Jeffrey M. 1998. *¡Que vivan los tamles!: Food and the Making of Mexican Identity.* Albuquerque: University of New Mexico Press.

Popkin, Barry. 2003. "The Nutrition Transition in the Developing World." *Development Policy Review* 21(5–6):581–97.

———. 2009. *The World is Fat: The Fads, Trends, Policies, and Products That Are Fattening the Human Race.* Toronto: Penguin Group.

Poppendieck, Janet. 1999. *Sweet Charity?: Emergency Food and the End of Entitlement.* New York: Penguin.

Power, Elaine, and Mustafa Koç. 2008. "A Double-Double and a Maple-Glazed Doughnut." *Food, Culture and Society* 11(3):263–7.

Preibisch, Kerry. 2007. "Local Produce, Foreign Labor: Labor Mobility Programs and Global Trade Competitiveness in Canada." *Rural Sociology* 72(3):418–49.

———. 2010. "Pick-Your-Own Labor: Migrant Workers and Flexibility in Canadian Agriculture." *International Migration Review* 44(2):404–41.

Qualman, Darrin, and Fred Tait. 2004. *The Farm Crisis, and the Myths of "Competition" and "Efficiency."* Ottawa: Canadian Centre for Policy Alternatives.

Ray, Krishnendu. 2004. *The Migrant's Table: Meals and Memories in Bengali-American Households.* Philadelphia, PA: Temple University Press.

Riches, Graham, and Tiina Silvasti, eds. 2014. *First World Hunger Revisited: Food Charity or the Right to Food?* London: Palgrave Macmillan.

Ritzer, George. 2001. *Explorations in the Sociology of Consumption: Fast Food, Credit Cards and Casinos.* London: Sage.

Rothblum, Esther, and Sondra Solovay, eds. 2009. *The Fat Studies Reader.* New York: New York University Press.

Rousseau, Signe. 2012a. *Food Media: Celebrity Chefs and the Politics of Everyday Interference.* New York: Berg.

———. 2012b. *Food and Social Media: You Are What You Tweet*. Lanham, MD: Rowman & Littlefield.

Rudolph, Karlah Rae, and Stephane M. McLachlan. 2013. "Seeking Indigenous Food Sovereignty: Origins of and Responses to the Food Crisis in Northern Manitoba, Canada." *Local Environment* 18(9):1079–98.

Scrinis, Gyorgy. 2008. "On the Ideology of Nutritionism." *Gastronomica* 8(1):39–48.

Shapiro, Laura. 1986. *Perfection Salad: Women and Cooking at the Turn of the Century*. New York: Farrar, Straus, and Giroux.

Simun, Miriam. 2011. *The Human Cheese Project*. Installation. New York: Michael Mut Gallery.

Singer, Peter. 1975. *Animal Liberation: Towards an End to Man's Inhumanity to Animals*. New York: HarperCollins.

Steiner, Rudolf. 2004. *Agriculture Course: The Birth of the Bio-dynamic Method*. Forest Row, UK: Rudolph Steiner Press.

Tarasuk, Valerie, and Joan M. Eakin. 2005. "Food Assistance through 'Surplus' Food: Insights from an Ethnographic Study of Food Bank Work." *Agriculture and Human Values* 22:177–86.

Thompson Jr, Charles D., and Melinda F. Wiggins, eds. 2009. *The Human Cost of Food: Farmworkers' Lives, Labor, and Advocacy*, 2nd edn. Austin, Texas: University of Texas Press.

Van der Ploeg, Jan Douwe. 2010. "The Peasantries of the Twenty-First Century: The Commoditisation Debate Revisited." *The Journal of Peasant Studies* 37(1):1–30.

———. 1986. *Much Depends on Dinner*. Toronto: HarperCollins.

Visser, Margaret. 1991. *The Rituals of Dinner: The Origins, Evolution, Eccentricities, and Meaning of Table Manners*. Toronto: HarperCollins.

Wallerstein, Immanuel. 2004. *World-systems Analysis: An Introduction*. Durham: Duke University Press.

Walters, Krista. 2012. "'A National Priority': Nutrition Canada's *Survey* and the Disciplining of Aboriginal Bodies, 1964–1975." Pp. 433–52 in *Edible Histories, Cultural Politics: Towards a Canadian Food History*, ed. Franca Iacovetta, Valerie J. Korinek, and Marlene Epp. Toronto: University of Toronto Press.

Warnock, John. W. 1978. *Profit Hungry: The Food Industry in Canada*. Vancouver: New Star Books.

———. 1987. *The Politics of Hunger*. Toronto: Methuen.

Weis, Tony. 2013. *The Ecological Hoofprint*. New York: Zed Books.

White, Ben. 2012. "Agriculture and the Generation Problem: Rural Youth, Employment and the Future of Farming." *IDS Bulletin* 43(6):9–19.

——— and Anirban Dasgupta 2010. "Agrofuels Capitalism: A View from Political Economy." *The Journal of Peasant Studies* 37(4):593–607.

Wilk, Rick. 2012. "The Limits to Discipline: Towards Inter-disciplinary Food Studies." *Physiology and Behaviour* 107(4):471–5.

Williams-Forson, Psyche A. 2006. *Building Houses out of Chicken Legs: Black Women, Food, and Power*. Chapel Hill: University of North Carolina Press.

Winson, Anthony. 1993. *The Intimate Commodity: Food and the Development of the Agri-Industrial Complex in Canada*. Toronto: University of Toronto Press.

———. 2004. "Bringing Political Economy into the Debate on the Obesity Epidemic." *Agriculture and Human Values* 21:299–312.

———. 2008. "School Food Environments and the Obesity Issue: Content, Structural Determinants, and Agency in Canadian High Schools." *Agriculture and Human Values* 25:499.

———. 2013. *The Industrial Diet: The Degradation of Food and the Struggle for Healthy Eating*. New York: New York University Press.

———, Rod MacRae, and Aleck Ostry. 2012. "The Obesogenic Environment and Schools: Have CSOs Played a Role in Shifting the Debate from Individual Responsibility to Structural Factors?" Pp. 204–22 in *Health and Sustainability in the Canadian Food System: Advocacy and Opportunity for Civil Society*, ed. Rod MacRae and Elisabeth Abergel. Vancouver: UBC Press.

Wiskerke, Johannes. 2009. "On Places Lost and Places Regained: Reflections on the Alternative Food Geography and Sustainable Regional Development." *International Planning Studies* 14(3):369–87.

Wolfe, Cary. 2012. *Before the Law: Humans and Other Animals in a Biopolitical Frame*. Chicago: University of Chicago Press.

2 Changing Food Systems
from Top to Bottom
Political Economy and Social
Movements Perspectives

Harriet Friedmann

Learning Objectives

Through this chapter, you can

1. Gain an appreciation of the social context surrounding the study of food systems
2. Understand the strengths and shortcomings of commodity studies
3. Explain global change through the food regimes approach

Introduction

The study of food systems takes a broad view of all dimensions of food from soil to stomach, and all scales of organization, from gardens, farms, and cooking pots to international organizations. The social and political context for the academic field was a series of "food crises" beginning in 1973, which created a period of volatile prices after decades of stability, and which raised issues of hunger and food security. The same period saw an ongoing farm crisis and environmental critiques of industrial agriculture. Academically, national studies were proving too limited as trade grew, culminating in the 1990s in international agreements that changed food production and consumption in all countries. One transnational approach was commodity studies, in which researchers track patterns of production, trade, consumption, and ideas about a single commodity such as wheat, milk, or tomatoes. A larger approach called **food regimes** combines commodity studies with world-systems analysis

to identify long periods of stability and change in agri-food systems.

This chapter first explores the social context of the study of food systems, followed by an overview of commodity studies. It then discusses food regimes as a way to understand global change, and concludes by focusing on the concept of "communities of food practice."

Social Context for the Study of Food Systems

In the 1970s, big changes brought food to the forefront of world affairs for the first time in decades. The first "world food crisis" was declared in 1972–3 when the prices of the most important traded food crops of the time—soy, maize, and especially wheat—doubled or tripled. This change interrupted a long period of low and declining prices, in which even poor people could afford to eat and Third World countries happily became dependent on food imports while they fostered the growth of cities and industries. High prices suddenly confronted those relying on cheap food and imports with the prospect of growing hunger; even middle-class people complained about the high cost of meat, which became more expensive because of feed-grain prices. Yet farmers did not benefit from these prices; it was corporations, especially those in international trade, that profited. Prices fell at the end of the decade, but they remained volatile. "Food crises" marked by dramatic, sudden price rises have recurred ever since. The world of food became unstable and unpredictable.

The first World Food Summit was held in Rome in 1974 in response to the crisis, launching national and international movements for **food security**. The "right to food" had been agreed to by governments in 1948 in Article 25 of the Universal Declaration of Human Rights (UNHCR 1948), but had not been top of mind as long as hunger seemed on a steady decline. Agreeing that a food crisis existed, governments signed commitments in 1974 to ensure food security for their populations. Commitments to reduce hunger have been undertaken again and again (most recently in the United Nations Sustainable Development Goals), but have not been met either in Canada or in many other countries (Friedmann 2005). The goal of food security, however, provided focus for social movements advocating social welfare, equality, and justice, including a new set of **social movements** and institutions focused specifically on hunger. It was complemented by the farmer-led goal of **food sovereignty** in response to the trade agreements of the 1990s.

Promoting Food Security

The United Nations World Food Programme (WFP) was founded in 1974 to promote the new idea of food security through multilateral food aid. Food aid up to that time had been provided from one country to another. As a result, humanitarian motives were mixed with the need

to dispose of surplus farm products and requirements that recipients buy farm machines, fertilizers, and pesticides from the donor country. This form of food aid thus did harm as well as good. The WFP is multilateral and focuses on food emergencies. Nonetheless, subsidized exports continue, and the European Union countries joined the United States as major donors of surplus agricultural products. These donations were referred to as "dumping" rather than "aid" in international trade negotiations in the 1990s and after (Friedmann 2005)—though it is important to note that emergency aid today usually takes the form of buying food from farmers in distressed areas rather than sending food that undercuts their prices and incomes. Fearing that pending trade deals would worsen their situation, small farmers across the world (who are also many of the world's poor), including Canada's National Farmers Union, launched the largest social movement in the world, La Vía Campesina (McMichael 2010; Patel 2007; Desmarais 2002; and this volume), and defined a new goal of food sovereignty. Meanwhile, the goal of ending hunger, despite regular restatements, receded ever farther into the future (Friedmann 2004).

Hunger was hardly restricted to the global South. Food insecurity came to so-called rich countries, including Canada, as incomes grew more unequal. In the 1980s, Canada's first food banks were created (Riches 1986). As hunger worsened, especially among families and children, it became clear that food banks were not, as everyone had hoped, temporary. When politicians noticed that hunger had become a permanent fact for many Canadians, some of the most creative community organizations of our time began to emerge. Notable were FoodShare Toronto and the Toronto Food Policy Council, recognized across North America as pioneer non-profit and municipal organizations. FoodShare was created in 1985 by Toronto mayor Art Eggleton as an alternative to food-bank charity, and has fostered innumerable individual and organizational initiatives. The Toronto Food Policy Council, a volunteer citizen council established in 1991 and supported by Toronto Public Health staff, has facilitated and coordinated numerous food-related initiatives in the non-profit, public, and private sectors. Its innovative Food Charter has been adopted by cities across the continent, and its Food Strategy promises to spark another wave of innovation. Another large non-profit, The Stop, grew from a food bank (which it still is) into a complex organization devoted to empowering people and communities through community food centres (Saul and Curtis 2013). Since agriculture and food are both an economic sector as well as a social movement, innumerable creative individuals have formed successful for-profit and non-profit social enterprises (Murray 2009).

Meanwhile, similar initiatives have been growing across the country, showing how regional food systems can pursue goals of sustainability, food security, and food justice. Food Secure Canada was created in 2006, the culmination of almost a decade's efforts to bring together food security initiatives across the country. Soon after, it led a project to update the popular cross-country research of the 1970s called "The Land of Milk and Money." The People's Food Policy Project, which was the work of many writers and editors based on "kitchen table talks" around the country, was launched during the federal election in 2011. This was the first time that all political parties (except the Conservatives, the party that won) had a **food policy**. The Greens, with the most extended food policy of any party, elected their first member of Parliament in that election; the Liberals and New Democratic Party (NDP) each had excellent food policies, which, despite some differences, shared a focus on health as the link between farming and food. As this is being written, the Liberal Party won a majority in the federal election of 2015 and has taken the first steps to fulfill its election promise to create a national food policy.

Promoting Healthy Food

Not only quantity but also quality of food became important in the 1970s. "Organic agriculture" and "health foods," as well as concern for global food security, were popularized by writers such as Frances Moore Lappé in *Diet for a Small Planet* (1975 [1971]) and *Food First: Beyond the Myth of Scarcity* (Lappé et al. 1977), Susan George in *How the Other Half Dies* (1976), and Wendell Berry in *The Unsettling of America: Culture and Agriculture* (1977). Of the many youth rebellions against the individualism and alienation of industrial capitalist society, one strand aimed to create communities centred on growing, cooking, and sharing food. Its proponents were early critics of industrial food and agriculture, focusing on soil loss, water pollution, dangers to wildlife from agricultural chemicals (Carson 2002 [1962]), and dangers to human health from additives and the environmental and health dangers of industrial animal production. Later critiques emphasized the dangers of sugar, fat, and salt in processed foods (Winson 2013). They experimented with conscious ways of returning to farming without chemicals and to cooking fresh meals from scratch. Vegetarianism, hardly a new phenomenon, took on new meaning in an era that also witnessed the emergence and rapid growth of standardized fast-food chains, led by McDonald's and Kentucky Fried Chicken, and early confined animal feeding operations. People formed food co-operatives as an alternative to the growing dominance of supermarkets that accompanied the growth of suburbs and the dependence on cars. Several food co-ops, such as Karma Co-op and the Big Carrot in Toronto, are still active, and the number of health-food stores has multiplied. Serving many small co-ops was the Ontario Natural Food Co-op, which still connects small, diversified farms, health-food stores, and consumers. In addition, a number of civil society organizations, such as FoodShare and The Stop, took on the role of promoting healthy food through education and advocacy.

Commodity Studies

The growing interest in food studies ushered in a wave of new research on specific foods, beginning in the 1980s. In a groundbreaking article,

Counihan (1984) showed how changes in the ways that bread is produced, distributed, and consumed could serve as a "lens" to understand massive changes in family, community, and work in a small community in Italy. Complementing this microcosmic view, other scholars traced complex global patterns by following a single food making its way through a food system. Two books set the standard for many to come.

In the pioneering work *Sweetness and Power: The Place of Sugar in Modern History* (1985), anthropologist Sidney Mintz shed new light on capitalism and colonialism. Mintz showed how the African slave trade and New World sugar plantations underpinned industrial capitalism in England by making possible new foods for emerging working classes, such as jams, which were rich in calories but poor in nutrition. He showed how sugar reshaped culture both of the rich—for example, through astoundingly complicated giant sugar sculptures for entertaining guests—and the poor—for example, through combining the energy boost of sugar with other colonial imports such as tea and opium to compensate for the suffering caused by appalling living conditions, diets, health, and work. The book is written in a lively, accessible manner, and is still a staple of food courses in history, anthropology, sociology, and other disciplines.

In the same decade, sociologist William Friedland and his colleagues produced a trailblazing book called *Manufacturing Green Gold: Capital, Labor, and Technology in the Lettuce Industry* (Friedland et al. 1981). Building on Friedland's earlier research into migrant labour in the eastern United States and Carey McWilliams's study of the structure of California agriculture, called *Factories in the Field* (1939), they showed how systems of large-scale crop production in California were fully industrial in their labour relations, finances, and distribution systems.

This work opened up two important directions. First, sociology of agriculture broadened beyond "family farms" to study all the determinants of agriculture, including inputs, such as machinery and chemicals, and sales, which were coordinated on a continental scale. Lettuce was bred to be easily harvested by machines and shipped across the continent. Labour was not family labour, except that of families of migrant Mexican and Hispanic labourers with limited rights. Canadian contributions to the literature on the role of migrant farm labour include Basok (2002), Wall (1994), and Preibisch (2007, 2010). The low cost made possible by industrial systems (through hidden subsidies of oil and water, as well as through exploited labour) allowed lettuce—and many other crops—to become concentrated in California in large monocropping operations at the expense of small and mixed farms closer to urban consumers. Durability and ease of shipping and storing took precedence over consumption; thus, varieties such as iceberg lettuce (rather than multiple varieties better for health or taste) became dominant in supermarkets, shaping consumer choice.

In the second direction, researchers began to reinterpret the history of the capitalist world-system through a food lens, focusing on the worldwide wheat, meat, and dairy trade of the 1800s made possible by European settlement of (mainly) British colonies in North America, Australia, New Zealand, and South America. McMichael (1984) shows how the class structure, land ownership, exports, and eventually independence of Australia were shaped by migration from Britain, British investment, and most important, the monetary system (gold standard) that favoured Britain and underpinned its rule. Friedmann (1978) shows how family farms in Canada, the United States, Argentina, Australia, and other parts of the world were caught up in the changing diets of industrial workers in England—a paradoxical link between family labour on one side of the world and wage labour on the other. This situation was partly due to migration, railway building, new forms of credit, and so on. But it all began with an 1840s policy decision by the British government, then the centre of a dominant world empire, to sacrifice its own farmers for cheaper imports. A world market in staple foods, as Steel (2009) recently emphasized, was something quite new. Not since the Roman Empire, which had ended more than a thousand years earlier, had any government felt so confident of its ability to control a world-system that it could risk the food supply of its people. Since then, there have been periods of national management of food and agriculture, followed by periods of increased trade. The present era forced the opening of national markets and a shift toward exports through the World Trade Organization, but these efforts are faltering over agriculture.

Many commodity studies draw on the research tradition of Canadian Harold Innis (1956 [1930], 1940), whose *staples theory* inspired others such as Vernon Fowke (1944), who traced the role of wheat in Canadian political-economic history. Commodity or value chain studies are now proliferating because they allow researchers to follow the food wherever it goes, to understand the food systems at all scales, and thus to discern larger patterns of production, distribution, and consumption (Collins 2005; Bernstein and Campling 2006a; 2006b). Among these are Sanderson's 1986 study of the "world steer," Wells's 1996 study of strawberries, and DuPuis's (2002) study of milk. In the Canadian context, MacLachlan (2002) has contributed a valuable study on the beef commodity chain. Barndt's 2008 study of the tomato chain from Mexico to Canada is another particularly important Canadian contribution.

Food Regimes: Understanding Global Change

Are **commodity chains** related through a global food system? How can analysts link not only all stages of specific production-distribution-consumption of commodities such as wheat, beef, tomatoes, and fish, but all those **commodity systems** too? Commodity studies show how specific changes in food systems happen globally and historically; by tracking commodities along supply chains we get a picture of regional specialization,

class relations in production and consumption, and interstate power, but only as these shape each specific food. Putting them together is an approach to the study of food systems called food regimes, defined as a "rule-governed structure of production and consumption of food on a world scale" (Friedmann 1993:30–31). The most important historical food regimes were those centred on imperial power under British hegemony (1870–1914) and on national regulation of food and agriculture under US hegemony (1947–73) (McMichael 2009).

Food regime analysis combines the "bottom-up" approach of commodity studies with the "top-down" approach of world-systems theory. In **world-systems theory** (Wallerstein 1974; Arrighi 1978, 1994) it is argued that capitalism is not something that emerges in any one country and then spreads to others. Rather, the capitalist era began when countries and states became related in a world market through colonial expansion about 500 years ago; the world market ever since is bigger than any state, and the hierarchy of power among states both shapes the market and is shaped by it. In other words, capitalism emerged on a world scale in the years after 1500, because of the *relationships* among industrial wage labour in England, slavery in the Caribbean, servitude in Eastern Europe, and sharecropping in Italy; each region and each commodity complex (sugar, cotton, textiles, iron, wheat) existed only because of the relations among them, including the differences in the powers of states. These relations are the spatial dimension of the world-system. The time dimension of the world-system is equally important. Researchers have documented how the world-system as a whole goes through phases of economic expansion and contraction, and how contractions coincide with shifts in power among states (Arrighi 1994; Arrighi and Silver 1999). These shifts are called *transitions between hegemonic powers*.

Food regimes built on world-systems theory tend to make two major contributions. First, following the great theorist Karl Polanyi (1944), researchers show through food regime analysis how "markets" (with their specific mix of commodity prices) are shaped by historically specific rules governing power, money, trade, labour, and more (Magnan 2012; Pritchard 2009b). Food regimes are *relatively* stable periods in which all actors, whether they like it or not, can predict the outcome of their actions with reasonable accuracy. There are tensions, even contradictions, but these are stabilized during the regime; but when old tensions and new issues cannot be handled within institutions of the regime, actions become unpredictable, and the regime goes into crisis.

Second, food regime analysis shows that periods of crisis (or "transition") last as long as periods of stability do. The transition between British- and US-centred food regimes lasted more than three turbulent decades. It began in 1914 with the outbreak of the First World War, which disrupted the New World market even as that world market affected the outcome of the war (Offer 1989); encompassed the Great Depression of the 1930s; and ended in 1947. A new regime emerged after 1947, when a wartime plan to manage international food trade was defeated. In the same year, a clause excluding agriculture was added to the General Agreement on Tariffs and Trade (GATT), allowing nationally regulated production and consumption to become the implicit principle of the regime (Friedmann 1993).

The Current Transition

The crisis of the US-centred food regime, beginning with the food crisis of 1973–4, has not so far been accompanied by dramatic wars of the earlier transition. However, no stable, agreed rules and institutions governing global food relations have emerged. Food and agriculture have been a source of conflict and confusion ever since 1973 since the creation of both the World Trade Organization (WTO) and the North American Free Trade Agreement (NAFTA) in the 1990s, food safety and agricultural trade have been major sources of international and class conflict, including a transnational organization of small

farmers leading a new food sovereignty movement (McMichael 2010; Patel 2007; Desmarais 2007). Cascading financial, ecological, energy, and health problems have afflicted the food system, and disagreements multiply about what system is desirable and which rules will secure it (e.g., Campbell 2009; Dixon 2009; Pritchard 2009a; Lang and Heasman 2015). Indeed, Lang and Heasman see "food wars" between two possible futures: the "industrial life science" route based on genetic technologies and "functional foods" by private industries versus the "ecological public health" route based on public policies.

This long crisis has led to many changes in the food system since the 1980s. First, new corporate sectors have become powerful. Supermarkets dominate the food sector, and are more influential than branded manufacturers, such as Kraft and Nestlé, which prevailed in all countries in the US-centred food regime. Canadian supermarkets led the trend in offering their own brands such as Loblaws' President's Choice (Winson 1993; Barndt 2008). Since then, supermarkets have moved into financial and real-estate markets, too (Burch and Lawrence 2007, 2009). With social changes in work and family, supermarkets have also replaced mothers and grandmothers as a source of advice on what to eat (Dixon 2003). Governments turned over many of the responsibilities for regulating food quality to the ever-larger corporations formed through mergers and acquisitions (Lang et al. 2009; Marsden, Flynn, and Harrison 2000). Supermarkets began to make their own food quality regulations and enforce them on farmers and manufacturers around the world (Friedmann 2005). Other corporations controlling agriculture gained considerable power through new intellectual property rules of the WTO, including rules that, for the first time, allowed patenting of life forms (Tansey and Rajotte 2008). Genetic technologies became a new source of profit and a new basis for mergers and acquisitions, eventually repositioning agriculture with its seeds, chemicals, and pharmaceuticals as part of a new "life sciences industry" (see chapter 17 in this volume).

Second, new commodities have become important in international trade, creating new relations between North and South. Debt collection in the 1980s forced countries in Africa, Asia, and South America to shift from national food and agriculture policies to promotion of exports to (privileged) Northern consumers. Fresh vegetables, fruits, fish, and shrimp began to appear year-round in supermarkets, made available through the retailers' transnational commodity chains. Instead of growing food crops for domestic consumption, farmers began to shift to export commodities ranging from mangoes to shrimp to cut flowers, and consumers began to buy imported processed foods rather than fresh local products. In recent years, these supermarkets have begun to dominate food retailing in the global South as well (Reardon et al. 2005; Friedmann 2004).

Third, completely new problems have arisen that cannot be solved by existing divisions of government. The policies of the food regime that lasted until 1973 were designed to address food scarcity for consumers and low prices for farmers during depression and war. The goal was to help farmers produce lots of grains and livestock (and support their prices) to ensure that people would get adequate calories and protein. This goal was achieved: the glut of grains made it cheap to feed them to animals (and eventually to produce fuels for cars), and the hamburger became the iconic food of the regime. By-products of subsidized corn made high-fructose corn syrup a cheap sweetener in processed foods, and the raw materials for expanding processed foods, such as palm oil most recently, is transforming whole ecosystems. But the subsidy regime to increase availability of grains and meats succeeded all too well: nutrient-poor products now saturate food environments (Winson 2004, 2013). Costly health problems caused by industrial diets heavy in fats, sugar, and salt have become a burden on individuals and on health-care budgets, while public health and medicine are only beginning to incorporate diet into health care (Baker et al. 2010). Now processed foods, along with chronic

diseases related to obesity, are spreading to the global South (Hawkes 2010; Popkin 1998; Winson 2013: ch. 11). More immediately, lapses in food safety have caused public fears and become the focus of consumer politics (Blay-Palmer 2008).

Another new set of problems is the compounding environmental costs of the industrial food system, which now outweigh the advantages of past productivity gains (Sustainable Development Commission 2011). Between the clearing of forests in the Amazon and elsewhere for farming, and the massive use of fossil fuels on industrial farms and feedlots, agriculture is now understood to contribute substantially to greenhouse gases and global warming, to pollution and overuse of water, to loss of precious soil, and to drastic loss of species, both wild and cultivated. Today's farmers, who have inherited the wisdom of those who managed ecosystems and helped crops and livestock co-evolve with humans for 10,000 years, are being displaced in frightening numbers (Araghi 1995). Yet they are also resisting and adapting (van der Ploeg 2008) and have many allies among people advocating for healthy food and farming (IAASTD 2008; De Schutter 2011).

Toward a New Food Regime

While some assert the existence of a "corporate food regime" (McMichael 2013), others criticize this view (Bernstein 2016). One area of conflict is certification systems and standards. Certification systems began outside governments, to promote qualities beyond those traditionally regulated by governments such as the permitted levels of contaminants (e.g., from agricultural chemicals or animal manure) in food or water. The earliest certifications were for *organics*, created by "alternative" farmers to help their customers identify their products, and for *fair trade*, created by social justice organizations to help farmers in the global South get better prices for products such as coffee and cocoa. As demand for these certified, value-based products grew, however, corporations increasingly had a role in shaping them to become profitable niche markets (Guthman 2004). And as certifications multiply, from seafood- to forest- to animal-friendly products, consumers are in danger of both "label fatigue" (Goodman 2003) and uncertainty that any certifications really deliver promised benefits.

As problems of health and environment have multiplied, governments have found it increasingly difficult to keep up. Corporations, led by supermarkets, are taking on the role of making, implementing, and monitoring quality standards, and social movements have shifted their advocacy from public policy to corporations; for instance, Greenpeace and Environmental Defense Fund have pioneered tactics to shame corporations into adopting better practices. Not only do governments lag behind the social and private sectors, but also the certification game is open to anyone to play. Although corporate self-regulation has arguably not stabilized a new regime (Friedmann 2016), public policy to address this issue is as important as it is elusive. In Canada, a national food policy, which has long seemed distant, may come; its success will depend on how well it can cross issues such as health, agriculture, and social services, and how it negotiates the conundrums of trade, sustainability, poverty, and most of all, saving land for farming.

One innovative policy strategy has been put forward by Morgan and Sonnino (2008), who advocate the "power of the public plate" to encourage schools, hospitals, and municipal agencies to provide healthy meals for students, patients, and workers, and at the same time create demand for local ingredients grown by sustainable farmers. Alliances between non-profit food advocacy organizations and public institutions are effective means to this end. For example, in Canada, Local Food Plus was one such non-profit that grew very quickly after its founding in 2006 to facilitate public procurement of local, sustainable foods (Friedmann 2007), and although its nonprofit form did not allow it to endure, the organization has left a legacy of certified suppliers and instilled an understanding of the value of public procurement of healthy local food by universities, government agencies, and even perhaps hospitals.

School meals have been publicly shown to be inadequate and unhealthy in the United States and the United Kingdom, as well as in Canada (see, for example, the work of Marshall 2006, Taylor et al. 2005, and Winson 2008). Shamefully, Canada is the only so-called rich country that has never had a national school meal program; fortunately, if the government creates one now, it can learn from the experiences, good and bad, of all the other countries. As well, FoodShare Toronto is pioneering a multi-stakeholder campaign to make healthy meals and food literacy, including hands-on gardening and cooking skills, part of the school curriculum from kindergarten to graduation.

These are only two of many strategies adopted by a growing food movement to bring together the fragments of a dying food regime to find synergistic solutions to many social problems. Food regimes is a perspective that focuses attention on food as a lens, to see ways to address many social problems at once, from promoting health to managing ecosystems, and to move toward a wise agri-food system as the foundation for a sustainable and just society.

Thinking about Food System Change

Analysis of how the food system is changing in Canada, in its regions, and in the world involves at least two questions: What is changing? How does change happen? Food regime analysis can guide research to answer these questions. In addition, we need to think about how economic actors, social movement organizations, and public agencies are linked through **communities of food practice**.

What Is Changing?

Food system change is at once a social movement and a set of practical activities to transform the food sector of the economy (Baker 2009). From a food regimes perspective, specific historical social movements have been agents of large-scale change or transitions from one regime to another (Friedmann 2004). Seeing how these changes happened can help us ask useful questions about change today. As mentioned earlier, the first food regime began when the British government removed tariffs on grain in the early 1840s, sacrificing its own powerful farm sector to imports, and promoted grain production in its colonies, including Canada, by encouraging huge populations to migrate. At one stroke, these two policies created a world market in wheat and quelled unrest and demands for bread in the working classes of Great Britain. Together, these international movements of wheat and settlers created the first food regime of 1870–1914, which, in turn, created new classes of specialized export wheat farmers in the United States, Canada, and other settler regions.

When the world wheat market collapsed in the 1920s, it heralded a decade of general crisis called the Great Depression. Prairie wheat farmers were hardest hit, since they depended on export markets which had failed. Farmers created strong social movements, such as the Co-operative Commonwealth Federation in Canada, which later joined with labour to become the NDP. Such political coalitions were key to defining the policies and rules of the second food regime, especially (but not only) in the United States (Winders 2009). These included price supports, marketing boards, supply management, import controls, and the whole array of programs now called subsidies, including export subsidies. In this regime, agrifood corporations became large and powerful through industrialization of agriculture and food manufacturing with the creation of the GATT in 1947. When in turn the second regime began to falter about 25 years later in 1973, it ushered in another period of transition, in which social movements arose in the 1980s to criticize the industrial food system; these movements comprised consumers, environmentalists, alternative agriculture practitioners, and advocates for food

security, food safety, and healthy food. The newest of these is the food sovereignty movement of small farmers around the globe—possibly the largest social movement in the world (Patel 2007; McMichael 2008).

These new movements can be studied through food regime analysis. They seek creative ways to live within natural limits, which the industrial food system tends to override (Weis 2007). Food scholars study both these change initiatives and the industrial food system itself, examining, for example, how to measure and evaluate risks related to hormones and antibiotics in livestock, to pesticides and genetically modified crops, to food system workers and consumers, and to health systems. These initiatives include certifications for fair-trade and organic products, and new networks of production and distribution, such as food co-ops, farmers' markets, and **community-supported agriculture** (CSA). The CSA is an innovation that came of age during the 1990s, in which customers buy a farmer's crops in advance of the growing season and receive produce throughout the season (see Fieldhouse 1996). CSAs help farmers invest and plant without borrowing from a bank and allow customers to share the risks and benefits of agriculture.

New distribution systems create closer connections—food networks near home for both farmer and eater—and combine social (market) with natural (crops, animals, weather) factors. They support a revival of small, artisanal processors of foods made from local farm products. In other words, they create short, local, alternative supply chains (Marsden, Banks, and Bristow 2000). Social movements recreating the infrastructure of a regional food economy (Baker et al. 2010) thus provide opportunities for entrepreneurs from farm to table. These movements may be the seeds of a democratic rather than corporate food regime.

How Does Change Happen?

Change always involves tensions. One tension in the food movement exists between alleviating injustices in the current food system and building a new food system. On one side, the food-bank communities, which form the front line of emergency help for hungry people, would like to end hunger, and they advocate for better incomes so that everyone can afford to buy food. On the other side, organizations like FoodShare and The Stop, which also guide people to food banks or even operate food banks themselves, nonetheless focus on helping people become self-reliant through education and through community gardens and kitchens. Even "middle-class" organizations such as Slow Food advocate for food that is "good, clean, and fair." But although this tension persists, most organizations are converging on a concept of **food citizenship** (Lang et al. 2009; Hinrichs and Lyson 2007).

Another tension exists between farm renewal and meeting the needs of an increasingly urban and diverse population of eaters. Waves of immigrants, from the founding of Canada until the middle of the last century, arrived in a rural country. Many became farmers; the rest were closely connected to the farms and ate what local farmers grew and sold. Historically, most immigrants came from Europe. About 30 years ago, immigrants began to arrive in large numbers from all over the world, mostly settling in large cities. As these cities grew, sprawling across farmland, the new residents found themselves very far from remaining farming areas both geographically and culturally. These recent immigrants began arriving as food markets were becoming global in the crisis of the US-centred food regime. It was easy, therefore, for them to import their familiar cultural foods. Meanwhile, local vegetable farmers, such as those in the fertile Holland Marsh near Toronto, began to specialize in two crops—carrots and onions—and export them, while nearby supermarkets were importing them. As wheat farmers before them had discovered, growing for export is not a reliable livelihood. We now have an economic problem: How can farming be renewed so that farmers can have a decent livelihood? How can good incomes for farmers be reconciled with solving hunger (Friedmann 2011)? There is also a cultural problem: How can farmers discover what foods consumers want and learn how to grow them?

Two other important tensions are less frequently noticed. First, much of the revival of local food production has relied on temporary migrant workers. These workers lack the rights of citizens (Sharma 2006; Barndt 2008). Organizations such as Justice for Migrant Workers are just beginning difficult conversations with other food citizenship organizations. Second, Indigenous people, who have been displaced and marginalized since the first food regime, have by far the deepest knowledge of how to live in each ecosystem of Canada. The resurgence of First Nations, both in cities and on reserves, embraces farming and healthy food as part of their pursuit of justice and sustainability. First Nations are potentially the centre in Canada of better ways of using land to create a better food system.

Communities of Food Practice

Economic and social movement initiatives for food citizenship are linked in communities of food practice (Friedmann 2007). These consist of networks of individuals and organizations—public, private, and non-profit—engaged in creating a regional, integrated, inclusive agri-food economy. Recent research illustrates the richness and diversity of this phenomenon in Ontario, for example (see Blay-Palmer et al. 2013; Ballamingie and Walker 2013; Fridman and Lenters 2013; Campbell and MacRae 2013; Nelson et al. 2013; Mount and Andrée 2013; Mount et al. 2013; Hayhurst et al. 2013; and Stroink and Nelson 2013).

A community of food practice is most successful when it is anchored by creative, values-based organizations. Individuals within these organizations—founders, staff, and volunteers—can trust others in the food community even if it is too large for everyone to be personally acquainted. Food change organizations tend to be fluid and to encourage individual creativity, including assisting individuals to move through and beyond them, leaving behind (and taking with them) experiences and projects that foster the movement as a whole. These individuals in turn help the organizations to evolve quickly and encourage others to emulate successful experiments. Many of these organizations are non-profits, with an increasing number of small, values-based businesses that respond to opportunities within an emerging food system based on social economy (Murray 2009). At the centre of such a network, however, we often find a public organization. For example, the Toronto Food Policy Council (TFPC) straddles the line between municipal government and citizen organizations, and facilitates and anchors networks of individuals and organizations. This role has made it an acknowledged pioneer in food system change.

Communities of food practice support creative solutions to a food regime in crisis. The future of food can go one of two ways. Either large-scale food production units will continue to dominate, with their hierarchies of a few good jobs and many poor jobs, including those of migrant workers with few rights; or local communities of food practice will connect and form a "joined-up food economy" (Roberts 2008).

The growing number of people in communities of food practice cannot know each other—there are too many. But they can easily meet each other and trust each other to work together to improve and innovate (People's Food Policy Project 2011). Trust is especially important in easing the tensions among movements, which will test the communities of food practice in coming years. The most important insight of the concept "community of food practice" is that by training ourselves to see the links among many diverse initiatives and individuals and organizations, we can discover deep changes underway in the food system.

Conclusion

This chapter has described the food regimes approach to the study of food systems. To provide background to and a holistic view of this approach, the chapter first explored the social context of food studies. The chapter then outlined commodity studies, which provided groundbreaking research on specific foods within a food system. The main focus, however, was on food regimes as a way to understand changes in the global food system. The chapter concluded by introducing the concept of "communities of food practice," which support creative solutions to a food system in crisis.

Discussion Questions

1. Why is social context important to the study of food systems?

2. What are commodity studies? Describe the strengths and weaknesses of using this approach to study food.

3. Define the term *food regime* and explain the advantages and challenges of using this approach to study food.

4. How are communities of food practice linked to food system change?

Further Reading

1. Barndt, Deborah. 2008. *Tangled Routes: Women, Work, and Globalization on the Tomato Trail*, 2nd edn. Lanham, MD: Rowman & Littlefield.

Using commodity chain analysis, Barndt follows the trail of two tomatoes from field to table through stories and photographs. The first tomato is "corporate": a standardized fruit designed to grow, travel, and be sold in large-scale operations, originating in a Mexican field and ending up in a Canadian supermarket. Workers along the commodity chain are organized by gender, race, class, and nationality. The other tomato is called by the Indigenous word *tomatl*: gardeners and small farmers across the world today continue the centuries-long adaptation of tomatoes. They save and exchange seeds and thus increase the genetic, cultural, and culinary diversity of the plant.

2. Lang, Tim, and Michael Heasman. 2015. *Food Wars: The Global Battle for Mouths, Minds and Markets*. London: Earthscan.
   Although its data are from the United Kingdom, this book offers such a clear analysis of present dilemmas and choices about food systems that it is a good starting point for understanding Canada, too. Lang and Heasman show how the "productionist paradigm" that dominated national food systems for decades is no longer viable because it took no direct account of human or ecosystem health. They outline two trajectories for a new food system: the "life sciences integrated paradigm" and the "ecological public health paradigm."

3. McMichael, Philip. 2009. "A Food Regime Geneaology." *Journal of Peasant Studies* 36(1): 139–69.
   A good place to get an up-to-date overview of food regimes approaches, their origins, and their evolution.

4. Morgan, Kevin, Terry Marsden, and Jonathan Murdoch. 2006. *Worlds of Food: Place, Power, and Provenance in the Food Chain*. Oxford: Oxford University Press.
   The authors use actor-network theory and political economy to compare three regional farming systems, in California (industrial–export); Tuscany, Italy; and Wales (a "placeless foodscape" with "short supply chain" alternatives—much like most regions of Canada). These international comparisons together show how a global economy of values-based, short supply chain, networked regions could work.

5. Weis, Tony. 2007. *The Global Food Economy: The Battle for the Future of Farming*. London: Earthscan and Halifax, NS: Fernwood.
   Weis uses food regime analysis to show the ecological and social consequences of linking North and South through commodities. Two main commodity chains are the foundation of most global food trade: wheat and livestock. Since most grains in fully commercial systems like North America are fed to animals, corn and soy are part of the livestock complex. In both systems production of grains and meat is concentrated in a few regions, and neither are sustainable. As international trade and investment organize the global South along the lines of the global North, the world food supply becomes increasingly vulnerable.

Video Suggestions

1. Wagenhofer, Erwin. *We Feed the World*. www.we-feed-the-world.at/en/film.htm. 96 min.

2. Woolf, Aaron, Curt Ellis, and Ian Cheney. *King Corn*. www.kingcorn.net/. 1 hr, 28 min.

References

Araghi, F. 1995. "Global De-Peasantization, 1945–1990." *The Sociological Quarterly* 36(2):337–68.

Arrighi, Giovanni. 1978. *Geometry of Imperialism: The Limits of Hobson's Paradigm*. London: Verso.

———. 1994. *The Long Twentieth Century: Money, Power and the Origins of Our Times*. London: Verso.

——— and Beverly Silver. 1999. *Chaos and Governance in the Modern World System*. Minneapolis: University of Minnesota Press.

Baker, Lauren E. 2009. *Emerging Biocultural Agrifood Relations: Local Maize Networks in Mexico*. Unpublished PhD thesis. York University.

———, Philippa Campsie, and Katie Rabinowicz. 2010. *Menu 2020: Ten Good Food Ideas for Ontario*. Toronto: Metcalf Food Solutions. Metcalf Foundation.

Ballamingie, P., and S. Walker. 2013. "Field of Dreams: Just Food's Proposal to Create a Community Food and Sustainable Agriculture Hub in Ottawa, Ontario." *Local Environment* 18(5):529–42.

Barndt, Deborah. 2008. *Tangled Routes: Women, Work, and Globalization on the Tomato Trail*. Lanham, MD: Rowman & Littlefield.

Basok, Tanya. 2002. *Tortillas and Tomatoes. Transmigrant Mexican Harvesters in Canada*. Montreal: McGill-Queen's University Press.

Bernstein, Henry. 2016. "Agrarian Political Economy and Modern World Capitalism: The Contributions of Food Regime Analysis," *Journal of Peasant Studies* 43(3):611–47.

Bernstein, Henry, and Liam Campling. 2006a. "Commodity Studies and Commodity Fetishism I: Trading Down," *Journal of Agrarian Change* 6(2):239–64.

———. 2006b. "Commodity Studies and Commodity Fetishism II: Profits with Principles?," *Journal of Agrarian Change* 6(3):414–47.

Berry, Wendell. 1977. *The Unsettling of America: Culture and Agriculture*. San Francisco: Sierra Club Books.

Blay-Palmer, Alison. 2008. *Food Fears: From Industrial to Sustainable Food Systems*. Aldershot, UK Burlington, VT: Ashgate.

———, K. Landman, I. Knezevic, and R. Hayhurst. 2103. "Constructing Resilient, Transformative Communities through Sustainable 'Food Hubs.'" *Local Environment* 18(5):521–8.

Burch, David, and Geoffrey Lawrence, eds. 2007. *Supermarkets and Agri-food Supply Chains: Transformations in the Production and Consumption of Food*. Cheltenham/Camberley UK/Northampton MA: Edward Elgar.

———, and ———. 2009. "Towards a Third Food Regime: Behind the Transformation." *Agriculture and Human Values* 26(4):267–79.

Campbell, A., and R. MacRae. 2013. "Local Food Plus: The Connective Tissue in Local/Sustainable Supply Chain Development." *Local Environment* 18(5):557–66.

Campbell, Hugh. 2009. "Breaking New Ground in Food Regime Theory: Corporate Environmentalism, Ecological Feedbacks and the 'Food From Somewhere' Regime?" *Agriculture and Human Values* 26(4):309–19.

Carson, Rachel. 2002 [1962]. *Silent Spring*. Boston: Houghton Mifflin.

Collins, J. 2005. "New Directions in Commodity Chain Analysis of Global Development Processes." Pp. 3–17 in *New Directions in the Sociology of International Development: Research in Rural Sociology and Development*, ed. F.H. Buttel and P. McMichael. Amsterdam: Elsevier.

Counihan, Carole. 1984. "Bread as World: Food Habits and Social Relations in Modernizing Sardinia." *Anthropological Quarterly* 57(2):47–59.

De Schutter, Olivier. 2011. "Agro-ecology and the Right to Food." Report of the United Nations Special Rapporteur on the Right to Food presented at the 16th Session of the United Nations Human Rights Council [A /HRC /16/49]. www.srfood.org/index.php/en/documents-issued. Accessed 21 June 2011.

Desmarais, Annette Aurélie. 2002. Peasants Speak—The Vía Campesina: Consolidating an International Peasant and Farm Movement." *Journal of Peasant Studies* 29(2): 91–124.

———. 2007. *La Vía Campesina: Globalization and the Power of Peasants*. London: Pluto Press.

Dixon, Jane. 2003. "Authority, Power and Value in Contemporary Industrial Food Systems." *International Journal of the Sociology of Agriculture and Food* 11(1):31–9.

———. 2009. "From the Imperial to the Empty Calorie: How Nutrition Relations Underpin Food Regime Transitions." *Agriculture and Human Values* 26(4):321–33.

Dupuis, Melanie. 2002. *Nature's Perfect Food: How Milk Became America's Drink*. New York: New York University Press.

Fieldhouse, Paul. 1996. "Community Shared Agriculture." *Agriculture and Human Values* 13(3):43–7.

Fowke, Vernon. 1944. *National Policy and the Wheat Economy*. Toronto: University of Toronto Press.

Fridman, J., and L. Lenters. 2013. "Kitchen as Food Hub: Adaptive Food Systems Governance in the City of Toronto." *Local Environment* 18(5):543–56.

Friedland, William H., Amy E. Barton, and Robert J. Thomas. 1981. *Manufacturing Green Gold: Capital, Labor, and Technology in the Lettuce Industry*. Cambridge/New York: Cambridge University Press.

Friedmann, Harriet. 1978. "World Market, State, and Family Farm: Social Bases of Household Production in the Era of Wage Labor." *Comparative Studies in Society and History* 20(4):545–86.

———. 1993. "International Political Economy of Food: A Global Crisis." *New Left Review* 197:29–57.

———. 2004. "Feeding the Empire: The Pathologies of Global Agriculture." Pp. 124–43 in *Socialist Register 2005*, ed. Leo Panitch and Colin Leys. London: Merlin.

———. 2005. "From Colonialism to Green Capitalism: Social Movements and the Emergence of Food Regimes." Pp. 227–64 in *New Directions in the Sociology of International Development. Research in Rural Sociology and Development*, ed. Frederick H. Buttel and Philip D. McMichael. Amsterdam: Elsevier.

———. 2007. "Scaling Up: Bringing Public Institutions and Food Service Corporations into the Project for a Local, Sustainable Food System in Ontario." *Agriculture and Human Values* 24(3):389–98.

———. 2011. "Food Sovereignty in the Golden Horseshoe Region of Ontario." Pp. 169–89 in *Food Sovereignty in Canada*, ed. Hannah Wittman, Annette Aurélie Desmarais, and Nettie Wiebe. Halifax, NS: Fernwood.

———. 2016. "Commentary: Food Regime Analysis and Agrarian Questions: Widening the Conversation," *The Journal of Peasant Studies* 43(3): 671–92

George, Susan. 1976. *How the Other Half Dies: The Real Reasons for World Hunger*. Harmondsworth/New York: Penguin.

Goodman, David. 2003. "The Quality 'Turn' and Alternative Food Practices: Reflections and Agenda." *Journal of Rural Studies* 19(1):1–7.

Guthman, Julie. 2004. *Agrarian Dreams: Paradoxes of Organic Agriculture in California*. Berkeley: University of California.

Hawkes, Corinna. 2010. "The Influence of Trade Liberalization and Global Dietary Change: The Case of Vegetable Oils, Meat and Highly Processed Foods." Pp. 35–59 in *Trade, Food, Diet, and Health: Perspectives and Policy Options*, ed. Corinna Hawkes, Chantal Blouin, Spencer Henson, Nick Drager, and Laurette Dube. Oxford: Blackwell.

Hayhurst, R.D., F. Dietrich-O'Connor, S. Hazena, and K. Landman. 2013. "Community-based Research for Food System Policy Development in the City of Guelph, Ontario." *Local Environment* 18(5):606–19.

Hinrichs, Clare, and Thomas A. Lyson, eds. 2007. *Remaking the North American Food System: Strategies for Sustainability*. Lincoln: University of Nebraska Press.

IAASTD. 2008. *Agriculture at a Crossroads*. International Assessment of Agricultural Knowledge, Science and Technology for Development. Washington, DC: Island Press.

Innis, Harold. 1940. *The Cod Fisheries: The History of an International Economy*. New Haven, CT: Yale University Press.

———. 1956 [1930]. *The Fur Trade in Canada: An Introduction to Canadian Economic History*. Toronto: University of Toronto Press.

Lang, Tim, David Barling, and Martin Caraher. 2009. *Food Policy: Integrating Health, Environment, and Society*. Oxford: Oxford University Press.

———, and Michael Heasman. 2015. *Food Wars: The Global Battle for Mouths, Minds and Markets*. 2nd edn. London: Taylor and Francis.

Lappé, Frances Moore. 1975 [1971]. *Diet for a Small Planet*. New York: Ballantine.

———, Joseph Collins, and Cary Fowler. 1977. *Food First: Beyond the Myth of Scarcity*. Boston: Houghton Mifflin.

MacLachlan, Ian. 2002. *Kill and Chill: Restructuring Canada's Beef Commodity Chain*. Toronto: University of Toronto Press.

Magnan, André. 2012. "Food Regimes." Pp. 370–88 in *The Oxford Handbook of Food History*, ed. Jeffrey M. Pilcher. Toronto: Oxford University Press.

Marsden, Terry, Andrew Flynn, and Michelle Harrison. 2000. *Consuming Interests: The Social Provision of Foods*. London: UCL Press.

———, Jo Banks, and Gillian Bristow. 2000. "Food Chain Supply Approaches: Exploring Their Role in Rural Development." *Sociologia Ruralis* 40(4):424–38.

Marshall, Amanda. 2006. *Best Practices in Farm to School*. Report prepared for the Ontario Farm to School Network.

McMichael, Philip. 1984. *Settlers and the Agrarian Question: Capitalism in Colonial Australia*. Port Melbourne, Au.: Cambridge University Press.

———. 2008. "Peasants Make Their Own History, but Not Just as They Please . . . ." *Journal of Agrarian Change* 8(2/3):205–28.

———. 2009. "A Food Regime Genealogy." *Journal of Peasant Studies* 36(1):139–69.

———. 2010. "Food Sovereignty in Movement: Addressing the Triple Crisis." Pp. 168–85 in *Food Sovereignty: Reconnecting Food, Nature and Community*, ed. Hannah Wittman, Annette Aurélie Desmarais, and Nettie Wiebe. Halifax, NS: Fernwood.

———. 2013. *Food Regimes and Agrarian Questions*. Halifax, NS: Fernwood.

McWilliams, Carey. 1939. *Factories in the Field: The Story of Migratory Farm Labor in California*. Boston: Little, Brown.

Mintz, Sidney. 1985. *Sweetness and Power: The Place of Sugar in Modern History*. New York: Viking.

Morgan, Kevin, and Roberto Sonnino. 2008. *The School Food Revolution: Public Food and the Challenge of Sustainable Development*. London: Earthscan.

Mount, P. and P. Andree. 2013. "Visualising Community-Based Food Projects in Ontario." *Local Environment* 18(5):578–91.

———, S. Hazen, S. Holmes, E. Fraser, A. Winson, I. Knezevic, E. Nelson, L. Ohberg, P. Andree, and K. Landman. 2013. "Barriers to the Local Food Movement: Ontario's Community Food Projects and the Capacity for Convergence." *Local Environment* 18(5):592–605.

Murray, Robin. 2009. *Danger and Opportunity; Crisis and the New Social Economy*. London: National Endowment for Science, Technology, and the Arts (NESTA). www.youngfoundation.org/files/images/Prov_09_-_Danger_and_Opp_v9_methods.pdf.

Nelson, E., I. Knezevic, and K. Landman. 2013. "The Uneven Geographies of Community Food Initiatives in Southwestern Ontario." *Local Environment* 18(5):567–77.

Nelson, C.H. and M.L. Stroink, 2013. "Northern Ontario." Pp. 16–67 in *Models and Best Practices for Building Sustainable Food Systems in Ontario and Beyond*, eds. I. Knezevic, K. Landman A. Blay-Palmer, and E. Nelson. Guelph, ON: Ontario Ministry of Agriculture, Food and Rural Affairs.

Offer, Avner. 1989. *The First World War: An Agrarian Interpretation*. Oxford: Clarendon Press.

Patel, Raj. 2007. *Stuffed and Starved: Markets, Power and the Hidden Battle for the World's Food System*. Toronto: HarperCollins.

People's Food Policy Project. 2011. *Resetting the Table: A People's Food Policy for Canada*. http://peoplesfoodpolicy.ca/files/pfpp-resetting-2011-lowres_1.pdf.

Polanyi, Karl. 1944. *The Great Transformation*. New York: Rinehart.

Popkin, B.M. 1998. "The Nutrition Transition and Its Health Implications in Lower-Income Countries." *Public Health Nutrition* 5:205–14.

Preibisch, Kerry. 2007. "Local Produce, Foreign Labor: Labor Mobility Programs and Global Trade Competitiveness in Canada." *Rural Sociology* 72(3):418–49.

——. 2010. "Pick-Your-Own Labor: Migrant Workers and Flexibility in Canadian Agriculture." *International Migration Review* 44(2):404–41.

Pritchard, Bill. 2009a. "The Long Hangover from the Second Food Regime: A World-Historical Interpretation of the Collapse of the WTO Doha Round." *Agriculture and Human Values* 26(4):297–307.

——. 2009b. "Food Regimes." Pp. 221–5 in *The International Encyclopedia of Human Geography*, ed. Rob Kitchin and Nigel Thrift. Amsterdam: Elsevier.

Reardon, Thomas, C. Peter Timmer, and Julio A. Berdegué. 2005. "Supermarket Expansion in Latin America and Asia." In *New Directions in Global Food Markets*, ed. Anita Regmi and Mark Gehlhar. USDA, 47–61. www.ers.usda. gov/publications/aib794/aib794.pdf.

Riches, Graham. 1986. *Food Banks and the Welfare Crisis*. Ottawa: Canadian Council on Social Development.

Roberts, Wayne. 2008. *The No-Nonsense Guide to World Food*. Toronto: New Internationalist/Between the Lines.

Sanderson, Steven. 1986. "The Emergence of the 'World Steer': Internationalization and Foreign Domination in Latin American Cattle Production." Pp. 123–47 in *Food, the State and International Political Economy*, ed. F.L. Tullis and W.L. Hollist. Lincoln: University of Nebraska Press.

Saul, Nick, and Andrea Carter. 2013. *The Stop: How the Fight for Good Food Transformed a Community and Inspired a Movement*. Toronto: Random House.

Sharma, Nandita. 2006. *Home Economics: Nationalism and the Making of "Migrant Workers" in Canada*. Toronto: University of Toronto Press.

Steel, Carolyn. 2009. *Hungry City: How Food Shapes Our Lives*. Vintage.

Sustainable Development Commission. 2011. *Looking Back, Looking Forward: Sustainability and UK Food Policy 2000–2011*. London.

Tansey, Geoffrey, and Tasmin Rajotte, eds. 2008. *The Future Control of Food: A Guide to International Negotiations and Rules on Intellectual Property, Biodiversity, and Food Security*. London/Sterling, VA: Earthscan.

Taylor, J.P., S. Evers, and M. McKenna. 2005. "Determinants of Healthy Eating in Children and Youth." *Canadian Journal of Public Health* 96(suppl. 3):S20–6.

UNHCR. 1948. Universal Declaration of Human Rights. Accessed 2 April 2011. http://daccess-dds-ny.un.org/doc/RESOLUTION/GEN/NR0/043/88/IMG/NR004388.pdf ?OpenElement.

van der Ploeg, Jan Douwe. 2008. *The New Peasantries: Struggles for Autonomy and Sustainability in an Era of Empire and Globalization*. London/Sterling, VA: Earthscan.

Wall, Ellen. 1994. "Farm Labour Markets and the Structure of Agriculture." *The Canadian Review of Sociology and Anthropology* 31(1):65–81.

Wallerstein, Immanuel. 1974. *The Modern World-System, Volume 1: Capitalist Agriculture and the Origins of the European World-Economy in the Sixteenth Century*. New York/London: Academic Press.

Weis, Tony. 2007. *The Global Food Economy: The Battle for the Future of Farming*. London/Halifax, NS: Earthscan/Fernwood.

Wells, Miriam. 1996. *Strawberry Fields: Politics, Class, and Work in California Agriculture*. Ithaca, NY: Cornell University Press.

Winders, Bill. 2009. *The Politics of Food Supply: U.S. Agricultural Policy in the World Economy*. New Haven, CT: Yale University Press.

Winson, Anthony. 1993. *The Intimate Commodity: Food and the Development of the Canadian Agro-Industrial Complex*. Toronto: Garamond Press.

——. 2004. "Bringing Political Economy into the Debate on the Obesity Epidemic." *Agriculture and Human Values* 21(4):299–312.

——. 2008. "School Food Environments and the Obesity Issue: Content, Structural Determinants and Agency in Canadian High Schools." *Agriculture and Human Values* 25(4):499–511.

——. 2013. *The Industrial Diet: The Degradation of Food and the Struggle for Healthy Eating*. Vancouver and New York: UBC Press and New York University Press.

3 You Are What You Eat
Enjoying (and Transforming) Food Culture

Josée Johnston and Sarah Cappeliez

Learning Objectives

Through this chapter, you can

1. Explore the role culture plays in everyday food choices
2. Appreciate the tension between individual agency and culture that shape food choices
3. Recognize how consumers try to balance ethics and pleasure in their shopping experiences
4. Learn about the motivations underlying alternative food cultures

Introduction

It has become a truism that *culture* shapes how we eat. Our culture tells us how meals are prepared, what foods are enjoyable, and which are taboo. We criticize fast-food culture and praise slow-food cultures that promise meaningful, sustainable sustenance. Culture is the linchpin between the physical, material dimension of food and its more ephemeral existence as norms, ideals, and phobias.

Culture seems an obvious and important influence on our food choices, but what exactly do we mean by *culture*? The great British scholar Raymond Williams famously observed that "culture is one of the two or three most complicated words in the English language" (1976:87). While culture clearly affects how we eat, the meaning of a **food culture**, particularly as it operates in daily life, is nebulous. Does culture dictate our food decisions? To what extent can individuals resist unhealthy or unsustainable food cultures? Food culture is even more perplexing when we consider the highly individualized ideas of eating

that dominate the **foodscape**. Today's eaters are continually reminded about the importance of individual choice and personal responsibility. Individuals are encouraged to eat mindfully to avoid overeating (Roth 2010), obese bodies are linked to personal failings (Saguy and Gruys 2010), and individual dietary changes are lauded as solutions to social and environmental problems (Bittman 2008; Pollan 2006). Given the prominence of these individualized understandings, it is important to think about what exactly is meant by food "culture" and use cultural analyses to move beyond simplistic understandings of individual choice and willpower.

A basic definition of culture is useful to get us started and move toward an analysis of food culture more specifically. We rely on a working definition of culture as "human processes of meaning-making generating artifacts, categories, norms, values, practices, rituals, symbols, worldviews, ideas, ideologies, and discourses" (Spillman 2010:113). The cultural process of meaning-making can happen in a specific institution (e.g. a gourmet food magazine), be applied to a specific, defined group (e.g. the food culture of immigrant Somalis), or be part of everyday life interactions (e.g. the culture of shame that exists around overeating). A key phrase in this discussion of culture is "meaning-making"—how social interactions convey meaning, and how we interpret meaning. The realm of *meaning* signals that culture is present and that culture matters to our understanding. Food scholars interested in culture are interested in the *meaning* of different food choices, habits, restrictions, and policies.

In this chapter we first suggest ways to understand food culture as something that shapes us but that we also participate in through our everyday lives of eating and drinking. To do this, we introduce conceptual tools that clarify how people use food culture and are in turn used by food culture. Our second goal is to showcase how food culture can be a flashpoint for critique. People are increasingly dissatisfied with the dominant food culture and associated industrial food system: they associate it with threats and risks like toxic chemicals, overeating, the fear of fat, genetic engineering, and food industry manipulation. As a result, people actively work to change food culture. To shed light on alternative food culture, we examine interviews with consumers at Whole Foods Market (the world's largest natural-food retailer) and Karma Co-op (a small consumer co-op in downtown Toronto).[1] These comparative case studies showcase two different efforts to transform food culture through food shopping, demonstrating how shoppers engage with food culture in diverse ways that are influenced by the norms and pleasures of **consumer culture**.

Using (and Being Used by) Food Culture

Cultural sociologists have encouraged scholars to move away from an idea of culture as a single, unified, monolithic "thing" that determines social action (DiMaggio 1997). Stepping away from such a model requires that we appreciate the creative ways people selectively use culture to make sense of their actions. One influential contribution here is the idea of cultural "tool kits" developed by sociologist Ann Swidler (1986, 2001). Seeing culture as a "tool kit" is an important way to avoid seeing people as either manipulated by culture or entirely free agents. Swidler argues that culture should be viewed as a collection of culturally defined elements that make up a tool kit or repertoire (1986:277). From this repertoire, individuals can pick elements that sustain habitual behaviours (e.g. cooking from an old family recipe) or can select tools to explore new ways of acting in the world (e.g. trying a new cuisine) (Swidler 2001:24). By viewing culture this way, scholars can appreciate the complex ways culture is used by individuals in daily life.

Insights from cultural sociologists like Swidler match up with the work of food scholars who have long recognized that there is no singular food culture dictating diet and that there is ample room for agency when it comes to making dinner (DeVault 1991:12). At the same time, it is important not to overstate people's agency—their capacity to actively shape a food culture. As Swidler notes, not only do people use culture, but culture in turn "uses people" (2001:24). Applying this idea to food, we see that people have some agency about what they eat, but culinary tastes and ideas about "good" food are also shaped by ethnic background, social class, family socialization, and gender (see Beagan and Chapman in this volume; Cairns, Johnston, and Baumann 2010; Bourdieu 1984). In addition, food scholars have documented how political-economic and institutional forces (e.g. markets, transnational corporations, global brands) control key parts of the food system and influence many aspects of our food culture (e.g. Winson 1993, 2004). Powerful political-economic forces shape available cultural repertoires about food, but their influence is not always clear to the casual eater (Moss 2013). Furthermore, people's stated ideas and knowledge about food do not always match up with their actual food habits and behaviours (e.g. Caplan 1997:5–6). As a result, people often have good intentions to eat a salad for dinner, but the pull of fast-food culture remains deeply appealing, fast, and economical.

How then does culture work at a less conscious level to influence our food choices? Sociologists have made key insights about how this works. In *Distinction* (1984), a seminal study of culture and class in France, Bourdieu argues that people's desire to appreciate culture (like fine art and good food) is not always consciously developed but reflects a less conscious desire to reproduce their class status. Bourdieu developed the influential concept of the **habitus** to reflect how certain tastes and preferences become "internalized, and converted into a disposition that generates meaningful practices and meaning-giving perceptions" (1984:170). Bourdieu noted that the habitus typically translates people's social class into their **embodied** taste preferences that may give them advantages later on in life. For example, an upper-middle-class Canadian child who is socialized to have a taste for sushi, oysters, pork belly, and French cheese may grow up to feel comfortable and natural in a variety of cosmopolitan food settings (Cappeliez and Johnston 2013). This may give the upper-middle-class child advantages later in life, for example, allowing her to feel comfortable travelling around the world or ordering food with her employers in an expensive restaurant.

One critique of the habitus concept is its "black box" quality (e.g. Boudon 1998): how do we know if this is how culture works, and what processes are involved in the construction of habitus? Research in social psychology gives empirical force to the idea of habitus and the idea that we make many choices on a habitual, embodied, less conscious level. Giddens (1984) distinguishes between "practical consciousness," which involves tacit understandings and intuitive decisions, and "discursive consciousness," which involves people's formal articulations and rationalizations for their actions. Together, this research suggests that our thoughts have a dualistic quality: there is a deliberate, conscious process that is slow and reflexive, and a practical, automatic process that is fast and intuitive (Chaiken and Trope 1999). Incorporating insights about our semi-conscious, intuitive thoughts appears essential for understanding how culture works (Vaisey 2008, 2009). We argue that this is especially true for food culture—a fact well appreciated by fast-food advertisements and marketers (Moss 2013). Not only is automatic consciousness influential in what we think, feel, and do, most of our thinking occurs "below the level of conscious awareness" (Vaisey 2009:1681). A useful metaphor is one of an elephant (the automatic or practical consciousness) and a rider (the deliberate or discursive consciousness) (Haidt 2001). While the rider might *think* she is in charge of the thinking process—training and steering the elephant—the elephant is ultimately "larger and stronger than the rider" (Vaisey 2009:1683). In the context of food culture, we may feel as though we have complete control over our food preferences, but research on cognitive processes suggests otherwise.

Research on culture, cognition, and consciousness is important for food scholarship because it provides insights on how our food choices may not always be processed at a fully conscious, discursive level. Put simply, what we eat may be based more on habits, hunches, and emotional associations than reasoned arguments. But where do our food habits and hunches come from? This is where cultural "schemas" come into play. Schemas are taken-for-granted frameworks for understanding our place in society. Schemas are not actively "deployed" like cultural tools, but represent "deep, largely unconscious networks of neural associations that facilitate perception, interpretation and action" (Vaisey 2009:1686). Gender schemas, for instance, unconsciously organize thoughts and expectations of how men and women should behave, and maternal schemas shape our ideas of mothers as caring and nurturing (de Laat and Baumann 2014). Schemas emerge from experience and allow people to act in more automatic ways in their daily lives (Vaisey 2009:1686). Like Bourdieu's habitus, schemas are connected to our emotions and motivate actions even if they are not consciously articulated (ibid). In our earlier example of the cosmopolitan upper-middle-class child who loves oysters and can appreciate French cheese, we can imagine that this child may come to develop a schema of everyday eating that includes fish, fibre-rich carbohydrates, and vegetables at every meal based on her class habitus. These unconscious associations not only shape her choices but also provide status in social settings, as well as protective health benefits in a "fat-sugar-salt"–dominated food environment (Moss 2013; Winson 2004).

We are particularly interested in the cultural schemas surrounding food and food shopping. While people deliberately and consciously select cultural tools for eating (e.g. intentionally buying vegetables to be healthier), cultural schemas also influence food behaviours at less conscious levels (e.g. an ice-cream advertisement can kick-start associations between sugar and pleasure). We argue that consumer culture, with all of its attendant institutions, norms, markets, and habits, is a central and powerful influence on the cultural schemas shaping food choices. We can understand consumer culture as emphasizing the satisfaction of private needs and desires through the purchase of commodities. Consumer culture tends to focus on individual consumer choices as a central terrain for cultivating individual pleasures, identities, and the good life in general (Cohen 2003:18–19). In consumer culture, we absorb cultural schemas around shopping that are central to consumers' expectations. For grocery shopping, consumers believe that the ideal experience should be aesthetically pleasing (e.g. attractive displays), be convenient, involve a wide range of choices, and be relatively cheap (Johnston and Szabo 2011; Johnston 2008). Many of us have strong, schematic beliefs about how much food should cost and react negatively when food no longer feels "cheap"—even though cheap food can have a high social and environmental price tag (see Carolan 2011).

Past generations of critical cultural theorists pointed out the ways consumer culture influenced and even manipulates consumer desires (e.g. Adorno 1975; Marcuse 1991 [1964]). While these critiques of capitalist manipulation were powerful, more recent cultural theorists want to resist the idea of consumers as unthinking "dopes." Incorporating cultural sociology's insights about cognition (e.g. Vaisey 2008, 2009) can refine critical theory's critiques of capitalism and better our understanding of consumer "choice" within consumer society. Ultimately, we want to shed light on how our consumer culture shapes shopping choices in ways that are not fully understood by consumers themselves, while also recognizing consumers' deliberate thought processes. Paying attention to the cultural schemas of consumer culture can help us better understand how food culture gets "inside us" and serves as a foil to the popular—but unrealistic—idea of individuals as fully and completely in charge when it comes to making food choices.

Challenging and Transforming the Dominant Food Culture: The Ethical Foodscape

Food culture is continually evolving. In 1960s hippie food culture, the "countercuisine" emerged to challenge the white-bread, processed-cheese North American food culture of the mainstream and offered up macrobiotic food and tofu casseroles (Belasco 1989). Today, numerous challengers have emerged against the dominant corporate-industrial food culture: healthy eating movements and organic, local, and fair-trade foods, among others. Corporate food culture has proven adept at incorporating critical voices into the commercial mainstream (e.g. organic food at Walmart) (Frank 1997; Johnston and Cairns 2012; Johnston, Biro, and MacKendrick 2009). We view this process of social critique and market adaptation as a fundamental feature of the foodscape. The foodscape is a concept that captures the ways we understand food consumption as well as our relationship to the material reality of food systems (Johnston and Goodman 2015). In the **ethical foodscape**, food is not simply considered an individual right but is being connected to collective issues like sustainability, animal welfare, hunger, labour rights, and social justice (Goodman et al. 2010). Corporate entities, food celebrities, and social movement actors co-exist in the ethical food-scape, sometimes uneasily, making it difficult for consumers and food scholars to identify possibilities for transforming an unsustainable and unjust global food system (Johnston and Goodman 2015). Put differently, it is often hard for consumers to identify what aspects of food culture significantly challenge the status quo, and what is simply a "radical" new product line promising you great taste *and* a chance to "save the world" (Johnston and Cairns 2012).

Philosopher Kate Soper identifies possibilities for transforming the food system through cultural challenges with her concept of **alternative hedonism** (2009:4). The idea of alternative hedonism involves "new conceptions of the good life" and finding pleasure in alternative ways of living—like biking (instead of driving) or eating home-cooked meals from your garden (instead of a TV dinner). Crucially, alternative hedonism is not just about buying different stuff (e.g. substituting organic for regular milk). Alternative hedonism critiques commodity solutions and draws attention to consumer dissatisfaction with high-consumption lifestyles (Soper 2008). Soper proposes that consuming differently can create pleasures that are not reducible to the moral satisfactions of "doing right." Soper also suggests that hedonistic approaches are necessary to woo consumers away from unsustainable living standards in affluent societies (2009:3–4). In other words, you have to offer people some kind of *pleasure* if you want to attract them to an ethical foodscape and convince them to make more sustainable, humane, socially just food choices (See Lorenzen 2014).

We have argued that sociological debates about culture and **consumerism** help critical food scholars understand the limits and possibilities of food cultures. We have put forward a view of food culture that people actively use in daily life but that also constrains and shapes everyday food choices. In this conceptualization, people have agency selecting the cultural tools that shape how and what they eat, but do not always completely control the cultural repertoires available to them. While the deliberate nature of some food choices is important, we equally emphasize how people's food decisions are influenced by less conscious, habitual ways of being. Bourdieu used the term *habitus* to refer to these embodied, habitual influences on our tastes preferences and their roots in our class upbringing. We can bolster Bourdieu's concept by identifying how cultural schemas and our practical consciousness shape the habitus and by identifying the habits and hunches that shape what feels enjoyable in the realm of food and food shopping. We have also argued that ideas and values about eating are influenced by consumer culture and its prioritization of choice, convenience, and sensory pleasures. The dominant consumer culture actively shapes our schemas of food and food shopping, but it is not unchallenged or static. Critiques continually emerge and are articulated through struggles in the ethical foodscape. Market actors must react to these critiques, and they frequently incorporate critiques of the food system into their product lines (e.g. fair-trade Kit Kat; organic hot dogs).

In the next section, we use consumer interviews to clarify these cultural concepts, especially those relating to consumer motivations in the ethical foodscape. At an empirical level, we want to document shopping at two different shopping sites—a Whole Foods megastore and a small-scale food co-op. More theoretically, we examine how both shopping experiences involve a goal of improving the food system while drawing from and developing distinctly different kinds of food culture in the process.

Food Culture in Action: Whole Foods Market and Karma Co-op

Next, we examine food consumers in two different settings: Whole Foods Market (WFM) and Karma Co-op. Both stores can be understood as actors within the ethical foodscape, but they operate on different scales and employ very different philosophies. WFM is the world's largest natural-food retailer, with over 360 locations in North America and the United Kingdom (see Johnston and Rodney 2015). WFM dominates the retail environment for natural foods while encouraging consumers to "feel good" about where they shop (Johnston 2008). Karma Co-op is a small member-owned food co-operative in downtown Toronto in operation since 1972. Karma attempts to satisfy the demands of older members who do not want the co-op to grow or change while keeping the space attractive enough to draw new members and stay fiscally solvent. Based on an interpretive reading of interviews with shoppers at both stores, we explore the ways deliberative food consciousness can contradict (and affirm) automatic thoughts, habits, and feelings about food shopping.

Whole Foods Market: Enjoying the Pleasures of Consumer Culture (Sometimes Guiltily)

Situated in the tony Yorkville neighbourhood in Toronto, WFM is an epicurean paradise. Pyramids of brightly coloured produce can be found alongside aged balsamic vinegar, exotic cheeses, eco-friendly laundry soap, and organic meat. Despite its busy downtown location, WFM is large and spacious, and offers free parking. The store seems to offer shoppers the possibility to shop ethically, responsibly, and healthily without sacrificing pleasures like delicious food, choice, and convenience.

Consumer pleasure is central to the WFM shopping experience (Johnston and Szabo 2011; Johnston 2008). The idea of aesthetically appreciating and prioritizing culinary pleasures in daily life is strongly associated with the cultural repertoires of gourmet or "foodie" culture (Cappeliez and Johnston 2013; Johnston and Baumann 2015). Most shoppers interviewed mentioned the aesthetic appeal of WFM and emphasized the allure of an enjoyable and attractive shopping setting: the cleanliness, open layout, natural lighting, extensive selection, and the overall play of colours and products were all part of participants' pleasurable experience. These pleasures were presented as primary reasons to shop at WFM but also frequently prioritized over other concerns, like ethically sourced products and environmentally sustainable practices (Johnston and Szabo 2011). A particularly prominent element of consumer culture at WFM is the idea of *choice* (Johnston 2008), an ideal that is central to modern consumer culture (Slater 1997:61). Rather than being overwhelmed with the extensive selection of goods on offer (e.g. 72 types of bottled water were available at one store visit), almost all interviewees valued and enjoyed the range of choices available. Several shoppers suggested that the selection at WFM was more important than sourcing ethical products. These consumers did not deliberately seek out *unethical* products, nor do we want to suggest that interviewees were heartless. Instead, we propose that the idea of maximum choice is so central to underlying cultural schemas of pleasurable shopping that restricting choice in the name of ethics was intuitively understood as diminishing the shopping experience.

Another key element of cultural schemas around food shopping expressed in our interviews was the valuation of a luxurious and elite shopping experience. This value operated on a relatively intuitive plane; not only was it obliquely referenced, but it frequently co-existed (and contradicted) an egalitarian ethos articulated in other parts of the interview. Respondents would decry the fact that WFM was snobby and too expensive, but in the same interview they would describe the store's luxurious and upscale environment as highly appealing. For example, Steve critiqued WFM for its high prices and elitism, but also spoke positively about its luxurious atmosphere, indicating that it made him "feel special." Mary, a 62-year-old teacher who had an interest in social justice, insisted "nobody needs to go to Whole Foods. There's nothing at Whole Foods that anybody couldn't do without"; still, she described WFM as a space to feel the thrill of "rubbing shoulders" with elites. While Mary clearly experienced WFM as pleasurable, she also indicated she did not want to think about *why* it is pleasurable: "I'm trying not to analyze it, I'm not the sociologist doing this research." Mary's comments suggest that cultural schemas around food shopping can generate strong pleasures, even though conscious thought processes might reject these pleasures as elitist.

The idea of shopping at WFM as an "escape" from everyday life also appeared central to underlying cultural schemas about shopping pleasures. Almost half of the respondents framed shopping at WFM as a leisure activity, using words like *destination*, *outing*, *vacation*, and *escape*. However, the idea of a shopping "vacation" generated feelings that were in tension with normative visions of leisure and community. Olivia described visiting WFM as a

> little mini vacation. . . . I like to troll the aisles and look at the 20 different kinds of teas because that is my outlet right now. . . . my outlet right now is shopping. . . . Which is a sad commentary but that is the truth.

Olivia clearly understood shopping at WFM as a pleasurable form of entertainment. However, her observation that it represents a "sad commentary" demonstrates that she is simultaneously critical, and does not see the food consumer culture available at WFM as straightforwardly positive.

Like Olivia, other interviewees acknowledged their attraction to WFM's consumer pleasures while identifying ambiguities and contradictions. Put differently, the pleasurable cultural schemas of shopping, so attractively presented at WFM, were often described as intuitively and automatically enjoyable but were critically evaluated when the interviewee was asked to think more deliberately and consciously. This trend clearly shows the ability of consumers to draw from multiple cultural tools, to alternately emphasize shopping pleasures and critique consumer culture. This juxtaposition of intuitive pleasures and critical thinking was clearly articulated by Julie, a 34-year-old lawyer with one small child, who described a profound enjoyment of the shopping experience at WFM, as long as she minimized "thinking" about "political matters": "I really enjoy it. . . . *if I feel like not thinking* politically, it's kind of fun" [emphasis ours].

Respondents like Julie were openly skeptical of WFM's corporate practices and questioned the firm's commitment to social and environmental issues, but admitted that they were nonetheless drawn to WFM's pleasurable atmosphere and products. Despite some less agreeable "political" aspects, the store was associated with "fun"—a place where "thinking" could be put on hold. Julie and her husband Hugh describe how they have tried to go to WFM less frequently but find the store difficult to resist. In Hugh's words, "You kind of get sucked in." The phrase *sucked in* indicates for us an intuitive level of attraction based on underlying cultural schemas of shopping as eminently pleasurable. Similarly, Chris, a participant in our sample who was highly politicized about food issues and critical of WFM policies and practices, still felt vulnerable:

> You walk into Whole Foods and you're in the bakery section and you smell the cookies, you smell the cakes and you see all the breads and all the cheese laid out. You walk in a little further and you see the sushi bar

and the hot food and *you're basically sucked into that experience.* [emphasis ours]

Both participants allude to the feeling of being compelled by a shopping environment where the pull of consumer pleasures is difficult to resist, even when ideological contradictions and critiques are present at the level of discursive consciousness. While we observed many instances where consumers straightforwardly pursued culinary pleasures and interests at WFM, the excerpts above suggest that ideas of food pleasure are formed neither in a cultural vacuum nor purely at the level of discursive consciousness. Instead, food practices are shaped by influential cultural schemas linked to consumer culture (and related ideals of choice, luxury, and escape) and generate behaviours and pleasures that can contradict some consumers' political and ethical beliefs.

Feelings of guilt and anxiety were the by-products of a tension between consumer pleasures intuitively valued at WFM and normative commitments articulated more deliberately at the level of discursive consciousness. For Hugh, a 32-year-old physician who works with economically disadvantaged patients, the abundance and exclusivity that are hallmarks of the consumer culture on offer at WFM created feelings of ambivalence: "I walk in there and I definitely get a bit of a sick feeling in my stomach and sometimes *a lot* of a sick feeling in my stomach, you know, especially when I walk through and just look at the kind of prices they're charging." Hugh's remarks stand somewhat apart from those of most of the interviewees, who generally found pleasurable the very elements that Hugh found nauseating, but they also bring nuance to our analysis. While most shoppers framed their WFM experience as enjoyable (e.g. WFM's extensive product selection and feelings of luxurious exclusivity), not all consumers wholeheartedly embraced the shopping experience on offer. For those who experienced a tension between intuitive pleasures and political beliefs, shopping at WFM was fun but not a guilt-free experience.

The ambiguity expressed by some WFM consumers suggests that engagement with food culture is more complicated than a simple enjoyment of consumer pleasures. Consumers' engagement with food culture involves multiple (often competing) motivations, values, and norms. Specifically, we observed a complex relationship between the intuitive cultural schemas that generate consumer pleasure and the processes of deliberative consciousness that question or disrupt these pleasures. The attractive shopping environment at WFM is intended to make a banal household task like grocery shopping feel luxurious, fun, and "guilt-free." However, this strategy can backfire when consumer pleasures are examined at a critical discursive level. For some respondents, the by-products of the food culture on display at WFM—the higher prices, the exclusive atmosphere—were a source of discontent that pushed them to question their decision to shop there. In the next section, we examine how shoppers at Karma Co-op critique conventional consumer food culture but still experience pleasures associated with grocery shopping.

Resistance, Shopping Deliberately, and Alternative Hedonism: Karma Co-op

Compared to WFM, Karma Co-op is a much smaller, more democratic, and humbler market actor in the ethical foodscape. Member-owned and co-operatively managed, Karma Co-op is situated in a back alley in the Annex neighbourhood in downtown Toronto. Despite its smaller size, Karma stocks many staples of health-conscious and green lifestyles—soy milks, soba noodles, supplements, and local produce. Bulk goods and produce are weighed by members, and the checkout is usually staffed by a member doing their monthly work shift. Karma Co-op has existed in this guise since 1972 and currently has about 1,000 active member households.

We examine here how some Karma shoppers articulate a conscious decision to oppose the harmful aspects of the food system. They describe their food pleasures as alternatives to conventional consumer culture—a phenomenon we understand using the concept of alternative hedonism outlined in our introduction (Soper 2008). Karma shoppers' purposeful decisions to participate in and promote a different kind of food culture are sustained by the alternatively hedonistic pleasures they experience while shopping. We also explore some limitations to this consciously transformative food culture—namely, the persistence of dominant cultural schemas around food shopping.

A majority of the Karma shoppers interviewed expressed concerns about social and environmental issues in the food system and viewed Karma as a more ethical option than conventional grocery stores. Some respondents talked explicitly about their desire to resist consumer culture through shopping at Karma, commenting on how it exposed their families to "anti-consumerism ideals," for example. Shopping at Karma was also described by members as a way to avoid the feeling of manipulation in conventional shopping contexts and reclaim a sense of control. For Michela, a 31-year-old PhD student who noted feeling like a "puppet" in big supermarkets, Karma is different:

> I have my brain, I have my mind, I have my conscience and I feel not anyone is sending me in any direction. Actually, I'm more pro-active. . . . I know that there is something, like I'm conscious, like I'm not a puppet—I'm a member.

Michela's description of deliberate participation in the food culture at Karma contrasts with the remarks of WFM shoppers that describe feeling "sucked in" to a consumerist culture that some found politically problematic. Lorn, a 51-year-old graphic designer, reasoned that his appreciation of Karma resulted precisely from the potential for control, community, and connection: "It's 'cause I have some control over what's going on in [Karma]. . . . Like I'm involved and I have a stake and it's part of my community. There's connection there." Shopping at Karma involves engaging in the more labour-intensive food culture on offer at Karma through membership privileges and responsibilities (e.g. paying an annual membership fee, volunteering on committees, and for some, working shifts in the store). For many of the Karma interviewees, their participation with Karma involved a relatively high level of deliberate decision making, and fewer automatic, "non-thinking" pleasures that feel uncomfortable or contradictory (as we saw in the WFM case study).

This is not to say that Karma shoppers were ascetics who described lives devoid of culinary pleasures. A key aspect of alternative hedonism is the idea that disaffected consumers are not simply motivated by the moralistic satisfaction of "doing the right thing," but that consuming in an "alternative" way generates new pleasures that sustain greener lifestyles (Soper 2007:211). Based on our Karma interviews, we suggest that these kinds of "alternative hedonism" food cultures involve a dual cognitive process: a deliberative thought process (e.g. intentionally going out of one's way to choose Karma over a more convenient grocery chain), yet the ensuing pleasures are often experienced at the level of automatic consciousness and create positive associations. Without these automatic pleasures, it is not clear that deliberative consumer practices can become routine habits (see Soper 2009:3–4). More concretely, consumers may need some kind of hedonistic pay-off to make sense of shopping choices that are less convenient, cost more, or require more effort.

To explore this idea, we examine how Karma members discussed the pleasures of engaging with an alternative food culture. First we note that some Karma shoppers derived satisfaction from *not* consuming. Alternative hedonism draws attention not only to the pleasures obtained from new forms of consumption but also to the idea that non-consumption is gratifying (Soper 2007, 2008). Joschka, an 18-year-old teaching assistant, displayed this idea when he positively reflected on his consumption practices as "*not* doing stuff, that's basically what my kind of consumption is. Like *not* buying certain things."

Pleasures at Karma were not just about avoiding or minimizing consumption. For half of the shoppers interviewed, the sense of community and connection at Karma was described as an important source of pleasure and a primary reason for shopping at the co-op. Karma was described as a friendly place where members and staff greeted each other openly. Renee, a 28-year-old who works at a local college, summed up this common sentiment: "The people [at Karma] are friendlier. . . . And it's a lot easier here to have a quick chat with somebody." For Orly, a 23-year-old student, her desire for a shared community motivated her decision to join the co-op: "I wanted to [join] Karma because you're not just passing through, you know, you're making relationships and you're with people that want to make relationships with you." In these quotations, we see the dual-process dialectic of food culture at Karma: it is inspired by deliberative thought processes and intentional actions but sustained and associated with pleasures of community experienced at the level of practical, everyday consciousness.

Almost half of participants also identified pleasures in the co-op's shopping environment, even though it contrasts with the deluxe environment at WFM. While the Karma experience is less luxurious and more labour intensive (e.g. shoppers

Tara Walton/Toronto Star via Getty Images

Karma Food co-op employee Paul Dixon stocks the produce shelves. How do the supermarkets in your area differ in terms of what products are sold, how they have been sourced, and how they are laid out in the store? How might these differences impact a customer's decision to purchase food there?

weigh produce, pack groceries, and often clean up spills), shoppers identified precisely these characteristics as sources of pleasure. For Joschka, the laid-back attitude at Karma was enjoyable because "you don't feel so much as a customer as in different stores." Hong's comments suggest the automatic cognitive processes involved with going to Karma—an environment that he connected with the pleasures of being "home":

> It's just like going home, you know. . . . I don't know how to explain it. It just feels right when you go there. You work twenty-four hours a day, your energy's all drained, you go there, you look at the smiling faces, you feel good about it.

Hong's words suggest that his decision to go to the co-op is sustained at the level of practical consciousness: "it just feels right." Hong's sentiment partly echoed those of WFM shoppers, for whom shopping at WFM also felt deeply enjoyable though he emphasized the "smiling faces" of people at Karma and how shopping "feels right," rather than the massive selection or plush environment WFM shoppers enjoy (sometimes guiltily) as a vacation from everyday life. Karma members emphasized the *social* rather than the *aesthetic* qualities of the shopping environment. When Karma members did mention aesthetic qualities of Karma, these were often things that *did not align* with conventional aspects of consumer culture such as Karma's less polished decor, complete with mismatched light fixtures and exposed concrete floor.

Besides the pleasurable countercultural associations of the shopping environment, another source of pleasure for some Karma participants came from feeling more connected to their food source. Respondents spoke enthusiastically about the pleasure they felt supporting small, green, local producers at Karma, but they also commented about how these foods *tasted* good. By consuming foods that are both "good to think" and "good to eat" (Lévi-Strauss 1962), Karma shoppers aligned conscious thought processes to consume differently with more automatic culinary pleasures. Other Karma members described how shopping at Karma made them feel more balanced and harmonious. Moral values linked to "doing good" were intimately tied to the personal benefits of *feeling* good because of one's actions. In Joschka's words: "It gives you a new kind of pleasure knowing that you don't have such an impact on the world, meaning like negative impact. . . . generally, you feel more in harmony with the world."

In short, people's account of why they shop at Karma Co-op is evident at the level of deliberative consciousness—the intentional decision to shop differently and avoid big-box grocery stories—but is also based on pleasures experienced at the level of practical consciousness. The social (and sometimes aesthetic) pleasures of shopping at a small-scale, local co-op like Karma reinforces people's commitments to engaging with and contributing to an alternative food culture. However, not all Karma members saw the shopping experience as uniformly pleasurable or convenient. In some instances, Karma members expressed desires for aspects of consumer culture that are *less* available at Karma—elements that are generally associated with dominant cultural schemas around food and food shopping. In these cases, people seemed less able to detach themselves from the dominant cultural schemas of food shopping. For example, some shoppers who were very committed to the co-op acknowledged that the choice of products at Karma was limited. Lorn commented that "Karma's doesn't have the space to give members the choices that a lot of them want." Lorn's words recognize that the alternative pleasures available at Karma may be insufficient to attract and keep members at the co-op. For other members, pricing was an issue, especially for products like organic and free-range meats. Renee mentioned that she finds the high price of "happy meat" at Karma to be "quite difficult," and noted, "sometimes I decide that going conventional—like going to Sobey's and picking up some chicken breast is a better option for me that day."

Some respondents described Karma's shopping space as less convenient and efficient than a regular grocery store. The co-op's more restricted store hours (closed Mondays), limited parking (only two spots), and store organization were all identified as problematic. Lara, a 42-year-old member was frustrated by the lack of information about the ordering process, showing that the limited schedules of the co-op staff responsible for special ordering could be difficult to negotiate for a newcomer and a busy professional.

While the majority of respondents expressed positive feelings about shopping at Karma, the comments above show that consumer culture and the cultural schemas around food and food shopping—expectations of convenience, bountiful selection, and inexpensive meat—still reside in the cultural consciousness of Karma members. We have seen how the deliberate decision to consume differently at Karma is maintained through alternatively hedonistic culture of community and a feeling of hominess. However, dominant cultural schemas around food and shopping also compete for members' attention—especially when they suggest easier, less costly grocery options. In some cases, the alternatively hedonistic pleasures offered at Karma are insufficient, and shoppers decide to make more conventional shopping choices. For these shoppers, the decision to continue supporting Karma Co-op may be re-examined in the long term, especially as big-box grocery chains offer more "green," "feel-good" options (e.g. organic milk, fair-trade coffee, local produce) that seem cheaper and more convenient.

Conclusion

Building a more sustainable and equitable food system is an economic and political as well as a *cultural* project. While agency is undeniably involved in our food choices, we have drawn from cultural sociology to suggest that food culture both enables and constrains our eating practices. More specifically, the cultural schemas of a dominant consumer culture exert tremendous influence on food habits, desires, and preferences—often in ways that reside at the level of practical consciousness, and thus are not fully examined or articulated by consumers. Challenging the schematic assumptions of the dominant food culture (e.g. that food should be cheap and bountiful regardless of seasonality) is key to food system transformations; however, these challenges take shape within a larger capitalist context where corporate actors often incorporate cultural resistance into their brands (e.g. Frank 1997; Johnston et al. 2009).

We have looked at two cases that illustrate both sides of a dual-process understanding of culture and the idea that culture is both constraining and enabling. The WFM case demonstrates how consumers seek out consumer pleasures at WFM while being shaped by a food culture that prioritizes consumer choice, convenience, luxury, and sensory indulgences. Even highly politicized shoppers found it difficult to

resist the pull of WFM, a finding we interpret by examining dominant cultural schemas around shopping. Some WFM consumers experienced a contradiction between their political *ideas* and the sensory pleasures they enjoyed at WFM, and reported feelings of guilt, anxiety, and ambiguity. In these cases, the cultural schemas supporting an automatically pleasurable response to WFM are challenged and overshadowed by more deliberative cognitive processes (e.g. asking questions about who can access healthy, sustainable food). Our interviews confirm that consumers experience corporate food cultures in multi-faceted ways that may resist the framing presented by corporations. However, our findings also suggest that corporate food cultures within a broader ethical foodscape can be immensely attractive at the level of practical consciousness, even to people who have highly developed political critiques of a corporate-dominated food system. In short, the WFM case speaks to how the dominant food culture can "use" us, potentially constraining and lessening our desires for food system transformation.

Our Karma Co-op interviews prominently featured deliberate efforts to create an alternative food culture: members intentionally choose to shop in a less convenient place with less product selection and a less glamorous environment. Karma members described efforts to resist the dominant corporate food culture, which they understood as unsustainable and unjust, and to support an alternative food culture more in keeping with their political principles. While we observed deliberative consciousness at work in Karma members' thoughtful ideas and actions, we also saw ample evidence of pleasures automatically experienced—a sense of community among like-minded people, delicious local products, and a feeling of "harmony" achieved when one's principles matched up with culinary pleasures. While motivations for shopping at Karma varied, the lens of alternative hedonism is an apt concept for understanding many of the pleasures discussed. As noted, these pleasures were not completely in line with conventional consumer pleasures—they represented an attempt to support a deliberately transformative food culture by consuming differently or by not consuming at all. However, we are careful not to paint a monochromatic picture of Karma shoppers, since dominant cultural schemas of shopping (as convenient, cheap, abundant) were evident in some member's critiques of Karma.

The question that our WFM and Karma interviews raise about food cultures is a daunting one: How can food consumers build a more deliberative, reflexive food culture? In popular discourse, this question is often discussed in simple, individualized, and moralistic terms: either a consumer chooses "good food" (e.g. sustainable, non-exploitative, local, organic, grass-fed), or they ignore ethics and make "bad" food choices (e.g. fast food). Looking at the influence of culture on food choices allows us to frame the issue with greater nuance, empathy, and sensitivity to culture's constraining dimensions. Not only does culture interact with inequalities of race, class, and gender, but *multiple* cultural factors shape food choices, tastes, and culture. For example, powerful political-economic actors shape our food culture, creating a food system dominated by unhealthy, unsustainable foods that most of us develop a taste for (Carolan 2015). In addition, people's food tastes are shaped by their classed upbringing

and their habitus (Bourdieu 1984). Cultural schemas around food shopping and food prices further shape our tastes, and are in turn influenced by a broader consumer culture valorizing cheap prices and convenience. Our consumer case study has also shown that individual food commitments do not seamlessly match up with food practices and routines; all food consumers live with multiple contradictions in their everyday lives (e.g. Do you buy the *organic* strawberry? The non-organic *local* strawberry? Or the cheapest non-organic, non-local strawberry option available?).

Put simply, food consumers do not live in a bubble of rational economic decision-making. They—we—live in a specific cultural (and political-economic) context where dominant schemas around food shopping make corporate supermarket shopping feel immensely attractive and appealing. Certainly, the pleasures of alternative hedonism at places like Karma are a hopeful sign in the ethical foodscape, and a necessary fuel sustaining efforts to build a more sustainable, socially just food culture. Still, Karma is a very small and relatively unusual player in the larger foodscape. This suggests that food scholars and citizens alike need to devote more attention to understanding how alternative hedonism can move beyond specific subcultures and become a mass movement of delicious, sustainable, and accessible food pleasures.

Discussion Questions

1. How does culture influence eating practices? More concretely, what kinds of food culture promote healthy, environmentally friendly food choices? What kinds of food culture undermine these choices?

2. When (and how frequently) do food choices involve practical consciousness (e.g. habits, emotional eating)? When (and how frequently) do people draw on a deliberative level of consciousness to make food choices, and why?

3. What factors motivate consumers to consume sustainable foods produced with fair labour practices (e.g. fair-trade chocolate)? Do you agree with Kate Soper that *pleasurable* rewards are necessary to sustain alternative food practices?

Further Reading

Alternative Hedonism

1. Soper, Kate. 2007. "Re-thinking the 'Good Life': The Citizenship Dimension of Consumer Disaffection with Consumerism." *Journal of Consumer Culture* 7(2):205–29.

   An introduction to the concept of "alternative hedonism" and how it fits into the larger context of an analysis of contemporary consumption.

How Culture Works

2. Swidler, Ann. 1986. "Culture in Action: Symbols and Strategies." *American Sociological Review* 51:273–86.

   Swidler argues that culture is not a singular force, but should be viewed as a mixed bag of tools that individuals select either to sustain habitual action or to explore new ways of being in the world.

3. Vaisey, Stephen. 2009. "Motivation and Justification: A Dual-Process Model of Culture in Action." American Journal of Sociology 114(6):1675–715.

   Finding the idea of culture as repertoire insufficient, Vaisey develops the dual-process model that posits that culture both motivates (i.e. pushes one toward) and justifies (i.e. explains) action.

Consumer Culture and Ethical Eating

4. Johnston, Josée. 2008. "The Citizen-Consumer Hybrid: Ideological Tensions and the Case of Whole Foods Market." *Theory and Society* 37:229–70.

   This article explores the tensions between the competing and often contradictory dimensions of "consumerism" and "citizenship" using the case of Whole Foods Market.

5. Sassatelli, Roberta. 2007. *Consumer Culture: History, Theory and Politics.* Thousand Oaks, CA: Sage.

   A highly nuanced "introduction" to consumer culture, this book masterfully incorporates economic, institutional, historical, theoretical, and political analyses.

Video Suggestion

1. Kenner, Robert. 2008. *Food Inc.* www.takepart.com/foodinc. 93 min.

   An excellent overview of the forces behind the dominant corporate foodscape, and the subsequent rise of an ethical foodscape populated by greener, organic, local alternatives.

Note

1. The data in this chapter is based on semistructured one-hour interviews with 20 Karma Co-op shoppers and 20 Whole Foods Market shoppers, recorded and transcribed verbatim by Michelle Szabo. We gratefully acknowledge the invaluable assistance she provided carrying out this research.

References

Adorno, Theodor W. 1975. "Culture Industry Reconsidered." *New German Critique* 6:12–19.

Belasco, Warren. 1989. *Appetite for Change.* Ithaca, NY: Cornell University Press.

Bittman, M. 2008. *Food Matters: A Guide to Conscious Eating with More than 75 Recipes.* Toronto: Simon & Shuster.

Boudon, Raymond. 1998. "Social Mechanisms without Black Boxes." Pp. 172–203 in *Social Mechanisms: An Analytical Approach to Social Theory*, ed. P. Hedström and R. Swedberg. New York: Cambridge University Press.

Bourdieu, Pierre. 1984. *Distinction: A Social Critique of the Judgement of Taste.* Cambridge, MA: Harvard University Press.

Cairns, Kate, Josée Johnston, and Shyon Baumann. 2010. "Caring about Food: Doing Gender in the Foodie Kitchen." *Gender & Society* 24:591–615.

Caplan, Pat. 1997. "Approaches to the Study of Food, Health

and Identity." Pp. 1–31 in *Food, Health and Identity*, ed. Pat Caplan. New York: Routledge.

Cappeliez, Sarah, and Josée Johnston. 2013. "From Meat and Potatoes to 'Real-Deal' Rotis: Exploring Everyday Culinary Cosmopolitanism." *Poetics* 41(5):433–55.

Carolan, Michael. 2011. *The Real Cost of Cheap Food*. NY: Taylor and Francis.

———. 2015. "Affective Sustainable Landscapes and Care Ecologies: Getting a Real Feel for Alternative Food Communities." *Sustainablility Science* 10(2):317–29.

Chaiken, Shelly, and Yaacov Trope. 1999. *Dual-Process Theories in Social and Cognitive Psychology*. New York: Guilford.

Cohen, Lizabeth. 2003. *A Consumer's Republic: The Politics of Mass Consumption in Postwar America*. New York: Knopf.

de Laat, Kim, and Shyon Baumann. 2014. "Caring Consumption as Marketing Schema: Representations of Motherhood in an Era of Hyperconsumption." *Journal of Gender Studies* (February):1–17.

DeVault, M. 1991. *Feeding the Family*. Chicago: University of Chicago Press.

DiMaggio, P. 1997. "Culture and Cognition." *Annual Review of Sociology* 23:263–87.

Frank, Thomas. 1997. *The Conquest of Cool*. Chicago: University of Chicago Press.

Giddens, Anthony. 1984. *The Constitution of Society: Outline of a Theory of Structuration*. Berkeley: University of California Press.

Goodman, Mike, Damian Maye, and Lewis Holloway. 2010. "Ethical Foodscapes?: Premises, Promises and Possibilities." *Environment and Planning A* 42(8):1782–96.

Haidt, Jonathon. 2001. "The Emotional Dog and Its Rational Tail: A Social Intuitionist Approach to Moral Judgement." *Psychological Review* 108(4):814–34.

Johnston, Josée. 2008. "The Citizen-Consumer Hybrid: Ideological Tensions and the Case of Whole Foods Market." *Theory and Society* 37:229–70.

——— and Shyon Baumann. 2015 [2010]. *Foodies: Democracy and Distinction in the Gourmet Foodscape*. 2nd edn. New York: Routledge.

———, Andrew Biro, and Norah MacKendrick. 2009. "Lost in the Supermarket: The Corporate Organic Foodscape and the Struggle for Food Democracy." *Antipode: A Radical Journal of Geography* 41(3):509–32.

——— and Kate Cairns. 2012. "Eating for Change." Pp. 219–39 in *Commodity Activism: Cultural Resistance in Neoliberal Times*, ed. Sarah Banet-Wiser and Roopali Mukherjee. New York: New York University Press.

——— and Michael Goodman. 2015. "Food Celebrities and the Politics of Lifestyle Mediation in an Age of Inequality." *Food, Culture and Society* 18(2):205–22.

——— and Michelle Szabo. 2011. "Reflexivity and the Whole

Foods Market Consumer: The Lived Experience of Shopping for Change." *Agriculture and Human Values* 28(3):303–19.

——— and Ali Rodney. 2015. "Whole Foods Market." *Blackwell Encyclopedia of Sociology*, ed. George Ritzer. Malden, MA: Blackwell.

Lévi-Strauss, Claude. 1962. *La pensée sauvage*. Paris: Plon.

Lorenzen, Janet. 2014. "Convincing People to Go Green: Managing Strategic Action by Minimising Political Talk." *Environmental Politics* 23(3):1–19.

Marcuse, Herbert. 1991 [1964]. *One Dimensional Man*. NY: Beacon Press.

Moss, Michael. 2013. *Salt, Sugar, Fat: How the Food Giants Hooked Us*. Toronto: McClelland & Stewart.

Pollan, Michael. 2006. *The Omnivore's Dilemma: A Natural History of Four Meals*. New York: Penguin.

Roth, Geneen. 2010. *Women, Food and God: An Unexpected Path to Almost Everything*. Toronto: Scribner.

Saguy, Abigail, and Kjerstin Gruys. 2010. "Morality and Health: News Media Constructions of Overweight and Eating Disorders." *Social Problems* 57(2):231–50.

Slater, Don. 1997. *Consumer Culture and Modernity*. Cambridge, MA: Blackwell.

Soper, Kate. 2007. "Re-thinking the 'Good Life': The Citizenship Dimension of Consumer Disaffection with Consumerism." *Journal of Consumer Culture* 7(2):205–29.

———. 2008. "Alternative Hedonism, Cultural Theory and the Role of Aesthetic Revisioning." *Cultural Studies* 22(5):567–87.

———. 2009. "Introduction: The Mainstreaming of Counter-Consumerist Concern." Pp. 1–24 in *The Politics and Pleasures of Consuming Differently*, ed. K. Soper, M. Ryle, and L. Thomas. London: UK: Palgrave.

Spillman, Lyn. 2010. "Culture." *Blackwell Concise Encyclopedia of Sociology*, ed. George Ritzer and Michael Ryan. Malden, MA: Blackwell.

Swidler, Ann. 1986. "Culture in Action: Symbols and Strategies." *American Sociological Review* 51:273–86.

———. 2001. *Talk of Love: How Culture Matters*. Chicago: University of Chicago Press.

Vaisey, Stephen. 2008. "Socrates, Skinner, and Aristotle: Three Ways of Thinking About Culture in Action." *Sociological Forum* 23(3):603–13.

———. 2009. "Motivation and Justification: A Dual-Process Model of Culture in Action." *American Journal of Sociology* 114(6):1675–715.

Williams, Raymond. 1976. *Keywords: A Vocabulary of Culture and Society*. London: Fontana.

Winson, Anthony. 1993. *The Intimate Commodity: Food and the Development of the Agro-Industrial Complex in Canada*. Toronto: University of Toronto Press.

———. 2004. "Bringing Political Economy into the Debate on the Obesity Epidemic." *Agriculture and Human Values* 21(4):299–312.

4 Canada's Food History through Cookbooks

Nathalie Cooke

Learning Objectives

Through this chapter, you can

1. Discover some of Canada's most important historical cookbooks

2. Recognize that cookbooks offer valuable insight into changing social roles (particularly within families and communities) and food tastes over time, in addition to information about food preparation

3. Identify ways and moments in which cookbooks identify their strategic objectives in order to sensitize readers to ways of decoding ideologically charged information contained in cookbooks

4. Understand moments of pivotal social change as identified by Canadian cookbooks

Introduction

What factors have influenced our eating habits over time in Canada? The question is not an innocent one, posed out of idle curiosity. Rather it is an urgent question, posed during a time when, despite the increasing knowledge about nutrition and health, we are unable to stem rising obesity rates and illnesses born of poor dietary habits. Yet we cannot identify how we make **food choices** today and improve our choices without understanding how and why we made food choices in the past. After all, most would agree that the goal of the home food provider is to serve fare that promotes health and well-being. But in the twentieth century alone, perceptions of how to achieve health and well-being have varied dramatically. For early settlers, for example, well-being meant a full belly. In the 1920s it depended upon milk, the "perfect" food. By 1942, when

Canada's dietary guidelines were introduced, it was perceived as resulting from a varied, full diet. By the 1980s, cookbook writers were promoting "lighter fare" and guidelines to limit, rather than increase, Canadians' food intake. For those of us interested in charting the history and shaping of taste, food choices indicate changing tastes and signal key factors motivating and defining moments of pivotal change. Canadian cookbooks, first published in 1840, are a window through which to glimpse changing food tastes and habits over the last 150 years.[1]

Overview

Canadian **foodways** have involved a fine balance between change and continuity, adoption or refusal of exotic foods and food innovations.

However, since a comprehensive overview of Canadian foodways is beyond this study's scope, this chapter addresses the question—"What factors have influenced our eating habits over time in Canada?"—by looking closely at cookbooks, which are rich resources of information about foodways at a given time and place.

In *À table en Nouvelle-France*, Yvon Desloges, looking specifically at the foodways of New France and later Quebec, posits and credibly defends a framework of five periods of culinary practice:

1. 1605 to 1690, beginning when the first French settlers arrived and encountered Amerindian food practices
2. 1690 to 1790, when one ate "à la française," or in the French style
3. 1790 to 1860, when there was an exchange between French and British foodways resulting from the influx of British in Quebec city following the battle on the Plains of Abraham in 1759
4. 1860 to 1960, when one ate "à la canadienne," and the Dominion of Canada set about establishing its own distinctive traditions
5. 1967 to the present, when Canadian foodways were shaped by international culinary influences (2009:145)

Desloges's model is effective in part because of its clear focus. However, as one ponders ways to expand the model beyond New France to reference Canadian foodways more generally, the notion of a singular Canadian culture becomes increasingly problematic. Under what conditions can we justifiably use the first-person plural—"we Canadians"—about a country of such diversity? Given a multicultural population formed by successive waves of immigrants from around the world, as well as the land's First Nations, skepticism about a singular culinary culture is understandable. Nevertheless, Canadian cookbook bibliographer Elizabeth Driver finds varying degrees of similarity in cookbooks across regions and over time. She writes, "I looked at over 2,200 individual works and noticed little regional variation in the form and content of the daily meal in works published before 1950" (Driver 2008:198). Certainly, since the 1950s, considerable energy has been spent articulating a distinctively Canadian culinary tradition—with emphasis on the **connotation** of commensality evoked by such a shared tradition. As Rhona Richman Kenneally points out, the 1967 centennial celebrations prompted an outpouring of nationalistic narratives, ironically at a time when Canada was recognizing not only its multicultural heritage but also its pride in the cultural wealth it afforded (2009:168–9). These narratives evoke national distinctiveness through reference to shared foodways traditions as well as reliance on specific and readily available ingredients (for example, the bacon colloquially dubbed "Canadian bacon" outside Canada, salmon, maple syrup). Today, we might add a number of distinctively Canadian foods to the list because of their recent rise to **iconic** status: butter tarts; Nanaimo bars, named after a town on Vancouver Island; poutine, the cheese-curd delicacy from Quebec that gained culinary celebrity in New York in 2007; deep-fried, yeast-raised beaver tails, best enjoyed in winter when skating on the Rideau Canal in Ottawa; or Tim Hortons doughnuts, named after the hockey legend.

The first pulse of Canada's project to identify distinct food practices was felt in the nineteenth century, which saw the rise of the printing industry and literacy rates, and the emergence of cookbooks published in Canada and aimed at a specifically Canadian audience. This desire to distinguish things Canadian can be found in the title of one of the earliest cookbooks, *La cuisinière canadienne* (1840), as in many subsequent ones, including the classic 1923 *Canadian Cook Book* (the first edition of many). Also promoting a taste of place were recipes using locally sourced foods, such as those recorded by Lynn Thornton for rhubarb juice and partridge pie in *From the Kitchens of Kings Landing* (1995), a collection of recipes dating from nineteenth-century New Brunswick. This focus on local produce is all the more significant since ingredients such as pineapple and recipes for curry in the "Indian mode" in Mrs Margaret Leighton McMicking's *The King's Daughters Cookery Book* (1904) suggest diverse influences and plentiful supplies of exotic foods relatively early, at least on the Pacific coast of British Columbia.

By the mid-twentieth century, it seems that many cookbook authors, in addition to assuming or identifying a national cuisine, wanted to share distinctive foodways traditions. Best known, perhaps, are the Mennonite cookbooks of Edna Staebler, including *Food That Really Schmecks* (1968). However, as Driver has found, cookbooks as early as the 1940s began to define ethnic foodways, either in distinct sections in mainstream texts or in recipe manuals produced by ethnic groups. By the 1950s Canada's cookbooks revealed a wealth of diverse food traditions through recipes for distinctive ethnic dishes appearing alongside those for the Anglo-Scots' fare familiar to early twentieth-century readers of Canadian cookbooks (Driver 2009:206–7). Certainly by 1970, Canadian cookbooks catering to divergent palates and inclinations were the norm, and one must assume that Canadian meals featured an extraordinary diversity of food items as well.

Interestingly, there is considerable evidence to suggest that the sea change in food practice in the mid-twentieth century—from homogeneity to diversity or from shared to distinctive tastes and habits—was rooted not in Canada's growing multiculturalism and its eventual official recognition, but rather in the contemporary zeitgeist more generally, both in North America and abroad. In the years following the Second World War, soldiers who had tasted the culinary fare of other countries returned home. At the same time, Canadians prospered and began to travel for leisure; they also began to explore the world through their television screens. Despite a prescriptive emphasis on the nuclear family and traditional values in magazine articles and advertisements, change was in the air. In an insightful analysis of New Zealand foodways, Michael Symons points to the 1960s as a time when the "food industry shifted into a new mode" and suggests that 1963 marked a significant turning point in international culinary traditions (2006:180–1).

Paradoxically, while Canadians increasingly tasted different foods from around the world, the rise of corporate advertising and technological innovation enabled efficient and affordable production of processed foods—big business promoting big brands. This development increased normalization of food tastes and practices. For example, gelatin powder, introduced at the beginning of the twentieth century, dramatically reduced the preparation time of jellies. Not only was the gelatin powder produced and sold in Canada and the United States similar to that in New Zealand, but so too were the cookbooklets promoting the "dainty" dishes that could be prepared with this versatile product.[2] Similarly, cake mixes were carefully developed to produce a successful cake in a variety of conditions; one wonders if there was a difference between a cake made from a mix north of the forty-ninth parallel and one to the south. Certainly companies developing packaged foods were often multinational, with satellite or branch offices in various countries.

Policy and technology innovations affecting Canadian foodways can be traced through Canadian cookbooks. For example, Canadian cookbooks record Canada's adoption of the metric system in the 1970s. New cooking technologies were quickly followed by cookbooks to train home food providers in their use, such as *Speed Cooking with Your New General Electric GE Range* (1948), and the many works of Quebecers Norene Gilletz and Jehane Benoît introducing Canadians to cooking methods for the microwave oven and the food processor. Today's readers will find it ironic that *The Modern Cook Book*, compiled in 1923 by the Imperial Order Daughters of the Empire, looks to the past and the future through ads lauding the "modern" convenience of the electric range in addition to ones extolling the virtues of gas and coal-fired stoves. Perhaps it was "modern" precisely because the future was to be seen in comparison with the past?

Promotional cookbooks document the introduction and use of specific food products. Companies produced and distributed these cookbooks, incorporating recipes designed to highlight their own products, which were often featured in advertisements with the books. Published by the Kellogg Company, for example, *The Housewife's Almanac: A Book for Homemakers* (1938) advocates a regular diet of Kellogg's All-Bran cereal, along with a number of tips for homemakers in sections entitled "How to Acquire and Develop Winning Ways" and "The Canadian Wedding."

Review of Literature and Commentary

Canada's 1967 centennial celebrations, including Montreal's Expo '67, gave impetus to food studies in Canada by launching a period of intense introspection that continues today. Canadians began to review and revise past and present culinary practices—to figure food (sometimes retrospectively) as a symbol of self, community, and nation. Cookbooks began to appear on bedside tables and desks as well as on kitchen counters, and they gained currency as signifiers of societal change rather than being merely culinary handbooks.

During the past few decades, much light has been shed on Canada's food history to identify moments of pivotal change and continuity: first by cookbook writers and cooks in historical kitchens tasked with understanding and reproducing historical recipes; next by bibliographers and **culinary historians**; and, most recently, by scholars in such diverse disciplines as anthropology, cultural and communications studies, economics, geography, gastronomy, history, sociology, social studies of medicine, and women's studies.

How can we trace and precisely identify changes in the ways Canadians eat? Exploring the relationship between food choices and larger patterns of taste must rely on a wide and diverse range of cultural artifacts, as well as discursive and visual texts: recipes and cookbooks, novels, journals, maps, menus, product packaging and advertising, photos, postcards, and floor plans, to name only a few. Always present for the researcher is the danger of confusing **prescriptive practice**—what people are told or advised to do—with **descriptive practice**—what they actually do.

While such an open set of possibilities was daunting to those determined to categorize and quantify, for those eager to pioneer the new field of Canadian food studies and to explore food and the shaping of taste in the latter decades of the twentieth century, such breadth of possibility was nothing short of exhilarating. Certainly an enthusiasm for the range of possibilities is evident in the pioneering publication *A Century of Canadian Home Cooking* by Carol Ferguson and Margaret Fraser (1992). Pat Beeson's *Macdonald Was Late for Dinner* (1993) is another labour of love, containing historical photographs, menus, and recipes. Such enthusiasm was crucial in sustaining Driver in her quest to identify every cookbook longer than 16 pages published in Canada before 1950 (the final count was 2,276 titles, many published in several editions) for *Culinary Landmarks: A Bibliography of Canadian Cookbooks, 1825–1949*.

The number of courses, colloquia, and publications relating to food history has increased exponentially during the past two decades, which should not distract from the significant role played earlier in the twentieth century by those passionate about teaching and learning about food and its history in Canada. Well known were individuals who took on iconic status, such as Kate Aitken, Jehane Benoît, Soeur Sainte-Marie Edith, Soeur Berthe, Soeur Angèle, Elizabeth Baird, Anne Lindsay, and Rose Murray. Others appeared on stage or penned articles using pseudonyms including Edith Adams for the *Vancouver Sun*, Penny Powers for the Saskatchewan Power Corporation, Marie Fraser for the Dairy Food Services Bureau, Brenda York for Canada Packers, and Rita Martin for Robin Hood Multifoods.

Food writers and journalists also played a crucial role in cementing the link between food and its various contexts, including Margo Oliver, author of *Classical Canadian Recipes* (1993), and food columnist Julian Armstrong, author of *A Taste of Quebec* (1990). Incidentally, that Armstrong is a food writer using her own name, while her aunt a generation earlier wrote about food under a pseudonym, indicates the rapidly changing norms surrounding women's roles in the workforce in mid-century Canada. *A Taste of History, the Origins of Quebec's Gastronomy* (1989) by historians Yvon Desloges and Marc Lafrance is another important source of information about Quebec foodways.

A key forum of discussion was the 1993 conference "Northern Bounty," which gave rise to a collection of essays by culinary professionals and writers, edited by Jo Marie Powers and Anita Stewart (1995). It also served to launch the organization Cuisine Canada. Carol Ferguson and Margaret Fraser's *A Century of Canadian Home Cooking* (1992) and Dorothy Duncan's *Canadians at Table* (2006) represent the most comprehensive discussion of Canadian foodways to date. While Ferguson and Fraser provide an illustrated overview of what was happening in Canadian kitchens through the twentieth century—in a remarkably handsome book that, admittedly, first piqued my interest in the subject—Duncan provides an accessible and engaging introduction to food's role in Canadian history. For example, she explains how the outcome of competition between the two titans of the fur trade—the North West Company and the Hudson's Bay Company—hinged on pemmican, a food substance invaluable to those travelling great distances, made from powdered dried meat mixed with berries and sealed in a bag with grease (2006:49–50). This analysis stands in my mind as one of the best examples of how focusing on an often-overlooked food item can give rise to profound insights.[3]

Canada is also lucky to have a number of cookbook writers whose work provides readers with a glimpse into regional history: Marie Nightingale's *Out of Old Nova Scotia Kitchens* (1971) is a fine example. Beulah (Bunny) Barss, through illustrated cookbooks, draws her readers into an understanding of pioneering foodways in Alberta (see, for example, the 1988 *Alberta Pictorial Cookbook*). More recently, in *Flavours of Canada* (2000), Anita Stewart provides an updated and lavishly illustrated overview of Canada's diverse bounty and the recipes developed to celebrate it, a theme also emerging in *Anita Stewart's Canada—the Food, the Recipes, the Stories* (2008), *From Pemmican to Poutine* by Suman Roy and Brooke Ali (2010), and *True North* by Derek Dammann and Chris Johns (2015). Rose Murray's *A Taste of Canada* (2008) provides an enjoyable and educational introduction to the regional variety of Canada's foods and fascinating insights into Canada's food history. It is from Murray that we learn that canning was revolutionized and popularized by the patenting of the Mason jar in 1858 (2008:161) and that buffalo hump and moose nose featured on the Christmas menu served at Fort Edmonton in 1847 (2008:59).

Most recently, the Internet has provided us with unprecedented access to historical cookbooks; blogs and Twitter feeds also provide valuable insights into treasures emerging from the pages of both published and unpublished manuscript cookbooks. The virtual library tool provided by Library and Archives Canada's *Early Canadiana Online*[4] is at the forefront of open-access resources, while public and research libraries are gradually digitizing their cookbook collections, providing digital access to texts no longer under copyright restriction and also highlighting insights through blogs and Twitter feeds. The Toronto Public Reference Library, for example, provides a downloadable version of the first edition of Catharine Parr Traill's *The Female Emigrant's Guide* (1854).[5] At the time of printing there is no Canadian equivalent to the Manuscript Cookbooks Survey, a searchable database of manuscript cookery books held in a consortium of public institutions in the United States.[6] However, major print collections of Canadian cookbooks are housed in the libraries of the Universities of Guelph, Alberta, and Toronto, as well as McGill University, and all are embarking on dissemination and digitization initiatives.

The Form and Function of Cookbooks

Astonishingly, only very recently have commentators in Canada and elsewhere begun to scrutinize the form and function of cookbooks, posing such questions as: What is a cookbook? Is a collection of recipes different in degree or in kind from a single recipe? What kinds of meaning do cookbooks convey?

One wonders whether the lack of a clear definition for the cookbook **genre** is less the result of scholarly trepidation than of scholarly elitism. After all, cookbooks do not participate in what Anne Bower (1997) calls the "status-bearing" forms of literature. Nor is a particular cookbook yet identified as a "classic" in the literary sense: "a work considered excellent of its kind, and therefore standard, fit to be used as a model or imitated."[7] Certainly, Ann Mendelson's *Stand Facing the Stove* (2003) strives to bestow status upon the American favourite, *The Joy of Cooking* (Rombauer 1931). However, her argument focuses on the attributes of this cookbook that rendered it more popular than its peers, thereby asserting its authority as a bestseller rather than as a classic. Further, since cookbooks strive to be timely as well as timeless, it is difficult for such a genre to produce a classic work, which, by definition, transcends time.

Thus positioned outside or, at best, on the margins of the literary taxonomy, cookbooks have not been deemed worthy of literary scrutiny—that is, until relatively recently. Two discussions of a key component of cookbooks—the recipe—surfaced in *PMLA*, the journal of the Modern Language Association of America. The first was Susan Leonardi's "Lobster à la Riseholme" (1989) and the second was David Herman's "Scripts, Sequences, and Stories: Elements of a Postclassical Narratology" (1997).

Neither one mentions earlier attempts to define the recipe, thus clearly distinguishing their particular literary inquiry from earlier approaches. Of these very few earlier commentaries, perhaps the most influential was M.F.K. Fisher's project of describing the three distinct parts of the "modern" recipe's "anatomy": the name, the ingredients, and the method (1968:23).

What Is a Recipe?[8]

In her influential article, Leonardi looks at the contexts of recipe giving, and in so doing, affords us a sense of what a recipe is. She begins by arguing that recipes are a form of "embedded discourse" that generally stems from a particular context. She states that her focus is on the "giving of the recipe" rather than on the list of ingredients and the directions for assembling them because, as she puts it, "such a list alone is, in fact, surprisingly useless, even for a fairly experienced cook, and surprisingly seldom encountered" (1989:340). This narrative frame constitutes what linguist Colleen Cotter calls "orientation components" (1997:60). Leonardi points out that "like a **story**, a recipe needs a recommendation, a context, a point, a reason to be" (1989:340). For Leonardi, then, the conventions of the recipe genre include

- "a persona" for the recipe giver with whom "readers could identify and trust" (1989:347)
- "the possibility of literalization outside the text" (1989:346)
- the use of second-person address, of the "you" (1989:347)

While Leonardi focuses on the recipe as a way of connecting people, narratologist David Herman focuses on the recipe as something that can make things happen, that can function as an agent of transformation. For Herman, a recipe, such as:

Remove pizza from box and inner wrapper . . . [and] place on preheated cookie sheet.

Bake for 16–18 minutes or until center cheese is melted and edges are golden brown.

is a sequence that can be identified as a recipe because it "tells not how something happened, in the manner of a story, but rather how to make something (good) happen, in the manner of a prescription or, more precisely, a recipe" (1997:1047). Thus, for Herman, the conventions of a recipe include

- prescriptive language that anticipates, describes, and directs literalization beyond the text
- "telling narratives," "describing," "arguing," and "greeting"—this prescriptive language allows the reader or recipient to reconcile "emergent with prior knowledge" (1997:1048)

Leonardi and Herman agree that recipes direct attention beyond their texts to the possibility of a future event—the preparation of the described dish. In so doing, they establish an affective relationship with the recipient. The two scholars differ in their location of agency, that is, their sense of where the action in and of a recipe takes place.

What Is a Cookbook?

Drawing on Leonardi's and Herman's observations, we could define a cookbook as a sequence of prescriptive narratives that both

- anticipate culinary realization outside the text
- are disseminated within a particular context that is signalled by the text in the form of an implied author (via the first-person pronoun) and implied reader (signalled and actualized by the second-person pronoun "you")

Thus, a primary emphasis on the dissemination of practical information seems to distinguish cookbooks from other forms of food-related texts,

including the four categories of "literary-culinary offspring" informally defined by Anne LeCroy: "general histories of human cuisine; essays with illustrative recipes; recipes introduced by metaphysical commentary; and fiction using recipes as vehicles for plot, character, or setting development" (1989:8). As Lynette Hunter observes, "any literary study of cookery books comes up against the fact that they exist primarily to communicate information and opinion, not as literary objects in and of themselves" (1980:19). A primary emphasis on prescription, then, seems to distinguish cookbooks from *literary* texts, which privilege aesthetic over practical concerns or, in other words, art over science. Nonetheless, commentators cannot ignore how recipes prompt readers to react and to act. Colleen Cotter, for example, acknowledges "one way to look at a recipe is as a form of narrative—a particular kind of storytelling—and viewing it formally and structurally as a narrative enriches our reading of it" (1997:52). If a recipe is so framed and mediated, then how much more so must be a collection of recipes, organized by prefatory comments? If a recipe can call up a cast of at least two characters, then how many more can be conjured in a whole cookbook?

If, however, one scrutinizes Canadian cookbooks' own claims about the genre (often articulated in a preface or introduction), one finds claims and aspirations that challenge the privileging of practical concerns over aesthetic ones. The most explicit assertions that cooking is an art, and not a mere skill or craft, appear in the French-language cookbooks. For example, in the 1957 edition of *La cuisine raisonnée*, cooking is described as a science and an art, related to the sciences of anatomy, physics, and chemistry, as well as hygiene. This cooking manual insists that cooking, albeit a science, is also an aesthetic outlet for women, who can exercise their aesthetic tastes (1957:vii). The tenth edition of the same cookbook elevates Canadian cuisine to an art form that accounts for emergent scientific and nutritional knowledge, as well as cultural values and socio-economic norms (1967:11).

If *La cuisine raisonnée* seems to put a heavy onus on the woman of the house to practise the art of cooking, it is nothing compared with the responsibilities bestowed by that formidable pillar of virtue, Mère Caron. As the figurehead of the Institute of Providence community at Longue-Pointe, Montreal, Quebec, the Reverend Mother urges women not only to practise the culinary art but also to become the model of Christian virtue. She stresses that a cook can be "truly Christian" because cooking requires patience, and that in old religious communities, the cook was the perfect model of all saintly virtues (1878:7). These precepts appear in the 1878 edition and in subsequent editions. In other words, they are aspirations unchanged by changing times.

Aesthetic aspirations, however, are not exclusive to the French-language cookbooks. In her domestic science textbook, Nellie Lyle Pattinson emphasizes the "art of cooking," instead of positioning cooking as "only one more job to be done" (1923:v). While English-language cookbooks also claim in their introductions that giving practical instructions is a means to higher ends, these ends are typically ideological rather than purely aesthetic.

One of those ideological ends is the promotion of Canadian nationalism. However, the first Canadian cookbook published (*The Cook Not Mad; or Rational Cookery*) was a reprint of an American book, whose authority depended on its wholesome "Americanness"; it contains "Good *Republican dishes* and garnishing, proper to fill an every day bill of fare" (1831:7). Another US import was a community cookbook entitled *The Home Cook Book*. It was nonetheless substantially revised by a committee of Toronto ladies and includes an introductory letter to the publisher by prominent Canadian editor and author George Stewart Jr. He suggests that the book has the potential to "supply the place of the Academy," which is crucial, he argues, because "the subject of cookery is of *national* importance" (1877:v).

These preliminary observations not only suggest that cookbooks lay heavy expectations upon the home food producer's shoulders but also signal that Leonardi's sense that recipes need "a recommendation, a context, a point, a reason to be" rings true for both cookbooks and recipes (1989:127). More generally, our understanding of the cookbook genre must enable us to understand it as a strategy rather than as a category of textual communication, one that is ideologically loaded rather than neutral.

Exceptions or Further Evidence?

Before accepting the conclusion that cookbooks employ rhetorical techniques to achieve aesthetic or ideological ends rather than merely giving instructions to achieve a tangible and practical goal, we should pause to scrutinize two seeming exceptions, both important to the Canadian cookbook canon.

The first of these is a group of cookbooks whose authority resides in the personal cooking experience of their authors, following in the tradition of Catharine Parr Traill's *The Female Emigrant's Guide* (1854). These books resist elevating culinary responsibilities to the realm of higher aesthetic or ideological purposes; yet, they comply with Leonardi's sense that recipes need to be "given," insofar as they contextualize their contents in a way that affects the reader. These cookbooks offer knowledge garnered from practical experience and invite readers to accept their authors as authorities because of that experience. For example, in *Mrs. Clarke's Cookery Book* (1883), Anne Clarke provides recipes that are "useful." In *The Dominion Home Cook Book*,[9] the anonymous author provides recipes of "practical utility" and, ironically, adds that "*every recipe,—every advice—every little piece of information, is the result of personal experience*" (1868:4). Mrs Flynn claims that her Charlottetown cookbook of about 1930 is "thoroughly practical" (Driver 2008:70), and it provides the "choicest bits of the best experience of those who have long traveled the daily round of household duties" (Lewis 1981:3). Even the title page of a francophone cookbook, the 1825 third edition of *La cuisinière bourgeoise* (first published in 1746), notes that a housewife has reviewed the text. In some ways, these claims are less modest than those made by cookbook authors who invite readers to join with them in their struggle to achieve religious, aesthetic, and nationalistic goals. But there is something very engaging about the first-person appeal of a cookbook author who claims first-hand kitchen know-how, even if her readers discover that she is skilled working with both words and food.

The second exception includes some of the most significant cookbooks in the Canadian canon, if one judges success on the basis of sales and successive new editions alone: namely, corporate cookbooklets.[10] This type of cookbook emerged with the rise of food manufacturing in the twentieth century, and it often featured "personal" testimonies of fictional corporate "spokespersons," some of whom, like the well-known North American Betty Crocker, actually "author" the cookbooks that contain "their" recipes and advice.[11] Although these were not real people, they put a human face on the corporate identity, and they created the illusion of being trustworthy and personable advisers for the home food provider. Speaking for Maple Leaf Foods, Anna Lee Scott claimed to have been "a dietitian, lecturer and adviser on household science" for many years (Scott, n.d., n.p.); while Rita Martin appears as a friendly and approachable woman—"just drop me a line. . . . I'd love to hear from you" (*The Velvet Touch*, n.d.). Martha Logan writes, "We . . . I mean myself and the other Home Economists who assist me . . . spend most of our time in the kitchen just as you do" (1942:3).

Rather than privileging a particular claim to authority, these cookbooks claim *multiple* authoritative sources, such as

- objective authority of science and innovation
- first-hand experience in the kitchen
- rigorous tests performed in industry food laboratories
- intimate understanding of the tastes and inclinations of the home food provider and her family

They also take advantage of the affective aspects of conventional cookbooks and exaggerate them by fabricating a fictional cookbook author. For example, Mary Blake of Carnation explains in "her" 1924 cookbook: "My own favorite recipes are contained here-in, one hundred of them, and I can promise that you will find them all thoroughly practical."[12] The introduction is signed by Blake, who allegedly works for the Domestic Science Department of Carnation Milk Products Company. Mary maintains her professional role but engages the attention of her readers by employing the first-person singular: "All of these recipes have been carefully tested in the Carnation kitchen, I am sure you will like them" (1924:2). This sense of certainty results both from the corporate backing of a company that tests its products and recipes extensively and from a culture awed by technology and the promise of modernity. The popular Five Roses cookbooks also tread a fine line between personal experience and corporate collaboration. One notes that recipes are drawn from "successful users of Five Roses Flour throughout Canada," but the author also maintains that they are "carefully checked and re-checked by [a] competent authority" (*Five Roses Cook Book* 1913). The fictitious Anna Lee Scott is the authority for both Maple Leaf Milling's brand, Monarch Flour, and Purity Flour in the late 1950s. "She" claims authority not only on baking, but also, as the title of her book *51 Ways to a Man's Heart* suggests, on things beyond the cooking world. A letter on the book's back cover, which bears an illustration of Scott and her "signature" reads: "It is many years since I began as a dietitian lecturer and adviser on household science." Rita Martin, with a name that translates into French easily with a shift in pronunciation, plays a similar role for Robin Hood Flour. Only Ogilvie Flour resisted this trend of putting a name, signature, or face to a corporation, as they provided an unnamed "expert woman" to give advice for *Ogilvie's Book for a Cook* (1905:5). Ironically, Ogilvie claimed to be both the manufacturer of flour of royal households and the publisher of recipes that suit the needs of the "average housekeeper . . . without calling too much upon her means" (1905:2).

Thus we find two seeming exceptions to the rule that cookbooks are highly mediated forms of communication—the cookbook author's claim to first-hand experience, and the multiple, often paradoxically conflicting claims such as those appearing in the corporate cookbooks. But, as further scrutiny here shows, these examples reinforce my suggestion that a cookbook is a strategic offering of a collection of recipes within a particularized context, and they further illustrate the constructed and contrived nature of that context.

Historical Transformation of the Cookery Books

As we view Canadian history through the lens of cookbooks, then, it is with the understanding that cookbooks are consciously shaped communications. In this way, five distinct periods emerge, each with its canon of prescriptions for the way a Canadian kitchen and household might best be managed: contact and settlement; consolidation; affiliation; articulation; and differentiation.[13] Rising literacy rates coincided with the first waves of Canadian immigration and settlement; thus cookery that declared itself to be distinctively "Canadian" was largely founded on the printed page rather than passed down through generations by word of mouth. As such, its formational history differs significantly from its culinary forebears—the Old World traditions of French and British cuisines, and American cuisine—and indeed from the long transmission of Indigenous knowledge of the Aboriginals of North America.

Contact and Settlement

In the mid-nineteenth century, the first Canadian cookbooks emerged as guidebooks for newly arrived Canadians, the best known being Catharine Parr Traill's *The Female Emigrant's Guide* (1854) and A.B. of Grimsby's *Frugal Housewife's Manual* (1840), as well as *La cuisinière canadienne* (1840) and *La nouvelle cuisinière canadienne* (1850). While immigrants certainly carried with them cookbooks from the Old World, these first Canadian cookbooks were self-conscious about their role as texts constructed for those intending to make a life in the New World. Traill writes, "[I] confine my recipes to dishes that are more peculiar to the cookery of Canada" (1854:126) and "This is not a regular cookery book; but is confined to the preparing of food, as practiced in this country" (1854:153).

Consolidation

During the last decades of the nineteenth century, cookbooks consolidated knowledge gleaned from various sources for Canadian home cooks. The best known of these include *The Home Cook Book* (1877), *Canadian Housewife's Manual of Cookery* (Richards and Richards 1861), *Mrs. Clarke's Cookery Book* (Clarke 1883), and *Directions diverses données par la Rev. Mère Caron* (Caron 1878). The consolidation of culinary knowledge in this period was intended to serve the Canadian cook in her kitchen, but it was also the first step in a larger program of consolidation that would both give rise to a sense of a distinctly Canadian cuisine and position cookbooks as vehicles for articulating Canadian tastes and values. In some ways, then, the period of consolidation might be seen to extend to the latter half of the twentieth century, reaching a crescendo in 1967.

As guides on household management, these books often contain advice on decorum. *The Home Cook Book*, a fundraising project for the Hospital for Sick Children in Toronto, and notable as the first example of the fundraising genre of cookbooks in Canada, has sections on "Housekeeping," "Table Talk," "The Little Housekeepers," and "Social Observances." Although intended as practical manuals for household management in the nineteenth century, for twenty-first-century readers they provide valuable insights into domestic ritual, supplies and their availability in different regions of Canada and at different times in its history, advances in technology and nutritional science, and shifts in taste and philosophy.

Affiliation

At the beginning of the twentieth century, many cookbooks were affiliated with institutions rather than individuals. Such corporate cookbooks as *Five Roses Cook Book/La cuisinière Five Roses* (1913), as well as those of the Purity and Ogilvie Flour companies, became valued resources in Canadian homes. Further, single-author cookbooks gained credibility from their association with educational institutions. Nellie Lyle Pattinson, for example, developed the trusted *The Canadian Cook Book* (1923) as a textbook for the cooking school of which she was director; similarly, in Quebec the popular *Manuel de cuisine raisonnée* (1919) was used in homes and classrooms.

These textbooks found audiences outside the classroom throughout the twentieth century. In October 2004, the Quebec newspaper *La Presse* surveyed readers about their favourite cookbooks. Both the classic *Five Roses Cookbook* and the 1945 classic *La cuisine raisonnée* made the shortlist, with rationales explaining their trustworthy and timeless recipes. One reader comments:

> My preferred book is *La cuisine raisonnée* by the Congrégation Notre-Dame. I have had it since 1962. I find it practical, with simple and economical recipes. I raised my daughters with this cooking, and if somebody asks me for cooking tips, this is where I find them. This book is invaluable. It is the oldest one I have. (as cited in Marquis 2009:221)

Articulation

Home economics was professionalized in Canada in 1939. As home economists took up positions not only as teachers and dieticians but also as corporate and public spokespeople, cookbooks—alongside radio and, later, television

shows—channelled the articulation of Canadian identity. Cookbooks by Kate Aitken (fondly known as "Mrs A." to her audiences), such as *Kate Aitken's Canadian Cook Book* (1945), and by Jehane Benoît (or "Mme B."), such as *L'encyclopédie de la cuisine canadienne* (1963), stirred an emerging sense of shared national identity. At first glance, then, what characterizes this period is the clear vision of a distinctively Canadian cuisine. Another form of articulation appeared in this period, one that has received virtually no scrutiny to date. Culinary authorities of this time—and both Mrs A. and Mme B. are excellent examples—began to establish themselves as significant forces in the culinary scene in their own right under their own names, instead of being the public face of a corporate or educational institution, as in the period of affiliation. Kate Aitken, for example, used her own name and became one of the best-known and best-loved cookbook writers and radio personalities of her day. Jehane Benoît was notable for her ability to reach beyond Quebec to an English-language audience; she became a trusted adviser for Canadians from coast to coast. During a period of transition in women's roles during the mid-twentieth century, it is fascinating to note that one saw fictional corporate spokespersons sharing the spotlight, quite literally, with their "real-life" counterparts who worked under their own names. Christine Hindson, who portrayed Swift's Martha Logan, explained to me in a 2003 telephone conversation: "I did cooking schools in Vancouver [and the] Montreal Forum with Jehane Benoît with 10 000 people at each of those shows. Stores selling our products would give out the tickets, and the grand prize would be a stove. Overhead cameras. . . . a very exciting time. I never imagined myself spinning these wonderful tales and making a pie at the same time."

Differentiation

During a time of increasing normalization of foodways traditions internationally, the distinctive food traditions of French-speaking Canadians highlighted the differences between Canada and other countries—most obviously its neighbour to the south. Indeed, Canada's centennial celebrations ushered in an era of cultural branding north of the forty-ninth parallel. The appearance of *Canadian* in cookbook titles from around 1967 may have underlined a shared sense of identity, but the 1960s also introduced increasing differentiation, evident in cookbooks that focused on regional and cultural variations in foodways practices. These competing drives—toward identification and differentiation—are always at play to some degree in the shaping of foodways, but their co-existence was most visible in Canadian cookbooks of the 1960s and 1970s (Cooke 2009:4–6).

Conclusion

Why, then, should we attend to books that describe what Canadians have eaten in bygone days? One compelling answer is surely that cuisine is a story told through the medium of food. Cookbooks, by recording and attempting to shape the cuisine of a community or region at a particular time, tell us the diverse stories of the lived history of a people. If we pay attention to the stories about the foods Canadians have chosen to eat and to share with those around them, and if we learn to read and make sense of them, then our culinary storytelling will become increasingly rich and complex, as will our sense of who Canadians have wanted to be.

Discussion Questions

1. Identify some key factors influencing Canadians' food choices.

2. How have Canadian cookbooks changed since their first appearance in mid-nineteenth century?

3. What are some of Canada's iconic foods?

4. Give one example of how one might view Canadian history through the lens of a particular food item.

5. How might one define "Canadian cuisine"?

Further Reading

1. Cooke, Nathalie, ed. 2009. *What's to Eat?: Entrées in Canadian Food History.* Montreal: McGill-Queen's University Press.
   A collection of articles focusing on Canadian food history—what foods Canadians chose to eat and the meanings ascribed to particular food choices. The introduction offers a way of glimpsing Canadian history through the lens of Canadian cookbooks, developing the five-stage framework introduced here.

2. Desloges, Yvon. 2009. *À Table en Nouvelle-France.* Quebec: Septentrion.
   Drawing on primary archival research, Desloges provides a close reading of the foodways of New France from the moment of first contact between North American Aboriginals and European explorers in what is now Quebec through the Conquest of 1760. For those requiring information in English, see Desloges and Lafrance (1989).

3. Driver, Elizabeth. 2008. *Culinary Landmarks: A Bibliography of Canadian Cookbooks, 1825–1949*. Toronto: University of Toronto Press.
The first and only bibliography of Canadian cookbooks, this is an indispensable resource tool.

4. Ferguson, Carol, and Margaret Fraser. 1992. *A Century of Canadian Home Cooking: 1900 through the '90s*. Scarborough, ON: Prentice-Hall.
An illustrated guide to the shifting food tastes in each decade of the twentieth century.

Video Suggestion

1. Provencher, Richard, and Betty Geraldes. 2015. *Celebrating Canadian Cookbooks*. Library and Archives Canada. www.bac-lac.gc.ca/eng/news/videos/Pages/celebrating-Canadian-cookbooks.aspx. 3 min.
The fifth in a series of 12 videos launched in 2015 entitled *On the Road to 2017 with Library and Archives Canada*, this video with full transcription celebrates Canada's cookbooks by revisiting a historical recipe for ginger cake from *The Frugal Housewife's Manual* (1840). It references the challenges and rewards of working with historical cookbooks.

Notes

1. For additional perspectives on the (hi)stories Canadian cookbooks tell, see Cooke (2002).
2. For further scrutiny of similarities and differences between corporate cookbooklets across continents, see Cooke (2010a).
3. Bernard Assiniwi's historical perspective on Aboriginal cuisine, the illustrated *Recettes indiennes et survie en forêt*, provides additional insights.
4. See http://eco.Canadiana.ca/?usrlang=en.
5. See http://www.torontopubliclibrary.ca/detail.jsp?R=DC-37131055380711D.
6. See http://www.manuscriptcookbookssurvey.com/catalogue/.
7. See "classicism, classic," p. 139 in *The Concise Oxford Companion to English Literature*. 2007. Margaret Drabble and Jenny Stringer, eds. (New York: Oxford University Press). Originally, the term *classic* referred to the writer rather than to the work. "A classic, according to the usual definition, is an old author canonised by admiration, and an authority in his particular style" (Charles Augustin Sainte-Beuve, 1909, "What Is a Classic?," p. 14 in *Literary and Philosophical Essays*, Vol. XXXII. New York: P.F. Collier & Son). Interestingly, individuals have been identified as authorities in the culinary world (Julia Child and Fannie Farmer in the United States; Mère Caron and Jehane Benoît in French Canada) in a way that particular cookbooks have not.
8. For a discussion relating these definitions of the recipe to the genre of poetry, see Cooke (2010b:65–82).
9. This is the title of some later editions of Clarke's cookbooks, but this particular *Dominion Home Cook Book* is unrelated to Clarke's text.
10. For a discussion of the form and function of the implied author in corporate cookbooks, see also Cooke (2010a:22–26).
11. For a more detailed discussion of the corporate spokespersonalities or "fictional food folk" see Cooke (2003).
12. Mary Blake is of course "American" (if a fictitious person can indeed have a nationality) as indicated by the American spelling of favorite; however, through the Carnation Company's publication and dissemination of corporate ephemera in Canada, she was a well-known visitor to Canadian homes.
13. See also the Introduction of Cooke's *What's to Eat?* (2009) for a more expansive discussion of this concept and the way it gives rise to our current culinary introspection.

References

A.B. of Grimsby. 1840. *The Frugal Housewife's Manual*. Toronto.

Aitken, Kate. 1945. *Kate Aitken's Canadian Cook Book*. Montreal: The Standard.

Armstrong, Julian. 1990. *A Taste of Quebec*. Toronto: Macmillan.

Assiniwi, Bernard. 1972. *Recettes indiennes et survie en forêt*. Montreal: Leméac.

Barss, Bunny. 1988. *Alberta Pictorial Cookbook*. Halifax, NS: Nimbus.

Beeson, Patricia. 1993. *Macdonald Was Late for Dinner: A Slice of Culinary Life in Early Canada*. Peterborough, ON: Broadview Press.

Benoît, Jehane. 1963. *L'encyclopédie de la cuisine canadienne*. Montreal: Les Messageries de Saint-Laurent.

——. 1979. *La cuisine canadienne*. Montreal: Éditions du Jour.

Berg, Jennifer. 2002. "Icon Foods." Pp. 243–4 in *Encyclopedia of Food and Culture*, Vol. 2. New York: Charles Scribner's Sons.

——. 2006. "From Pushcart Peddlers to Gourmet Take-Out: New York City's Iconic Foods of Jewish Origin, 1920 to 2005." PhD dissertation, Department of Nutrition, Food Studies and Public Health, New York University.

Blake, Mary. 1924. *My Hundred Favorite Recipes*. Toronto: Carnation.

Bower, L. Anne. 1997. "Bound Together: Recipes, Lives, Stories, and Readings." Pp. 1–14 in *Recipes for Reading: Community Cookbooks, Stories, Histories*, ed. Anne L. Bower. Amherst: University of Massachusetts Press.

The Carnation Year Book of Menus and Recipes. n.d. [likely 1935–1937; see Driver, *Culinary Landmarks*] Toronto: Carnation.

Caron, [Emmelie]. 1878. *Directions diverses donées par la Rev. Mère Caron pour aider ses soeurs à former de bonnes cuisinières*. 1st edn. Montreal: n.p.

Clarke, Anne. 1883 *Mrs. Clarke's Cookery Book*. Toronto: Grip.

Clow, Meribeth, Dorothy Duncan, Glenn J. Lockwood, and Lorraine Lowry, eds. 1990. *Consuming Passions: Eating and Drinking Traditions in Ontario*. Willowdale: Ontario Historical Society.

The Cook Not Mad; or Rational Cookery. 1831. Kingston, ON: James Macfarlane. Reprint. ed. Roy Abrahamson. 1973. Toronto: Cherry Tree Press.

Cooke, Nathalie. 2002. "Cookbooks and Culture." *Encyclopedia of Literature in Canada*, ed. W.H. New. Toronto: University of Toronto Press.

——. 2003. "Getting the Mix Just Right for the Canadian Home Baker." *Essays on Canadian Writing* 78:192–219.

——. 2009. "Introduction." Pp. 3–17 in *What's to Eat?: Entrées in Canadian Food History*, ed. Nathalie Cooke. Montreal: McGill-Queen's University Press.

——. 2010a. "Cookbooklets and Canadian Kitchens." *Material Culture Review* 70:22–33.

——. 2010b. "Poems and Recipes: What Do These Two Magpie Modes Have in Common?" *Ranam, recherches anglaises et nord américaines* 43:65–82.

Cotter, Colleen. 1997. "Claiming a Piece of the Pie." Pp. 51–72 in *Recipes for Reading*, ed. Anne L. Bower. Amherst: University of Massachusetts Press.

La cuisine raisonnée. 1957. 8th edn (first edition 1919). Quebec: Congrégation de Notre-Dame de Montreal.

La cuisine raisonnée. 1967. 10th edn (first edition 1919). Montreal: Éditions Fides.

La cuisinière bourgeoise. 1825. 3rd edn (first edition 1746). Quebec: Augustin Germain.

La cuisinière canadienne. 1840. Montreal: Louis Perrault.

Dammam, Derek, and Chris Johns. 2015. *True North*. Toronto: HarperCollins.

Davidson, Alan. 1999. *The Oxford Companion to Food*. Oxford: Oxford University Press.

Desloges, Yvon. 2009. *À table en Nouvelle-France*. Quebec: Septentrion.

—— and Marc Lafrance. 1989. *A Taste of History, the Origins of Quebec's Gastronomy* [*Goûter à l'histoire, les origines de la gastronomie québécoise*]. Ottawa: Service canadien des parcs et les Éditions de la Chenelière.

The Dominion Home Cook Book. 1868. Toronto: Adam Miller.

Driver, Elizabeth. 2008. *Culinary Landmarks: A Bibliography of Canadian Cookbooks, 1825–1949*. Toronto: University of Toronto Press.

——. 2009. "Regional Differences in the Canadian Daily Meal? Cookbooks Answer the Question." Pp. 197–212 in *What's to Eat?: Entrées in Canadian Food History*, ed. Nathalie Cooke. Montreal: McGill-Queen's University Press.

Duncan, Dorothy. 2006. *Canadians at Table: Food, Fellowship and Folklore: A Culinary History of Canada*. Toronto: Dundurn.

Farmer, Fannie. 1896. *The Boston Cooking-School Cook Book*. Boston: Little, Brown.

Ferguson, Carol, and Margaret Fraser. 1992. *A Century of Canadian Home Cooking: 1900 through the '90s*. Scarborough, ON: Prentice-Hall.

Fisher, M.F.K. 1968. "Anatomy of a Recipe." *With Bold Knife and Fork*. Ed. M.F.K. Fisher. New York: G.P. Putnam's Sons.

Five Roses Cook Book. 1913. Montreal: Lake of the Woods Milling.

The Grist. 1951. Published for all employees by International Milling Company, Robin Hood Flour Mills Limited, 8.

A Guide to Good Cooking from the Makers of Five Roses Flour. 1938. Rev. and enl. edn. Montreal: Lake of the Woods Milling Company.

A Guide to Good Cooking with Five Roses Flour. 1954. Rev. edn. Montreal: Lake of the Woods Milling Company.

Herman, David. 1997. "Scripts, Sequences, and Stories: Elements of a Postclassical Narratology." *PMLA* 112(5):1046–59.

The Home Cook Book. 1877. Toronto: Belford Brothers.

The Housewife's Almanac. 1938. London: Kellogg Company of Canada.

Hunter, Lynette. 1980. "Cookery Books: A Cabinet of Rare Devices and Conceits." *Petits Propos Culinaires* 5:19–34.

Kenneally, Rhona Richman. 2009. "'There *Is* a Canadian Cuisine, and It Is Unique in All the World': Crafting National Food Culture During the Long 1960s." Pp. 167–96 in *What's to Eat?: Entrées in Canadian Food History*, ed. Nathalie Cooke. Montreal: McGill-Queen's University Press.

La nouvelle cuisinière canadienne. 1850. Montreal: Louis Perrault.

LeCroy, Anne. 1989. "Cookery Literature: Or Literary Cookery." Pp. 7–24 in *Cooking by the Book*, ed. Mary Anne Schofield. Bowling Green, OH: Bowling Green State University Press.

Leonardi, Susan. 1989. "Recipes for Reading: Summer Pasta, Lobster à la Riseholme, and Key Lime Pie." *PMLA* 104(3):340–47. Reprinted (1989) as pp. 126–38 in *Cooking by the Book*, ed. Mary Anne Schofield. Bowling Green, OH: Bowling Green State University Press.

Lewis, Katherine C. 1981. *Mrs. Flynn's Cookbook.* Charlottetown: Ladies of St. Vincent's Orphanage and Society in Aid of St. Vincent's Orphanage. Reprint. Charlottetown: PEI Heritage Foundation.

Logan, Martha. 1942. *Meat Complete, a Handbook of Meat Cookery.* Toronto: Swift Canada Co. Ltd.

Manuel de cuisine raisonnée adapté aux élèves des cours élémentaires de l'école normale classico-ménagère de Saint-Pascal. 1919. Quebec: Imprimerie l'Action sociale ltée.

Marquis, Marie. 2009. "The Cookbook Quebecers Prefer: More than Just Recipes." Pp. 213–27 in *What's to Eat?: Entrées in Canadian Food History*, ed. Nathalie Cooke. Montreal: McGill-Queen's University Press.

McDougall, Elizabeth J. 1997. "Voices, Stories, and Recipes in Selected Canadian Community Cookbooks." Pp. 105–17 in *Recipes for Reading: Community Cookbooks, Stories, Histories*, ed. Anne L. Bower. Amherst: University of Massachusetts Press.

McMicking, Mrs Margaret Leighton, compiler. 1904. *The King's Daughters Cookery Book.* Victoria: Banfield.

Mendelson, Ann. 2003. *Stand Facing the Stove.* New York: Scribner.

Moodie, Susanna. 1989 [1852]. *Roughing It in the Bush; or, Life in Canada.* Toronto: McClelland & Stewart.

The Modern Cook Book. 1923. Calgary, Alberta: Armistice Chapter IODE.

Murray, Rose. 2008. *A Taste of Canada: A Culinary Journal.* Vancouver: Whitecap Books.

Nightingale, Marie. 1971. *Out of Old Nova Scotia Kitchens: A Collection of Traditional Recipes of Nova Scotia and the Story of the People Who Cooked Them.* Toronto: Pagurian Press.

Ogilvie's Book for a Cook. 1905. Montreal: Ogilvie.

Oliver, Margo. 1993. *Classical Canadian Recipes.* Montreal: OptimumPublishing.

Pattinson, Nellie Lyle. 1923. *The Canadian Cookbook.* Toronto: McGraw-Hill.

———. 1947. *Canadian Cook Book.* Rev. edn. Toronto: Ryerson.

Powers, Jo Marie, and Anita Stewart, eds. 1995. *Northern Bounty: A Celebration of Canadian Cuisine.* Toronto: Random House.

Richards, Henry Ilett, and Elizabeth Richards. 1861. *The Canadian Housewife's Manual of Cookery Compiled from the Best English, French and American Works.* Hamilton, ON: William Gillespie.

Rombauer, Irma. 1931. *Joy of Cooking.* St Louis: A.C. Clayton Printing.

Roy, Suman, and Brooke Ali. 2010. *From Pemmican to Poutine, A Journey Through Canada's Culinary History.* Toronto: Key Publishing House.

Sainte Marie Edith, Soeur. 1928. *The Secrets of Good Cooking.* Montreal: The Canadian Printing and Lithographing Company.

Scott, Anna Lee. n.d. *51 Ways to a Man's Heart.* Maple Leaf Milling.

Speed Cooking with Your New General Electric Range. 1948. Toronto: General Electric.

Staebler, Edna. 1968. *Food That Really Schmecks: Mennonite Country Cooking.* Toronto: McGraw-Hill Ryerson.

Stewart, Anita. 2000. *Flavours of Canada.* Vancouver: Raincoast.

———. 2008. *Anita Stewart's Canada—the Food, the Recipes, the Stories.* Toronto: HarperCollins.

Symons, Michael. 2006. "Grandmas to Gourmets: The Revolution of 1963." *Food, Culture and Society* 9(2): 179–200.

Thornton, Lynn. 1995. *From the Kitchens of Kings Landing.* Fredericton: Kings Landing Historical Settlement.

Traill, Catherine Parr. 1854. *The Female Emigrant's Guide, and Hints on Canadian Housekeeping.* Toronto: Maclear. Early Canadiana Online. 7 September 2007. http://www.Canadiana.org/ECO/mtg?doc=41417.

The Velvet Touch. n.d. Robin Hood.

5 Constructing "Healthy Eating"/ Constructing Self

Brenda L. Beagan and Gwen E. Chapman

Learning Objectives

Through this chapter, you can

1. Understand "healthy eating" as diverse ways of thinking about and relating to food, influenced by media, government policies, and the food industry as well as personal and cultural traditions.

2. Reflect upon how food practices are one of the ways people "produce" or portray their social identities as men and women, teens and adults, members of ethnic, racial, or class groups, and represent their moral worth in relation to others.

3. Reflect upon how social identities—such as gender, ethnicity, social class, age—influence people's relationship to "healthy eating."

Introduction

A Canadian national newspaper recommends that to boost nutrient intake and improve health, Canadians should cut out processed foods and refined starches, cook from scratch, reduce sugar intake, and eat more vegetables (Beck 2015). A research article in *Circulation: Journal of the American Heart Association* reports that women who eat less red meat and more nuts, poultry, fish, and low-fat dairy products have significantly lower risk of coronary heart disease (Bernstein et al. 2010). Health Canada advises that, "A healthy diet rich in a variety of vegetables and fruit may help reduce the risk of some types of cancer" (Health Canada 2011).

These kinds of messages from the media, researchers, government websites, and nutrition and health educators are everywhere, constantly informing Canadians that the food choices we make as individuals affect our health. Most Canadians understand basic nutrition, are confident in their knowledge, and take healthfulness into consideration when deciding what to eat (Canadian Foundation for Dietetic Research 2014). Nonetheless, Canadians' diets do not measure up to current nutrition recommendations (Garriguet 2009).

Clearly, there is no simple relationship between what people think and know about nutrition and what they actually eat. Health educators have developed a variety of models to understand the complexity of this relationship. The population health approach points to a variety of individual, interpersonal, and environmental factors that determine **healthy eating** (Raine 2005). The Food Choice Model describes how food decisions are shaped by values and beliefs, as people balance food preferences, cost, convenience, healthfulness, and social relationships (Sobal and Bisogni 2009). For social scientists, "healthy eating" is understood as a socially constructed, shifting **discourse** that shapes and is shaped by what people say and do in relation to food, and that is specifically implicated in the ways people understand and perform their social identities. For example, women and men think and talk about "healthy eating" differently largely because social definitions of masculinity and femininity construct certain ways of being in relationship to food. Similarly, being a teenager means talking and acting in relation to "healthy eating" in different ways than adults.

This chapter explores relationships between "healthy eating" and how people construct and convey their social identities. We argue that contemporary understandings of "healthy eating" influence the ways Canadians engage with food and eating because of discourses that link health and eating practices to **identity** categories defined by **gender**, life stage, **ethnicity**, and social class. We draw on a number of qualitative studies we have conducted exploring how everyday food practices and concerns are shaped by understandings of food, health, bodies, and identities. While other discourses, social structures, and systems—such as food policies and characteristics of the food system—are equally important influences on food practices, here we focus only on discursive social influences, specifically the relationships among healthy eating, food practices, and social identities. How Canadians simultaneously "do food," "do health," and "do self" are central to everyday eating practices.

The chapter begins with an introduction to healthy eating discourses and a discussion of the nature and content of contemporary healthy eating discourses in Canada. We then discuss how people's engagements with healthy eating are implicated in the construction of four identity categories: gender, life stage (teen/adult), ethnicity, and social class. Although we treat each of these facets of identity in separate sections of the chapter, obviously they intersect within each

individual, shifting people's everyday experiences and practices.

Healthy Eating—Discourses of Food, Consumption, and Health

When we interview people in our research about food, almost everyone refers at some point to the healthfulness of food patterns—accepting messages about healthy eating, adapting those messages, refuting them, or resisting them, but nevertheless engaging with the idea of healthy eating. Other ideas about food also come up, such as ethical or environmental concerns about food production, processing, and transportation (Beagan, Ristovski-Slijepcevic, and Chapman 2010; Beagan, Chapman, Johnston, et al. 2015), but these issues are not raised as frequently, and many people do not address them at all. Healthy eating is currently one of the dominant discourses—if not *the* dominant discourse—concerning food.

"Discourses" refers to pervasive ways of thinking that over time come to define what can be said about something or even considered possible. Discourses influence and determine how people are expected to think or act in a given society (Foucault 1979). The power of discourses works through setting social standards that influence behaviour and ways of thinking. For example, healthy eating discourses construct some foods and practices as "healthy" or "unhealthy," "good" or "bad." Such assessments are promoted through avenues like *Canada's Food Guide* and nutritional advice from the Heart and Stroke Foundation, the Canadian Diabetes Association, and other health agencies. Healthy eating messages are then dispersed through newspapers, television, magazines, the Internet, and educational institutions. They are further promoted every day through informal channels as people talk with each other about food and health and observe others enacting or resisting healthy eating practices.

The discourses that are used most frequently, that are most widespread in a particular place and time, are considered dominant. The dominance of healthy eating as a way of thinking and talking about food in Western societies is well documented (Biltekoff 2013). The effect of this dominant discourse on what people eat, however, is not simple. While social discourses shape and constrain individual actions, individual actions (and inactions) simultaneously shape social discourses, expectations, and practices. As people alter or actively resist thinking and acting in ways that conform to dominant discourses, alternative discourses begin to circulate through society and may gradually shift the dominant discourse. More marginal discourses may gain strength in different times or places, or may dominate for specific social groups according to age, ethnicity, gender, education, or social class.

Thus, multiple discourses relating to healthy eating may circulate within a society at any given time. Several of our studies in Canada have uncovered distinct ways of knowing and thinking about healthy eating (e.g. Ristovski-Slijepcevic, Chapman, and Beagan 2008; Beagan, Chapman, Johnston, et al. 2015). A discourse we have called "mainstream" healthy eating emphasizes consumption of fruits and vegetables, grains, poultry, some low-fat meat, and dairy products. With a focus on broad nutrition principles of balance, moderation, and variety, as well as physical activity, this perspective fits well with current official nutrition guidelines. Study participants talk about specific nutrients and food components such as protein, vitamins, and minerals, and emphasize control and monitoring food intake. As one 16-year-old boy said, "Getting all your vitamins and nutrients, and just staying healthy and active. I would put it under the category of eating right" (Beagan, Chapman, Johnston, et al. 2015:39). Other researchers have also found Canadians are well versed in the mainstream healthy eating discourse, with children as young as 11 years able to cite the food groups defined in *Canada's Food Guide* and discuss the pros and cons of fibre, produce, and dietary fat and sugar (Protruder et al. 2010).

A co-existing more "traditional" discourse of healthy eating emphasizes consumption of home-cooked meals based on meat, potatoes, and vegetables, as well as unprocessed foods. Food is described as natural, and is rarely dissected into component nutrients, or associated with specific health risks. As one 50-year-old woman in one of our studies said, "I don't think it matters about fat content. . . . It's the processed food that I think is a problem, even if it's diet [food]—Processed food, I just don't think the body was meant to eat that stuff" (Beagan, Chapman, Johnston, et al. 2015:41). People talk about learning healthy eating from the way they ate as children, from their elders, and from their own bodily experiences. In some ethno-cultural groups, people refer to traditional cultural cuisines, and to the strength-giving properties of specific foods. The clearest distinction between "traditional" and "mainstream" discourses lies in how meat is described: while the traditional view sees meat as a key component of healthy eating, the mainstream view sees meat, particularly red meat, as unhealthy. A review of qualitative research exploring how people interpret "healthy eating" has noted similar contrasts in views about meat, ranging from those who see it as essential to proper eating to those who believe it makes them ill (Bisogni et al. 2012).

In our research, we have identified an "alternative" healthy eating discourse that also emphasizes natural unprocessed foods but focuses more on toxins and carcinogens in food, as well as protective factors such as micronutrients and phytochemicals. People using this discourse talk about organic food production, the risks of synthetic pesticides and fertilizers, and compounds in particular foods that boost the immune system or combat environmental toxins. They often express outright distrust of dominant nutrition messages and suspicion of additives in processed foods as well as environmental contamination, monoculture, and factory farming practices. Toxins in foods are seen as causing immediate and long-term negative health effects such as food intolerances and cancer. For example, one 13-year-old girl in our recent study prefers organic foods "because there's not all those steroids and stuff in it; I guess your body would digest them but the toxins would be in your body." People tend to learn about this healthy eating discourse from naturopaths, other alternative health practitioners, health-food stores, books, magazines, and nutritional supplement literature.

Healthy eating discourses are strongly connected to body weight. Currently, a major focus in North America concerns body weight and the "obesity epidemic" (Biltekoff 2013). A variety of health promotion initiatives encourage Canadians to take responsibility for preventing future health issues by achieving and maintaining a "healthy" body weight. Not surprisingly, Canadians tend to conflate healthy bodies with slender bodies and healthy eating with maintaining low body weight (Beagan, Chapman, Johnston, et al. 2015). Healthy eating is seen as a lifestyle that entails "watching what you eat" as a never-ending practice of self-surveillance, a practice embraced as an individual responsibility by good and moral citizens. Critical research in a number of fields challenges the taken-for-granted "truth" that obesity is directly linked with poorer health (Kramer, Zinman, and Retnakaran 2013), though these messages are far less available through mainstream media. Such accounts point to the socially constructed nature of current approaches to health and body weight.

In this section, we have introduced the notion of healthy eating discourses: multiple, shifting understandings of how eating practices affect well-being. These understandings are socially constructed through the ways people engage with, support, and resist messages promoted by government, science, health professionals, the media, and each other. What we have particularly explored here are some variations in how healthy eating is currently understood in Canada. Certain ways of thinking about healthy eating seem to be articulated more or less frequently by certain groups of people, for example by women rather than men, or by people from different ethnic groups. We explore these differences in more depth in the remainder of this chapter, examining how people interact with healthy eating discourses differently as they construct and convey self-identities through food practices and their interactions with healthy eating discourses.

Gendered Interactions with Healthy Eating Discourses

Canadians tend to believe that gender does not shape our lives or our practices, including our food practices. As in all liberal democracies, there is a strong impetus to believe that individuals exercise free choice in the context of equal opportunity. Thus any inequalities are individualized, seen as the result of individual choices rather than systematic and historically rooted oppressions. Denying the potential impacts of gender, then, becomes part of constructing images of ourselves as liberal, equality-minded individuals (McPhail, Beagan, and Chapman 2012).

Yet decades of scholarship have shown that food practices are highly gendered. Many foods are well understood to be "feminine" (e.g. ice cream, chocolate, salads, vegetables, and "light" foods) or "masculine" (e.g. steak and other red meat, "heavy" and rich foods). Vegetarians are perceived to be less masculine than omnivores (Ruby and Heine 2011). The relationship between women and "light" foods largely centres on desire to maintain low body weight (Beagan, Chapman, Johnston, et al. 2015). While some have argued that obsession with body image is a distinctly feminine preoccupation, others have countered that men's body image concerns are simply less well understood, and that it is less socially acceptable for men to admit to concern with body image (Norman 2011).

In a recent study, we explored how men, women, and teens engaged with food discourses by asking them about their own food habits and preferences, then asking them to categorize photographs of a variety of foods as associated more with women or with men (McPhail, Beagan, and Chapman 2012). Regardless of age or gender, the participants strongly denied that foods were in any way gendered, then proceeded to sort the photographs into highly consistent categories of masculine (bacon cheeseburger, Beef Wellington, pot roast, hot dog, pizza, and macaroni and cheese) or feminine (sushi, stir-fry, couscous, chicken soup, Korean food, fish, and spring green salad). Women's foods were seen as prettier, fancier, more "delicate," and healthier. Masculine eating was described as centred on meat, heavy and filling, and unconcerned with health. Further exploring participants' own eating practices revealed that most did in fact adhere to at least some aspects of the stereotyped gendered food practices they denied exist.

The association of women's eating with health concerns and men's eating as unconcerned with health demonstrates the significant interactions between gender and healthy eating. Numerous studies have shown that men typically are uninterested in healthy eating, and in fact lack of concern for health is almost a defining characteristic of masculinity (Beagan, Chapman, Johnston, et al. 2015; Norman 2011; Sloan, Gough, and Conner 2011). Men who do deliberately engage in healthy eating usually have other means of securing their masculinity, such as high levels of education or income. They are also more likely to engage as kitchen "helpers," constructing their wives or female partners as the experts on health and nutrition (Mróz et al. 2011). Our recent study, however, suggests a discursive shift may be underway. While healthy eating, body image, and weight were decidedly the preoccupation of women and girls, we did find some men and boys engaged with those discourses, specifically through the language of health:

Boys and men tended to relate to obesity and weight loss through the discourse of healthy eating, particularly through and for sport. This provided boys with an avenue through which they could perform weight loss and maintenance regimes without appearing overly feminine. (Beagan, Chapman, Johnston, et al. 2015:130–131)

The language of an obesity epidemic may be making it more possible for boys and men to engage with healthy eating—as well as engage in monitoring and attempting to control their bodies—which were previously feminine domains.

For women, healthy eating discourses make it possible to construct or convey particular versions of femininity, most notably through supervising healthy eating within the family. Mothers are understood to have a critical role in children's nutrition education; preparing healthful meals for children and male partners is one way women can fulfill the social role of "good mother" (Beagan, Chapman, D'Sylva, and Bassett 2008; Beagan, Chapman, Johnston, et al. 2015). While feeding the family has long been understood as one way women can construct themselves as good women and good mothers (DeVault 1991), today there is an added requirement of healthy eating expertise. Good mothers are those who care for their children's health by providing healthy food, learning about healthy eating and educating family members about it, monitoring what is eaten, and guiding their children and protecting them from unhealthy influences (Ristovski-Slijepcevic, Chapman, and Beagan 2010). As a mother in one of our studies said about serving foods she considered unhealthy, "I don't think I would get very much satisfaction from throwing fish sticks and McCain fries on the table for my kids. I think I would feel like a terrible parent" (Beagan, Chapman, and Power, 2016: 59).

The perceived healthfulness of foods served to families is one of the many ways people critique and judge one another through food (Beagan, Chapman, Johnston, et al. 2015). While the woman above says "parent," this is a decidedly gendered discourse. Women who do not (cannot, choose not to) feed their children foods considered "healthy" are considered "failed mothers" in a way that men who do not feed their children "healthy" foods are never considered "failed fathers." Similarly, women's mothering skills are increasingly criticized if their children do not present optimally slender bodies. The provision of foods considered healthy is a distinctively feminine (maternal) expectation (Cairns and Johnston 2015). It has become one of the major rationales people offer for why women continue to do most of the work associated with food within families (Beagan et al. 2008).

In summary, it is clear that the different ways that individuals engage with and resist "healthy eating" practices are strongly implicated in how they develop and portray social identities as men or women. Its strongly gendered character makes it readily available for disparaging those who do not meet (or who choose to resist) gender role expectations.

Age and Life Stage— Interacting with Healthy Eating Discourses

Children are routinely described as being either "good eaters" who readily eat a variety of food or "picky eaters" whose narrow food repertoires require considerable managing in relation to healthy eating (Johnson et al. 2015). As children age, parents struggle to enforce healthy eating standards, while granting increasing autonomy to adolescents, who often prefer to seek out "junk food" associated with freedom from parental control and allegiance with a peer group. One of our studies documented the complex family negotiations through which parents (especially mothers) tried to encourage teens to eat healthy foods (Bassett, Beagan, and Chapman 2008). As discussed above, this may be one means for women to establish themselves as "good mothers." Strategies for encouraging healthy eating included coaching, coaxing, and coercing, though they also controlled consumption to some extent through food purchasing and meal preparation. They made space for teens to develop a growing sense of autonomy by allowing them to

choose from the foods in the house, while enforcing healthy eating by purchasing predominantly healthy foods. Many parents emphasized they would never force their teens to eat particular foods, emphasizing support for teen autonomy as a particular approach to "good parenting."

Meanwhile, teens pestered, cajoled, coaxed, and manipulated parents to get foods they liked. They were forging autonomous identities in relation to healthy eating, at times ignoring their parents' nutrition advice, at times taking up healthy eating as their own responsibility. One 14-year-old said, "I don't think, 'Should I be eating this?' or 'Could I find a better restaurant?' I'll get whatever tastes good and probably with the highest fat content on the menu" (Bassett, Beagan, and Chapman 2008:329). In contrast, an 18-year-old stated, "I definitely keep learning things [about healthy eating]. Mom mentions things and I pick up on them" (Bassett, Beagan, and Chapman 2008:329). Some frustrated parents reported that their teens seemed to use food to convey an adult identity only outside the home:

> There's things, like, that [my son has] learned to like that he would never have tried here. I could strangle him. He complained and complained when we'd have them. Next thing he'd say, "Oh, I had such-and-such at somebody's house and it was really good." (Bassett, Beagan, and Chapman 2008:329)

In our recent study with families across Canada, foods most likely to be seen as "teen foods" (as opposed to "adult foods") were almost identical with those foods perceived by adults and teens as "unhealthy." Stressing that, in addition to lack of concern about health, teens *like* convenient and tasty foods, one 16-year-old girl said, "It's easier, it's tastier, it's badder for you" (Beagan, Chapman, Johnston, et al. 2015:54). One mother taught her son her version of healthy eating until he went to school: "I didn't have the control. [He would] come home with ideas about food and say, 'I don't really want tofu. I want a hamburger.' . . . The exposure at school changed everything" (Beagan, Chapman, Johnston, et al. 2015:214). Despite widespread perceptions that teens eat unhealthy foods, many of the teens in our study themselves reported having very healthy eating habits. Some were pressuring their parents to adopt healthy eating practices learned in school. Some families experienced considerable tension when parents were separated or divorced, with teens caught between what they considered healthy eating in one household and not-so-healthy fare in the other. One 16-year-old described her father as "a very unhealthy eater. So whenever I went over to his house, it would be just kind of be the junk food weekend" (Beagan, Chapman, Johnston, et al. 2015:223).

Consumption of fast food has been strongly linked with teens and with unhealthy eating, raising significant concern regarding the implications for health and obesity (Bugge 2011; Weeks 2009). In our interviews with 132 Canadian teens, we found that only 25 considered fast-food consumption completely unproblematic (McPhail, Chapman, and Beagan 2011). Most teens regarded fast food as unhealthy yet continued to consume it, albeit with guilt. They also levelled considerable negative judgment against others who ate fast food:

> The fact that teens regarded fast food as unhealthy and judged those who ate it as "unknowledgeable," "out of control," "disgusting" people that made poor and unhealthy food choices did not translate neatly into behavior; some teens who believed fast food to be unhealthy and bad avoided fast food, while other teens, even though they also judged fast food as unhealthy, ate it frequently. (McPhail, Chapman, and Beagan 2011:304)

Most teens who ate fast food despite considering it unhealthy passed equally harsh judgments on themselves, labelling themselves and their food choices as "good" or "bad." Unlike an earlier UK study, we found that teens from all social class categories used disparagement of fast food as a means of judging; this was not a tool exclusively employed by upper-class teens to mark their moral worth (Wills, Backett-Milburn, Lawton, and Roberts 2009). Nor did we find rural–urban differences in teens' engagement with healthy eating or perceptions of fast food (McPhail, Chapman, and Beagan 2013).

In some families, teens are the ones attempting to introduce healthy eating to the family. When teens adopt vegetarianism—sometimes for health reasons, sometimes for ethical concerns, sometimes for both—there is potential for intra-family conflict with parents potentially refusing to accommodate the change. In our study with Canadian families, 22 teens had become vegetarian. Parents who were supportive of this were more likely to be middle or upper-middle class, with access to material resources for experimental cooking, and a general approach to food that emphasized creativity and flexibility, as well as an approach to "good parenting" that emphasized teen autonomy (Beagan, Chapman, Johnston, et al. 2015). Several had previously been vegetarian themselves. Parents who resisted teen vegetarianism were all low income, lacking the material resources to accommodate their children's vegetarian preferences through purchasing vegetarian foods or preparing vegetarian options to the main family meal. Equally importantly, however, they resisted teen vegetarianism on the basis of health concerns, fearing their children would face nutritional deficiencies and inadequate calorie intake through not eating meat. In these families, many teens discontinued vegetarian eating.

In this section we have explored some of the tensions experienced as family members negotiate individual and collective identities through the ways they take up or resist specific eating practices considered healthy. Teens convey adolescent identities through resisting "healthy eating" in some settings and adopting it in others. They and their parents negotiate around food, as adults may attempt to convey "good parenting" through encouraging "healthy eating" while still allowing teens autonomy in food choices.

Ethnicity and Race Interacting with Healthy Eating

Food is a highly significant cultural symbol of ethnicity and an important means for constructing ethnic identities. For many members of migrant communities, food and food preparation are central mechanisms in the transmission and maintenance of culture as well as in the process of acculturation, adaptation to the new culture (e.g. Lawton et al. 2008). Women often pass along cultural values, norms, expectations, stories, and skills through cross-generational work in the kitchen. Many families experience tensions between the desire to maintain traditional foods as part of ethnic identity and the desire to incorporate "new" foods (D'Sylva and Beagan 2011). There are often intergenerational conflicts, as youth seek to solidify Canadian identities through eating "Western" foods, while elders may prefer to eat the foods of "home." In one of our studies, a mother described constant struggle with her children, who resisted "brown food"—their term for Pakistani food—preferring "Canadian" food (Beagan, Chapman, Johnston, et al. 2015:194).

Some studies suggest eating in ways that maintain ethnic identity may conflict with healthy eating (Lawton et al. 2008), while others have suggested that Western diets adopted after migration significantly increase nutrition-related illnesses (e.g. Lesser, Gasevic, and Lear 2014). What seems clear is that the meanings of food in relation to health differ by ethnicity. In one of our studies, Canadians of European heritage in both Vancouver and Halifax thought about food and eating primarily through a lens of mainstream healthy eating discourses, with an emphasis on minimizing risk of chronic diseases. Punjabi Canadians who were relatively recent migrants (one to three generations) and African Canadians whose families had been in Canada for centuries tended to employ broader understandings of health and well-being in relation to food (Ristovski-Slijepcevic, Chapman, and Beagan 2008). They incorporated more

than prevention of physical illnesses, emphasizing spiritual wellness, family and community well-being, and cultural well-being. While the latter two groups knew and understood dominant discourses, many of them focused on other attributes of foods, rather than depicting certain foods as increasing disease risk. Foods were described as strength-giving, energy-providing, healing, and improving resistance to disease. Healthy eating knowledge was not only that learned in school or through the media, but also that passed down through generations.

In the Punjabi families, young people particularly sought out "Western" foods and understood healthy eating in terms of dominant discourses, highlighting Canadian identity. Punjabi elders tended to think about healthy eating in more traditional terms, focusing on cultural heritage. As one man stated, "I have learnt from the old and wise people of my village. They say that heavy food is not good for health; we can even get some diseases from eating it, as we are unable to digest it" (Chapman and Beagan 2013:379). Participants in the middle generations generally moved smoothly between traditional and scientific discourses of healthy eating, displaying an integrated identity (Chapman, Ristovski-Slijepcevic, and Beagan 2011).

In the African Canadian families, adults and youth all showed familiarity with mainstream healthy eating discourses, yet also displayed resistance to them. To some extent, this reflected cultural ways of eating that people did not see reflected in healthy eating guidelines (Beagan and Chapman 2012), as well as culturally specific body-size preferences. Many saw the slender body type promoted in the media and through healthy eating discourses as too thin for health. One woman said, "I'm supposed to be like 150 pounds. I don't want to be no 150 pounds. . . . It's too small. . . . you need something to lean on when you get sick" (Ristovski-Slijepcevic et al. 2010:323). Participants spoke of distrust in health professionals, healthy eating discourses, and discourses concerning body size. They contested the validity of nutritional advice and standardized measures such as the body mass index. Participants knew and understood mainstream healthy eating discourses, but believed nutrition guidelines were based on research with Euro-Canadians, not taking into account African-heritage cultures, body types, or lifestyles (Beagan and Chapman 2012). Some argued explicitly that "healthy eating" is a white way of eating.

While for recent migrants to Canada, foods considered healthy may be in conflict with eating patterns grounded in ethnic and cultural traditions, for long-established racialized groups like African Canadians, resisting mainstream healthy eating may be part of resisting racism. The healthy eating discourse which has been so strongly connected to an "obesity epidemic" discourse in recent years has disproportionately targeted women, people from racialized groups, Aboriginal people, immigrants, the working class, and those living in poverty (Biltekoff 2013; Fee 2006; Herndon 2014). And if watching what we eat is a sign of moral goodness and responsibility, marking us as worthy citizens, then fatness and overweight (taken as signs of "unhealthy eating") are read as markers of immorality, irresponsibility, and lack of moral worth. Herndon (2005:219) notes that anti-obesity rhetoric further casts already-marginalized groups as second-class citizens. Writing about Aboriginal Canadians, Fee suggests the war on obesity waged in the name of health constructs "an 'us/them' divide, in this case between the good thin people and the bad fat ones" (Fee 2006:2993).

In summary, the mainstream "healthy eating" discourse is associated with the dominant culture and Euro-Canadian ethnic identity, leaving others to negotiate relationships to it. Young people from migrant families may be quick to adopt this dominant discourse as part of their Canadian identity, but this may be in tension with their elders and with food discourses associated with their cultural heritage. In the case of long-standing racialized communities, resistance to "healthy eating" may be—at least in part—a form of resistance to historical and ongoing racism and colonialism.

Social Class Interactions with Healthy Eating Discourses

Social class concerns not only income but also education and type of job, as well as the education and employment of one's parents and of their parents. While the upper class live mainly on inherited wealth, the middle class has at least high school education and works in professional or semi-professional jobs, considered "white-collar" work or mental labour. The working class conducts manual labour in skilled or unskilled trades, or service, retail, and clerical work. The working poor hold one or more minimum wage jobs, while an impoverished "underclass" may receive income assistance such as disability pension or welfare, or have no source of income.

Income is obviously related to diet. People with higher incomes have diets closer to mainstream healthy eating guidelines (e.g. Mark, Lambert, O'Loughlin, and Gray-Donald 2013), particularly concerning consumption of fruit, vegetables, and dairy products. In some provinces minimum wage simply does not provide enough income for a nutritious diet. Consequently, some 13 per cent of Canadian households lack adequate and secure access to food (Tarasuk, Mitchell, and Dachner 2014). The lowest-cost diets are considered least healthy, featuring calorie-dense, shelf-stable foods (such as pasta) rather than nutrient-dense foods (Williams et al. 2012). Low-income families and individuals are typically caught between competing priorities, having to decide whether to use scarce dollars to pay for food, or pay rent or utilities (Clark et al. 2011; Williams et al. 2012). They are often compelled to emphasize quantity and value over healthfulness (Beagan, Chapman, and Power 2016). Lower-income shoppers are also less likely to have access to transportation and often cannot afford the costs associated with getting to a supermarket outside of their immediate neighbourhood, forcing them to prioritize convenience over cost and quality (Walker, Keane, and Burke 2010).

The lower nutritional quality of diets identified by nutrition and health researchers as common among low-income households is frequently assumed to be a product of poor education or the inability to prioritize health over taste and convenience. The appropriate "solution" is assumed to be more or better nutritional education. In fact, research shows knowledge of nutritional guidelines is widespread among people living with low incomes; people simply cannot afford to eat the way they would prefer (Clark et al. 2011; Williams et al. 2012). As a mother in one of our studies commented, "You can go buy a bag of chips cheaper than you can an apple. It's just the way it is" (Beagan, Chapman, and Power 2016:61). Whether for ethical reasons or health, low-income participants in that study also showed very high commitment to buying organically produced foods, though they could not always afford them. One woman, for example, bought only organic foods, including flour, though her annual income was below $10,000.

Beyond the direct relationship between money and food access, social class affects eating in far more complex ways. In the 1960s sociologist Pierre Bourdieu (1984) documented the way food can distinguish between social classes. He argued that for lower classes, food has been a means of sustenance, while for upper classes it has been aesthetic, both in the presentation of food and in a focus on self-discipline to maintain a particular body aesthetic. Engaging with food from a position of aesthetics, seeing food not as fuel but as an arena of stylistic distinction, pleasure, and appreciation, enables elite social classes to demonstrate their distance from necessity. In contrast, the lower classes may focus on value for dollar, food that is plentiful, tasty, and filling. Such deeply held relationships to food may be difficult to change, even when financial circumstances are altered.

While it appears that families may use particular approaches to ethical eating and may emphasize a cosmopolitan, sophisticated palate as markers of higher social class status, the role of healthy eating as a marker of class is less clear (Beagan, Power, and Chapman 2015). Research in the UK suggests that middle-class parents focus

far more on the healthfulness of teen diets, while working-class parents seek less control, emphasizing that young people's food preferences are their own concern (Backett-Milburn et al. 2010; Wills et al. 2011). A US study found families that had fallen into poverty still emphasized nutrition and preparing food from scratch, even though they no longer had the time or money for those food practices (Gross and Rosenberger 2010). The authors argue that those families sought to display their (former) middle-class affiliations. In Northern England, Shildrick and MacDonald (2013) found people living in (often extreme) poverty routinely described themselves as healthy eaters, and other (less deserving) "poor people" as unhealthy eaters. They suggest this is a means of distancing from the stigma of poverty.

In our own research we have found Canadians from all income levels express strong knowledge of and commitment to mainstream healthy eating, but not all can afford to indulge those food preferences (Beagan, Chapman, Johnston, et al. 2015). We have also found, however, that endorsement of healthy eating is definitely used to judge others across class categories. When we explored the food patterns of people who have changed class locations over a lifetime—either upward or downward—we found healthy eating is one way to show class affiliation. People who grew up in poverty but now live in relative affluence tended to disparage the eating patterns with which they grew up, emphasizing the lack of healthfulness, describing food practices as "awful" and "disgusting." At the same time, people who grew up in relative affluence but now live in poverty tended to speak with disdain of the food practices of others in their current income bracket. For example, one woman described the typical diet of other people on welfare as consisting of fast food, processed cheese, white bread, Kraft Dinner, hot dogs, and bologna, with no fruits or vegetables; she saw this as "horrible, really, really bad" (Beagan, Power, and Chapman 2015:88).

At this time, the mainstream healthy eating discourse enjoys almost uncontested dominance in Canada. This lends it considerable moral weight and enormous social power to dictate standards for everyday living (Foucault 1979). Not only can this discourse be used to mark one's own identity as distinct from less-virtuous (and perhaps mythical) "poor people" (see Shildrick and MacDonald 2013), but it can also be used to judge and belittle those whose eating patterns are deemed "unhealthy." In our study, inexpensive foods often associated with the lower social classes were routinely scorned by people from all income levels. While this rejection was usually in the name of healthy eating, "rejecting these foods suggests a moral condemnation that may extend beyond the foods themselves, to include the people who regularly eat these foods" (Beagan, Chapman, Johnston, et al. 2015:153). Poverty makes it very difficult to engage in mainstream healthy eating, and when healthy eating is routinely used to judge and disparage, poverty also makes it very difficult to eat with dignity in Canada.

In short, social class interacts with eating practices in multiple ways. Current income status affects access to high-quality foods deemed healthy, potentially affecting long-term health. At the same time, food practices can also be a means of conveying social class identities. Judgments concerning the healthfulness of one's own or someone else's diet are employed every day to bolster one's own identity construction and to distinguish from others deemed lesser in social hierarchies.

Conclusion

In this chapter, we have argued that "healthy eating" discourses play a major role in shaping how Canadians engage with food and eating and that the ways people think, talk, and act in relation to healthy eating are entwined with various facets of their social identities. We have specifically explored variations in how healthy eating is currently understood, including mainstream discourses that reflect nutritional science approaches, discourses grounded in tradition and cultural histories, and alternative discourses that emphasize food system concerns. We have examined the interplay with gender, demonstrating

how healthy eating is primarily constructed as a feminine pursuit, placing demands on women to not only take care of their own bodies (especially bodily appearance) but also manage their families' nutritional well-being. Though the gendered nature of healthy eating discourses has historically limited men's uptake of healthy eating, since lack of interest in health, food, and nutrition help define masculinity, this may be shifting. The language of an obesity epidemic may be facilitating an expansion of attention to body weight and appearance to boys and men, couched in the language of health. Nonetheless, it is a particularly strong discursive tool used to police adherence to gender role expectations.

We have also explored how healthy eating discourses are negotiated within families. While youth may seek to be "independent teens" through resisting parental influence over eating patterns, adults may strive to establish themselves as "good parents" through promoting healthy eating. We then examined how ethnic identities may be preserved and shifted by the different ways people "do" healthy eating, and relationships to health and well-being. While mainstream healthy eating may be employed to display assimilation into Western culture, alternative discourses of health and eating may be used to signal resistance. More pointedly, among racialized groups with long histories in Canada, healthy eating discourse may be experienced as another form of racism and colonialism. Finally, we explored the ways healthy eating is understood and engaged with across social classes, yet remains a powerful means of judging others and marking one's own social class status.

It is not possible, of course, to address in one chapter all the ways healthy eating discourses intersect with social identities. However, the examples that we have chosen illustrate multiple complex influences of the social on people's everyday food practices. One of our aims in presenting this argument has been to challenge individualistic assumptions about nutrition behaviours. Both the lay public and health professionals often assume that what people eat is shaped primarily by individual factors such as nutrition knowledge, beliefs, and motivations. There is less understanding of how food practices and ideas about healthy eating are structured by social identities and discourses. As a core part of our everyday lives, we think about, talk about, and consume food multiple times a day, alone or with others. Food is pragmatic but also symbolic, individual yet social, mundane yet also tied to ritual and occasion.

Certain food practices are continually being constructed as morally commendable (desirable, beneficial for well-being, responsible), while other food practices are constructed as morally reprehensible (irresponsible, disdainful, and fat-promoting). These distinctions are very much about maintaining distinctions of class, age, ethnicity, race, and gender. Food discourses like "healthy eating" carry intense symbolic weight enabling all of us to easily—and apparently innocently—reinforce existing social inequities through simple everyday food choices, and the ways we talk about food. All nutrition advice is a social, cultural and political construction and should be read with critical awareness of its potential use in judging and marginalizing individuals and groups.

Discussion Questions

1. How does "healthy eating" influence your family and friends differently, depending on age, gender, race/ethnicity, and social class?

2. If food is so strongly influenced socially, how is it people believe so strongly that eating is guided by individual food tastes and preferences?

3. In what ways do people use food to convey particular social identities?

4. Working in a group, make a list of 25 foods. Next to each item individually note whether that food is associated with males or females, teens or adults, higher or lower social classes. Discuss your agreements and disagreements.

Further Reading

1. Biltekoff, C. 2013. *Eating Right in America: The Cultural Politics of Food and Health.* Durham, NC: Duke University Press.
A powerful and accessible book that looks at how dietary reform movements through history have used nutritional science in service of the politics of race, class, and nation. It traces the rise of nutrition, domestic science, and home economics in the late 1880s, through World War II nutrition-as-patriotism, and the 1980s–90s alternative food movements, to the anti-obesity discourse of the 1990s and 2000s.

2. Cairns, K., and J. Johnston. 2015. *Food and Femininity.* New York: Bloomsbury.
A very current tracing of the relationships between gender and food for women in Canada. It explores the social roles and expectations women face in relation to food, such as good mother, expert cook, and nutritionist, careful consumer, and embodiment of healthy (weight-conscious) eater. They argue that doing food "inadequately" is perceived as doing femininity inadequately.

3. Lupton, D. 2013. *Fat.* Abingdon, UK: Routledge.
Examines the stigma, social marginalization, derision, and revulsion currently attached to fatness in Western societies. Challenges the scientific singularity of the "obesity epidemic," critically reviewing research on obesity discourse and politics, including fat activism and movements for accepting a range of body sizes.

4. Metzl, J.M., and A. Kirkland, eds. 2010. *Against Health: How Health Became the New Morality.* New York: New York University Press.

A collection of articles that explore the social judgments, hierarchies, and privileges enforced through a range of health discourses. Some chapters address healthy eating, fat panic, and obesity.

Video Suggestions

1. British Nutrition Foundation. 2011. *Ethnic Diet & Health.* www.foodafactoflife.org.uk/VideoActivity.aspx?siteId=20&sectionId=84&contentId=505. 11 min.

A podcast exploring the diets of minority ethnic groups in the UK in relation to health.

2. Cornejo, Luis, John Sanderson, and Bahar Tussi. 2013. *Food for Thought.* www.youtube.com/watch?v=vN8Vjxnbfp8. 5 min.

Beautifully filmed, without a word of dialogue, presents dramatic differences in diet shaped by wealth and poverty.

3. Hoffman, John, and Dan Chaykin. 2012. *Poverty and Obesity: When Healthy Food Isn't an Option.* http://theweightofthenation.hbo.com/films/bonus-shorts/poverty-and-obesity-when-healthy-food-isnt-an-option. 24 min.

Explores relationships between poverty, geographic location, health, and obesity.

4. Lee, Jennifer 8. 2008. *The Hunt for General Tso.* www.ted.com/talks/jennifer_8_lee_looks_for_general_tso. 16.5 min.

A humorous exploration of the relationships among food, ethnicity, and identity in a global context, through tracing Chinese food in America. It raises wonderful questions of "authenticity" and shows how racism and ethnocentrism can operate through food.

5. Ramsey, Meaghan. 2014. *Why Thinking You're Ugly Is Bad For You.* www.ted.com/talks/meaghan_ramsey_why_thinking_you_re_ugly_is_bad_for_you. 12 min.

Biting analysis of the messages girls—and now boys—face that entrench the links between "healthy eating" and body-image concerns. It shows the negative effects on health and well-being, understood holistically.

References

Bassett, R., B.L. Beagan, and G.E. Chapman. 2008. "Autonomy and Control: Parents, Teens & Resistance." *Appetite* 50(2/3):325–32.

Backett-Milburn, K.C., W.J. Wills, M.L. Roberts, and J. Lawton. 2010. "Food, Eating and Taste: Parents' Perspectives on the making of the Middle Class Teenager." *Social Science & Medicine* 71(7):1316–23.

Beagan, B.L., and G.E. Chapman. 2012. "Meanings of Food, Eating and Health in African Nova Scotian Families: 'Certain Things Aren't Meant for Black Folk.'" *Ethnicity & Health* 17(5):513–29. http://dx.doi.org/10.1080/13557858.2012.661844

——, ——, D'Sylva, and R. Bassett. 2008. "'It's Just Easier for Me to Do It': Rationalizing the Family Division of Foodwork." *Sociology* 42(4):653–71. http://dx.doi.org/10.1177/0038038508091621.

——, ——, Johnston, D. McPhail, E.M. Power, and H. Vallianatos. 2015. *Acquired Tastes: Why Families Eat the Way They Do.* Vancouver: UBC Press.

——, ——, and E.M. Power. 2016. "Cultural and Symbolic Capital with and without Economic Constraint: Food Shopping in Low-Income and High-Income Canadian Families." *Food, Culture & Society* 19(1):45–70.

——, E.M. Power, and G.E. Chapman. 2015. "'Eating Isn't Just Swallowing Food': Food Practices in the Context of Social Class Trajectory." *Canadian Food Studies* 2:75–98.

——, S. Ristovski-Slijepcevic, and G.E. Chapman. 2010. "'People Are Just Becoming More Conscious of How Everything's Connected': Ethical Food Consumption in Two Regions of Canada." *Sociology* 44:751–69.

Beck, L. 2015. "Five Strategies to Help You Adopt a Clean-Eating Lifestyle." *Globe and Mail*, 4 January. Accessed

23 January 2015. http://www.theglobeandmail.com/life/health-and-fitness/health/five-strategies-to-help-you-adopt-a-clean-eating-lifestyle/article22276823/.

Bernstein, A.M., Q. Sun, F.B. Hu, M.J. Stampfer, J.E. Manson, and W.C. Willett. 2010. "Major Dietary Protein Sources and Risk of Coronary Heart Disease in Women." *Circulation* 122:876–83.

Biltekoff, C. 2013. *Eating Right in America: The Cultural Politics of Food and Health*. Durham, NC: Duke University Press.

Bisogni, C.A., M. Jastran, M. Seligson, and A. Thompson. 2012. "How People Interpret Healthy Eating: Contributions of Qualitative Research." *Journal of Nutrition Education and Behavior* 44:282–301.

Bourdieu, P. 1984. *Distinction: A Social Critique of the Judgement of Taste*. Cambridge, MA: Harvard University Press.

Bugge, A.B. 2011. "Lovin' it? A Study of Youth and the Culture of Fast Food." *Food, Culture & Society* 14(1):71–89.

———, A.B., and R. Lavik. 2010. "Eating Out: A Multifaceted Activity in Contemporary Norway." *Food, Culture & Society* 13:215–40.

Cairns, K., and J. Johnston. 2015. *Food and Femininity*. New York: Bloomsbury.

Canadian Foundation for Dietetic Research. 2014. "CFDR Presents Tracking Nutrition Trends 2013." Accessed 20 February 2015. https://www.cfdr.ca/Downloads/CCFN-docs/TNT-2013-Summary-Report.aspx.

Chapman, G.E., and B.L. Beagan. 2013. "Food Practices and Transnational Identities: Case Studies of Two Punjabi Canadian Families." *Food, Culture & Society* 16(3):367–86.

———, S. Ristovski-Slijepcevic, and B.L. Beagan. 2011. "Meanings of Food, Eating, and Health in Punjabi Canadian Families." *Health Education Journal* 70(1):102–12.

Clark, A.M., A.S. Duncan, J.E. Trevoy, S. Heath, and M. Chan. 2011. "Healthy Diet in Canadians of Low Socioeconomic Status with Coronary Heart Disease: Not Just a Matter of Knowledge and Choice." *Heart & Lung* 40(2):156–63.

DeVault, M.L. 1991. *Feeding the Family: The Social Organization of Caring as Gendered Work*. Chicago: University of Chicago Press.

D'Sylva, A., and B.L. Beagan. 2011. ""Food is Culture, but It's Also Power": The Role of Food in Ethnic and Gender Identity Construction among Goan Canadian Women." *The Journal of Gender Studies* 20:279–89.

Fee, M. 2006. "Racializing Narratives: Obesity, Diabetes and the 'Aboriginal' Thrifty Genotype." *Social Science and Medicine* 62:2988–97.

Foucault, M. 1979. *Discipline and Punish: The Birth of a Prison*. New York: Random House. (French original published in 1975).

Garriguet, D. 2009. "Diet Quality in Canada." *Health Reports* 20(3):41–52.

Gross, J., and N. Rosenberger. 2010. "The Double Binds of Getting Food among the Poor in Rural Oregon." *Food, Culture & Society* 13(1):47–70.

Health Canada. 2011. "Canada's Food Guide." Accessed 23 January 2015. http://www.hc-sc.gc.ca/fn-an/food-guide-aliment/index-eng.php.

Herndon, A.M. 2005. "Collateral Damage from Friendly Fire?: Race, Nation, Class and the 'War against Obesity.'" *Social Semiotics* 15(2):127–41.

———. 2014. *Fat Blame: How the War on Obesity Victimizes Women and Children*. Lawrence: University Press of Kansas.

Johnson, S.L., L.S. Goodell, K. Williams, T.G. Power, and S.O. Hughes. 2015. "Getting My Child to Eat the Right Amount. Mothers' Considerations When Deciding How Much Food to Offer Their Child at a Meal." *Appetite* 88:24–32.

Kramer, C., B. Zinman, and R. Retnakaran. 2013. "Are Metabolically Healthy Overweight and Obesity Benign Conditions? A Systematic Review and Meta-analysis." *Annals of Internal Medicine* 159:758–69.

Lawton, J., N. Ahmad, L. Hanna, M. Douglas, H. Bains, and N. Hallowel. 2008. "'We Should Change Ourselves, but We Can't': Accounts of Food and Eating Practices amongst British Pakistanis and Indians with Type 2 Diabetes." *Ethnic Health* 13:305–19.

Lesser, I.A., D. Gasevic, and S.A. Lear. 2014. "The Association between Acculturation and Dietary Patterns of South Asian Immigrants." *PLOS ONE* 9, 2:e88495.

Mark, S.. M. Lambert, J. O'Loughlin, and K. Gray-Donald. 2013. "Household Income, Food Insecurity and Nutrition in Canadian Youth." *Canadian Journal of Public Health* 103:94–99.

McPhail, D., B.L. Beagan, and G.E. Chapman. 2012. "'I Don't Really Want to Be Sexist But–': Denying Gender, Reinscribing Gender through Food." *Food, Culture and Society* 15:473–89.

———, G.E. Chapman, and B.L. Beagan. 2011. "'Too Much of That Stuff Can't Be Good': Canadian Teens, Morality, and Fast Food Consumption." *Social Science & Medicine* 73:301–7.

———, ———, and ———. 2013. "The Rural and the Rotund? A Critical Interpretation of Food Deserts and Rural Adolescent Obesity in the Canadian Context." *Health & Place* 22:132–9.

Mróz, L.W., G.E. Chapman, J.L. Oliffe, and J.L. Bottorff. 2011. "Gender Relations, Prostate Cancer and Diet: Re-inscribing Hetero-Normative Food Practices." *Social Science and Medicine* 72:1499–1506.

Norman, M.E. 2011. "Embodying the Double-Bind of Masculinity: Young Men and Discourses of Normalcy, Health, Heterosexuality, and Individualism." *Men & Masculinities* 14:430–49.

Protruder, J.L.P., G. Marchessault, A.L. Kozyrskyj, and A.B. Becker. 2010. "Children's Perceptions of Healthful Eating and Physical Activity." *Canadian Journal of Dietetic Practice and Research* 71:19–23.

Raine, K.D. 2005. "Determinants of Healthy Eating in Canada: An Overview and Synthesis." *Canadian Journal of Public Health* 96: S8–14.

Ristovski-Slijepcevic, S., K. Bell, G.E. Chapman, and B.L. Beagan. 2010. "Being 'Thick' Indicates You Are Eating, You Are Healthy and You Have an Attractive Body Shape: Perspectives on Fatness and Food Choice amongst Black and White Men and Women in Canada." *Health Sociology Review* 19(3):317–29.

———, G.E. Chapman, and B.L. Beagan. 2008. "Engaging with Healthy Eating Discourse(s): Ways of Knowing about Food and Health in Three Ethnocultural Groups in Canada." *Appetite* 50(1):167–78.

———, ———, and ———. 2010. "Intergenerational Transmission of Healthy Eating Knowledge in Three Ethnocultural Groups in Canada." *Health: An Interdisciplinary Journal for the Social Study of Health, Illness and Medicine* 14(5):467–83.

Ruby, M.B., and S.J. Heine. 2011. "Meat, Morals, and Masculinity." *Appetite* 56:447–50.

Shildrick, T., and R. MacDonald. 2013. "Poverty Talk: How People Experiencing Poverty Deny Their Poverty and Why They Blame 'The Poor.'" *The Sociological Review* 61:285–303.

Sloan, C., B. Gough, and M.T. Conner. 2011. "Healthy Masculinities? How Ostensibly Healthy Men Talk about Lifestyle, Health and Gender." *Psychology & Health* 25(7):783–803.

Sobal, J., and C.A. Bisogni. 2009. "Constructing Food Choice Decisions." *Annals of Behavioral Medicine* 38(Suppl. 1): S37–46.

Tarasuk, V., A. Mitchell, and N. Dachner. 2014 *Household Food Insecurity in Canada 2012.* Toronto: PROOF.

Walker, R.E., C.R. Keane, and J.G. Burke. 2010. "Disparities and Access to Healthy Food in the United States: A Review of Food Deserts Literature." *Health & Place* 16(5):876–84.

Weeks, C. 2009. "More Young Canadians at Risk for Heart Disease." *Globe and Mail* 21 July, L1.

Williams, P.L., R.B. MacAulay, B.J. Anderson, et al. 2012. "'I Would Have Never Thought That I Would Be in Such a Predicament': Voices from Women Experiencing Food Insecurity in Nova Scotia, Canada." *Journal of Hunger & Environmental Nutrition* 7(2/3):253–70.

Wills, W., K. Backett-Milburn, J. Lawton, and M.-L. Roberts. 2009. "Consuming Fast Food: The Perceptions and Practices of Middle-Class Young Teenagers." Pp. 52–68 in *Children, Food and Identity in Everyday Life*, ed. A. James, A. T. Kjorhold, and V. Tingstad. Houndsmills, Basingstoke, Hampshire: Palgrave Macmillan.

———, ———, M. Roberts, and J. Lawton. 2011. "The Framing of Social Class Distinctions Through Family Food and Eating Practices." *The Sociological Review* 59(4):725–40.

Part II

Analytical Perspectives in Food Studies

What are the components of a food system and how do they relate to each other? What explains some of the food-related problems such as hunger, obesity, and the farm crisis? While answers to these questions are unique to their historical and geographical contexts, there are broader social forces that reveal similarities in patterns and explain interrelations among food-related social problems and various social forces, processes, and institutions. Analytical explanations allow us to understand and explain these broad patterns and interrelations among different parts that compose the whole. In part II we will present four analytical perspectives that have influenced many researchers in food studies.

In chapter 6, Brady, Power, Szabo, and Gingras tell us what we can learn about food, foodwork, and food studies by looking through a feminist lens. Feminists pay specific attention to the causes and consequences of inequalities of power between men and women and the division of labour at home and in the workplace. They argue that much of the earlier social science and food studies literatures have neglected gender analysis. They contend that scholarly analyses of food must pay attention to gender because of the centrality of women to foodwork and the resulting gender inequalities in matters of food, foodwork, and bodies.

In chapter 7, Gingras, Asada, Brady, and Aphramor provide us with insights on the historical conditions that led to the rise of the critical dietetics movement. The chapter expands on the debate on critical thinking that was discussed in chapter 1 of this volume, providing links between critical dietetics and critical literatures of other health professions, namely nursing and critical social theory. Questioning the limitations of their professional education and training, critical dietitians provide a critique of the pedagogies and training of professionals in the food system.

In chapter 8 Albritton offers us an account of the historical transformation of the agri-food system from the political economy perspective. Emphasizing the significance of relations of production in human history, the political economy perspective underlines the historical specificity of each epoch with a dominant mode of production and corresponding patterns of class relations and social organization in society. Using this perspective, Albritton examines the impacts of two great revolutions in the agri-food system. The first revolution brought us agriculture and animal husbandry about 10,000 years ago. The second one—the "Industrial Revolution"—combines the mechanical, chemical, and biotech revolutions in agriculture. Albritton argues that the second revolution enabled global capitalism to increasingly enter and control the food system, which explains many of the problems associated with the modern agri-food system.

In the final chapter of part II, Weis looks at the environmental problems associated with the agri-food system from the political ecology perspective. Political ecology borrows insights from political economy by looking at political-economic tendencies and power imbalances, but also pays special attention to ecological instabilities in how systems operate. Looking through the political ecology lens, Weis identifies the hidden environmental costs of cheap food by focusing on the industrial grain–oilseed–livestock complex and examines how the pressures to standardize and mechanize agriculture magnify biological and physical problems.

6 Still Hungry for a Feminist Food Studies

Jennifer Brady, Elaine Power, Michelle Szabo, and Jacqui Gingras

Learning Objectives

Through this chapter, you can

1. Appreciate what **feminist analyses** have contributed to food studies
2. Consider how **feminism** could continue to strengthen, deepen, and politicize the field of food studies in the areas of domestic foodwork and critical health studies
3. Understand the significance of feminist food studies as an area of inquiry

Introduction

Whether or not we like to admit it, our food practices remain profoundly gendered (Cairns and Johnston 2015; McPhail, Beagan, and Chapman 2012; Beagan et al. 2015). Despite important changes in the **gendered division of household labour**, women continue to perform the majority of **foodwork** in Canadian families (Beagan et al. 2008) and tend to do certain types of foodwork, such as planning, more than men do (Cairns and Johnston 2015). Moreover, ideas about food and foodwork are still tightly tied to how we think about femininity—our generally accepted, socially constructed ideas about the attributes and practices associated with being a woman (Cairns and Johnston 2015). As a result, women generally *care* more about food than men do, because there is so much more at stake for women in terms of their identities as women, mothers, consumers, and citizens who meet—or fail to meet—dominant social expectations.

In this chapter, we are interested in what we can learn about food, foodwork, and food studies

by looking through a feminist lens. We focus particularly on women because of the close connections between femininity and food, foodwork, and **the body**. We also focus on women because of the persistence of sharp gender inequities related to paid and unpaid foodwork and the ways in which women continue to be oppressed by gendered ideas about food and bodies. This includes profound dissatisfaction among women about their bodies, resulting in high rates of disordered eating, anorexia, bulimia, and dieting.

The chapter introduces some of the key facets of feminist thinking as it relates to food production, distribution, preparation, and consumption from a structural perspective. That is, this chapter considers how food and women, as two stable categories of analysis, interact and are informed by wider systems of power. We acknowledge the profound impact on feminist thinking of established and emerging area studies including queer studies, critical Indigenous studies, settler colonial studies, disability studies, and critical race studies but do not engage with this work directly here. Meaningfully engaging with these post-structural approaches would require a fuller discussion that is beyond the scope of this chapter.

A Feminist Lens on Food Studies

Until recently, the relationship between food studies and gender studies has been somewhat obscure. First, although feminists have long had an interest in food-related topics, much feminist food scholarship has been conducted outside of the new interdisciplinary field of food studies and within more traditional disciplines. For example, feminist psychologists and health scholars have critiqued the dominant (white, upper-middle-class) cultural obsession with thinness and the ways that this obsession keeps women perpetually dissatisfied with their bodies, promotes pathological relationships with food, and benefits capitalism by encouraging women to buy products and services to achieve the elusive "perfect body" (Avakian and Haber 2005). Feminist sociologists and anthropologists have anayzed domestic foodwork (e.g. meal planning, cooking) as an axis of oppression in the gendered division of labour, in which women's work in social reproduction is largely invisible, unpaid, and undervalued (e.g. DeVault 1991; Murcott 1982). Feminist scholars of political economy, sociology, and rural studies have also noted the largely unrecognized contributions of female farmers and migrant farm workers to farming economies (Barndt 2008; Preibisch and Grez 2011; Shortall 2006). Secondly, given the association between foodwork and women's oppression, which was highlighted in the 1960s and 1970s, some feminists spurned scholarly analyses of food and rejected domestic foodwork in their personal lives (Avakian 1997). It was not until the twenty-first century that feminist scholars began to publicly reclaim foodwork as a potential source of power, resistance, political activism, creativity, and positive emotions (Cairns and Johnston 2015; D'Sylva and Beagan 2011; Hollows 2003a; Williams-Forson 2006). Thirdly, feminist food scholarship is not always taken seriously, preventing feminist analyses of food and identity from gaining entry to scholarly venues. For example, Arlene Avakian's 1997 anthology of feminists' reflections on their relationships to food, *Through the Kitchen Window*, was regularly shelved in the cookbook sections of bookstores rather than in academic ones (Avakian and Haber 2005). In sum, feminist scholars have both embraced and avoided food-related scholarship, but the work that has been produced has not always been considered "food studies."

On the other side, food studies scholarship has often neglected gender analysis (Avakian and Haber 2005). In writing on food studies and the historical lack of food scholarship, Warren Belasco (2008) notes that food, or more specifically **food production**, has been a topic of concern for particular disciplines, including economics, chemistry, agronomy, engineering, marketing, and labour relations. In addition to the emphasis on food production, it is significant to note that these disciplines are traditionally male dominated and mainly privilege positivist ways of knowing which do not cohere with the types of knowledge involved in elaborating the social, cultural, and emotional meaning of food and cooking. Belasco argues that the oversight of critical analyses of food lies in a historical context in which "women [scholars] have been hesitant to write on food topics for fear of being relegated to a pink ghetto of domestic scholarship, while men have avoided the topic because they fear their work will be dismissed as scholarship lite" (cited in Deutsch and Miller 2007). In other words, the structural and cultural organization of the academy has curtailed feminist food scholarship.

It is also important to note that the food movement and unreflexive food scholarship may in fact exacerbate gender inequities. Advocates of initiatives like "slow food" and "eco-eating" (e.g. Pollan 2008) often call for the public to "re-engage" with their food by doing things like cooking more from scratch or shopping at farmers' markets. However, advocates often fail to take into account the fact that convenience food and supermarkets became popular in part because they helped women entering the work-force juggle the dual responsibilities of employment and unpaid work in the home. In other words, those calling for "re-engagement" with food often fail to consider not only *who* would likely do the extra work involved (i.e. women), but *how* they would do it, given the already significant pressures of balancing paid and unpaid work (Szabo 2011). Furthermore, many analyses of food practices consider gender in isolation from other social positions (Avakian and Haber 2005), neglecting how women's unpaid food-work is part of the complex "doing" of *intersecting* identities of gender, class, race, ethnicity, and sexuality (West and Fenstermaker 1995). In other words, women do foodwork not just as people with a particular gender identity, but *also* as people of particular classes, races, ethnicities, and sexualities.

Since the publication of the first edition of this volume, we are pleased to see that gender has become more significant to food scholarship. This happened in large part because scholarly disciplines such as sociology, women's and gender studies, philosophy, and cultural studies, which already had well-formed theoretical concepts that dealt with identity and power such as gender, race, and class, have taken up the topic of food. Conversely, food studies has less thoroughly amalgamated these critical theoretical tools to expand its scholarship in this area, which has meant a dearth of conversations and critical perspectives regarding gender in food studies forums.

Still, analyses of the relationship between gender and food do not necessarily approach this topic with a feminist lens. Feminist analyses of food and gender seek to expose, critique, and ultimately change the systems of power that lead to gender oppression as it intersects with racism, classism, homophobia, ableism, weight stigma, and other axes of oppression that maintain narrow possibilities for the expression of masculinity and femininity. This point highlights one key theory that has been developed by feminist writers and that is vital to food studies, **intersectionality**. Intersectionality urges scholars to attend to the way in which various oppressions are interwoven and produce unique experiences of subjugation for different individuals and groups. For example, the gender-based oppression faced by Asian women is different than that faced by black women, which is again, different than that experienced by Hispanic women. If we are to envision an **emancipatory** future in which food is produced, distributed, and prepared equitably, we must first appreciate the ways in which oppression operates to prevent all people from participating in that future.

As feminist food studies scholars, we appreciate the increased popularity of gender analyses within the scholarly food literature, but more specifically call on our fellow food studies colleagues to attend to the theoretical tools that feminist scholarship has to offer analyses of food. In this chapter, we ask, "What happens to food studies when we look at it through a feminist lens?" We have three intertwined goals: (a) to make visible the complex relationships that women have with food, foodwork, and the body; (b) to highlight the need for food scholars to pay more attention to gender; and (c) to deepen, strengthen, and politicize food studies by highlighting relations of power and social inequalities related to food, foodwork, and the body. We consider the intimate spaces of women's unpaid foodwork, the body, and the household. While recognizing its importance, we leave aside women's paid food-work in the agri-food system because of space limitations. We have used a feminist analysis to map food, body, and unpaid foodwork, working from the personal to the political, from the micro to the macro, and from the individual to the collective, weaving them together, recognizing that each pole of these analytical dualities contains and creates the other. In so doing, the message is clear: people's relationships with food are felt intimately; at the same time these relationships are partly constituted by "the power that society allocates or denies to men and women through their access to and control of one essential resource: food" (Counihan and Kaplan 1998:2).

Moral Imperatives of Food and Eating

Coveney (2000) aptly describes the dominant contemporary moral imperative facing women with respect to food: "good food requires one to show less concern with the physical pleasure of eating, and more interest in the good health that results from our dietary habits" which, in turn, serves as "the basis for the moral judgment we make about ourselves and others" (p. viii). Because of this moral impetus, food in Canadian culture is, today, predominantly viewed through a paradigm known as **nutritionism**. Nutritionism is a reductionist and technical way of thinking about food that assumes that food's role in promoting bodily health is more important than any other (Scrinis 2013). This dominant approach to food promotes a simplistic way of engaging with food that ignores its multiple symbolic dimensions, such as those related to family, community, and ethnic identity (Beagan and Chapman 2012; Beagan et al. 2015), as well as the pleasures and satisfactions of food, cooking, and eating (Mudry 2009; Pollan 2008). Under nutritionism, eating and feeding others has taken on a specific, singular, and moralistic purpose. Food is seen as simply a vector of nutrient delivery that eaters consume mainly to maintain their health and feeders provide to maintain the health of others.

When viewed through a feminist lens, it becomes clear that nutritionism has particular consequences for women. To challenge nutritionism, we encourage a critical, feminist theoretical standpoint for food studies scholars, informed by related perspectives from fat studies and **critical dietetics**. Nutritionism represents a significant cultural shift in how modern Western society understands food and eating. Because women continue to perform the majority of paid and unpaid food work, it is women who bear the brunt of the additional work involved in satisfying not only the new expectations for food preparation brought by nutritionism but also the moral judgments if they fail to meet them. For example, for women who care for others in the household, such as children, partners, elderly parents, and other dependants, nutritionism holds them responsible for their loved ones' health and nutritional well-being. Even Scrinis himself does not attend to the importance of gender, or other forms of oppression such as racism or classism, in understanding how nutritionism works. However, we assert that Scrinis' **nutricentric person** is not genderless, but must be understood as situated within various intersecting forms of oppression that texture their experiences of food and eating as well as their bodies. It is this kind of analysis that a feminist lens brings to food studies.

Emerging Theories of the Body: Fatness and Embodiment

It is not surprising that many feminist writers have taken the body into account, because "feminism is concerned with the historical, social, and political meanings of sexual difference in the human body, and the spectrum of experiences those meanings produce" (Kevin 2009:1). We take a broad view in that we cannot consider food without feminism, and we cannot consider feminism without the body. Hence feminism, food, and the body are inextricably connected.

Contemporary fat studies scholars have taken up the feminist challenge of considering the ways in which society's obsession with the thin body has disciplined women and regulated their relationships with food. Since the publication of the first edition of this volume, fat studies has established itself as interdisciplinary field of study, "marked by an aggressive, consistent rigorous critique of the negative assumptions, stereotypes, and stigma placed on fat and the fat body" (Rothblum and Solovay 2009:2). Fat studies seeks to break the links between body size, health, and moral worthiness (i.e. thin = healthy = good versus fat = unhealthy = bad). Fat studies also exposes the dominant **discourse** on the body as racist and classist. For example, those who identify with some cultural groups (e.g. those of African descent) put a higher value on rounded, plump bodies than do white people, or at least are less obsessed by thinness (Hughes 1997; Ristovski-Slijepcevic et al. 2010).

Scholars of fat studies and critical dietetics urge us to resist the wave of fat panic that has been buttressed by public-health policy (Kirkland 2011; Beausoleil and Ward 2010). Even feminists have been swept up in fat panic, echoing the public-health call for changes to support healthy eating and increased physical activity through urban planning, taxation, agricultural policy, and so on (Guthman, 2011). Writing from the context of the United States, Kirkland (2011) questions what seems to be feminists' heartfelt, well-meaning desire to help low-income minority groups, especially women and children, who have poor access to fresh food and recreational facilities, and who have higher rates of fatness. She argues, "It is unethical and self-defeating to ride anxiety about fatness to fulfill political goals that actually call for a sustained commitment to economic redistribution for their long-term success" (p. 481). The public-health stance toward "obesity" that some feminists have adopted can appear to be caring and compassionate, but their arguments can be moralizing and unreflexive, with the unintended consequence of adding another layer of marginalization (fatness) to bodies that are already marked by poverty and racialization. Fat studies scholars urge us to consider: Why are we so fixated on body size instead of attending to other, more important determinants of health like racism and poverty?

Gender and Unpaid Foodwork

Just as fat studies scholars have drawn attention to the political nature of the body, feminist activists and researchers highlight the political nature of foodwork, drawing attention to its inequitable distribution and the resulting gender-based oppression at every level, from the household to global food systems (Allen and Sachs 2007).

Unpaid Foodwork and the Public–Private Dichotomy

The ideological dichotomy of **public and private spheres** mirrors dominant gender ideologies and underpins the gendered division of labour. The binary arrangement that organizes gender into two categories, men and women, corresponds with the dichotomy of the public sphere and the private sphere. Dominant gender ideologies associate men and the public sphere with independence, power, paid employment, and financial support of the family. Conversely, women and the private sphere are coupled with dependence, vulnerability, care giving, and feeding the family (DeVault 1991). The private sphere of home and family has been seen as inherently less important than the public sphere of "real" work of measurable economic value. Real work is viewed as remunerated, happening in the public sphere, and the purview of men. On the other hand, women are assumed to be innately inclined to nurture, and responsibilities like unpaid foodwork are viewed as a "labour of love" rather than as the "real work" done by men (Smith 1987; Swenson 2009). The gendered division of labour thus hinges on the socially constructed, binary ideological grouping of men–paid employment–public sphere versus women–unpaid foodwork–private sphere.

Not acknowledging unpaid foodwork as work trivializes the knowledge, skill, and effort it requires and contributes to gender inequality (Oakley 1974). Since unpaid foodwork is not remunerated, it is erroneously considered of little economic consequence to family well-being or the functioning of society at large. DeVault (1991) notes that the work of feeding a family is often unnoticed or mistaken for other, more leisurely tasks: "managing a meal looks like simply enjoying the companionship of one's family . . . and learning about food prices can look like reading the newspaper. The work is noticeable when it is not completed (when the milk is all gone, for example, or when the meal is not ready on time), but cannot be seen when it is done well" (p. 56). This disregard for unpaid foodwork as real work renders the persons held responsible for it (mainly women) of less consequence than those who are ideologically positioned as family breadwinners (traditionally men).

Feminist scholarship has challenged the ideological dichotomies of gender and social space to argue that "unpaid foodwork" is indeed real work and invariably bridges public and private space (DeVault 1991; Smith 1987). Unpaid foodwork involves tasks and processes carried out in the public sphere and which influence and are influenced by it. To illustrate, unpaid foodwork includes budgeting financial, human, and material resources; assessing, purchasing, and transporting food; seeking out and using knowledge of nutrition; planning and preparing meals; juggling the schedules, likes, dislikes, health concerns (e.g. diabetes, low-sodium diet) and dietary needs (e.g. allergies, vegetarian/vegan) of family members; and cleaning up. Clearly, many of these tasks do not occur exclusively within what is usually considered domestic space. Moreover, unpaid foodwork produces goods not only for family members to consume at home (family meals) or away from home (packed lunches, snacks), but also for extended kinship and community networks (entertaining guests, school bake sales, pot lucks). In addition, unpaid foodwork is central to the physical reproduction of family members who live and work outside of the home as well as the reproduction of their social and cultural identities, which marks their membership in a wider community. For example, the preparation of a Passover Seder, Thanksgiving meal, or Eid feast provides sustenance for family members' bodies and sustains their affiliations with their cultural, religious, and social communities. In this light, the tasks and outcomes of unpaid foodwork trouble the notion that the public sphere and the private sphere are distinct realms.

A recent Statistics Canada report suggests that the division of housework among young dual-earner heterosexual couples is becoming more equitable (Marshall 2011). However, once couples have children, women's contribution to housework becomes larger (Marshall 2011) and overall, women still spend more than double the average time that men spend on child care, and more than one and a half times the amount of time that men spend on unpaid domestic work (Milan, Keown, and Robles Urquijo 2011). As Cairns and Johnston (2015) explain, just because men and women are more aware of gendered inequities in housework does not mean that it is easy to change them. But why does this gendered division of domestic foodwork persist—especially in a modern context when male cooks are ubiquitous on food TV?

Four main theories have been put forward to explain women's larger contribution to household work: relative resources; time constraints; gender **ideology**; and gender construction theory. Haddad (1996) classifies such theories into two groups: "pragmatic strategies" and "patriarchal dynamics" based on the underlying thrust of each theory. The "pragmatic strategies," which include relative resources and time constraints, propose that co-habitating couples rationally allocate the distribution of household work, including foodwork, based on their relative material and social resources and availability. Relative resources theory is based on the idea that in the interests of maximizing available resources, the partner with greater socio-economic status (financial resources, education, and occupational prestige) will wield greater interpersonal bargaining power to get out of doing household chores (Erickson 2005; Kroska 2004; McFarlane, Beaujot, and Haddad 2000). The time constraints theory posits that men's and women's participation in unpaid work is a function of the time spent in paid work: as the time spent in paid employment increases, the time spent in unpaid work in the home decreases (Erickson 2005; Kroska 2004; Sayer 2005). Studies have shown however, that even in households where both partners spend an equal number of hours per day in paid work, women still contribute more time to unpaid household work (Shelton and John 1996; Sullivan 2000).

The problem with the theories of relative resources and time constraints is that neither attends to the underlying ideologies that underpin the inequitable distribution of unpaid work. This is particularly so in light of studies that have found that factors related to the relative resources and time constraints theories do not equally impact men's and women's participation in household work (Bittman, England, Folbre, Sayer, and Matheson 2003; McFarlane, Beaujot, and Haddad 2000). Gender ideology theory posits that gender is not determined at birth, but through various socialization experiences is fixed at an early age (cf. West and Zimmerman 1987). Gender ideology theory hypothesizes that in couples that hold more traditional gender ideologies, women perform more of the household work (Erickson 2005; Sullivan 2000). Conversely, partners who hold more liberal gender attitudes will share household work more equally. Studies have shown that men's gender role attitudes have a stronger influence than women's on the division of household work (Kroska 2004; Shelton and John 1996); however, research also indicates that attitudes are generally unreliable predictors of individuals' behaviour (Shelton and John 1996; Cairns and Johnston 2015).

Because of the problems in the above-mentioned theories, many feminist scholars have turned to gender construction theory to explain the fact that women continue to do more housework (including foodwork) than men in North America. Gender construction theory departs from gender ideology theory in seeing gender as an impermanent aspect of identity that is continuously produced through individuals' everyday activities. According to gender construction theory, performing household work is significant beyond individuals' socio-economic worth, availability, or ideological values because it is implicated in the very constitution of individuals' gender identities (Erickson 2005). That

is, gender construction theory proposes that "the gendered allocation of household labour remains unchanged because it signals the extent to which husbands and wives have constructed gender 'appropriately'" (Erickson 2005:340). In other words, it is (in part) by allocating household work unequally that individuals make themselves out to be proper women and men. For example, a woman might choose to cook more than her male partner to signal her femininity; a man might cook less to avoid being seen as "unmasculine."

Foodwork and Gender as Iterative Processes

In line with gender construction theory, some scholars contend that gender is neither a biologically determined nor a socially fixed identity category, but is a matter of individuals' everyday activities and interactions with their social environments (Butler 1990; West and Fenstermaker 1995; West and Zimmerman 1987). Berk explains, "Simultaneously, [household] members 'do' gender, as they 'do' housework and childcare, and what [has] been called the division of labor provides for the joint production of household labor and gender; it is the mechanism by which both the material and symbolic products of the household are realized" (as quoted in West and Zimmerman 1987:144).

For women, unpaid foodwork is a central part of how they "do" gender in ways that fit with prevailing gender norms. DeVault (1991) notes that "It is not just that women do more of the work of feeding, but also that feeding work has become one of the primary ways that women 'do' gender . . . By feeding the family, a woman conducts herself as recognizably womanly" (p. 118). Based on their research of young mothers' dinner practices, Bugge and Almas (2006) support DeVault's (1991) claim in arguing that "women's dinner practice should be understood not only as an act of caring for others (care work), but also something they do for themselves, a kind of identity work" (p. 204; see also McIntyre,

Thille, and Rondeau 2009; Cairns and Johnston 2015). To contravene these normative expectations of being a woman is to risk illegitimacy as a properly gendered individual. By conducting themselves as "recognizably womanly," women's unpaid foodwork iteratively reinforces the gendered assignment of these tasks as feminine, while also constituting those who perform these tasks as feminine subjects. Thus foodwork is too symbolically loaded and emotionally binding for women to simply step back from it (Cairns and Johnston 2015). The iterative construction of foodwork and femininity is also supported by research on same-sex families, where gay men may see foodwork as potentially emasculating, and lesbians may see not doing foodwork as a threat to feminine identity (Carrington 2008).

Overall, "doing" masculinity has received considerably less attention in the literature concerned with gender and foodwork (Julier and Lindenfeld 2005). Of the small pool of published works, many focus on celebrity chefs from television cooking shows (Hollows 2003b; Smith and Wilson 2004; Swenson 2009). For example, Hollows (2003b) explores how celebrity chef Jamie Oliver pulls off an acceptably masculine identity while cooking homestyle food in the domestic setting of his television kitchen. She says that he accomplishes this by "disavowing the extent to which cooking is a form of labour and constructing it as a 'fun' leisure and lifestyle activity" (p. 229). Hollows (2003b) adds that is it this element of performance that keeps men's cooking at home and for others at a safe distance from the sense of obligation and drudgery associated with women's everyday foodwork. However, men in different life circumstances do masculinity differently in relation to cooking. In her examination of men's domestic cooking in Toronto, Szabo (2014) finds that men who are the primary cooks in their households often see cooking as a family responsibility rather than a leisurely pastime.

That men in different circumstances "do" gender differently builds on more recent work suggesting that the practices of "doing" gender (West and Zimmerman 1987) actually constitute

a multiplicity of gender identities (Sobal 2005). Swenson (2009) describes gender as "an activity that is performed in response to institutional and social norms and is capable of pluralities" (p. 39). In other words, the practices by which individuals "do" gender are not prescribed and therefore, neither are masculinity or femininity. Moreover, gender identity is cross-cut by the ways in which people simultaneously engage in practices involved in "doing" other social identities, such as class, race, ethnicity, and sexuality, which further diversifies doable gender identities. Rather than "doing gender," people's relational and interactive everyday practices may be more aptly described as "doing gender(s)."

In their study on women's dinner practices, Bugge and Almas (2006) also found that, although women rationalized the unequal distribution of foodwork between themselves and their male partners based on "pragmatic strategies" (i.e. time constraints), their talk was underpinned by intersecting ideological constructions of gender and class that were enacted by purchasing certain kinds of foods and preparing certain kinds of meals for their families. Study participants explicitly distanced themselves from women seen as not appropriately "doing" their roles as wives and mothers, that is, from those who purchased and cooked primarily prepackaged convenience foods (which have often been associated with working-class diets). For these women, preparing "proper meals" and purchasing the right kinds of high-quality, healthy foods are part of "doing" a particularly gendered, class identity.

Cairns and colleagues (2010) explored how intersectionalities of gender and class are enacted through "foodie discourse" by women and men who self-identified as "foodies" (p. 596). The men and women interviewed spoke similarly about cooking and food as means of seeking pleasure, knowledge, and expertise. For women this seems to challenge traditional gender norms that associate femininity with self-denial rather than desire and expertise. While men and women converged on their discussion of food as a source of pleasure, how they talked about feeding others diverged and tended to reinforce traditional gender norms. The female participants described cooking primarily as a means of caring for their partners and children, fostering family connection, and safeguarding family health. Conversely, men discussed cooking as a leisure activity; preparing food for others was performative and used to showcase their talents. For both the women and men, practices of "doing" class were inseparable from their practices of "doing" gender. Constructing a foodie identity by spending family resources such as time and money on purchasing certain foods, entertaining guests, and pursuing specialized knowledge and skill iteratively constructs the participants' class privilege.

In another study that highlighted the intersectionalities of gender and race, Beagan, Chapman, D'Sylva, and Bassett (2008) found that while the rationale offered by Punjabi-, African-, and European-Canadian families for the unequal distribution of foodwork among their members differed, the underlying reasons were very similar in that all appealed to traditional notions of gender-appropriate work roles. When asked how foodwork responsibilities are divided among family members, Punjabi families explicitly cited gender role expectations (i.e,. foodwork is women's work), while African and European families rationalized men and women's unequal foodwork in ways that concealed the gender discourse that underpinned their reasoning. To illustrate, African and European families often noted women's greater availability of time, despite the fact that in most of these families women were employed full-time. Moreover, women's interest in healthier foods, higher standards for cleaning up, and inclination to keep the peace among family members were cited by African and European participants as additional reasons why women were tasked with the majority of foodwork. The authors added however, that these additional explanations implicitly appeal to gender role expectations, such as women's responsibility for managing the health, well-being, and contentment of family members. These expectations set up standards by

which women, not men or teenaged family members, are judged. Based on this research, Beagan, Chapman, D'Sylva, and Bassett (2008) conclude, "For decades, scholarship in the area of domestic labour has assumed gender inequities will diminish over time, yet this does not appear to be happening. Rather, traditional gender roles seem to reinvent themselves in new guises" (p. 668).

For some marginalized groups, unpaid foodwork may be an important part of resistance to acculturation and oppression by dominant groups. Discussion of resistance movements generally situates action within the public sphere (e.g. demonstrations, labour strikes) rather than in the intimate spaces of the home. For example, the Gullah are African-Americans descended from slaves, who live along the coast of South Carolina and Georgia. In exploring Gullah women's unpaid foodwork, Beoku-Betts (2002) finds that food preparation, including the type of foods prepared, the methods, and the flavourings used, is part of women's conscious effort to resist the racist past of their ancestors and demarcate and maintain a group identity distinct from the surrounding dominant culture. Similarly, Narayan (1995) explores the role of food in negotiating Indian identity for expatriates living in Britain and shows how foodwork was a practice of resistance during British rule and was used to set Indians' identities and communities apart from their British colonizers.

However, for women who are economically marginalized, lack of money to feed oneself and one's family adds new levels of complexity and stress to foodwork and contributes to the misery and suffering of poverty. Inadequate money to buy food brings into sharp relief all the invisible work involved in feeding the family and adds to that workload. Food providers who have experienced periods of low income describe the more careful budgeting and planning needed at those times, including checking flyers, clipping and keeping track of coupons, comparison shopping, and keeping a running tally of the cost of the food in the grocery cart so as not to go over budget. With financial constraints, women must be more resourceful in their cooking: cooking more often from scratch; altering menus to "stretch" the meal; making low-cost meals that use a minimum of ingredients; and serving only food that the family likes so that none is wasted. Under financial duress, women will serve themselves lower-quality food or smaller portions, sometimes skipping meals entirely, to ensure that their children are not hungry or their male partners are satisfied. They will also swallow their pride and endure the demeaning experience of receiving food from charitable sources such as food banks (DeVault 1991; Hamelin, Beaudry, and Habicht 2002; Power, Beagan, Salmon, and McPhail 2010). Attesting to the invisibility of this work, food providers who had never been short of money for food were asked to imagine what would change if they were. They never mentioned the extra practical work listed above, thinking instead of the food items and restaurant meals they would no longer be able to afford (Power et al. 2010). Layered onto these practical tasks are intense emotions: the worry and anxiety of juggling which bills will get paid and how much money will be left over for groceries; the heartbreak of refusing children's requests so often that eventually they stop asking; the fear of not being able to properly provide for one's children and failing as a mother; the sinking feeling in the gut when what is left in the cupboard and fridge is inadequate to make a satisfying meal (Hamelin et al. 2002; Power et al. 2010; Power 2005). For women living on inadequate incomes, food is hardly the source of pleasure that highly resourced "foodies" describe (Cairns et al. 2010; Cairns and Johnston 2015); instead it is a constant source of stress and anxiety, limiting women's ability to properly feed themselves and their families, and thus their ability to live up to standards of acceptable femininity.

Conclusion

As we finish this manuscript in the spring of 2016, and reflect on the earlier version of this chapter written in 2011, we see that the crises facing our world have intensified. The environmental crisis, particularly global climate change, is one of the most prominent, but there are crises in every realm, from the economic and political to the religious, cultural, and social arenas. The natural and social worlds cry out for caring and nurturing, values associated with the feminine (in both men and women), and with women's foodwork.

It is our profound hope that food studies can contribute to building a better, more just world by analyzing the ways in which food, foodwork, and bodies produce, reproduce, and resist forms of inequality and oppression. We will thus make our scholarship useful, because clear understandings and thoughtful analysis are critical to promoting change. Like Avakian and Haber (2005), Allen and Sachs (2007), Cairns and Johnston (2015), and other feminist food scholars, we encourage food studies to become inherently feminist, to know that we cannot claim to understand food, foodwork, or the food system without considering gender and gender inequities. Food studies can also learn from feminism to consider other ways in which power operates to re-inscribe—or resist—relations of inequality and oppression.

On the other hand, food studies is already helping bring feminists back in touch with food, as highly attuned producers (locavores), distributors (fair-trade doyennes), and consumers (customers of organic products and foodies) (Cairns et al. 2010; Cairns and Johnston 2015). And, perhaps women are more politically involved in environmental issues (Micheletti 2004), especially those that concern the food supply, bringing feminists and their theories closer to the earth, sustenance, nourishment, and longing. A feminist perspective positions food studies at the promising and visceral edge of integrating embodiment, food, emotionality, and social trust (Beasley and Bacchi 2007; Hayes-Conroy and Hayes-Conroy 2010), a crucial step in doing a better job of caring for and nourishing ourselves, others, and the planet. Lupton (1996) argues that "devoting attention to embodiment indeed confounds the entire logocentric project of philosophy; the drive to rationalize the emphatic separation of the mind from the body, the elevation of thought over embodiment" (p. 2). Such confounding is exactly what we wish to imagine for future iterations of food studies, theory, and practice.

Discussion Questions

1. A key tenet of feminism is that the personal is political, meaning that in addition to the political proceedings we most commonly associate with the public sphere (i.e. policy, laws, government, the economy), the events and relationships that take place in our everyday lives also shape and are shaped by political currents. How do the issues discussed in this chapter affect your everyday life? How is your relationship to food, foodwork, and the body shaped by dominant ideologies about health, nutrition, gender, and class?

2. One goal of this chapter is to deepen, strengthen, and politicize your understanding of food studies by drawing lessons from feminism and other related critical scholarly fields. If your primary discipline is not gender studies, how does your field of study or area of interest contribute to the discussion of feminist perspectives of food studies presented here?

3. The first part of this chapter discusses the impact of nutritionism on women's relationships to food, eating, and their bodies. How might nutritionism affect women as those responsible for unpaid foodwork, as discussed in the second part of the chapter?

4. Recognizing the following, how might we, individually and collectively, reduce gendered inequities in foodwork?
   a. the symbolic links between foodwork and femininity, and the positive associations that many women have with foodwork
   b. some women who do foodwork in families saying that "it is just easier to do it myself" rather than following through on a more equal gendered division of food labour
   c. ideals and principles about gender equity in foodwork often not translating into practices

Further Reading

1. Allen, P., and C. Sachs. 2007. "Women and Food Chains: The Gendered Politics of Food," *International Journal of Sociology of Food and Agriculture* 15(1):1–23.
This article offers a review of the feminist literature on food and gender, and explores the ways in which the contemporary food system begets gender inequality. Allen and Sachs argue that feminist food studies researchers must explore and theorize how the material, socio-cultural, and corporeal domains of the contemporary food system are interconnected and how each is implicated in women's subordination and their acts of resistance. The authors also review how women are organizing to create change within the food system to promote gender equity.

2. Bordo, S. 1993. *Unbearable Weight: Feminism, Western Culture, and the Body.* Berkeley: University of California Press.
This is an important feminist text for those interested in understanding the (female) body as a social construction. In a collection of delightfully written and accessible essays, Bordo examines the cultural, social, and media influences on Western women's bodies.

3. **Cairns, K. and Johnston, J. 2015. *Food and Femininity*. London: Bloomsbury.**

   This book, which draws on Canadian research, explores women's experiences of food and foodwork in depth. It explores how notions of "femininity" (and related notions such as "motherhood") shape and are shaped by food practices, including dieting, cooking, food shopping, eating, and engaging in food activism. The authors give attention to both the emancipatory and pleasurable aspects of food and its oppressive and marginalizing potential. Drawing out the intersections of gender and class, the book highlights how women with low incomes are particularly affected by the pressures of "femininity" around food.

4. **Counihan, C., and S. Kaplan. 1998. *Food and Gender: Identity and Power*. Amsterdam: Harwood Academic Publishers.**

   In this edited volume, Counihan and Kaplan present articles that explore various perspectives of food and gender. On the whole, this volume addresses questions about the roles of food production, consumption, and distribution in constructing gender identity and the gendered distribution of social and personal power.

5. **DeVault, M. 1991. *Feeding the Family: The Social Organization of Caring as Gendered Work*. Chicago: University of Chicago Press.**

   In this food studies and feminist classic, DeVault reports on her analysis of interviews with those most responsible for foodwork (30 women and 3 men) in 30 economically, culturally, and ethnically diverse households in the United States. DeVault sheds light on the often invisible, gendered organization of foodwork and its significance in constructing gender and class identities in the context of the North American family. *Feeding the Family* has stood the test of time and is an essential resource for food studies students and scholars.

Video Suggestion

1. **Nash, Terre. 1995. *Who's Counting? Marilyn Waring on Sex, Lies and Global Economics*. www.nfb.ca/film/whos_counting. (94 min).**

   Former New Zealand MP Marilyn Waring uses a feminist lens to deconstruct the myths and assumptions of the global economic system, which ignores the unpaid and invisible work of women and counts socially and environmentally destructive activities as economically productive. Waring's vision of an alternative economic system uses time as currency instead of money.

References

Allen, P., and C. Sachs. 2007. "Women and Food Chains: The Gendered Politics of Food." *International Journal of Sociology of Food and Agriculture* 15(1):1–23.

Avakian, A.V. 1997. *Through the Kitchen Window: Women Writers Explore the Intimate Meanings of Food and Cooking*. Boston: Beacon.

——— and B. Haber. 2005. "Feminist Food Studies: A Brief History." Pp. 1–28 in *From Betty Crocker to Feminist Food Studies: Critical Perspectives on Women and Food*, ed. A. Avakian and B. Haber. Boston: University of Massachusetts Press.

Barndt, Deborah. 2008. *Tangled Routes: Women, Work and Globalization on the Tomato Trail*. Lanham, MD: Rowman & Littlefield.

Beagan, B., and G. Chapman. 2012. "Meanings of Food, Eating and Health among African Nova Scotians: 'Certain Things Aren't Meant for Black Folk.'" *Ethnicity & Health* 17(5):513–29.

———, ———, A. D'Sylva, and B. Bassett. 2008. "'It's Just Easier for Me to Do It': Rationalizing the Family Division of Foodwork." *Sociology* 42(4):653–72.

———, ———, J. Johnson, D. McPhail, E. Power, and H. Vallianatos. 2015. *Acquired Tastes: Why Families Eat the Way They Do*. Vancouver: UBC Press.

Beasley, C., and C. Bacchi. 2007. "Envisaging a New Politics for an Ethical Future: Beyond Trust, Care and Generosity—Towards an Ethic of 'Social Flesh.'" *Feminist Theory* 8(3):279–98.

Beausoleil, N., and P. Ward. 2010. "Fat Panic in Canadian Public Health Policy: Obesity as Different and Unhealthy." *Radical Psychology* 8(1). http://www.radicalpsychology. org/vol8-1/fatpanic.html.

Belasco, W. 2008. *Food: The Key Concepts*. Oxford: Berg.

Beoku-Betts, J. 2002. "'We Got Our Way of Cooking Things': Women, Food, and Preservation of Cultural Identity among the Gullah." Pp. 277–94 in *Food in the USA: A Reader*, ed. C. Counihan. New York: Routledge.

Bittman, M., P. England, N. Folbre, L. Sayer, and G. Matheson. 2003. "When Does Gender Trump Money? Bargaining and Time in Household." *The American Journal of Sociology* 109(1):186–214.

Bugge, A.B., and R. Almas. 2006. "Domestic Dinner: Representations and Practices of a Proper Meal among Young Suburban Mothers." *Journal of Consumer Culture* 6(2):203–28.

Butler, J. 1990. *Gender Trouble: Feminism and the Subversion of Identity*. New York: Routledge.

Cairns, K., and J. Johnston. 2015. *Food and Femininity*. London: Bloomsbury.

———, ———, and S. Baumann. 2010. "Caring about Food: Doing Gender in a Foodie Kitchen." *Gender and Society* 24(5):591–615.

Carrington, C. 2008. "Feeding Lesbigay Families." Pp. 259–86 in *Food and Culture: A Reader*, 2nd edn, ed. C. Counihan and P. van Esterik. New York and London: Routledge.

Counihan, C., and S. Kaplan. 1998. *Food and Gender: Identity and Power*. Amsterdam: Harwood Academic Publishers.

Coveney, J. 2000. *Food, Morals, and Meaning: The Pleasure and Anxiety of Eating*. New York: Routledge.

Deutsch, J., and J. Miller. 2007. "Food Studies: A Multidisciplinary Guide to the Literature." *Choice* 45(3):393–401.

DeVault, M. 1991. *Feeding the Family: The Social Organization of Caring as Gendered Work*. Chicago: University of Chicago Press.

D'Sylva, A., and B. Beagan. 2011. "'Food Is Culture, but It's Also Power': The Role of Food in Ethnic and Gender Identity Construction among Goan Canadian Women." *Journal of Gender Studies* 20(3):279–89.

Erickson, R.J. 2005. "Why Emotion Work Matters: Sex, Gender, and the Division of Household Labor." *Journal of Marriage and Family* 67(2):337–51.

Guthman, J. 2011. *Weighing In: Obesity, Food Justice, and the Limits of Capitalism*. Oakland: University of California Press.

Haddad, A. 1996. *The Sexual Division of Household Labour: Pragmatic Strategies or Patriarchal Dynamic? An Analysis of Two Case Studies*. PhD thesis. York University.

Hamelin, A.-M., M.Beaudry, and J.-P. Habicht. 2002. "Characterization of Household Food Insecurity in Quebec: Food and Feelings." *Social Science and Medicine* 54(1):119–32.

Hayes-Conroy, J., and A. Hayes-Conroy. 2010. "Visceral Geographies: Mattering, Relating, and Defying." *Geography Compass* 49:1273–83.

Hollows, J. 2003a. "Feeling Like a Domestic Goddess: Postfeminism and Cooking." *European Journal of Cultural Studies* 6(2):179–202.

———. 2003b. "Oliver's Twist: Leisure, Labour and Domestic Masculinity in *The Naked Chef*." *International Journal of Cultural Studies* 6(2):229–48.

Hughes, M.H. 1997. "Soul, Black Women and Food." Pp. 272–80 in *Food and Culture: A Reader*, ed. C. Counihan and P. V. Esterik. New York and London: Routledge.

Julier, A., and L. Lindenfeld. 2005. "Mapping Men onto the Menu: Masculinities and Food." *Food and Foodways* 13(1):1–16.

Kevin, C. 2009. *Feminism and the Body: Interdisciplinary Perspectives*. Newcastle, UK: Cambridge Scholars.

Kirkland, A. 2011. "The Environmental Account for Obesity: A Case for Feminist Skepticism." *Signs: Journal of Women in Culture and Society* 36(2):463–85.

Kroska, A. 2004. "Division of Domestic Work: Revising and Expanding the Theoretical Explanations." *Journal of Family Issues* 25(7):900–32.

Lupton, D. 1996. *Food, the Body, and the Self*. London: Sage.

Marshall, K. 2011. "Generational Change in Paid and Unpaid Work." *Canadian Social Trends* 92 (Winter). Statistics Canada catalogue 11-008-x.

McFarlane, S., R. Beaujot, and T. Haddad. 2000. "Time Constraints and Relative Resources as Determinants of the Sexual Division of Domestic Work." *Canadian Journal of Sociology/Cahiers Canadiens de Sociologie* 25(1):61–82.

McIntyre, L., P. Thille, and K. Rondeau. 2009. "Farmwomen's Discourses on Family Food Provisioning: Gender, Health-ism, and Risk Avoidance." *Food and Foodways* 17:80–103.

McPhail, D., B. Beagan, and G. Chapman. 2012. "'I Don't Want to Be Sexist But . . .': Denying and Re-inscribing Gender through Food." *Food, Culture & Society* 15(3):473–89.

Micheletti, M. 2004. "Why More Women? Issues of Gender and Political Consumerism." Pp. 245–64 in *Politics, Products, and Markets: Exploring Political Consumerism Past and Present*, ed. M. Micheletti, A. Folesdal, and D. Stolle. Piscataway, NJ: Transaction.

Milan, A., L.-A. Keown, and C. Robles Urquijo. 2011. "Families, Living Arrangements and Unpaid Work." *Women in Canada: A Gender-Based Statistical Report*. Statistics Canada Catalogue 89-503-X.

Mudry, J. 2009. *Measured Meals: Nutrition in America*. Albany: State University of New York Press.

Murcott, A. 1982. "'It's a Pleasure to Cook for Him': Food, Meal Times and Gender in South Wales Households." Pp.78–90 in *The Public and The Private*, ed. E. Gamarnikow, D. Morgan, J. Purvis, and D. Taylorson. London: Heinemann.

Narayan, U. 1995. "Eating Cultures: Incorporation, Identity and Indian Food." *Social Identities* 11:63–86.

Oakley, A. 1974. *The Sociology of Housework*. New York: Random House.

Preibisch, K., and E. Grez. 2011. "Re-examining the Social Relations of the Canadian 'Family Farm': Migrant Women

Farm Workers in Rural Canada." Pp. 91–112 in *Reshaping Gender and Class in Rural Spaces*, ed. Barbara Pini and Belinda Leach. Farnham, UK: Ashgate.

Pollan, M. 2008. *In Defense of Food: An Eater's Manifesto*. New York: Penguin.

Power, E. 2005. "The Unfreedom of Being Other: Canadian Lone Mothers' Experiences of Poverty and 'Life on the Cheque.'" *Sociology* 39(4):643–60.

———, B. Beagan, N. Salmon, and D. McPhail. 2010. "'And Then the Broccoli Crept into Our Life': Imagined and Real Impacts of Changes in Income on Food & Eating Practices." Paper presented at the Association for the Study of Food and Society. 3–6 June, Bloomington, IN.

Ristovski-Slijepcevic, S., K. Bell, G. Chapman, and B. Beagan. 2010. "Being 'Thick' Indicates You Are Eating, You Are Healthy and You Have an Attractive Body Shape: Perspectives on Fatness and Food Choice amongst Black and White Men and Women in Canada." *Health Sociology Review* 19(3):317–29.

Rothblum, E., and S. Solovay, eds. 2009. *Fat Studies Reader*. New York: New York University Press.

Sayer, L.C. 2005. "Gender, Time and Inequality: Trends in Women's and Men's Paid Work, Unpaid Work and Free Time." *Social Forces* 84(1):285–303.

Scrinis, G. 2013. *Nutritionism: The Science and Politics of Dietary Advice*. New York: Columbia University Press.

Shelton, B.A., and D. John. 1996. "The Division of Household Labor." *Annual Review of Sociology* 22:299–322.

Shortall, S. 2006. "Gender and Farming: An Overview."

Pp. 19–26 in *Rural Gender Relations: Issues and Case Studies*, ed. B.B. Bock and S. Shortall. Wallingford, UK: CABI.

Smith, D.E. 1987. *The Everyday World as Problematic: A Feminist Sociology*. Boston: Northeastern University Press.

Smith, G.M., and P. Wilson. 2004. "Country Cookin' and Cross-Dressin': Television, Southern White Masculinities, and Hierarchies of Cultural Taste." *Television & New Media* 53:175–95.

Sobal, J. 2005. "Men, Meat and Marriage: Models of Masculinity." *Food & Foodways* 13(1):135–58.

Sullivan, O. 2000. "The Division of Domestic Labour: Twenty Years of Change?" *Sociology* 34(3):437–56.

Swenson, R. 2009. "Domestic Divo? Televised Treatments of Masculinity, Femininity and Food." *Critical Studies in Media Communication* 26(1):36–53.

Szabo, M. 2011. "The Challenges of 'Re-engaging with Food': Connecting Employment, Household Patterns and Gender Relations to Convenience Food Consumption in North America." *Food, Culture & Society* 14(4):547–66.

———. 2014. "Men Nurturing through Food: Challenging Gender Dichotomies around Domestic Cooking." *Journal of Gender Studies* 23(1):18–31.

West, C., and S. Fenstermaker. 1995. "Doing Difference." *Gender & Society* 9(1):8–37.

——— and D.H. Zimmerman. 1987. "Doing Gender." *Gender & Society* 1(2):125–51.

Williams-Forson, Psyche A. 2006. *Building Houses out of Chicken Legs: Black Women, Food, and Power*. Chapel Hill: University of North Carolina Press.

7 Critical Dietetics
Challenging the Profession from Within

Jacqui Gingras, Yuka Asada, Jennifer Brady,
and Lucy Aphramor

Learning Objectives

Through this chapter, you can

1. Describe the critical dietetic movement including its core framework, goals, and historical context
2. Discuss what we see as the key areas of this theoretical framework and what implications the framework would have for dietetic education, practice, and research
3. Discuss the relevance of the critical dietetics movement to food studies scholarship

Introduction

This chapter discusses the background, main constructs, and implications of the **critical dietetics**[1] movement. Critical dietetics is a dynamic movement that continues to grow as dietitians question the limitations of their professional education and training, and as the movement reaches out to other groups involved in critical work related to food, eating, and the body, such as food studies. This chapter begins by briefly visiting the history of dietetics to provide context for the state of the dietetic profession today, as well as the critical dietetics movement. Next, we show how the seeds of critical dietetics have grown out of many contexts and disciplinary perspectives, including critical literatures of other health professions—namely nursing—and critical social theory. The following section discusses the implications of critical dietetics for the dietetic profession, as well as for food studies and contemporary perspectives of food, eating, and nutrition. We conclude that critical dietetics

offers an approach for current and future dietitians—practitioners, educators, researchers, and students—as well as those who work closely with dietitians to recreate the future of the dietetic profession: a future that better serves those in search of nutrition support and that helps to contribute to a socially just food system.

Historical Context in Canada

According to Dietitians of Canada, the primary organization that represents and advocates for the interests of the dietetic profession in Canada, "dietitians are highly qualified professionals educated in science, management, human development, and health of populations" (Dietitians of Canada 2015). Dietitians work in many different settings including clinical roles (i.e. hospitals and other treatment centres), public health and community nutrition, sport and recreation facilities, policy and government, food industry, food service (i.e. cafeterias), nutrition communication and journalism, research, and education.

In Canada, Dietitian or Registered Dietitian (RD) is a protected title that may only be used by members of provincial regulatory bodies.[2] **Dietetics** is self-regulated through a provincial college or professional association, which is granted oversight of its members by a provincial act. In Ontario the scope of practice for dietetics is defined in the 1991 Dietetic Act as: "the assessment of nutrition and nutritional conditions and the treatment and prevention of nutrition-related disorders by nutritional means." However, there is some variation in the scope of practice statements, as well as the practices and procedures among the provinces (Sellinger and Berenbaum 2015). Dietetics is not a regulated profession in any of the three territories.

The education and training required to become a dietitian includes a four-year undergraduate degree in human nutrition plus a period of practical internship training in four key areas of dietetic practice (clinical, community, food service, and research), which is supervised by dietitian preceptors. Upon completion of these requirements, individuals must pass the Canadian Dietetic Registration Examination to be granted a licence to practice. Central to the education and training of dietitians, as well as all areas of practice, is a primary focus on evidence-based nutrition science. This focus, which has been critiqued for its narrow scope (Clarke 2011; Cuddy 2012; Gingras and Brady 2009) is key to understanding the values and culture of dietetics and to its emergence and development as a profession. The education and registration system for dietitians in the UK follows the same pathway. However, before we further explore this focus and the significance to dietetics, it is important to sketch out another profession that gave rise to dietetics—home economics (Cassell 1990).

In Ontario, Alberta, New Brunswick, British Columbia, and Manitoba, the title Professional Home Economist (PHEc) is protected and home economics is self-regulated by provincial associations (Ontario Home Economics Association 2015). In the workplace, home economists are involved in a wide range of practice areas including health and nutrition, clothing and textiles, family relationships, and consumer issues, and are employed in various roles in the private and public sectors such as advertising, media and public relations, communications, teaching, fashion design and textile development, national and international development, policy creation, and advocacy. Home economists complete a four-year degree program comprising study in pure, applied, and social sciences in housing and consumer studies, food and nutrition science, childhood development and family studies, and clothing and textiles, which reflects PHEc's breadth of employment areas and workplace roles (Ontario Home Economics Association 2015).

At the heart of home economics is a philosophical, conceptual, and practical commitment to a human ecology model of understanding the world and the role of home economists. The human ecology model sees "humans as social, physical, biological beings in interaction with each other and with their physical, socio-cultural, aesthetic, and biological environments, and with the material and human resources of these environments" (Bubolz and Sontag 1988:3). The spirit of the human ecology model is captured in the widely accepted mission statement of home economics penned by Brown and Paolucci (1979):

> the purpose of home economics is to "enable families, as individual units and generally as a social institution, to build and maintain systems of action which lead 1) to maturing in individual self formation, and; 2) to enlightened, cooperative, participation in the critique and formulation of social goals and the means of accomplishing them" (p. 23)

Although the theory and practice of home economics includes a commitment to evidence-based science, like dietetics, particularly in the area of food and nutrition, the human ecology model places the evidence base alongside the social, cultural, economic, and relational aspects of food and eating within the human ecosystem that comprises the individual, the family, and the surrounding society (Bubolz and Sontag 1988).

Even though today home economics and dietetics are distinct professions with separate educational paths and credentials, as well as their own regulating bodies and workplace roles, the history of these two professions is very much intertwined. Dietetics emerged from home economics, at first as a subspecialty in food and nutrition, but gradually became the distinct profession that we know today. It is important to understand the emergence of home economics and dietetics throughout the mid-nineteenth and early twentieth centuries within the context of the sweeping societal changes happening at the time. The Industrial Revolution was bringing massive changes in labour arrangements that were accompanied by rapid urbanization and immigration. Interest in science, efficiency, and mechanization exploded, and with it came the rise of nutrition science as a field of study. It was during this period that vitamins were discovered—vitamins A and B in 1914 and 1911 respectively, and then vitamins C, D, E, and K; riboflavin (B_2); folic acid (B_6); and beta-carotene throughout the 1920s and 1930s (Ostrowski 1986). The interest and growth in science and technology led to new and expanding areas of knowledge, which prompted growth of many different professions, including home economics and dietetics (Bright-See 1998). Home economics was originally seen as a field through which women could access opportunities that were generally off limits to them at this time, namely post-secondary education, particularly in the sciences, and paid professional employment (Stage 1997).

One of the first areas of employment for women trained in home economics was in hospitals as dietitians preparing food for staff and patients and instructing nurses in "sick room" or "invalid cookery"—the preparation and service of meals and special diets for the sick (Lang and

Upton 1973; Reddin 2006). By the 1910s home economics recognized the opportunity for training dietitians to its future growth as a profession and to the continued advancement of women's access to paid careers (Nyhart 1997; Reddin 2006). Increasingly dietitians' duties expanded to include implementing doctor's orders for special therapeutic diets (mainly diabetes), diet teaching to patients at discharge, planning and overseeing dietary kitchens, and purchasing supplies (Lang and Upton 1973). As the technical knowledge of dietetics grew throughout the early 1900s with the continued growth of nutrition science, dietetics continued to gained prestige.

A key event in the development of home economics and dietetics was the commencement of the First World War in 1914. By the advent of the war, dietitians trained in home economics were downplaying their role in nurse training to seek out new opportunities for growth, which they found in hospital food administration in the newly formed Canadian military hospitals (Nyhart 1997). These practitioners' background in home economics translated well to this new role since the hospital could be easily framed as a large household (Nyhart 1997). Dietitians were appointed to direct and manage the food service in approximately half of the 50 military hospitals with plans to extend appointments to all institutions when trained dietitians could be found (Lang and Upton 1973; Ryley 1918). In these roles dietitians were tasked with budgeting and accounting; planning menus; managing all kitchen and service staff; overseeing quality control for the food, the service, and the equipment and facilities; and instructing and supervising student dietitians.

While these developments advanced the professionalization of home economics, they also set in motion the eventual splitting of dietetics from home economics as a distinct area of practice. The American Dietetic Association (ADA), which granted credentials to both American and Canadian dietitians until the Canadian association was established in 1917 just as dietitians took the helm of food services for the military hospitals across Canada. The purpose of the ADA was to set educational standards for dietitians' membership to the organization and for employment in military hospitals which made dietitians' roles more exclusive and, consequently, more prestigious. Initially ADA membership required members to have a two-year college-level course in a home economics–related program, but educational standards continued to increase so that by the mid-1920s membership required a four-year degree with a major in foods and nutrition. In contrast, the American Home Economics Association had no requirements for membership and accepted anybody interested in joining, including "corporate home economists" who were widely seen as "company flacks" (Stage 1997:11). The split between home economics and dietetics in the United States and Canada continued to deepen with the commencement of the Second World War and the founding of Canadian provincial and national dietetic associations.

We wish to recognize the hard work and milestones accomplished by dietitians in the past and look to address how their work, and dietetics' **gendered history**, may shed light on the values, culture, and status of the profession today, and may inform the future direction of the profession. The gendered history of dietetics is seen today: 98 per cent of dietitians are women, yet fewer women than men are involved in nutritional research, and fewer men are front-line practitioners (Pollard et al. 2007). It is important to note that dietetics' body of knowledge was founded upon research that, at times, neglected the voice of women (Liquori 2001), an implication that remains unexamined today in dietetic education and training (Gingras 2005, 2008b). As Erickson-Weerts (1999) states, "Our forbearers' tribute to us might be: Your efforts to help the public achieve optimum nutritional health should intensify and be informed, not replaced, by prudence and therapeutics" (p. 293). Critical dietetics asks the kinds of questions that bring to light the ways in which dietetics' beginnings and ecological worldview have been supplanted by "prudence and therapeutics." What—if anything—does it mean

for dietitians to be disseminating knowledge and practising within frameworks mainly generated by men? How we can balance this emphasis on science with other valuable perspectives toward health? What perspectives are missing?

What Is Critical Dietetics?

Critical dietetics is an initiative that is rooted in **critical social theory** and urges the dietetic profession to broaden its lens beyond its traditional, dominant paradigms that are rooted in positivist science. Critical dietetics was born from a growing recognition that the current approach to nutrition generally, and dietetic practice more specifically, does not attend to the multiple meanings of food and the complex and contextual nature of health and illness (Aphramor and Gingras 2009). Critical dietetics calls on the dietetic profession to embrace both new ways of understanding its practice and its role in creating a socially just world, beyond nutrition. One aspect of this work that we urge dietetics to undertake includes building a food system that attends to social and cultural factors that negatively impact the physical, emotional, spiritual, and relational health of all people, as well as the natural world. Some criticize the ability of critical social theory to invoke "communicative action" between theory and practice (Cole 1993). In other words, these critiques raise questions about the ability of a movement such as critical dietetics to effect real change outside of academic theorizing. However, Steinvorth (2008) reminds us that critical theory actually prioritizes action and practical solutions over theorizing. Yet, like food studies, critical dietetics takes up critical social theory, not as an end point, but as an addition to the activism from which this movement grew.

As practitioners, we have experienced the sorrow, frustration, and burnout that comes with trying to effect change in the lives and communities of those we serve, only to be troubled by our lack of resources to do so and sometimes silenced by our colleagues. To move forward, we have reached out to the critical literature produced by other health professions that questioned the values and practices of their discipline, as elaborated upon below. We discuss how new ways of thinking and asking questions may help to expose our assumptions and familiar ways of practice in our profession. Like the critical bodies of work developed from within other health professions, critical dietetics is framed by the critical literature produced by areas of study that have emerged from activist movements and from within the academy. For example, critical dietetics draws on feminist and critical social theory (Hayes-Conroy and Hayes-Conroy 2013), critical race theory (White 2013); queer studies (Atkins and Brady 2016); fat studies (Rochefort, Senchuk, Brady, and Gingras 2016), food studies (Aphramor, Brady, and Gingras 2013), ecofeminism (Aphramor 2012), and critical nutrition studies (Biltekoff 2013).

Many before us have called for change to the theoretical frameworks and practices that are rooted in dietetics' history (Devine, Jastran, and Bisogni 2004; Buchanan 2004; Kent 1988; Puckett 1997; Gingras 2009; Mosio and Eide 1984). Others have shown that feeling of frustration and burnout among dietitians arises from the ambiguity about our professional identity and capabilities (Waterlow 1981; Erickson-Weerts 1999; Politzer 1996), as well as narrow scopes of education and training that are insufficient for the challenges faced in work settings (Jarratt and Mahaffie 2007; Puckett 1997; Gingras 2009; Florencio 2001). Others have urged dietetics to adopt a more holistic view of food, eating, and nutrition, which includes a critical "examination of the world which generates nutrition problems" (Kent 1988:3), thereby advocating for more social, political, and economic understandings of health into our practice (Mosio and Eide 1984).

As seen in dietetics' history, the field of nutrition has traditionally been grounded in **biomedical, positivist science**—a loyalty that sees other ways of understanding food, eating, and nutrition, such as their social, cultural, economic, and historical aspects, as "unprofessional or unscientific" (Mosio and Eide 1984:68). This commitment to biomedical, positivist science has acted as a barrier toward redefining new ways of practice. Our intention is not to reject this paradigm altogether; we recognize that empirical, scientific research and its methods have allowed the discovery and treatment of serious nutritional concerns (e.g. nutrient deficiencies such as scurvy). However, these and many other problems require different paradigms to better understand and respond (Aphramor et al. 2009; Kent 1988; Mosio and Eide 1984). Problems such as food security, urban agriculture, overfishing, climate change, food waste, precarious and underpaid employment in food work, the **food sovereignty** of Indigenous people, and **fat phobia** require multiple frameworks to elucidate and ameliorate. Hence, a key goal of the critical dietetics movement is to shed light on the problematic aspects and limitations of **positivism**, the first of which is a belief in a reality or truth as that which is derived from the scientific method, and which consequently excludes or devalues other forms of knowledge generation (Duchscher 1999). A significant implication of positivism is that it often serves the interests of those creating the knowledge—those in power—while ignoring other necessary forms of knowledge (Thomas 1995; Grundy 1987). Critical dietetics recognizes that scientific knowledge is always social knowledge and that, far from being neutral, the belief in value-free science arises from a particular ideological position.

Another assumption that underlies a positivist worldview is that knowledge can be hypothesized, tested, and subsequently predicted to anticipate future behaviours or environments (Grundy 1987). Shuftan problematizes this view and shows why dietetics would benefit from a broader paradigm to better answer our questions:

> The social reality is not like a laboratory; many variables in it are unknown and unforeseen and when we look at them it is often in the wrong way, searching for the statistical "whats" instead of analyzing the human "whys." (1982:163)

Buchanan also highlights the problematic nature of reducing human behaviour "to the kind of general laws that we observe in the natural world" (2004:147). He argues that by attempting to understand human behaviour in a decontextualized, linear relationship, we fail the public by suppressing awareness of the world that perpetuates nutrition problems (Buchanan 2004). When applied to nutrition, positivism tends to highlight the quantifiable and measurable aspects of food and eating (i.e. calories, macronutrients, vitamins, minerals), while overshadowing the social, cultural, economic, and relational dimensions. Scrinis (2013) has coined the term *nutritionism* to described this reductive view of food as simply a vector for nutrient components rather than as an object of desire, pleasure, and disgust; a sensory experience; and so on. Critical dietetics promotes an acceptance of different paradigms in research and practice as a means to better understand the human condition beyond predictable behaviours and outcomes, and people's experiences with health and nutrition. By adopting a paradigm that values other forms of knowledge and methods of knowledge generation, we create the possibility of gaining a better understanding of how to best respond to nutrition-related issues more comprehensively.

Critical dietetics looks to critical social theory as a way to elucidate the problems related to dietetics' positivist worldview and to provide new ways of incorporating a more holistic or ecological approach to practice. Key constructs of critical social theory may prove useful for dietetics in several ways. First, critical social theory aims to shed light on the assumptions of objective or "non-position" claims of traditional science, by reformulating questions and calling attention to how the knowledge was created, whose interests it served, and the historical path in which it came to be (Hoy and McCarthy 1994; Holstein and Minkler 2003). A useful tool in this epistemologic process is the practice of **reflexivity**—a practice that allows

for self-understanding and critical consciousness. Power (2005) describes reflexivity as developing an understanding of one's own position in order to gain insight into the perspectives of others. Critical social theory also emphasizes the "situatedness of knowledge" and the possibility of knowledge that is generated broadly: in other words, knowledge that is socially constructed outside of science (Hoy and McCarthy 1994:15). For example, critical theory may value knowledge created through literature, personal narrative, and lived experience—all sources that shed insight and increase understanding of the human condition. Often these forms are not considered to be valid in positivistic paradigms (Holstein and Minkler 2003). Despite critique that suggests self-reflexivity precludes political action (Kobayashi 2003), critical social theorists argue that empirically determined "truths" are important; however, their relevance is realized through people's lived experience and meaning making (Duchscher 1999). Finally, through these former two practices, critical social theory seeks to create knowledge for the purposes of human emancipation (Murray and Poland 2006). Emancipation is described as "autonomy from all that is outside the individual," which requires both individual freedom and freedom from one's society (Grundy 1987:16). These freedoms are born from a consciousness of the power differences that pervade society (Grundy 1987).

The core framework of critical dietetics comprises four key tenets that are informed by critical social theory and that are of relevance to food studies. In what follows we outline these four tenets and the potential applications in four areas of the field. Critical dietetics promotes education, research, practice, and scholarship that engage in:

1. *Multiple dimensions of rigour.* Acceptance of knowledge that is socially constructed outside of the scientific arena. Critical dietetics understands that "facts" or truths produced through all forms of knowledge generation

are made relevant in human subjectivity: in other words, in the lived experience of persons (Campbell and Bunting 1991). Therefore, the movement promotes a "constructivist" approach to knowledge generation, whereby the possibility of many truths is embraced. In valuing other epistemologies, we seek not to neglect empirical science but to emphasize that "additional dimensions of rigour are required" (Murray and Poland 2006:383) in order to respond to the complex issues facing society today.

2. *Transdisciplinary scholarship.* Waterlow (1981) describes dietetics as situated in a "middle place" and charges dietitians with the responsibility to connect issues of biology and social sciences in order to respond to issues of human welfare. This requires us to expand to issues—often directly impacting our work—that the profession has historically not addressed (Gingras 2008a).

3. *Reflexivity.* Reflexivity is the vehicle that allows for "wide awakeness" or "critical consciousness" that questions traditional paradigms and reconstructs assumptions, leading to generation of new knowledge that is subsequently rechallenged (Duchscher 1999). This iterative process is crucial to the application of critical theory in everyday practice (Duchscher 1999). Critical health professions have identified reflexive practice as a means to avoid the "detached, objective technician of the scientist-practitioner model into a reflexive, engaged and invested social actor" (Hepworth 2006:338).

4. *Emancipatory, participatory, socially just, and socially accountable practices.* Critical theory is thought to be "inherently productive of enlightenment and emancipation" due to its emphasis on reflection of one's true situation that is free from institutional, cultural and social ideologies (Campbell and Bunting 1991:2). The movement promotes practices that seek empowerment and participation for all those involved.

Implications of Critical Dietetics for the Dietetic Profession and Food Studies

Critical dietetics has wide-reaching potential to influence all areas of dietetic practice including education, research, and individual patient and client care. In discussing critical pedagogy Ellsworth contends, "It is possible to teach students [in a way] that doesn't require them to assume a fixed, singular, unified position within power and social relations" (Ellsworth 1997:7). Similarly, we believe that dietetic education must adopt the lessons offered by critical and feminist pedagogy in the education and training of new dietetic practitioners. Even though some have long called for dietetic scholarship to include **transdisciplinary** studies such as culture, religion, philosophy, and psychology, these topics have yet to be included in dietetic curriculum (Puckett 1997). When these areas of study are included in dietetic curriculum, it is often in parallel to courses that teach about the pure sciences rather than as integrated topics that contextualize lessons in chemistry, biology, and nutritional science. Harding (1994) contends that by treating natural sciences and humanities as parallel subjects, science students are taught that areas outside of sciences are not as important or necessary to make educated, practice-based decisions. This situation is concerning especially when these decisions inherently have social, political, and cultural implications, and often affect the public on a wider level when they lead to policy or public-health interventions. Critical dietetics suggests that the dietetic curriculum be reimagined, similar to curriculum changes in nursing, to embrace **transdisciplinary scholarship** and explore both quantitative and qualitative conversations of gender, poverty, human rights, race, class, sexual orientation, ability, size, art, poetry, and so on (Gingras 2008b; Florencio 2001). In addition, to introduce students to social action, education that raises awareness of policy and community action will allow dietitians to become more effective agents of socially just change (Yarker-Edgar and Forster-Coull 2009). Broadening our scope does not necessarily imply that nutrition professionals become "super experts capable of dealing with all factors contributing to nutrition" (Mosio and Eide 1984:67). Rather, an expansion of our understanding of these factors would improve our analysis and actions in our work.

Another outcome of such curriculum changes is that the educative process may be emancipatory for nutrition students (Duchscher 1999; Gingras 2008b). Critical pedagogy has the potential to be emancipatory through egalitarian approaches and a focus away from the student as passive receiver of knowledge (Duchscher 1999). Educators working from this approach aim to be open to learning alongside their students as co-learners, and explore the creation of socially constructed knowledge together. The most significant implications of this dynamic are that it creates awareness of power imbalances among educators and learners and honours learners' contributions to knowledge.

Throughout this process, both student and teacher may engage in an iterative process between self-reflection and action, which may eventually lead to transformation (Grundy 1987). Cargill (2007) provides one example of students using a reflective process to examine their relationship to food through autobiographical narrative. This process strengthened self-awareness by allowing students to explore political, cultural, racial, and gender identities in the context of food (Cargill 2007). Fade (2004) also supports reflective practice in dietetics curriculum, providing several models for adopting it into the classroom. Both Fade (2004) and nursing critical theorists describe challenges such as lack of time and lack of comfort/familiarity with facilitating reflexive practice. They also caution that, initially, students may have difficulty coping with this shift in the learning process, especially for those who are outcome oriented; however, this can be overcome with further exploration

of dominant paradigms and implicit assumptions, which potentially leads to transformation (Duchscher 1999).

Adopting new paradigms toward teaching require courage to change practice and an emotional readiness that may first be met with disorientation and feelings of vulnerability. Bevis (1989) describes the challenges of restructuring curriculum; often it is met with cultural shock from departing from the norm and anxiety from feelings of loss and the unknown future, as well as faculty power struggles over course structure, specialties, and contrasting philosophical views. However, appropriate training for staying with the vulnerability leads to faculty who are more self-aware and "display a professional confidence balanced by a knowledge of their own fallibility; they can reveal themselves without jeopardizing mutual respect" (Duchscher 1999:459). In short, critical practice generates a new, expanded dietetic practice both within and outside of the classroom.

Research is another important area that critical dietetics seeks to transform. We believe, as Waterlow states, "To discuss research strategies without considering the researcher is to omit a crucial element from the debate" (1981:198). This does not mean that critical dietetics discourages science, measurement, or empirical research. As Cole (1993) states, measurement is necessary in health research. Rather, for critical dietetics the issues lie in our approach to research and the practices of meaning making that follow the gathering and interpretation of data. In critical dietetics, a measurement or response may be treated as "*both* a variable and a voice, an activity of dialogue—susceptible to interpretation . . . the telling of the story becomes part of the story itself" (Cole 1993:24). In other words, the researcher becomes part of the dialogue; her or his presence is inseparable from the meanings and knowledge that are generated from the research. By acknowledging the impossibility of an objective science, critical dietetics seeks to place researchers within a reflexive process that understands research as a practice of storytelling or dialogue among themselves, the participants, and the wider community (Campbell and Bunting 1991). These approaches expose any assumptions and perspectives that are inherent to the process.

Another important implication of critical dietetics for dietetic research is a call for the diversification of research methodologies that more comprehensively address the many realities that face individuals and society with respect of food, eating, and nutrition. Inter- and transdisciplinary scholarship within dietetics may invite other methodologies from both qualitative and quantitative backgrounds, drawing upon narratives, discourse analysis, and institutional ethnographies, to name a few. Landman and Wootton argue that in order for dietetics to best respond to societal problems, we must continue "further debate about how to combine—some would say reconcile—the epistemologies of a quantitative nutrition science with qualitative profession-related social sciences" (1997:73). This comment directly ties to dietetic education and the way students learn about various epistemic positions: students often graduate with a better understanding of quantitative science and tend to lean toward this type of research when continuing in research or utilizing research in practice.

Critical dietetics also proposes that research has the potential to directly serve the communities studied, by connecting lived experience with social environments and structures (Travers 1997a). Research for social action—such as community-based participatory research (CBPR)—aims to involve communities in addressing their own barriers to health (Travers 1997b). Critical dietetic scholars can follow the example of critical health psychologists, who view themselves as "scholar activists" rather than "scientist-practitioners" (Murray and Poland 2006:383), and thus emphasize the importance of social action within communities.

Dietitians provide nutrition support in a wide range of clinical settings including hospitals, family health teams, community care centres, long-term care centres, mental health facilities, and private practice. One of the responsibilities of any dietitian in clinical practice includes the teaching and education of those who use dietetic services. Critical dietetics has significant implications for this area of practice in highlighting the issues involved in providing nutrition care beyond the simple transfer of information from practitioner to client. Kent (1988) notes that nutrition education can empower people or communities to drive their own actions for change. Travers (1997b) cautions, however, that by merely educating without social context, such as teaching clients how to eat on a budget without considering the roots of poverty, actually perpetuates social inequities. Power (2005) contends that all dietitians have a responsibility to address issues of food security by, at minimum, remaining cognizant of social policies. She makes several recommendations about how dietitians may do so, such as engaging in reflexive practice, collaborating with community organizations, conducting research that support social safety nets, and voting (Power 2005).

Carlos Osorio/Toronto Star via Getty Images

Dietitians provide nutritional support in a range of contexts. Here Karolina Otto, a dietitian at a Superstore in Oakville, Ontario, guides a group of students through the grocery store as part of a program designed to help children learn how to make healthy food choices.

Critical dietetics also offers a way for practitioners to be more cognizant of the "expert"–"client" power imbalance that is imposed by traditional biomedical models of nutrition education (Buchanan 2004). Humans are assumed to have an inherent set of resources and ability to be self-reliant; the educator's goal is to allow the participant to realize and develop these skills (Arnold et al. 2001). Thus, we support people to "improve their own skills of practical autonomy, rather than categorizing them in terms of preconceived theories with resulting automatic formulas for treatment" (Buchanan 2004:152). Implications of this approach to practice cannot be understated: vulnerability and tolerance to a certain level of uncertainty will be required as practitioners remove the "expert" hat and work alongside people in mutual dialogue to aid in the search for social solutions (Gingras 2008a; Buchanan 2004; Travers 1997a; 1997b). Arnold and colleagues (2001) also cite difficulties for participants, such as negative views and lack of confidence and trust toward available support. The researchers provide examples for fostering self-sufficiency in low-income participants, such as building trust and group support, as well as a strong focus on both individual and community-level empowerment (Arnold et al. 2001).

What implications does critical dietetics have for food studies, and vice versa? We believe that collaboration between the two fields would lead to synergistic gains in knowledge and power sharing for each, ultimately enhancing health equity. As the self-acclaimed "experts" in food and nutrition, dietitians should be well positioned to respond to pressing social, cultural, economic, and political food issues. The reality is that, outside of food security, dietitians' contribution to advancing food justice is not on a par with that made by food studies with its well-developed scholarly and activist knowledge, analyses, and methods. As accredited health professionals, dietitians possess socially and legally sanctioned power within the Canadian food system, influencing how food and nutrition are discussed and valued in the popular consciousness. The narrative they have constructed to date is a reductionist one: a critical dietetic narrative, informed by food studies activists and scholars, is needed to re-orient public-health nutrition for socially just change.

Conclusion

Berenbaum proposes that in order to nourish the dietetic profession, we need "to think outside the box, to take risks, to challenge the status quo" (2005:196). Critical dietetics offers a way to ask questions of "business as usual"—the ideas offered in this paper are only the beginnings—and we are excited about the potential to use our imaginations and stir up dialogue about the possibilities in field. The movement arose from questions born through practice and research and is grounded in "theory from doing," embracing **praxis**. We hope to collectively answer these questions, and generate more, in ways that are empowering for the profession, as well as for those we serve.

Discussion Questions

1. What are the intersections between critical dietetics and food studies?

2. Has there ever been a time when you were asked to transform your worldview? What was that experience like for you?

3. What has the gendered history of dietetics done to shape the field of dietetics?

4. What does a feminist theoretical analysis do to define the field of critical dietetics?

Further Reading

1. Buchanan, D. 2004. "Two Models for Defining the Relationship between Theory and Practice in Nutrition Education: Is the Scientific Method Meeting Our Needs?" *Journal of Nutrition Education & Behavior* 36:146–54.
Despite the scientific method bringing much significant information to the field of nutrition, the contributions of science have overshadowed most of everything else. Buchanan presents a clear critique of the overreliance on the scientific method for understanding the social aspects of food and eating.

2. DeVault, M. 1999. "Whose Science of Food and Health? Narratives of Profession and Activism from Public-Health Nutrition" Pp. 166–83 in *Revisioning Women, Health, and Healing: Feminist, Cultural, and Technoscience Perspectives,* ed. Adele E. Clarke and Virginia L. Olsen. New York and London: Routledge.
This chapter represents one of the first sociological inquiries with nutritionists as the focus. DeVault brings a much-needed sociological frame to this professional field from which the critical dietetics movement was created.

3. Ellsworth, E. 1989. "Why Doesn't This Feel Empowering? Working through the Repressive Myths of Critical Pedagogy." *Harvard Educational Review* 59(3):297–324.
This germinal article by Ellsworth outlines the challenges and critique with critical approaches to education using examples from teaching critical pedagogy. In the context of this chapter, we note that questions require asking of our intended efforts to "be critical" so as not to reproduce "oppressive myths" about critical pedagogy.

4. Travers, K.D. 1997. "Nutrition Education for Social Change: Critical Perspective." *Journal of Nutrition Education* 29:57–62.
Along with Travers's chapter "'Do You Teach Them How to Budget?' Professional Discourse in the Construction of Nutritional Inequities" from Jeffrey Sobal and Donna Maurer's edited volume *Eating Agendas* (Piscataway, NJ: Transaction, 1995), this article represents the first and most influential writing by a scholar within the field about the negative impact of not taking a critical perspective toward nutrition inequities. Travers proposes the early outlines of critical dietetics by linking critical perspectives with positive social change.

Video Suggestions

1. Drinkwater, Kelli Jean. 2013. *Aquaporko!* http:// aquaporkofilm.com. 22 min.
2. Hamer, Bent. 2003. *Kitchen Stories.* www. youtube.com/watch?v=sKYyHJFxmVA (film trailer). 96 min.
3. Wyman, Julie. 2012. *Strong!* http://strongthefilm .com. 76 min.

Notes

1. In June 2009, an invitation-only research workshop entitled "Beyond Nutritionism: Rescuing Dietetics through Critical Dialogue"—funded by the Social Sciences and Humanities Research Council (SSHRC) of Canada—established the beginning of a movement named "critical dietetics." A declaration was published to commemorate the birth of the initiative, and to invite colleagues to join in the process of exploring the movement (Aphramor et al. 2009).

2. In Canada the authority to regulate health professions is exercised through the provinces via provincial Acts, which set out policies and procedures for various tasks including registration

of members, oversight of education and training, protection of professional titles, definition of the scope of practice, creation of a code of ethics and standards of practice, and investigation and discipline of members further to complaints (Alliance of Canadian Dietetic Regulatory Bodies 2006).

References

Alliance of Canadian Dietetic Regulatory Bodies. 2006. "Statement of Purpose." http://www.dieteticregulation.ca/en/#regulatedprof.

Aphramor, L. 2012. "Field Notes from a Forager." Presented at Second International Critical Dietetics Conference, Law School, Sydney University. 1 September.

———, Y. Asada, J. Atkins, et al. 2009. "Critical Dietetics: A Declaration." *Practice* 48:1–2. www.criticaldietetics.org.

———, J. Brady, and J. Gingras. 2013. "Advancing Critical Dietetics, Theorising Health at Every Size." Pp. 85–102 in *Why We Eat, How We Eat: Contemporary Encounters Between Foods and Bodies*, ed. A. Lavis and E. Abbots. London; Routledge.

———, and J.R. Gingras. 2009. "That Remains to Be Said: Disappeared Feminist Discourses on Fat in Dietetic Theory and Practice." Pp. 97–105 in *Fat Studies Reader*, ed. E.D. Rothblum and S. Solovay. New York: New York University Press.

Arnold, C.G., P. Ladipo, C.H. Nguyen, P. Nkinda-Chaiban, and C.M. Olson. 2001. "New Concepts for Nutrition Education in an Era of Welfare Reform." *Journal of Nutrition Education* 33(6):341–46.

Atkins, J., and J. Brady. 2016. "Queering Dietetic Epistemology." *Journal of Critical Dietetics* 3(1):24–34.

Berenbaum, S. 2005. "Imagination Nourishes Dietetic Practice." 2005 Ryley-Jeffs Memorial Lecture. *Canadian Journal of Dietetic Practice and Research* 66(3):193–6.

Bevis, E.O. 1989. *Curriculum Building in Nursing: A Process*. Toronto, ON: Jones and Bartlett Publishers.

Biltekoff, C. 2013. *Eating Right in America: The Cultural Politics of Food and Health*. Durham, NC: Duke University Press.

Bright-See, E. 1998. "Human Ecology/ Home Economics An Introduction to the Professions and to Becoming a Professional." Unpublished manuscript. Department of Human Ecology, Brescia University College, University of Western Ontario, Waterloo, ON, Canada.

Brown, M., and B. Paolucci. 1979. *Home Economics: A Definition*. Washington, DC: American Home Economics Association.

Bubolz, M.M., and M. Suzanne Sontag. 1988. "Integration in Home Economics and Human Ecology." *Journal of Consumer Studies and Home Economics* 12:1–14.

Buchanan, D. 2004. "Two Models for Defining the Relationship between Theory and Practice in Nutrition Education: Is the Scientific Method Meeting Our Needs?" *Journal of Nutrition Education & Behavior* 36:146–54.

Campbell, J.C., and S. Bunting. 1991. "Voices and Paradigms: Perspectives on Critical and Feminist Theory in Nursing." *Advances in Nursing Science* 13:1–15.

Cargill, K. 2007. "Teaching the Psychology of Food and Culture." *Teaching of Psychology* 34(1):41–5.

Cassell, J. 1990. *Carry the Flame: The History of the American Dietetic Association*. American Dietetic Association.

Clarke, S. 2011. "A Politics of Knowledge: Reviewing the Dietetics Curriculum." *Journal of Critical Dietetics* 1(1):4–9.

Cole, T.R. 1993. *Voices and Visions of Aging: Toward a Critical Gerontology*. New York: Springer Publishing.

Cuddy, A. 2012. "A Recipe for Obsolescence: The Troubling Divide between Food and Nutrition, Part 2." *Journal of Critical Dietetics* 1(2):40–5.

Devine, C.M., M. Jastran, and C.A. Bisogni. 2004. "On the Front Line: Practice Satisfactions and Challenges Experienced by Dietetics and Nutrition Professionals Working in Community Setting in New York State." *Journal of the American Dietetic Association* 104:787–92.

Dietitians of Canada. 2015. "What Does a Dietitian Do?" http://www.dietitians.ca/Your-Health/Find-A-Dietitian/What-does-a-Dietitian-do.aspx

Duchscher, J.E. 1999. "Catching the Wave: Understanding the Concept of Critical Thinking." *Journal of Advanced Nursing* 29(3):577–83.

Ellsworth, E. 1997. *Teaching Positions: Difference, Pedagogy, and the Power of Address*. New York: Teachers College Press.

Erickson-Weerts, S. 1999. "Past, Present, and Future Perspectives of Dietetic Practice." *Journal of the American Dietetic Association* 99(3):291–3.

Fade, S.A. 2004. "Reflection in the Dietetic Curriculum." Pp. 76–81 in *The Development of Critical Reflection in Health Professions*, ed. S. Tate and M. Sills. North Yorkshire, UK: Learning and Teaching Support Network, Centre for Health Sciences and Practice.

Florencio, C.A. 2001. "Rights-Based Food and Nutrition Perspective: 21st Century Challenge for Dietetics." *Journal of Human Nutrition and Dietetics* 14:169–83.

Gingras, J. 2005. "Evoking Trust in the Nutrition Counselor: Why Should We Be Trusted?" *Journal of Agricultural and Environmental Ethics* 18:57–74.

———. 2008a. "The Vulnerable Learner: Moving from Middle to Margin in Dietetic Education." Accessed 21 January 2010. http://www.kwantlen.ca/__shared/assets/gingras_vulnerable_learner7424.pdf.

———. 2008b. "Sacra conversazione—A Tender Dialectic Invoking an Arts Practice–Based Autoethnography to Bridge Language and Silence in Dietetics." *Educational Insights* 12(2). http://www.ccfi.educ.ubc.ca/publication/insights/v12n02/articles/gingras/index.html.

———. 2009. "The Educational (Im)possibility for Dietetics: A Poststructural Discourse Analysis." *Learning Inquiry* 3(3):177–91.

———, and J. Brady. 2009. "To Be Other: Relational Consequences of Dietitians Feeding Bodily Difference." *Radical Psychology* 8(1). www.radicalpsychology.org.

Grundy, S. 1987. *Curriculum: Product or Praxis?* Oxford: Routledge Falmer.

Harding, S. 1994. "Is Science Multicultural? Challenges, Resources, Opportunities, Uncertainties." *Configurations* 2:301–330.

Hayes-Conroy, A. and J. Hayes-Conroy. 2013. *Doing Nutrition Differently: Critical Approaches to Diet and Dietary Intervention.* Farnham, UK: Ashgate.

Hepworth, J. 2006. "The Emergence of Critical Health Psychology: Can It Contribute to Promoting Public Health?" *Journal of Health Psychology* 11(3):331–41.

Holstein, M.B., and M. Minkler. 2003. "Self, Society and the 'New Gerontology.'" *The Gerontologist* 43(6):786–96.

Hoy, F.C., and T. McCarthy. 1994. *Critical Theory.* Oxford: Blackwell.

Jarratt, J., and J. Mahaffie. 2007. "The Profession of Dietetics at a Critical Juncture: A Report on the 2006 Environmental Scan for the American Dietetic Association." *Journal of American Dietetic Association* 107:S39.

Kent, G. 1988. "Nutrition Education as an Instrument of Empowerment." *Journal of Nutrition Education* 20(4): 193–95.

Kobayashi, A. 2003. "*Gender, Place and Culture* Ten Years On: Is Self-Reflexivity Enough?" *Gender, Place and Culture* 10(4):345–49.

Landman, J.P., and S.A. Wootton. 1997. "Curriculum Design for Professional Development in Public Health Nutrition in Britain." *Public Health Nutrition* 1(1):69–74.

Lang, M., and E. Upton. 1973. *The Dietetic Profession in Canada.* Toronto: Canadian Dietetic Association.

Liquori, T. 2001. "Food Matters: Changing Dimensions of Science and Practice in the Nutrition Profession." *Journal of Nutrition Education* 33:234–46.

Mosio, M., and W.B. Eide. 1984. "Toward Another Nutrition Education." International Foundation for Development Alternatives, IFDA Dossier 40: 63–9. Accessed 25 May 2010. http://www.dhf.uu.se/ifda/readerdocs/pdf/doss_40.pdf.

Murray, M., and B. Poland. 2006. "Health Psychology and Social Action." *Journal of Health Psychology* 11(3):379–84.

Nyhart, L.K. 1997. "Home Economists in the Hospital, 1900–1930." Pp. 125–44 in *Rethinking Home Economics: Women and the History of a Profession*, ed. S. Stage and V.B. Vincenti. New York: Cornell University Press.

Ontario Home Economics Association. 2015. "What is a Professional Home Economist?" http://www.ohea.on.ca/what-is-a-phec.html.

Ostrowski, P. 1986. "Who Discovered Vitamins?" *The Polish Review* XXXI(2–3):171–83.

Politzer, E. 1996. "Defining Dietetics Practice for Today and Tomorrow: An International Perspective." *Nutrition* 12(2):141–2.

Pollard, P., M. Taylor, and M. Daher. 2007. "Gender-Based Wage Differentials among Registered Dietitians." *The Health Care Manager* 26(1):52–63.

Power, E.M. 2005. "Individual and Household Food Insecurity in Canada: Position of Dietitians of Canada." *Canadian Journal of Dietetic Research and Practice* 66(1):43–6.

Puckett, R.P. 1997. "Education and the Dietetics Profession." *Journal of the American Dietetic Association* 97(3):252–3.

Reddin, J. Estelle. 2006. "Who We Are, Our Heritage and Horizons: Home Economics in Prince Edward Island in the Twentieth Century." Charlottetown: Home Economics Publishing Collective, University of Prince Edward Island.

Rochefort, J., A. Senchuk., J. Brady, and J. Gingras. (2016). "Spoon Fed: Learning about 'Obesity' in Dietetics." In *Obesity in Canada: Historical and Critical Perspectives*, ed. W. Mitchinson, D. Macphail, and J. Ellison. Toronto: University of Toronto Press.

Ryley, V. 1918. "The Work of the Dietitian in the Canadian Military Hospitals." *Journal of Home Economics* 10(3): 108–13.

Scrinis, G. 2013. *Nutritionism: The Science and Politics of Dietary Advice.* New York: Columbia University Press.

Sellinger, M., and S. Berenbaum. 2015. "Dietetic Scopes of Practice across Canada." *Canadian Journal of Dietetic Practice and Research* 76(2):64–9.

Shuftan, C. 1982. "Ethics, Ideology and Nutrition." *Food Policy* 7(2):159–64.

Stage, S. 1997. "Introduction: Home Economics, What's in a Name?" Pp. 1–14 in *Rethinking Home Economics: Women and the History of a Profession*, ed. S. Stage and V.B. Vincenti. New York: Cornell University Press.

Steinvorth, U. 2008. "On Critical Theory." *Analyse & Kritik* 30:399–423.

Thomas, L.W. 1995. "A Critical Feminist Perspective of the Health Belief Model: Implications for Nursing Theory, Research, Practice and Education." *Journal of Professional Nursing* 11(4):246–52.

Travers, K.D. 1997a. "Reducing Inequities through Participatory Research and Community Empowerment." *Health Education & Behavior* 24(3):344–56.

———. 1997b. "Nutrition Education for Social Change: Critical Perspective." *Journal of Nutrition Education* 29:57–62.

Waterlow, J.C. 1981. "Crisis for Nutrition." *Proceedings of the Nutrition Society* 40(2):195–207.

White, J. 2013. "Cultural Dominance in Dietetics; Hearing the Voices, African American Nutrition Educators Speak." *Journal of Critical Dietetics* 1(3):26–35.

Yarker-Edgar, K., and L. Forster-Coull. 2009. "Being Strategic: Providing Dietetic Students with the Skills to be Effective Agents of Change." Paper presented at Beyond Nutritionism: Rescuing Dietetics through Critical Dialogue Research symposium, Toronto.

8 Two Great Food Revolutions
The Domestication of Nature and the Transgression of Nature's Limits

Robert Albritton

Learning Objectives

Through this chapter, you can

1. Understand the centrality of profit to capitalism and how this centrality affects agricultural production

2. Understand the immense significance of the original domestication of plants and animals in comparison to the previous gathering and hunting

3. Examine manual field labour and conditions for agricultural workers

4. Look at how the increased turnover of agricultural capital may increase profits and examine some of the negative consequences

5. Understand why excluding the costs of externalities from capitalist market prices makes it difficult to address health and sustainability in connection with the food system

Introduction

Historians and anthropologists often claim that the most important change in human history was the domestication of plants and animals that started around 15,000 BCE (before the common era) and was more or less complete by 5000 BCE. The changes in food provision that have occurred since the Second World War, however, may be even more important. I refer to these recent changes as the "second great food revolution."

The first revolution gave us agriculture and animal husbandry. It may seem strange to refer to changes that occurred slowly over 10,000 years as a "revolution," but sometimes deep, restructuring changes that have a monumental impact do take a long time. Fifteen thousand years

ago change proceeded very slowly compared to today. The second revolution, which began in 1945 and continues to the present, is both deep and, in world-historic time, quite fast. This revolution combines the mechanical, chemical, and biotech revolutions, which together enable global **capitalism** to increasingly enter and control the food system. It is this second revolution, agriculture becoming more capitalist, that is the primary focus of this chapter.

The approach to understanding capitalism in this chapter is strongly influenced by Karl Marx's important insights into the nature of capitalism and into how a society could be more egalitarian and democratic (Albritton 2009,

2011). As the analysis unfolds, it will become clearer why I refer to the current food revolution as "capitalist." This chapter will begin with an examination of gathering and hunting, then move to the first great food revolution—the domestication of plants and animals. It will then discuss the second great food revolution—the capitalist takeover of agriculture. It will conclude with some brief thoughts about how to move forward and deal with the problems caused by capitalist agriculture.

Gathering and Hunting (2 million BCE to 15,000 BCE)

Food provisioning stands at the very centre of human evolution. Over the millions of years of this evolution, nearly all of what might be called "work" was preoccupied with satisfying the basic human needs to eat and drink. *Homo erectus*, one of modern humankind's ancestors, began to slowly move outward from their African home about 1.5 million years ago. They remained in the tropics and semi-tropics where food was plentiful year round and easily extracted directly from nature through what came to be known as hunting and gathering. It is no accident that *hunting* typically precedes *gathering* in the traditional term *hunting and gathering*; for a long time anthropologists seemed to agree that hunting played a far more important role in human evolution than gathering, and that men did the hunting and women the gathering. On the contrary, we now know that in most cases far more food was supplied by gathering than by hunting, and that sometimes males gathered and women hunted. No doubt hunting did influence human evolution, but it is likely that gathering was more influential. A more accurate term, then, would put *gathering first as in gathering and hunting*.

For a very long time humans lived in this way, in groups of 25 to 50. When nature's food supply diminished, a group would simply move on to a more plentiful environment. Over most of this evolution there were no techniques for

storing or conserving food, so there was no motivation to accumulate more food than could be consumed before it spoiled. Since the tropics were highly productive ecosystems, early hominids and humans had much more leisure time than modern humans. For example, they might very well have taken only two or three days to provide food needed for a week; since they had few needs other than food, the remaining time was leisure time. As anthropologist Marshall Sahlins (1972:1–5, 14) has claimed, if leisure time is the measure of an affluent society, then, ironically, these early societies were far more affluent than ours. According to Marx and Friedrich Engels (1978:734–59), the most interesting point about this early period is the general absence of any surplus over and above subsistence and thus the absence of **class relations** that an ongoing surplus makes possible. For once there is a surplus, a dominant class may take control of most of it, and thereby take control of socio-economic life.

The First Great Food Revolution (15,000 BCE to 5000 BCE)

The domestication of plants and animals may be the most important development in human history. Improvements in gathering and hunting would entail simply finding better ways of taking food from the wild; domestication, by contrast, involves the taming and shaping of the wild itself, presumably to better serve human needs. Words like *cultivate* and *agriculture* imply the entry of other living and growing things into human *culture*. Indeed, since its development, agriculture has formed the basis of human food provisioning, though there are exceptions, such as in far northern societies where agriculture is not possible.

The first farmers were groups or extended families who developed more or less co-operative divisions of both the labour and the products. There would have been no strong sense of private property; rather, an extended family or group of families might farm in a particular area, giving it some sense of property based on use, while a particular area might be considered a "commons" where all families would graze animals or gather wood co-operatively. Thus, while early agriculture might have given rise to the first weak sense of private property, it would not typically be the strong sense that develops later with capitalism, in which a single owner of a piece of land could in principle have a total monopoly over access, control, and use.

As the domestication of plants and animals spread and developed, food productivity gradually increased, generating a relatively stable and growing surplus. It is this surplus that opened the door to radical changes in social and economic structures. First, a food surplus made it possible for increasing numbers of people to be freed from the work of food production, who might then focus on, for example, craft production, art, politics, religion, or war.

Second, surplus food enabled the population to grow in relatively permanent settlements that could trade food and crafts with other settlements and thus develop a degree of specialization. The global population never exceeded 4 million people during the very long era of gathering and hunting. Between 10,000 BCE and 500 BCE, the domestication of nature enabled the global population to increase from 4 million to 100 million; compare this growth to that associated with the post–Second World War capitalist food revolution, which allowed the global population to increase from 2.55 billion in 1950 to 7.4 billion in 2016. Demographers expect the global population to level off at around 9 billion by 2050, though such predictions are always subject to fairly large variations.

Third, food surpluses presented the possibility of class **stratification**. In other words, by systematically taking over most social surplus, one class could come to be dominant. At first this would likely have been a warrior class, institutionalizing itself as an economic master class that also controlled the state.

Fourth, state functions could begin to emerge, as the dominant class generated a key decision-making group that would make and enforce laws, collect taxes, promulgate religion, and make war.

These four changes are fundamental to the evolution of human societies to this day. Today in the most advanced capitalist countries farm productivity is high enough that typically in industrialized countries less than 3 per cent of the population work in the farming sector. This percentage is continuously decreasing, particularly in places like the United States and Canada where a long tradition of family farming is being undermined by large corporate-controlled modes of agriculture.

In the ancient world, a major reason for the decline of civilizations was the degradation of soil caused by lack of knowledge of how to replenish the soil's fertility, by deforestation, or sometimes by salination (the buildup of salts in the soil due to irrigation). Today, civilization is threatened not only by soil degradation (although this is occurring), but also by global warming, generalized pollution, and the depletion of non-renewable resources, most notably fossil fuels and fresh water, but also many other resources such as helium, phosphorous, and copper.

The Second Great Food Revolution: Capitalism Takes Over Food Production

Though capitalism first developed in England as early as the seventeenth and eighteenth centuries, and has been the predominant economic system globally for at least two centuries, agriculture came under its control in the United States and Canada only after the Second World War (Albritton 1993). Capitalism gained control over agriculture very late in its history because some general features of capitalism do not fit well with agriculture, and because some general features of agriculture in the United States and Canada made it resistant to capitalism until after the Second World War.

Capitalism and Agriculture

The most basic aim of capitalism is to accumulate the greatest **profit** in the least time. This is done by maximizing the spread between the production cost and the selling price of a commodity, by expanding the market for the profitable commodity as quickly as possible, and by increasing the speed at which a unit of capital turns over. Maximizing profit overrides all other goals or values in a capitalist system, for a capitalist's very survival as such depends upon making a profit. A strong though arguable case can be made that ultimately profits depend on getting workers to give maximum effort for minimum pay, so that each worker produces more value than he or she receives back in the form of wages. Marx called the difference between value created by workers and the value they receive back as wage **exploitation**, such that the higher the rate of exploitation, the greater the profits (Marx 1976: parts II–IV).

Another important dimension of profit making is the speed of **circuits of capital** or **turnover time** between purchase of inputs and sale of outputs (Marx 1978: part II). For example, if one unit of capital turns over five times a year and a second, similar unit turns over once a year, then the first will earn five times more profit than the second. Each instant that capital is idle or its circuit slows down means profit lost forever. In short, time is money; the goal is the fastest turnover, and hence the greatest profit. There are other important principles inherent to capitalism, but for now we will take these three (profit, exploitation, fast turnover) as central.

These principles can help us understand capitalism's difficulties with agriculture. Suppose a capitalist finds the rate of profit in corn production attractive. Unlike factory production, which in principle requires only buying the needed raw materials, tools, and labour, agriculture poses specific problems. Fertile land may be hard to buy, and access to sufficient water may pose problems. Because temperate farming is seasonal, a given crop can be planted and harvested only once or twice a year (depending on how long it takes to grow); thus, there is a natural limit on speeding up turnover time. It may be difficult to find enough workers at harvest time if hand-picking is required. Transportation and storage of crops may be costly. Finally, because agricultural commodities are so dependent upon unpredictable natural forces such as weather, diseases, or insect infestations, prices can vary widely, causing large unexpected losses or gains.

Capitalism's emphasis on profit means human health, environmental health, and social justice are ignored unless they affect profit or unless laws require that these be considered. The problem here is that capitalist markets by themselves do not measure long-term social and ecological costs or benefits, which are dumped into the theoretical black box that economists call **externalities**. If the costs of externalities, such as considerations of long-term human flourishing, far exceed profits, then capitalist markets can be considered irrational, meaning that very large costs and benefits are excluded from prices. And this is precisely what is happening. The growing irrationality of our capitalist economic system needs to be fully recognized if we are to deal with the pressing, mutually exacerbating crises of, for example, economy, health, food, water, petroleum (and other non-renewable resources), and climate change. Long-term, global, systemic problems require long-term, global, systemic solutions, although global solutions may often get their start at a local level.

Let me explain briefly why I prefer to name the main problem *capitalism* and not *globalization* or *industrialization*. If the main problem that agriculture faces is globalization or industrialization, then strategies of change are likely to be different than if the main problem is seen to be capitalism. Globalization emphasizes the spatial aspect, arguing that too much control is wielded at a global level rather than at the state, regional, or local level. Industrialization emphasizes the large factory-like units of production that are coming to dominate in the global food system. While both of these perspectives underline important problems with current agriculture, neither is as broad nor as meaningful as the capitalism perspective.

Arguably it is capitalism that is the main cause of both the globalization and the industrialization of food production. Capitalism emphasizes the profit motive that underlies both the exploitation of workers up and down the food chain and efforts to continuously speed up the food chain. And, as already mentioned, capitalism helps us to understand why long-range social and environmental costs are often ignored in favour of short-term profits. Thus, for example, it may be profitable in the short term to replace rain forests with monocultures such as the palm oil plantations now expanding in Indonesia and Malaysia, but the long-term costs of climate change, health problems for plantation workers, species loss, and land degradation make the profits negligible in comparison. If we were more critical of capitalism, we could more actively intervene in markets to make the prices of commodities reflect real long-term social and environmental costs or benefits. If we did this, palm oil plantations would not exist on the scale and in the locations that they do, because they would not be profitable. In short, we need prices that take into account long-run human and environmental flourishing and that are not based narrowly on short-term production costs and selling prices.

A proto-capitalist agriculture first developed in Britain in the seventeenth and eighteenth centuries, followed by a long history of capitalism's alternating attraction to and repulsion from agriculture. I strongly believe that it makes sense to claim that full-fledged capitalist agriculture first developed in the United States after the Second World War and subsequently has become the dominant type of agriculture globally. While it exists in its most unadulterated form in the United States, the world domination by capitalist agriculture means not only that it is the predominant form of agriculture globally but also that it tends to shape other forms of agriculture more than it is shaped by them. Thus global agriculture is dominated by capitalist corporate farming, which in turn shapes all other modes of farming that still exist to some extent in the world, such as capitalist collective farming, capitalist state farming, capitalist family farming, capitalist co-operatives, capitalist slavery, and capitalist feudalism (and various permutations and combinations of these). I place *capitalist* in front of each type of farming to emphasize the formative powers of capitalism over it. In other words, each mode of production or set of property relations is modified in varying degrees by the dominant capitalist system. At the same time there are many movements to break free from capitalist agriculture that are gradually gaining strength.

From a global perspective, agriculture can be viewed as having multiple dimensions interconnected by a capitalism that asserts various degrees of control and domination in different parts of the world and in different agricultural and food sectors. Note that the focus here is on agriculture as a whole and not specifically on food provisioning. Agriculture can be considered to consist of "commodity chains" that start with crop production and end up as cotton shirts, cigars, ethanol, roast beef, or waste.

Agriculture in North America

The family farm rooted itself deeply in the culture of the United States and Canada, where, in contrast to Britain, there was no landlord **class** that centralized landownership into large estates and therefore into a few hands. In the United States and Canada, family farmers, with military backing, pushed the Aboriginal peoples off the land and into reservations, and typically set up farms that one family could manage with existing technology. Further, since much of the soil had not been previously farmed, it tended to be fertile. In the middle of the nineteenth century, North American farms became larger with the introduction of horse-drawn machinery, which was particularly effective on prairie flatlands. Better storage and transportation meant that the increasing grain surpluses could be traded abroad, so that by the second half of the nineteenth century a global market for basic grains was created—for wheat in particular. Prairie grain, with high yields at lower cost, quickly took over the growing global market, and capitalists discovered ways of profiting from family farms from the outside, thereby avoiding the risks and difficulties of farming itself.

Family farmers may have occasionally hired a few farmhands, but for the most part they relied on family labour and not the wage labour that is the basis of capitalist profits. If they exploited anyone's labour it was their own and not that of others. Family farmers may try to maximize profits, but not by the basic capitalist activity of exploiting wage labour. Also, because family farms are usually relatively permanent settlements, farmers would tend not to maximize short-term profits if in doing so they would undermine the long-term fertility of the soil or other basic conditions of sustainable farming.

A family farm, therefore, would typically not be capitalist unless it were to hire a significant number of wage labourers. Since family farmers are self-employed, their labour cannot be directly exploited by capitalists, but it can be exploited at arm's-length or indirectly. Storage and transportation companies, merchants, and bankers can exploit farmers by charging high fees for their services. Because crops can be wiped out by floods or droughts, because farm machinery can be expensive, and because income arrives in lumps when harvests are sold, farmers are particularly dependent upon banks or other creditors who can ultimately foreclose if debts go unpaid. For these reasons, various economic safety nets have been devised and legislated for farmers, but in many cases they are far less supportive than required, especially when smaller farms need help.

Further, it is necessary to emphasize the extent to which the family farm has been replaced by industrial agriculture. For example, in Canada the number of small farms was reduced by half in the 10-year period spanning 2001–2011, and paralleling this change, the government allowed agricultural producers to import 39,700 migrant farm workers in 2012 to meet the demand of a doubling of large-scale industrial farms. The problem is that temporary migrant labourers in the agricultural sector lack many of the rights and protections allotted to other workers in Canada, and as a result they lack the powers to resist the many dimensions of exploitation (low wages, poor working conditions, etc.) that increase the profits of agricultural capitalists. For example, "Labour is cheap when the worker has few or no alternatives and the employer has many" (UFCW 2015:11).

The phase of capitalism that developed after the Second World War is labelled in various ways; the label depends upon the theoretical emphasis. One such label, *Fordism*, emphasizes the mass production and consumption of consumer durables, named for Henry Ford's manufacturing and selling of cars. Mass consumption of such products required significant increases in working-class income. Because mass consumption was a novel economic concept and was so important to this phase of capitalism, I like to use the label *consumerism* (Albritton 1991: Ch. 8). In order for consumerism to work, workers needed to spend far less of their total income on food and drink, leaving them more disposable income to buy houses, cars, and appliances. Therefore, capitalism had to find ways to decrease the price of food through large increases in productivity, large decreases in production costs (particularly the cost of labour), or both.

The numerous uncontrollable risk factors that always threatened farm profit margins began to be sharply diminished by the mechanization, chemicalization, biological manipulations, irrigation, increase in size, and general industrialization that became widespread after the Second World War. Before these innovations, the high risks and low gains of traditional agriculture made it uninviting to capitalists, who had oriented most of their profit-making activities toward factory production. But the technological revolutions after the Second World War promised significant economies of scale (through mechanization and monocultures), less dependence on the weather (through irrigation), less dependence on soil fertility (through petrochemical-based fertilizers), less risk of pest invasions (through petrochemical-based pesticides), and more rapid crop turnover (through improved hybrid seeds that sometimes allowed for more harvests in a year). Many of these changes were based on the incredible release of energy made possible by cheap petroleum (as cheap as US$2 a barrel in the 1960s, compared to prices in the US$40 range today, prices that are bound to rise in the future). Today the food system has become so dependent on petrochemicals that the resulting foods have been called "petro-foods" (meat is particularly "petroleum dense," and there has been an accelerating and unsustainable "meatification" of the world's diet) (Weis 2013). In general, then, cheap energy, control over risk factors, and productivity increases made agricultural profit rates increasingly inviting to capitalism.

Given that agriculture could generate higher profit rates, capital could expand to this sector by creating new corporate farms, buying up family farms and expanding them into corporate farms, or by controlling family farms from the outside. If the family farm becomes simply one link in a very long food chain (or value chain) controlled by large capitalist corporations, then it loses much of its autonomy. In other words, family farms would become almost completely dependent on capitalist corporations: buying all their inputs from them, being guided by their production norms, and selling all their crops to them. It is as if the family farm becomes one station on a long factory assembly line. To put it strongly but accurately, capitalism's seemingly friendly embrace of family farming is really a strangulation, as on average 20,000 farms go out of business each year in the United States, and between 2006 and 2008, Canada lost 10,000 farmers (Rosset 2006:49; Cook 2004; Heaps 2010:30).

Capitalist industry has penetrated the once relatively autonomous family farm in several major ways:

- It provides the farm machinery and the petrochemicals needed to run them. Running a giant high-tech, custom-made combine, sometimes costing more than half a million dollars, requires significant petroleum inputs.

- It provides the petrochemical fertilizers that increase yields and can create a treadmill effect (the more you use, the more you have to increase the use). When a soil's fertility depends on chemicals and little organic matter is returned to it, chemical fertilizers tend to run off as water drains from the soil. It provides pesticides, the use of which has skyrocketed, also due to a treadmill effect, as the pests build resistance to them and as huge monocultures set the table for pests to devour their favourite crop.

- It provides seeds that are increasingly costly (especially **genetically modified seeds**) and that need to be bought anew for every crop. Further, as in many sectors of the food system, a handful of giant corporations control production and marketing. For example, the top three seed companies (Monsanto, DuPont, Syngenta) control 35 per cent of the global seed market (Dalle Mulle and Ruppanner 2010:3). Such concentration of power is particularly disturbing here, because seeds are fundamental to the whole food system.

- US government subsidies go mainly to the largest farms, thus undermining the smaller family farms.

- Large farms are in a better position to win the lucrative contracts with the suppliers of supermarkets and fast-food chains that need standardized produce in large quantities, which only large capitalist farms can provide. For example, as is typical in the food system, in 2003 the largest fast-food company in the world, Yum! Brands (which owns KFC, Pizza Hut, Taco Bell, and other restaurants) bought all of its American produce from one company, Unified Foodservice Purchasing Co-op, which in turn bought all of its tomatoes from six growers (Ahn, Moore, and Parker 2004:3).

- In addition to outside control, anything that favours larger farms can ultimately require that farmers hire significant numbers of wage labourers and thus become capitalist farmers. This is particularly the case when a farm is not fully mechanized, and harvesting, packing, or other agricultural processes are done at least partially by hand, as with most fruits and vegetables. The intense competition of capitalism drives the system toward larger units of production. Added to this force is the system of government farm subsidies that rewards sheer size rather than the promotion of human and environmental health.

Conclusion

This chapter can be read as an introduction to a political economy approach to the study of food production. In order to emphasize the immensity of the changes that have occurred in food production since the Second World War, I have compared them to the original development of agriculture and animal husbandry that occurred over a much longer time span far in the past. I have argued that capitalist market prices have become increasingly irrational because they exclude most social and environmental costs, and that capitalism's orientation toward short-term profits is also irrational, when what is needed is long-range democratic planning informed by the best science available to bring prices into line with real social and environmental costs and benefits.

There are many ways of moving forward to deal with the kinds of problems created by capitalist agriculture. While it is not my purpose in this chapter to present an extended discussion of alternatives, such a critique as this does invite at least some mention of general directions toward alternatives. Many problems would be alleviated if we moved toward more organic forms of production and reduced our dependence on petrochemicals. One of the main arguments against

this position is that yields would be reduced. But even assuming this to be the case, do we really need so much of certain types of crops, such as corn? For example, more than 36 per cent of the current corn crop goes to the meat industry as animal feed. However, cattle's natural diet is not corn but grass, so it is not only possible but desirable that farmers raise grass-fed beef. No longer using corn to manufacture **agrofuel** (a sensible move given that it takes more energy to produce agrofuel than it yields), would free up 40 per cent or more of the corn crop that is now converted into ethanol to fuel cars. Radically reducing the amount of high-fructose corn syrup in our diet, which we should do for our health, would free up another 5 per cent. In short, we could easily get by with 45 per cent or less of the current corn crop, an amount that could be grown using farming techniques that either are organic or need far fewer petrochemical or biotech inputs, and also an amount that would free up arable land to grow many other crops.

If we intervene in markets to make prices approximate real long-term social and environmental costs and benefits, then some prices would go up and others down, and people would consume less of the costly and more of the cheaper food commodities. Let's say for the sake of argument that the price of beef quadruples as a result of pricing that includes externalities. This might mean that only the rich could afford beef, which seems unfair. One way to make fair the including of "externalities" in market prices is to redistribute wealth on a massive scale in order to promote greater equality. Nationally this could in principle be achieved by highly progressive taxation on incomes, wealth, and profits. Internationally we would need a taxing authority that does not yet exist, but changes could also be made in existing international practices that would make a big difference. For example, we could crack down on the tax evasion arising from one-third of all global assets being held in tax havens (Kohonen and Mestrum 2009:xiii). The resulting funds could contribute to advancing equality by giving everyone a basic income well above the poverty line, and giving anyone who works full-time at least twice the basic income. In our capitalist economy this is a radical proposal, but from the point of view of ethics, it is simply putting into practice the ancient principle that each human life should be equally valued. Further, it is a way of linking sustainability with social justice, a linkage that is essential if we are to avoid advancing sustainability at the cost of social justice or vice versa (Albritton 2011).

It should be possible to devise a system in which subsidies would go to those farmers attempting to use methods that improve the soil, save water, favour local markets, and reduce petrochemical inputs, because these practices would reduce long-run social and environment costs. Similarly, farming practices that increase social and environmental costs could be discouraged by placing surtaxes on them. In this way the price of food could come to approximate its real social costs and benefits, and price structures could actually encourage both a good diet and ecological farming practices. Junk food would become much more expensive, while healthy food would become much cheaper.

This essay has made the great leap from taming the wild through the domestication of plants and animals, to a wildly unsustainable and irrational capitalism, to a bare mention of a socially just and ecologically friendly food system. This happier future is increasingly unlikely unless we mobilize massively to bring about change. To turn things around, we will need to continually expand our scientific knowledge, our practical wisdom, and our ability to organize in the face of powers both corporate and political that are caught up in capitalist structures, which tend to undermine the possibilities of a better future.

Discussion Questions

1. What are some of the most important changes in social life made possible by the domestication of plants and animals?

2. What role have food surpluses played in agricultural societies?

3. What is capitalism? How did the rise of a capitalist economy affect agricultural production and access to food?

4. What are externalities, and why should they be included in the price of commodities?

Further Reading

1. Magdoff, F., and B. Tokar. 2010. *Agriculture and Food in Crisis: Conflict, Resistance, and Renewal.* New York: Monthly Review Press.
   This is a good collection of different approaches to the political economy of agriculture and food, a collection that is unified by its analysis of many of the currently most crucial crises and their interconnections. Further, there is analysis of efforts toward the sort of radical transformations required to deal with them.

2. Pollan, M. 2006. *Omnivore's Dilemma: A Natural History of Four Meals.* New York: Penguin.
   This is a widely read and influential book on the centrality of corn to the US food system. Readers may be surprised at the extent to which corn and corn by-products are part of most processed food, meat, and soft drinks.

3. Ponting, C. 1991. *A Green History of the World: The Environment and the Collapse of Great Civilizations.* New York: Penguin.

This classic ecological history is particularly interesting because of its recognition of the role of unsustainable food provisioning in the collapse of great civilizations.

4. Smolker, R., B. Tokar, A. Peterman, E. Hernandes, and J. Thomas. 2008. "The Real Cost of Agrofuels: Impacts on Food, Forests, People, and Climate." www.globalforestcoalition.org/wp-content/uploads/2010/10/Truecostagrofuels.pdf.

This is an excellent in-depth study of the short- and long-term impact of the recent turn to agrofuel production as a means of dealing with the looming shortage of fossil fuels and of the power that this shortage gives to petroleum-producing countries.

5. Worldwatch Institute. 2011. *The State of the World: Innovations that Nourish the Planet.* New York: W.W. Norton.

See also *State of the World* for 2012, 2013, 2014, and 2015. The Worldwatch Institute publishes valuable updated volumes of *State of the World* every year, and they all address issues of agriculture and food to some extent.

Video Suggestions

1. BBC. 2014. *Jimmy's Food Price Hike.* http://tvo.org/programs/jimmys-food-price-hike. 48 min (each episode).

A three-part series in which farmer Jimmy Doherty travels the globe to find out why the price of our food is spiralling out of control.

2. Hozer, Michèle. 2015. *Sugar Coated.* http://sugarcoateddoc.com. 90 min.

Examines the consequences of a sugar-heavy diet.

References

Ahn, C., M. Moore, and N. Parker. 2004. "Migrant Farm Workers: America's New Plantation Workers," Food First *Backgrounder* 10(2). www.foodfirst.org/en/node/45.

Albritton, Robert. 1991. *A Japanese Approach to Stages of Capitalist Development.* London: Macmillan.

———. 1993. "Did Agrarian Capitalism Exist?" *Journal of Peasant Studies* 20:419–41.

———. 2009. *Let Them Eat Junk: How Capitalism Creates Hunger and Obesity.* London: Pluto Press.

———. 2011. "A Practical Utopia for the 21st Century." In *Existential Utopia: New Perspectives on Utopian Thought*, ed. M. Marder and P. Vieira. London: Continuum Press.

Cook, Christopher D. 2004. "Thanksgiving's Hidden Costs." Alternet. 23 November. www.alternet.org/story/20556.

Dalle Mulle, Emmanuel, and Violette Ruppanner. 2010. *Exploring the Global Food Supply Chain: Markets, Companies, Systems.* 3D–Trade–Human Rights–Equitable Economy. www.3dthree.org/pdf_3D/3D_ExploringtheGlobalFoodSupplyChain.pdf.

Heaps, T. 2010. "The Killer Kernel." *Corporate Knights* 33 (Fall). http://www.corporateknights.com/channels/food-beverage/killer-kernel-2-12856849/.

Kohonen, M., and F. Mestrum. 2009. *Tax Justice.* London: Pluto Press.

Marx, Karl. 1976. *Capital*, Vol. I. New York: Penguin.

———, 1978. *Capital*, Vol. II. New York: Penguin.

———, and Friedrich Engels. 1978. *The Marx-Engels Reader*, ed. Robert Tucker. New York: W.W. Norton.

Rosset, Peter. 2006. *Food is Different: Why We Must Get the WTO out of Agriculture.* Halifax, NS: Fernwood.

Sahlins, Marshall. 1972. *Stone Age Economics.* New York: Aldine Press.

United Food and Commercial Workers (UFCW). 2015. "The Status of Migrant Farm Workers in Canada." http://www.ufcw.ca/templates/ufcwCanada/images/directions15/october/1586/MigrantWorkersReport2015_EN_email.pdf.

Weis, T. 2013. *The Ecological Hoofprint: The Global Burden of Industrial Livestock.* London and New York: Zed Books.

9 A Political Ecology Approach to Industrial Food Production

Tony Weis

Learning Objectives

Through this chapter, you can

1. Understand the problems associated with cheap industrial food and the central place of food and agriculture in global environmental problems and solutions

2. Examine a conceptual framework for understanding the resource budgets and pollution loads—and, by extension, unvalued and undervalued environmental costs—embedded in high-yielding monocultures and factory farms, which are at the heart of the world food system

3. Recognize why the system is becoming increasingly unstable

4. Appreciate the environmental motivations for people turning away from cheap industrial food and seeking to support alternatives that connect them to the earth and to farmers in more sustainable ways

Introduction

Industrial capitalist agriculture has generated ever more and cheaper food. Production comes from fewer and larger farms, while fewer and larger firms dominate agricultural inputs and food processing, distribution, and retail networks. On the consumption side, people's interaction with food in wealthy countries like Canada is overwhelmingly mediated by opaque market forces, from giant supermarkets to super-sized "value" meals in fast-food restaurants. Together, the low prices, bounty, and opacity of the modern food system have undoubtedly obscured its environmental foundations, limits, and vulnerabilities for many people. The more food gets severed from time and space, the less eating is appreciated as a powerful bodily interaction with the earth, for good or ill.

As with all commodities, food is shrouded in mystery, in that consumers have limited knowledge about the array of social and ecological relations that went into making the things (and their prices) that they encounter in markets, and the many costs that are unvalued or undervalued in this process. The fact that these relations and costs are hidden and largely incomprehensible is something Marx called **commodity fetishism**. Put another way, most consumers see food as having a price, a brand, and a country of origin, but would find it difficult or impossible to answer a host of basic questions about most of what they eat with any precision. What part of the country was it grown in? What agro-inputs were used, how were these made, and where did they come from? How and when was the food harvested and processed? What routes did it travel from land to retail outlet? Beyond these questions lie even more complex ones: How do these matters affect soils, water, biodiversity, energy consumption, and the atmosphere?

To begin to unpack the environmental costs embedded in our cheap food supply, we start by examining how the imperatives of industrial capitalism have transformed agriculture as a biological and physical process. The general approach taken is called **political ecology**, which gives attention to the political-economic tendencies, power imbalances, and ecological instabilities in how systems operate.

Agriculture as a Relatively Closed-Loop System

For the vast majority of our history, humans acquired the energy and nutrients produced by photosynthesis and accumulated in plant, animal, and marine life through gathering, hunting, and fishing. In effect, this meant that the products of photosynthesis were harvested from ecosystems, with humans taking a minute part of net primary production. The rise of agriculture 10,000 years ago represented an enormous shift in how human societies obtained energy and nutrients. It meant that the photosynthetic activity of plants was first *organized*—by managing biodiversity, plant and animal interactions, nutrient flows, and water supplies—before the products of photosynthesis were appropriated. While agriculture obviously increased the usability of these products for humans, the displacement of more biologically productive ecosystems reduced the volume of photosynthetic activity. Over millennia then, agricultural expansion was the biggest factor in the slow but steady increase in the **human appropriation of the net primary product (of photosynthesis) (HANPP)**, though this remained very small prior to the modern era.

The limits of technology, surpluses, and storage and the large "friction of distance" meant that until very recently agricultural societies were predominantly localized. In other words, it was hard to move anything in bulk across significant distances when dependent upon human, animal, or wind power, especially something as perishable as food. Problems of soil loss, pests, and drought had to be mitigated using nearby resources and by fostering complementary biological interactions, such as **intercropping** patterns (planting multiple crops in mutually beneficial combinations). Agricultural innovation—including, at its core, the selection of seeds geared toward long-term improvements—was deeply rooted in cultures and bioregions, apart from episodic dispersions of seeds and animals. Long-distance trade had to be confined to a small number of commodities, generally those prized for flavouring, preservation, and medicinal effects rather than sustenance.

Another way of appreciating these imperatives was that agricultural landscapes had to be based upon relatively "closed-loop" cycles of biological and physical materials:

- Most organic wastes and nutrients had to be returned to land close to where they were withdrawn.
- Biodiversity in the soils enhanced the breakdown and recycling of nutrients.
- Biological approaches (and in some cases extensive terracing) were needed to limit soil erosion and enhance moisture retention.
- Biological approaches were needed to suppress undesirable organisms.
- The sun was the sole external source of energy, fuelling photosynthesis and through this animal power and human labour (Sage 2012; Altieri 1999; Jackson 1985).

Although more closed-loop cycles tended to promote crop protection as well as the long-term stability of the resource base, this does not mean that all short-term vulnerabilities were eliminated or that this loop was ever entirely closed, in particular with respect to soil. Soil is the "living skin of the earth," a combination of biological and physical materials that ultimately underpins all human civilizations; without great care it tends to be lost far more quickly than it develops.

Some societies have managed the balance of soil loss versus soil formation more effectively than others, thus enhancing their stability, but failure to maintain soil fertility has had a recurring central role in the decline of civilizations throughout history (Montgomery 2007).

In short, non-industrial agricultural systems contain a range of lessons and applied knowledge about managing diversity, much of which is very valuable in thinking about sustainability, but it does little good to romanticize a pre-industrial golden age.

The Industrial Revolution in Agriculture: Scale, Mechanization, and Standardization

The scope of traded food increased with the onset of European colonialism and the rising movement both of tropical commodities (e.g. sugar, coffee, tea, and cocoa) from parts of the Caribbean, Central and South America, Africa, and Asia, and of temperate grain and livestock products from places such as the United States, Canada, Argentina, and the Punjab region of India. These trade patterns were linked to momentous social and ecological changes and enduring inequalities, as Indigenous peoples across vast areas were displaced by large plantations, farms, and pastures.

While colonialism established new trade patterns and dependencies—and novel long-distance flows of food in bulk—we need to recognize how thoroughly the biological and physical nature of agricultural production has been transformed by capitalist imperatives and industrial methods. The distinctive capitalist imperatives of incessant competition, growth, and accumulation are entwined with the pressure to achieve **economies of scale**: in essence, to increase output per worker in order to reduce the relative cost of labour in production. In uncritical accounts (i.e. mainstream economics), economies of scale are primarily attributed to the wonders of technological innovation, while another crucial element is left out or downplayed: the essential role of fossil fuels in running machines and factories and in reducing the friction of distance in moving commodities around—sometimes described as the compression of time and space. Oil, natural gas, and coal account for roughly four-fifths of the world's total primary energy supply (i.e. the energy used in production, households, and transportation), with oil providing virtually all of the liquid fuel that powers transportation systems (IEA 2014; Heinberg 2005).

Remarkable economies of scale have been achieved in agricultural systems across the industrialized world, with fossil-fuel-powered machines, factories, and transportation systems central to the increasing output per worker. Whereas for most of agrarian history a large majority of the population has had to work the land, today farmers make up only about 4 per cent of the workforce across the countries of the Organisation for Economic Co-operation and Development. Economies of scale in agriculture are most advanced in the United States and Canada, the world's largest surplus-producing and exporting region. There farmers make up only 2 per cent of the workforce—and only 1 out of every 400 farmers in the world—yet they accounted for more than one-tenth of total world agro-exports by value in 2011, and an even greater volume of basic food staples. In the United States, the number of farms has declined precipitously, together with a remarkable polarization of landholding. In 2012, almost 70 per cent of all US farmland was controlled by only 8 per cent of landholders, and more than 82,000 farms were larger than 800 hectares. In Canada, the number of farms peaked in 1941 and then fell almost fourfold in only 70 years, declining from 732,832 to 205,730 in 2011 (USDA NASS 2013; Statistics Canada 2012).

In a general sense, in order for technology (and capital) to progressively displace human labour, the production process must be standardized in terms of both physical space and the nature of work. In agriculture, small fields with a range of different crops and small animal populations are obviously not conducive to large, labour-saving machinery. Rather, large machines demand big volumes of the same thing. The basic imperative is thus to reduce **biodiversity** in terms of the numbers of plant and animal species on farms, the ways they interact, and the biological structure of individual species. Thus the loss of biodiversity can be seen from the large scale of **monoculture** (single crop) fields down to the microscopic scale of plant and animal genetics.

Scientific innovation aimed at standardizing plants and animals has been entwined with efforts to increase their size and/or rate of growth, and thus increase their yield. Conventional **genetic enhancement** of seeds and livestock breeds— improvements made by crossing varieties within the same species—is a pivotal dimension of both the biological narrowing and the rising productivity of industrial capitalist agriculture.

The Industrial Grain-Oilseed-Livestock Complex

Today only 10 crops account for roughly three-quarters of humanity's plant-based calories, and only five livestock animals are responsible for virtually all meat, eggs, and milk consumed on a global scale. Industrial agriculture in temperate climates is dominated by a few grain and oilseed monocultures and a few livestock species reared in high-density factory farms and feedlots. This system, referred to as the **industrial grain–oilseed–livestock complex** (Weis 2013, 2010; Friedmann 1993), is principally focused on

- maize and wheat, and a few secondary grains
- soybeans and secondarily canola (or rapeseed)
- pigs, poultry, and cattle

Industrially reared livestock consume more than a third of the world's grain harvest, and a much greater share of all oilseeds, with the ratios of cycling feed through livestock the highest in industrialized countries like the United States and Canada.

As noted, the separation of livestock from farmland has enabled increasing scale and mechanization, and the productivity gains of industrial grain and oilseed monocultures have allowed livestock populations to grow far beyond their former densities on small integrated farms. At the same time, the cycling of large volumes of grains and oilseeds through livestock greatly expanded profit-making opportunities for cheap surpluses—enhancing markets for grain and oilseed processors and distributors and increasing value-added possibilities in meat, milk, and eggs. Concentrated feed combined with confinement and breeding innovations have also accelerated livestock weight gain and milk and egg productivity, or what might be understood as speeding up the "turnover time" of animals (Mann and Dickinson 1978).

Thus, while physically separated in landscapes, industrial monocultures and livestock production are bound together by an economic logic that has transformed both (Weis 2013). The industrial grain–oilseed–livestock complex is at the centre of the global livestock revolution, a term that marks the dramatically rising scale at which animal flesh and derivatives are produced (Steinfeld et al. 2006). Animal flesh was on the periphery of human diets for most of the history of agriculture, but these transformations have driven it to the centre, a process described as the "meatification" of diets. Incredibly, the average person today eats twice as much meat as the average person only three generations ago, in spite of the more than doubling of the human population over this period. This colossal shift has, of course, been highly uneven on a world scale, tightly correlated to affluence. The average person in an industrialized country consumes over two and a half times more meat than an average person in a developing country. The United States and Canada are at the apex of this trend, consuming roughly four times more poultry, three times more beef, and six times more cheese per capita than the world average—along with one-third more calories, 50 per cent more protein, and nearly 100 per cent more fat. Fast-industrializing countries, foremost China, are moving quickly toward these consumption patterns (Weis 2013; Nierenberg 2005).

The United States and Canada illustrate the grain–oilseed–livestock complex in its most productive and technologically developed form. Together, in 2013, they produced roughly

- 18 per cent of the world's total cereal production (the United States alone accounts for more than one-third of all maize)
- 34 per cent of the world's soybeans (mainly in the United States) and 25 per cent of the world's canola (mainly in Canada)
- 15 per cent of the world's meat by volume (including roughly one-fifth of all poultry and beef)

Factory farming and industrial feedlots originated in the United States and are most extensive there. In 2012, over 90 per cent of all pigs in the United States were confined in operations with "inventories" of more than 2,000 animals, and 99 per cent of all meat chickens (called broilers) are raised in operations which sell more than 100,000 birds a year. Since 2001, nearly 9 billion chickens have been killed every year in the United States alone, more in a single day today than were killed in an entire year less than a century ago (FAOSTAT 2015; USDA NASS 2013).

Agriculture as a Through-Flow Process

This booming productivity and the accompanying meatification of diets are widely taken for granted across the industrialized world, along with the long-term decline in the average share of income devoted to food. However, this increased output is only one side of the story; on the other side, much less acknowledged, are the increasing external inputs needed to produce it. To appreciate this, it helps to understand the range of ways that biological and physical problems are magnified or created. Key dynamics include

- reduced fallowing (leaving fields unplanted for a time to let them regain fertility) and shorter time horizons driven by competitive pressures, often linked to the scale of capital investment and debt on farms
- reduced recycling of organic material on farms as a result of the decline in soil biodiversity, fallowing, and scavenging by small livestock populations
- reduced soil moisture retention and increased erosion as a result of the elimination of ground cover between planted rows in monocultures
- damage done to soil biota (the living component of soil) from increased tillage (plowing) and compaction by large machinery
- increased opportunities for weeds and insects to thrive and spread amid monocultures
- "thirstier" enhanced seeds, compared with lower-yielding traditional varieties
- increased risks of animal health problems, diseases, and neurotic behaviours as a result of their intensive confinement and large concentrations in factory farms
- increased food safety concerns associated with foodborne bacteria and viruses in concentrated animal production facilities

The net result is a system with deep biological and physical instabilities, which hinges on its ability to override them with a host of inputs (which therefore might be understood as **biophysical overrides**), such that it comes to resemble a through-flow process.

As human labour and animal traction are displaced with machinery, the principal source of energy on farms shifts from the sun to fossil fuels—in other words, from renewable stores of photosynthesized solar energy (i.e. plants) to ancient and irreplaceable stores of compressed, photosynthesized solar energy (i.e. oil). The movement of animals into factories further extends this dependence upon external sources of energy (although, as we will see in the following section, the dependence upon fossil fuels and derivatives does not end with the on-farm energy supply).

One of the most fundamental problems in industrial agriculture is the speed at which key nutrients and soil organisms are lost, which has been called **soil mining**. Though soil degradation has an old history, it is greatly accelerated by reduced soil biodiversity and ground cover in monocultures, repeated cycles of tillage and compaction, and heavy chemical use. Soil mining in industrial agriculture is primarily overridden with three fertilizers—nitrogen, phosphorous, and potassium—from inorganic sources (Sage 2012; Pimentel 2006; McKenney 2002; Warshall 2002). The increased pest problems also stem from the fact that many organisms which once had complementary, beneficial roles within more diverse agro-ecosystems become problematic within industrial monocultures. The risks are overridden with a large volume of chemical pesticides, the umbrella term for herbicides (targeting weeds), insecticides, fungicides, and disinfectants. The voracious appetite for inputs in industrial monocultures is reflected in the fact that United States and Canada together consumed 14.4 million tonnes of nitrogen, phosphate, and potash fertilizer in 2012, about 12 per cent of the world total (FAOSTAT 2015).[1]

As discussed below, the total volume of fertilizers and chemicals consumed in industrial monocultures expands with the rising volumes of grains and oilseeds fed to growing livestock populations. Further, the health and behavioural problems caused by the unnatural densities of animals in factory farms involve their own chemical overrides: the proliferation of animal pharmaceuticals (with antibiotics and hormones also serving to enhance yields) and of disinfectants, which are used with large amounts of water to clean factory farms and industrial abattoirs. These overrides do not, however, stem the persistent disease threats associated with industrial livestock, such as H1N1 (or swine flu), H5N1 (or avian flu), listeriosis, *E. coli*, and bovine spongiform encephalopathy (a.k.a. mad cow disease).

Un-anaesthetized mutilations are another means for overriding behavioural problems, as in the rapid debeaking lines for poultry or tail docking for pigs (Weis 2013; Mason and Singer 1990).

While agricultural societies have long relied on irrigation to varying degrees, high-yielding monocultures have significantly increased the scale of irrigation infrastructure and freshwater diversions. Agriculture is by far the largest consumer of water in industrial countries (Hoekstra 2013), and its consumption reflects the polarization of productivity described earlier. In the United States, for instance, 72 per cent of all irrigated land is contained on farms greater than 1,000 acres (405 hectares), which represent just 8 per cent of all farms (USDA NASS 2013).

In sum, although the industrial revolution in agriculture has brought great gains in terms of output per worker, along with increased yields from each plant and animal, the flipside is that these have been accompanied by tremendous increases in the resources going into farms (Weis 2007). The dependence upon these biophysical overrides—which must often be sourced across great distances—constitutes a historic rupture of agriculture from relatively closed-loop cycles to a through-flow process, as depicted in figure 9.1.

The Hidden Environmental Costs of Cheap Food

The previous section examined how industrial capitalism has radically reconfigured agriculture into a through-flow process, with the great productivity gains enabled by a large range of inputs or biophysical overrides. This through-flow process depends upon a large budget of non-renewable resources and is implicated in a multidimensional environmental burden. To appreciate the environmental costs of food, then, it is necessary to understand these overrides both in terms of their resource budget and their pollution burden: that is, to assess what inputs go into the process and what wastes come out of the process. The fact that this burden does not register as costs

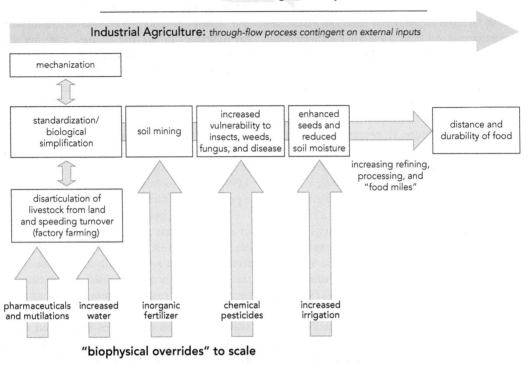

Non-industrial Agriculture: *relatively closed-loop cycles of biological and physical materials and managed diversity*

Industrial Agriculture: *through-flow process contingent on external inputs*

mechanization

standardization/ biological simplification

soil mining

increased vulnerability to insects, weeds, fungus, and disease

enhanced seeds and reduced soil moisture

distance and durability of food

increasing refining, processing, and "food miles"

disarticulation of livestock from land and speeding turnover (factory farming)

pharmaceuticals and mutilations

increased water

inorganic fertilizer

chemical pesticides

increased irrigation

"biophysical overrides" to scale

Figure 9.1 The Through-Flow of Industrial Agriculture

within the prevailing economic system—and is largely externalized—is a major reason why industrial food has long been so cheap.

Food Miles

The industrial transformation of agriculture is entwined with the increasing distance and durability of food (Friedmann 1993). As scale and mechanization expand, landscapes are specialized to produce large quantities of a few crops, rural populations decline, communities are separated from their surrounding countrysides, control is centralized in large corporate intermediaries, and food travels farther from land to mouth. This distance is popularly referred to as **food miles**, and cheap and abundant oil coupled with processing and transportation innovations

have been essential to reducing the friction of distance. Much of the growing popular awareness about food miles has focused on the resulting carbon emissions, which makes this concept a very visible marker for how the food system is linked to climate change. Rising concern is reflected in things like the "100-mile diet" (Smith and McKinnon 2007) and related "locavore" movements to "eat local" or, as Kloppenberg et al. (1996) put it, to "move in to the foodshed."

Soil Mining

If food miles are one of the most popularly recognized environmental costs in the industrial food system, soil mining is one of the least. This is not an entirely new problem; as noted, soil degradation has repeatedly played a significant part in the decline of civilizations, although unfolding too gradually to be appreciated. What is new is that this loss is comprehensively understood and has sped up to an extent that some place this among the most worrisome of all global environmental problems (Shiva 2008; Montgomery 2007; Pimentel 2006; Jackson 1985). But rather than responding to the causes of soil degradation and finding ways to restore organic content and enhance soil formation, the primary industrial response has been the repeated, short-term fix of industrial fertilizers to replace lost nitrogen, phosphorous, and potassium, which involves a host of environmental costs (Sage 2012; Pimentel 2006; McKenney 2002; Warshall 2002).

Fertilizers from Production to Farm

Synthetic nitrogen fertilizers are by far the greatest soil input by volume. They are primarily manufactured through the Haber-Bosch process for combining atmospheric nitrogen and hydrogen, with natural gas and coal the main feedstocks. Phosphorous and potassium fertilizers come from phosphate ore and potash mining, which depend upon fossil-fuel-powered machinery and refining, and result in a considerable pollution burden. The manufacture of phosphate fertilizer is implicated in highly acidic and toxic wastewater ponds. Potash mining occurs over large areas both above and below ground. Above ground, it leaves behind open-pit wastelands; below ground, extensive mines create risks of water table contamination and land subsidence. In addition to the manufacturing and mining processes, the transportation and application of industrial fertilizers require large volumes of oil, as fertilizers are bulky materials that often travel great distances. When this consumption is added up, from factories and mines to farms and tractor spreaders, fertilizers account for a significant share of both the overall fossil energy budget and of the carbon emissions in industrial agriculture (Sage 2012; Pimentel 2006; McKenney 2002). Nitrogen fertilizer is also a major source of nitrous oxide emissions, a significant greenhouse gas (GHG). Thus, if people are concerned

about how far their food has travelled (and the energy and atmospheric costs contained in this), they might also be asking, "How local was its fertilizer?". Shiva (2008) argues that there is a central, systematic link between soil degradation, oil dependence, and climate change, and that sustainable and just societies need to be built on the foundation of healthy "soil not oil."

Pesticides from Production to Farm

As with fertilizers, the proliferation of chemical pesticides is a short-term fix that not only fails to resolve the basic dynamic of why monocultures face greater pest problems, but worsens it over time. These inputs thus have a treadmill effect. The **pesticide treadmill** means that more or newer pesticides are always needed as natural predators and controls are eliminated, pests and disease organisms develop resistance over time, and localized ecological knowledge and the ability to use non-chemical responses are lost (sometimes referred to as "knowledge erosion"). In *Silent Spring*, a book which helped give rise to the modern environmental movement, Carson (1962) highlighted the basic dynamics of this treadmill with the powerful metaphor of a low-intensity chemical war on ecosystems and other species. This situation was more than metaphorical: much of the incredible surge in agro-chemicals after the Second World War was manufactured in reconstituted war munitions plants. Many pesticides are petrochemical based, and like fertilizers they involve an energy budget in their manufacture, transport, and application which is seldom recognized (although they are less bulky than fertilizers). Extensive use of chemical pesticides also contributes to the destruction of soil microorganisms and thus to the decline of soil fertility.

GMO Risks

In contrast to conventional genetic enhancement where varieties *within* the same species are crossed, **genetic modification** is the term given to the technological combination of genetic traits from different species that could not cross naturally (which is why this process is also described as genetic engineering). Somewhat ironically, the same companies that control pesticide production on a global scale seek to justify the expansion of genetically modified organisms (GMOs), which they also dominate, partly by claiming that this innovation can reduce overall chemical use in agriculture through building pest resistance into the genetic makeup of crops. The predominant corporate actor here is Monsanto, followed by DuPont and Syngenta. The other key trait associated with most GMO crops is their tolerance for a particular chemical, which links seed and chemical purchase in a very powerful way—as in Monsanto's Roundup Ready seed varieties (Robin 2010).

GMOs pose complex, long-term contamination risks to ecosystems, which has led many countries to take a strong regulatory position against their use. They have also led to a tremendous amount of environmental activism, from public education and lobbying campaigns to direct actions like setting fire to GMO crops. However, permissive regulatory regimes in a few countries have allowed the widespread diffusion of GMOs ahead of comprehensive long-term impact assessments, most notably in the United States, Canada, Argentina, and Brazil, four of the world's most important agro-exporting nations. In these countries, a small number of genetically modified grains and oilseeds now pervade agricultural landscapes and the food system, outside of much public awareness and scrutiny (Druker 2015; see also chapter 16 in this volume).

Factory Farms and Feedlots

Throughout most agrarian history, small livestock populations had roles in nutrient cycles on fallowed land and small pastures, and in scavenging organic wastes on the margins of farm households, by providing fecal matter (manure) for nourishing the soil. Today, in stark contrast, the huge concentrations of animals in factory farms and feedlots produce fecal waste on a scale far greater than what nearby landscapes can absorb.

Making matters worse, this waste is also laden with residues from the antibiotics and hormones that the animals are routinely given, and from the agro-chemicals in concentrated feeds (Weis 2013; Imhoff 2010; Mason and Singer 1990). Landscapes dotted with factory farms and feedlots are marked by "manure lagoons" of untreated waste, which not only create wretched "smell-scapes" but also release methane, another potent GHG. The growth of factory farming, with its heating, ventilation, and machinery, also increases energy consumption and GHG emissions (depending on which energy sources supply the local electrical grid).

Factory farms also raise profound ethical questions, as animals are transformed from sentient beings into pure commodities—inanimate objects whose treatment is shaped almost entirely by market imperatives. This can be seen in the both the episodic violence (e.g. mutilations, transport, fast-paced slaughter lines) and the chronic misery in intensive confinement (e.g. battery cages, broiler houses, gestation crates). The ethical dimensions of these spaces also extends to health concerns facing workers in factory farms and slaughterhouses, who have to cope with the severe psychological trauma of routinely inflicting suffering and death, as well as high incidences of repetitive stress and accidental injuries (Weis 2013; Eisnitz 1997; Mason and Singer 1990).

The Downstream Pollution Burden

Industrial farms, factories, and feedlots place a large pollution burden on downstream water bodies and groundwater supplies, which necessitate increased investment, technology, and energy in water treatment facilities. However, excess nutrients, chemicals, and pharmaceuticals are much too diffuse to contain residues on food and in water supplies end up creating untold risks for ecosystems, animal life, and ultimately human bodies (Steingraber 2010; Moore 2002). One of the largest burdens on ecosystem health comes from the run-off of nutrients from fertilizers and from the waste of concentrated animal populations. These excess nutrients cause widespread **eutrophication** (oxygen-depleting algae blooms) in freshwater bodies and around coastal riverheads, which can have a devastating impact on aquatic life. The most infamous case is the giant dead zone in the Gulf of Mexico, the by-product of run-off from the US agricultural heartland deposited by the Mississippi River, but there are now many such zones of varying sizes in coastal areas around the world (Sage 2012; Mitchell 2009; Schindler and Vallentyne 2008; MEA 2005; McKenney 2002).

The persistent toxins that are released into the environment bio-accumulate in higher life forms as they move through aquatic and terrestrial food chains, a problem to which Carson (1962) was the first to draw widespread attention. Though there are more controls on releasing chemicals today than when *Silent Spring* was published (when such controls were virtually non-existent), many would argue that regulatory regimes still generally favour the early release of new chemicals (Moore 2002). Environmentalists argue for chemical regulation to be guided by the precautionary principle, which places a strong, pre-release burden of proof on demonstrating that a given chemical is benign in the long term.

Freshwater Diversions and Over-Consumption

On a global scale, agriculture is responsible for almost three-quarters of all freshwater consumption, and irrigated land—although a relatively small percentage of all cultivated areas—accounts for two-fifths of the world's food production. Industrial monocultures are central to this discrepancy, with their heightened productivity enabled, in part, by drawing on freshwater withdrawals disproportionately to the land area (Hoekstra 2013; Sage 2012; Briscoe 2002).

Large-scale irrigation projects together with hydroelectricity drove the era of mega-dam–building in the twentieth century, which wrought massive transformations to riverine ecosystems around the world (McCully 1996). One of the greatest examples of this is in the American West. In *Cadillac Desert*, Reisner (1993) describes how natural watercourses, from the Columbia to the Colorado Rivers, were comprehensively transformed by massive engineering schemes to make highly productive industrial agricultural landscapes in dry areas with little natural irrigation. Other irrigation systems depend upon the unsustainable consumption of underground aquifers, drawing water from them faster than they are recharged. Nowhere is this overdraft more precarious than with the great Ogallala Aquifer, which irrigates much of the arid American Midwest, the world's most important grain producing and exporting region, and which is being used at a rate that effectively amounts to mining a non-renewable resource (Opie 2000). There is also an energy cost; while many irrigation diversions are linked to hydroelectric generation at some point in the system, fossil energy powers a great deal of irrigation pumping.

Prolonged irrigation often contributes to problems of waterlogging, nutrient leaching, and **salinization**. Soil becomes salinized when the dissolved salt in water is left behind after evapotranspiration (water evaporating from the land or transpiring from plants). Salts build up over time, and beyond a certain point salinization has large negative impacts on moisture uptake by plants and thus on crop yields (Sage 2012; Briscoe 2002).

Magnifying the Costs: Reverse Protein Factories

A very important dynamic of global agriculture is that rising volumes of monoculture grains and oilseeds are being fed to intensively reared livestock. This trend is led by industrialized countries, where increasingly meat-centred diets are held as one marker of modernization and development (Weis 2013). The cycling of grains and oilseeds through livestock is an inefficient way to produce food, as large amounts of useable protein, carbohydrates, and fibre are lost in the metabolic process of animals converting grains and oilseeds to flesh. In *Diet for a Small Planet*, Lappé (1971) first drew attention to the environmental implications of this wastefulness, which she called "reverse protein factories." Different animals have different conversion ratios, with the pinnacle of inefficiency being the grain-fed steer, but the basic point is that as the proportion of meat rises in a society's diet, so too does the overall land area that must be devoted to grain and oilseed production. Thus, in addition to the direct pollution burden associated with factory farms and feedlots, the process of cycling of feed through livestock acts like a magnifying lens for the many environmental costs of industrial monocultures (Weis 2013).

This magnifying lens ultimately has a powerful impact on energy consumption and GHG emissions, as much more energy goes into a unit of edible protein contained in factory-farmed meat than goes into a unit of edible protein in industrial grain or oilseed. Rising livestock populations are implicated in the carbon emissions from the conversion of biodiverse ecosystems to additional cultivation and pasture, as well as in the resulting reduced capacity for sequestering carbon that follows. The global ruminant population is also a major source of methane emissions. When these atmospheric effects are added up, global livestock production has one of the largest impacts on climate change of all economic sectors (Weis 2013; McIntyre et al. 2009; Steinfield et al. 2006; Nierenberg 2005). Finally, the overall energy and atmospheric budgets are further stretched by the fact that most animal flesh and derivatives have a greater dependence upon both mobile and in situ refrigeration units.

The Loss of Biodiversity

The United Nations *Millennium Ecosystem Assessment* (2005:777) describes agriculture as the "largest threat to biodiversity and ecosystem function of any single human activity." This report also highlights how the destruction of natural ecosystems for agriculture accelerated dramatically in the second half of the twentieth century, with more land converted to cropland in only three decades (1950–80) than occurred during a century and a half of widespread colonial transformations (1700–1850) (MEA 2005).

The expansive footprint of industrial monocultures in landscapes, magnified by factory-farmed livestock, reduces the space for natural ecosystems and other species. The shrinking of ecosystems and the extirpation, endangerment, and extinction of species have both immeasurable dimensions (What is the ethical cost of a species going extinct?), and ones that more directly impair human economies. These effects on human economies are sometimes discussed in terms of ecosystem services to highlight the underappreciated ways in which economies depend upon natural processes and to translate their degradation into measurable economic costs. Ecosystem services can be understood through a range of biophysical processes and scales, such as the roles of forests in the carbon cycle, watershed health in freshwater supplies, bees and other pollinators in plant reproduction, and micro-organisms in soil formation.

The radical reduction of biodiversity on farms and the consolidation of control over the world's seed markets are destroying the environmental conditions which gave rise to agricultural diversity. Biodiversity loss at the scale of soils has also reduced the nutritional content of industrial foods (Pollan 2008). For most people, however, the biological narrowing of the food supply is partially obscured by the endlessly creative ways it is refined, mixed, coloured, flavoured, and packaged.

From Hidden Costs to Crisis: Accelerating Instabilities

The previous section examined the many hidden environmental costs in industrial capitalist agriculture; these costs effectively subsidize the cheap bounty industrial agriculture generates. A pivotal, recurring aspect is the intractable dependence upon fossil fuels, which can be viewed as a powerful current coursing across the through-flow process (as depicted in figure 9.2), from the running of heavy machinery and of factory farms, to the production, transport, and application of fertilizers and chemical pesticides, to irrigation pumping and added water treatment, to the increasing processing, packaging, and long-distance movement of food durables. In short, when we eat industrial foods we are "eating fossil fuels," as many calories of fossil energy are contained in a single calorie of industrial food (Sage 2012; Shiva 2008). This dependence on fossil energy, and in particular oil, connects the industrial grain–oilseed–livestock complex and the associated meatification of diets

to the long, sordid history of Western political manipulation in the Middle East and the deeply entrenched US military presence there—and a set of unaccounted political, economic, and social costs that might be seen as a "geopolitical externality" (Weis 2010). The energetic budget of industrial food is also a significant reason why countries like the United States and Canada have per capita GHG emissions far greater than the world average.

The earth's climate history has had long periods of both major cooling and major warming, a fact which climate change skeptics sometimes cite in order to downplay threats and justify inaction. However, there is overwhelming

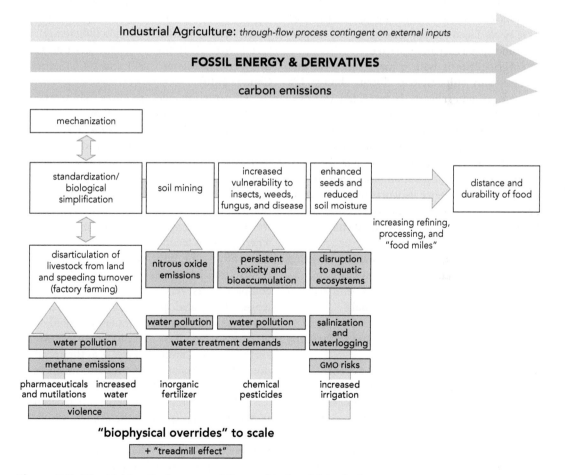

Figure 9.2 The Hidden Environmental Costs of Industrial Agriculture

scientific evidence that the trajectory of current warming falls outside of any natural variability and is attributable to human economies increasing GHG concentrations in the earth's atmosphere. For a number of reasons, including the persistence of GHGs in the atmosphere, the thermal lag of the oceans, and a variety of positive feedbacks (e.g. less ice in polar and alpine regions means less reflected solar radiation and more absorption of heat), the earth is already committed to a significant amount of warming. The extent of this warming could well be pushing the earth out of the **Holocene**, the short geological period of relative climatic stability in which agriculture and human civilization arose (IPCC 2013). In other words, while agricultural societies have always faced climate variability, they have never faced climate change on the magnitude and speed that are projected.

Agriculture is both a major cause of and exceptionally vulnerable to climate change. On balance, climate change is projected to negatively affect agricultural projection on a global scale, but with an incredible regressivity: while rich countries are most responsible, the world's poorest countries (which have by far the highest shares of their population in agriculture) are expected to experience its worst impacts (UNDP 2007). Among projected changes, some of the threats to agricultural production include

- hotter average temperatures increasing evaporation and reducing soil moisture
- increased heat waves, aridity, and risks of heat stress for crops and animals
- more variable rains
- declining freshwater yields due to changing rainfall and ice patterns
- more intense extreme weather events
- enhanced conditions for the movement and reproduction of pests and pathogens (IPCC 2013; Hertel et al. 2010; McIntyre et al. 2009)

There is, of course, inevitable uncertainty about the magnitude and interactions of different changes. There is also the possibility that warmer temperatures and extended growing seasons could enhance agricultural productivity along the cooler margins of temperate regions and extend potential arable land northward in a few countries like Canada.

But even in the areas which might benefit, there are fears that gains would be cancelled out by new dynamics, to say nothing of the disastrous climatic implications of further deforestation to expand the land area in cultivation or pasture. Further, increased aridity coupled with significantly reduced river run-off and water availability are anticipated to present a very serious threat to agricultural productivity in the drier mid-latitude regions, and there is extensive evidence that this is already unfolding (Cook et al. 2015; IPCC 2013). The overall water yield in southern Canada (where agriculture is overwhelmingly concentrated) declined by 9 per cent between 1971 and 2004 (Statistics Canada 2010).

Climate change requires simultaneous action on two fronts: mitigation and adaptation. **Climate change mitigation** means making urgent efforts to reduce the scale of change, first through drastic cuts to GHG emissions and second by increasing GHG sequestration in ecosystems. The immediacy of this challenge is impossible to overstate, as climate scientists are warning of an impending "point of no return" where positive feedbacks take on an irreversible momentum. The imperative of mitigation challenges the industrial grain–oilseed–livestock complex to its very core. Reflecting this challenge, the global peasant movement La Vía Campesina has begun to argue that small-scale, biodiverse farms have a role in "cooling down the earth" (La Vía Campesina 2007), as they produce much less emissions and promote much more sequestration than do industrial farms.

Along with mitigation efforts, there is a need to plan for and respond to the changes which are unfolding and projected, broadly encapsulated in the concept of **climate change adaptation**. In no other sector is adaptation more critical or challenging than in agriculture, as changing physical parameters (e.g. temperatures, evaporation rates, rainfall patterns, watershed yields) affect a range of biological responses (e.g. crops, soil organisms, insects, undesirable and invasive species), which themselves interact in complex ways (Howden et al. 2007). Research and scientific innovation are obviously very important, but ultimately the prospects for adaptation are heavily contingent on the extent of mitigation.

Another dynamic making industrial capitalist agriculture more unstable is the fact that human economies are at, near, or have just passed the halfway point in the consumption of all "conventional" oil reserves—the point of **peak oil**. This implies that

- the world's most accessible (and hence lowest cost) oil reserves have already been discovered
- low-cost conventional reserves are all in marked decline
- extracting the remaining conventional reserves will become ever more difficult, costly, and energy intensive (e.g. further offshore, at the poles)
- the second half of the world's oil supply will be consumed much faster than the first half was (Heinberg 2005, 2007)

In the face of declining conventional reserves, there has been a major increase in the extraction of "unconventional" oil, including the mining of bitumen (the biggest frontier being the Canadian tar sands) and kerogen shale and hydraulic fracturing for "tight" oil (a process commonly known as "fracking" that is also increasingly used to extract natural gas). The extraction of unconventional oil reserves entails much greater energy expenditures than with conventional oil, and hence greater GHG emissions, as well as posing a range of other serious environmental health risks.

The decline of conventional oil reserves has also spurred a very contradictory dynamic: a sharp increase in the conversion of grains and oilseeds to industrial agrofuels (or biofuels) over the past decade. On one hand, the agrofuel boom reflects the desire to find new sources of renewable liquid energy as oil declines. On the other hand, nearly as much (or sometimes more) fossil energy goes into the growing and processing of industrial grains and oilseeds as comes out in ethanol or biodiesel. Beginning around 2000, the United States led the global surge in agrofuel production, which constitutes an important and growing dynamic influencing the prices of basic foodstuffs (Houtart 2010; Giampietro and Mayumi 2009).

In the longer term, the pressures associated with the extraction of costlier and more polluting oil production will inevitably reverberate in the through-flow process of industrial agriculture, reducing the implicit subsidy that relatively cheap oil has long provided to cheap food. The peaks and declines in other key non-renewable resources will complicate matters further, with the decline of high-grade phosphorous ore ("peak phophorous") threatening the industrial fertilizer override (Cordell and White 2011; Heinberg 2007). In short, the continuing displacement of labour with technology will become more problematic as current biophysical overrides break down, posing more foundational problems for industrial capitalist agriculture. This is likely to impel either more technological responses or a movement to rebuild agricultural systems in ways that re-centre human labour and skill, localized ecological knowledge, and functional diversity on farms.

Conclusion

This chapter has examined the hidden environmental costs of cheap food by focusing on the industrial grain–oilseed–livestock complex, the productive foundation of the food system in the United States, Canada, and other temperate countries. It explored how the pressures to standardize and mechanize agriculture magnify biological and physical problems and create new ones, how these problems get overridden, and how these overrides involve a large resource budget and pollution burden (amplified by increasingly meat-centred diets), with fossil fuels playing an integral part in all of these matters. When the through-flow process of industrial agriculture is understood, it becomes clear that cheap food depends upon many costs not being counted, and that, in spite of its productive bounty, the system is environmentally unstable. Industrial capitalist agriculture is at once deeply implicated in and threatened by climate change, as well as in soil degradation and the overconsumption and pollution of water. In different ways, climate change and the looming scarcity of oil each present fundamental challenges to the continuation of the system—climate change begs for major restructuring of food economies, and peak oil could well force it.

Fortunately, as people increasingly recognize the environmental costs embedded in cheap food, many are creating alternatives to the industrial grain–oilseed–livestock complex. In the struggles of ecological farmers, consumers' rising demand for local, organic food, and new economic networks linking the two supported by food-centred education and political activism, we find both mounting critical recognition of the problems in the dominant system and hope that it can be rebuilt in more sustainable ways.

Discussion Questions

1. Explain what is meant by the conception of agriculture as a relatively *closed-loop system*, and by agriculture as a *through-flow process*. Discuss what the transformation from closed-loop system to through-flow process has meant for soil in particular, and how ensuing problems have been overridden.

2. Identify and discuss three major aspects of the "resource budget" of the modern food system.

3. Explain how the modern food system is a major factor in climate change, giving attention to the expansion of livestock production.

4. How will the inevitable scarcity and rising costs of oil affect the modern food system?

Further Reading

1. McIntyre, B.D., H.R. Herren, J. Wakhungu, and R.T. Watson, eds. 2009. *International Assessment of Agricultural Knowledge, Science and Technology for Development: Synthesis Report.* Washington, DC: Island Press.
   This was an expansive project (involving over 400 experts from 110 different countries) that examined the role of agricultural knowledge, science, and technology in shaping development policies over the past half century, and the implications for hunger, poverty, nutrition, human health, rural development, and the environment. It identifies many unaccounted costs associated with great productivity gains and argues that new approaches are needed to simultaneously reduce hunger and poverty and build more sustainable agricultural systems.

2. Sage, C. 2012. *Environment and Food.* New York: Routledge.
   An outstanding overview of the environmental dimensions of agri-food systems, which is rich in scope yet highly accessible. Sage moves from processes of production to changing consumption patterns, assessing implications for water, soil degradation, biodiversity, climate change, and energy consumption, and raising questions about the instability of cheap industrial food and long-distance supply chains.

3. Steinfeld, H., P. Gerber, T. Wassenaar, V. Castel, M. Rosales, and C. de Haan. 2006. *Livestock's Long Shadow: Environmental Issues and Options.* Rome: FAO.

A major FAO report examining the central role of global livestock production in an array of pressing environmental problems, including climate change, land degradation, water pollution, and the loss of biodiversity. It had a major role drawing attention to impacts of global livestock production on climate change.

4. Weis, T. 2013. *The Ecological Hoofprint: The Global Burden of Industrial Livestock.* London: Zed Books.

The Ecological Hoofprint examines the industrialization of livestock production, the driving force behind the phenomenal and uneven increase in global meat consumption, and the momentous implications of this trajectory with respect to environmental change, human inequality, and soaring populations of concentrated and commodified animals.

Video Suggestions

1. Geyrhalter, N. 2005. *Our Daily Bread.* www.ourdailybread.at/jart/projects/utb/website.jart?rel=en. 92 min.

2. Kenner, R. 2009. *Food Inc.* www.takepart.com/foodinc. 93 min.

3. Robin, M.-M. 2008. *The World According to Monsanto.* http://www.nfb.ca/film/world_according_to_monsanto/trailer/monsanto-trailer/. 3 min.

4. Worcester, T. 2009. *Pig Business.* www.pigbusiness.co.uk/resources/pig-business/. 58 min.

Note

1. Global statistics are much patchier for pesticide consumption than they are for fertilizer consumption.

References

Altieri, M.A. 1999. "The Ecological Role of Biodiversity in Agroecosystems." *Agriculture, Ecosystems & Environment* 74 (1–3):19–31.

Briscoe, M. 2002. "Water: The Overtapped Resource." Pp. 181–90 in *The Fatal Harvest Reader: The Tragedy of Industrial Agriculture*, ed. A. Kimbrell. Washington, DC: Island Press.

Carson, R. 1994[1962]. *Silent Spring.* Boston: Houghton Mifflin.

Cook, B.I., T.R. Ault, and J.E. Smerdon. 2015. "Unprecedented 21st Century Drought Risk in the American Southwest and Central Plains." *Science Advances* 1(1). doi: 10.1126/sciadv.1400082

Cordell, D. and S. White. 2011. "Peak Phosphorus: Clarifying the Key Issues of a Vigorous Debate about Long-Term Phosphorus Security." *Sustainability* 3(10):2027–49.

Druker, S. 2015. *Altered Genes, Twisted Truth: How the Venture to Genetically Engineer Our Food Has Subverted Science, Corrupted Government, and Systematically Deceived the Public.* Fairfield, IA: Clear River Press.

Eisnitz, G. 1997. *Slaughterhouse: The Shocking Story of Greed, Neglect, and Inhuman Treatment Inside the US Meat Industry.* New York: Prometheus.

Food and Agriculture Organization of the United Nations Statistics Division (FAOSTAT). 2015. "Production and Trade Statistics Calculator." http://faostat3.fao.org/home/E.

Friedmann, H. 1993. "The Political Economy of Food: A Global Crisis." *New Left Review* 197:29–57.

Giampietro, M., and K. Mayumi. 2009. *The Biofuel Delusion.* London: Earthscan.

Heinberg, R. 2005. *The Party's Over: Oil, War, and the Fate of Industrial Societies.* 2nd edn. Gabriola Island, BC: New Society Publishers.

———. 2007. *Peak Everything: Waking up to the Century of Declines.* Gabriola Island, BC: New Society Publishers.

Hertel, T.W., M.B. Burke, and D.B. Lobell. 2010. "The Poverty Implications of Climate-Induced Crop Yield Changes by 2030." *Global Environmental Change* 20:577–85.

Houtart, F. 2010. *Agrofuels: Big Profits, Ruined Lives and Ecological Destruction.* London: Pluto Press.

Hoekstra, A.Y. 2013. *The Water Footprint of Modern Consumer Society*. London: Routledge.

Howden, M.S., J.-F. Soussana, F.N. Tubiello, et al. 2007. "Adapting Agriculture to Climate Change." *Proceedings of the National Academy of Sciences of the United States*, 104(50):19691–6.

Imhoff, D., ed. 2010. *The CAFO Reader: The Tragedy of Industrial Animal Factories*. Berkeley: University of California Press.

Intergovernmental Panel on Climate Change (IPCC) 2013. *Climate Change 2013: The Physical Science Basis*, Contribution of Working Group I to the Fifth Assessment Report of the Intergovernmental Panel on Climate Change. Cambridge: Cambridge University Press.

International Energy Agency (IEA) 2014. *Key World Energy Statistics 2014*. Paris: OECD/IEA. http://www.iea.org/publications/freepublications/publication/keyworld2014.pdf.

Jackson, W. 1985. *New Roots for Agriculture*. San Francisco: Friends of the Earth.

Kloppenberg, J., J. Hendrickson, and G.W. Stephenson. 1996. "Coming in to the Foodshed." *Agriculture and Human Values* 13(3):33–42.

Lappé, F.M. 1991[1971]. *Diet for a Small Planet*. New York: Ballantine.

La Vía Campesina. 2007. "Small Scale Sustainable Farmers Are Cooling Down the Earth." November 2007. http://www.viacampesina.org/main_en/index2.php?option=com_content&do_pdf=1&id=457.

McCully, P.M. 1996. *Silenced Rivers: The Ecology and Politics of Large Dams*. London: Zed Books.

McIntyre, B.D., H.R. Herren, J. Wakhungu, and R.T. Watson, eds. 2009. *International Assessment of Agricultural Knowledge, Science and Technology for Development: Synthesis Report*. Washington, DC: Island Press.

McKenney, J. 2002. "Artificial Fertility: The Environmental Costs of Industrial Fertilizers." Pp. 121–9 in *The Fatal Harvest Reader: The Tragedy of Industrial Agriculture* , ed. A. Kimbrell. Washington, DC: Island Press.

Mann, S., and J. Dickinson. 1978. "Obstacles to the Development of a Capitalist Agriculture." *Journal of Peasant Studies* 5(4):466–81.

Mason, J., and P. Singer. 1990. *Animal Factories*. 2nd edn. New York: Harmony Books.

Millennium Ecosystem Assessment (MEA). 2005. *Ecosystems and Human Well-Being: Synthesis*. Washington: Island Press.

Mitchell, A. 2009. *Sea Sick: The Global Ocean in Crisis*. Toronto: McClelland & Stewart.

Montgomery, D.R. 2007. *Dirt: The Erosion of Civilizations*. Berkeley: University of California Press.

Moore, M. 2002. "Hidden Dimensions of Damage: Pesticides and Health." Pp. 130–47 in *The Fatal Harvest Reader: The Tragedy of Industrial Agriculture*, ed. A. Kimbrell. Washington, DC: Island Press.

Nierenberg, D. 2005. *Happier Meals: Rethinking the Global Meat Industry*. Washington: WorldWatch Paper #171.

Opie, J. 2000. *Ogallala: Water for a Dry Land*. 2nd edn. Lincoln: University of Nebraska Press.

Pimentel, D. 2006. "Soil Erosion: A Food and Environmental Threat." *Environment, Development and Sustainability* 8(1):119–37.

Pollan, M. 2008. *In Defence of Food: An Eater's Manifesto*. New York: Penguin Books.

Reisner, M. 1993[1987]. *Cadillac Desert: The American West and Its Disappearing Water*. 2nd edn. New York: Penguin.

Robin, M.-M. 2010. *The World According to Monsanto*. New York: New Press.

Sage, C. 2012. *Environment and Food*. New York: Routledge.

Schindler, D.W. and J.R. Vallentyne. 2008. *The Algal Bowl: Overfertilization of the World's Freshwaters and Estuaries*. Edmonton: University of Alberta Press.

Shiva, V. 2008. *Soil Not Oil: Environmental Justice in an Age of Climate Crisis*. Boston: South End Press.

Smith, A., and J.B. McKinnon. 2007. *The 100-Mile Diet: A Year of Local Eating*. Toronto: Random House.

Statistics Canada. 2010. "Freshwater Supply and Demand in Canada." *Human Activity and the Environment*. Ottawa: Government of Canada.

———. 2012. *2011 Census of Agriculture*. Government of Canada, Ottawa. Accessed 15 May 2015. http://www.statcan.gc.ca/eng/ca2011/index.

Steinfeld, H., P. Gerber, T. Wassenaar, et al. 2006. *Livestock's Long Shadow: Environmental Issues and Options*. Rome: FAO.

Steingraber, S. 2010. *Living Downstream: An Ecologist's Personal Investigation of Cancer and the Environment*. 2nd edn. Cambridge, MA: Da Capo Press.

United Nations Development Programme (UNDP). 2007. *Human Development Report 2007–8: Fighting Climate Change: Human Solidarity in a Divided World*. New York: Palgrave Macmillan.

US Department of Agriculture, National Agricultural Statistics Service (USDA NASS). 2013. *The Census of Agriculture, 2012*. Accessed 15 May 2015. http://www.agcensus.usda.gov/Publications/2012/Full_Report/Volume_1,_Chapter_1_US/usv1.pdf.

Warshall, P. 2002. "Tilth and Technology: The Industrial Redesign of Our Nation's Soils." Pp. 167–80 in *The Fatal Harvest Reader: The Tragedy of Industrial Agriculture* , ed. A. Kimbrell. Washington, DC: Island Press.

Weis, T. 2007. *The Global Food Economy: The Battle for the Future of Farming*. London: Zed Books.

———. 2010. "The Acclerating Biophysical Contradictions of Industrial Capitalist Agriculture." *Journal of Agrarian Change* 10(3):315–41.

———. 2013. *The Ecological Hoofprint: The Global Burden of Industrial Livestock*. London: Zed Books.

© Jim West/Alamy Stock Photo

Part III

Crises and Challenges in the Food System

As food issues come to be central in public discourse, it is clear that part of the reason for this focus is the perception of a crisis in our food system. The recent manifestation of this crisis was the escalation of food prices around the globe, particularly in 2010–11. The dramatic price increases we saw in a whole range of food commodities aggravated the misery of hundreds of millions of the poorest people around the globe and were credited with providing oxygen to the democratic struggles in the Middle East characterized as the "Arab Spring." Price spikes for food commodities are essentially "conjunctural" crises, that is, of a limited time frame, and in hindsight we now see how speculation, notably by the world's largest grain-trading companies, fuelled price hikes while millions suffered.

Although raw food prices have moderated somewhat, retail prices for food have continued to climb because powerful actors in the food system are able to prevent price declines in raw commodities from being transferred to consumers. The issue of powerful actors in the food system is dealt with in more detail in the chapters by Wiebe and Winson.

In addition to conjunctural crises, the food system is beset with other crises that are arguably much more serious. These crises are of a more structural nature, in that they are rooted in the very structures that make up the food economy as we know it. In other words, they are more deep-seated—embedded in the way in which our economy and society are organized—and require careful analysis to really understand how they are generated and what their consequences are.

In this part of the book, various contributors have provided multiple insights into a number of structural crises that characterize our food system today. To begin the inquiry, the chapter by Wiebe provides a clear analysis of how our political economy is shaping the prospects for those producing food on the land—farm operators and their families. The "cost–price squeeze" is a central process negatively impacting agricultural producers and leading to extraordinary debt loads in recent times.

The crisis in our food system is arguably much more than an economic one. As Kornelsen makes abundantly clear, this crisis also has clear ethical and moral dimensions. A major part of our food production system is concerned with the production of animal protein in the most profitable manner possible. The logical outcome of a meat production system dictated by lowest costs and profit maximization is the spread of intensive confined animal feeding operations, or factory farming. Not only does this have grave consequences of an environmental nature, but it typically subjects sentient animal species we choose to raise for food to a number of painful mutilating procedures that, while not widely known, are being questioned by a growing number of Canadians. Kornelsen's chapter is must-reading for any responsible person who intends to have meat protein as a regular part of their meal plans.

The Sundar chapter, on the other hand, examines the serious degradation of our marine environment and of the populations of animal species that we depend upon for foods that emanate from the sea. She also considers the problems associated with aquaculture as a solution to the decline in wild marine food species, as well as more long-term solutions to the ongoing crisis in global fisheries.

Moving away from the production of food, Winson, and Martin and Amos, discuss separate dimensions of the crisis that characterizes some aspect of food consumption. Among the crises characterizing our food system is a crisis of nutrition. While a growing number of Canadians are facing an insecure food supply, the majority of adult Canadians are now overweight or obese, and dramatic increases in weight gain have occurred among children and youth. This situation is especially disturbing because of the host of chronic diseases that medical science has established are associated with being overweight. Winson brings a political-economic perspective to the analysis of food environments to shed light on this situation and to help us understand why these food environments are so saturated with nutrient-poor "pseudo foods" and junk foods. He brings to bear empirical evidence from two key food environments—supermarkets and schools—to support his argument.

Martin and Amos's chapter probes the nutritional transition taking place in Canada's Aboriginal communities and the heavy burden of chronic disease that has been associated with this transition. They present a strong case for the need to consider the social, economic, and political context as crucially shaping this nutrition transition and, in particular, to consider the impact of *colonization* on the way this nutrition transition has unfolded in these communities and the chronic food insecurity that many Aboriginals face. Integral to their analysis of the food crisis in Aboriginal communities is their critique of nutritionism, with its focus on specific ingredients in diet and stress on individual responsibility around diet rather than a more comprehensive understanding of the broader socio-economic, cultural, and political contexts of diet and nutrition. Stressing the traditional importance of food in the production of community among Aboriginal cultures, they argue that respect for the traditional cultural practices around food must be part of the nutritional solutions so badly needed in many Aboriginal communities.

The crisis in food security is explored by Dachner and Tarasuk, who highlight the alarming rise of *food insecurity* in Canada and the increasing recourse to food banks for a growing number of Canadian adults and their children. They note that some 4 million Canadians experience some degree of food security, with rates considerably higher in the Maritimes, the Yukon, and the Northwest Territories. It is in Nunavut where food insecurity reaches deplorable levels, however, where they observe that in 2012 some 45 per cent of households were food insecure. They detail research on the health consequences of food insecurity before looking at the variety of grassroots, community-based approaches to ending food insecurity, and the very limited though promising programs fostered by both local and government interventions around the matter of school nutrition programs. As they make clear, however, there still exists no clear federal or provincial policy intervention explicitly directed to reducing household food insecurity in Canada.

These chapters do not exhaustively explore the crises facing our food system, but they do give the reader a good idea of their breadth, provide crucial analytical tools for understanding their root causes, and offer some revealing insights into the policy initiatives that will have to be vigorously pursued if viable solutions are to be found.

10 Crisis in the Food System
The Farm Crisis[1]

Nettie Wiebe

Learning Objectives

Through this chapter, you can

1. Gain a critical understanding of the key forces that have changed farming and food production in Canada

2. Evaluate the advantages and dangers posed by the transition from family farming to corporate dominance in the food system

3. Articulate the primary causes of the farm crisis

4. Name some ecological and social advantages of small-scale farming

Introduction: Images of Farming

A summer drive through the countryside in much of settled Canada offers a picturesque and reassuring view. The landscape is dotted with farmsteads, and herds of cattle and even the occasional flock of sheep can be spotted, along with a variety of field and horticultural crops. The practised eye might observe some abandoned farms, clusters of grain bins without buildings nearby, or nearly empty villages, especially on the Prairies. But for the most part, "farming country" looks as if it is doing just fine.

These impressions are reinforced by any food-product advertising that links food to its sources. The key images connecting food to farming in the popular imagination are rustic, serene, and healthy. Wholesome healthy food, whether butter, burgers, lettuce, or breakfast cereal, is claimed to come from grandpa and grandma's **family farm** where you are apt to see chickens running in the yard, apples hanging from trees in the garden, or golden wheat waving

in the prairie wind. The farming folk are hard-working, hearty, and honest. The countryside might be rugged in places, but it is mostly benign and welcoming.

The publicity directed at farmers themselves, however, has an entirely different tone. The prevalent advertising for farm products such as chemical pesticides[2] and farm machinery is overwhelmingly focused on their awesome power and efficacy. The images tend to be masculine and victorious, portraying wiping out the "enemy" pests and getting the job done. Chemical names include Avenge, Achieve, Fulfill, Fortress, Leader, Liberty, Pinnacle, Sharpshooter, and Touchdown. To farmers who may feel oppressed and financially insecure, chemical companies market promises of power and profit.

The story of agriculture and farming in Canada is a story of change and movement. From the immigrant farmers for the most part displacing hunter–gatherer food systems (Hurt 1987) to the current high-tech, high-input, corporate-controlled agriculture in turn displacing family farming,[3] the food system has changed more fundamentally than most sectors of our society and economy. These changes have largely been driven by technology, trade, urbanization, and the politics of agriculture. People and jobs have moved from rural to urban areas, reducing the social, economic, and political importance of rural populations. And the political and economic power within the sector has shifted from the family farm and rural community to corporate agri-business and international markets.

This chapter examines the values and forces driving some of the key changes that have occurred in Canadian agriculture, focusing on what these changes have done to the family farm. I begin with an overview of the trade and technology agendas that have moved food production from small family-owned businesses to corporate enterprises. Far from benefiting family farms, increases in food production and trade, greater efficiencies, and more investments have led to higher debt loads, lower net earnings, and a shrinking, aging farming population. Understanding the causes and outcomes of the crisis in farming explored in this chapter can help us see how to stem and reverse many of the other crises in our current food system. In the final section of this chapter, I argue for a fundamental reorientation of food production—food sovereignty. This initiative moves control over food-producing resources and markets back into local domains, where the primary responsibility for and control over food is in the hands of small-scale growers and those who put this food on our tables.

Redesigning Canadian Farming: External Forces

The industrialization of farming, which began more than two centuries ago in Western economies, gained velocity and momentum as horses were replaced by tractors in many parts of North America. This trend began in the decades following the First World War, with particularly rapid changes occurring during and immediately after the Second World War (Olmstead and Rhode 2001; Winson 1985). As in other sectors, replacing animal power with engines increased the speed, power, and output of farm operations exponentially. A team of horses could cultivate a few acres in a day of hard work; tractors raised that limit dramatically, with far fewer person-hours required, and made larger farms possible. Exchanging the hay and grain that fed horses for tractor fuel had several other effects on the farm. What was essentially solar power was displaced by oil, increasing greenhouse gases and making food production vulnerable to the risks inherent in dependence on non-renewable resources.[4] Also, the breeding and feeding of draft horses was agricultural work, mostly done on the farm. By contrast, tractors are designed and built in industrial plants, and the oil that runs them is extracted and refined by oil companies. The cost of purchasing these sources of power made larger farms necessary. A more subtle cost of technological advances is farmers' loss of self-reliance as farming increasingly depends on the industrial corporate sector for key inputs. This shift has had dramatic effects on family farming, rural communities, the environment, and rural cultures, as discussed below.

The changes that came with the adoption of engine-driven farm equipment were rapidly augmented by the widespread introduction of hybrid seeds, chemical fertilizers, and pesticides. These technological advances fundamentally changed farming and food production methods. For example, planting farm-saved seed or seed acquired through purchase or exchange within farming communities had been the norm since the beginning of cultivated crop production; new technologies and regulatory regimes changed those practices. Seed is increasingly purchased from seed companies, who own patent rights to the new varieties. Plant breeders' rights legislation enacted in Canada in 1990 curtailed farmers' rights to sell seeds to each other and gave powerful new profit-protection tools to seed development companies. Repeated efforts to further curtail farmers' abilities to save and reuse their seeds were pushed back by farmer and citizen outcry (Canadian Organic Growers 2005). However, with the passage of Bill C-18, the Agricultural Growth Act, in February 2015, farmers' seed rights have been reduced to "privileges" while the corporate ownership and control over seeds and seed patents has been strengthened. Hybridization, long used in breeding corn, is now being expanded to canola and other crops; farmers must purchase new hybrid seed each year, because subsequent generations of the seed lose their "hybrid vigour." The most recent shift to **genetically modified (GM) seeds** and their patented genes, which began with the commercialization of Roundup Ready canola in 1996, has eliminated the option to save or trade seeds altogether for farmers who use this seed. The purchase of GM seeds (mostly canola, corn, and soybeans in Canada) comes with a technology-use agreement prohibiting the planting of seeds harvested from these crops. New seed must be purchased from the patent-holding corporation every year.

Much of the touted efficiency of high-input, intensive agriculture stems from its ability to produce a uniform, standardized product with greater speed and in higher volume than would be possible on smaller-scale diversified farms. Industrial production demands standardization. But food comes from living organisms, and biological diversity can be forced into uniformity only with a great deal of control and manipulation. The drive to achieve massive production of uniform product, whether pigs or tomatoes, can be successful only if genetic diversity is suppressed or eliminated, growing environments are artificially controlled, and all inputs such as feed or fertilizer are standardized and uniform. In short, the natural diversity of living, interacting organisms has to be ruthlessly thwarted to achieve the industrial uniformity desired for the shelves of the supermarket. In contrast, small-scale farmers can work within more natural contexts and enhance the diversity of the food they produce. They seldom have the capacity to impose the strict controls of industrial-scale operations, even if they should wish to do so.

The introduction of chemicals to the farm has driven major changes in on-farm practices and in the way food is produced. The promise of greater control and higher productivity, coupled with little critique about environmental impacts or long-term outcomes for biodiversity, non-targeted species, soils, and water, has won the day. Canadian farming now relies very heavily on chemical interventions to control diseases in livestock, poultry, and crops of every variety. The use of broad-spectrum and targeted herbicides, along with fungicides and insecticides, is an integral part of conventional farming. The sprayer has become as essential for crop and horticultural operations as the seeding and harvesting implements. The push for higher yields requires increasing use of chemical fertilizers, so that Canadian farmers are using 56 per cent more fertilizer today than they did 20 years ago (1993–4 compared to 2013–14) and farm fertilizer use has more than tripled since the early 1970s (Statistics Canada, n.d.b., n.d.c.). Nationwide, Canadian farmers now apply just over 3.7 megatonnes of fertilizer nutrients per year. Pesticide purchases are up almost sixfold, based on inflation-adjusted values, between 1973 and 2013 (Statistics Canada, n.d.e.). Farmers have become so reliant on chemical inputs that many can no longer conceive of farming without them. When we converted our own prairie grain and cattle farm from conventional to organic production more than a decade ago, many of our farming neighbours and peers expressed skepticism that it would even be possible to grow crops without the use of chemicals.

The key objective for redesigning food production, as articulated in much of the information, advertising, and agriculture policy directives, is to increase efficiency and maximize production and thereby enhance profitability.

Canadian farms have certainly become steadily more efficient as measured by output per farm, farmer, hour, animal, and acre. With the use of sophisticated technologies such as automatic-steering global positioning systems for tractors, robotic milking machines, and computerized feed-ration mixers, productivity has risen while the number of farms and farmers has declined. In the 25 years between 1989 and 2014 Canada's production of corn, wheat, oats, barley, canola, soybeans, and other major grains increased by approximately 40 per cent (Statistics Canada, n.d.a.). Although production of beef cattle and calves had become 20 to 40 per cent higher than in 1989 those increases disappeared after 2011 as the size of the Canadian herd shrank with farmers selling down herds to capture higher prices (Statistics Canada, n.d.h.). Canadian hog production is up 56 per cent since 1989 (Statistics Canada, n.d.i.). Overall, Canadian farm production revenues (adjusted for inflation and not counting support program payments) are up 59 per cent in two-and-a-half decades: an estimated $54.5 billion in 2014 versus an inflation-adjusted $34.4 billion in 1989 (Statistics Canada, n.d.d.; Agriculture and Agri-Food Canada 2015a).

The drive to greater efficiency and productivity, which in very simple terms are labour expended and volumes produced, has necessarily led to greater specialization. Instead of producing a variety of plants and animals, efficiency and productivity dictate that only those products which can be produced with the highest yields or fastest gain should be grown in any one operation. Not only is it too labour intensive to have a variety of production systems on one farm, but also neither economies of scale nor adequate investment in new technologies is likely to be achieved in any one of those endeavours. A few chickens, a pen with a half-dozen pigs, and a small dairy herd along with field crops and gardens—the kind of "mixed" family farm that I grew up on—cannot compete on price in any one of those products. Intensive chicken or hog operations housing tens of thousands of birds or thousands of pigs have lower costs per pound of meat raised. Thus, we see the end of the mixed farm and the growing trends toward large-scale operations and monocultures.

Abandoning or being forced out of mixed farming has changed the lives of farming families. The increased use of technology has lightened the physical labour demanded by farming and changed the nature of the work. The sheer range of skills and knowledge required for raising a variety of animals and crops is no longer demanded. However, new skills for operating equipment, mixing chemicals, doing advanced accounting, navigating government programs, and running computers are now required along with the general traditional knowledge about soils and climate conditions. As well, producing fewer products on larger farms has undermined on-farm food self-sufficiency. Prairie farm families that produce thousands of tonnes of canola or barley are as reliant on the grocery store for food as any household living in an inner-city apartment.

Technology advances have made many of the changes in farming possible. But the rate of uptake and the usage of new technologies is a function of the values, politics, and culture of a society. The shift in Canadian agriculture away from small-scale, family farms to large-scale, intensive, high-input operations bespeaks a change in how food and farming is viewed and valued. Viewing the growing of food primarily as the production of commodities for profit and trade, rather than as an essential ingredient in nurturing people, catapults agriculture into the marketplace on a par with other commodities. The pressures for competitiveness and increased market share militate against small-scale, diverse, ecologically and culturally sensitive farming practices in favour of concentrated industrial operations maximizing the production of standardized products. This focus on maximizing production, lowering price per unit, and increasing market share reflects and enhances the global neo-liberal trade agenda.

Policy Changes: Trade-Driven Agriculture

When the first farming settlers arrived in Canada early in the seventeenth century, they concentrated on subsistence agriculture, but even then fishing for export on the Grand Banks near Newfoundland was already underway. Vast food-producing resources of fertile land, fresh water, and well-stocked fisheries coupled with sparse populations resulted in a pattern of surplus food production. Much of western Canada was settled with the express purpose of developing agriculture for export out of the region or across the ocean. Thus, growing more food than we need for our own consumption and exporting the surplus is not a new phenomenon.

However, the more recent shift to growing food primarily for export while importing food from other countries to meet our own needs has changed the focus of agriculture policy and purpose. The inclusion of agriculture in the General Agreement on Tariffs and Trade negotiations in the 1980s made this changed perspective official and global. This move was welcomed by food-exporting countries such as Canada and the United States and advocated by agri-business corporations. But it proved to be contentious as many countries balked at the risks of putting such a key sector under the control of external markets. Farmers and peasants protested the extreme dangers the liberalization of agriculture trade posed for local markets, rural livelihoods, cultures, and environments (La Vía Campesina 1996). However, the forces pushing for the liberalization of trade in agricultural goods prevailed. Agricultural goods have become one of the key commodities in the global marketplace, although this trade remains subject to an array of concessions, exceptions, qualifications, and distortions. The new trade policies signalled the changing place of food and farming and the attendant displacement of farmers, both here in Canada and elsewhere.

Although Canada has been an exporter of grains and other foods for a long time, the trade agreements opened a new era. The rate of export growth increased dramatically and Canadian agri-food exports have tripled (values adjusted for inflation) since the 1989 implementation of the Canada–United States Free Trade Agreement, the 1994 implementation of the North American Free Trade Agreement, and the 1995 implementation of the World Trade Organization Agreement on Agriculture. These pacts have been followed by the implementation of numerous other bilateral and multilateral investors' rights and trade agreements that are aimed at gaining greater market access and erasing whatever barriers to trade in foodstuffs remain. As currently negotiated, the Comprehensive Economic and Trade Agreement (CETA) with the European Union entails even more measures, such as further curtailing farmers' rights to save and reuse seeds (Boehm 2010).

Individual farmers do not trade in the global marketplace. They are excluded by the scope, risks, expertise, and power required. Nor, for the most part, do nations trade. Agricultural trade is largely given over to agri-business corporations operating in multiple jurisdictions. Thus, it is not Canada versus Brazil versus the United States when it comes to international agricultural trade, but rather Cargill Canada, Cargill Brazil, and Cargill US "competing" against each other to make a sale.

The **Canadian Wheat Board (CWB)**, western Canadian farmers' collective marketing agency for wheat and barley, stood out as one of the key exceptions within this transnational-controlled trading system. However, it was effectively dismantled when the Conservative government ended its monopoly and dismissed its farmer-elected board of directors in August 2012. In April 2015, controlling ownership (50.1 per cent) was given to G3 Global Grain Group, a joint venture between US corporate giant Bunge and SALIC Canada, a subsidiary of the state-owned Saudi Agricultural and Livestock Investment (Atkins 2015). The policy directives that privatized the CWB removed the last remaining farmer agency from the international grain trade (Magnan 2014).

Other sectors of Canadian food production that continue to operate as exceptions to the dominant liberalized trade rules are poultry, egg, and dairy farms. Canadian farmers collectively secured their domestic market for these products with a legislated **supply management** system that matches production to the needs of that market. Under this system farmers are rewarded for the discipline of limiting their production with the assurance that their production costs are met by the prices they receive. This is possible only because of negotiated trade restrictions prohibiting the importation of cheaper products, which would undercut the domestic prices based on production costs and displace Canadian products. It is noteworthy that supply-managed farms maintain high productivity, adopt new technological advances, and produce high-quality foods without being subjected to the global market forces. Furthermore, these farms are among the few in Canada that despite increasing in size continue to operate as family farms, successfully managing generational transfers, attracting younger farmers, and garnering viable farm incomes.

Under the neo-liberal policy agenda, Canadian agriculture is subsumed under trade policy whose key goal is to increase both the volume and the value of exports. Ensuring that Canadians enjoy food security, that farmers prosper, or that food-producing resources are protected and enhanced may figure as subsidiary interests in agriculture policy, but these are overridden by the primary goals of increasing production, global market share, and trade. These goals are being successfully met. Over the past two decades, Canadian governments and transnational agri-business corporations have set aggressive food-export targets, and they have met them—tripling our agri-food exports between 1989 and 2014 (AAFC 2010a; 2015b).

Canadian agricultural trade policy is developed in concert with transnational agri-business corporations whose interests in increasing trade are clearly linked to their own profitability and global market power. Corporate profitability is a function of buying products at the lowest price, processing and transporting them, and then selling them into the highest-paying market available. So, with the exception of intellectual property rights, where patent holders profit from the restrictions imposed, agriculture clauses in trade agreements have focused almost exclusively on deregulating the industry and removing domestic restrictions on exporting or importing food.

The overarching goals for Canadian agriculture, as set out by governments and industry organizations, are to increase production, competitiveness, exports, and market share. Agriculture policies and trade agreements are shaped to achieve these goals. The project has been a brilliant success on all these counts. As Agriculture Canada boasts:

> Almost 45 per cent of [Canada's] domestic food and agricultural production . . . is exported either directly as primary products or indirectly as part of processed products. In 2008 we exported $42.8 billion (Cdn) worth of food and agriculture around the world! We were also the 4th largest exporter in the world! (AAFC 2010a)

These statistics, highlighting the achievements of growth and competitiveness in the agriculture industry, might evoke the skeptical question: What crisis?

Down on the Farm: Growing More, Losing Ground

The phenomenal growth in investment, productivity, and trade in agriculture is mirrored by an equally dramatic decline in the fortunes of family farms in Canada. As the "agricultural industry" is doing better and better, its primary stakeholders, farmers, are doing worse and worse. Export success, for example, has not benefited farmers. In fact, as figure 10.1 illustrates, net farm income has fallen as agriculture exports have risen.

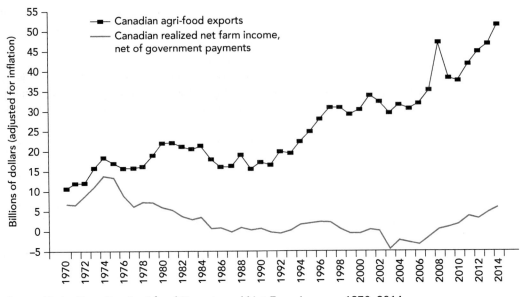

Figure 10.1 Canadian Agri-food Exports and Net Farm Income, 1970–2014

Sources: Agriculture and Agri-Food Canada (AAFC), *Agri-Food Export Potential for the Year 2000*; AAFC, *Canada's Trade in Agricultural Products*, various years; AAFC, "Import and Export Data: Canada—At a Glance." http://www5.agr.gc.ca/resources/prod/Internet-Internet/MISB-DGSIM/ATS-SEA/PDF/4679.pdf.

To understand the apparent paradox of higher productivity and more trade resulting in lower farm incomes, we must consider how the structural changes in agriculture marginalize and exploit small- and medium-sized farms to the advantage of intensive, large-scale production and corporate profit. A complex array of interrelated factors could be named, but the most destructive ones are the **cost–price squeeze**, (higher input costs coupled with lower farm-product prices), overweening corporate power within the food system, and hostile agriculture policies that aid and abet the forces undermining family farming and local food systems.

Cost–Price Squeeze

Canadian farmers have been and continue to be willing adopters of new technologies. These include ever-larger and increasingly complex (and expensive) machinery; new seed varieties; updates to and new inventions of chemicals, antibiotics, and animal health and growth products; and sophisticated, computerized farm management and accounting systems. All these items are manufactured externally to the farm and are costly purchases. Higher yields, better production and growth rates, and labour savings are all incentives for making these expenditures.

The financial problems on many farms stem from the imbalance between the cost of these technical advances and inputs and the remuneration received from selling the farms' products. While the prices paid for inputs continually rise, the farm-gate price of many of the key products has either remained stagnant or fallen. For example, over the past 50 years, farm-input prices have increased nearly twice as fast as farm-product prices (e.g. fertilizer and chemical prices have gone up twice as much as corn and feeder-calf prices) (AAFC 2009:115). Prices for grains, potatoes, other crops, and other farm products are well below even the most efficient farmer's costs of production. This is the cost–price squeeze that is eliminating many family farms.

Writing about agriculture policy, US economist Richard Levins says: "The shortest possible economic history of . . . agriculture during the twentieth century would be this: non-farmers learning how to make money from farming" (Levins 2000:8). This quip sums up the past 25 years of Canadian farming. From 1989 to 2014, Canadian farmers, employing world-leading productivity and efficiency, managed to produce and sell $1.05 *trillion* worth of grains, livestock, potatoes, vegetables, milk, and other farm products (government payments excluded and all values adjusted for inflation). But over that same two-and-a-half decades, farmers' net farm income (again, government payments excluded and values adjusted for inflation) was only $14 billion—about $3 per acre per year and less than 1.5 per cent of gross revenues. This means that 98.5 per cent of the money farmers generated as gross revenues, that is, almost the entire trillion dollars, was captured by the agri-business transnational corporations that sell farmers fuel, chemicals, fertilizer, veterinary drugs, machinery, technology, and other products and supplies. (Statistics Canada 2011b, 2014a, 2014b, and n.d.d.) To survive financially, most farm families have been forced to rely on off-farm income, taxpayer-funded farm-support programs, and borrowed money.

Downsides of Trade Dependence

Most non-farming people hear about variable weather and its effects such as droughts, floods, or early frosts reducing the quality and quantity of harvests. However, the weather risks are paralleled by growing uncertainty about markets and fluctuating prices. While farmers can buy crop insurance to help them survive weather-related yield losses, farmers have few tools to deal with market risks. Price fluctuations are considered useful "price signals" for farmers to use in their production decisions. But as more Canadian products move into a global marketplace, the vicissitudes of global demand and pricing can come home to roost on the farm with dire results. For example, when the United States closed its border to Canadian beef in 2003 due to the discovery of a cow in Alberta with bovine

spongiform encephalitis (BSE), the farm-gate price for prairie beef cattle plummeted, throwing many cattle farmers and ranchers into a financial crisis (NFU 2008). With the exception of the supply-managed sectors, marketing uncertainties and product price fluctuations have to be absorbed on the farm.

As the BSE example shows, greater reliance on offshore markets, even a nearby market such as the United States, increases the risks for farmers. The underside of the glowing agricultural export numbers and increased reliance on exports is the higher risks that farmers face in these markets. As well, in the global agricultural marketplace Canadian farmers are competing with growers who produce in more favourable climates using low-cost farm labour and production systems and, in some cases, with government-subsidized producers. All these factors contribute to low and declining farm-gate prices.

Sized to Succeed?

In the face of this economic reality, governments and agricultural economists advise farm families to make up for the lower margins by making the farms bigger and producing more. This advice is based on the view that economies of scale deliver efficiencies that can compensate for lower prices. Canadian farmers have complied. Whether it is potato farms in Prince Edward Island, orchards in British Columbia's Okanagan Valley or greenhouses in Essex County in southwestern Ontario, every kind of farm has increased in size. Whereas a large cow-calf operation might have had 100 cows a generation ago, today 300-cow operations are not uncommon. Feedlots are even larger; several single-location feedlots in Canada boast throughput of 100,000, 200,000, or more cattle per year. Grain and oilseed farms, especially in western Canada, routinely encompass thousands of acres, with some very large farms covering 10,000 or 20,000 acres or more.

In 2011, farms with $1 million or more of annual revenues produced 49 per cent of Canadian food, by value. Those million-dollar-plus farms made up just 5 per cent of farms overall (AAFC 2013:22). Thus, approximately 10,300 production units produced nearly half of Canadian food output. The focus on expanding and intensifying production has worked—but not for family farms. While some of these large operations, such as the intensive hog barns, are owned by individuals or communally on Hutterite colonies, most of the large intensive operations are owned by outside investors and rely on hired labour and management. Following the 2008 financial crisis, institutional and corporate investors are also buying large tracts of agricultural land in some parts of Canada (NFU 2015a; Desmarais 2015). These investor and management structures are characteristic of industrial plants, not family farms.

Perverse Programming

The productivity of large-scale operations succeeds in driving down prices per unit and driving out smaller-scale producers. For example, intensive hog operations in the Prairie region have succeeded in displacing virtually all family-farm hog production—two-thirds of Canada's independent family-farm hog producers have been forced to cease production during this consolidation (Statistics Canada, n.d.j.; Statistics Canada 2010a, 2010b). But this has resulted in neither profitability nor stability. The farm types that have been most aggressive and successful in expanding, such as grain and oilseed farms and hog farms, also suffer the largest farm losses (Statistics Canada 2009). Large farms are getting billions of dollars in tax-funded farm-program payments in order to remain solvent. Based on Statistics Canada farm tax-filer data from 2004 to 2008, approximately 64 per cent of program payments—about $2.2 billion annually—went to the 27 per cent of Canadian farms with gross revenues over $250,000 per year (AAFC 2009:105). The payment imbalance becomes even more disproportionate at the top end. Approximately 28 per cent of program payments—about $1 billion annually—went to the 5 per cent of

Canadian farms with gross revenues over $1 million per year (Statistics Canada 2009). Canada's largest farms are by far the largest recipients of publicly funded farm-support payments, presumably because they are the neediest. It may seem counterintuitive that these large operations are granted public money while family farms are suffering severe losses. However, because agriculture subsidy programs are primarily based on payment per unit of production, with very high caps on the total amount of program money any single operation can receive, the largest producers get most of the funds.[5] Federal and provincial governments have increased caps on maximum payments to agricultural operations; they now stand at $3 million per year. As this policy of "backing the winners" subsidizes products that will be exported, it enhances agri-business profitability while in effect subsidizing foreign buyers of our pork, soybeans, wheat, and other farm products. A further perverse outcome for family farms is the added resources and incentives that these subsidies provide for further buyouts and displacement of small farms.

Killer Debts

To pay for rising input, machinery, and land costs, to expand operations, or to simply stay in farming, families are borrowing money. Canadian farm debt is increasing rapidly, rising from $64 billion in 2010 to about $78 billion by 2013 (Statistics Canada, n.d.f.; NFU 2015a).

The debt loads on many farms make them very vulnerable to rises in interest rates—and contribute to a great deal of anxiety. The farm financial crisis of the 1980s was brought on by sharp increases in interest rates, which made farm debts unpayable. Thousands of farm families saw generations of their work, history, and hopes disappear in the wake of foreclosures and forced sales (Pugh 1987).

Family farms are even more vulnerable now than they were in the 1980s because the current ratio of debt to net income is higher. In the 1970s farm families bore $3.40 worth of debt for each dollar of net income; by the 1980s, this ratio had risen to $7.42. In the 1990s, for each dollar of net income, farmers carried $10.47 in debt. During the first decade of the twenty-first century, farmers were carrying more than $23 in debt for each dollar of net income. Because, in effect, farm families must now borrow and risk seven times as much debt as in the 1970s and three times as much as in the 1980s, they are that much more vulnerable to losing the farm if interest rates go up, prices go down, or they suffer a bad crop year (Qualman 2011).

Corporate Takeover

As farm families struggle to make ends meet, other parts of the food system are highly profitable. Farmers buy fuel, fertilizers, chemicals, antibiotics, seeds, and equipment from corporations at the demanded prices. These inputs are sold by some of the world's most powerful and profitable corporations: fuel by Exxon and Shell; fertilizer by Potash Corporation, Cargill, Mosaic, Yara, and Agrium; chemicals by Bayer, Syngenta, Dow, Monsanto, and DuPont; and seeds by Monsanto, DuPont, Syngenta, and Bayer. Farmers have virtually no bargaining power on any of those items.

The industrialization and globalization of agricultural trade has also been a bonanza for the agri-business transnationals such as Monsanto, Cargill, ADM, and others who buy, process, market, and increasingly produce agricultural products. Although they tend to eschew the risks and low returns of actually producing raw foodstuffs, corporations are making some strategic intrusions into production where upstream profitability can be enhanced. For example, beef processors are taking ownership of more of the cattle being finished in feedlots for slaughter in order to use this captive supply to depress the price of cattle they have to buy for their packing plants. Farmers delivering cattle to the auction ring have no choice but to sell at the prices offered. With two beef packers, Cargill and JBS (formerly XL Foods) owning almost 90 per cent of the industry in Canada, their market power

allows them to control prices. So, while the inflation-adjusted price Canadians are paying for ground beef in the grocery store is up by more than 100 per cent compared to 25 years ago, the inflation-adjusted prices farmers are getting paid for slaughter cows and other cattle are up by just 50 per cent, meaning that packing companies and retailers are taking an ever-larger share of Canadians' grocery store dollars (Statistics Canada, n.d.g. and n.d.k.). As corporate power becomes more concentrated, the handful of transnational agri-business firms that farmers rely on are able to extract all the potential revenue from farming (Qualman 2001). As these corporate players are thousands of times bigger than the biggest family farm, the market–power imbalance is overwhelming.

Policy Failure

Although farm families cannot successfully challenge large corporate interests, government policies can rebalance the relative power and profitability of farmers vis-à-vis the large corporate players in the system. Unfortunately, despite rhetoric touting support for farmers, agriculture policies over the last three decades have done much to undermine and erase family farming in Canada.

Program payments, the most obvious and public "aid to farmers," fail to secure small- and medium-scale farms, although they are clearly a crucial component of net farm income. As noted above, the money goes disproportionately to large-scale operations when the payouts are based on production and revenues.

Government failures to limit corporate power and regulate the industry to support family farming have had devastating effects on farming families and rural communities. Instead of protecting them, the government has created a regulatory framework that is entirely and increasingly hostile to small-scale diversified farms. For example, the reregulation of grain transportation in the latter half of the 1990s, giving Canada's two major railways leave to offer favourable rates to unit trains (large blocks of cars) and abandon branch lines, had a domino effect throughout the rural Prairies. Grain co-operatives and companies that had located elevators in hundreds of communities along these branch lines consolidated their operations. Functioning elevators in many communities were demolished in order to force grain into higher-throughput, centralized elevators. This forced grain from railcars onto trucks, adding road costs and greenhouse gas emissions to the equation. These regulatory changes have also had multiple on-farm effects. Along with making transportation one of the highest expenses for grain farms, the trucking requirements have forced farmers to either invest in larger trucks or hire truckers to haul their grain. The policy changes did not offer any new revenue streams to compensate for these added expenses.

Farmers were supposed to be able to share the benefits of these so-called efficiencies. Canadian legislation sets the amounts Canadian National and Canadian Pacific railways can charge farmers for transporting western grain. These rates are fixed at levels that cover railway costs and allow for appropriate profits for the rail companies. Moreover, those regulated rates increase each year to account for inflation. In addition to this inflation-adjustment mechanism, however, a second mechanism—a costing review—is supposed to assess actual railway costs and to reduce rates as efficiency gains and other cost-saving measures lower the actual costs of moving grain. In effect, costing reviews are meant to ensure both that railways continue to earn reasonable profits and that farmers share in system-wide efficiency gains. The federal government has refused, however, to hold a costing review since 1992. Thus, farmers' freight rates have increased year after year. A recent independent study (Travacon 2010) has calculated that the lack of such a review is costing western grain farmers an extra $200 million per year—money transferred from hard-pressed farm families to railway executives and shareholders.

Government policy that dismantled the CWB eliminated the single-desk marketing power, price pooling, and oversight of transportation logistics. While the CWB supported family farms by ensuring equitable delivery opportunities and returning the export price (minus operating costs) to prairie grain farmers, the transnational grain traders focus on corporate profits. The loss of the CWB has been described as "the biggest transfer of wealth away from farmers in the history of Canada," having cost farmers more than $7 billion in less than three years (NFU 2015b).

Regulations on meat processing offer another example of how policy undermines small-scale, local food production. Most local abattoirs in Canada have gone out of business. Along with price competition from large corporate processors selling through supermarkets and undercutting smaller operations, further impediments introduced as food-safety requirements make it virtually impossible for many to continue. In response to the food dangers inherent in large plants, many food-safety regulations have been imposed that are both inappropriate and unaffordable for smaller operations. By opting for a one-size-fits-all regime, the Canadian Food Inspection Agency has in fact harmed local butchers and taken away a market option for small-scale farmers. As these examples illustrate, hostile agriculture policies that increase costs and fail to enhance revenues harm the prospects of making a living on the family farm.

The cost–price squeeze has meant that farmers' net incomes from the marketplace have been negative in most of the first decade of the twenty-first century. Farm families are caught in the tightening grip of the cost–price squeeze. Extraordinary commitment, adaptability, some government aid, and, most importantly, non-farm income, account for the survival of those families who continue in farming. Because the market fails to allow farmers to profit from producing food, off-farm income and farm-support payments now make up 100 per cent of most farm families' net income. This is the reality for farm families in every part of the country, although not in every sector—supply-managed farms are consistently the exceptions. In general however, the investments in, labour for, and costs of growing food do not return enough for farmers to live on, so wages from other employment are needed to meet family living expenses.

Sadly, working longer hours and doing more jobs, along with getting the farm work done, has not been enough to save many farms. Agriculture census data indicate that Canada lost 27 per cent of its farms and farm families between 1991 and 2011 (Statistics Canada 1992, 2011a). However, this number does not tell the whole story. It leaves out the troubling fact that many of the surviving farms are in a holding pattern with little likelihood of a long-term future. This situation is reflected in the statistics on young farmers, on whom that future depends. According to Statistics Canada's Census of Agriculture, in 1991 Canada had 77,910 young farmers (those aged under 35). Twenty years later, in 2011, we had just 24,055—a drop of 69 per cent (Statistics Canada 2011a). In 1991, there was a young farmer on one farm in every four; today, just one farm in eight supports a young farmer. Aspiring young farmers are faced with almost insurmountable obstacles. The high debt loads required to start farming coupled with the lack of potential net earnings to meet those debts makes it virtually impossible for people to enter farming. And it is obvious that an aging farm population that is not being replaced by the next generation of young farmers spells the end of many family farms.

Rural Communities: Change and Decline

The aging farmer demographic affects not only the prospects of particular family farms, but also the dynamics, culture, and prospects of farming communities. The boarded-up buildings along the main streets of towns and villages stand as stark testimony to both the economic and the social losses of these communities. My own nearby village has declined from a thriving community, that in the 1940s boasted five grain elevators, stores, a church, an arena, a restaurant, and a bank, to a nearly deserted site today where the collapsing roof of the church and its precariously tilting steeple graphically paint the picture of the fate of many such communities. Small-town businesses that rely on farm trade become unviable unless non-farming customers move into the area to make up for the diminished and aging farm populations. Without young families to use the services, the schools, sports arenas, and social organizations in many rural communities have become unsustainable. Boarded-up hardware stores, defunct arenas, and empty schoolyards illustrate the lack of youth and renewal in many towns and villages.

Women in farming and rural women in general are differentially affected by the decline of rural communities and the loss of young people from these communities. As primary family caregivers, women often invest energy in maintaining the social and cultural life of their communities. The absence of young families and young women in rural communities is felt especially acutely. Although rural families share with their urban counterparts the common experience of having their own children move away from home when they reach adulthood, the move away from rural areas represents not only that particular loss but also a more general one. While urban centres experience an influx of young people seeking jobs and education, the departure of most rural youth from their homes and communities leaves a gap that is unlikely to be filled with incoming young people. This means that the energy and forward-looking dynamic of young people is permanently gone. It makes the social life, such as community events and services that rely on buoyant community spirit and volunteer energy, much more difficult to initiate and maintain. As women are often key initiators and volunteers for family-oriented community life and celebrations, the absence of young neighbours makes this social and cultural work more challenging, if not impossible, in aging and dying rural communities.

The cultural losses in rural communities, though most acutely experienced in those communities, accrue to the whole country. Just as biological diversity is necessary for healthy and sustainable biological life, so cultural diversity contributes to making societies more adaptive and sustainable. The displacement of traditional farming knowledge and skills has practical consequences. So does the loss of the wisdom and cultural nuances that are developed by communities of people who share a unique physical place and have learned to grow food, create meaning, and build social spaces adapted to and shaped by that particular place.

Conclusion: Changing Menus and Relationships

Farming does not have to be ecologically destructive and financially ruinous. Since the long-term sustainability of our food system affects us all, positive change is in our collective interest. Far more food could be grown and purchased locally. Prosperous, ecologically sound family farms could produce healthy food, and eaters could know what they are eating and where it comes from. Public policy could support and enhance small-scale farming, local food production, and markets rather than shoring up transnational agri-business. All this is possible.

In this final section of the chapter, I argue that the restoration, reinvigoration, and reinvention of small-scale family farming is at the crux of the solutions to many of the ecological, health, and social ills of our current food system.

Mixed family farms can use resources in an integrated way that enhances diversity, works with natural biological cycles, and decreases pollution. For example, raising cattle as well as cropping land allows us to integrate hay crops into our crop rotations, adding fertility to soils, controlling weeds, and producing feed for the animals. The cattle, while being fed to produce beef, generate manure which does the work of fertilizer. The hay rotation and manure eliminate the need to bring in external chemical inputs that require fossil fuels both to manufacture and to transport. Where the waste products from **intensive livestock operations** create dangerous water, soil, and air pollution and require careful management, less-concentrated animal waste

on small-scale integrated farms is a welcome resource. This is only one example of the complex ecological services small-scale, multipurpose, integrated food production offers.

In contrast to agricultural production that is owned by outside investors primarily interested in profits, family farms are, as the name indicates, *family* enterprises as well as business ones. Not only does the enterprise rely on family labour, management, and commitment, but its long-term success depends on cross-generational co-operation. Without generational transfers, either within or outside of the family, the individual farm disappears as a distinct entity. The tradition of retaining farms within families over many generations has various roots and reasons, not the least of which is the valuable local knowledge about growing food and living well in a particular place, which takes generations to accumulate. Also, knowing that the livelihoods and well-being of one's children and grandchildren depend on the condition of the farm is a great incentive to carefully enhance ecological resources for the next generation rather than depleting them for current profits.

Beyond the ecological benefits, family farms and local food production offer important benefits to everyone who eats. Many of the health and dietary problems caused by the current food system are explored in other chapters of this volume. Solutions and improvements are possible only if those who work for them have the power to effect changes. As long as agriculture is controlled by corporations and investors and regulated by governments to support corporate interests, the fundamental transformations that are needed for sustainable, healthy food production cannot be implemented. In order to reorient priorities and make the food system responsive to nutritional, cultural, environmental, and social needs, control of food-producing resources and markets must be handed back to local farmers, communities, and citizens. That is, food sovereignty must be achieved (see chapter 21 in this volume).

But in order to get there we need to be able to imagine and articulate new relationships to food, community, and ultimately the earth. Instead of the system where farmers are producing commodities that are transformed and transported to distant markets, the relationships among farmers, food, and eaters must be re-established. Food sovereignty begins from the position that citizens can and must be engaged in decisions about a life-sustaining good—food—within an ecological, social, and cultural context. It recognizes that the growing, buying, preparing, and eating of food are embedded in social and ecological relationships, rather than primarily functioning under market determinants.

Changing the role, purpose, and structure of agriculture by reasserting the importance of ensuring that everyone has healthy, culturally appropriate food produced in ecologically and socially sustainable ways requires the engagement of a movement of citizens. Although the number of family farms is declining, a growing number of non-farming people are engaging in actions that focus on food and farming issues, from buying local food at farmers' markets, to gardening, to social movement activism. More eaters are recognizing that family farming and local food are linked to eating well and having access to sustainably produced food from a known source. Solving the farm crisis requires many major changes in the food system. It begins with a new understanding of the key role of family farmers in solving many of the other crises in the food system.

Discussion Questions

1. How have industrialization and liberalized trade benefited the agriculture industry?

2. What benefits and harms have industrialization, technical advances, and liberalized trade afforded family farms?

3. How is it possible that the agriculture industry is experiencing growth and enhanced profits while family farms are suffering decline and financial losses?

4. Could Canadian agriculture policy support small-scale farming? If so, how?

5. What is the role of family farming in a sustainable food system?

Further Reading

1. Diaz, Harry P., Joanne Jaffe, and Robert Stirling, eds. 2003. *Farm Communities at the Crossroads: Challenge and Resistance*. Regina, SK: Canadian Plains Research Center.
    Essays on the politics, economics, and culture of rural communities.

2. Epp, Roger. 2008. *We Are All Treaty People: Prairie Essays*. Edmonton: University of Alberta Press.
    A personal and political exploration of rural communities and farm people whose livelihoods are under intense economic and cultural pressure.

3. Epp, Roger, and Dave Whitson, eds. 2001. *Writing Off the Rural West: Globalization,* *Governments, and the Transformation of Rural Communities*. Edmonton: University of Alberta Press & Parkland Institute.
    Essays on the changes and prospects for agriculture-, resource-, and tourism-dependent rural communities.

4. Ervin, Alexander M., Cathy Holtslander, Darrin Qualman, and Rick Sawa, eds. 2003. *Beyond Factory Farming: Corporate Hog Barns and the Threat to Public Health, The Environment, and Rural Communities*. Saskatoon, SK: Canadian Centre for Policy Alternatives—Saskatchewan.
    Experts and activists present a critical analysis of the impact of intensive hog operations.

5. Wittman, Hannah, Annette Desmarais, and Nettie Wiebe, eds. 2010. *Food Sovereignty: Reconnecting Food, Nature and Communities.* Halifax, NS: Fernwood; Oakland, CA: Food First; Cape Town, SA: Pambazuka.

Experts present in-depth analysis of key issues and trends in the global food system and explore the radical alternative options that a food sovereignty framework affords.

6. Wittman, Hannah, Annette Desmarais, and Nettie Wiebe, eds. 2011. *Food Sovereignty in Canada: Creating Just and Sustainable Food Systems.* Halifax, NS: Brunswick.

Canadian authors explore the current state of the Canadian food system, offering ways in which adopting food sovereignty as the operative framework would resolve key problems.

Video Suggestions

1. CBC. 2015. "Growing Concern." *Land and Sea* (series). www.cbc.ca/player/Shows/Shows/More+Shows/Land+and+Sea/ID/2648477575/. 22 min.
2. Lamont, Eve. 2005. *The Fight for True Farming.* www.nfb.ca/film/fight_for_true_farming. 90 min.

3. Springbett, David. 2008. *Hijacked Future.* www.cinemapolitica.org/film/hijacked-future. 43 min.
4. Suderman, Steve. 2012. *To Make a Farm.* http://tomakeafarm.ca. 74 min.

Notes

1. I want to thank Darrin Qualman for the key research and analysis he contributed to this chapter.
2. The term *pesticide* includes herbicides, fungicides, and insecticides.
3. The term *family farm* denotes a farming operation where the labour and management and much of the ownership investment are supplied by family members.

4. Wendell Berry notes that fossil-fuel-driven agriculture turns food production into an industrial project based on a non-renewable source of energy that uses up "in our own time the birthright and livelihood of posterity" (2009:59).
5. Margin-based programs such as AgriInvest pay on the basis of whole-farm losses which advantages single-commodity operations.

References

Agriculture and Agri-Food Canada (AAFC). *Canada's Trade in Agricultural Products.* various years. Ottawa: Supply and Services Canada.

——. 1996. *Agri-Food Export Potential for the Year 2000.* June. Ottawa: AAFC working paper.

——. 2009. *An Overview of the Canadian Agriculture and Agri-Food System: 2009.* May.

——. 2010a. "Canadian Trade Highlights." (Agri-Food Trade Service). ats-sea.agr.gc.ca.

——. 2010b. "Canada Brand International, Market Research in Key Export Markets." marqueCanadabrand.agr.gc.ca/research-etudes/research-etudes-eng.htm.

——. 2013. *An Overview of Canadian Agriculture: 2013.* March. marqueCanadabrand.agr.gc.ca/research-etudes/research-etudes-eng.htm.

——. 2015a. *Canadian Agricultural Outlook 2015.* February.

——. 2015b. "Import and Export Data: Canada—At a Glance." http://www5.agr.gc.ca/resources/prod/Internet-Internet/MISB-DGSIM/ATS-SEA/PDF/4679.pdf.

Atkins, Eric. 2015. "Canadian Wheat Board Deal with U.S., Saudi Group Ends an Era." *Globe and Mail*, 15 April. http://www.theglobeandmail.com/report-on-business/us-saudi-firms-to-buy-former-Canadian-wheat-board/article23966156/.

Berry, Wendell. 2009. "Energy in Agriculture." In *Bring It to the Table: On Farming and Food.* Berkeley, CA: Counterpoint.

Boehm, Terry. 2010. "Canada-EU Trade Agreement Damaging." *Western Producer*, 29 April:11.

Canadian Organic Growers. 2005. "A Response to the Proposed Amendments to Plant Breeders Rights Legislation and the Seed Sector Review." http://www.cog.ca/documents/COGrespPBRseeds_001.pdf.

Desmarais, Annette, Darrin Qualman, Andre Magnan, and Nettie Wiebe. 2015. "Land Grabbing and Land

Concentration: Mapping Changing Patterns of Farmland Ownership in Three Rural Municipalities in Saskatchewan, Canada." *Canadian Food Studies* 1(2):16–47. http://Canadianfoodstudies.uwaterloo.ca/index.php/cfs.

Hurt, R. Douglas. 1987. *Indian Agriculture in America: Prehistory to the Present.* Lawrence: University of Kansas Press.

La Vía Campesina. 1996. "The Right to Produce and Access to Land." http://www.connexions.org/CxLibrary/Docs/CX8459-1996DeclarationFoodSovereignty.pdf.

Levins, Richard. 2000. *Willard Cochrane and the American Family Farm.* Lincoln: University of Nebraska Press.

Magnan, Andre. 2014. "The Rise and Fall of a Prairie Giant: The Canadian Wheat Board in Food Regime History." Pp. 73–90 in *The Neoliberal Regime in the Agri-Food Sector: Crisis, Resilience, and Restructuring,* ed. Steven A. Wold and Alessandro Bonanno. New York: Routledge.

National Farmers Union (NFU). 2008. "The Farm Crisis and the Cattle Sector: Towards a New Analysis and New Solutions." Report by the National Farmers Union (Canada). 19 November.

———. 2015a. "Losing Our Grip: 2015 Update." Report by the National Farmers Union (Canada). March.

———. 2015b. "Ritz Locks Out Farmers, Hands CWB Keys to Bunge and Saudi King's Fund." Press release, 15 April.

Olmstead, Alan L., and Paul W. Rhode. 2001. "Reshaping the Landscape: The Impact and Diffusion of the Tractor in American Agriculture, 1910–1960." *Journal of Economic History* 61(3):663–98.

Pugh, Terry, ed. 1987. *Fighting the Farm Crisis.* Saskatoon, SK: Fifth House.

Qualman, Darrin. 2001. *The Farm Crisis and Corporate Power.* Ottawa: Canadian Centre for Policy Alternatives.

———. 2011. "Advancing Agriculture by Destroying Farms? The State of Agriculture in Canada." Pp. 20–42 in *Food Sovereignty in Canada: Creating Just and Sustainable Food Systems,* ed. Hannah Wittman, Annette Desmarais, and Nettie Wiebe, eds. Halifax, NS: Fernwood.

Statistics Canada. n.d.a. *Table 001-0017 Estimated Areas, Yield, Production, Average Farm Price and Total Farm Value of Principal Field Crops.* CANSIM (database). http://www5.statcan.gc.ca/cansim/a26?lang=eng&id=10017.

———. n.d.b. *Table 001-0065 Fertilizer Shipments to Canadian Agriculture Markets, by Nutrient Content and Fertilizer Year.* CANSIM (database). http://www5.statcan.gc.ca/cansim/a26?lang=eng&id=10065.

———. n.d.c. *Table 001-0069 Fertilizer Shipments to Canadian Agriculture Markets, by Nutrient Content and Fertilizer Year, Cumulative Data.* CANSIM (database). http://www5.statcan.gc.ca/cansim/a26?lang=eng&id=10069.

———. n.d.d. *Table 002-0001 Farm Cash Receipts.* CANSIM (database). http://www5.statcan.gc.ca/cansim/a26?lang=eng&id=20001.

———. n.d.e. *Table 002-0005 Farm Operating Expenses and Depreciation Charges.* CANSIM (database). http://www5.statcan.gc.ca/cansim/a26?lang=eng&id=20005.

———. n.d.f. *Table 002-0008 Farm Debt Outstanding, Classified by Lender.* CANSIM (database). http://www5.statcan.gc.ca/cansim/a26?lang=eng&id=20008.

———. n.d.g. *Table 002-0043 Farm Product Prices, Crops and Livestock.* CANSIM (database). http://www5.statcan.gc.ca/cansim/a26?lang=eng&id=20043.

———. n.d.h. *Table 003-0026 Cattle and Calves, Farm and Meat Production.* CANSIM (database). http://www5.statcan.gc.ca/cansim/a26?lang=eng&id=30026.

———. n.d.i. *Table 003-0028 Hogs, Sheep and Lambs, Farm and Meat Production.* CANSIM (database). http://www5.statcan.gc.ca/cansim/a26?lang=eng&id=30028.

———. n.d.j. *Table 003-0089 Hogs Statistics, Number of Farms Reporting and Average Number of Hogs per Farm.* CANSIM (database). http://www5.statcan.gc.ca/cansim/a26?lang=eng&id=30089.

———. n.d.k. *Table 326-0012 Average Retail Prices for Food and Other Selected Items.* CANSIM (database). http://www5.statcan.gc.ca/cansim/a26?lang=eng&id=3260012.

———. 1987. *Census, Canada 1986, Agriculture.* Cat. No. 96-102. December. Ottawa: Ministry of Supply and Services.

———. 1992. 1991 Census of Agriculture. *Agricultural Profile of Canada,* Cat. No 93-350. June. Ottawa: Minister of Industry, Science, and Technology.

———. 2009. *Statistics on Income of Farm Families.* Cat. No. 21-207-E. 26 June.

———. 2010a. Historical Overview of Canadian Agriculture, Cat. No. 93-358-XPB.

———. 2010b. "Hog Statistics," Cat No. 23-010, 28 October, third quarter.

———. 2011a. 2011 Census of Agriculture. Cat. No. 95-629-XWE. http://www.statcan.gc.ca/pub/95-640-x/95-640-x2011001-eng.htm and http://www5.statcan.gc.ca/cansim/a03?C2DB=PRD&pattern=0040200..0040242&p2=50&retrLang=eng&CII_SuperBtn=Search&copyVersion=0&lang=eng&typeValue=1.

———. 2011b. "Farm Cash Receipts—Agriculture Economic Statistics." Cat. No. 21-011. November.

———. 2014a. "Net Farm Income—Agriculture Economic Statistics." Cat. No. 21-010. November.

———. 2014b. "Direct Payments to Agriculture Producers—Agriculture Economic Statistics." Cat. No. 21-015. November.

Travacon Research Limited. 2010. *Estimating Contributions Earned by Railways from Handling of Statutory Grain and Grain Products 2007/2008 and 2008/2009.* Prepared for the Canadian Wheat Board. May.

Winson, Anthony. 1985. "The Uneven Development of Canadian Agriculture: Farming in the Maritimes and Ontario." *Canadian Journal of Sociology* 10(4):411–38.

11 The Welfare of Farm Animals on Intensive Livestock Operations (ILOs) in Canada

Shannon Kornelsen

Learning Objectives

Through this chapter, you can

1. Understand the ILO as the dominant mode of production for animal foods in Canada
2. Examine the standard industry practices of ILOs and the impacts they have on farm animal welfare
3. Appreciate the motivations for people choosing to eschew industrial animal foods and support alternative sources of nourishment

Introduction

The past 60 years have witnessed the large-scale industrialization of Canadian agriculture, driven by an increase in mechanization, external inputs, and biological manipulation. Since 1956, the total number of farms has decreased by around 65 per cent, while the size of the average farm has increased by more than 158 per cent (Statistics Canada 2012a).

Despite this shift, when Canadians think of farming, many still picture a bucolic countryside characterized by "small farms surrounded by field crops and . . . livestock in fields and barns," but in reality this is "more the stuff of childhood bedtime picture books" (Government of Canada 2008a:35).

Nowhere is this more obvious than on **intensive livestock operations** (ILOs), which currently produce 95 per cent of the nearly 700 million animals killed for food each year in Canada. The

goal of ILOs are identical to that of intensive agriculture as a whole: to produce the greatest quantity of sellable product for the lowest cost.

In order to achieve this goal, ILOs are "characterized by high stocking densities and/ or close confinement, forced growth rates, high mechanization and low labour requirements" (WSPA 2012:14). This shift in production allowed producers:

> to put animals into environments for which they were ill-suited, yet still assure production and profitability . . . in modern systems, the loss of welfare does not always entail a loss in economic productivity. (Duncan and Rollin 2012:135)

With profit no longer directly tied to **animal welfare**, and in many cases opposed to it,

ILOs have been increasingly criticized for their **standard industry practices**. In response to this scrutiny, the animal foods industry has taken strong measures to prevent consumers from questioning the "good stewardship" of the animals in their care, including extensive marketing and PR campaigns, strategic lawsuits, and aggressive lobbying.

As a result of these measures, and coupled with the ever-increasing urbanization of the population, few Canadians are aware of what life is like for the animals whose meat, eggs, and dairy they consume, instead assuming that producers prioritize animal welfare and that strict laws and regulations are in place to ensure that farm animals are well cared for.

Laws, Regulations, and Codes of Practice

Of the three federal acts that can be used to protect farm animals in Canada, the Health of Animals Act and the Meat Inspection Act focus solely on animals during transport and slaughter, leaving only "Section 445.1—Cruelty to Animals: Causing unnecessary suffering" of the federal Criminal Code to protect animals on the farm. It prohibits "unnecessary pain, suffering or injury to an animal or a bird" that is "willful or without lawful excuse" (GC 2008b). This makes prosecution difficult, since intent must be proven.

Enforcement agencies strongly favour the use of provincial Acts, since they require a lower burden of proof for laying charges and obtaining convictions. However, since all but one province (New Brunswick) have exemptions for "generally accepted practices of animal husbandry, management, slaughter, etc." (Canadian Food Inspection Agency 2014), enforcement activities, which can only be initiated once a complaint is received, are typically "only used to prosecute livestock producers in cases of rare and egregious abuse, such as when animals are neglected to the point of starvation" (Canadian Federation of Humane Societies, n.d.b.).

In response to pressure from various animal welfare organizations about this gap in protection, in the early 1980s the government proposed that national **Codes of Practice (COP)** be developed for each species, with the hope that they would encourage producers to maintain a minimum standard of welfare. The development of the COP brought together stakeholders from various producer groups, as well as veterinarians, scientists, government, and one animal welfare organization. Unsurprisingly, the resulting COP merely reinforced standard practices, focusing exclusively on rudimentary needs like adequate water and feed, safe housing, and basic health care, and adherence was voluntary.

Pressured again by animal advocates to create a more stringent, transparent, and science-based process for COP development, in 2002 the National Farm Animal Care Council (NFACC) was formed. However, with only three animal welfare groups out of the more than 30 partners (NFACC 2015), there remain legitimate concerns "that NFACC is dominated by producer organizations" and that "the only way it ever comes to the attention of animal welfare authorities that a farmer is not meeting a standard . . . is when a member of the public makes a complaint" to appropriate authorities (CFHS, n.d.a.); a rare occurrence given that the majority of farm animals are kept in windowless buildings on private, rural property.

Given the legal and regulatory exemptions afforded to standard industry practices, and the largely voluntary, complaint-based nature of the COP, it is perhaps unsurprising that undercover investigations of Canadian ILOs and slaughterhouses have consistently demonstrated routine violations of the COP as well as rampant animal cruelty.[1]

The Animals

From an animal welfare perspective, the industrialization of animal farming has demonstrated that profit margins and quality of life are often mutually exclusive. In order to maximize efficiency, farm animals are routinely confined in ways that deny proper movement and inhibit natural behaviours; mutilated in ways that produce both acute and chronic pain; and genetically manipulated in ways that increase physical and/or psychological suffering. The purpose of this section is to highlight the impacts that ILOs have on the welfare of each farm animal species,[2] with an emphasis on standard industry practices.

Chickens and Turkeys

The domestic chicken is descended from the red jungle fowl, a species indigenous to India and Southeast Asia. Despite intensive selection for increased egg production and rapid growth, domestic chickens have retained the instincts of their wild counterparts and are considered the same species (*Gallus gallus*). When given the opportunity, domestic chickens partake in a wide range of natural behaviours: spending the greater part of their day in small social groups, foraging for food, preening, dust-bathing,[3] and roosting.

Once ready to lay her eggs, a hen will find a secluded site to build her nest. There, she will sit over her eggs (or brood) for three weeks, leaving it once per day to quickly find food and water, and to dust-bathe (Duncan, Savory, and Wood-Gush 1978). For the first several days after hatching, chicks remain close to their mother, who crouches over them to keep them protected. When necessary, a hen will draw predators toward herself to divert attention from her chicks.

Similar to chickens, ancestors of the domestic turkey (*Meleagris gallopavo*) live in small family flocks, where they forage, dust-bathe, and roost. While modern turkeys have difficulty running or flying due to intensive breeding for accelerated growth, they have retained key ancestral instincts, including the drive to brood.

Of the 700 million farm animals killed last year in Canada, more than 640 million were broiler chickens and about 20 million were turkeys (AAFC 2015b). Additionally, there are more than 25 million egg-laying hens in Canada at any given time. While chickens and turkeys can live for more than a decade, on Canadian ILOs broiler chickens are slaughtered at 42 days of age or less, turkeys are slaughtered at 12 to 26 weeks, and egg-laying hens are slaughtered at around 18 months.

Egg-Laying Hens

Bred in commercial hatcheries and hatched by the thousands in industrial incubators, the first day of a chick's life involves being separated by sex. Male chicks, who cannot lay eggs, are killed upon hatching. Typically, they are deposited fully conscious into a macerator, a form of euthanasia considered acceptable under the COP.

Female chicks are selected for production and begin laying eggs at 18 to 20 weeks of age, laying an average of 305 eggs per year (AAFC 2013b). The hen's high rate of productivity is a result of genetic selection; her jungle fowl ancestors lay about 4 to 6 eggs annually. After approximately one year, a hen's productivity declines and she is sent to slaughter for processed chicken products.

Of the more than 25 million egg-laying hens in Canada, 95 per cent spend their lives in battery cages: small, barren, metal enclosures with sloped wire mesh floors that allow eggs to roll to the front of the cage for collection and excrement to fall through to the floor below. With five to seven birds per cage and cages stacked up to eight units high (CCFA 2005:3), the average Canadian farm holds 22,255 hens, with the largest holding 400,000 hens (AAFC 2013b). The primary benefit of the battery cage system is low labour costs.

Canada's current COP require 432–483 square centimetres of space per hen, which is smaller than an average sheet of paper. More than two-and-a-half times that amount of space would be required for a hen to perform even the most basic activities, like flapping her wings. The wire mesh floors commonly cause "lesions, fissures, hyperkeratosis on the feet, and twisted, broken or overgrown claws" (Street 2012:4).

In a natural setting, hens partake in a range of instinctive behaviours, including foraging, dust-bathing, perching, and building nests. The drive to fulfil these urges is so strong that in

ILOs, hens will "vacuum" dust-bathe[4] in their barren cages.

Another frustration response to confinement is feather-pecking, which can cause open wounds that become infected and may also trigger cannibalism, a major cause of death for egg-laying hens. In order to mitigate these economic losses, ILOs debeak hens within the first week of life using no anesthesia or analgesia, a procedure that causes both acute and chronic pain (Duncan and Rollin 2012:146).

As a result of calcium depletion from intensified egg production, hens also suffer from osteoporosis, which makes them more susceptible to injury at the time of transport to slaughter. An estimated 30 to 50 per cent of hens suffer from one or more fractures during loading and unloading (CCFA 2005:5).

Broiler Chickens and Turkeys

Virtually all the 640 million broiler chickens (raised for meat) and 21 million turkeys killed annually in Canada spend their lives in large, barren, windowless sheds with thousands of other birds; a large broiler farm can house 500,000 birds or more. By the time a broiler chicken is sent to slaughter at five to six weeks of age, they will have half a square foot of space, or less than the size of a computer mouse pad. When a turkey is sent to slaughter at 12 to 26 weeks of age, they will have about two square feet of space, or less than the size of a newspaper.

A key element of intensive poultry production is a highly controlled environment, where food, water, temperature, and lighting are optimized for maximal weight gain at minimal cost. In broiler barns, lights are kept on for up to 23 hours a day to stimulate appetite and faster weight gain. This disrupts the chickens' natural circadian cycle and can result in the birds feeling permanently "jet-lagged."

Air quality is another major concern for broiler chickens and turkeys, as the litter on the barn floors will not be changed until the birds have been removed for slaughter. The result is an ever-increasing accumulation of excreta (feces and urine), which generates irritating chemicals including hydrogen sulphide, methane, and ammonia. This leads to breast blisters, hock burns, contact dermatitis, foot ulcerations, and lameness. Ammonia, dust, and micro-organisms circulating in the air can also cause inflammation of the eyes and respiratory system.

Another consequence of high-density housing is that birds are unable to establish a natural pecking order. This causes social frustrations that can lead to aggressive pecking. Producers seek to prevent this via debeaking, dubbing (cutting off the comb on a chicken's head), desnooding (cutting off the wattle on a turkey's upper beak), and detoeing (cutting off portions of a turkey's three anterior toes). All procedures are performed without anesthesia or analgesia (Duncan and Rollin 2012:146).

Another tool used by producers to maximize gains is genetic selection. Growth rates for broiler chickens have increased by 300 per cent in the past 50 years, with today's broiler chickens reaching a market weight of 2 kilograms in just 32 to 36 days. Turkeys have also more than doubled in growth rate during the same period.

These unnatural growth rates come with a number of significant welfare concerns, including skeletal and joint disorders that can lead to pain, lameness, and death. Tibial dyschondroplasia (TD), a cartilage disease, is a leading cause of lameness, mortality, and carcass condemnations, affecting 30 to 49 per cent of broilers (Tablante, Estevez, and Russek-Cohen 2003:53) and over 80 per cent of turkeys (Halls 2009:4).

As a result of TD and other joint and leg issues, the vast majority of broilers have an abnormality in their gait. They will spend 76 to 86 per cent of their time lying down (Weeks et al. 2000), suggesting significant pain and discomfort. The joints and muscles of turkeys also have difficulty supporting their weight, leading to degenerative lesions of the hip joints (Duncan and Rollin 2012:150).

Rapid growth also leads to a number of heart-related issues, including ascites, a condition in which fluids leak into the body cavity, as well as acute heart failure (also known as sudden death syndrome). These two conditions can account for up to 90 per cent of on-farm mortality (Olkowski 2009).

Pigs

The domestic pig (*Sus scrofa*) is descended from the Eurasian wild boar. Despite intensive selection for rapid growth, it has retained the instincts of its wild counterparts. When observed in natural environments, domestic pigs display a wide array of behaviours, including rooting for food, building nests, wallowing in mud, and forming small social groups. Pigs have a natural lifespan of 12 to 15 years.

In the artificial environments of ILOs, confinement in barren crates and crowded pens thwarts pigs from engaging in many of these instinctual behaviours, including proper socialization. Coupled with the negative side effects of genetic selection, these living conditions often lead to increased disease, injury, stress, and aggression. In an attempt to mitigate the most costly of these symptoms, the majority of pigs are subjected to a number of painful procedures that cause both acute and chronic pain.

In 2014, more than 20 million pigs were killed in Canada, the majority of them market pigs raised for meat (AAFC 2015a). These pigs are prematurely weaned from their mothers at 10 to 21 days of age and moved to small pens where they remain until they reach market weight. At around six months old, they are killed. Canada's 1 million breeding sows (Statistics Canada 2015) will have approximately two pregnancies per year, giving birth to 19 to 22 piglets. The average sow has around three litters before her productivity declines and she is sent to slaughter at around 24 to 30 months of age.

Sows

The vast majority of breeding sows in Canada are confined to gestation and/or farrowing crates: barred stalls only slightly bigger than themselves where they eat, sleep, urinate, and defecate on a slatted floor. Sows may take one step forward or backward and lay down, but they cannot turn around. Crates are said to increase a sow's pregnancy rate and litter size while also keeping labour costs down.

When a sow is around one year of age, she is put into a gestation crate. Just before giving birth, she will be moved to a farrowing crate, where she will nurse her piglets for 10 to 21 days through a guardrail, before being returned to a gestation crate and re-impregnated (CCFA 2006).

In a natural environment, prior to giving birth, sows gather appropriate materials to build a nest, where they will nurse for 14 to 15 weeks. Gestation and farrowing crates prevent sows from fulfilling these basic instincts and behaviours, causing both physical and psychological suffering.[5]

A sow's lack of exercise leads to muscle atrophy, joint damage, and decreased bone density, which contribute to abrasions, bruising, damaged ligaments, and broken bones while in the crate. It also puts her at "greater risk of bone fracture when transported for slaughter" (WSPA 2012:23). As many as 94 per cent of sows are estimated to have hoof lesions and 54 per cent are lame (Seddon and Brown 2014).

The psychological effects of confinement result in more than 90 per cent of confined sows (Duncan and Rollin 2012:140) displaying stereotypic behaviours (e.g. bar biting, "vacuum" chewing, rooting at the bare floor), which are indicative of mental suffering.

Market Pigs

The vast majority of Canada's 20 million market pigs are raised in small pens with 15 to 30 other animals and thousands of other animals under the same roof. The largest known pig operation in Canada produces 1.4 million pigs annually. Weaned prematurely at 10 to 21 days of age, domestic pigs will reach market weight after five to six months.

Feral pigs travel several kilometres each day, and domestic pigs in extensive environments will average 3.8 metres from their nearest neighbour (Stolba and Wood-Gush 1989). In contrast, required space for a 200 pound (91 kilogram) pig on a Canadian farm is 0.67 square metres, with an additional permitted space reduction of 15 per cent (NFACC 2014). This high-density housing leads to increased risk of injury, disease, and social disorders.

Modern pig barns feature small metal pens with slatted, concrete floors, which allows manure to fall through to a pit below; bedding is typically not used "due to cost, difficulty of cleaning, and incompatibility with slatted floors" (Holden and Ensminger 2006:375–8). This form of flooring leads to foot lesions, injuries, and lameness at a herd prevalence of up to 30 per cent (Ellingson et al. 2012).

Air quality is a major issue in modern pig barns, with high concentrations of dust, moisture, micro-organisms, and gases (hydrogen sulphide, carbon monoxide, methane, and ammonia) leading to compromised immunoresponse and increased transmission of infectious disease. Conditions commonly linked to compromised air quality include pleuritis, atrophic rhinitis, swine influenza, and pneumonia—which has been measured at a prevalence of 80 per cent in Canadian pig herds (Gardner and Hird 1990). Respiratory problems cause the majority of on-farm deaths (Knetter et al. 2014).

Another common cause of on-farm mortality in pigs is gastric ulcers, which are strongly linked to the finely ground, pelleted feed that has replaced the pigs' natural diet of small amounts of high-fibre food. Herd prevalence has been reported as high as 94 per cent, causing up to 27 per cent of total on-farm mortality (Melnichouk 2002).

Social disorders are another major impact of the crowded, barren environment in modern pig barns. In extensive environments, pigs spend more than 50 per cent of their time engaging in foraging-related activities (Stolba and Wood-Gush 1989) and can easily prevent confrontation by avoiding one another. Close confinement in barren pens results in a redirection of foraging behaviour and aggression toward the ears and tails of other pigs (Duncan and Rollin 2012:147).

These biting behaviours can also be an attempt to suckle another pig due to premature weaning. In addition to causing acute pain and frustration, tail-biting can also result in serious wounds, infection, spinal abscess, paralysis, and in extreme cases, death (NFACC 2014:34).

In order to mitigate potential economic losses associated with these adaptive behaviours, young piglets have their deciduous teeth clipped and the lower half of their tails removed. Piglets are also castrated in order to reduce aggression and to prevent "boar taint."[6] Until 2014, these procedures were performed without the use of any anesthesia or analgesia. The latest COP now requires that piglets have some form of pain control when being castrated or having their tails docked, but only when older than 10 days for the former, and 7 days for the latter.[7] After July 2016, tail docking or castration will require analgesics (but not anesthesia). No pain control is required for teeth clipping (NFACC 2014).

Due to selective breeding for large litters, sows routinely give birth to more piglets than they have teats for. These "excess" piglets are commonly killed using a method known as PACing (pounding against concrete) (CCFA 2015), which the most recent COP consider an acceptable method of euthanasia for piglets up to 20 pounds (9 kilograms).

Cows

The domestic cow (*Bos taurus*) is descended from the auroch (*Bos primigenius*), a long-horned wild ox that once inhabited Europe, Asia, and North Africa. Like their ancestors, cows are social and prefer to live in established herds, where females share the responsibility of caring for young. As ruminants, their natural diet consists of grass and other plant materials.

When given the opportunity, cows raise their calves like any wild ungulate and engage in a wide range of maternal behaviours, including licking, nuzzling, and maintaining close physical contact. The bond between calf and mother is formed within minutes of birth (Enríquez,

Hötzel, and Ungerfeld 2011) and is reinforced throughout the 7 to 14 months a calf will spend reliant on his mother for protection and sustenance (Reinhardt 2002). Weaning occurs gradually over several months, during which the calf begins to graze. After weaning, mother and calf remain bonded and prefer one another as grazing partners (Reinhardt and Reinhardt 1981).

In 2014, there were 2,752,000 beef cattle slaughtered across Canada (AAFC 2013a), and about 300,000 veal calves (Farm and Food Care Ontario n.d.). There are also more than 1.4 million dairy cows and heifers[8] in Canada at any given time (Canadian Dairy Information Centre 2014). While cows can live up to 25 years, on ILOs dairy cows are typically slaughtered between four and five years of age, beef cattle between one and two years, and veal calves anywhere from two days to 28 weeks old.

Dairy Cows

Like all mammals, cows produce milk for their newborns and must give birth in order to lactate. Dairy production exploits this process via highly controlled breeding, early weaning, and genetic selection. As a result, the average Canadian dairy cow now produces 9,780 kilograms of milk per lactation (305 days) (CDIC 2015), about 10 times more than she would naturally (Van Doormaal et al. 2005). Dairy cows are artificially inseminated for the first time at around 15 months of age, and, after giving birth nine months later, are inseminated again after 60–90 days (BCSPCA 2009a).

More than 500,000 dairy calves are born in Canada each year. Approximately half are female, who join/replace existing cows in the milking herd. The other half are male, a few of whom are kept for breeding purposes, with the rest becoming veal (Statistics Canada 2012b). In order to accelerate rebreeding (Enríquez, Hötzel, and Ungerfeld 2011), modern dairy production separates calves from their mothers as soon as possible: within 24 hours of birth for female calves, and within a few hours of birth for male (veal) calves.

After being separated from their mother, female calves are moved to individual pens, where they are prevented from socializing with other calves or moving freely. Premature weaning poses a number of welfare concerns, including stress to both mother and calf, as characterized by anxious vocalizations of mothers and calves calling for one another. Because producers take their mother's milk for human consumption, the calf is fed a milk replacement diet. Calves in a natural setting nurse 5 to 10 times per day; the urge to suckle is so strong that isolated calves routinely perform sucking behaviours on objects in their environment. Forced weaning is associated with increased rates of coccidiosis, viral diarrhea, respiratory disease, and premature death (Reinhardt 2002). At 6 to 12 weeks of age calves are then abruptly weaned onto solid food (BCSPCA 2009a) and moved to group housing, "a very stressful time for calves" during which "disease outbreaks are common," with infectious diseases like pneumonia sometimes reaching 100 per cent morbidity (Leslie and Todd 2007). At about 15 months of age, 10 months sooner than studies indicate may be natural, young heifers are artificially impregnated. Before they begin to produce milk, they will be confined to either a tie- or a free-stall system.

Around 72 per cent of dairy cows in Canada are confined using a tie-stall system (CDIC 2013). Typically, this means that they are tethered by the neck to an individual stall 24 hours per day, preventing them from performing basic movements or behaviours, including turning around, grooming, and socializing. Lying down can also prove difficult.

Twenty-three per cent of dairy cows in Canada live in free-stall systems, which consist of pens with access to bed stalls, food, and water (CDIC 2013). Overstocking is a common problem, resulting in cows having to wait long periods to eat or for a place to lie down, which is stressful as dairy cows prefer to spend 12 to 14 hours per day resting (BCSPCA 2009a).

Cows forced to stand on concrete floors for extended periods are at higher risk of developing lameness, which is found in up to 30 per cent of the Canadian dairy population (Weary, Rushen, and Crabtree 2010). Feet and leg problems are a common reason for culling in Canadian dairy herds (CDIC 2014).

Another side effect of intensive production and a primary reason for culling is mastitis, a painful infection of the udder linked to contact with manure. While rates as high as 97 per cent have been reported in some Canadian herds (Riekerink et al. 2007), it is widely accepted that at least 20 per cent of dairy cows suffer from mastitis (Derakhshani et al. 2015), which is estimated to cost producers $300 million per year (Dairy Farmers of Canada, n.d.).

In an attempt to lower mastitis rates by reducing potential contact with manure, tail docking is routine, despite the fact that research has shown it does not improve rates of mastitis and can lead to infection and chronic pain (NFACC 2009:34).[9] Performed without anesthesia or analgesia, the procedure involves cutting off blood supply to the tail, causing it to eventually fall off.

Slaughtered after an average of 2.7 lactations, or at approximately four years old, (Duncan and Rollin 2012:154), Canadian dairy cows are most commonly culled due to reduced fertility, followed by mastitis, feet and leg problems, and reduced milk production (CDIC 2014). Due to the lower quality of their carcasses, meat from dairy cows is used predominantly for ground beef.

Veal Calves

A by-product of the dairy industry, more than 300,000 male calves (Canadian Meat Council 2013) are killed in Canada each year for veal (FFCO n.d.). Separated from their mothers shortly after birth, most male dairy calves are sold at auction or to dealers for bob veal,[10] grain-fed veal, or milk-fed veal, and will be slaughtered at anywhere from a few days to 28 weeks old.

In a natural environment, calves spend one to two years alongside their mother in the herd, nursing up to 10 times a day for 7 to 14 months. On modern veal farms, calves are denied this experience and confined for much or all of their lives in individual crates or stalls. Under the current COP (1998), the recommended width of a crate or stall is 70–90 centimetres (CARC 1998), which prevents the calf from walking, running, turning around, or even lying laterally with his legs extended, which is a normal resting position for cows. Some calves are also tethered at the neck, restricting movement even further. This confinement keeps the calf's muscles undeveloped, which in turn produces the tender quality that veal is known for.

Grain-fed veal calves spend the first 6 to 8 weeks of their lives confined to individual stalls or crates, after which they are moved into group housing, where they will share a pen with up to 10 other calves (Lang 2010) for the remaining 18 to 20 weeks before they are slaughtered. Milk-fed veal calves, who make up one-third of the veal calves in Canada, will not leave their individual crates until they are sent to slaughter at around 16 weeks of age.

Prolonged confinement leads to numerous physical issues, including muscle atrophy, wounds from rubbing against the crate, knee lesions, leg and joint disorders, and lameness. They also routinely demonstrate separation-induced behaviours including excessive vocalizing, licking, self-cleaning, and sucking (Greter and Levison 2012).

On-farm mortality rates of veal calves are as high as 20 per cent (Livestock Research Innovation Corporation 2013). Calf deaths are largely attributable to diarrhea and pneumonia, with multiple contributing factors, including the stress of transport from dairy farm to purchaser, group housing, and high stocking densities. Another major factor is inadequate access to their mother's colostrum, which provides the necessary antibodies for a strong immune system. As a result of premature weaning, it is estimated that 35 to 40 per cent of calves experience "failure of passive transfer" of these vital antibodies, putting them at a much greater risk of mortality (Lang 2010).

Substituting their mother's milk with milk replacer also limits proper gut development, predisposing calves to metabolic and digestive conditions, including abomasal ulcers, which have been reported to affect as many as 87 per cent of veal calves (Welchmen and Baust 1987). Milk-fed veal calves, whose liquid diet is intentionally formulated for low iron to ensure that their meat has a pale appearance, are commonly found to be anemic, with up to 35 per cent presenting with marginal or clinical anemia (Stull and McDonough 1994).

Beef Cattle

Approximately 2,750,000 beef cattle are slaughtered in Canada every year, at ages ranging from 12 to 24 months. When given the opportunity, domestic cows reach full maturity at 4 to 5 years of age and can live for an additional 15 to 20 years.

Much like market pigs and broiler chickens, beef cattle are not confined to individual stalls since this would impede the muscle growth for which they are bred. Canadian beef cattle typically spend their first six to eight months on pasture with their mothers until they reach a minimum weight of 160 kilograms, at which point they may be transferred to a backgrounding lot intended to increase their weight as quickly as possible (CBI 2012a). At about 400 kilograms, the majority of calves are sent to a feedlot (or finishing lot).

This premature, abrupt weaning leads to physiological and psychological distress characterized by suppressed immunoresponse, increased heart rate and cortisol levels, increased vocalizations, reduced play, and increased aggression (Enríquez, Hötzel, and Ungerfeld 2011). Transfer to feedlots also causes anxiety by destroying the secure social groups that cows established while in pasture.

Confining up to 40,000 cows at a time (CBI 2012b), feedlots pose significant health risks, with overcrowding and waste accumulation leading to significant eye, skin, and respiratory issues. Of particular concern is bovine respiratory disease (BRD), which has prevalence rates of up to 64.4 per cent (Schneider et al. 2009) and causes 45 to 75 per cent of deaths on some feedlots (Jelinski and Janzen 2014).

The high incidence of BRD is also associated with the grain-based food given to feedlot cows, whose natural diet consists almost entirely of grass. This concentrated feeding regimen also leads to acidosis (grain overload) and other severe digestive disorders, which account for about one-third of feedlot mortalities (Galyean and Rivera 2003).

Starting as early as one week of age, male calves are castrated to reduce aggression, prevent unwanted impregnation, and improve the perceived quality of the meat (Duncan and Rollin 2012:144). Castration, which is typically done without anesthesia or analgesia,[11] not only causes acute pain and distress, but can also lead to infection and the need for more complicated surgeries.

Beef calves are also disbudded[12] or dehorned in order to minimize potential losses due to carcass bruising (NFACC 2013:22). Disbudding is performed at two to three months of age, with a knife or caustic paste, before the horns have fully attached to the skull. Dehorning is performed when the horns have attached to the skull and must be cut or gouged out. Both procedures cause pain and distress, with dehorning also increasing risk for numerous infectious diseases including tetanus and bovine leukemia virus (American Veterinary Medical Association 2014).

Transport and Slaughter

Before the industrialization of agriculture, most Canadian farm animals were born, raised, and slaughtered on or close to the farms they lived on. Due to industry concentration, today most of the 700 million Canadian farm animals slaughtered annually will be transported long distances, in many cases out of province or country. Spent egg-laying hens, for example, have been transported as far as 2,400 kilometres (Newberry et al. 1999:20).

The Health of Animals Regulations (HAR) place no upper limit on how long an animal's entire journey can be, with some of the longest transportation allowances in the industrialized world. Pigs, horses, and birds may be transported continuously for up to 36 hours with no food, water, or rest; cattle and sheep may be transported for up to 52 hours. Rest periods can be as short as five hours, even following maximum continuous travel times (GC 2014a). Transport is permitted at any time of day and in any weather conditions, and drivers require no special training in the handling and care of animals.

Because the COP for transport are voluntary (CARC 2001), the HAR is the primary enforcement tool for Canadian Food Inspection Agency (CFIA) inspectors, whose responsibilities include ensuring humane transport. These regulations do not address loading density, specify health conditions that would prohibit an animal from being humanely transported, or mandate that trucks come equipped with automatic cooling and heating systems for varied weather conditions.

The number of inspectors is also limited; for example, in one Ontario municipality, a single inspector is responsible for 14 facilities, and as such, cannot be present for the unloading of most animals (WSPA 2010:10). As a result, employees are often left to "police themselves" (p. 8). Even when inspectors observe gross violations, a common course of action is to issue warnings or provide educational pamphlets instead of taking the appropriate punitive measures (p. 10).

As a result of these and other factors, farm animals en route to slaughter "stand or lie in their own waste in overcrowded conditions, and endure extreme weather conditions without adequate protection, ventilation or nesting materials" (WSPA 2010:4), with the CFIA estimating that between 2 and 3 million animals die during transport each year. Countless others arrive emaciated, sick, downed, or severely injured.

Hours or even days after being loaded for transport, farm animals arrive at the slaughterhouse,[13] where they are unloaded by handlers who, like livestock transporters, require no specialized training. They move the animals using sticks, canes, and/or electric prods, resulting in stress, injury, and bruising severe enough to consistently impact carcass values (Grandin 2007).

Once ready for slaughter, the Meat Inspection Regulations (MIR) require that animals be stunned (rendered unconscious) prior to "being bled" (with exceptions for halal and kosher slaughter) (GC 2014b). Stunning methods vary between species.

The most common method for stunning poultry is electrified stun-baths. Birds are hung by their feet on metal shackles attached to a conveyor; their heads are then immersed in an electrified water tank to render them unconscious before they proceed to the neck cutter. Dead birds are then moved to the "scald" tank for feather removal. This method of slaughter poses numerous welfare issues, including leg amputations during shackling (Francois 2009a:3), inadequate voltage in the water tank to stun the birds (Francois 2009b:7), and shackled birds thus entering the scald tank fully conscious. Large poultry slaughterhouses can kill 100,000 chickens per day.

The most common stunning methods for pigs are electrocution and carbon dioxide gas. After stunning, pigs are chained by the leg and hung on a conveyor, where their throats are cut; the pig then moves to the scalding tank for hair removal before butchering. A 1999 audit (in which slaughterhouses were given prior notice of inspection) gave two slaughterhouses failing grades for improper stunning, with 23 per cent of pigs in one facility regaining sensibility prior to bleed out (Grandin 1999). Large pig slaughterhouses can kill 15,000 pigs per day.

The most common method for stunning cattle is captive bolt, which penetrates the cow's skull and renders them unconscious in preparation for shackling and bleed out. In the same 1999 audit referred to above, 37 per cent of audited beef slaughterhouses (including federally inspected plants) failed to properly stun at least 1 in 20 cows, with the auditor commenting that some of the treatment she witnessed "would probably constitute abuse and cruelty" (Grandin 1999). Large cattle slaughterhouses can kill 4,500 cows per day.

Conclusion

ILOs severely impact the welfare of Canadian farm animals, with standard industry practices justified by producers in order to meet consumer demand for a large, cheap, and steady supply of animal products.

But what sort of shift needs to take place if animals are to be spared the frustration, discomfort, pain, suffering, and disease that typifies intensive animal agriculture? Critics argue that it would be economically unfeasible to raise and slaughter 700 million farm animals annually in Canada using alternative systems that prioritize animal welfare. Such a shift would not only necessitate dramatically more land, enrichment, high-quality food, and veterinary care, it would demand genetic deselection for rapid growth, further decreasing efficiency. Animal products generated in this way would be almost entirely unaffordable.

Fortunately, another shift is already taking place that is decreasing the demand for cheap animal products: the move toward plant-based eating. In addition to significant increases in the percentage of Canadians following vegetarian or vegan diets, general consumption of plant-based alternatives to animal foods has been steadily on the rise, with per capita consumption of meat and milk declining.

Laying the foundation for this shift are advancements in nutritional science proving that animal products, once considered the building blocks of a healthful diet, are neither necessary nor optimal. According to the Dietitians of Canada, "a healthy vegan diet has health benefits including lower rates of obesity, heart disease, high blood pressure, high blood cholesterol, type 2 diabetes and certain types of cancer" (2014).

Underscoring the health benefits of plant-based eating is a growing awareness of the environmental impacts of food choices. According to the UN FAO, livestock production is "one of the top contributors to . . . land degradation, climate change and air pollution, water shortage and water pollution, and loss of biodiversity. . . . The impact is so significant that it needs to be addressed with urgency" (2006:xx).

The industrialization of animal agriculture has had significant consequences for Canada's rural communities, who have been forced to witness "the boarding-up of main street windows, a rural-youth diaspora, and the destruction of family farms—with the expulsion of farmers most rapid in sectors where ILO production expanded most aggressively" (Qualman 2012:85).

But nowhere have the consequences been more strongly felt than in the cages, crates, stalls, pens, and feedlots where hundreds of millions of Canadian farm animals are forced to spend their lives. Fortunately, despite decades of sustained effort to keep the realities of ILOs behind closed doors, the impact on farm animals is starting to be realized.

Discussion Questions

1. When considering humane treatment, why is relying on the codes and regulations for farm animals problematic?

2. What are the three key ways that ILOs frustrate and harm animals?

3. Does understanding standard industry practices on ILOs encourage Canadians to make more ethical food choices? Discuss why or why not.

Further Reading

1. National Farm Animal Care Council (NFACC). 2015. "Codes of Practice for the Care and Handling of Farm Animals." https://www.nfacc.ca/codes-of-practice.

The COP for each species of farm animal offers a detailed look at standard industry practices, as well as required/recommended practices for each species.

2. World Society for the Protection of Animals (WSPA). 2012. *What's on Your Plate? The Hidden Costs of Industrial Animal Agriculture in Canada.* Toronto. http://www.worldanimalprotection.ca/our-work-0/animals-farming/whats-your-plate.

This report examines the impacts that ILOs have on the environment, public health, rural communities, and animals, featuring experts from across Canada from multiple disciplines and backgrounds.

Video Suggestions

1. Canadian Coalition for Farm Animals. 2005. *The Truth about Canada's Egg Industry.* www.humanefood.ca/batterycagevideo.html. 4 min.
2. Francois, Twyla. 2009. *The Secret Lives of Sows.* www.youtube.com/watch?v=cmQfZTSNwuc. 3 min.
3. Mercy for Animals. 2012. *Crated Cruelty.* http://pigcruelty.mercyforanimals.org/. 4 min.

Notes

1. Canadians for the Ethical Treatment of Food Animals and Mercy for Animals have conducted numerous investigations across Canada.
2. Due to space constraints, a discussion of hatcheries and the farming of ducks, geese, rabbits, lambs, sheep, goats, boars, and horses could not be included.
3. A practice which allows the hen to remove the stale oil she produces to waterproof and condition her feathers by bathing in dry, dusty substrate.
4. "Vacuum" dust-bathing refers to a hen performing the act, but without the required substrate to make it effective.
5. The latest recommended COP (2014) states that a "ban on conventional stall systems" will go into effect in July 2024. After 2024, sows must be housed in groups or in individual pens or stalls, provided they are increased in size enough to allow sows to turn around, and that sows have access to "exercise" periodically. Critics feel the deadline is too far off, and leaves too much time to potentially dilute the future requirement (NFACC 2014:11).
6. An odour and taste in the meat that some consumers are said to find objectionable.
7. The COP recommends that tail docking be done at 24–72 hours of age, which would make pain control not a "requirement" for producers.
8. A heifer is a cow that has not yet had her first calf.
9. The latest COP (2009) states that dairy cattle must not be tail docked "unless medically necessary," a confusing distinction as industry has long claimed that tail docking was necessary to prevent mastitis, a medical issue.
10. Newborn calves slaughtered at less than four weeks of age.
11. As of 2016, pain control will be required when castrating bulls older than nine months. As of 2018, it will be required when castrating bulls older than six months (NFACC 2013).
12. As of 2016, pain control will be required when dehorning (but not disbudding) calves (NFACC 2013).
13. Once inside the slaughterhouse, under the "Meat Inspection Regulations" (MIR), an animal may be placed in a holding pen for 24 hours without food (GC 2014b:60). This is in addition to the 36–52 hours they may be transported without food, water, or rest.

References

Agriculture and Agri-Food Canada (AAFC). 2013a. "Annual Canada and United States Cattle and Beef Comparison 2011–2013." Government of Canada. www.agr.gc.ca/eng/industry-markets-and-trade/statistics

-and-market-information/by-product-sector/red-meat -and-livestock/red-meat-market-information-Canadian -industry/by-sector-reports/cattle-and-calves/Canada -and-united-states-cattle-and-beef-comparison/2011 -2013/?id=1415860000064.

———. 2013b. "Canada's Table and Processed Egg Industry . . . at a Glance." Government of Canada. www.agr.gc .ca/eng/industry-markets-and-trade/statistics-and-market-information/by-product-sector/poultry-and -eggs/poultry-and-egg-market-information-Canadian -industry/sub-sector-reports/table-and-processed-eggs/ ?id=1384971854396.

———. 2015a. "Origin of Hog Slaughtered in Canadian Plants—Annual Summary." Government of Canada. www.aimis-simia.agr.gc.ca/rp/index-eng.cfm?action= pR&PDCTC=&E=1&R=93.

———. 2015b. "Poultry Production Report by Month/Year." Government of Canada. www.aimis-simia.agr.gc.ca/rp/ index-eng.cfm?action=ePR&PDCTC=&R=6.

American Veterinary Medical Association. 2014. "Literature Review on the Welfare Implications of the Dehorning and Disbudding of Cattle." American Veterinary Medical Association Animal Welfare Division.

British Columbia Society for the Prevention of Cruelty to Animals (BCSPCA). 2009a. "Dairy Production in British Columbia." British Columbia.

Canada Beef Inc. (CBI). 2012a. "Backgrounding." Our Industry. www.Canadabeef.ca/ca/en/beef_export/industry/ backgrounding.aspx.

———. 2012b. "Feedlot Finishing." Our Industry. www .Canadabeef.ca/ca/en/beef_export/industry/finishing .aspx.

Canadian Agri-Food Research Council (CARC). 1998. "Recommended Code of Practice for the Care and Handling of Farm Animals." Guelph, ON: Ontario Veal Association.

———. 2001. "Transportation." Recommended Code of Practice for the Care and Handling of Farm Animals. Ontario: Canadian Food Inspection Agency.

Canadian Coalition for Farm Animals (CCFA). 2005. Battery Cages and the Welfare of Hens in Canada: A Summary of the Scientific Literature. http://www.humanefood.ca/ pdf%20links/BatteryReport.pdf.

———. 2006. Gestation Stalls and the Welfare of Sows in Canada: A Summary of the Scientific Literature. http:// www.humanefood.ca/pdf%20links/SowReport.pdf.

———. 2015. "Sow Stalls." Facts About Our Food. http://www. humanefood.ca/pdf%20links/Sow%20Stalls%202015.pdf.

Canadian Dairy Information Centre (CDIC). 2013. "Dairy Barns by Type in Canada." Government of Canada. www.dairyinfo.gc.ca/index_e.php?s1=dff-fcil&s2= farm-ferme&s3=db-el.

———. 2014. "Culling and Replacement Rates in Dairy Herds in Canada." Breed Improvement and Genetic Evaluation. Government of Canada. www.dairyinfo.gc.ca/index_e.php ?s1=dff-fcil&s2=mrr-pcle&s3=cr-tr.

———. 2015. "Canada's Dairy Industry at a Glance." Government of Canada. www.dairyinfo.gc.ca/index_e. php?s1=cdi-ilc&s2=aag-ail.

———. "D042—Number of Dairy Cows and Heifers by Province." Government of Canada. www.aimis-simia -cdic-ccil.agr.gc.ca/rp/index-eng.cfm?action=pR&PDCTC =&E=1&R=219.

Canadian Federation of Humane Societies (CFHS). n.d.a. "Codes of Practice and the National Farm Animal Care Council." Animals on the Farm. www.cfhs.ca/farm/codes_of_practice.

———. n.d.b. "Realities of Farming in Canada." Animals on the Farm. www.cfhs.ca/farm/ farming_in_Canada.

Canadian Food Inspection Agency (CFIA). 2014. "Provincial and Territorial Legislation Concerning Farm Animal Welfare." Government of Canada. www.inspection.gc .ca/animals/terrestrial-animals/humane-transport/ provincial-and-territorial-legislation/eng/1358482954113/ 1358483058784.

Canadian Meat Council. 2013. "Fact Sheet on Dairy Cows in Canada." Ottawa. http://www.cmc-cvc.com/sites/default/ files/files/Fact%20Sheet%20Cull%20Dairy%20Cattle% 20November%202013.pdf

Canfax Research. 2014. "Statistical Research." Alberta. www .canfax.ca/samples/statbrf.pdf.

Dairy Farmers of Canada. n.d. "Common Health Issues." www .dairyfarmers.ca/what-we-do/animal-health-and-welfare/ animal-health/common-health-issues.

Derakhshani, Hooman, Christine Rawluk, Kees Plazier, and Ehsan Khafipour. 2015. "New Microbiome Research for Tackling Mastitis on Manitoba Dairy Farms." National Centre for Livestock and the Environment newsletter (January/February):1–2. https://umanitoba.ca/faculties/ afs/ncle/pdf/Jan-Feb_2015_NCLE_Newsletter.pdf.

Dietitians of Canada. 2014. "Healthy Eating Guidelines for Vegans." www.dietitians.ca/your-health/nutrition-a-z/ vegetarian-diets/eating-guidelines-for-vegans.aspx.

Duncan, Ian J.H., and Bernard E. Rollin. 2012. "Farm Animal Welfare in Canada: Major Problems and Prospects." Pp. 133–60 in What's on Your Plate? The Hidden Costs of Industrial Animal Agriculture in Canada. Toronto: WSPA.

———. C.J. Savory, and D.G.M. Wood-Gush. 1978. "Observations on the Reproductive Behaviour of Domestic Fowl in the Wild." Applied Animal Ethology 4:29–42.

Ellingson, Joshua S., Locke A. Karriker, Matthew H. Borgmann, and Alexandra C. Buckley. 2012. "Finishing Lameness— What Do We Know?" Search and Summary of Current Evidence. Swine Medicine Education Center. http:// www.pic.com/Images/Users/1/salesportal/newsletters/ enewsletterarchive/FinishingLamenessWhatDoWeKnow2 .pdf.

Enríquez, Daniel, Maria J. Hötzel, and Rodolfo Ungerfeld. 2011. "Minimising the Stress of Weaning of Beef Calves: A Review." Acta Veterinaria Scandinavica 53(28). www .actavetscand.com/content/53/1/28.

Farm and Food Care Ontario (FFCO). n.d. "Facts and Figures about Canadian Veal." www.ontarioveal.on.ca/pdfs/Farm-and-Food-Care-Veal-Factsheet.pdf.

Food and Agriculture Organization of the United Nations (FAO). 2006. "Executive Summary." Pp. xx–xxiv in *Livestock's Long Shadow: Environmental Issues and Options*. Rome.

Francois, Twyla. 2009a. *Broken Wings: The Breakdown of Animal Protection in the Transportation and Slaughter of Meat Poultry in Canada*. Vancouver: Canadians for the Ethical Treatment of Animals.

———. 2009b. *The Electrified Stun Bath: Canada's Outdated Method of Stunning Poultry. Canadians for the Ethical Treatment of Animals*. http://www.humanefood.ca/pdf%20links/Taskforce%20Report%20Tour%20of%20CAK%20at%20Vleesch%20du%20Bois.pdf

Galyean, M.L., and J.D. Rivera. 2003. "Nutritionally Related Disorders Affecting Feedlot Cattle." *Canadian Journal of Animal Science* 83(1):13–20.

Gardner, I.A., and D.W. Hird. 1990. "Host Determinants of Pneumonia in Slaughter Weight Swine." *American Journal of Veterinary Research* 51(8):1306–11.

Government of Canada (GC). 2008a. *Beyond Freefall: Halting Rural Poverty*. Final Report of the Standing Senate Committee on Agriculture and Forestry. 39th Parl., 2nd Sess. Ottawa. http://www.parl.gc.ca/content/sen/committee/392/agri/rep/rep09jun08-e.pdf

———. 2008b. Section 445.1, Criminal Code. R.S., c. 12, s. 1. www.laws-lois.justice.gc.ca/eng/acts/c-46/page-209.html.

———. 2014a. "Health of Animal Regulations." Justice Laws Website. C.R.C., c. 296. www.laws-lois.justice.gc.ca/eng/regulations/C.R.C.%2C_c._296.

———. 2014b. "Meat Inspection Regulations, 1990." Ottawa: Ministry of Justice. www.laws-lois.justice.gc.ca/pdf/sor-90-288.pdf.

Grandin, Temple. 1999. "Canadian Animal Welfare Audit of Stunning and Handling in Federal and Provincial Inspected Slaughter Plants." Colorado: Grandin Livestock Handling Systems.

———. 2007. *Livestock Handling and Transport*. 3rd edn. Cambridge, MA: CABI.

Greter, A., and L. Levison. 2012. "Calf in a Box: Individual Confinement Housing Used in Veal Production." *Farm Sense: BCSPCA Farm Animal Welfare News* (June). http://www.spca.bc.ca/assets/documents/welfare/farm/farmsense/june-2012-feature-story.pdf.

Halls, Amy E. 2009. "Tibial Dyschondroplasia." *At a Glance* (Winter/Spring):4–5.

Holden, P.J., and M.E. Ensminger. 2006. *Swine Science*. 7th edn. Upper Saddle River, NJ: Pearson Prentice-Hall.

Jelinski, Murray, and Eugene Janzen. 2014. "Bovine Respiratory Disease." Beef Cattle Research Council. www.beefresearch.ca/research-topic.cfm/bovine-respiratory-disease-38.

Knetter, S.M., C.K. Tuggle, M.J. Wannemuehler, and A.E. Ramer-Tait. 2014. "Organic Barn Dust Extract Exposure Impairs Porcine Macrophage Function in Vitro: Implications for Respiratory Health." *Veterinary Immunology and Immunopathology* 157(1–2):20–30.

Lang, B. 2010. "Management of Grain-Fed Veal Calves." Ontario: Ministry of Agriculture, Food and Rural Affairs. www.omafra.gov.on.ca/english/livestock/beef/facts/06-083.htm.

Leslie, Ken E., and Cynthia G. Todd. 2007. "Keeping Your Calves Healthy." *WCDS Advances in Dairy Technology* 19:285–300.

Livestock Research Innovation Corporation (LRIC). 2013. "Ontario Veal Industry 'Fact Pack.'" www.livestockresearch.ca/documents/vealfactpack.pdf.

Melnichouk, Sergey I. 2002. "Mortality Associated with Gastric Ulceration in Swine." *Canadian Veterinary Journal* 43(3): 223–5.

National Farm Animal Care Council (NFACC). 2009. "Code of Practice for the Care and Dairy Cattle." Ottawa: Dairy Farmers of Canada.

———. 2013. "Code of Practice for the Care and Beef Cattle." Ottawa: Canadian Cattlemen's Association.

———. 2014. "Code of Practice for the Care and Handling of Pigs." Ottawa: Canadian Pork Council.

———. 2015. "Partners." National Farm Animal Care Council.

Newberry, Ruth C., A. Bruce Webster, Nora J. Lewis, and Charles Van Arnam. 1999. "Management of Spent Hens." *Journal of Applied Animals Welfare Science* 2(1):13–29.

Olkowski, Andrzej. 2009. "Cardiac Disease in Meat Type Chickens." Poultry Industry Council. www.poultryindustrycouncil.ca/pdfs/factsheets/fs_110.pdf.

Qualman, Darrin. 2012. "The Expulsion of Farm Families." Pp. 85–96 in *What's on Your Plate? The Hidden Costs of Industrial Animal Agriculture in Canada*. Toronto: WSPA.

Reinhardt, Viktor. 2002. "Artificial Weaning of Calves: Benefits and Costs." *Journal of Applied and Animal Welfare Science* 5(3):251–5.

———, and A. Reinhardt. 1981. "Cohesive Relationships in a Cattle Herd (*Bos indicus*)." *Behaviour* 77(3):121–51.

Riekerink, R.G.M., H.W. Barkema, D.F. Kelton, and D.T. Scholl. 2007. "Incidence Rate of Clinical Mastitis on Canadian Dairy Farms." *Journal of Dairy Science* 91:1366–77.

Schneider, M.J., R.G. Tait Jr., W.D. Busby, and J.M. Reecy. 2009. "An Evaluation of Bovine Respiratory Disease Complex in Feedlot Cattle: Impact on Performance and Carcass Traits Using Treatment Records and Lung Lesion Scores." *Journal of Animal Science* 87(5):1821–7.

Seddon, Y.M., and J.A. Brown. 2014. "Quantifying the Prevalence of Lameness and Hoof Lesions in Canadian Nucleus Herds." Pp. 11–12 in *Prairie Swine Centre Annual Research Report 2013–14*.

Statistics Canada. 2012a. "2011 Census of Agriculture." 2011 Farm and Farm Operator Data. Catalogue 95-640-X. Ottawa.

———. 2012b. "Cattle Industry Review, January 1, 2011." Cattle Statistics. www.statcan.gc.ca/pub/23-012-x/2010002/part-partie1-eng.htm.

———. 2015. *Table 003-0100—Hogs Statistics, Number of Hogs on Farms at End of Semi-Annual Period, Semi-Annual (Head)*. CANSIM (database).

Stolba, A., and D.G.M. Wood-Gush. 1989. "The Behaviour of Pigs in a Semi-Natural Environment." *Animal Production* 48:419–25.

Street, Brandy R. 2012. "The Future of Confinement Housing for Egg-Laying Hens." *Farm Sense: BCSPCA Farm Animal Welfare News* (April):1–11.

Stull, C.L., and S.P. McDonough. 1994. "Multidisciplinary Approach to Evaluating Welfare of Veal Calves in Commercial Facilities." *Journal of Animal Science* 72(9):2518–24.

Tablante, N.L., I. Estevez, and E. Russek-Cohen. 2003. "Effects of Perches and Stocking Density on Tibial Dyschondroplasia and Bone Mineralization as Measured by Bone Ash in Broiler Chickens." *Journal of Applied Poultry Research* 12:53–9.

Van Doormaal, Brian, F. Miglior, G. Kistemaker, and Peter Brand. 2005. "Genetic Diversification of the Holstein Breed in Canada and Internationally." University of Guelph.

Weary, Dan, Jeffrey Rushen, and Shelley Crabtree. 2010. "Healthy Hooves." *The Milk Producer* (May):20.

Weeks C.A., T.D. Danbury, H.C. Davies, P. Hunt, and S.C. Kestin. 2000. "The Behaviour of Broiler Chickens and Its Modification by Lameness." *Applied Animal Behaviour Science* 67:111–25.

Welchmen, D.D., and G.N. Baust. 1987. "A Survey of Abomasal Ulceration in Veal Calves." *Veterinary Record* 121:586–90.

World Society for the Protection of Animals (WSPA). 2010. *Curb the Cruelty: Canada's Farm Animal Transport System in Need of Repair*. Toronto.

———. 2012. "Executive Summary." Pp. 14–26 in *What's on Your Plate? The Hidden Costs of Industrial Animal Agriculture in Canada*. Toronto.

12

The Food System in the Fisheries
Crisis and Alternatives

Aparna Sundar

Learning Objectives

Through this chapter, you can

1. Understand the nature of the food system in the fisheries, in Canada and globally
2. Understand the relationship of food security, sustainability, and equitable development in the fisheries
3. Understand the multiple dimensions of the crisis in the fisheries
4. Become aware of the main institutions and actors involved in fisheries governance
5. Become familiar with key frameworks and approaches addressing fisheries sustainability

Introduction

The 2014 *State of World Fisheries and Aquaculture* (*SOFIA*) Report of the United Nations Food and Agriculture Organization (FAO) notes: "Never before have people consumed so much fish or depended so greatly on the sector for their well-being" (FAO 2014: III). According to the report, world per capita apparent fish consumption increased from an average of 9.9 kilograms in the 1960s to 19.2 kilograms in 2012. In Canada and the United States, as in other wealthy countries, fish and seafood are popular as healthy protein alternatives to red meat, and as the source of important omega-3 acids, or as "brain food." They also continue to be the major source of animal protein for low-income populations across the global South. Although world fish production has been rising steadily since the 1960s to meet this demand, there has been a decline of crisis proportions in significant marine fishing

stocks and a levelling off of total catches since the early 1990s. A growing proportion of the fish and seafood consumed in North America comes from elsewhere (Greenberg 2014)—fish and seafood are among the most highly traded food commodities in the world, and this trade continues to grow despite declining stocks. The gap between the growing demand for fish and the decline of wild stocks is being met to some extent by the growth of **aquaculture**, which now supplies over 40 per cent of all fish and seafood and is the fastest-growing form of agriculture in the world. Aquaculture, however, raises a whole new set of problems related to food safety and environmental impact.

The issues affecting the food system in the fisheries are multi-dimensional, having to do with food supply and food security, and also with food safety, the North–South dimension of the food trade, the survival of livelihoods and communities, biodiversity, and ecosystem stability. Both because fish do not respect national boundaries and because of the highly globalized trade in fisheries products, local and national approaches to fisheries sustainability must necessarily have a global perspective. Even more fundamentally, the state of the fisheries forces us to confront larger questions about our relationship to nature as the source of our food and about how we might draw upon it more sustainably in the future.

This chapter seeks to provide an understanding of the food system in the fisheries and the multiple dimensions of the crisis affecting it. The first two sections describe the nature and extent of the declining fisheries, along with an overview of the fisheries food chain. The third section traces the history of the current crisis, and the fourth discusses various solutions to it. The final section before the conclusion focuses on the growing importance of aquaculture as one solution.

Defining the Crisis

The growth rate of global marine fish catches, after rising rapidly through the 1960s and 1970s, began to slow in the 1980s, reaching its peak at the end of that decade. In Canada, this decline came dramatically to national attention when the Atlantic cod was declared "commercially extinct" by the end of the 1980s, and the East Coast cod fishery was closed in 1992.

Fisheries scientists work with the concept of **maximum sustainable yield (MSY)** to determine the size of the catch of a particular species of fish in any one year that will not impair its ability to reproduce itself and generate the same level of catch in subsequent years. If fishing has exceeded this level, the stock is deemed to have exceeded its MSY, and is declared overfished or over-exploited. When the drop in catches is so significant that the catch is unlikely to recover to financially viable levels in the foreseeable future, the species is declared "commercially extinct," a point reached well before that of biological extinction.

The 2014 *SOFIA* report states that the proportion of assessed marine fish stocks fished within biologically sustainable limits declined from 90 per cent in 1974 to 71.2 per cent in 2011. This means that 28.8 per cent of assessed stocks are overfished, or biologically unsustainable. A further 61.3 per cent are fully fished and therefore producing catches at or close to their MSY, with no room for further expansion. Only 9.9 per cent are under-exploited, meaning that catches have not yet reached the MSY levels established for those species and could perhaps produce more. Thus, overall, only about 10 per cent of global stocks still have room to provide increasing catches in coming years, while 90 per cent of the world fish stocks for which data are available are fully exploited or over-exploited. This is especially true for high-sea fish resources. The 2014 *SOFIA* report further notes that stocks of the 10 most productive species which account for 24 per cent of world marine capture fisheries production in 2011 are now fully fished or overfished. A 2006 study (Devine et al. 2006) classified five popular North Atlantic deep-sea species as biologically endangered, since these species grow and mature slowly and have been fished to the point where there are few juvenile fish left. The overfishing of the larger predator fish such as cod has complex impacts (Myers and Worm 2003). A phenomenon called **fishing down the marine food web** has been noted: as larger fish are depleted, a greater proportion of the catch consists of smaller fish of lower weight and density. Excessive fishing of these smaller fish in turn takes away the food source of the larger fish and prevents their regeneration, as well as threatening the food source of human populations who eat the smaller fish (Pauly et al. 1998). It also creates uncertainty about how different stocks will fare and points to the importance of biodiversity.

In addition to sustaining food supply, marine biodiversity is increasingly recognized as providing important **ecosystem services**, such as helping with waste detoxification and reducing floods. The Halifax-based authors of an important study conclude: "marine biodiversity loss is increasingly impairing the ocean's capacity to provide food, maintain water quality, and recover from perturbations" (Worm et al. 2006:787), although their data suggest that these trends are as yet reversible. As Alanna Mitchell found to her astonishment when talking to a marine biologist, "Life on land is utterly dependent on the life and chemistry in the ocean." Ocean plankton are "the real lungs of our planet," producing half the oxygen we breathe. "The ocean controls climate and temperature and the carbon and oxygen cycles of the planet, as well as other chemical systems that give all living creatures life—including us" (Mitchell 2009:12). Loss of ocean biodiversity due to overfishing might have graver consequences for us than we realize.

The social costs of the commercial or biological extinction of a species are complex and uneven. In Canada, when 30,000 fishermen in Newfoundland were thrown out of work upon the collapse of the cod fishery in the 1990s, the Department of Fisheries and Oceans (DFO) encouraged a shift to harvesting shellfish such as lobsters and crab, and later, Northern shrimp. Shellfish fetch a high price and now compensate to a large extent for the decline of groundfish such as cod in national production figures (DFO 2008). In this case, the crisis affected those dependent on the cod fishery for their livelihood more than it affected the Canadian economy as a whole. Canadian consumers are also sheltered from the effects of the crisis by the almost immediate availability of new species in the market when a popular species becomes rare (Jacquet and Pauly 2007, 2008), by their ability to buy food produced in all parts of the world, and by the increasing supply from aquaculture. For instance, the disappearing Atlantic cod was replaced in North American markets by Alaskan pollock, and then by farmed African tilapia and Vietnamese tra to provide the firm white flesh for fish sticks and battered fried fish that consumers were used to (Srinivasan, Watson, and Sumaila 2012:548). Thus, the social effects of the fisheries crisis are felt unevenly across regions and nations and can be understood only by paying attention to the various points of the fisheries food chain.

The Fisheries Food Chain

This section paints a broad-brush picture of production, trade, and consumption patterns in the fisheries. Table 12.1 provides an overview of production and employment in the different sectors of Canada's fisheries.

The proportion of marine versus inland catch in Canada is similar to the global pattern, where 87 per cent of all fish captured is from the seas and only 13 per cent from inland waters (FAO 2014). Discussions on the fisheries crisis tend to focus on the marine fisheries because of their overwhelming dominance and because available figures suggest that inland overfishing has generally not been a problem. We must nevertheless remember that inland water bodies are also complex ecosystems and susceptible to a range of pressures, including land reclamation and pollution.

In 2012, an estimated 58.3 million people were directly engaged in primary production of fish, either in capture from the wild or in aquaculture; 84 per cent of this number were in Asia. Fisheries and aquaculture now account for 4.4 per cent of the 1.3 billion people active in the agriculture sector, from 2.7 per cent in 1990. Counting employment in the secondary sector—processing, marketing, and service industries—and the households of those employed in the sector, it is estimated that some 10 to 12 per cent of the world population is economically dependent upon the fisheries and aquaculture sector (FAO 2014:6).

In Canada, the industry's economic contribution, including employment, is relatively more important at the regional and community levels than at the national: 75 per cent of all those employed in fish harvesting, processing, and aquaculture in 2013 were in Atlantic Canada (DFO 2014: "Employment"). Three-quarters of the country's total exports of fish and fish products originate from the Atlantic region, where the seafood sector is the second-largest exporting

Table 12.1 Employment, Landings, and Production Values for the Commercial Fisheries, Aquaculture, and Processing in Canada, 2013

Industry	Volume of Landings and Production (metric tonnes)	Gross Production Value ($ millions)	Employment
Marine fisheries	838,482	2,252	45,904 (including freshwater)
Freshwater fisheries	28,329	61	
Aquaculture	172,097	963	2,980
Seafood product preparation and packaging	Not available	4,557*	33,034*
Total	1,038,908	7,833	81,918

*2012 figures.
Source: Adapted from DFO (2014).

industry in terms of value, after refined petroleum products (DFO 2004).

Most fishers and fish farmers around the world are small-scale fishers. In 2012, about 79 per cent of the world's motorized fishing vessels were less than 12 metres long overall (FAO 2014:33). In Canada too, 92 per cent of fishing vessels are inshore vessels less than 45 feet (13.7 metres) long that each have two to three crew members including the skipper. However, larger vessels that operate further out in the ocean capture a far greater proportion of the catch by value because of the types of gear they use and their ability to traverse greater distances; large vessels made up only 8 per cent of all vessels but took 43 per cent of all catch in Canada in 2006 (DFO 2008:7). This is an important statistic to keep in mind in our subsequent discussion about how to achieve a sustainable fishery.

Fish and seafood are among the most-traded food commodities, with 37 per cent of all production entering international trade (FAO 2014:7). The highly globalized nature of the fish trade can be seen at the Tsukiji market in Tokyo, the world's largest wholesale seafood market, where almost $6 billion worth of fish changes hands every year. Here tuna from Massachusetts is sold beside octopus from Senegal, eel from Guangzhou in China, crab from the Russian island of Sakhalin, salmon from British Columbia and the Japanese island of Hokkaido, and abalone from California

(Bestor 2004; Grescoe 2008). Bestor (2000) provides a fascinating account of the trading process for bluefin tuna, a fish that on average weighs 500 pounds, and which in the late 1990s sold at over $35 wholesale per edible pound. He describes how, in a fishing village in Maine, 20 tuna buyers, half of them Japanese, inspect three bluefin tuna caught by local fishers. The buyers check the tuna, call Japan by cellphone to get the morning prices from the Tsukiji market, then place their bids on the fish. Once the deals are made, the fish are loaded onto trucks in crates of crushed ice, driven to New York's John F. Kennedy airport, and air-freighted to Tokyo. The prepared sushi using these fish may then be shipped back to restaurants in New York or elsewhere.

It is not only high-value fish like bluefin tuna that are globally traded. Small, low-value fish such as anchovy, which is used for fishmeal in aquaculture, animal feed, and pet food, are also highly traded items. The high volume of trade in fish raises two kinds of concerns: traceability and food security.

The concern over traceability arises because globalization in the fish trade occurs not only at the point of sale but also further back in the production chain. Fish caught in one place might be processed in a quite distant place: a significant amount of Canadian imports come directly to the processing plants, where they are processed, packaged, and re-exported. In such cases, the label might be quite confusing. For example, cans of "wild Alaska salmon" found in US supermarkets have been found to be labelled "product of Thailand" (Jacquet and Pauly 2008:310). The labelling of fish by their country of processing rather than of capture may disguise the fact that they were caught in a declining fishery. In other cases, fish that are on "red lists" (lists of endangered fish species) may be served up under another name, or an unfamiliar and lower-value species may be deliberately mislabelled as a popular, higher-value fish. For instance, American restaurant-goers continued to be served fish passed off as grouper long after the fish itself disappeared from American waters, leaving them oblivious to the fact that overfishing had destroyed grouper stocks (Jacquet and Pauly 2007, 2008). Mislabelling and the lack of traceability reduce consumers' ability to make choices around food safety and sustainability.

Turning to food security, the role of fish and seafood, especially as a source of animal protein and other important micronutrients, varies by region based on location, availability, and traditional patterns of food consumption. The largest import markets for fish and seafood are the European Union, Japan, the United States, and China, while the largest exporters are China, Norway, Thailand, and Vietnam. Canada imports far less fish than it exports, ranking as the world's seventh-largest fish and seafood exporter (FAO 2014:50). (In 1990, Canada was the second-largest seafood exporter in the world, behind the United States, but the collapse of the groundfish catches in Canada, combined with increased aquaculture production in China and elsewhere, has led to a drop in Canada's rank.) Even though fish is an important source of animal protein for low-income food-deficient countries (LIFDCs), these countries are net exporters of fish. Because they are not highly industrialized, they rely heavily on agricultural exports for their foreign exchange earnings, and fisheries products are now the single most valuable agricultural commodity exported by developing countries, as demonstrated in figure 12.1

(FAO 2014:50). In an analysis of the distribution of ecological impacts from human activities, Srinivasan et al. show that middle- and high-income countries consumed 85 per cent of the products fished in their waters, whereas low-income countries retained only 15 per cent. Furthermore, fishing in the high seas was almost entirely done by middle- and high-income countries, who captured 32 per cent and 68 per cent respectively (Srinivasan et al. 2008:1771).

Some 14 per cent of fish production is directed to non-food uses, down from 29 per cent in the 1980s (FAO 2014:42). Fish such as sardine, anchovy, mackerel, and other small pelagic fish (those that live at the ocean's surface) are fit for human consumption and are relatively cheap in LIFDCs, but are often converted to fishmeal because of the global demand for fishmeal for animal feed, including in aquaculture, for fish oil, and other non-food uses. While the decline in conversion to non-food uses is to be welcomed, the increasing use of fish residues and other substitutes in fishmeal and fish oil can have potential health impacts as they work their way up the aquaculture food chain (FAO 2014:44).

The Origins of the Crisis

There is historical evidence of excessive fishing leading to the decline and even extinction of fish species, such as in the Wadden Sea off northwest Europe between the fifth and the fifteenth centuries (Mitchell 2009:125). But there is no historical parallel to the speed and scale of the decline witnessed over the last century. The factors leading to the falling catch figures and virtual extinction of some species are a complex interplay of modern production technologies, growing demand, and inadequate governance structures, all based on the dangerous assumption that marine resources are virtually inexhaustible.

European fishers and sailors coming to Newfoundland in the 1600s wrote of seas so thick with cod that the fish could be scooped up in baskets (Kurlansky 1997:49). The Aboriginal fisheries that sustained numerous communities

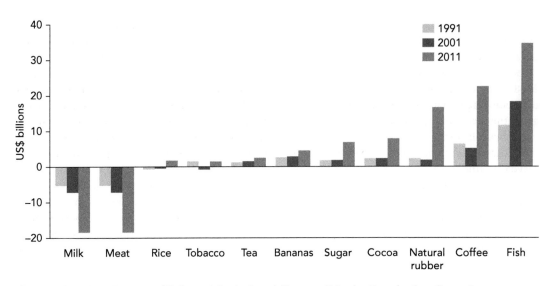

Figure 12.1 Net Exports of Selected Agricultural Commodities by Developing Countries

Source: FAO 2014. *State of World Fisheries and Aquaculture* 2014. Rome: FAO.: 50. Reproduced with permission.

across what is now Canada were for the most part freshwater fisheries, fishing salmon in rivers such as the Fraser River in British Columbia (Claxton 2008:52). Mark Kurlansky (1997) documents the role of the cod fishery in the development of an increasingly international pattern of settlement, colonization, and trade. The arrival of the Spanish, the French, and especially the English, led to the establishment of seasonal settlements in what is now Newfoundland and permanent settlements in the more temperate climate of New England. Here, cod was caught and dried by European fishing expeditions and supplied initially to Europe and later also to feed England's colonies in the Caribbean.

The expansion of markets and the increased profitability of the fishery led to two new developments in the Industrial and Scientific Revolution of the nineteenth century. One was the technological development of craft and gear, and the other was the establishment of fisheries science. The need to better predict the returns for capital invested in the fisheries put pressure on governments to focus scientific efforts on the study of fish patterns. This requirement became urgent by the middle of the 1800s, as catches began to

fluctuate dramatically and fishers reported the disappearance of cod from inshore waters and the need to go farther offshore. Techniques based on human demography and statistics were used to establish the dynamics of particular fish species (Bavington 2010:18–35).

The use of steam to power fishing craft by the late 1800s in Europe, the development of freezing technology, and the invention of the bottom trawling net all served to revolutionize fishing (Kurlansky 1997:112–25). The combination of more "efficient" craft (able to travel longer distances in less time and with less human effort) and more "efficient" gear such as the trawl net (able to scoop up larger quantities of fish in less time and with less human effort) marked a qualitative and quantitative shift in the nature of fishing in the early decades of the twentieth century, from a reliance on "passive" technologies that had to wait for the fish, to more "active" ones by which fish could be chased and scooped up aggressively.

The greatest expansion in fishing took place after the Second World War, when the fisheries became harnessed to the goal of national economic development, both in postwar Europe, North America, and Japan, and in the newly independent nations of Asia, Africa, and the Caribbean. In these latter parts of the world, fishing had been carried on for centuries by craft with limited propulsion power, using wind and human effort. Under the modernization approach that shaped most post-colonial development plans, efforts were made to introduce mechanized, fuel-dependent propulsion craft and fishing gear like trawlers and purse seiners (Kurien 1985).

In the decades following the Second World War the industrial fishery expanded and became firmly established in the temperate regions. During the war, the three innovations—powerful ships, onboard freezing facilities, and massive dragging nets—had come together in the huge factory ship. Today's factory ship may be 450 feet (140 metres) or longer, powered by twin diesel engines of more than 6,000 horsepower, pulling a trawl net with an opening large enough to swallow a jumbo jet. The trawl net is hauled up every four hours, 24 hours a day. "Tickler chains" hang from the net to stir up the bottom, making noise and clouding the water, thus forcing the groundfish such as cod that hide at the bottom of the ocean to flee into the net. The net catches everything in its way, and leaves behind a desert on the ocean floor (Kurlansky 1997:139–40). Modern devices such as global positioning systems and echo-sounders further enable ships to chase and locate fish more efficiently.

The postwar expansion took place along three dimensions—geographical, to more coastlines and continental shelves; *bathymetric*, to greater depths, especially in the high seas, due to new technologies like trawlers and long lines; and *taxonomic*, to include all kinds of new species, several of which were earlier rejected for food purposes (Pauly 2009:216). Pauly notes that at this time the fishery appeared to behave like any other sector of the economy, with increased inputs leading to increased outputs. Catch figures grew exponentially around the world. In Atlantic Canada, annual cod catches that had fluctuated from less than 100,000 tonnes to a maximum of 300,000 tonnes up to the 1940s expanded to

a historical high referred to as the "killer spike" in 1968, when over 800,000 tonnes of cod were landed (Bavington 2010:17).

The emphasis on the fisheries as a source of national revenue led to another development. The freedom of the seas (*mare liberum*), a key principle of the international law that had evolved in Europe since the seventeenth century, had allowed ships belonging to European and other fishing nations like Japan to fish unchallenged in seas distant from their own coasts. With fish and mineral resources under the sea becoming important national assets, more and more nations declared sovereignty over their territorial seas. This became codified in the **UN Convention on the Law of the Sea** (UNCLOS) of 1982, under which each nation-state had sovereignty over an **exclusive economic zone** (EEZ) extending 200 miles from its coast. The EEZ boundaries enclosed some 90 per cent of the world's fishing grounds, and coastal states were given the responsibility for their conservation (Allison 2001:937–9). But, as Seckinelgin (2006:15) notes, the fact that "throughout the convention, marine living resources are recognized as an agent of development," and that the "ecological life of the resources is subsumed under the *raison d'etat* in relation to 'development,'" meant that maximizing the exploitation of fisheries resources, rather than conservation, became the primary goal of states.

With the declaration of EEZs, countries acted swiftly to evict foreign fishing vessels from their territorial waters, as Canada did with the French and Spanish fleets fishing in the Grand Banks off Newfoundland. Canada then encouraged domestic investment to enable exploitation of the resources, because the UNCLOS dictated that fish within an EEZ should be harvested at their maximum sustainable yield. Any country unable to do so should allow other states access to their waters (Bavington 2010:32).

This requirement to harvest fish at their MSY within an EEZ also set in motion a North–South dynamic peculiar to the fisheries. Most newly independent states in the South lacked both the fishing capacity to harvest their own resources fully and the data collection and surveillance capacity to keep poachers out of the vast 200 mile EEZ. Many of them therefore signed Fisheries Access Agreements with countries of the North, such as that between the African–Caribbean–Pacific (ACP) Group of States and the European Union, inviting the EU's distant-water fleets to continue to operate in ACP waters in exchange for a fee. These agreements enable industrialized countries to use their advantages in technology and finance to keep their access to developing countries' fisheries (Kaczynski and Fluharty 2002).

The UNCLOS failed at conservation in part because it attempted to manage ecological zones through the creation of political boundaries, whereas living resources have their own spatial extents and logics that do not always follow national EEZ boundaries (Seckinelgin 2006). This can be seen in the challenge of managing deep-sea species that straddle EEZs or are highly migratory, such as the world's highest-value fish, the bluefin tuna: the Atlantic bluefin tuna ranges from the equator to Newfoundland, from Turkey to the Gulf of Mexico (Bestor 2000); a single Pacific tuna was tracked crossing the Pacific Ocean three times, covering a distance of 25,000 miles (40,000 kilometres) (Grescoe 2008). The International Commission for the Conservation of Atlantic Tunas, which has representation from all states that fish in the Atlantic or trade in its fish, has failed miserably to manage the tuna sustainably. This failure is due to the low deterrence cost of violating quotas compared to the potential profit from this highly valuable species.

The difficulties of international coordination can also be seen in the problem of **illegal, unregulated, and unreported** (IUU) fishing, especially in the high seas. Catch may be landed on shores of countries where regulation is minimal or processed offshore on factory ships. Where there is a fixed quota of a species, by-catch of lower-value fish other than the target species may be dumped at sea. Part of the recent growth in IUU fishing is due to large factory

ships subsidized by rich states but unable to find enough fish in their own waters (Jacquet and Pauly 2007:310; Pauly 2009).

Factors other than overfishing also contribute to the depletion of marine life. These include chemical and organic pollution and the destruction of habitats, such as mangroves and other coastal wetlands, for agriculture, aquaculture, urbanization, and industrialization. The effects of climate change are also beginning to be seen in the heating of the ocean, rising acidity levels, and falling metabolism rates of marine life. While destruction of habitat has been the major factor for the decline of freshwater species (Hutchings 2013:497), for marine species there is compelling evidence that the advent of industrial fishing and the intensification of fishing around the world have been the largest factors in the declining catches beginning in the early 1990s (Ward and Myers 2005). Since that time, efforts have been underway to arrest this decline and address the growing crisis in the marine fisheries. The next section will review some of these efforts and their effectiveness.

Solutions to the Crisis: Dilemmas of Scale, Authority, and Knowledge

The above sections indicate the complexities of fisheries governance, given the mobile and interdependent nature of the resource and the variety of scales—international, national, and local—at which there has to be coordination. The challenge is not simply to sustain the fish stocks and the marine ecosystem, but to do so in a way that continues to provide a healthy source of protein for millions and employment to large numbers of relatively low-income people around the world.

Part of the complexity of governance also arises from the fact that different actors involved in the fisheries bring very different, often conflicting, perspectives regarding the causes of declining catches and how best the goals of providing food and jobs might be met. The fisheries are studied by ecologists, marine biologists, economists, fisheries scientists (who combine biological knowledge and statistical skills), and social scientists such as anthropologists and geographers. Fishers and the community organizers who work with them are also important sources of knowledge. The chief debates occur around two related questions: Where should the locus of governance lie—in the state and its experts, the market and consumers, or producers and their communities? What knowledge is needed for effective governance?

The traditional approach to fisheries governance, especially in advanced industrial countries like Canada, placed it in the hands of the government. Government ministries like Fisheries and Oceans Canada (DFO) employ fisheries scientists to work out the MSY and **total allowable catch (TAC)** for particular species, monitor the catch, and set other regulations such as closed seasons. The TAC is then divided up between individual fishers in the form of an individual quota (IQ): the right to catch a certain quantity of each species each year within a given area. Since the 1980s, these quotas have been designated as assets that can be bought, sold, or transferred. Management through quota systems is the dominant mode in the Atlantic and Pacific fisheries in Canada, where quotas are sold for all the major fisheries, such as cod, salmon, and snow crab (Bavington 2010; DFO 2008).

Individual quotas are a form of private property rights in the fishery, created in response to an influential argument made by economists that overfishing occurs because of the absence of those rights in the fishery, or what they call the "tragedy of the commons" (Hardin 1968). As Bavington (2010) argues, however, the Atlantic cod fishery was managed according to these measures—it was not an unmanaged or open fishery—and yet it collapsed, in part because there is nothing in the logic of IQs to prevent overfishing. Quota owners may find it makes more economic sense during a bumper harvest to exceed the quota and pay the fine. The species-specific approach means that there is no way of measuring the harm done

to non-target species (by-catch) which are often dumped in order to meet the quota of the target species (Copes 1999). There is some recent evidence, however, that countries like Norway, Iceland, the United States, Canada, Australia, and New Zealand have implemented sustainable fishery management practices using quotas and fleet-reduction programs which may have stabilized or even reversed their losses due to overfishing, though in some cases the reduction of fishing pressure has been achieved by increasing imports (Srinivasan, Watson, and Sumaila 2012:548).

The difficulties of state-controlled fisheries management, coupled with the rise of neo-liberal policies that entail a reduced role for the state in the economy, have led to three parallel shifts since the late 1980s: adoption of international codes and conventions, increased influence of consumers and the marketplace, and increased influence of fishing communities and organizations.

International Codes and Conventions

States are the signatories to international codes and conventions, but the more recent ones all recognize the important role of non-state actors in the fisheries. These include chapter 17 of Agenda 21, the plan of action adopted at the first UN Conference on Environment and Development (UNCED) held in Rio de Janeiro in 1992, the **FAO Code of Conduct for Responsible Fisheries** of 1995, the 2001 UN **Fish Stocks Agreement on Straddling Stocks and Highly Migratory Fish Stocks**, and the 2003 Cartagena Protocol on Biosafety. These, along with the UNCLOS and many bilateral and multilateral regional fisheries agreements, constitute the normative framework for the management of marine resources.

These international agreements have led to the establishment of **Regional Fisheries Management Organizations (RFMOs)** such as the International Commission for the Conservation of Atlantic Tunas, mentioned earlier in the chapter, and are especially important in trying to address problems related to straddling and highly migratory stocks and to IUU fishing. But they are non-binding for the most part and, like all international treaties and agreements, very hard to enforce. Nevertheless, these agreements—the FAO Code of Conduct in particular—are significant in enshrining two important principles that have become the reference point for sustainable fisheries: the **precautionary principle**, which states that "the absence of adequate scientific information should not be used as a reason for postponing or failing to take conservation and management measures"(Article 7.5); and the **ecosystem approach**, which moves away from modelling individual stocks to recognizing the interdependence of marine flora and fauna and their sensitivity to many influences from destructive fishing gear to land-based pollution.

Consumers and the Marketplace

The second shift is seen in consumers' greater role in regulating fishing practices through the mechanism of the market, a perhaps logical shift given that fish and seafood are now the most-traded food commodities in the world, and that over a third of production in this sector enters international trade. Campaigns around overfishing, led by NGOs like Greenpeace, combined with growing consumer concern about the health effects and sustainability of fishing and aquaculture, have led to consumer-driven sustainability campaigns. In Europe, after Greenpeace launched its sustainable seafood campaign ranking supermarkets on the basis of their seafood sourcing policies, many of the largest supermarkets adopted seafood procurement policies which make sustainability a key criterion in their sourcing (Greenpeace 2008:31). A similar campaign in Canada saw supermarkets responding positively, although a Greenpeace report three years into the campaign suggested that only three of the eight major supermarkets received a grade of over 50 per cent on their sustainable sourcing efforts (Greenpeace 2011).

Consumer consciousness has led to the emergence of an increasingly popular form of labelling: **certification** or **eco-labelling**. This form of marketing incentive promotes consumer demand for fish caught or raised in environmentally and/or socially sustainable ways, and rewards producers for using responsible fisheries practices. The certifiers may be independent bodies such as the Marine Stewardship Council (MSC) or large supermarket chains such as Carrefour, a transnational chain based in France, which has its own *peche responsable* label (Sharma 2009).

However, market-based certification is no guarantee of reliable information for consumers or of sustainability. Certification bodies and schemes proliferate with no unanimity of criteria among them; some take into account only environmental sustainability, while others include food safety and social criteria such as labour standards (FAO 2009:96). The use of a quota system is often taken as evidence of sustainable management by certifying bodies; most fisheries certified as sustainable are industrial fisheries under quota management, rather than small-scale, community-based fisheries (Mathew 2011). Importantly, as Jacquet and Pauly (2007) note, in an era of increasing awareness that fisheries management must be ecosystem based, the species-specific approach of seafood campaigns and certification programs may represent a step backward.

Fishing Communities and Organizations

The third shift is toward a greater role for fishing communities and organizations in managing the fisheries. Organizations such as the Maritime Fishermen's Union in New Brunswick and Nova Scotia, the Canadian Council of Professional Fish Harvesters, the International Collective in Support of Fishworkers, and the World Forum of Fisher Peoples firmly assert a role for small-scale, community-based producers in fisheries production and governance. They argue that their reliance on smaller vessels that are less dependent on fossil fuels; their labour-intensive techniques that generate greater employment; their interest in the long-term survival of the fisheries, and their holistic, inherited, and experiential knowledge of the ecosystem allow for a more sustainable and equitable development of the fisheries than the destructive and overly efficient fishing techniques and the concentration of profits that characterize the industrial sector (Pauly 2007).

Small-scale fishers challenge the knowledge and approach underlying scientific fisheries management. The first element of this approach is the economists' assumption that the absence of private property rights is the chief cause of overfishing. The fishers' argument, backed by anthropological studies, is that much of the inshore fishery was historically governed by various community-based **common property resource** management regimes that regulated access and extraction (McCay and Acheson 1990), many of which were delegitimized as a direct outcome of the state's harnessing of fisheries management to national economic development after the Second World War (Allison 2001:938).

Fishers have also criticized the assumption, expressed in measures such as the MSY, TAC, and IQS, that increasingly sophisticated modelling and forecasting tools enable scientific prediction and control of the fishery. The failure of scientists to explain the recent disappearance and reappearance of the Fraser River salmon (Hume 2010; Hunter 2010) seems to back this critique. Fishers have argued instead for an ecosystem approach and an increased role for their own experiential knowledge in dialogue with the "expert" knowledge of scientists (Mathew 2010). Fishing people have historically held the sea in respect, seeing it as a powerful entity that must be propitiated and cared for in order for it to provide. The Aboriginal approach to the fishery (Claxton 2008; Metallic 2008) exemplifies this deep respect and sense of relationship. In Claxton's words:

> The W̱SÁNEĆ people successfully governed their traditional fishery for thousands of years, prior to contact. This was not just because there were laws and rules in place, and that everybody followed them, but there was

also a different way of thinking about fish and fishing, which included a profound respect. At the end of the net, a ring of willow was woven into the net, which allowed some salmon to escape. This is more than a simple act of conservation. . . . It represents a profound respect for salmon. It was believed that the runs of salmon were lineages, and if some were allowed to return to their home rivers, then those lineages would always continue. . . . The salmon are our relatives. (2008:54)

Collaboration and Conflict

In principle, and frequently in practice, states, multilateral institutions, private sector actors, and producer organizations work together in fisheries governance, with the FAO Code of Conduct and other international agreements providing the framework within which they work. The sustained advocacy by small-scale producers can be seen in sections of the Code, which recognizes their important contributions to employment and income and food security, and includes sections on the precautionary principle, the ecosystem approach to management, the mandatory use of selective fishing gear, and the traditional knowledge of fishers. The importance of the **small-scale fisheries** (SSF) in equitable and sustainable development and the need for special policies and strategies to strengthen it has been explicitly recognized by the FAO through the development of the Voluntary Guidelines for Securing Sustainable Small-Scale Fisheries in the Context of Food Security and Poverty Eradication (SSF Guidelines). Small-scale producers have also spearheaded attempts to evolve a form of collaborative or **co-management** between the state and fishing communities (World Bank 2004:37); sought to intervene in market-based management, proposing certification schemes in which the advantages of the small-scale sector, such as the use of less destructive gear, unique processing techniques, and sails (i.e. using wind power rather than fossil fuels), are given credit (Vandergeest 2007; Sharma 2009); and initiated experiments in **community-supported fishery** whereby producers directly supply consumers who wish to support sustainable fishing practices (Brown 2012).

Some states like the Scandinavian ones have chosen not to accept MSC certification and have created their own standards; others like Canada work closely with the MSC to get various fisheries certified as sustainable. Paul Foley shows how, in the process of certification of the Northern shrimp fisheries off Newfoundland and Labrador, the MSC worked closely with the state, drawing heavily on government agencies for data and self-evaluations, as well as on experts within government departments. While independent certification bodies like the MSC use the Code as the basis of their evaluation, states that have signed on to the Code may not always uphold it, as Canada's Fisheries Act of 2012 shows. The new Act removes protection for species that are not part of a commercial, recreational, or Aboriginal fishery, and habitat protection for fish more generally. In doing so, it undermines the ecosystem principle that calls for the protection not of individual species but of an entire ecosystem which may include commercially unimportant species and their habitat (Hutchings 2013). Critics have also argued that this Act, along with the use of private certifiers like the MSC; the 33 per cent reduction of DFO staff responsible for habitat protection (Hutchings 2013:499); and the closure of 7 of 11 of the DFO's fisheries libraries (Galloway 2014) are evidence of the state abdicating its responsibility for managing and protecting the fisheries and environment in the rush for economic development.

Is Aquaculture a Solution?

Aquaculture is a broad term that refers to a range of practices including the centuries-old carp farming in small ponds across China, the conversion of rice fields into shrimp farms across south and southeast Asia, the highly controlled marine salmon farms in Canada, and the marine pens in the Mediterranean where juvenile bluefin tuna captured in the wild are held and fattened for export to the Japanese market.

The FAO 2014 report notes that the supply from aquaculture more than compensates for the stagnation of capture fisheries and the growth of human population. Aquaculture now accounts for 42 per cent of all fish and seafood production for food, up from 13.4 per cent in 1990 and 25.7 per cent in 2000. It is set to overtake capture fisheries as a source of food fish, propelled by increased investment and further decreases in the stocks of wild fish. Asia already produces more from aquaculture than from capture fisheries; 54 per cent of all aquaculture production in 2012 came from Asia (FAO 2014:19–20). Globally, the number of people engaged in capture fisheries has declined while the number in aquaculture has gone up, from 17 per cent of all those engaged in the sector in 1990 to 32 per cent in 2012 (FAO 2014:27).

In Canada, aquaculture is a relatively new commercial activity, but by 2013 it already made up approximately 29 per cent of all Canadian fish and seafood production, with production going up from 10,000 tonnes in 1986 to 963,000 tonnes in 2013 (DFO 2014). The leading farmed marine species are Atlantic salmon, blue mussel, chinook salmon, Pacific oyster, and American oyster. Inland species like trout are also farmed (DFO 2008).

Some forms of aquaculture, especially that described as **intensive aquaculture**, where fish and shrimp are raised in industrial conditions, have proven to have several harmful effects. The high price fetched by shrimp in global markets has spurred the conversion of rice fields into shrimp farms across coastal south and southeast Asia, with obvious implications for the supply of rice (Flaherty et al. 1999). There, and in other places such as Ecuador, fragile coastal ecosystems such as mangroves and estuaries have been destroyed when converted to shrimp farms (Stonich et al. 1997). Problems with salination of inland areas and pollution by antibiotics and other organic pollutants have been noted in several parts of the world, including salmon farms in British Columbia and Atlantic Canada. There are also concerns around escaped farmed fish carrying sea lice and diseases into the wild (Young and Mathews 2010). Finally, the raising of carnivorous fish like salmon and tuna have created a phenomenon parallel to "fishing down the food web"—which has been labelled "farming up the food web" (Pauly 2009:219)—the use of captured smaller, lower-value fish to feed and fatten higher-value predator fish. Given that the smaller fish are often exported from LIFDCs where they would otherwise have been eaten, the net impact of this kind of aquaculture on global food security seems to be negative. But there are also examples of organic marine salmon farms that pay far greater care to ecosystem impacts (Halweil 2008).

There are fewer concerns with the **extensive aquaculture** that takes place in inland water bodies such as lakes, rivers, and ponds. The fish raised in these farms are largely herbivorous and tend to be less vulnerable to disease, thus requiring fewer antibiotics and chemicals. The bulk of the aquaculture carried out in China is of this kind, as is the trout farming in Canada's lakes.

For many, the shift to the culture rather than the capture of fish is the natural and long-overdue last step in our evolution from hunters and gatherers to settled agriculturalists. This progression is valid to the extent that it helps take pressure off marine stocks and gives them a chance to regenerate. However, our existing levels of urbanization and industrialization leave too little land for the amount of aquaculture necessary to substitute for the entire marine capture fisheries. Nor are there obvious solutions to the pollution, salination, and disease associated with intensive aquaculture. Further, a sustainable capture fishery remains vital for the employment and food security of millions of producers. An organic, ecologically friendly extensive system of farming small herbivorous fish in existing inland water bodies (an approach that Grescoe [2008] labels "bottomfeeding"), is probably the best option, but we must also reconcile ourselves to eating far smaller quantities.

Conclusion

As long as demand for fish and seafood remains high in world markets, production will continue to attempt to cater to it. Developing countries in particular are likely to direct more and more of their fish production to export in search of foreign exchange. Fishing access agreements and the reflagging of fishing vessels under the national flag of developing countries owning large fisheries resources are the equivalent of the purchase or lease of land in Latin America and Africa by agro-industrial corporations to supply food to wealthier countries. Unless serious attempts are made at generating alternative sources of employment and national income, the risk is that the fisheries resources of developing nations will remain under high pressure from international markets and the contribution of fish to local food security may decrease. Globally, as noted in the FAO's 2014 *SOFIA* report, the growth in the proportion of over-exploited or depleted fisheries is a matter of urgent concern. On the other hand, there is new evidence that management measures may have worked in some areas (Worm et al. 2009; FAO 2010:42; Srinivasan, Watson, and Sumaila 2012), and the rate of decline has been arrested.

It is possible that with increased consumer awareness of the need to limit demand, states' commitment to stop subsidizing large factory fleets and to regulate destructive technology more stringently, the shift to a governance approach that gives a leading role to small-scale fishers and to a perspective that respects the force and cunning of nature, and the judicious combination of capture fishery with extensive inland aquaculture of herbivorous species, we may yet be able to avert the crisis before it is too late.

This chapter has provided a picture of the crisis in the fisheries, arguing that it can be fully understood only in a global context. The crisis is multi-dimensional and affects not only food security but also ecological sustainability and social justice. While multiple factors have led to the crisis, central among them are the burgeoning demand for fish as both luxury food and fishmeal and the dominance of an industrial fishery using highly destructive craft and gear. The chapter explored diverse approaches to governing the fisheries and managing the crisis, and argued that an approach that gives priority in production and management to small-scale community-based fishers is most likely to achieve the related goals of food security, environmental sustainability, and equitable development. It concluded with a section on aquaculture, noting that while an extensive inland aquaculture of small, herbivorous fish could help compensate for the decline of the capture fisheries, it should not, for ecological and social reasons, be expected to replace it entirely.

Discussion Questions

1. What does "crisis in the fisheries" refer to?

2. What factors led to the decline of the cod fishery in Atlantic Canada?

3. To what extent can aquaculture replace capture fisheries?

4. What are the implications for food security of the high volume of trade in fish and seafood?

5. What are the most promising solutions to the crisis in the fisheries?

Further Reading

1. Bavington, Dean. 2010. *Managed Annihilation: An Unnatural History of the Newfoundland Cod Collapse.* Vancouver: UBC Press.
   An academic, but very accessible, study of fisheries policy and scientific management that makes a passionate argument for a less managerial approach to fishing and to nature.

2. FAO. The State of World Fisheries and Aquaculture. http://www.fao.org/fishery/sofia/en.
   A report which is released every two years, giving statistics and reports on trends and current issues.

3. Fisheries and Oceans Canada website. http://www.dfo-mpo.gc.ca/.
   Statistics and occasional reports on trends and current issues.

4. Grescoe, Taras. 2008. *Bottomfeeder: How to Eat Ethically in a World of Vanishing Seafood.* New York: Bloomsbury.
   Helps us think practically through a question that many of us are concerned with.

5. Halweil, Brian. 2008. "Farming Fish for the Future." *Worldwatch Report* 176. Washington, DC: Worldwatch Institute.
   Examines whether aquaculture is a sustainable and healthy alternative.

6. International Collective in Support of Fishworkers website and *Samudra Report.* http://icsf.net/.
   A gold mine for documents and resources on the fisheries worldwide.

7. Kurlansky, Mark. 1997. *Cod: A Biography of the Fish That Changed the World.* New York: Walker and Company.
   A highly readable, non-academic account of the rise and fall of the North Atlantic cod fishery.

8. Pauly, Daniel. 2009. "Beyond Duplicity and Ignorance in Global Fisheries." *Scientia Marina* 73(2):215–24.
   A short and excellent overview of the complex web of technology, markets, and management regimes that have contributed to the global crisis in the fisheries.

Video Suggestions

1. Hall, Mark. S. 2012. *Sushi: The Global Catch.* www
   .sushitheglobalcatch.com/. 75 min.
   An eye-opening documentary detailing the implications of sushi's growing popularity among bet-
   ter-off consumers.

2. Murray, Rupert. 2009. *The End of the Line.*
   http://endoftheline.com/. 85 min.
   A hard-hitting documentary on the crisis of

overfishing based on the book of the same name
by Charles Clover, although it does not address
issues of food security in the global South.

3. Thomas, Michelle. 2005. *Where's the Catch?
   Pacific Fishing in Crisis.* www.films.com/ecTitle
   Detail.aspx?TitleID=12299&r=. 27 min.
   A short film that also documents local activist
   responses to the growing crisis.

References

Allison, E.H. 2001. "Big Laws, Small Catches: Global Ocean Governance and the Fisheries Crisis." *Journal of International Development* 13:933–50.

Bavington, Dean. 2010. Managed Annihilation: An Unnatural History of the Newfoundland Cod Collapse. Vancouver: UBC Press.

Bestor, Theodore C. 2000. "How Sushi Went Global." *Foreign Policy* 121 (November/ December).

———. 2004. *Tsukiji: The Fish Market at the Center of the World.* Berkeley: University of California Press.

Brown, Patricia Leigh. 2012. "For Local Fisheries, A Line of Hope." *New York Times*, 1 October. Accessed 29 June 2015. http://www.nytimes.com/2012/10/03/dining/a-growing -movement-for-community-supported-fisheries.html?_r=0.

Claxton, N. X. 2008. "ISTÁ SĆIÁNEW̱, ISTÁ S̲X̲OLE 'To Fish as Formerly': The Douglas Treaties and the WSÁNEĆ Reef-Net Fisheries." Pp. 47–58 in *Lighting the Eighth Fire: The Liberation, Resurgence and Protection of Indigenous Nations*, ed. Leanne Simpson. Winnipeg, MB: Arbeiter Ring.

Copes, Parzival. 1999. "Coastal Resources for Whom?" *Samudra*, September 1999.

Devine, J.D., K.D. Baker, and R.L. Haedrich. 2006. "Fisheries: Deep-Sea Fishes Qualify as Endangered." *Nature* 439 (5 January).

DFO. 2004. "2004 Costs and Earnings Survey, Atlantic Region." Accessed 10 October 2010. http://www .dfo-mpo.gc.ca/stats/commercial/ces/content-eng.htm# n10AtlanticFishingIndustryOverview

———. 2008. *Canadian Fisheries Statistics 2008.* Ottawa: Fisheries and Oceans Canada. Accessed 29 June 2015. http://www.dfo-mpo.gc.ca/stats/commercial/cfs/2008/ CFS2008_e.pdf.

———. 2014. *Canada's Fisheries: Fast Facts 2014.* Accessed 24 June 2015. http://www.dfo-mpo.gc.ca/stats/stats-eng.htm.

Flaherty, M., P. Vandergeest, and P. Miller. 1999. "Rice Paddy or Shrimp Pond: Tough Decisions in Rural Thailand." *World Development* 27:12.

FAO. 1995. Code of Conduct for Responsible Fisheries. Rome: FAO.

———. 2010. State of World Fisheries and Aquaculture 2010. Rome: FAO.

———. 2009. State of World Fisheries and Aquaculture 2008. Rome: FAO.

———. 2014. State of World Fisheries and Aquaculture 2014. Rome: FAO.

Foley, Paul. 2013. "National Government Responses to Marine Stewardship Council (MSC) Fisheries Certification: Insights from Atlantic Canada." New Political Economy 18(2):284–307.

Galloway, Gloria. 2014. "Purge of Canada's Fisheries Libraries a 'Historic' Loss, Scientists Say." *Globe and Mail*, 7 January. Accessed 29 June 2015. http://www. theglobeandmail.com/news/politics/purge-of-Canadas -fisheries-libraries-a-historic-loss-scientists-say/article 16237051/.

Greenberg, Paul. 2014. *American Catch: The Fight for Our Local Seafood.* New York: Penguin.

Greenpeace. 2008. *Out of Stock: Supermarkets and the Future of Seafood.* Greenpeace Canada. Accessed 25 June 2015. http://www.greenpeace.org/Canada/en/campaigns/ ocean/Seafood/Resources/Reports/out-of-stock/.

———. 2011. *Emerging from the Deep: Ranking Supermarkets on Seafood Sustainability.* Accessed 25 June 2015. http:// www.greenpeace.org/Canada/en/campaigns/ocean/ Seafood/Resources/Reports/Emerging-from-the-deep/.

Grescoe, Taras. 2008. *Bottomfeeder: How to Eat Ethically in a World of Vanishing Seafood.* New York: Bloomsbury.

Halweil, Brian. 2008. "Farming Fish for the Future." *Worldwatch Report* 176. Washington, DC: Worldwatch Institute.

Hardin, Gareth. 1968. "The Tragedy of the Commons." *Science* 162:1243–8.

Hume, Mark. 2010. "Commission into Sockeye Salmon Stocks Releases Areas of Inquiry." *Globe and Mail*, 9 June.

Accessed 29 June 2015. http://www.theglobeandmail .com/news/national/british-columbia/commission -into-sockeye-salmon-stocks-releases-areas-of-inquiry/ article1597924/.

Hunter, J. 2010. "Surprising Salmon Run Masks an Industry in Crisis." *Globe and Mail*, 26 August. Accessed 29 June 2015. http://www.theglobeandmail .com/news/national/british-columbia/surprising-salmon -run-masks-an-industry-in-crisis/article1686603/.

Hutchings, Jeffrey A. 2013. "Gutting Canada's Fisheries Act: No Fishery, No Fish Habitat Protection." *Fisheries* 38(11): 497–501.

Jacquet, J.L., and D. Pauly. 2007. "The Rise of Seafood Campaigns in an Era of Collapsing Fisheries." *Marine Policy* 31:308–13.

———. 2008. "Trade Secrets: Renaming and Mislabelling of Seafood." *Marine Policy* 32:309–18.

Kaczynski, V.M., and D.L. Fluharty. 2002. "European Policies in West Africa: Who Benefits from Fisheries Agreements?" *Marine Policy* 26:75–93.

Kurien, John. 1985. "Technical Assistance Projects and Socioeconomic Change: Norwegian Intervention in Kerala's Fisheries Development." *Economic and Political Weekly* 20, 25/26:A77–79.

Kurlansky, Mark. 1997. *Cod: A Biography of the Fish That Changed the World.* New York: Walker and Company.

Mathew, Sebastian. 2010. "Fishery-Dependent Information and the Ecosystem Approach: What Role Should Fishers and Their Knowledge Play?" Keynote address to the FDI 2010 conference, Galway, Ireland, August.

———. 2011. "The Costs of Certification." *Samudra Report* 58:41–5.

McCay, Bonnie J., and James M. Acheson, eds. 1990. *The Question of the Commons: The Culture and Ecology of Communal Resources.* Tucson: University of Arizona Press.

Metallic, Fred (Gopit). 2008. "Strengthening Our Relations in Gespe'gewa'gi, the Seventh District of Mi'gma'gi." Pp. 59–72 in *Lighting the Eighth Fire: The Liberation, Resurgence and Protection of Indigenous Nations*, ed. Leanne Simpson. Winnipeg, MB: Arbeiter Ring Publishing.

Mitchell, Alanna. 2009. *Sea Sick: The Global Ocean in Crisis.* Toronto: McClelland & Stewart.

Myers, R.A., and J. Worm. 2003. "Rapid Worldwide Depletion of Predatory Fishing Communities." *Nature* 423(15 May):280–3.

Pauly, Daniel. 2007. "Small but Mighty: Elevate the Role of Small-Scale Fishers in the World Market." *Conservation Magazine* 8(3):25.

———. 2009. "Beyond Duplicity and Ignorance in Global Fisheries." *Scientia Marina* 73(2):215–24.

———, S. Christensen, J. Dalsgaard, R. Froese, and F.C. Torres Jr. 1998. "Fishing Down Marine Food Webs." *Science* 279:860–3.

Seckinelgin, H. 2006. *The Environment and International Politics: International Fisheries, Heidegger, and Social Method.* London and New York: Routledge.

Sharma, Chandrika. 2009. "Market-Driven Conservation: Social Issues in Certification Schemes for Capture Fisheries." Presentation to the National Seminar on Conservation and Sustainability of Coastal Living Resources of India.

Srinivasan, U. Thara, Reg Watson, and U. Rashid Sumaila. 2012. "Global Fisheries Losses at the Exclusive Economic Zone Level, 1950 to Present." *Marine Policy* 36:544–9.

———, Susan P. Carey, Eric Hallstein, et al. 2008. "The Debt of Nations and the Distribution of Ecological Impacts from Human Activities." *Proceedings of the National Academy of Sciences* 105(5):1768–73.

Stonich, S., J.R. Bort, and L.L. Ovares. 1997. "Globalization of Shrimp Mariculture: The Impact on Social Justice and Environmental Quality in Central America." *Society and Natural Resources* 10:161–79.

Vandergeest, Peter. 2007. "Certification and Communities: Alternatives for Regulating the Environmental and Social Impacts of Shrimp Farming." *World Development* 35(7):1152–71.

Ward, P., and R.A. Myers. 2005. "Shifts in Open-Ocean Fish Communities Coinciding with the Commencement of Commercial Fishing." *Ecology* 86(4):835–47.

World Bank. 2004. *Saving Fish and Fishers: Towards Sustainable and Equitable Governance of the Global Fishing Sector.* Washington, DC: The World Bank, Agriculture and Rural Development Department.

Worm, Boris, Edward B. Barbier, Nicola Beaumont, et al. 2006. "Impacts of Biodiversity Loss on Ocean Ecosystem Services." *Science* 314:787–90.

———, Ray Hilborn, Julia K. Baum, et al. 2009. "Rebuilding Global Fisheries." *Science* 325:578–85.

Young, Nathan, and Ralph Matthews. 2010. *The Aquaculture Controversy in Canada: Activism, Policy and Contested Science.* Vancouver: UBC Press.

13 Spatial Colonization of Food Environments by Pseudo Food Companies
Precursors of a Health Crisis[1]

Anthony Winson

Learning Objectives

Through this chapter, you can

1. Gain a better understanding of the political-economic determinants of key food environments such as supermarkets and schools.

2. Discover some novel conceptual tools to help understand what is driving unhealthy eating among Canadians.

Introduction

Canadian society today, as with most other developed countries, is facing a looming health crisis related to the characteristics of diets and lifestyles as they have evolved over the last several decades. Globally, obesity has doubled between 1980 and 2008 and today half a billion people, or 12 per cent of the world's population, are obese (see Kondro 2012).

The recent Canadian Health Measures Survey provides data on measured (as opposed to self-reported) body composition,[2] and gives us the most accurate picture for Canada in this regard to date. It indicates that between 1981 and 2009, the proportion of teen boys in the age group 15 to 19 who were classified as overweight or obese rose from 14 to 31 per cent. Among teen girls, this figure increased from 14 to 25 per cent. The survey also noted dramatic declines in fitness levels among younger adults age 20 to 39.

Moreover, during the 2007 to 2009 period, about 1 per cent of adult Canadians were underweight, 37 per cent were overweight, and 24 per cent were obese. The percentage of these adults with a waist circumference placing them at high risk for health problems more than quadrupled in this period, from 5 to 21 per cent among men and from 6 to 31 per cent among women.[3]

Serious chronic diseases such as type 2 diabetes are strongly correlated with excess weight and sedentary lifestyle. Canada, like many other countries, has seen a disturbing increase in the incidence of type 2 diabetes in recent years, and there is evidence that the rate of increase of this disease has been seriously underestimated (Lipscombe and Hux 2007). However, as a recent editorial in the *Canadian Medical Association Journal* has argued, the emphasis on individual initiatives and advice around diet and activity levels to combat obesity is not working. Rather, "obesity will only be curbed by population-level measures supported by legislation. Treating obesity does not work well; preventing it would be better" (Fletcher and Patrick 2014:1275). Unfortunately, the problematic nature of our contemporary food environment has not been tackled by policy makers, with very few exceptions. This is at least in part to do with the political sensitivity of the issue and the powerful vested interests that lie behind our food system.

While there are a variety of factors shaping eating behaviour, including individual psychological factors, family influences, peer pressures, the physical environment, and so on (see Raine 2005), political-economic determinants of diet have yet to receive the full attention they warrant. As Power has argued:

> it is important to explore how the food industry shapes social norms around eating in Canada; how those in different positions in social space (e.g. class, sex, ethnicity, age, etc.) are targeted by food marketers; and how people take up and act on those marketing messages and thus produce and reproduce food norms and culture.(2005:S40)

The present chapter considers the contemporary food environment as a problematic subject that is in need of critical analysis. It proposes to examine institutional food environments—specifically supermarkets and high schools—in the Canadian context with a view to understanding the key factors shaping their nutritional content. It draws on the author's own recent research and the research of others to make the case that the degradation of contemporary food environments in Canada plays a significant role in exacerbating weight gain and obesity in society and the serious health outcomes that have been linked to this.

Conceptual Issues

In previously published research the author has argued for the use of several concepts that aid in understanding the present content and factors shaping contemporary food environments. These concepts are food environments, pseudo foods, differential profits, corporate concentration, mass advertising and product differentiation, and spatial colonization (Winson 2004). These concepts will be discussed before considering how they may be utilized to critically analyze food environments.

Food environments, as the term is used here, are those institutional spheres where food is displayed for sale and/or consumed.[4] At one time in the not-too-distant past food was largely produced within the domestic unit in the countryside and largely consumed on site. This unity of production and consumption prevailed for thousands of years even though markets for food have existed at least since the times of the classical Incan and Mayan and Greco-Roman civilizations (see Garnsey 1999: Ch. 2). However, the rise of industrial capitalism undermined this unity in what became the developed world, as masses of people were forced off the land and into the industrializing cities. This has been the experience of much of the global South in recent times as well. The unity of production and consumption within the domestic unit that had been a central institution of agrarian societies for millennia has largely been broken. This fact alone has been fundamental to the development of the food industry. It has also provided processors and, more recently, retailers the conditions to dramatically shift food consumption patterns by modifying our food environments and thereby shaping mass diets. These processes have been largely neglected by food analysts and are in need of much more critical research.

Today there are some noticeable differences distinguishing the procurement of food from its consumption. Foodstuffs today have become some of the world's most valuable commodities to be bought, transported, and sold, and, indeed, a very significant proportion of our labour force is in some way involved with these commodity chains. For most people, and in keeping with the long-standing evolution of capitalist economies all over the world, food is procured from private, for-profit retail institutions which are now dominated by supermarket chain store operations that increasingly operate on a global scale (Reardon and Berdegué 2002; Reardon et al. 2003).

Unlike the realm of procurement, the realm of food consumption is still characterized by the continuing existence of not-for-profit institutional spheres. At-home consumption is one of the most obvious and important of these, and in this sphere pressures associated with the market are not yet as intrusive with respect to the shaping of the foods we consume. Another significant not-for-profit sphere of food consumption is the school, where food environments traditionally were run on a not-for-profit basis, although this is rapidly changing in many jurisdictions, with notable consequences. Even in institutional spheres where profit-making constraints do not hold sway, however, the influence of market pressures may be felt, as I will argue below. Overall, however, food consumption is increasingly taking place in *for-profit* institutional settings, as such factors as time constraints on family life, both parents working away from the home, and the loss of culinary skills, among other influences, determine that more and more people find they must eat away from the home or eat food prepared by others elsewhere that is then brought into the home. As Austin et al. (2005:1575) note, Americans now spend almost half of their food expenditures away from home, and "among youths aged 12 to 18 years, the percentage of total energy intake consumed from fast-food and other restaurants has increased from 6.5% in 1977–1978 to 19.3% in 1994–1996." This situation implies loss of control over nutritional content as decisions around ingredients (e.g. sugar and salt quantities) and preparation techniques (e.g. deep frying versus steaming of vegetables) are alienated to other actors in the food system.

Pseudo foods are those nutrient-poor edible products that are typically high in fat, sugar, and salt, and, other than the calories they provide, often in overabundance, are notably low in nutrients such as proteins, minerals, and vitamins essential for health. While pseudo foods include products more commonly known as "junk foods" (candy bars, chips, soft drinks, and the like), it is a more inclusive term in that it includes products not usually thought of as junk food. For example, many of the juice "beverages" sold today would qualify as pseudo foods because of their high sugar content and absence of the nutrients associated with products made from pure juices. Many of the frozen dairy products that are proliferating in supermarkets in recent years would be considered pseudo foods, because of their high fat and sugar content and low levels of essential nutrients. Ice cream, the dominant frozen dairy product in supermarkets and one that now occupies more shelf space than fluid milk, typically has around 50 per cent of its calories coming from fat, although some varieties reach 70 per cent (Nutribase 2001).[5] These and such high-profile supermarket products as pre-sweetened breakfast cereals, when added to the vast number of junk-food products, constitute a very substantial part of the modern supermarket food environment. They are ubiquitous in other food environments as well. Table 13.1 provides a graphic illustration of the nutritional differences underlying the pseudo food/food divide.

Differential profit is a concept that attempts to account for the fact that where foodstuffs are very highly commoditized, some food and beverage products attract higher returns, or profits, for their sellers than others. In a capitalist economy, profit and the rate at which it can be accumulated is the prime mover, the master compass that orients flows of investment, whether in the food business or in any other sector where market forces prevail. The rate of profit, or the more commonly used business euphemism *earnings*, plays a fundamental role in shaping the organization of food environments.

Generally speaking, more highly processed foodstuffs, goods with more "value added," have more attractive rates of return for retailers and processors. Foodstuffs that have undergone minimal levels of transformation, such as table potatoes, fluid milk, eggs, flour, and tomato paste,

Table 13.1 Nutrient Comparison of Pseudo Food Beverages with Real Food Beverages (Per 355 ml [12 oz.] serving)

	Coca-Cola	Pepsi	Orange Juice	1% Milk
Calories	154	160	168	153
Sugar, g	40	40	40	18
Vitamin A, IU	0	0	291	750
Vitamin C, mg	0	0	146	3
Folic acid, µg	0	0	164	18
Calcium, mg	0	0	33	450
Potassium, mg	0	0	711	352
Magnesium, mg	0	0	36	51
Phosphate, mg	54	55	60	353

Source: Adapted from Nestle (2002:198), Table 23.

referred to in the food business as "commodity" products, typically have thin profit margins, and are often sold below cost as "loss leaders" solely to attract customers to the store. On the other hand, products that have been created out of inexpensive (often subsidized, as with corn and sugar) raw ingredients, such as sugar, potatoes, wheat, and corn, with some processing and the addition of inexpensive chemical additives to create "value added," can be made into very profitable commodities.

Reports from the trade journals of the food retail industry give some idea of the profitability of pseudo food–type products. The *Canadian Grocer*, for example, reported that confectionery has grown to be one of the retailers' largest categories in Canada, at $2 billion in sales annually and growing at 5 per cent a year. It is also a category that has consistently had among the highest gross margins, averaging 35 per cent. It quotes an executive of one retail chain store operation as saying about confectionery, "healthy markups, good profits, reliable sales—there aren't many other grocery categories that can make the same claim" (Kahane 2000:59). Potato and corn chip products and the like, which the industry refers to as "salty snacks," are another high-profit product category for the food business. The main American grocery industry journal, *Progressive Grocer*, reports

that food retailers have indicated that salty snacks are the second-most profitable product category for them, only outpaced by bakery products (Centers for Disease Control 1997). The profitability of these pseudo foods is corroborated by a representative of one of the world's largest salty-snack manufacturers—PepsiCo's Frito Lay—who claimed that while his company's products represented only about 1 per cent of supermarket sales in 1998, they accounted for about 11 per cent of operating profits and 40 per cent of profit growth for the average American supermarket (cited in Wellman 1999).

The argument that pseudo foods are especially profitable is further corroborated by industry data from chain store companies that control convenience stores in the United States and reported in *Canadian Grocer*. While gross margins for all merchandise averaged 33 per cent, the gross margins for pseudo foods were notably higher, ranging from 35 per cent for cookies to 37 per cent for salty snacks, 39 per cent for ice cream, 43 per cent for candy and gum, and up to 59 per cent for soft drinks served in-store (Shoesmith 1992). Finally, it is noteworthy that in Canada the snack food industry has experienced much more rapid growth than has the food industry as a whole. In fact, its growth from 1988 to 1997, measured in constant 1992 dollars, was

56 per cent as compared to the overall growth of only 6 per cent for the entire food and beverage industry (Food Bureau 1998).

Corporate concentration helps to explain *why* these nutrient-poor products are so lucrative, beyond the fact that many of them are fabricated largely from cheap commodities, like sugar and wheat, and sold at a high return. The snack food industry, for example, is controlled by a very few multinational food manufacturers. In Canada the federal government reported that by 2015 only four firms controlled about 82 per cent of the value of all shipments of snack foods (Agriculture and Agri-Food Canada 2015). The breakfast cereal industry in North America is also highly concentrated with four firms having almost 80 per cent of the market (GAO 2009). A key benefit of this oligopoly situation, at least to these companies, is in the area of pricing, as corporate concentration confers considerable market power that allows corporations to avoid competition and set prices that ensure high profitability. In fact, corporate players who largely control the production and marketing of nutrient-poor pseudo food products are among the largest of all companies in the food and beverage sector. PepsiCo, for example, with worldwide revenue of $66.6 billion in 2014,[6] makes more in profits each year than the total sales of many prominent food companies.

Mass advertising is the process whereby a company's product becomes differentiated in the market place. The technologies and business strategies of mass advertising have enabled some companies to develop powerful branded products which, in turn, have historically allowed them to dominate their competition in the markets they sell in (Connor et al. 1985).[7] Mass advertising and corporate concentration in the food business go hand in hand, then—they are mutually reinforcing processes. The high cost of mass advertising on such media outlets as network television means that only the largest companies have the deep pockets to afford access in the first place. The benefits that come from such advertising can be immense, however, and its ability to create and strengthen a brand has made these same corporations even more powerful over time. Furthermore, there are economies of scale that come to companies that do the most advertising, enabling them to buy advertising time from media corporations more cheaply than competitors and gain market advantage. This process had progressed sufficiently far over the course of the twentieth century that even by the early 1980s, of the 1,100 food companies that were using major media sources to advertise their products, only 12 firms accounted for 45 per cent of all advertising expenditures (Connor et al. 1985: Ch. 3).

Food companies are intensive advertisers, and spending on pseudo foods takes a priority. As Taylor et al. (2005:S22) note, research supports the view that "food advertising promotes more frequent consumption of less healthy foods, including higher-fat, energy-dense snacks and rarely features healthy choices such as fruits and vegetables." According to Marion Nestle, of the astounding $33 billion spent by food companies on all their promotional campaigns by 2000, almost 70 per cent was spent on convenience foods, candy and snacks, alcoholic beverages, soft drinks, and desserts, whereas just 2.2 per cent was for fruits, vegetables, grains, or beans (2002).

Though such products are unnecessary and arguably damage health, a small number of corporations that market well-known branded pseudo food products spend an astounding amount of money each year to keep these products front and centre in the minds of consumers. For 2004, just the 10 most powerful companies marketing pseudo food products spent a total of $7.6 billion on advertising their brands in the United States, which was 119 times greater than the entire advertising budget for the US federal government's Department of Health and Human Services (*Advertising Age* 2005). In fact, in 2006 PepsiCo spent more than twice as much advertising its Tostitos brand of salty snacks alone as did the Department of Health and Human Services on all of its programs (*Advertising Age* 2007). Table 13.2 provides a breakdown of sales and ad expenditure by company, as well as advertising dollar spent per dollar of sales, for this group.

Table 13.2 Ten Largest Pseudo Food Manufacturers: US and World Sales and Expenditures on Advertising in the US, 2004 and 2006[1]

Company	US Sales (millions)			World Sales (millions)			US Ad Expenditures (thousands)		
	2004	2006	% change	2004	2006	% change	2004	2006	% change
Burger King	7,700	8,392	9.0	n/a	2,048	n/a	542,143	379,459	−30.0
Coca-Cola	6,643	6,662	0.3	21,962	24,088	9.7	540,551	740,824	37.0
General Mills	9,441	9,803	3.8	11,070	11,640	5.1	912,455	920,466	0.9
Kellogg's	5,968	7,349	33.2	9,614	10,907	13.4	647,097	765,089	18.2
McDonalds	6,525	7,464	14.4	19,065	21,586	13.2	1,388,862	1,748,345	25.9
Nestlé[2]	22,444	24,889	10.9	70,114	78,327	11.7	1,028,295	1,314,975	27.9
Pepsi	18,329	22,178	21.0	29,261	35,137	20.1	1,262,160	1,322,721	4.8
Wendy's (Tim Hortons)[3]	2,475	2,197	11.2	3,635	2,349	32.9	435,776	435,209	−0.1
Yum! Brands[4]	5,763	5,603	2.8	9,011	9,561	6.1	779,396	902,047	15.7

1. Figures in US dollars. Mars Inc. is a major manufacturer of pseudo foods but data on sales was not available. Expenditures on advertising in the US amounted to more than $658 million in 2006.
2. Sales are for the Americas (North and South). Ad expenditures are for the US.
3. Tim Hortons has become a separate corporate entity since this data was gathered.
4. Yum! Brands owns KFC, Taco Bell, Pizza Hut, and A&W restaurants.

Source: Advertising Age (2005, 2007).

Spatial colonization is a concept designed to help us understand how differential profits, corporate concentration, mass advertising, and market power come to affect the geography of food environments and the prominent role of pseudo foods within them. For profits to be realized, product must be sold. While intensive, incessant advertising has become a necessary investment for corporations marketing pseudo food products to maintain and expand their markets, it is not sufficient alone. To translate manufactured demand into sales, it is necessary to secure the *physical visibility and availability* of the product within a particular food environment. The process of spatial colonization refers to the power of food processors to place product *in the most visible and effective selling spaces* in a food environment. An industry spokesperson summed this process up concisely when commenting on the marketing of confectionery in supermarkets:

> Confectionery sells confectionery—you must have a variety of products and you must have a variety of locations in your store. You should use a combination of feature and display for maximum impact. . . . If it's not in the face of customers, it can't sell well. (Kahane 2000:59)

Ensuring a product's physical visibility and availability can take different forms. For fast-food corporations, spatial colonization is more about securing desirable real estate in high traffic urban locations, from busy city intersections to shopping malls, airports, or even public sector–controlled spaces such as schools, universities, and hospitals. For most pseudo food manufacturers, on the other hand, product visibility has to be secured first and foremost in the supermarket food environment, although other marketing channels, including convenience store chains and vending machines in a variety of institutional settings are very important as well. In the telling words of a Coca-Cola Company executive, "[T]o build pervasiveness of our products, we're putting ice-cold Coca-Cola classic and our

other brands within reach, wherever you look: at the supermarket, the video store, the soccer field, the gas station—everywhere" (cited in Nestle and Jacobson 2000:19).

In the remainder of this chapter, I will discuss some recent empirical research of the author that examines the spatial colonization of pseudo foods in the context of two essential institutional food environments: supermarkets and high schools.

Pseudo Foods and Private Sector Institutions: The Supermarket

As the most important food environment in terms of sales, supermarkets and their shelves are much-sought-after locations for pseudo food processors. Supermarket chain store companies, on the other hand, function as shelf space "landlords," renting out space in their store to those companies that can afford to pay. The fact that the supermarket retail sector has seen dramatic concentration in a number of countries, and particularly in Canada, gives the few retailers that dominate this sector a good deal of power over processors and what they can demand to display their products (Howe 1983). The special deals, discounts, rebates, and allowances that processors pay to "rent" the shelf space from the supermarket chains have, according to one analyst, allowed US food retailers to make up to one-third of their profits solely from these kinds of trade payments from processors to facilitate marketing of their products (Shapiro 1992). In Canada a report in the late 1980s by an industry analyst writing in the *Globe and Mail* estimated that these payments amounted to $2 billion of the $32 billion in annual food sales at that time (Matas 1987). Given the secretive nature of these payments, current data on them is hard to come by, but it can be assumed that they have grown as overall food sales have grown.

There is thus a considerable cost to a product being prominently displayed in the supermarket food environment. Increasingly fewer and fewer food processors are able to pay, and as a result in most product categories the products of smaller firms have all but disappeared. Hastening this trend has been the push since the early 1980s by most supermarket chain store companies to develop and market their own store brands (e.g. Loblaws' President's Choice) in the supermarkets they control. In this context, few companies can compete with the market power of the large concentrated corporations that dominate the production of pseudo foods.

The relationship between processor and supermarket chain is not simply a "landlord–tenant" relationship; it is more complex than that. The success of transnational processing giants in transforming the supermarket food environment would also appear to have much to do with their active promotion of the mutual benefits to be had with pseudo food sales to the retail chain stores. The largest companies, Nestlé and Coca-Cola among them, communicate regularly to retailers in such key trade journals as *Progressive Grocer* about preferred retail strategies to maximize sales and thus differential profits. For their part, supermarket retailers seem eager to steal business away from other non-food chain store operations, including drug store chains, when it comes to selling confectionery products, for example.

How is spatial colonization manifested in the geography of the supermarket? To begin, supermarket layout, the overall positioning of product categories, is noteworthy. Low-profit "commodity" items that most shoppers will purchase no matter what else they buy (milk, butter/ margarine, eggs, and often bread) are placed at the back of the store, as far as possible from the entrance, so that customers will have to pass by less essential but more profitable products first. Favoured locations in the supermarket include eye-level shelf location (as opposed to the much less favoured bottom shelf); unique product positioning, called special displays, that set product apart from competing brands and heighten visibility; and locations near store areas that must be passed by the customer, with the checkout counter being the most significant. In today's

supermarket, particularly in the "superstore" type formats, spatial colonization can take the form of massive island displays of a single product that are virtually impossible to ignore.

It might be asked, does the spatial manipulation of product have any real significance? Market research would suggest that it indeed has. Research indicates the powerful effect of shelf position on sales, for example, and studies have suggested that the use of special end-of-aisle displays in supermarkets can boost unit sales by several hundred per cent, even when no price reduction occurs (see Chevalier 1975; Cox 1970).

In 2001 and 2002 the author conducted a study that involved visits to a number of supermarkets in the cities of Kitchener, Waterloo, Cambridge, and Guelph in the south-central region of Ontario. Twelve of a total of 24 supermarkets existing in the region at that time were studied. While anecdotal evidence had suggested that nutrient-poor products had become more significant in modern retailing there was little research to document the situation. This study attempted to provide some data on the spatial colonization of pseudo food products in the supermarket food environment. The stores surveyed included stores owned by each of the three main supermarket chain store companies operating in Ontario. The study included both the smaller, more traditional, supermarket format stores and the largest superstore-type format that includes an in-store pharmacy, florist and electronic shops, furniture, and so on. It also included store formats that are marketed as lower-price "no-frills" stores. Because the industry is dominated by so few players, and because they tend to utilize fairly standard formats in organizing their stores, it is believed that the stores included in the study are reasonably representative of what is happening in the industry.

Measures were taken of the linear shelf space devoted to all food items in each of the main product categories (e.g. breakfast cereals; juices; bottled beverages; salty snack products; bakery; dairy; meats; fresh, frozen, and canned fruits and vegetables; etc.) and as well the linear shelf space devoted to nutrient-poor pseudo food products in each category was measured. In the end, for each store there were data on the total linear shelf space devoted to food and beverages (non-food and beverage items were not measured) and on the total linear shelf space devoted to pseudo foods. Data was also available by major product categories on the relative proportion of foods and pseudo foods. In some product categories, such as bottled beverages for instance, most of the shelf space was devoted to soft drinks. In others, such as breakfast cereals, a smaller portion of shelf space would be devoted to nutrient-poor products, in this case pre-sweetened breakfast cereals. In each store the number and content of all special displays were recorded, but the linear footage of these was not recorded. Since my study revealed that most of these displays market pseudo food products, the overall measure of pseudo food shelf space is a conservative one.[8]

Findings

In the supermarkets surveyed, the mean linear footage devoted to pseudo foods ranged from 26 to 37 per cent of the total of all linear footage devoted to edible goods in the store. For all 12 stores, the average proportion of pseudo foods of all foods measured was 31 per cent. The proportion of pseudo foods of all edibles was considerably higher for the shelves that constitute the central area of each store, ranging from 35 to 44 per cent. This is the part of most supermarket food environments where entire aisles are devoted to bulk candies and chocolates, to cookie displays, to soft drinks, and to potato and corn chip products. The area around the central aisles is typically a healthier place to shop, although this is changing with the rapid growth of extensive displays of high-sugar/high-fat products in this area as well.

Interestingly, there was no clear relationship between the prevalence of pseudo foods in the store and store ownership. All the chain store companies appeared to be employing the same marketing strategies as far as pseudo foods were

concerned. There was evidence that the newest stores in the study employed more prominent mechanisms to promote pseudo foods, however. This typically entailed the use of massive special displays to market nutrient-poor products rather than having a higher proportion of them on the regular store shelves. As well, some retailers are beginning to organize extra-wide aisles that are exclusively devoted to pseudo foods in some stores. This does seem to suggest the direction that food retailing is going in the future.

It was interesting to note that in the supermarkets under study, an entire shelf, and in the larger stores the equivalent of two entire shelves, extending the full length of the central retail space, are typically devoted to candies and chocolate bars, and these items were conspicuously displayed in many other locations in the store as well. In most stores a dairy case occupying an entire aisle was devoted to high-fat/high-sugar ice creams and other high-fat and high-sugar dairy products. This reflects the efforts by manufacturers and retailers to extend the consumption of "frozen snacks" from the traditional summer months to the entire year (Maclean 1992). The newer the store, typically the more extensive was the ice cream case.

With respect to some major product categories, it was typical, for example, to have over 90 per cent of the linear footage devoted to frozen juice drinks to be occupied by high-sugar beverages that contained 25 per cent or less, often much less, of real fruit juice. The situation with canned and Tetra Pak juices was not much different. In the ready-to-eat breakfast cereal category, from 55 to 80 per cent of total shelf space was devoted to pre-sweetened cereals, which represents a potent vehicle for getting sugar into children's diets.[9] The readiness of retailers to market pre-sweetened cereals aggressively is not surprising given that pre-sweetened cereals are the fastest-growing segment of the fastest-growing product category of 569 product categories tracked by the A.C. Neilsen Company (Burn 1993).

With consumer research indicating that as much as two-thirds of brand selection decisions being made *in the store* (A.C. Nielsen 1992), and impulse purchases being a significant part of overall profits for retailers, it is not surprising that stores, in conjunction with leading processors, have had increasing recourse to the use of special displays. It is well known that supermarkets have placed high-profit impulse items at the checkout, and indeed, in our survey candies, chocolate products, and salty snacks were present at 80 per cent or more of the checkout counters in a typical store. Impulse sales are driven throughout the modern supermarket operation today. Special display stands, hooks, and strips are now commonly positioned in the most visible locations throughout the store.

While special display devices can be utilized hypothetically to market any manner of goods normally found in supermarkets today, in practice we found they were overwhelmingly dominated by nutrient-poor products. The number of special displays of these pseudo foods in the sampled stores ranged from 8 to a high of 26, with the average number being 19. Figure 13.1 gives an idea of the extensive use of special displays in one of the supermarkets sampled, which was fairly typical of other stores as well. It also lists the products that were featured in these special displays.

The supermarket food environment today carries a range of foods from all parts of the globe that is unprecedented in human history. For those concerned with the lack of healthy nutritional offerings available to the poor and marginal populations in even the richest societies, the availability of a supermarket is often seen as a positive element for inner-city core populations and poor rural communities where little else than fast-food restaurants and convenience stores are to be seen (Cumins and MacIntyre 2006).[10] Supermarkets offer a *relative* diversity of foods and beverages, then, compared to what is on offer in the convenience chain stores that now colonize food environments. However, this relative diversity masks the drastic varietal simplification that has occurred with the industrial food system. In the expansive and often glamorous supermarket food environment today, an extremely small number of fruit and vegetable varieties are present compared to what exists in nature. I have explored this reality in more depth elsewhere, including what it might mean for our health (Winson 2013: Ch. 7). On the other hand, we have seen that certain types of products receive privileged treatment in the supermarket food environment in terms of visibility and promotional effort. These products are too often nutrient-poor edible commodities high in sugar, fat, and salt. Their presence in the supermarket is out of all proportion to their nutritional contribution to our lives.

Pseudo Foods and Public Sector Institutions: The High School

The high school is another institutional sphere worthy of study because of the evidence that youth today get a large portion of their daily energy needs while at school (French et al. 2004). Moreover, nutrient needs are higher in adolescence than at any other time in the life cycle (see Story et al. 2002). It has been noted that relatively little research has examined factors influencing adolescent eating behaviour (Shannon et al. 2002) and particularly in the Canadian context (see Taylor et al. 2005), and it is believed that food choices and eating patterns developed at this time are likely to influence long-term behaviour and help determine the vulnerability to chronic diseases such as heart disease, certain cancers, and osteoporosis later in life (Centers for Disease Control 1997). Nutritional authorities have argued that the schools can play a key role in reversing the trend toward childhood obesity (American Dietetic Association et al. 2003). For these reasons it is useful to know more about the role of pseudo foods in the high school food environment.

Given the relative dearth of concrete knowledge about the content of high school food environments in Canada and student food and

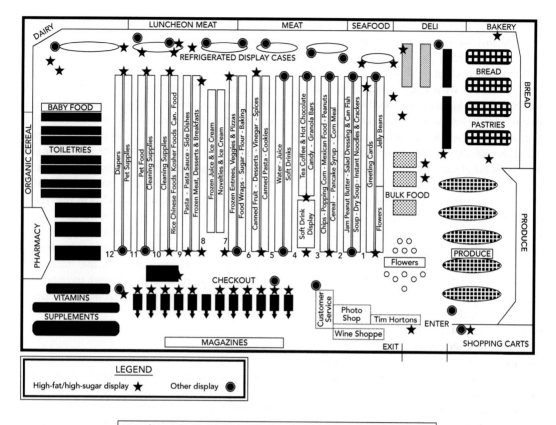

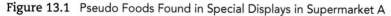

Figure 13.1 Pseudo Foods Found in Special Displays in Supermarket A

* Each listing represents a separate display in the store. Displays at checkout counters are *not* included.

beverage purchasing patterns while at school, the author and his research assistants undertook a pilot study of public high school food environments in 2004–5. The study had three basic objectives: (1) to provide some insights into the kinds of foods being purchased in Ontario schools; (2) gain insights into the factors that shape the high school food environment; (3) to discover whether formal or informal initiatives existed to improve the nutritional standard of the high school food environment.

The study took place in a school district encompassing three small cities and adjacent rural areas about one hour's drive west of Toronto, Ontario. A key reason this school district was chosen for study was because the majority of schools still controlled their cafeteria operations and thus offered better chances of access by the researcher than a situation where these operations were largely privatized.[11] In the end, interviews took place in 10 of the 12 schools in this school district.

To find out what kinds of foods were being purchased in these high schools (objective 1) face-to-face interviews were conducted that solicited detailed information regarding the quantities of various kinds of food stuffs and beverages purchased over the course of a week in each school cafeteria. At a minimum this allowed us to estimate the relative proportions of foods and beverages of different nutritional value being purchased by students (seasonal variations in food offerings were also recorded). Interviews took place with respondents overseeing cafeteria and vending machine operations in high schools, a group composed of teachers with special duties as "student activity directors," and/or cafeteria managers, depending on the school.

We surveyed all vending machines found in each school, as well as any tuck shops present, because the food environment of high schools includes more than cafeteria fare.

Early in the study, we found evidence suggesting that the food environment *external* to the school is an important determinant of what foods are sold in the schools. We thus endeavoured to map out the existence of food vendors within close proximity of the school, and the presence of fast-food vendors in particular. For each school, the variety of nearby food vendors and their distance from school property was recorded. Finally, we noted any implicit[12] or explicit nutritional policies that may have been adopted within a school.

Study Methods

To organize the data by nutritional content, we developed the following procedure. Data for units sold of various edible products on a daily basis were gathered from cafeteria staff. These data were organized into four basic categories: "main meals" (e.g. pasta plate, hamburger, stir fry, panzerotti), "side dishes" (e.g. french fries,

cut vegetables, salad), "desserts and snacks" (e.g. cookies, muffins, fresh fruit, fruit salad, brownies), and "beverages" (e.g. soft drink, chocolate milk, white milk, pure fruit juice, juice beverage, water).[13] These data were then organized according to three basic nutritional categories suggested by the Ontario Society of Nutrition Professionals in Public Health in an important recent report addressing nutrition in Ontario schools. These categories designated foods of "maximum," "moderate," and "minimum" nutrition (OSNPPH 2004: table 7). Foods in the "moderate" category were considered to have some positive nutritional value, but with higher than desirable levels of fat, sugar, and/or salt, often as a result of processing. Those in the "minimal" category are products typically high in sugar and fat and low in most nutritional areas, products termed *pseudo foods* above.

Findings

One notable finding was the popularity of high-sugar/high-fat foods—french fries, cookies, muffins, soft drinks, and fruit beverages—all of which were purchased in large quantities relative to other items in virtually all of the schools studied. These products are judged to be of "minimum" nutritional value by nutritionists (see OSNPPH 2004). Typically, these products were found as cafeteria side dishes and dessert or snack items. Outside school cafeterias, these nutrient-poor offerings dominated vending machines found in all schools and were available to students at any time of the school day.

Only "main meal" items could be considered of "maximum" or "moderate" nutritional value, and cafeteria staff typically made an effort to have nutritional options offered daily. Nevertheless, staff often felt obliged to cater to student demand for fast-food items as well (e.g. pizza, hamburgers), particularly when such items were easily available a short walk from the school, as was very often the case (see below).

We also found that the purchases of fresh fruit and vegetables were extremely low in almost all cases, and particularly so in the case of fruit. For example, in several of the surveyed high schools of 1,000 or more students, and in the context of the universal availability of fruit in these school cafeterias, as few as three to five pieces of fruit *in total* per week were purchased. All too often, when other low-nutrition snack and dessert products were available, the vast majority of students opted for them instead of fruit.

Students in the schools we studied purchased more products high in saturated fats and hydrogenated fats (trans fats) than desirable for a couple of reasons. One was the popularity of such main meal items as hamburgers that are high in saturated fat. Another was the popularity of industrial-baked goods (cookies, muffins, brownies, etc.) that were made with hydrogenated oils. Research over a number of years has established that trans fats in hydrogenated oils are even more harmful to health than saturated fats (Mozafarrian et al. 2006).

While a number of these schools had facilities to prepare baked goods from scratch on site, utilizing unsaturated and non-hydrogenized oils, and in fact had done so in the past, staff shortages in recent years made this impossible. Time constraints on the remaining staff forced the preparation of such items using semi-processed products made in factories. One positive feature of cafeteria kitchens in our study was that consumption of saturated fats in such perennial-favourite side dishes as french fries was reduced because of decisions in most of the schools surveyed not to purchase a deep fryer. Hamburgers, another popular main meal item, were baked rather than fried in most cases. Nevertheless, these are still high in fat.

Variations in the Schools

Some schools performed less well in the "main meals" category because they typically offered more fast-food items that were high in fat and refined carbohydrates (e.g. hamburgers and pizza) and fewer of the healthier main meals. With respect to the "side dish" and "snack/ dessert" categories, where pseudo foods tended to dominate, a couple of schools did relatively better in nutritional terms. These schools had made the choice not to offer such items as french fries and onion rings, but had placed more emphasis than was typical in offering instead healthier side-dish items such as well-prepared salads, cut-up vegetables, and egg rolls. The factors behind these nutritional decisions are discussed below.

With respect to beverages sold in cafeterias, we recorded a relatively high volume of "healthy" beverages sold compared to the less nutritious items. This is *not* an accurate reflection of beverage purchases in the schools, however. Rather, in nearly all cases a decision had been made not to offer soft drinks in the cafeteria, which is commendable, but in all but one case soft drinks were readily available in vending machines outside the cafeteria and in tuck shops, if present. The dismal nutritional picture that emerged from our survey of vending machines in high schools is illustrated in figure 13.2. Vending machines are a major mechanism for pseudo food manufacturers to market their products in these schools, a finding that Taylor et al. (2005) note has been reported in other Canadian research.

Determinants of the High School Food Environment

Why do student food-purchasing patterns in our study diverge so widely from what would be considered ideal from a nutritional perspective? Part of the explanation lies outside of the realm of schools entirely and has to do with the effects of aggressive mass advertising targeting children and youth by the corporate purveyors of junk foods and fast foods. Such advertising is a powerful force creating demand for these products, and students do not, of course, cease to be influenced by such advertising once they enter the school. However, there are other contributing factors that would seem to reinforce present food-purchasing patterns. Among the most important of these are factors that shape what food and beverages high schools *offer* students.

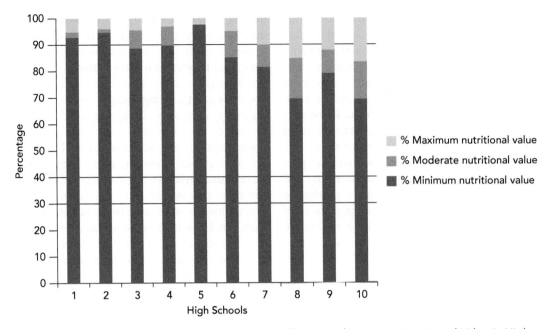

Figure 13.2 Percentage of Items of Maximum, Moderate, and Minimum Nutritional Value in High School Vending Machines

Since the era of Ontario provincial government cutbacks to education in the mid-1990s, school cafeterias and vending machines are expected to generate revenues to pay for a host of student activities and equipment needs and even essential parts of school infrastructure.[14] Fiscal restructuring by the provincial government under Progressive Conservative party rule (1995–2003) had largely eliminated monies coming from school boards for such expenses, according to respondents. Given the current fiscal realities, several schools have now assigned a teacher to spend significant time organizing the school food environment and accessing students' disposable income. As one of these teachers told the author, "All the money you need for student activities walks in the door each day, and walks right out again [to purchase food and drinks] unless you can capture it in the school." Today, schools are left to fend for themselves to cover a number of their costs. In effect, they have been forced to view their students as customers, and cafeterias and vending machines as "profit centres," to make up for lost government revenues.

Our interviews made it clear that additional factors shaped the food environment in the school as well. A crucial one is the food environment found in the immediate area *outside* the school. Respondents indicated to us that these outside-school food venues were well patronized by students. Mapping this outside-school food environment was clearly a necessary task to understand what was happening to food in the schools. When we did this we found that most schools, with the exception of two suburban schools and one rural school, were within easy walking distance of several fast-food outlets (see table 13.3). Why consider walking distance? Our reasoning was that with the elimination of grade 13 in Ontario schools, only a relatively small percentage of the school population is now of driving age and able to bring a vehicle to school.

Do purveyors of nutrient-poor edible products, such as fast-food corporations, explicitly target high schools as part of their locational strategies? This is an important question that has not been well studied. Our findings do indicate a pattern also found in one of the few other studies that has considered the relationship between schools and the fast-food industry. Austin et al. (2005) studying the Chicago area found that fast-food restaurants tended to be clustered around schools there as well. More recently, the impact of near-school food outlets on school food environments was corroborated by a study by Vine and Elliot (2013) in Ontario.

One inner-city school we studied that was in close proximity to several fast-food outlets and a deli in a large grocery store demonstrated the effects of nearby off-site fast-food vendors on the in-school food environment. The school had to compete on price and product offerings with outside vendors to capture students' disposable income, according to the respondent in this school. Given the price sensitivity of students generally (see Shannon et al. 2002), skewing the prices of unhealthy food and beverages in this manner is likely influencing food-purchasing patterns in the schools and contributing to unhealthy eating.

A further determinant of the in-school food environment was the cafeteria staff reductions deemed necessary because of funding cuts from the provincial government. Respondents in most schools reported that staff reductions made it difficult or even impossible to prepare meals, side dishes, and desserts from scratch. This led to a dependence on prepared or semi-prepared industrial food and a sacrifice in the nutritional quality of the food offered. When schools relied more on an outside supplier of a main dish, it was typically a "finger-food" type of item (panzerotti,

pizza) of only "moderate" nutritional value. In the case of cafeteria desserts prepared or semi-prepared off-site, the issue was excess trans fats and saturated fats in the products.

The Struggle to Promote Healthy Eating in Schools

When this study was undertaken, broader initiatives from government to deal with serious nutritional issues in high schools were largely non-existent.[15] In this policy vacuum it was left to *local* initiatives to improve the situation. One of these initiatives was the decision of staff in most of the schools surveyed not to purchase a deep fryer in the interests of avoiding the health perils of deep-fried food. Among the boldest of local initiatives was the elimination in one school of *all* soft drinks. This required the purchase of new vending machines, a considerable expense, so that healthier options could be offered (because the soft drink supplier had also provided vending machines). It is notable that the respondent at this school reported that no complaints had been received from students over the year since this change was made. While revenues from vending machines did decline with this decision, the healthier options that now filled the machines offset most of the decline that occurred.

There were a few other informal nutritional policies initiated by staff. These included concerted efforts made by staff to promote salad and vegetable options to students and to minimize junk foods in the cafeteria. Unfortunately these efforts to expand healthy eating in the schools were undermined by other factors. One was the perceived need to employ revenue generating vending machines to cover a host of student

Table 13.3 Extra–School Food Environment (n=10 schools)

	Number of Fast-Food Outlets and Distance from School				
	0–5 min. walk	6–10 min. walk	11–15 min. walk	16–20 min. walk	5 min. drive
Total all schools	16	25	3	1	10

activity expenses and even the cost of some basic infrastructure. Vending machines are the main mechanism that pseudo food companies presently have for entering public high school food environments.

Finally, a key factor appearing to undermine healthier eating in schools was the corporate food environment surrounding most schools. As with the Chicago schools studied by Austin et al. (2005), our schools were for the most part surrounded by several nutrient-poor fast-food vendors within easy walking distance.

In September 2011, the province of Ontario implemented a new School Food and Beverage Policy (PPM-150) in keeping with initiatives in several other Canadian provinces (Government of Ontario 2010). This policy was oriented to bring positive change to provincial school food environments. While a thorough assessment of the success of this initiative awaits further studies, a preliminary investigation of the impact of the new policy suggested that a number of barriers still exist to remaking school food environments as sites of healthy eating (see Vine and Elliot 2013).

Conclusion

We have argued that a powerful segment of the food industry controlling the production and promotion of nutrient-poor products we call pseudo foods has an inordinate impact on the content of contemporary food environments. The mutually reinforcing effects of corporate concentration and mass advertising in the food business via the process of spatial colonization of food environments by pseudo food-producing corporations is implicated in the undermining of healthy eating behaviours in society. Two institutional settings were examined in this study. In the private sector institution represented by the supermarket, our research suggests that both powerful pseudo food corporate processors and highly concentrated supermarket chain store companies engage in mutually beneficial behaviour to aggressively promote pseudo foods in the supermarket food environment. The spatial colonization of pseudo foods was well advanced in the sample of stores we studied.

In the public sector institution represented by the high school, our survey of high schools in one school district in southern Ontario indicated a high degree of penetration of pseudo foods as well, despite apparent efforts to encourage healthy eating there. Vending machines, school tuck shops, and to a lesser extent cafeterias were replete with nutrient-poor products, especially with respect to snack foods and side dishes served with main courses. Important factors shaping the high school food environment were (1) previous rounds of cutbacks by the Ministry of Education, which encouraged the use of vending machines to make up needed revenue; (2) kitchen staff shortages, also due to cutbacks, that resulted in the use of trans fat-laden baked goods prepared off-site; and (3) the food environment adjacent to schools, which was dominated by the presence of fast-food outlets and vendors of nutrient-poor products. The latter affected both the types of foods that schools could offer in order to compete effectively for students' disposable income and also the prices charged for pseudo foods available in school tuck shops where those existed.

Discussion Questions

1. What are key consequences of the rapidly increasing phenomenon of people eating away from the home?

2. How does the concept of *pseudo foods* differ from the commonly used term *junk foods*?

3. How does the concept of *spatial colonization* help us understand how powerful corporate pseudo food processors maintain and expand their dominance in our food environments?

4. What aspects of high school food environments were found to be most dominated by edible products of minimal nutritional value?

5. What were found to be the key determinants of the quality of high school food environments? Discuss how each had an influence on the results.

Further Reading

1. Kessler, David. 2009. *The End of Overeating.* Toronto: McClelland & Stewart.
   A remarkably accessible book that considers how the profit motive distorts modern restaurant meals and processed foods more generally. The book is particularly illuminating on the role of added salt, fats, and sugars in making processed foods so palatable, with an excellent and very readable discussion of the powerful neurological effects of these substances.

2. Nestle, Marion. 2007. *Food Politics: How the Food Industry Influences Nutrition and Health.* Berkeley: University of California Press.
   Probably the best-known person writing about nutritional matters in the world today, Nestle established her reputation with the earlier version of this book. With a title that says it all, Nestle has excellent chapters on shaping the diets of children and youth, school foods, and the role of food corporations in influencing the science of nutrition itself.

3. Pollan, Michael. 2006. *The Omnivore's Dilemma: A Natural History of Four Meals.* New York: Penguin.
   This book begins with an exposé of corn, which turns out to be, in its various forms, at the core of the modern industrial food system. Pollan's account of the transformation of this one-time mainstay of the Mexican diet into a feedstock of the contemporary food economy is exceptionally engaging, and leads to his examination of the meat industry as well.

4. Roberts, Wayne. 2013. *The No-Nonsense Guide to World Food*, 2nd edn. Toronto: Between the Lines.
   A wide-ranging and pioneering treatment of issues related to food by the former head of the Toronto Food Policy Council. Roberts's style is accessible and engaging, and challenges us to explore the surprising and disturbing contradictions that characterize the world of food, whether it be issues around food production and marketing, the reality of mass hunger in the world of food surpluses, or the amazing rise of food activism across the globe.

5. Winson, Anthony. 2013. *The Industrial Diet: The Degradation of Food and the Struggle for Healthy Eating.* Vancouver and New York: UBC Press and New York University Press.
   The industrialization of food beginning in the nineteenth century has had momentous implications for the nutritional quality of mass diets. This book argues that three industrial dietary regimes have shaped food environments since the last third of the nineteenth century. Food has been degraded via the processes of simplification, the speeding-up of food production, and the macro-adulteration of food with sugar, fat, and salt, among other additives. The intensification of the industrial diet and the proliferation of nutrient-poor pseudo foods in our food environments have had an important role in undermining our health. The final section of the book looks at various initiatives that have resisted the industrial diet and made healthy eating a priority.

Notes

1. The author would like to thank Maxine Fung, Chris Valiquet, and Anita Mahadeo for assistance with this research.
2. Body composition includes measures of BMI, waist circumference, and skin-fold tests. Previously Canadian data consisted largely of self-reported information, with the inherent biases this entails.
3. A summary of the "Canadian Health Measures Survey: Cycle 1 Data Tables, 2007 to 2009" was reported in Statistics Canada, 2010, "Health, 2007 to 2009," *The Daily*, 13 January, http://www.statcan.gc.ca/daily-quotidien/100113/dq100113a-eng.htm, accessed 6 January 2011.
4. While this term is used in the literature, it is not treated as a concept but typically used solely as a descriptive term.
5. "Light" ice creams tend to have substantially lower fat levels.
6. Pepsico Annual Report for 2014, http://www.pepsico.com/docs/album/default-document-library/pepsico-2014-annual-report_final.pdf, p. 12.
7. For a fuller discussion of this process, see Winson (1993:122–7).
8. For more details on the methodology of this study, see Winson (2004:305).
9. These cereals, a breakfast favourite of North American children and bestsellers in the prepared cereal category, have on average between four and five teaspoons of sugar for each single serving equivalent. Four grams of sugar are taken to be equivalent to one teaspoon (see Larsen 2003).
10. For more discussion of these "food deserts" see Alwitt and Donley (1997) and Nayga and Weinberg (1999).

11. In 2004 most but not all of the school boards in Ontario were phoned to assess the degree of privatization of food services. The great majority of those contacted had privatized their operations.
12. By "implicit" policy, I mean a decision regarding food and beverage offerings and/or their preparation that was made in the school and that was not explicitly designated as a nutritional policy, but which had obvious nutritional and therefore health implications for students.
13. What we have categorized as "side dishes," "snacks," and "beverage" items were almost always offered on a regular daily basis. "Main meals," on the other hand, were typically rotated through the week according to a fixed schedule in nearly all the schools sampled. Calculating units sold per day was not as straightforward with "main meals." Calculations were made on the following basis: if a pasta dish, for example, was usually offered once a week throughout the school year and typically sold 50 units on that day, we considered this as having sold 10 units per day (50 units/5 days =10 units/day). For further details on this study see Winson (2008).
14. In one school, for example, vending machine revenues went to replace the school clocks and complete the parking lot.
15. Since this research was completed sweeping new guidelines for school food have been implemented by the Ministry of Education, as in a number of other provinces. For an initial appraisal of the success of these guidelines in fostering healthy eating in schools, see Vine and Elliot (2013).

References

A.C. Neilsen Marketing Research. 1992. *Category Management: Positioning Your Organization to Win.* Chicago: NTC Business Books.

Advertising Age. 2005. "Special Report: Profiles Supplement." 27 June.

———. 2007. "Special Report: Profiles Supplement." 25 June.

Agriculture and Agri-Food Canada. 2015. *The Canadian Snack Food Manufacturing Industry.* http://www.agr.gc.ca/eng/industry-markets-and-trade/statistics-and-market-information/by-product-sector/processed-food-and-beverages/the-Canadian-snack-food-manufacturing-industry/?id=1172692863066.

Alwitt, L.F., and T.D. Donley. 1997. "Retail Stores in Poor Urban Neighbourhoods." *Journal of Consumer Affairs* 31(1):139–64.

American Dietetic Association. 2003. "Nutrition Services: An Essential Component of Comprehensive School Health Programs." *Journal of the American Dietetic Association* 103(4):505–14.

Austin, S. Bryn, Steven J. Melly, Brisa N. Sanchez, et al. 2005. "Clustering of Fast-Food Restaurants around Schools: A Novel Application of Spatial Statistics to the Study of Food Environments." *American Journal of Public Health* 95(9): 1575–81.

Burn, Douglas. 1999. "Thriving on Consumers' Hand to Mouth Existence." *Food in Canada* (January–February):16–17.

Burns, C., M. Jackson, C. Gibbons, and R.M. Stoney. 2002. "Foods Prepared Outside the Home: Association with Selected Nutrients and Body Mass Index in Adult Australians." *Public Health Nutrition* 5(3):441–8.

Carter, Mary-Ann, and Boyd Swinburn. 2004. "Measuring the 'Obesogenic' Food Environment in New Zealand Primary Schools." *Health Promotion International* 19(1):15–20.

Centers for Disease Control. 1997. "Guidelines for School Health Programs to Promote Lifelong Healthy Eating." *The Journal of School Health* 67(1):9–26.

Chevalier, Michel. 1975. "Increase in Sales Due to In-Store Display." *Journal of Marketing Research* 12:426–31.

Connor, John M., Richard T. Rogers, Bruce W. Marion, and Willard E. Mueller. 1985. *The Food Manufacturing Industries.* Toronto: Lexington Books.

Cox, Keith, 1970. "The Effect of Shelf Space on Sales of Branded Products." *Journal of Marketing Research* 7:55–8.

Crawford, Louise. 1977. "Junk Food in Our Schools? A Look at Student Spending in School Vending Machines and Concessions." *Journal of the Canadian Dietetic Association* 38(3):193–7.

Cumins, S., and S. McIntyre. 2006. "Food Environments and Obesity—Neighbourhood or Nation?" *International Journal of Epidemiology* 35(1):100–4.

Fletcher, John, and Kirsten Patrick. 2014. "A Political Prescription Is Needed to Treat Obesity." *Canadian Medical Association Journal* 186(17):1275.

Fontaine, Kevin R., and David B. Allison. 2004. "Obesity and Mortality Rates." Pp. 767–86 in *Handbook of Obesity: Etiology and Pathophysiology*, 2nd edn, ed. George Bray and Claude Bouchard. New York: Marcel Dekker.

Food Bureau. 1998. *The Canadian Snack Food Industry.* Ottawa: Market and Industry Services Branch. Accessed April 2003. www.agr.ca//food/profiles/snackfood/snack-food_e.html.

French, S., M. Story, J.A. Fulkerson, and P. Hannan. 2004. "An Environmental Intervention to Promote Lower-Fat Food Choices in Secondary Schools: Outcomes of the TACOS Study." *American Journal of Public Health* 94(9):1507–12.

Garnsey, Peter. 1999. *Food and Society in Classical Antiquity.* Cambridge: Cambridge University Press.

Government Accountability Office (GAO). 2009. *Agricultural Concentration and Agricultural Commodity and Retail Food Prices.* Briefing for professional staff, 24 April. http://www.gao.gov/assets/100/96258.pdf.

Government of Ontario, Ministry of Education. 2010. *School Food and Beverage Policy.* Policy/Program Memorandum No. 150. Toronto: Government of Ontario. http://www.edu.gov.on.ca/extra/eng/ppm/ ppm150.pdf.

Howe, D. 1983. "The Food Distribution Sector." In *The Food Industry: Economics and Politics*, ed. Jim Burns. London: Heinemann.

Kahane, Jack. 2000. "Sweet Opportunities: Maximize Your Profits in Confectionery." *Canadian Grocer* (September):57–61.

Kondro, Wayne. 2012. "Grim and Grimmer Global Health Statistics." *Canadian Medical Association Journal* 184(10): E506–E507.

Kramer-Atwood, J.L., J. Dwyer, D.M. Hoelscher, et al. 2002. "Fostering Healthy Food Consumption in Schools: Focusing on the Challenges of Competitive Foods." *Journal of the American Dietetic Association* 102:1228–33.

Larsen, Joanne. 2003. "Ask the Dietician: Junk Food." Accessed May 2003. http://www.dietitian.com/junkfood.html.

Lee, I-Min, JoAnn Manson, and Charles Hennekens. 1993. "Body Weight and Mortality: A 27-Year Follow-up of Middle-Aged Men." *Journal of the American Medical Association* 270(23):2823–7.

Levine, Barbara. 1997. "Childhood Obesity Associated with the Excessive Consumption of Soft Drinks and Fruit Juices." *Topics in Clinical Nutrition* 13 (1):69–73.

Lipscombe, Lorraine L., and Janet E. Hux. 2007. "Trends in Diabetes Prevalence, Incidence, and Mortality in Ontario, Canada, 1995–2005: A Population-Based Study." *Lancet* 369:750–6.

Ludwig, David S., Karen Peterson, and Steven Gortmaker. 2001. "Relations Between Consumption of Sugar-Sweetened Drinks and Childhood Obesity: A Prospective, Observational Analysis." *Lancet* 357:505–8.

Maclean, Susan. 1992. "Cold Comfort: A Frozen Novelty Is No Longer Just a Summertime Treat." *Canadian Grocer* 106(3):14–16+.

Manson, JoAnn E., Walter Willett, Meir Stampfer, et al. 1995. "Body Weight and Mortality among Women." *The New England Journal of Medicine* 333(1):677–85.

Marks, Ray, and John P. Allegrante. 2005. "Health Outcomes of Child, Adolescent and Adult Obesity: A Review of the Literature." Pp. 13–44 in *Body Mass Index: New Research*, ed. Linda A. Ferrera. New York: Nova Biomedical Books.

Matas, Robert. 1987. "Stocking Shelves Has a Hidden Cost." *The Globe and Mail*, 28 February.

Mozaffarian, Dariush, Martijn Katan, Alberto Ascherio, et al. 2006. "Trans Fatty Acids and Cardiovascular Disease." *New England Journal of Medicine* 354:1601–13.

Nayga, Rodolfo, and Zy Weinberg. 1999. "Supermarket Access to the Inner City." *Journal of Retailing and Consumer Services* 6 (3):141–5.

Nestle, Marion. 2002. *Food Politics: How the Food Industry Influences Nutrition and Health.* Berkeley: University of California Press.

—— and Michael Jacobson. 2000. "Halting the Obesity Epidemic: A Public Health Policy Approach." *Obesity* 115:12–24.

Nutribase. 2001. *Nutritional Facts: Desk Reference.* New York: Penguin Putnam.

Ontario Society of Nutrition Professionals in Public Health (OSNPPH). 2004. *Call to Action: Creating a Healthy School Nutrition Environment.* School Nutrition Workgroup Steering Committee. www.osnpph.on.ca.

Pi-Sunyer, F. Xavier. 2002. "The Obesity Epidemic: Pathophysiology and Consequences of Obesity." *Obesity Research* 10:97S–104S.

Power, Elaine. 2005. "Determinants of Healthy Eating among Low-Income Canadians." *Canadian Journal of Public Health* 96 (July–August suppl.):S38–S42.

Raine, K.D. 2005. "Determinants of Healthy Eating in Canada." *Canadian Journal of Public Health* 96(suppl. 3):S8-S14.

Reardon, Thomas, and Julio Berdegué. 2002. "The Rapid Rise of Supermarkets in Latin America: Challenges and Opportunities for Development." *Development Policy Review* 4:371–88.

———, Peter Timmer, Christopher Barrett, and Julio Berdegué. 2003. "The Rise of Supermarkets in Africa, Asia, and Latin America." *American Journal of Agricultural Economics* 85(5):1140–6.

Scherer, Frederic F. 1982. "The Breakfast Cereal Industry." Pp. 92–4 in *The Structure of American Industry*, 6th edn, ed. Walter Adams. New York: Macmillan.

Schlosser, Eric. 2001. *Fast Food Nation: The Dark Side of the All-American Meal*. New York: Houghton Mifflin.

Shannon, Christine, Mary Story, Jayne A. Fulkerson, and Simone French. 2002. "Factors in the School Cafeteria Influencing Food Choices by High School Students." *The Journal of School Health* 72(6): 229–34.

Shapiro, Eben. 1992. "P&G Takes on the Supermarkets with Uniform Pricing." *New York Times*, 26 April.

Shoesmith, John. 1992. "Changing the Way C-Stores Do Business: Gas, Deli, Fresh and Prepared Foods. Is This a Supermarket or a Convenience Store?" *Canadian Grocer* 106(10):30–4.

Statistics Canada. 2002. "National Longitudinal Survey of Children and Youth: Childhood Obesity, 1994–1999." *The Daily*, 18 October.

Story, M., D. Neumark-Sztainer, and S. French. 2002. "Individual and Environmental Influences on Adolescent Eating Behaviours." *Journal of the American Dietetic Association* 102(3):S40–S51.

Taylor, J., S. Evers, M. McKenna. 2005. "Determinants of Healthy Eating in Children and Youth." *Canadian Journal of Public Health* 96 (suppl. 3):S20-S26.

US Department of Health and Human Services. 2001. *The Surgeon General's Call to Action to Prevent and Decrease Overweight and Obesity*. Washington DC: United States Government Printing Office.

Vine, Michelle, and Susan Elliot. 2013. "Examining Local-level Factors Shaping School Nutrition Policy Implementation in Ontario, Canada." *Public Health Nutrition* 17(6): 1290–8.

Wechsler, Howell, Nancy D. Brener, Sarah Kuester, and Clare Miller. 2001. "Food Service and Foods and Beverages Available at School: Results from the School Health Policies and Programs Study 2000." *Journal of School Health* 71(7):313–24.

Wellman, David. 1999. "The Big Crunch." *Supermarket Business* 54 (3):46–8.

Winson, Anthony 1993. *The Intimate Commodity: Food and the Development of the Agro-Industrial Complex in Canada*. Toronto: University of Toronto Press.

———. 2004. "Bringing Political Economy into the Debate on the Obesity Epidemic." *Agriculture and Human Values* 21(4):299–312.

———. 2008. "School Food Environments and the Obesity Issue: Content, Structural Determinants, and Agency in Canadian High Schools." *Agriculture and Human Values* 25 (4):499–511.

———. 2013. *The Industrial Diet: The Degradation of Food and the Struggle for Healthy Eating*. Vancouver and New York: UBC Press and New York University Press.

14 What Constitutes Good Food?
Toward a Critical Indigenous Perspective on Food and Health

Debbie Martin and Margaret Amos

Learning Objectives

Through this chapter, you can

1. Develop a critical understanding of food security as it relates to Indigenous communities within Canada

2. Become aware of the role that nutritionism plays regarding food choices, and thus, health and well-being

3. Understand the diverse food systems that exist among Indigenous cultures within Canada, Indigenous food sovereignty, and the need for sustainable, just, and healthy ("good") food

Introduction

What constitutes "good food"? Is it food that is good *for* us? Food that fuels our well-being, along with our bodies? We contend that good food fits with these understandings but is also fundamentally about just, healthy, and sustainable food systems. For many, it is unfathomable that within a country as rich in economic, environmental, and human resources as Canada, there continue to be communities, disproportionately Indigenous, that experience problems attaining **food security**. Unfortunately, this is far too often the case. Food security is a serious and growing issue in Canada, particularly for Indigenous communities. For instance, the International Polar Year Inuit health survey (2007–08) indicates that Inuit in Canada face the highest documented rates of **food insecurity** of any Indigenous population living in the developed world. The causes of food insecurity are multiple and complex, but include processes such as colonialism and environmental dispossession, economic transitions and poverty, changing demographics, and logistical challenges (Council of Canadian Academies 2014). Clearly, concerted efforts are needed to achieve the goal of food security for all Canadians, but particularly for its Indigenous peoples.

If food security is understood as a goal to be achieved, then **food sovereignty** should be thought of as the means to achieve it (Council of Canadian Academies 2014). Food sovereignty involves providing increased involvement in and, therefore, control over the means through which food is procured. The increased involvement of Indigenous peoples in their food systems promotes healthier communities by decreasing dependency on globalized food systems and promoting traditional methods of harvesting and gathering foods that are sustainable and healthy. For many Indigenous peoples, increased involvement in the food system also means a decreased reliance on market foods and an increased ability to procure and prepare traditional foods. Local and traditional foods are often cited as alternatives to market foods, as they are healthier, sustainably sourced, and culturally appropriate, helping to combat food insecurity. However, many Indigenous communities in Canada face significant barriers that prevent them from accessing traditional foods, even when there are sufficient amounts of wild food sources available. In their research in two northern Ontario First Nations, Pal, Harman, and Robidoux (2013) note that resources needed to procure traditional foods are often prohibitively expensive for many and are often unavailable when needed. And, as these authors and many others point out, cost is not the only impediment for many, since traditional food procurement also requires that the *knowledge* of how to engage in these activities is passed from generation to generation, often made difficult by competing demands (e.g. full-time employment, child care, urban living). Such barriers indicate that a shift needs to occur at a systemic/policy level to support not only the ability to access the resources necessary to procure traditional foods, but also the corresponding sharing of knowledge necessary for the continuation of traditional food procurement practices.

The discussions and debates that occur around the issue of food security for Indigenous peoples and the best way to achieve it are often rationalized by assuming that improvements to an individual's health will occur simply through modifications to an individual's nutrition intake and diet. Indeed, nutrition is an essential component to proper growth and development and educational achievement, and is a requirement for the prevention of both chronic and infectious diseases, justifying the importance of food security. The diverse First Nations, Inuit, and Métis who make up the **Indigenous peoples of Canada** live within communities that are too often

characterized by high rates of chronic and infectious diseases, obesity, and even hunger, making food security a priority, but also a moving target. The causes of such issues are exceedingly complex, involving ongoing and problematic colonial relationships between Indigenous communities and the Crown, which manifests in deeply entrenched racialization of Indigenous communities (King et al. 2009; Loppie-Reading and Wien 2009; Power 2008). Such complexities, however, are incredibly difficult to tackle, and efforts to do so have often resulted in short-sighted solutions that target individual behaviours as opposed to the larger, more systemic issues that are causing them. This approach to food and eating, which distances individuals from the contexts in which their foods are eaten and reinforces a growing ignorance about the interconnectedness of the health of people and the health of the planet, has become so pervasive that it has been dubbed by its critics as **nutritionism**. Attempting to address complex issues such as food security within a nutritionism framework fails to account for Indigenous peoples' *perspectives* on how and why their communities are food insecure. Situating the argument for food security squarely within the realm of nutritionism to the exclusion of other important contexts—such as historical, social, and cultural circumstances—often limits the discussion of food security to one that only reflects the view that people need to make better food choices and to become more educated about what foods they should be eating, and that education about proper nutrition will somehow lead to better overall food security.

Focusing on the individual and failing to account for Indigenous peoples' collective perspectives about food and food systems, suggests, by default, that major contextual factors within a society—such as changing employment patterns, technological advancements, environmental destruction, and other associated measures of "progress"—are unavoidable by-products of development, as opposed to direct consequences of **colonization**, unfettered economic development, and the privileging of corporate interests in our global food systems over Indigenous knowledges (Kuhnlein et al. 2004; Lambden et al. 2006; Thow 2009; Winson 2004). The systematic exclusion of Indigenous peoples about discussions regarding food is a form of ongoing colonization—that is, the dismissal, under-representation, or complete undermining of Indigenous peoples' knowledge(s) regarding the important role of food within their communities in any discussions about their food systems (Smith 1999). This systematic exclusion of Indigenous peoples has been called into question in recent years, as Indigenous peoples and food researchers ranging from nutritionists to political economists have argued that for food security efforts to be effective, they must encompass the socio-political and community context in which foods are eaten. A more nuanced understanding sheds light on how an individual's food "choices" are often the complex by-product of various cultural practices, government policies, and marketing strategies (Thow 2009; Winson 2004). This suggests that food security is not inevitable, nor is it simply a matter of individual food choice (Delormier et al. 2009; Thow 2009). A more complex understanding that is broadened to include issues of food sovereignty, described later in this chapter, is warranted.

Before we move on to a discussion and further critique of nutritionism, it is important to note that although Indigenous collectives within Canada share an historical connection to the land and are each influenced, historically and presently, by the Canadian state, Indigenous peoples within Canada are incredibly diverse. In fact, Indigenous peoples worldwide, meaning all those who continue to hold an ancestral connection to a particular territory—Indigenous peoples of Canada included—share certain imperatives regarding the role of humans in relation to the world around them. These imperatives provide a framework that supports the food sovereignty of Indigenous peoples and includes an intimate connection and belonging to the environment, a sacred responsibility to the earth, and a respect for all things living and non-living.

Each of these imperatives manifests differently depending on the origins and experiences of particular Indigenous groups, but they all nevertheless reflect overarching themes consistent with Indigenous peoples worldwide (Clarkson et al. 1992).

Nutritionism: A Handmaiden of Colonialism

The past 40 years has witnessed significant changes to conventional ways in which people acquire food and make choices about what foods they should, and should not, be eating. Many argue that these changes have shifted the responsibility of food choices away from individuals and into the hands of large multinational corporations, whose interests are not so much about sustainable, just, and healthy foods as they are about ensuring that foods are marketable, produced in mass quantities, and profitable. Such changes represent a significant, and concerning, societal shift away from the cultural and contextual information that people have historically relied upon to make decisions about their foods. Scrinis (2008) labels this societal shift *nutritionism*, which he argues valorizes scientific and profit-driven understandings of food to the exclusion of the culture and context-specific knowledge that has characterized food and eating since time immemorial.

Such misconceptions about food included under the auspices of nutritionism may have particularly deleterious effects for Indigenous communities. Coupled with a shift toward a wage-economy and away from a subsistence way of life, many Indigenous communities (particularly in northern and remote places, but also in rural and urban locations) have experienced alarming increases in the availability and affordability of processed and prepackaged foods with low nutrient value (Lambden et al. 2006). This food transition has led to a corresponding increase in confusion about what to eat (Kuhnlein and Chan 2000), and a growing dependence on and a disenchantment with non-Indigenous nutrition "experts" for a one-size-fits-all approach to nutritional knowledge (Martin 2009). Efforts to address the resulting health effects of such dietary changes have often happened through educational and behaviour-change efforts. Although such efforts may help with respect to increasing nutritional literacy, it does little in terms of addressing underlying societal structures that are perpetuating food insecurity and the movement away from traditional foods.

The failure to address the underlying causes of food insecurity through the spread of nutritionism amounts to a cultural oppression of food. It does so by deepening the growing disconnection between food, people, and place, severing the important and integral relationships people once had with their foods (Scrinis 2008) and the environment. For example, whole foods procured from the land were once the trusted source of nourishment among Indigenous communities. Yet, increasingly research addresses dietary guidelines more concerned with consumption of food components such as fats, cholesterol, sugar, and carbohydrates, than with the overall foods themselves. Furthermore, under the influence of nutritionism, people tend to do a quick scan of food labels to judge them according to nutritional guidelines. But a food item that is low in fat, sugar, or sodium, for example, may contain a roster of other ingredients that may be as bad or worse for an individual's health. Nestle (2007) affirms that this confusion (what she refers to as "nutrition confusion") has led to the overeating of unhealthy foods and poor nutritional practices. As Sturdy and Scrinis (2014) suggests, nutritionism is not meant to bring people closer to understanding a healthy diet, nor does it provide recommendations for healthy eating. To the contrary, nutritionism highlights how distanced we have become from understanding our food and how the food industry has manipulated and marketed food for reasons that go beyond improving the health of people. We contend that there is an immediate and pressing need to question the assumptions inherent in nutritionism, and that Indigenous communities are uniquely positioned to challenge these assumptions because they often hold significant knowledge regarding traditional foods and all the associated values and norms that are attached to procurement, preparation, and consumption of traditional foods.

At face value, it might seem counterintuitive to seek nutritional advice from communities experiencing food crises at every end of the food security spectrum—ranging from hunger and poverty to nutritional deficiencies and obesity. However, if we view the foods we eat as inseparable from the social, cultural, political, and natural environment in which foods are procured and consumed (as is advocated by critics of the nutritionism paradigm), then we begin to see that Indigenous communities are perhaps best positioned to offer valuable advice on food and eating and indeed, what constitutes good food. Whereas the goal of nutritionism is to reduce foods to biochemical properties and categories (Lupton 1996; Scrinis 2002; Warde 1997), the goal of food and eating within many Indigenous communities is to provide a means to express culture, uphold cultural traditions, and strengthen cultural knowledge. A side effect of this intricate relationship is positive health outcomes. In fact, nutrition research that accounts for the wealth of knowledge held by Indigenous peoples who remain rooted to their traditional territories has arrived at interesting findings: Indigenous peoples who obtain the bulk of their nutrient energy from traditional sources get more essential nutrients than those who substitute traditional foods for market foods (Egeland et al. 2009; Hanrahan 2008). Although market foods tend to provide more energy, they have an overall lower density of essential nutrients than what is found in traditional foods (Egeland et al. 2009). This data offers support for the consumption of traditional foods and for the inclusion of Indigenous perspectives in conversations about what constitutes good food.

The idea that the foods we eat are linked to our health can be traced back thousands of years to cultures that identified eating certain foods with preventing or curing illness or enhancing one's overall health and sense of well-being (Trivedi 2006). Historically, however, the link between food and health has not focused on understanding how foods react within the body as much as needing to learn more about the types of foods that were necessary to avoid hunger or to prevent nutritional deficiencies (Cannon 2003; Hanrahan 2008). As such, what was known about food was also closely related to a particular culture's locale: through trial and error, experience, and circumstance, people engaged with their surroundings to grow, harvest, hunt, and gather foods as they were made available. Food allowed diverse cultures to survive in their particular localities and also to develop relationships with their surroundings that are expressed through culture (Martin 2009; Willows 2005). As a symbol of culture, food shapes the health of particular cultural groups, in ways that extend far beyond its importance for nutrition and sustenance, to include social, emotional, and spiritual health and well-being (Kuhnlein et al. 2004). For example, the ceremonies and activities related to acquiring, processing, and consuming food are integral for reinforcing cultural practices and norms that are important for overall health and well-being.

The Imperative of Indigenous Food Sovereignty

Food sovereignty, broadly speaking, has the aim of reclaiming a public voice on issues related to food. Supporters of the food sovereignty movement feel strongly that those who depend upon food systems should have a say in decisions about every element of its procurement, production, and consumption (Desmarais and Wittman 2014). Food sovereignty, as a concept, has its roots outside of Indigenous realities. Within Canada, the National Farmers Union (NFU) and the Union Paysanne (two members of La Vía Campesina) introduced the concept to the Canadian context in 2001. NFU works against the corporate

control of the food system and participated in the early debates about the emerging concept of food sovereignty, and Union Paysanne represents farmers of Quebec who joined together to build alternatives to industrial agriculture. Initially these discussions of food sovereignty were limited to agricultural production and trade policy issues, but this changed in 2007 when members of Food Secure Canada attended an international forum on food sovereignty, and where several Indigenous peoples and organizations also met to deepen their own knowledge about food sovereignty frameworks (Kneen 2011).

The term **Indigenous food sovereignty** holds special significance for Indigenous peoples, because although the concept itself is relatively new, it speaks to issues that Indigenous peoples and communities have been struggling with for many, many generations. It also differs somewhat from the larger food sovereignty movement that is happening globally, because although there are shared concerns over issues like environment degradation and industrialization of food systems, Indigenous food sovereignty advocates also stress the importance of decolonization and self-determination, and the inclusion of co-management strategies for resource development and food use. A critique of the global (non-Indigenous) food sovereignty movement suggests that its policy demands are very modest, often focusing on an *individual* ethic of making food choices that are local, organic, nutritious, and healthy to the exclusion of a broader discussion about structural changes that are needed in our food systems at the national or international level (Desmarais and Wittman 2014). To the contrary, those seeking Indigenous food sovereignty advocate for a more *collective, relational approach*, wishing "to honor, value and protect traditional food practices and networks in the face of ongoing pressures of colonization" (Desmarais and Wittman 2014:1165).

Thus, for those committed to Indigenous food sovereignty, there is a rejection of one, universal definition in favour of one "that respects the sovereignty of distinct nations to have their rights to lands and resources recognized" (Morrison 2011:98). To date, Indigenous peoples within Canada have, more often than not, been systematically excluded from discussions about their food systems, including decisions about when and how often to eat, and how much and even what types of food can be eaten. This represents a significant shift from only a generation or two ago, when Indigenous communities and families relied upon their own wherewithal to acquire, prepare, and store all the foods that were needed to live healthfully within a particular geographic area (Martin 2009).

Within Canada, the conversation about Indigenous food sovereignty has largely been spearheaded by the British Columbia Food Systems Network Working Group on Indigenous Food Sovereignty (Morrison 2011). Through their conversations with Indigenous Elders, traditional harvesters, and community members, they have identified four principles of Indigenous food sovereignty that will be explored here. They include: (1) food is sacred; (2) participation; (3) self-determination; and (4) legislation and policy reform.

1. Food Is Sacred

> Only after the last tree has been cut down.
>
> Only after the last river has been poisoned.
>
> Only after the last fish has been caught.
>
> Only then will you find that money cannot be eaten.
>
> —Cree Prophecy

Indigenous peoples' knowledge of the natural world has historically arisen in response to the need to find ways of addressing problems of hunger, thirst, shelter, and clothing. Learning about one's natural surroundings and how its bounties can provide for one's family and community was integral to life itself (Radkau 2008). The connection and belonging that Indigenous peoples have with their natural surroundings

is born not out of romantic notions of "living close to nature," as is often assumed, but rather, is viewed as a reciprocal relationship, where the earth provides resources for survival as long as people take care not to deplete their surroundings (Turner 2005). Similarly, the greater awareness that people have in caring for the lands and waters around them, the greater likelihood that the earth will continue providing food and other necessities for survival. This understanding of the fragile relationship between humans and nature created an indisputable maxim for sustainability that was not only premised on *not depleting* resources, but, in fact, was dedicated to improving the amounts and types of resources available for future generations (Turner 2005). This perspective aligns with the goals of Indigenous food sovereignty, which is to create the conditions necessary for people to procure food sources from the land in ways that do not separate the health of people from the health of the environment. As Kneen suggests:

> If food is sacred, it cannot be treated as a mere commodity, manipulated into junk foods or taken from people's mouths to feed animals or vehicles. If the ways in which we get food are similarly sacred, Mother Earth cannot be enslaved and forced to produce what we want, when and where we want it, through our technological tools. (2011:92)

For many Indigenous cultures, humans form an inseparable part of their physical surroundings; thus, all the foods that are eaten reaffirm a direct and intimate connection to the earth and all things living and non-living. Among Inuit, for example, there is a belief that the foods one eats become a part of you, and therefore, you are what you eat. Respecting the sacrifice that an animal makes to provide food is recognized as a necessary part of life and, thus, of overall health and well-being (Hanrahan 2008). The natural surroundings in which foods are obtained provide important ingredients for medicines, clothing, shelter, and, indeed, for overall health and well-being. For Inuit in particular, ensuring that all parts of an animal or plant were used largely stemmed from times when foods were scarce. For example, both Ackroyd (1930) and Howell (1998) note that Labrador Inuit women developed tonics of cod liver oil, bog bean, and various other locally derived remedies, undoubtedly preventing certain nutrition deficiencies. Indeed, Ackroyd (1930) finds that compared with their non-Indigenous counterparts in northern Newfoundland, Inuit of the south coast of Labrador exhibited far fewer incidents of food-deficiency diseases such as beriberi, rickets, and scurvy than their non-Indigenous counterparts, despite less access to fresh fruits and vegetables and higher levels of poverty. The foods eaten, therefore, are intimately connected to health; since foods come from lands and waters, the health of individuals and communities is dependent upon the health of those resources. Essentially, what we do to our physical surroundings, we ultimately do to ourselves. This very holistic definition of health accepts the interrelatedness of all things, since we all form an integral part of the ecosystems that make up our surroundings (Henderson 2000).

2. Participation (at an Individual, Family, Community, and Regional Level)

Humans cannot manage or even control land; therefore, we must manage and control our behaviours in relation to it (Morrison 2011). Transforming the food system to reflect this philosophy will require a significant departure from the current dominant framework that is shaping our food systems, one that supports a food production model that is geared toward industrial food production. Rather than being defined by industry, Indigenous food systems are defined to include all land, soil, water, air, plants, and animals, as well as Indigenous knowledge, wisdom, and values (Morrison 2011). Indigenous food systems are maintained through active

participation in cultural harvesting strategies, making individual and community involvement in food procurement, preparation, and consumption a necessary element of the sustainability of this type of food system. Indigenous food sovereignty asserts that sustainable and ecological approaches are an inherent part of Indigenous ecosystems, and that fostering this balance rather than disrupting it assists with the maintenance of the health and integrity of the food system.

Historically, the participation of one's family and community in the food system was a given; it was not a choice. Ensuring the replenishment of resources required many Indigenous groups to adopt lifestyles that accommodated the need to avoid depleting the resources in a particular area (Carter 1990; Turner 2005). Thus, intricate methods of crop rotation, nomadism, and seasonal transhumance were mechanisms that ensured the respectful and frugal use of precious resources. How groups of Indigenous peoples organized themselves varied according to geographic location and the ages and genders of the group members, as well as the roles and responsibilities assigned to each member. The pragmatic nature of Indigenous survival on the land demanded clearly defined roles for each group member, as people depended upon one another for the group's survival.

Food not only protected against nutritional deficiencies but also reinforced a collective solidarity, fostering emotional, mental, and spiritual health and well-being. In fact, many pre-Columbian Indigenous peoples of Canada did not exhibit signs of social stratification and hierarchies that are common in Western society today (Cruikshank 1998; Samson and Pretty 2003). Although each member of a community or tribe had specific roles and responsibilities, none were given priority over others and everyone participated equitably in ensuring the survival of the community (Cruikshank 1998; Gunn Allen 1986; Kelm 1998). For example, among the Inuit of southern Labrador there was always a tradition of sharing the first salmon caught in the spring with all members of a community (Hanrahan 2000; Martin 2009). This practice, arising from a collective history of benevolence and respect for others, ensured that even the young and frail had a meal and provided an important means to protect against hunger at a time of year when supplies of food were at their lowest, in addition to fostering an atmosphere of sharing and cohesion among community members.

In many Indigenous communities, men and women had roles and responsibilities that were clearly divided by gender (those with multiple genders often being viewed as providing additional value to communities), yet unlike the Western world's gendered divisions of labour, roles were given equitable value (Gunn Allen 1986). As the only ones able to bring life into the world, women were given special status in communities as caregivers and creators of life (Graveline 1998). Women were also charged with preparing meals and clothing for men, enabling the men to hunt, trap, and fish, thus providing the family and community with food (Goudie 1983; Hanrahan 2001). If anyone failed to accomplish their assigned duties or did so inadequately, the entire family and perhaps community might go hungry or starve. And since women played essential roles in food production and procurement, respect for women and their freedom from violence were necessary components of this gendered balance (Wittman et al. 2010). Young people were given the important role of gathering fuel and food for the family, and as they got older and learned about their environments, were expected to impart their knowledge to the next generation (Cruikshank 1998).

Community Elders have always been given a special place in Indigenous communities (Knudtson and Suzuki 1992). As the keepers of legends and stories, Elders were considered the very transmitters of culture and were expected to pass on their knowledge to younger generations through the provision of advice and guidance (Knudtson and Suzuki 1992). The accumulated wisdom and teachings of the Indigenous ancestors tell much about how to encourage plant and animal resources to thrive, so that they can continue to give life and support the needs of current and future generations (Knudtson and Suzuki 1992). Thus, interactions with the earth and the resources utilized from it must be carefully considered in order to ensure the survival and well-being of future generations.

This sense of responsibility for future generations has guided previous generations and offers guidance to the current generation. Respecting and honouring Elders and ancestors means listening carefully to their teachings, learning from their mistakes, and living in step with their wisdom. Accordingly, there is a responsibility for us all to take care to respect and honour the generations of the future, just as previous generations have honoured us by giving us life and taking care of our resources. Thus, the knowledge passed on through generations, whether through actions or words, must be given privilege and respect if there is to be greater understanding of our food systems. Viewing food and eating from this perspective, we can begin to think of our food systems as a series of processes that are profoundly infused with the culture in which they occur and which cannot be understood outside of a social, cultural, and political context.

3. Self-Determination

Within the context of food sovereignty, self-determination is the ability to make informed decisions over the amount, type, quality, and quantity of foods that are procured—hunted, fished, gathered, grown. Indigenous food sovereignty, then, offers a means through which Indigenous communities can regain control over their own food systems (Morrison 2011). And yet, many Indigenous peoples continue to face mounting pressures to end traditional practices of food gathering. These pressures come from all directions—through the decimation of Indigenous lands for industrial development, through conservation policies that undermine traditional practices of food gathering, and through the increasing corporate control of the food economy which undermines the value of traditional food-gathering practices (Damman et al. 2008). For example, some Cree and Inuit communities in northern Quebec can no longer access local country food from spoiled fish stocks or caribou that have taken to new ground as a result of inefficient mining practices. As a result, hunting becomes more of a challenge and less accessible because people have to absorb the costs of flying into areas where country food stocks have not been impacted by industrial development. Where nearby country food is available, Indigenous communities must weigh the benefits of maintaining traditional food-gathering practices against the increasing contamination of their local foods supplies from resource extraction and development activities (Kuhnlein and Chan 2000). Essentially, Indigenous peoples are fighting a tidal wave of pressure to end traditional practices of food gathering that are essential for the maintenance of Indigenous food systems and vital to preserving food sovereignty.

These battles, unfortunately, are not new, and in fact represent the modern-day version of colonization that has always undermined the ability for Indigenous peoples to uphold sovereignty over their own lands and resources. In her book *The Earth's Blanket* ethnobotanist Nancy Turner (2005:24) states that the "rich are those people who balance the benefits they receive in life with the responsibilities they assume for themselves, their families and communities and their environment." In the Western world, wealth is measured by the accumulation of possessions and more and more infrequently by the value placed upon traditions or the ability to care for and benefit from natural surroundings (Turner 2005). Such teachings suggest that "wealth dwells in people who know about, appreciate and respect the other life forms around them and who understand the importance of habitats for people and all living things" (Turner 2005:24–5).

Turner describes a letter written by James Douglas, who later became governor of the Colony of Vancouver Island, upon his first arrival from Europe at what is now the city of Victoria. He described the landscape that he first saw as "a perfect Eden in the midst of the dreary wilderness of the Northwest Coast" (as quoted in Turner 2005:147). Europeans' historical accounts about (what is now known as) Canada noted dramatically varied landscapes and climates, suggesting that diverse adaptations must have evolved among Indigenous peoples in order to survive in these varied locations. These adaptations corresponded with the biodiversity of the geographic regions, which is evidenced by the diversity of foods, languages, songs, clothing, ceremonies, and other practices that emerge directly from the intimate knowledge of the world around them. Important for understanding the historical context of food sovereignty are the accounts that demonstrate the commonly held assumption by European colonists that the lands and waters upon which they arrived were undiscovered and untouched by humans, *terra nullius*, and were therefore awaiting human intervention in the form of "development." Turner (2005) suggests that what was assumed to be untouched wilderness on Canada's west coast was interpreted as prime real estate by Europeans, when in fact such bounty was the result of years of carefully crafted resource management practices by the Coast Salish, who tended and cared for the land using centuries-old practices of burning, clearing, and harvesting. From this perspective, food for Indigenous peoples acts as far more than a means to ensure nutritional health or provide sustenance. Traditional practices of hunting, fishing, picking, trapping, and other forms of harvesting are also used to demonstrate an historical and ongoing connection to the land that has never been ceded.

4. Legislation and Policy Reform

Indigenous food sovereignty advocates for coordinated, cross-sectoral strategies that address food insecurity through such efforts as wildlife co-management strategies, asserting the harvesting rights of Indigenous communities, and taking a strong position on the cross-border trade of animal products (Desmarais and Wittman 2014; Morrison 2011). Even though mounting concerns about the diminishing food supply and the increasing burden of disease are attracting attention from Indigenous knowledge holders, researchers, and policy makers all over the world, there is very little in the way of cross-sectoral conversation among these key players regarding potential solutions to our shared ecological and human crises (Morrison 2011; Saul 2008). As examples, nutritionists remain isolated from sociologists and anthropologists, and public health officials are largely unaware of their counterparts who work in areas of political economy and environmental stewardship—to say nothing of key Indigenous knowledge holders whose voices are often completely absent from these discussions. The result is that policies and programs that rely upon the research advances within specific disciplinary fields are overlooking key areas of concern that exist across multiple disciplines, and that our efforts at addressing these crises are resulting in ongoing damage to our waters, soil, and air, which we ultimately depend upon for good food. Although certain policies and programs may legitimately address the concerns within a particular discipline or sector, such as the need to develop public health interventions and policies that halt growing rates of diabetes, the application of these policies may undermine, ignore, or contradict some of the fundamental concerns that exist within a different discipline or policy field. For example, when government policies regarding resource conservation infringe upon Indigenous peoples' right to access their traditional livelihoods and sources of income, the result may be an increased burden on health care as Indigenous peoples experience higher rates of chronic disease such as obesity and diabetes resulting from physical inactivity and poor food choices (Damman et al. 2008). In effect, policies and programs meant to address problems of environmental devastation or population health may contribute to the harm affecting the overall health of the environment and the people who

live in it, when they do not seek to more broadly understand issues that affect health outside of specific disciplinary silos.

Scratching the surface of the broader social, economic, political, and environmental crises in which food insecurity is occurring raises many more questions than answers for Indigenous communities. As Indigenous youth, our most precious resource, grow up to learn that traditional land use is not regarded as contributing to the economy in the same way as more conventional agricultural or industrial uses might be, they are discouraged from adhering to the ways of their Elders. Indeed, it is difficult for Elders to suggest otherwise, as they witness any direct dependence upon the natural world as making their people more vulnerable. This has created circumstances where some Indigenous youth, like other non-Indigenous youth, feel distanced from their Elders and in some cases are expressing reluctance to continue to engage in traditional food-procurement practices (Orchard 1998). Their vulnerabilities and subsequent disengagement prevent their knowledge from becoming part of the discourse about food systems (Damman et al. 2008).

Conclusion: What Constitutes Good Food?

Some of the greatest population and public health concerns being faced today are linked to over-consumption of nutrient-poor food (e.g. cardiovascular disease, obesity, diabetes) (WHO 2000). Yet, at the same time, the world is experiencing unprecedented inequalities with respect to food access and appropriate distribution, often leading to hunger. Clearly, there is a pressing need for solutions to food security around the world, and this issue is certainly not isolated to Indigenous communities within Canada. Indigenous communities are a microcosm of these global food security concerns, where both hunger related to maldistribution of foods and chronic diseases related to eating too many nutrient-poor foods can be simultaneously present. This might seem to make little intuitive sense at first glance. But, if we begin to look at these two health concerns as being related (in that one may still be undernourished, despite weight gain) and as each representing part of a growing crisis relating to our ability to access "good food," we can begin to view food as much more than providing people with too much or too little to eat, and more in terms of how social, economic, political, environmental, and cultural circumstances beyond the control of individuals affect how, how much, when, and even why certain foods are being eaten or not eaten across diverse populations.

Increasingly, our food systems are characterized by capitalist commodity exchange, which emphasizes profit over all else, including the health of people and the ecosystem. It does so by insidiously touting nutrient-poor "foods" (or food-like substances) as healthy (Scrinis 2008), by commodifying the practice of hunting (putting the cost of the hunt out of reach for those most reliant upon it), and perhaps most concerning, by doing irreparable damage to the natural world, making Indigenous food-gathering practices impossible due to contamination and disruption of the environment for the purpose of unfettered economic development (Grey, Mittenthal, and Stenbaek 2013). Thus, legitimate concerns regarding the equitable distribution of foods, the biodiversity of foods, and the importance of foods for cultural expression are minimized and ignored. Consequently, understanding the role that food plays in our health and well-being is about far more than simply having "enough" to eat or calculating nutritional content of foods; instead, it is essential, *critical*, to understand the social, economic, political, environmental, and cultural context in which foods are accessed and consumed.

The promotion and protection of Indigenous food systems within Canada, and indeed, the food systems of Indigenous peoples all over the world, needs to happen through the protection and promotion of diverse Indigenous cultures. This must occur through the inclusion of Indigenous peoples as a fundamental part of the decision-making process around food systems—which includes a far bigger conversation than what is currently happening at the political level, and one that positions Indigenous voices rather than corporate voices at the centre of food systems discussions. Only when Indigenous peoples are included as full and equal partners in key conversations that affect access to traditional foods might we recognize that creative solutions to worldwide food shortages and over-consumption hinges very largely upon the preservation of the cultural diversity of our world's Indigenous peoples. We stress that such solutions can come in the form of food sovereignty.

There is not one, catch-all solution to achieving food sovereignty for Indigenous peoples within Canada. Rather, solutions must come from Indigenous communities, who are best positioned to know what works and what does not within their specific social, political, and cultural locations. To this end, Wittman et al. (2010) discuss a vision of food sovereignty that views food as integral to local cultures and is based upon local knowledge. They go even further by suggesting that food sovereignty cannot be achieved without political sovereignty, aligning with Morrison's (2011) vision for Indigenous food sovereignty as fundamentally embracing self-determination as one of its key pillars.

Challenges to the achievement of Indigenous food sovereignty within Canada remain. The impact of historical colonial encounters continues to shape the types and amounts of foods that are eaten within Indigenous communities. And, it is also important to remember that colonization continues to exist, manifesting differently according to which community is affected. Indigenous peoples within Canada currently face struggles with respect to accessing and using their traditional territories for food procurement purposes like hunting, fishing, trapping, and growing. These struggles exist for a variety of reasons, all related to historical and ongoing colonial practices: strict government regulations that prevent traditional food-gathering practices from taking place, economic development processes that affect Indigenous communities but do not include them in decision making, environmental destruction resulting from unfettered development, and moral opposition to traditional food-gathering practices by non-Indigenous people who are unfamiliar with Indigenous livelihoods (Lynge 1992; Nuttall et al., 2005; Panelli and Tipa 2009; Radkau 2008; Samson and Pretty 2003). Failing to account for the existing wealth of knowledge about food from Indigenous people's perspectives perpetuates colonial assumptions about the unworthiness of Indigenous knowledge(s) (Smith 1999). Continued forms of colonization present new challenges for Indigenous peoples in procuring and consuming foods necessary to uphold, strengthen, and celebrate their diverse cultures.

In addition to these challenges, Indigenous communities are also facing the significant influence of Western values on traditional Indigenous norms. Many argue that this gives rise to cultural discontinuity among Indigenous communities, where youth, in particular, may feel distanced from the experiences of their Elders and thus increasingly shift away from traditional food procurement practices (Orchard 1998). Discussions of Indigenous food sovereignty should be expanded to consider what it means to be Indigenous in today's contemporary society and whether and how Indigenous peoples are able to remain connected (or to reconnect) with their traditional roots while also remaining part of a contemporary, Westernized society.

Despite these challenges, there have been significant strides made at international, national, and regional levels that each indicates that progress toward Indigenous food sovereignty is happening. Since 1976, Canada has been a signatory of the International Covenant on Economic, Social and Cultural Rights (ICESCR) and is legally bound by its provisions. Of relevance to this discussion, the Committee on Economic, Social and Cultural Rights defines the right to adequate food as "when every man, woman and child, alone or in community with others, has physical and economic access at all times to adequate food or means for its procurement." Furthermore, it states that "adequate food should not be interpreted in a narrow or restrictive sense which equates it with a minimum package of calories, proteins and other specific nutrients." As well, sections of the United Nations Declaration on the Rights of Indigenous Peoples (2008), of which Canada is also a signatory, are also relevant for addressing both food security and food sovereignty, including the right to the resources and territories Indigenous peoples have traditionally occupied and the right to own and develop lands by reason of their traditional ownership.

Morrison (2011) argues that even though there have been a number of examples where rights-based approaches to addressing food sovereignty within Canada have been successful, this is just one possibility and in fact, may not always be the most effective (citing the significant length of time and resources necessary for Indigenous communities to work through lengthy court proceedings in order to have their rights acknowledged). She suggests that alternatives that engage Indigenous peoples "in activities and policy creation that . . . learns from and is informed by the experiences and expertise gained through many millennia of practice" (Morrison 2011:111). Swanson and Bhadwal (2009) call this approach "adaptive" and suggest that such bottom-up approaches to policy development are an effective means to respond to complex and dynamic conditions.

To conclude, we end with the question that spawned this discussion of food security, nutritionism, and food sovereignty, which was: What constitutes good food? We believe that the growing networks of Indigenous peoples across the country who are working toward Indigenous food sovereignty will contribute to discussions and critiques of nutritionism and the devastating impacts such an approach can have on Mother Earth. As they are the keepers and providers of their traditional territories since time immemorial, it is prudent to look to Indigenous peoples for guidance on how best to protect and preserve our global food systems. Thus, what constitutes good food? Ultimately, we contend that there is no one recipe for good food; it is food that is harvested, prepared, and consumed according to the principles, values, and norms of the Indigenous peoples on whose territory that food has been acquired; it is about understanding the diversity of communities and the people within them as unique, understanding that their knowledge(s) about their own lands and waters, and thus, their foods is also unique; it is about education that does not present itself as a narrowly constructed, one-size-fits-all approach to promoting healthy decisions about food and eating; it is about trusting in the ancestral knowledge that diverse groups possess about food; and finally, it is at the root of bringing people together to celebrate culture.

Discussion Questions

1. What is nutritionism? How might understanding Indigenous cultures promote a better understanding of nutritionism? Is it possible to overcome nutritionism?

2. Think about the apparent contradiction between global food shortages and rising rates of obesity. What might Indigenous perspectives on food offer in terms of understanding the complexity of this contradiction?

3. Many Indigenous communities in Canada are fighting for greater control over their lands and resources. How and why might traditional food use and greater control over market foods be an important part of this fight?

Further Reading

1. Desmarais, A.A., and H. Wittman. 2014. "Farmers, Foodies and First Nations: Getting to Food Sovereignty in Canada." *The Journal of Peasant Studies* 41(6):1153–73.
    This scholarly journal article provides a rich and well-documented interpretation of food sovereignty in Canada, including debates regarding the tensions around defining the terms and policies that will support movements for Indigenous food sovereignty. The authors are experts in the areas of rural social movements and development, local and national politics, and collaborative research on local food systems both nationally and globally. This article provides a contextual framework that emphasizes the need to critically assess the food system of our country and argues for a national movement on food sovereignty and to move words to action beyond the stages of infancy. The authors leverage the demands and expertise of local players and equip the reader to further understand the existing challenges in the Canadian context among the National Farmers Union, Québec's Union Paysanne, Food Secure Canada, and movements toward decolonizing Indigenous food sovereignty from coast to coast to coast.

2. Morrison, D. 2011. "Indigenous Food Sovereignty: A Model for Social Learning." Pp. 97–113 in *Food Sovereignty in Canada: Creating Just and Sustainable Food Systems*, ed. H. Wittman, A.A. Desmarais and N. Wiebe. Halifax, NS: Fernwood.
    Morrison's chapter is one of a collection of poignant case studies in Wittman, Desmarais, and Wiebe's book. As a whole, this book examines how average people in communities throughout Canada are resolute in their efforts to gain control over food resources, develop sustainable food-producing models, provide socially just markets, and implement policies in an urgent

effort to reclaim food as healthy and safe for consumers. Achieving food sovereignty in Canada, as represented by Dawn Morrison, describes the sacredness of food along with an Indigenous eco-philosophy that underlies the ability of Indigenous peoples to maintain honourable relationships with the land. Morrison talks about four guiding principles recognized by Indigenous communities to reconnect and reclaim their food, push beyond the confines of food security, and strive for food sovereignty: (1) the understanding that food is sacred or divine; (2) sovereignty is action and participation; (3) self-determination that underlies the freedom to hunt as needed and to have access to quality food; (4) legislation and policy that is able to reconcile Indigenous ways of knowing and colonial knowledges. This book is requisite for anyone who wants to think beyond the general scope of food sovereignty and to understand the importance of eating well, and living well, as the basis for creating a healthy and sustainable food system or all.

Video Suggestions

1. Bissell, Mary. 2008. *My Big, Fat Diet.* www .mybigfatdiet.net/. 42 min.

   If you have encountered *Super Size Me* or *Fed Up*, then *My Big, Fat Diet*, directed by Mary Bissell, should also impress. This intimate made-in-Canada documentary is a raw account about how six people in the fishing village of Namgis First Nation, just off Vancouver Island, go head-to-head with the target culprits of obesity and diabetes—sugar and junk food—by choosing to eliminate them from their diets. This documentary looks at the problem of obesity through the lens of physician Dr. Jay Wortman, a local medical professional who aims to position himself between two often competing cultures, Western medicine and the Indigenous culture of the Namgis First Nation. This story uncovers a time and place when traditional food gathering was the norm, and shows how the health of people and the environment have been compromised as a result of the Western diet replacing a more traditional existence.

2. Thompson, Shirley. 2011. *Harvesting Hope: In Northern Manitoba Communities.* http://home .cc.umanitoba.ca/~thompso4/harvestinghope_ doc.html. 37 min.

   The sequel to *Growing Hope in Northern Manitoba.* Both videos, considered participatory, were developed to explore the issues around food selection, food insecurity, and the implications of policy at the community level for Indigenous people in rural Manitoba. *Harvesting Hope* documents First Nation and Métis people from Northern Manitoba, academics, and Ovide Mercredi, former chief of the Assembly of Manitoba Chiefs. With over three-quarters of the northern Manitoba population being identified as food insecure, this video is a candid depiction of how the market food system affects the procurement of country food, compromises quality food selection and availability, and overwhelms the health-care system in this part of the country, thus fuelling the cycle of poverty among Canada's rural Indigenous inhabitants, far outweighing the national average.

References

Ackroyd, W.R. 1930. "Beriberi and Other Food-Deficiency Diseases in Newfoundland and Labrador." *Journal of Hygiene* 30:357–86.

Cannon, G. 2003. *The Fate of Nations: Food and Nutrition Policy in the New World.* Royal Society, London: The Caroline Walker Lecture.

Carter, S. 1990. *Lost Harvests: Prairie Indian Reserve Farmers and Government Policy.* Montreal: McGill-Queen's University Press.

Clarkson, L., V. Morrissette, and G. Regallet. 1992. *Our Responsibility to the Seventh Generation: Indigenous Peoples and Sustainable Development.* A report of the International Institute for Sustainable Development. Winnipeg.

Condon, R., P. Collings, and G. Wenzel. 1998. "The Best Part of Life: Subsistence Hunting, Ethnicity and Economic Adaptation among Young Adult Inuit Males." *Arctic* 48(1):31–56.

Council of Canadian Academies. 2014. *Aboriginal Food Security in Northern Canada: An Assessment of the State of Knowledge*. The Expert Panel on the State of Knowledge of Food Security in Northern Canada, Council of Canadian Academies. Ottawa.

Cruikshank, J. 1998. *The Social Life of Stories: Narratives and Knowledge in the Yukon Territory*. Vancouver: UBC Press.

Damman, S., W.B. Eide, and H.V. Kuhnlein. 2008. "Indigenous Peoples' Nutrition Transition in a Right to Food Perspective." *Food Policy* 33:135–55.

Delormier, T., K.L. Frohlich, and L. Potvin. 2009. "Food and Eating as Social Practice—Understanding Eating Patterns as Social Phenomena and Implications for Public Health." *Sociology of Health and Illness* 31(2):215–28.

Desmarais, A.A., and H. Wittman. 2014. "Farmers, Foodies and First Nations: Getting to Food Sovereignty in Canada." *The Journal of Peasant Studies* 41(6):1153–73.

Egeland, G.M., G. Charbonneau-Roberts, J. Kuluguqtuq, et al. 2009. "Back to the Future: Using Traditional Food and Knowledge to Promote a Healthy Future among Inuit." Pp. 9–22 in *Indigenous Peoples' Food Systems: The Many Dimensions of Culture, Diversity and Environment for Nutrition and Health*, ed. H.V. Kuhnlein, B. Erasmus, and D. Spigelski. Rome: UN Food and Agriculture Organization.

Goudie, E. 1983. *Woman of Labrador*. Agincourt, ON: Book Society of Canada.

Graveline, F.G. 1998. *Circle Works: Transforming Eurocentric Consciousness*. Halifax, NS: Fernwood.

Grey, M., P. Mittenthal, and M. Stenbaek. 2013. *Voices and Images of Nunavimmiut: Environment (partie 2): Contaminants, Land Use & Climate Change*. Montreal: McGill-Queen's University Press.

Gunn Allen, P. 1986. *The Sacred Hoop: Recovering the Feminine in American Indian Traditions*. Boston: Beacon Press.

Hanrahan, M. 2008. "Tracing Social Change among the Labrador Inuit and Inuit-Metis: What Does the Nutrition Literature Tell Us?" *Food, Society and Culture: An International Journal of Multidisciplinary Research* 11(3):315–33.

———. 2001. "Salmon at the Centre: Ritual, Identity, and the Negotiators of Life Space in Labrador Métis Society." Pp. 146–65 in *From Red Ochre to Black Gold*, ed. D. McGrath. St. John's, NL: Flanker Press.

———. 2000. *Brooks, Buckets and Komatiks: The Problem of Water Access in Black Tickle*. St. John's, NL: Faculty of Medicine, Memorial University of Newfoundland.

Henderson, J.Y. 2000. "The Context of the State of Nature." Pp. 11–38 in Reclaiming Indigenous Voice and Vision, ed. M. Battiste. Vancouver: UBC Press.

Howell, J., transcribed by M. Hanrahan. 1998. "Taking Care of Each Other: The Relationship between the Labrador Metis and the Environment." *Terra Borealis* 1:26–8.

Inuit Health Survey 2007–2008. n.d. McGill University, Centre for Indigenous Nutrition and Environment. Accessed 12 March 2015. http://www.mcgill.ca/cine/resources/ihs.

Kelm, M.E. 1998. *Colonizing Bodies: Aboriginal Health and Healing in British Columbia, 1900–50*. Vancouver: UBC Press.

King, M., A. Smith, and M. Gracey. 2009. "Indigenous Health Part 2: The Underlying Causes of the Health Gap." *Lancet* 374(9683):76–85.

Kneen, C. 2011. "Food Secure Canada: Where Agriculture, Environment, Health, Food and Justice Intersect." Pp. 80–96 in *Food Sovereignty in Canada: Creating Just and Sustainable Food Systems*, ed. H. Wittman, A.A. Desmarais, and N. Wiebe. Halifax, NS: Fernwood.

Knudtson, P., and D. Suzuki. 1992. *Wisdom of the Elders: Native and Scientific Ways of Knowing about Nature*. Vancouver: Greystone.

Kuhnlein, H.V., and H.M. Chan. 2000. "Environment and Contaminants in Traditional Food Systems of Northern Indigenous Peoples." *Annual Review of Nutrition* 20:595–626.

———, O. Receveur, R. Soueida, and G.M. Egeland. 2004. "Arctic Indigenous Peoples Experience the Nutrition Transition with Changing Dietary Patterns and Obesity." *Journal of Nutrition* 134(6):1447–53.

Lambden, J., O. Receveur, J. Marshall, and H.V. Kuhnlein. 2006. "Traditional and Market Food Access in Arctic Canada Is Affected by Economic Factors." *Journal of Circumpolar Health* 65:331–40.

Loppie-Reading, C., and F. Wien. 2009. *Health Inequalities and Social Determinants of Aboriginal Peoples' Health*. Vancouver: National Collaborating Centre for Aboriginal Health.

Lupton, D. 1996. *Food, the Body and the Self*. London: Sage.

Lynge, F., trans. M. Stenbaek. 1992. *Arctic Wars, Animal Rights, Endangered Peoples*. Hanover, NH: University Press of New England.

Martin, D.H. 2009. "Food Stories: A Labrador Inuit-Metis Community Speaks about Global Change." Unpublished doctoral dissertation. Halifax, NS: Dalhousie University.

———. 2011. "'Now We Got Lots to Eat and They're Telling Us Not to Eat It': Understanding Changes to South-East Labrador Inuit Relationships to Food." *International Journal of Circumpolar Health* 70(4):384–95.

Morrison, D. 2011. "Indigenous Food Sovereignty: A Model for Social Learning." Pp. 97–113 in *Food Sovereignty in Canada: Creating Just and Sustainable Food Systems*, ed. H. Wittman, A.A. Desmarais, and N. Wiebe. Halifax, NS: Fernwood.

Nestle, M. 2007. *Food Politics: How the Food Industry Influences Nutrition and Health*. Berkeley: University of California Press.

Nuttall, M., F. Berkes, B. Forbes, et al. 2005. "Hunting, Herding, Fishing and Gathering: Indigenous Peoples and Renewable Resources Use in the Arctic." Pp. 662–95 in *Arctic Climate Impact Assessment Scientific Report*, ed. C. Symon, L. Arris, and B. Heal. Cambridge: Cambridge University Press.

Orchard, T. 1998. "Teenagers of the Tundra: The Teenage Experience among the Naskapi of Kawawachikamach, Quebec." MA thesis, Memorial University of Newfoundland.

Pal, S., F. Harman, and M.A. Robidoux. 2013. "The Costs of Local Food Procurement in Two Northern Indigenous Communities in Canada." *Food and Foodways* 21(2): 132–52.

Panelli, R., and G. Tipa. 2009. "Beyond Foodscapes: Considering Geographies of Indigenous Well-Being." *Health Place* 15:455–65.

Power, E. 2008. "Conceptualizing Food Security for Aboriginal People in Canada." *Canadian Journal of Public Health* 99(2):95–7.

Radkau, J. 2008. *Nature and Power: A Global History of the Environment*. New York: Cambridge University Press.

Samson, C., and J. Pretty. 2003. "Environmental and Health Benefits of Hunting Lifestyles and Diets for the Innu of Labrador." *Food Policy* 31:528–53.

Saul, J.R. 2008. *A Fair Country: Telling Truths about Canada*. Toronto: Viking Canada.

Scrinis, G. 2002. "Sorry, Marge." *Meanjin* 61(4):108–16.

———. 2008. "On the Ideology of Nutritionism." *Gastronomica: The Journal of Food and Culture* 8(1):39–48.

Smith, L.T. 1999. *Decolonizing Methodologies: Research and Indigenous Peoples*. New York: Zed Books.

Sturdy, S., and G. Scrinis. 2014. "Nutritionism: The Science and Politics of Dietary Advice." *Food Security* 6(1):153–5.

Swanson, D., and S. Bhadwal. 2009. *Creating Adaptive Policies: A Guide for Policymaking in an Uncertain World*. Ottawa and New Delhi: Sage and IDRC.

Thow, A.M. 2009. "Trade Liberalization and the Nutrition Transition: Mapping the Pathways for Public Health Nutritionists." *Public Health Nutrition* 12(11):2150–8.

Trivedi, B. 2006. "The Good, the Fad and the Unhealthy." *New Scientist* 191(2570):42–9.

Turner, N. 2005. *The Earth's Blanket: Traditional Teachings for Sustainable Living*. Vancouver: Douglas and McIntyre.

United Nations. 2008. Assessment of the World Food Security and Nutrition Situation. 34th Committee on World Food Security. Rome: UN Food and Agriculture Organization.

———. 2009. The State of Agricultural Commodity Markets 2009: High Food Prices and the Food Crisis—Experiences and Lessons Learned. Rome: UN Food and Agriculture Organization.

———. 2014. The State of Food Insecurity in the World 2014. UN Food and Agricultural Organization. Accessed 8 March 2015. http://www.fao.org/publications/sofi/2014/en/.

Wadden, J. 2010. "De-linking from Dependency: Indigenous Food Sovereignty Brings Together Land, Food and Health." *Briar Patch* 39(5):35–6.

Warde, A. 1997. *Consumption, Food and Taste*. London: Sage.

Willows, N.D. 2005. "Determinants of Healthy Eating in Aboriginal Peoples in Canada." *Canadian Journal of Public Health* 96: S32 S36.

Winson, A. 2004. "Bringing Political Economy into the Debate on the Obesity Epidemic." *Agriculture and Human Values* 21:299–312.

Wittman, H., A.A. Desmarais, and N. Wiebe. 2010. *Food Sovereignty: Reconnecting Food, Nature and Community*. Halifax, NS: Fernwood.

World Health Organization (WHO). 2000. Obesity: Preventing and Managing the Global Epidemic. WHO Technical Report Series. Geneva.

———. 2015. *Global Strategy on Diet, Physical Activity and Health*. Accessed 6 March 2015. http://www.who.int/dietphysicalactivity/childhood/en/.

15 Origins and Consequences of and Responses to Food Insecurity in Canada

Naomi Dachner and Valerie Tarasuk

Learning Objectives

Through this chapter, you can

1. Understand the scope and nature of food insecurity in Canada
2. Develop an appreciation of the limitations of community responses to local problems of food insecurity
3. Recognize the critical role of public policy in relation to household food insecurity

Introduction

A growing number of Canadians are struggling to afford the food that they need. This problem is popularly referred to as "hunger" but also termed **household food insecurity**, and it constitutes a serious social problem and population health concern in Canada. In 2012, food insecurity affected more than 4 million Canadians (Tarasuk, Mitchell, and Dachner 2014). In this chapter, we review the origins of our current awareness of "hunger" in Canada, describe the scope and nature of household food insecurity from a population health perspective, and critically examine policy and programmatic responses to it.

Awareness of "Hunger" as a Problem in Canada

Our current awareness of food insecurity as a problem in Canada has its origins in the early 1980s when communities across the country began to establish ad hoc **charitable food assistance** programs in response to concerns that people in their midst were going hungry (Riches 1986). These programs took the form of "food banks," community organizations established to collect donated foodstuffs and redistribute them to the "needy." They were patterned after similar initiatives in the United States (Riches 1986). Although initially construed as temporary "emergency" responses to problems of hardship caused by the economic recession of the early 1980s, food banks rapidly proliferated through the 1980s and 1990s, and the number of people using these services skyrocketed. The trend paralleled broad-sweeping social policy reforms at the federal and provincial/territorial levels that effectively weakened Canada's social safety net (Riches 1986; Riches 2002; Davis and Tarasuk 1994). In 1989, the Canadian Association of Food Banks released its first *HungerCount*, reporting that 378,000 Canadians used food banks nationally in March of that year (Davidson 1989). Within 10 years, this number had almost doubled (Canadian Association of Food Banks 2005), and it has remained above 800,000 since 2010 (Food Banks Canada 2014).

Through their continual public appeals for food donations (i.e. "food drives"), food banks have rendered problems of "hunger" in Canada visible. They have also become the public face of hunger and food insecurity in Canada with their highly publicized campaigns for donations and regular reports on food bank usage through the annual release of *HungerCount* and countless local reports and press releases issued by individual food banks and provincial associations.

The first national survey to include any questions about food insecurity was the National Longitudinal Survey of Children and Youth, begun in 1994 with a sample of almost 23,000 families (McIntyre, Connor, and Warren 2000). Survey respondents were asked if their child had "ever experienced being hungry because the family had run out of food or money to buy food," and if so, how often, and how did they cope with feeding their child when this happened. Only 1.2 per cent of the families interviewed in 1994 reported child hunger, perhaps because this represents such a severe state of household food insecurity and its reporting is highly stigmatized (McIntyre, Connor, and Warren 2000). Nonetheless, the portrait of vulnerability that emerged from McIntyre et al.'s analysis of these data is prescient, pinpointing the particularly high risk of child hunger among single-parent families, those on social assistance, and off-reserve Aboriginal families. Several other investigations of this phenomenon followed.

The Experience of Food Insecurity

The need to better understand the phenomenon of "hunger" gave rise to several qualitative studies of the lived experiences of those directly affected by "hunger" (Campbell and Desjardins 1989;

Dachner and Tarasuk 2002; Hamelin, Beaudry, and Habicht 1998; Hamelin, Habicht, and Beaudry 1999; Hamelin, Beaudry, and Habicht 2002; Tarasuk and Maclean 1990), and some detailed assessments of the nutritional vulnerability and household circumstances of particular vulnerable groups (Jacobs Starkey, Kuhnlein, and Gray-Donald 1998; Jacobs Starkey, Gray-Donald, and Kuhnlein 1999; McIntyre et al. 2003; McIntyre et al. 2002; Tarasuk and Beaton 1999a; Tarasuk, Dachner, and Li 2005; Tarasuk et al. 2009; Tarasuk and Beaton 1999b). This research has continued to evolve, and today there is extensive understanding of the problem popularly referred to as *hunger* but now more commonly termed *food insecurity*. Food insecurity, defined as inadequate or insecure access to food due to financial constraints, is understood to be a managed process, whereby the quality of foods consumed is likely to be compromised before any substantial reductions in the total amount of food eaten occur (i.e. "going hungry"). There are also disruptions in familial eating patterns, as adults limit their own food intakes as a way to free up scarce resources for younger children (Hamelin, Beaudry, and Habicht 2002; McIntyre et al. 2003). Research from the United States suggests that older children also try to minimize their own food needs during times of food shortages (Fram et al. 2011).

Food insecurity occurs in the context of severe financial constraints, and the food problems that have come to define this condition are essentially manifestations of **material deprivation**. As resources dwindle, people mount extensive efforts to "stretch" what food they have and augment their existing supplies so as to minimize experiences of food deprivation. This might entail seeking charitable food assistance from a food bank or charitable meal program in the community, but coping with food insecurity more commonly includes a myriad of more "private" strategies. It is a condition characterized by social isolation and feelings of marginalization and alienation (Hamelin, Beaudry, and Habicht 2002). In their efforts to obtain needed food or money for food, people who are food insecure often delay bill and rent payments; put off filling prescriptions for needed medications; try to borrow food or money for food from relatives and friends; purchase food on credit; sell or pawn any possessions they have that can net some money; terminate telephone, Internet or cable services; and even obtain food through illegal means (McIntyre, Connor, and Warren 2000; Kirkpatrick and Tarasuk 2009; Hamelin, Beaudry, and Habicht 2002; Tarasuk and Beaton 1999a). Thus the experience of food insecurity extends well beyond food, ultimately impacting all aspects of one's life.

Food Insecurity Measurement and Monitoring

In 1996, questions about household food insecurity began to appear on the National Population Health Survey and then on its successor, the **Canadian Community Health Survey (CCHS)**. Unfortunately, it was not until 2004 that food insecurity began to be measured consistently on CCHS using a standardized, validated questionnaire. This questionnaire, the **Household Food Security Survey Module** (HFSSM), assesses *households'* experiences of food insecurity over the previous 12 months (Health Canada 2007). This survey module was developed by the US Department of Agriculture and has been used since 1995 to monitor food insecurity in that country. The module consists of 18 questions asking the respondent whether he/she or other household members experienced the conditions described, which range in severity from experiences of anxiety that food will run out before household members have money to buy more, to modifying the amount of food consumed, to experiencing hunger, and finally, to going a whole day without eating. These questions differentiate the experiences of adults and children, recognizing that in households with children, adults may compromise their own food intake as a way to reallocate scarce resources for children.

CCHS, the survey platform for food insecurity monitoring in Canada, is a cross-sectional survey administered by Statistics Canada that collects health-related information from about 60,000 Canadians per year. The food security survey module is only part of the common content of CCHS on alternate two-year "cycles" of the survey. During cycles of CCHS when the module has been optional, there have always been some provinces and territories that have chosen not to collect data on food insecurity. Thus national data are only available on alternate two-year periods (e.g. 2011–12, 2015–16, 2019–20).

The CCHS sample is designed to be representative of the 10 provinces and three territories, but it excludes individuals who are full-time members of the Canadian Forces and those living on First Nations reserves, in some remote areas of Quebec, or in prisons or care facilities. Because CCHS is limited to Canadians with domiciles, it also excludes homeless people. Although on-reserve First Nations people and homeless people make up relatively small proportions of the total population in Canada, their extremely high levels of vulnerability to food insecurity must mean that the true **prevalence** of food insecurity in Canada is to some extent underestimated because of their omission.

The Prevalence of Food Insecurity in Canada

Our most recent, nationally representative measure of food insecurity in Canada comes from 2012. That year, 12.6 per cent of Canadian households experienced some degree of food insecurity; over 4 million Canadians were affected (Tarasuk, Mitchell, and Dachner 2014). As illustrated in figure 15.1, this represents a significant increase since 2007 (the first year for which nationally representative data are available), when 11.4 per cent of households were food insecure. Although food insecurity is monitored in the United States using the same questionnaire, the terminology and classification schemes differ in that country.

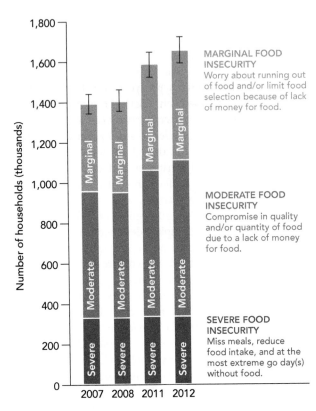

Figure 15.1 Household Food Insecurity

Source: Tarasuk, Mitchell, and Dachner (2014).

is where the bulk of the problem resides. Four provinces—Ontario, Quebec, Alberta, and British Columbia—accounted for 84 per cent of food insecurity households in Canada in 2012 (Tarasuk, Mitchell, and Dachner 2014).

Food insecurity is most prevalent among households characterized by social and economic disadvantage. The single strongest predictor of food insecurity is low income, but being reliant on social assistance, being black or of Aboriginal status, renting rather than owning one's home, and being a lone-parent female-led household also increase the probability of food insecurity (Che and Chen 2001; Tarasuk, Mitchell, and Dachner 2014; Ledrou and Gervais 2005; McIntyre, Connor, and Warren 2000; Office of Nutrition Policy and Promotion 2010b; Office of Nutrition Policy and Promotion 2010a; Tarasuk and Vogt 2009; Vozoris and Tarasuk 2003; Willows et al. 2009). While these household characteristics denote elevated risk of food insecurity, they do not necessarily describe the majority of food-insecure households in Canada. Consider the main source of income of food-insecure households, for example (figure 15.3). While those dependent on social assistance are most at risk of food insecurity, they make up only 16 per cent of food-insecure households in the country. Almost two-thirds of food-insecure households in Canada depend on employment. Those most at risk are workers with low-waged, part-time, and/or short-term employment and multi-person households with only one earner (McIntyre, Bartoo, and Emery 2012).

Food Insecurity and Health

Food insecurity is tightly intertwined with individuals' health and well-being. Among children, food insecurity has been linked to poorer health status (McIntyre, Connor, and Warren 2000)

Both countries apply comparable definitions of food insecurity, but the prevalence of food insecurity in the United States in 2012 is almost three times higher than the rate in Canada (Tarasuk, Mitchell, and Dachner 2014).

There is considerable variation in rates of food insecurity across the country (figure 15.2). The problem is worst in Nunavut where, in 2012, 45.2 per cent of households were food insecure, and 62.2 per cent of children were living in food-insecure families (Tarasuk, Mitchell, and Dachner 2014). More focused surveys of Inuit children have charted even higher prevalence rates (Egeland et al. 2010). About 15 to 20 per cent of households in Yukon, Northwest Territories, and the Maritime provinces were food insecure in 2012. While the rate of food insecurity is typically lower in central and western Canada, this

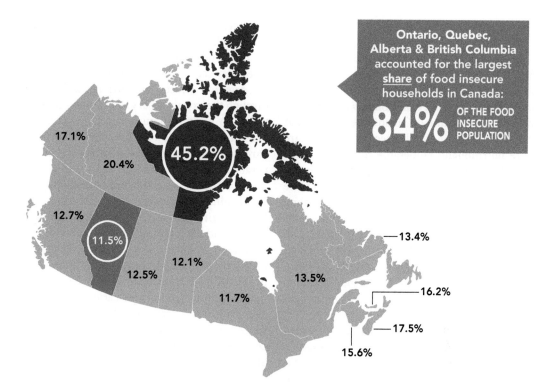

Figure 15.2 Household Food Insecurity by Province and Territory

Source: Tarasuk, Mitchell, and Dachner (2014).

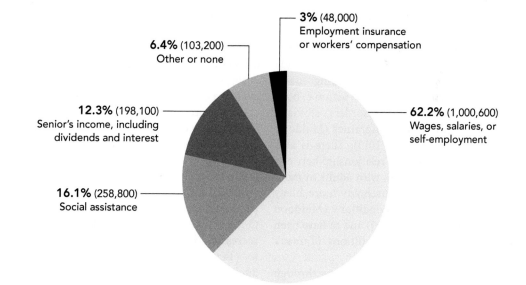

Figure 15.3 Food-Insecure Households' Main Source of Income

Source: Tarasuk, Mitchell, and Dachner (2014).

and the subsequent development of a variety of chronic health conditions, including asthma and depression (Kirkpatrick, McIntyre, and Potestio 2010; McIntyre et al. 2012). While some of the observed effects of food insecurity on children's health may arise from compromises in nutrition, in fact there is limited Canadian evidence that young children in food-insecure families are more nutritionally vulnerable than other children (Kirkpatrick and Tarasuk 2008). However, household food insecurity appears to increase the **likelihood** of nutritional deprivation among older children and adolescents in this country (Kirkpatrick and Tarasuk 2008; Mark et al. 2012). And, irrespective of whether children and youth experience nutritional compromises as a result of living in families that are food insecure, being in such deprived settings clearly takes a toll on their health.

Household food insecurity is a potent marker of nutritional inequities in the Canadian adult population (Kirkpatrick, Dodd, Parsons, et al. 2015), with adults in food-insecure households less likely to meet their nutrient requirements for good health (Kirkpatrick and Tarasuk 2008). In addition, food insecurity is associated with poorer physical and mental health among adults. Adults in food-insecure households are much more likely than food-secure adults to report having been diagnosed with a wide variety of chronic diseases, including mood and anxiety disorders, arthritis, asthma, back problems, diabetes, bowel disorders, stomach and intestinal ulcers, and migraines (Muldoon et al. 2012; Tarasuk et al. 2013). There is also some evidence of a graded relationship between food insecurity and health, with adults in more severely food-insecure households more likely to report chronic health conditions (Muldoon et al. 2012; Tarasuk et al. 2013) and to have been diagnosed with multiple conditions (Tarasuk et al. 2013).

While the biological mechanisms through which food insecurity affects health are not well understood, the relationship between household food insecurity and adults' health appears to be bidirectional (Tarasuk et al. 2013; Anema et al. 2009; Heflin, Corcoran, and Siefert 2007). On the one hand, chronic and severe household food insecurity can erode individuals' health through its negative effects on dietary intakes and through the extraordinary stress that comes with trying to cope with such hardships (Seligman and Schillinger 2010). On the other hand, adults' chronic ill-health appears to increase their vulnerability to food insecurity (Tarasuk et al. 2013). There are three potential mechanisms through which adults' health can impact their household food security status: (1) chronically poor health impedes adults' earning power, increasing their likelihood of having low incomes; (2) it places additional financial demands on the household as people who are chronically ill may require more money for prescription medications, special dietary needs, transportation, etc.; and (3) chronic illness can limit adults' abilities to manage in the context of scarce resources (Heflin, Corcoran, and Siefert 2007).

Irrespective of whether food insecurity compromises adults' health or whether the poor health of adults increases the probability that they and their families will be food insecure, once people are in food-insecure circumstances, they are unquestionably less able to manage chronic health problems (Anema et al. 2009; Gucciardi et al. 2009; Seligman and Schillinger 2010; Seligman et al. 2012). Similarly, there is evidence of poorer disease management among children with diabetes in food-insecure families (Marjerrison et al. 2010).

The deleterious effects of household food insecurity on the health of Canadians are apparent in the increased health-care costs associated with this condition. A recent examination of provincial health-care expenditures for adults in Ontario revealed a sharp gradient in costs with increasing severity of household food insecurity (Tarasuk et al. 2015). In a 12-month period, adults in severely food-insecure households cost the province, on average, more than twice as much in health-care dollars as those who were food secure.

Responses to Problems of Hunger and Food Insecurity

There has been considerable activity at the community level to provide charitable food assistance and a variety of other food programs. The bulk of this activity is extra-governmental, and there is no indication that these efforts effectively address problems of household food insecurity.

Community-Based Responses

Charitable Food Assistance

Charitable food assistance, primarily in the form of food banks, but also meal programs, is currently the only direct response to household food insecurity in Canada. These forms of assistance typically emerged on an ad hoc basis, as members of communities came together to deal with hunger in their area. A recent examination of charitable food assistance in five Canadian cities (Victoria, Edmonton, Toronto, Quebec City, and Halifax) revealed extensive engagement by a broad spectrum of agencies and organizations (Tarasuk et al. 2014). Food charity is distributed by faith groups, faith-based social service agencies (e.g. the Salvation Army), multi-service agencies (e.g. drop-in centres), health centres, colleges and universities, and a variety of standalone programs established for the sole purpose of providing food assistance (Tarasuk et al. 2014). Although new charitable food programs open up each year, the "system" as a whole is deeply entrenched, with more than two-thirds of food assistance programs in the five cities studied in operation for at least a decade.

Food banks and meal programs have evolved over time in ways that are, in part, unique to the features of the particular community, yet they share many fundamental characteristics. Almost all are heavily reliant on food donations and volunteer labour. In most regions of Canada, there is a provincial or city-wide organization that coordinates the collection and distribution of donated foods to local food banks and meal programs, and links to the national food sharing program of Food Banks Canada (e.g. Toronto's Daily Bread Food Bank, Feed Nova Scotia, Edmonton Food Bank, etc.). In spite of this centralized coordination, many food banks and meal programs also solicit donated food from local business and hold events to raise funds for their food assistance programs to increase the assistance they are able to offer (Tarasuk et al. 2014). Only about half of food banks and two-thirds of meal programs have any paid staff; the provision of food assistance hinges on the work of thousands of volunteers (Tarasuk et al. 2014; Pettes et al., in press).

The voluntary, donor-driven nature of charitable food assistance in many ways dictates program operations, as the scheduling of services and provision of food assistance are constrained by these practical realities. Despite program operators' best efforts to amass sufficient food supplies to serve those who seek their assistance, the stock of food available for distribution is ultimately a function of donations, not the needs in the community. This sets the stage for program workers to ration food and restrict access to it. Food banks contain demand by imposing eligibility requirements (e.g. limiting their service to people living in a particular catchment area, with income below a certain threshold, etc.) and limiting the frequency with which any one person or household can obtain assistance. Meal programs and food banks also keep demands for food assistance in check by restricting their hours of operation. Nonetheless, it is common for food program operators to report sometimes having to reduce the amount and/or quality of food given as a way to stretch limited supplies; at times, they even turn people away or reduce service hours because of a shortage of food (Tarasuk et al. 2014; Food Banks Canada 2013; Pettes et al., in press). In fact, the harder food banks try to meet needs in their community (e.g. by serving more people, serving people more often, and scheduling their services in relation to times of particular need), the more likely they are to encounter difficulties in maintaining whatever standards of service they have set (Tarasuk et al. 2014). Not surprisingly, interviews with people who use food banks continually highlight the limited amount, selection, and quality of food obtainable from these programs (Hamelin, Beaudry, and Habicht 2002; Loopstra and Tarasuk 2012; Tsang, Holt, and Azevedo 2011; Williams, McIntyre, and Glanville 2010; Williams et al. 2012), and evaluations of the food provided by food banks and meal programs document limited quantities and poor nutritional quality (Bocskei and Ostry 2010; Irwin et al. 2007; Tse and Tarasuk 2008; Willows and Au 2006).

While the high public profile of food banks gives the impression that these programs are a mainstay for those in need, only 20 to 30 per cent of people experiencing food insecurity report seeking charitable food assistance (Rainville and Brink 2001; Vozoris and Tarasuk 2003; McIntyre, Connor, and Warren 2000). Food charity is most likely to be accessed by those facing severe food insecurity (Kirkpatrick and Tarasuk 2009; Rainville and Brink 2001; Tarasuk et al. 2009; Tarasuk and Beaton 1999a), but even among this group, food bank usage is very low (Kirkpatrick and Tarasuk 2009). Even when children are at risk, only about one-third of households reporting food insecurity seek food bank assistance (McIntyre, Connor, and Warren 2000). Moreover, it is common for people who use food banks or eat in charitable meal programs to still report going hungry, despite receiving food assistance (Kirkpatrick and Tarasuk 2009; Tarasuk and Beaton 1999a; Tarasuk et al. 2009; Hamelin, Mercier, and Bedard 2007; Hamelin, Beaudry, and Habicht 2002), with directors of charitable food assistance programs themselves reporting that the people they serve need more food than they are able to provide (Tarasuk et al. 2014). In part, the failure of charitable food assistance programs to prevent people from going hungry speaks to the extraordinary levels of vulnerability of those who seek their assistance. It also reflects the limited assistance that individuals can receive from what has evolved to be a highly fragmented, resource-constrained system of food relief.

Food banks are aware that they are unable to address the root causes of hunger and food insecurity. Since their inception, many food charities have worked to advocate for social policy changes to address the poverty underpinning the food problems that their clients face. Some organizations like Daily Bread Food Bank in Toronto regularly publish reports drawing attention to the social and economic conditions that cause people to turn to food banks for help (Daily Bread Food Bank 2015). Another recent and inspiring example of advocacy in this sector is the work of the Meal Exchange, a national charity working with college and university students to engage in public education and advocacy activities related to problems of food insecurity experienced by vulnerable post-secondary students across Canada (please see http://mealexchange.com).

Children's Nutrition Programs

Alongside the rise of food banks and charitable meal and snack programs has been the growth of children's nutrition programs in schools, originally serving breakfast and increasingly offering lunch (Hyndman 2000). Over the past two decades, these programs have proliferated through community-based voluntary efforts (Public Health Agency of Canada 2008), occasionally receiving funding support from school boards or municipalities (Henry, Allison, and Garcia 2003). As they have evolved from a focus on "hungry" children to a more inclusive healthy eating function, and most recently as an obesity prevention strategy (Vogel 2010), there have been increasing investments by the provinces and territories and repeated calls for a universal school nutrition program. Every province and territory is now investing in school nutrition programs, in some instances with funds allotted as part of provincial poverty reduction initiatives (Editeur officiel du Quebec 2002; Government of Ontario 2010). The success of these programs in reaching hungry children has not been demonstrated (Hay 2000; Kirkpatrick and Tarasuk 2009; Raine, McIntyre, and Dayle 2003), although there is some evidence of positive effects on children's nutrition and body weights (Mullaly et al. 2010; Veugelers and Fitzgerald 2005). In addition, a study of food assistance programs in secondary schools in disadvantaged neighbourhoods in Quebec suggests that these programs may improve the scholastic performance of adolescents in food-insecure families, mitigating difficulties typically associated with household food insecurity (Roustit et al. 2010).

Community Food Security Initiatives

While charitable food assistance through food banks, meal programs, and school programs remains the mainstay of community responses to household food insecurity, several other types of food programs have emerged in recent years. Community kitchens, community gardens, alternative food distribution networks (e.g. the "good food box"), and neighbourhood-level interventions to improve food retail access (e.g. farmers' markets) have been established in many jurisdictions, often under the rubric of public health or health promotion. Some of these initiatives have evolved in part from a critique of the adequacy and appropriateness of charitable food assistance as a response to problems of household food insecurity and a quest to find more lasting, long-term solutions. Increasingly however, this work is also being shaped by a growing interest in local food production and sustainable agriculture and the promotion of healthy eating, with programs designed to embrace all members of the community, not just those with low incomes. These programs typically operate on a much smaller scale than charitable food assistance programs (Johnston and Baker 2005) and involve only a small fraction of those at risk of food insecurity (Kirkpatrick and Tarasuk 2009). There has been considerable research to suggest that by design, such initiatives do not, and cannot, respond to the immediate food needs that define problems of severe food insecurity (Crawford and Kalina 1997; Hamelin, Mercier, and Bedard 2008; Engler-Stringer and Berenbaum 2005; Engler-Stringer and Berenbaum 2007; Power 2005; Tarasuk and Reynolds 1999; Tarasuk

2001), though it is important to recognize that this is typically not the goal.

Despite the ever-evolving landscape of charitable food assistance programs and **community food security** initiatives, there is widespread consensus that such community efforts do not and cannot tackle the root causes of food insecurity in Canada. Since their inception, many food banks have been staunch advocates for social policy reforms to address the structural underpinnings of food insecurity. Food Banks Canada's annual *HungerCount* routinely includes public policy recommendations to address key issues affecting food bank clientele (Food Banks Canada 2014). In recent years, several diverse civil society groups have begun to work in coalition under the auspices of "Food Secure Canada" to advocate for "zero hunger" among other policy goals. In addition, professional groups like the Dietitians of Canada have taken strong public positions in favour of public policy interventions to reduce food insecurity in this country (Power 2005). To date, however, such calls for action have yielded little response from governments at either the federal or the provincial/territorial level.

Government Responses

Historically, Canada's approach to social welfare has been a social safety net, created to protect citizens from the devastating effects of extreme poverty through income transfer programs such as social assistance, employment insurance, and old age security. Thus, unlike the United States which has national- and state-level food assistance programs (cf. the Supplemental Nutrition Assistance Program) to target the food needs of vulnerable groups, Canada does not. We have no dedicated federal policy intervention to address household food insecurity and very few initiatives provincially, although school nutrition programs and some community-based food programs targeting low-income groups are supported to some extent by public funds. Additionally, food insecurity has been on the national and provincial public health agendas, but incorporating effective interventions has been difficult, in part because policy solutions to the problem appear to lie outside core public health and health promotion mandates (Mah et al. 2014).

On the international stage, Canada was a key player at the Food and Agriculture Organization's 1996 World Food Summit, affirming food as a human right and committing to a plan of action to address food insecurity within and across countries (Food and Agriculture Organization 1996). However, since that time no national plan to address food insecurity has been put into place. To the contrary, Mah and colleagues' critical frame analysis of World Food Summit documents and subsequent progress reports (1996–2008) revealed a decline in the importance of government involvement and policy intervention in addressing food insecurity (Mah et al. 2014). Over the period of documentation, the link between poverty and food insecurity was de-emphasized, and the concept of the right to food completely disappeared. With the recent (2012) visit of Olivier De Schutter, the United Nations Special Rapporteur on the Right to Food, Canada's international legal obligations were brought to the fore again, but to date there are no government mechanisms in place to ensure the right to food for Canadians.

Notwithstanding the lack of social policies targeting food insecurity in Canada, much has been learned about the relationship between household food insecurity and our social programs through analyses of national population health data. Social assistance and seniors' benefits—programs which have contrasting effects on food insecurity—are two policy arenas in which the sensitivity of food insecurity to social policy and the potential of policy intervention in addressing food insecurity have been demonstrated.

Social Assistance

Social assistance includes "welfare," the last-resort support program meant to provide for the basic necessities in life, as well as "disability," the income assistance program available to working-aged adults who are permanently unable to work for medical reasons. In 2012, food insecurity affected 70 per cent of Canadian households reliant on social assistance, six times higher than the rate of households reliant on employment (Tarasuk, Mitchell, and Dachner 2014). Social assistance programs fall under provincial/territorial jurisdiction, and the prevalence of food insecurity among social assistance recipients varies accordingly, from a low of 46 per cent of social assistance households being food insecure in Newfoundland and Labrador to a high of 79 per cent in Alberta, as illustrated in figure 15.4.

Comparisons of welfare incomes with food and shelter costs in many jurisdictions suggest that the assistance provided is insufficient to enable many recipients to meet basic needs (Alberta Community/Public Health Nutritionists Food Security Subcommittee and Dietitians of Canada 2009; Dietitians of Canada 2012; Association of Local Public Health Agencies 2009; Nova Scotia Food Security Network and the Food Action Research Centre (FoodARC) 2013; New Brunswick Common Front for Social Justice Inc. 2011). In most jurisdictions, rates are not indexed to inflation and access to additional resources is curtailed through the program's eligibility criteria which severely restrict social assistance recipients from maintaining assets and earnings from employment.

The experience of food insecurity among social assistance recipients in Newfoundland and Labrador is one important exception to the deleterious relationship between food insecurity and social assistance in Canada. From 2007 to 2012, the rate of food insecurity among social assistance recipients in this province dropped by nearly 50 per cent, demonstrating that food insecurity is sensitive to changes in social policy (Loopstra, Dachner, and Tarasuk 2015). Over this period, Newfoundland and Labrador implemented a Poverty Reduction Strategy which included a series of policy reforms to increase the income support rates, allowable earnings and assets, and the low-income tax threshold, as well

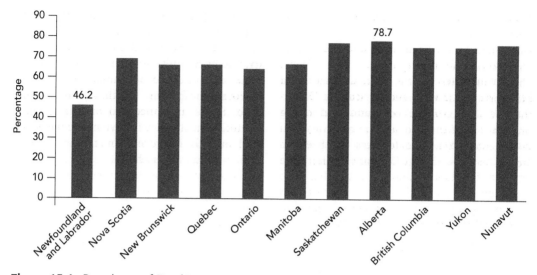

Figure 15.4 Prevalence of Food Insecurity among Households Whose Main Source of Income Is Social Assistance, 2012

Note: Results for PEI and Northwest Territories are not shown as the sample sizes in these jurisdictions were too small to derive reliable estimates.

Source: Tarasuk, Mitchell, and Dachner (2014).

as provide more affordable housing and health benefits. The changes improved the material circumstances and well-being of social assistance recipients, which improved their food security status. The experience in Newfoundland and Labrador indicates that policy reforms to improve the incomes and expand the benefits for people on social assistance will improve their food security.

Seniors' Benefits

At the age of 65, individuals in Canada become beneficiaries of Canada's public pension system consisting of the universal old age security program, the means-tested Guaranteed Income Supplement, and the contributory Canadian Pension Plan. These programs create an income floor for adults 65 years and older that has been linked to a dramatic reduction in poverty rates among Canadian seniors; Canada now boasts one of the lowest rates of elder poverty in the world (Emery, Fleisch, and McIntyre 2013). Similarly, the rate of food insecurity is relatively low among seniors. For example, the prevalence

of food insecurity for households with children is 16 per cent, whereas for elderly individuals living alone the rate is 7 per cent (Tarasuk, Mitchell, and Dachner 2014).

In an examination of the impact of the income floor created by the seniors' support programs on household food insecurity, Emery and colleagues (Emery, Fleisch, and McIntyre 2013) found that the prevalence of food insecurity among low-income Canadians living alone decreased by nearly 50 per cent at the age of 65. This research suggests that a **guaranteed annual income (GAI)** ensuring that all Canadians have enough money to afford basic needs for food and shelter could be a powerful intervention to reduce household food insecurity. A GAI would remove the extraordinarily high vulnerability to food insecurity experienced now by individuals and families with very low incomes. That group includes not only people who are in the workforce but unable to earn enough money to cover their basic needs, but also people on employment insurance, worker's compensation, and social assistance.

Conclusion

Household food insecurity is a serious social and population health problem in Canada. There has been rigorous measurement and monitoring of food insecurity since 2005, and the sociodemographic correlates and health implications of this problem are now very well documented. Yet, to date there has been no federal or provincial policy intervention with the explicit goal of reducing household food insecurity. The primary response has been food charity, delivered through a massive and diverse array of community programs, conditional on donations and volunteer labour. While these efforts are incapable of tackling the root causes of food insecurity, national data is enabling identification of policy interventions that would fundamentally improve the material well-being of food-insecure households.

Discussion Questions

1. Should food be a right in Canada?

2. What is the role of community action around food insecurity?

3. If you were advising government, what do you see as the key ways forward to address food insecurity in Canada?

4. Given the intersection of food insecurity and health, what should the role of health professionals be in combating food insecurity?

5. Given the limitations of food banks, what should their role in the future be?

Further Reading

1. Emery, J.H., Fleisch, V., and L. McIntyre. 2013. "How a Guaranteed Annual Income Could Put Food Banks out of Business." *School of Public Policy Research Papers* 6(37):1–20.
This paper compares food insecurity rates between low-income Canadians aged 65 to 69 years and those aged 60 to 64, revealing that the rate is half for the older group. The authors suggest that this finding can be explained by the guaranteed annual income afforded to Canadians 65 years and older and argue that expanding guaranteed income programs to younger Canadians would be beneficial to public health.

2. Loopstra, R., N. Dachner, and V. Tarasuk. 2015. "An Exploration of the Unprecedented Decline in the Prevalence of Household Food Insecurity in Newfoundland and Labrador, 2007–2012." *Canadian Public Policy* 41(3):191–206.
This study explores the unprecedented decline in household food insecurity in Newfoundland and Labrador, from 2007 to 2011 (15.7 to 10.6 per cent), a period of time coinciding with that province's poverty reduction strategy. Food insecurity fell most dramatically among social assistance recipients, possibly reflecting the cumulative impact of the poverty reduction strategy on the material circumstances of households receiving social assistance.

3. Loopstra, R., and V. Tarasuk. 2012. "The Relationship between Food Banks and Household Food Insecurity among Low-Income Toronto Families." *Canadian Public Policy* 38(4):497–514.
This study examines food bank use among low-income families in Toronto, finding that less than one-quarter (23 per cent) had used a food bank while three-quarters of the families had experienced food insecurity. Perceptions of stigma, the

suitability of the food available, and a mismatch between need and what the food bank offered, as well as barriers to access, were cited as reasons for non-use.

4. Tarasuk, V., J. Cheng, C. De Oliveira, N. Dachner, C. Gundersen, and P. Kurdyak. 2015. "Health Care Costs Associated with Household Food Insecurity in Ontario." *Canadian Medical Association Journal* 187(14):E429–E436.

This study examines the health-care costs associated with food insecurity among adults in Ontario. Costs systematically increased with severity of household food insecurity, with adults in severely food-insecure households costing more than twice as much as those who were food secure. This paper provides evidence that reducing household food insecurity could offset public expenditures in health care.

Video Suggestion

1. Tarasuk, V. 2015. *Association between Household Food Insecurity and Annual Health Care Costs.* www.cmaj.ca/content/187/14/E429/suppl/DC2. 9 min.

    This podcast is an interview between the deputy editor of the *Canadian Medical Association Journal*, Dr. Matthew Stanbrook, and Professor Valerie

Tarasuk, lead author of a research paper on the health-care costs associated with household food insecurity in Ontario. In addition to discussing the study findings, Professor Tarasuk speaks to the nature, magnitude, and problem of food insecurity in Canada.

References

Alberta Community/Public Health Nutritionists Food Security Subcommittee and Dietitians of Canada. 2009. "Cost of Eating in Alberta 2008." https://www.dietitians.ca/Downloads/Public/Alberta-Cost-of-Eating-2008.aspx.

Anema, A., N. Vogenthaler, E.A. Frongillo, et al. 2009. "Food Insecurity and HIV/AIDS: Current Knowledge, Gaps, and Research Priorities." Current *HIV/AIDS* Reports 6:224–31.

Association of Local Public Health Agencies. 2009. "Nutritious Food Basket Survey. Final Report." Toronto. www.alphaweb.org/resource/resmgr/nfb_summary_report_2009apr.pdf.

Bocskei, E., and A. Ostry. 2010. "A Survey of Charitable Feeding Programs for Poor and Homeless People in Victoria, BC." *Canadian Journal of Dietetic Practice and Research* 71(1):46–8.

Campbell, C.C., and E. Desjardins. 1989. "A Model and Research Approach for Studying the Management of Limited Food Resources by Low Income Families." *Journal of Nutrition Education* 21(4):162–71.

Canadian Association of Food Banks. 2005. "HungerCount 2005. Time for Action." Toronto. https://www.banquesalimentaires.org/wp-content/uploads/2015/08/hungercount-2005.pdf.

Che, J., and J. Chen. 2001. "Food Insecurity in Canadian Households." *Health Reports* 12(4):11–22.

Crawford, S.M., and L. Kalina. 1997. "Building Food Security through Health Promotion: Community Kitchens." *Journal of the Canadian Dietetic Association* 58(4):197–201.

Dachner, N., and V. Tarasuk. 2002. "Homeless 'Squeegee Kids': Food Insecurity and Daily Survival." *Social Science & Medicine* 54(7):1039–49.

Daily Bread Food Bank. 2015. "Who's Hungry? A Tale of Two Cities, 2015 Profile of Hunger in Toronto." Toronto. http://www.dailybread.ca/wp-content/uploads/2015/09/2015-WH-FINAL-WEB.pdf.

Davidson, B. 1989. "March 1989 HungerCount Report." Toronto: Canadian Association of Food Banks.

Davis, B., and V. Tarasuk. 1994. "Hunger in Canada." *Agriculture and Human Values* 11(4):50–7.

Dietitians of Canada. 2012. "Cost of Eating in British Columbia 2011." http://www.dietitians.ca/Downloads/Public/CostofEatingBC2011_FINAL.aspx.

Editeur officiel du Quebec. 2002. "Loi visant a lutter contre la pauvrete et l'exclusion sociale." Projet de loi no 112. http://www.mess.gouv.qc.ca/telecharger.asp?fichier=/publications/pdf/GD_Loi.pdf.

Egeland, G., A. Pacey, Z. Cao, and I. Sobol. 2010. "Food Insecurity among Inuit Preschoolers: Nunavut Inuit Child Health Survey, 2007–2008." *Canadian Medical Association Journal* 182(3):243–8.

Emery, J.H, V. Fleisch, and L. McIntyre. 2013. "How a Guaranteed Annual Income Could Put Food Banks out of Business." *SPP Research Papers* 6(37):1–20. The School of Public Policy, University of Calgary.

Engler-Stringer, R., and S. Berenbaum. 2005. "Collective Kitchens in Canada: A Review of the Literature." *Canadian Journal of Dietetic Practice and Research* 66(4):246–51.

—— and ——. 2007. "Exploring Food Security with Collective Kitchens Participants in Three Canadian Cities." *Qualitative Health Research* 17(1):75–84.

Food and Agriculture Organization. 1996. "Rome Declaration on World Food Security and World Food Summit Plan of Action." http://www.fao.org/docrep/003/w3613e/w3613e00.HTM.

Food Banks Canada. 2013. *HungerCount 2013.* Toronto. http://www.foodbanksCanada.ca/FoodBanks/MediaLibrary/HungerCount/HungerCount2013.pdf.

——. 2014. *HungerCount 2014.* Toronto. https://www.foodbanksCanada.ca/getmedia/d8b36130-cc83-46ba-8183-d33d484c7591/HungerCount2014_revised.pdf.aspx?ext=.pdf.

Fram, M., E. Frongillo, S.J. Jones, et al. 2011. "Children Are Aware of Food Insecurity and Take Responsibility for Managing Food Resources." *Journal of Nutrition* 141(6):1114–19.

Government of Ontario. 2010. "Breaking the Cycle: The Second Progress Report. Ontario's Poverty Reduction Strategy 2010 Annual Report." https://www.ontario.ca/document/poverty-reduction-strategy-2010-annual-report.

Gucciardi, E., M. DeMelo, J. Vogt, and D. Stewart. 2009. "Exploration of the Relationship between Household Food Insecurity and Diabetes Care in Canada." *Diabetes Care* 32:2218–24.

Hamelin, A.M., M. Beaudry, and J.P. Habicht. 2002. "Characterization of Household Food Insecurity in Quebec: Food and Feelings." *Social Science & Medicine* 54(1):119–32.

——, ——, and ——. 1998. "La vulnerabilite des menages a l'insecurite alimentaire." *Revue canadienne d'etudes du developpement* 19:277–306.

——, J.P. Habicht, and M. Beaudry. 1999. "Food Insecurity: Consequences for the Household and Broader Social Implications." *Journal of Nutrition* 129:525S–8S.

——, C. Mercier, and A. Bedard. 2007. "The Food Environment of Street Youth." *Journal of Hunger & Environmental Nutrition* 1(3):69–98.

——, ——, and ——. 2008. "Perceptions of Needs and Responses in Food Security: Divergence between Households and Stakeholders." *Public Health Nutrition* 11(12):1389–96.

Hay, D.I. 2000. "School-Based Feeding Programs: A Good Choice for Children?." Victoria, BC: Information Partnership. http://foodsecureCanada.org/sites/default/files/hay_-_2000.pdf.

Health Canada. 2007. "Canadian Community Health Survey, Cycle 2.2, Nutrition (2004)—Income-Related Household Food Security in Canada." 4696. Ottawa: Health Canada Office of Nutrition Policy and Promotion, Health Products and Food Branch.

Heflin, C.M., M.E. Corcoran, and K. Siefert. 2007. "Work Trajectories, Income Changes, and Food Sufficiency in a Michigan Welfare Population." *Social Service Review* March:3–25.

Henry, C., D. Allison, and A. Garcia. 2003. "Child Nutrition Programs in Canada and the United States: Comparisons and Contrasts." *Journal of School Health* 73(2):83–5.

Hyndman, B. 2000. "Feeding the Body, Feeding the Mind: An Overview of School-Based Nutrition Programs in Canada." http:/breakfast4learning.com/reports/litreview.htm.

Irwin, J.D., V.K. Ng, T.J. Rush, et al. 2007. "Can Food Banks Sustain Nutrient Requirements?" *Canadian Journal of Public Health* 98(1):17–20.

Jacobs Starkey, L., H. Kuhnlein, and K. Gray-Donald. 1998. "Food Bank Users: Sociodemographic and Nutritional Characteristics." *Canadian Medical Association Journal* 158(9):1143–9.

——, K. Gray-Donald, and H.V. Kuhnlein. 1999. "Nutrient Intake of Food Bank Users Is Related to Frequency of Food Bank Use, Household Size, Smoking, Education and Country of Birth." *Journal of Nutrition* 129:883–9.

Johnston, J., and L. Baker. 2005. "Eating Outside the Box: FoodShare's Good Food Box and the Challenge of Scale." *Agriculture and Human Values* 22:313–25.

Kirkpatrick, S., K.W. Dodd, R. Parsons, et al. 2015. "Household Food Insecurity Is a Stronger Marker of Adequacy of Nutrient Intakes among Canadian Compared to American Youth and Adults." *The Journal of Nutrition* 145(7):1596–1603.

——, and V. Tarasuk. 2008. "Food Insecurity Is Associated with Nutrient Inadequacies among Canadian Adults and Adolescents." *Journal of Nutrition* 138:604–12.

——, 2009. "Food Insecurity and Participation in Community Food Programs among Low-Income Toronto Families." *Canadian Journal of Public Health* 100(2):135–9.

——, McIntyre, and M. Potestio. 2010. "Child Hunger and Long-Term Adverse Consequences for Health." *Archives of Pediatrics and Adolescent Medicine* 164(8):754–62.

Ledrou, I., and J. Gervais. 2005. "Food Insecurity." *Health Reports* 16(3):47–50.

Loopstra, R., N. Dachner, and V. Tarasuk. 2015. "An Exploration of the Unprecedented Decline in the Prevalence of Household Food Insecurity in Newfoundland and Labrador, 2007–2012." *Canadian Public Policy* 41(3):191–206.

——, and V. Tarasuk. 2012. "The Relationship between Food Banks and Household Food Insecurity among Low-Income Toronto Families." *Canadian Public Policy* 38(4):497–514.

Mah, C., C. Hamill, K. Rondeau, and L. McIntyre. 2014. "A Frame-Critical Policy Analysis of Canada's Response to the World Food Summit 1998–2008." *Archives of Public Health* 72(41):1–7.

Marjerrison, S., E. Cummings, N.T. Glanville, et al. 2010. "Prevalence and Associations of Food Insecurity in Children with Diabetes Mellitus." *Journal of Pediatrics* 158(4):607–11.

Mark, S., M. Lambert, J. O'Loughlin, and K. Gray-Donald. 2012. "Household Income, Food Insecurity and Nutrition in Canadian Youth." *Canadian Journal of Public Health* 103(2):94–9.

McIntyre, L., A. Bartoo, and J. Emery. 2012. "When Working Is Not Enough: Food Insecurity in the Canadian Labour Force." *Public Health Nutrition* 17(1):49–57.

——, S.K. Connor, and J. Warren. 2000. "Child Hunger in Canada: Results of the 1994 National Longitudinal Survey of Children and Youth." *Canadian Medical Association Journal* 163(8):961–5.

——, T. Glanville, S. Officer, et al. 2002. "Food Insecurity of Low-Income Lone Mothers and Their Children in Atlantic Canada." *Canadian Journal of Public Health* 93:411–15.

——, K.D. Raine, et al. 2003. "Do Low-Income Lone Mothers Compromise Their Nutrition to Feed Their Children?" *Canadian Medical Association Journal* 168(6):686–91.

——, J. Williams, D. Lavorato, and S. Patten. 2012. "Depression and Suicide Ideation in Late Adolescence and Early Adulthood Are an Outcome of Child Hunger." *Journal of Affective Disorders* 150(1):123–9.

Muldoon, K., P. Duff, S. Fielden, and A. Anema. 2012. "Food Insufficiency Is Associated with Psychiatric Morbidity in a Nationally Representative Study of Mental Illness among Food Insecure Canadians." *Social Psychiatry and Psychiatric Epidemiology.* doi: 10.1007/s00127-012-0597-3.

Mullaly, M., J. Taylor, S. Kuhle, et al. 2010. "A Province-Wide School Nutrition Policy and Food Consumption in Elementary School Children in Prince Edward Island." *Canadian Journal of Public Health* 101(1):40–3.

New Brunswick Common Front for Social Justice Inc. 2011. *Sharp Hike in the Cost of Food: Results of a 2011 N.B. Survey.* http://www.frontnb.ca/document/food-cost-report.pdf

Nova Scotia Food Security Network and the Food Action Research Centre (FoodARC). 2013. Can Nova Scotians Afford to Eat Healthy? Report on 2012 Participatory Food Costing. Mount Saint Vincent University. http://foodarc.ca/wp-content/uploads/2013/05/NSFoodCosting2012_Report.pdf.

Office of Nutrition Policy and Promotion. 2010a. "Household Food Insecurity in Canada in 2007–08: Key Statistics and Graphics." Ottawa: Health Canada. http://www.hc-sc.gc.ca/fn-an/surveill/nutrition/commun/insecurit/key-stats-cles-2007-2008-eng.php.

——. 2010b. "Summary Tables on Household Food Insecurity in Canada in 2007–08." Ottawa: Health Canada.

Pettes, T., N. Dachner, S. Gaetz, and V. Tarasuk. In press. "An Examination of Charitable Meal Programs in Five Canadian Cities." *Journal of Health Care for the Poor and Underserved.*

Power, E. 2005. "Individual and Household Food Insecurity in Canada: Position of the Dietitians of Canada." Dietitians of Canada. https://www.dietitians.ca/Downloads/Public/householdfoodsec-position-paper.aspx.

Public Health Agency of Canada. 2008. "The Chief Public Health Officer's Report on the State of Public Health in Canada 2008." Cat. HP2-10/2008E. Ottawa: Minister of Health.

Raine, K., L. McIntyre, and J.B. Dayle. 2003. "The Failure of Charitable School- and Community-Based Nutrition Programmes to Feed Hungry Children." *Critical Public Health* 13(2):155–69.

Rainville, B., and S. Brink. 2001. "Food Insecurity in Canada, 1998–1999." R-01-2E. Hull, QC: Human Resources Development Canada.

Riches, G. 2002. "Food Banks and Food Security: Welfare Reform, Human Rights and Social Policy. Lessons from Canada?" *Social Policy & Administration* 36(6):648–63.

——. 1986. *Food Banks and the Welfare Crisis.* Ottawa: Canadian Council on Social Development.

Roustit, C., A.M. Hamelin, F. Grillo, et al. 2010. "Food Insecurity: Could School Food Supplementation Help Break Cycles of Intergenerational Transmission of Social Inequalities?" *Pediatrics* 126:1174–81.

Seligman, H.K., E. Jacobs, A. Lopez, et al. 2012. "Food Insecurity and Glycemic Control among Low-Income Patients with Type 2 Diabetes." *Diabetes Care* 35:233–38.

——, and D. Schillinger. 2010. "Hunger and Socioeconomic Disparities in Chronic Disease." *New England Journal of Medicine* 363(1):6–9.

Tarasuk, V. 2001. "A Critical Examination of Community-Based Responses to Household Food Insecurity in Canada." *Health Education & Behavior* 28(4):487–99.

—— and G.H. Beaton. 1999a. "Household Food Insecurity and Hunger among Families Using Food Banks." *Canadian Journal of Public Health* 90(2):109–13.

—— and ——. 1999b. "Women's Dietary Intakes in the Context of Household Food Insecurity." *Journal of Nutrition* 129:672–9.

——, J. Cheng, C. De Oliveira, et al. 2015. "Health Care Costs Associated with Household Food Insecurity in Ontario." *Canadian Medical Association Journal* 187(14):E429–E436.

——, N. Dachner, A.M. Hamelin, et al. 2014. "A Survey of Food Bank Operations in Five Canadian Cities." *BMC Public Health* 14:1234.

——, ——, and J. Li. 2005. "Homeless Youth in Toronto Are Nutritionally Vulnerable." *Journal of Nutrition* 135:1926–33.

——, ——, B. Poland, and S. Gaetz. 2009. "Food Deprivation Is Integral to the 'Hand to Mouth' Existence of Homeless Youth in Toronto." *Public Health Nutrition* 12(9):1437–42.

—— and H. Maclean. 1990. "The Food Problems of Low-Income Single Mothers: An Ethnographic Study." *Canadian Home Economics Journal* 40(2):76–82.

——, A. Mitchell, and N. Dachner. 2014. *Household Food Insecurity in Canada, 2012.* Toronto: Research to Identify

Policy Options to Reduce Food Insecurity (PROOF). http://proof.utoronto.ca/

——, ——, L. McLaren, and L. McIntyre. 2013. "Chronic Physical and Mental Health Conditions among Adults May Increase Vulnerability to Household Food Insecurity." *Journal of Nutrition* 143:1785–93.

—— and R. Reynolds. 1999. "A Qualitative Study of Community Kitchens as a Response to Income-Related Food Insecurity." *Canadian Journal of Dietetic Practice and Research* 60:11–16.

——, and J. Vogt. 2009. "Household Food Insecurity in Ontario." *Canadian Journal of Public Health* 100(3):184–8.

Tsang, S., A. Holt, and E. Azevedo. 2011. "An Assessment of the Barriers to Accessing Food among Food-Insecure People in Cobourg, Ontario." *Chronic Diseases and Injuries in Canada* 31(3):121–8.

Tse, C., and V. Tarasuk. 2008. "Nutritional Assessment of Charitable Meal Programs Serving Homeless People in Toronto." *Public Health Nutrition* 11(12):1296–305.

Veugelers, P.J., and A.L. Fitzgerald. 2005. "Effectiveness of School Programs in the Prevention of Childhood Obesity." *American Journal of Public Health* 95:432–5.

Vogel, L. 2010. *Canadian Medical Association Journal* 182(17):E779–E780.

Vozoris, N., and V. Tarasuk. 2003. "Household Food Insufficiency Is Associated with Poorer Health." *Journal of Nutrition* 133:120–6.

Williams, P.L., R. Macaulay, B.J. Anderson, et al. 2012. "I Would Have Never Thought That I Would Be in Such a Predicament": Voices from Women Experiencing Food Insecurity in Nova Scotia, Canada." *Journal of Hunger & Environmental Nutrition* 7:253–70.

——, L. McIntyre, and N.T. Glanville. 2010. "Milk Insecurity: Accounts of a Food Insecurity Phenomenon in Canada and Its Relation to Public Policy." *Journal of Hunger & Environmental Nutrition* 5:142–57.

Willows, N.D., and V. Au. 2006. "Nutritional Quality and Price of University Food Bank Hampers." *Canadian Journal of Dietetic Practice and Research* 67(2):104–7.

——, P. Veugelers, K. Raine, and S. Kuhle. 2009. "Prevalence and Sociodemographic Risk Factors Related to Household Food Insecurity in Aboriginal Peoples in Canada." *Public Health Nutrition* 12(8):1150–6.

Part IV

Challenging Food Governance

Although the term *governance* had become obsolete by the 1950s, it has made a comeback in the age of globalization. Considered by some to be synonymous with *government*, the term is, however, generally understood to have a broader meaning that encompasses power both within and beyond the nation-state. From a critical perspective, the rejuvenation of *governance* highlights a shift in the patterns and processes of governing from the public sector to the private sector. The emerging public–private partnerships, free-trade agreements, codes of corporate social responsibility, and non-democratic, supranational institutions like the World Trade Organization are all evidence of a structural shift to create the infrastructure to support a liberalized market economy that denounces social and environmental considerations as barriers to trade. This shift is opposed by social movements around the world that have sprung up in resistance to the marketization of all aspects of life.

Not surprisingly, the tensions of governance are evident in the area of food and food systems. The enclosure of common land, the rise of fast food, the effects of industrial agriculture, the spread of global food, and the consolidation of the food system under corporate control are all opposed by grassroots food movements such as the international peasant movement called La Vía Campesina, the Slow Food movement, the organic farming movement, and the local food movement.

The chapters in part IV reflect the tensions surrounding food system governance and raise questions about who wins and who loses in the new governance climate. In chapter 16, Knezevic examines food labelling as one contentious area in **food system governance**. Rather than informing consumers so they can make rational choices in the marketplace, labels hide more than they reveal. In essence, the chapter argues that labels serve to subdue consumer questions and concerns while perpetuating a questionable food system that has been criticized for myriad social and environmental costs.

Chapter 17 addresses another area of struggle—genetically modified crops. Clark analyzes the 35-year-old decision to tie the success of genetic modification (GM) to Canada's national interest. In essence, GM was touted as a springboard to enhance Canadian competitiveness in world markets. The result is the current domination of Canadian field crop agriculture by GM, all predetermined by government policy. Illuminating this decision is key to understanding the expansion of GM and government behaviour toward GM in subsequent decades.

In chapter 18, Margulis and Duncan introduce the concept of global food security governance. Recent decades have brought dramatic changes in the governance of the production, distribution, and access of food that crosses borders. Since these changes fundamentally shape the larger structures within which food systems operate, understanding them is crucial to envisioning the prospects and challenges of moving to sustainable food systems.

The governance of urban food systems is Mendes's subject in chapter 19. In cities around the world, millions of hungry people depend on food that has often travelled thousands of kilometres to reach supermarket shelves. Until recently, however, few of us questioned the conditions under which that food was grown, processed, and transported in and out of our cities, let alone considered the far-reaching social, economic, and environmental impacts on our communities and our planet. Today, Mendes maintains, food is reappearing on the agenda of a growing number of municipal governments, becoming an issue for city planners, and emerging as a pressing concern for urban dwellers. As a result, new forms of municipal governance are being expressed through urban food system policies and programs.

16 Making Wise Food Choices
Food Labelling, Advertising, and the Challenge of Informed Eating

Irena Knezevic

Learning Objectives

Through this chapter, you can

1. Consider food labelling through a critical lens
2. Explore the links between food, advertising, and health
3. Examine connections between the **industrial food system** and public policy

Introduction

As we wade through the problems of the contemporary global **foodscape**, as in this volume, many of the criticisms seem to identify the same culprit. Whether the critiques address environmental problems of food production, the alarming trends in human health, or the inequities inherent to the dominant food economy, they all point to the industrial food system as being largely responsible for these woes. The model is profit driven, is based on free-market principles of efficiency, and, critics argue, treats food as just another commodity (Winson 1993; Shiva 1999; Lang and Heasman 2003). In contrast, the critiques call for a recognition that food is a human right as well as a social and cultural artifact and thus should not be merely a commodity (Shiva 1999; Kent 2005; Patel 2007; Tansey and Rajotte 2008). Because of its free-market foundations, the industrial food system is incapable of accommodating such demands. It is likewise inadequate in addressing the concerns regarding its social and environmental costs, except to the extent that

changing practices to accommodate those concerns can sometimes mean profits, when such changes allow price premiums.

Large-scale food scares have plagued the industrial food system in recent years with everything from mad-cow disease to *E. coli* outbreaks. The spread of the problems brought into question the overall safety of the wide geographical distribution of food that is essential to the industrial model. Questionable practices abroad, such as the melamine contamination of some pet foods manufactured in China, discovered in 2007, also prompted consumers to distrust the global economic system that brings food from all corners of the world to the North American consumer. Such incidents were accompanied by a flood of academic literature, and now a growing body of popular literature, exposing problematic industry practices and their consequences (e.g. Schlosser 2001; Pollan 2006; Patel 2007; Kenner 2008). In turn, these exposés resulted in a better-informed public and a new breed of discriminating consumers who demand more information about their food (Caswell 1998; Hobbs 2002; Roosen et al. 2003).

In addition to years of tweaking mandatory nutritional information requirements, governments are now also overseeing an increasing flow of information from the food industry to the consumer. The current nutrition label modernization initiative in Canada aims to create a "modern food labelling system that responds to current and future challenges" and in doing so the Canadian Food Inspection Agency (2014) is removing the mandatory requirements for information on vitamins A and C. The justification is that these are no longer public-health issues, but what the change reveals is both the level of information clutter around food (which requires the regulators to weed out what they no longer consider critical information) and the highly selective nature of food labelling information presented to us. The clutter is made messier by an onslaught of new labelling initiatives—for example, the US-based chain Whole Foods is now rolling out their "Responsibly Grown" label that will evaluate environmental impact of produce and flower growing practices associated with the products they carry. In a system where the supplier of food is most commonly a vague corporate entity, **food labels** are the link between that entity and the consumer, and this link is becoming increasingly complex. Consumer demand has led to a greater number of more detailed labels on industrial food. Yet, as this chapter reveals, rather than holding the industrial food system to account, labels are themselves tools of the industry. They ensure that while small adjustments are implemented, the system's foundations remain intact and unchallenged. The symbolic power of labels shapes our **discourse** on food and hence our understanding of it. Sophisticated marketing practices ensure that the products are always presented in a positive light, so labels commonly advertise much more than they reveal.

In shaping the discourse, labels also play political and ideological roles by helping the industry appear properly regulated, thus making radical policy changes appear unnecessary. Finally, in their role as representations of standards and regulation, labels assist the industry in **co-opting** and commercializing alternative food models. In doing so, labels minimize the effects of alternatives on the industry. As this chapter demonstrates, labels help turn those alternatives from attempts at undermining the industrial food system into profitable niche markets. A selected sample of a broad set of data on food labelling and advertising (collected randomly over the last decade or so), including a brief discussion of organic labelling, is used to illustrate the complex nature of labels and the way in which they mediate the relationships between food and consumers.

Labels as Discourse

In 2009, a provincially run liquor store in North York, Ontario, featured an end-of-aisle display that exclaimed "GO LOCAL!" to advertise a celebrity-label wine from the Niagara region. While the winery was a mere 130 kilometres from North York, the product on display was only "cellared in Canada." In other words, up to 70 per cent[1] of the wine in the bottles was not from Canada, but from some other part of the world where labour and grapes are cheaper. "Cellared in Canada" is a legitimate label, but it does misleadingly suggest that the wine is Canadian and, teamed with the distributor's shameless advertising, is a perfect ploy to attract consumers looking for wine from local vineyards. The irony of this marketing move is that the label was in fact addressing those who could be seen as discriminating customers.

A variety of "in Canada" labels target consumers looking for Canadian products. Following several 2007 media exposés of the problematic "product of Canada" label, the Canadian government changed the label regulation. Previously that label meant only that more than half of production capital was supplied by a Canadian company, allowing Russian fish processed in China and then packaged in Canada to be labelled "product of Canada" (CBC 2007). The public outcry following the media reports caused the Canadian Food Inspection Agency to stipulate that for the label to be used "all or virtually all of the significant ingredients, components, processing and labour used in the food product must be Canadian" (2008:1). Instead of causing the industry's practices to change, the new labelling regulation resulted in a number of new variations of the claim—"prepared in Canada," "manufactured in Canada," and so on. Such vague and misleading claims are not exceptions in the world of food labels, and they are commonly used to attract consumers to products about which they essentially know nothing.

Labels on food products are the communicative bridge between the producer/processor and the consumer in a food system in which the two may never otherwise communicate. While most effective when presented as simple and straightforward messages, labels are inherently never just that. As Cook and O'Halloran write, "food labels bring together within a very small space and short text, the interests of major discourse communities. On a food label, the discourses of business, marketing, aesthetics, law, science, health, environmentalism, and the family, all meet, intermingle and compete" (1999:148). The content of a label then, complex as it is, is never a simple message, and its loaded meaning is further complicated by its interaction with other labels on the same product. In theory, labels inform and reassure the consumers that their food is monitored, nutritionally analyzed, and held to a variety of safety and quality standards. In practice, they are more of an opportunity to advertise and make glowing claims about products. They are the tool of the packaged food industry, necessitated and developed by it, and as such can really only serve one master faithfully—the industry that needs them for its very existence.

And labels do more than just promote and perpetuate the processed food industry. They also determine the boundaries of discourse. By giving us "need to know" information, they also indicate what should not be of concern to us. The messages conveyed by labels obscure more than they declare, by selectively providing the information the manufacturers want us to know. They shape our understanding of the food items we buy and consequently our understanding of the food system. They tap into what we want to hear (and read) by providing constant reassurance that the food system is under control and functioning. In the long run, they assist the industrial food system in minimizing criticism and challenges. For most consumers, who can devote only a fraction of their time to making food-purchasing decisions, they provide a sense of security and knowledge and at the same time discourage questioning of the food system. Most of all they assure us that is acceptable to not know where our food comes from.

Distancing from Food

In his *Scavenger's Guide to Haute Cuisine* Steven Rinella writes, "A historian could make a good argument that human history is just a long story of depersonalization of food production" (2005:12). Critiquing the food system in which consumers have little or no personal connection to their food is not a nostalgic cry for pastoral images of agrarian idyll. Rather, it is a warning bell to citizens who want to eat fresh and healthy foods produced in a sustainable manner, within the context of a system where few food items can be described as such. Various chapters in this volume outline the shortcomings of the dominant food system. Other critiques of the industrialized, intensive mass production of food also encompass a range of concerns relating to the health of societies: human (Nestle 2002; Pilcher 2005), environmental (Altieri and Nicholls 2005), and economic (Perelman 2003). Those problems persist virtually unchallenged in large part because they happen outside of consumers' immediate environments.

Brewster Kneen uses the term **distancing** to describe the process of "separating people from the sources of their food and nutrition with as many interventions as possible" (1995:11). Distance is both physical and informational. Consequently, consumers' purchasing decisions are informed mainly through the labels on the packaging. Without any connection to the field or the farmer who produced the food, consumers are prompted to associate their food with brands, such as the friendly faces of Aunt Jemima and the Pillsbury Doughboy. They are also prompted to rely on the labels to tell them how one product can be a better choice than the next and to assure them that the product meets some set of standards of quality and safety. The industrial food system depends on these messages to communicate with consumers and provide them with a sense of trust and reassurance. It also depends on them to maintain the distancing without major objections.

Food labels can be mandatory or voluntary, and both types can distance people from their food. Mandatory labels are the ones required by the extensive regulatory framework imposed on the agri-food companies to ensure certain standards are met and that certain information (such as the nutritional breakdown or expiry date) is available to the consumer. The regulatory framework is overseen by government agencies (such as Health Canada and the Canadian Food Inspection Agency) that set the standards, and while it determines many of the safety and quality requirements, it does nothing to remedy the "distance." Instead, the regulatory framework provides us with what Laura B. DeLind describes as a "surrogate for trust," explaining that:

> Standards and certification processes, whatever their scope, cut two ways. They are restrictive as well as enabling. While they function as a form of interest-group insurance and assurance, they also insert themselves between individuals and direct experience and responsibility. They substitute for, indeed, they become a surrogate for personal awareness and judgement. In what we are told is an ever expanding universe, we are continually asked to place our trust in standards and certification processes at the expense of our trust in interpersonal relationships and daily interactions informed by wisdom locally generated and grounded in place. . . . Even at the local level there is a tendency for standards and certification to

become more significant than the principles they are designed to uphold. (2002:200)

In other words, labelling (and its regulation) not only fails to address many of the shortcomings of the industrial food system, it also facilitates the system by providing few and easily surmountable obstacles, which, rather than significantly challenging the system, actually provide it with a cloak of legitimacy. Whereas a mandatory label such as a nutrition table can tell us about the level of sodium in a food item, the manufacturer is not required to explain how it treats its labour force or how it disposes of its waste. In fact, the existence of standards and labels that represent manufacturers mediate the economic and environmental consequences of industrial food production (Deaton and Hoehn 2005). What labels do not tell us can sometimes be even more significant than what they say.

Voluntary labelling, on the other hand, refers to the labels that the manufacturer can choose to apply, usually because such a label extols some virtue of the product, such as "low in fat," "no sugar added" or the above-noted labels of origin. They can also be labels associated with a certification process that differentiates the product from others in the same category, for instance "organic" or "fair trade." Voluntary labels are still somewhat regulated—though not required, their use is restricted at times and some of the claims are carefully defined. Government agencies, industry associations, and advertising councils all have a say in what voluntary labels can claim and under what circumstances. Certification procedures for voluntary labels are often designed by third parties (e.g. Fairtrade Canada) or a combination of third-party and industry collaboration (e.g. the Rainforest Alliance) and in some cases by producer associations and government agencies (e.g. Canada Organic). Often associated with noble causes and aimed at consumers concerned with the shortcomings of industrial food production, voluntary labels nevertheless, as the next section describes, are often used to advertise rather than inform.

Moreover, voluntary labels fragment the information surrounding food. They can really convey only one or two messages at a time, allowing for distancing to continue. Fair-trade certification says nothing about pesticide use, organic labelling says nothing of food miles, food-miles/carbon-footprint labels tell us nothing of labour conditions, and so on. Even in cases of multiple labels, the distance remains, because the labels themselves are merely representations of those interventions. They tell the concerned consumer that the interventions are up to their higher-than-average standards, deflecting suspicion that the interventions themselves may be problematic.

Advertising and Labels

Through their selective nature food labels try to highlight information that can sell the product while obscuring the information that may make us question the product. Packages of Kraft Singles processed cheese, for example, emphasize the product's calcium content, and each package bears a very visible stamp stating that the product is "A source of calcium." The product is indeed a source of calcium, providing 6 per cent of recommended daily value in one slice, compared to a cup of average yogourt which provides nearly 50 per cent. Processed cheese is also a source of saturated fat (13 per cent), sodium (15 per cent), and cholesterol (3 per cent), and one-half of the total calories in a slice come from fat. This information, though available in the nutrition table, is something that the potential buyer has to look for, as it is less immediately visible than the calcium-boasting claim. Similarly, Nature Valley granola bars packaging touts a "Made with 100% whole grains" label in addition to its healthy-sounding name, but tells us in small print that the whole-grain oats are in fact only the second ingredient; the first is corn syrup, and the third and fourth are sugar and glucose-fructose. The whole grains in the product provide only 1 gram of fibre in a 35 gram bar, compared to 14 grams of sugar, and the entire nutrition table suggests that the nutritional value of a Nature Valley granola bar is about the same as that of 35 grams of the proverbial junk snack—the Pop Tart.[2]

Nutrition tables are still useful for the concerned consumer, but a 2008 US Department of Agriculture (USDA) Economic Research Service study indicates that fewer than two-thirds of consumers use nutritional information in making their purchasing decisions, and that even those numbers have been declining, particularly among young adults. While the numbers may indicate consumer skepticism, they also mean that flashy messages are more likely to reach consumers than the information provided in mandatory nutrition tables.

In addition to this imbalance in how messages are conveyed, some labelling can confuse the consumer when, instead of informing, it actually creates new questions. For instance, a package of seasoned Ontario-processed shish kebabs informs the buyers that the product is of "Mediterranean quality" and that it is "authentic." There is nothing that explains what is authentic about it, nor what "Mediterranean quality" means, and there is certainly no standardized meaning for those labels in the food industry.

In all the above examples, while the mandatory information is still provided to the consumer, the voluntary labels that cast the product in a positive light are significantly more pronounced and more likely to be noticed by the potential buyer. On a bottle of PurOliva cooking oil, for instance, the large-letter product name is accompanied by a similarly large picture of olives, and it is only in much a smaller and quite ornamental (and therefore more difficult to read) font that the product admits to being "A perfect blend of canola oil & extra virgin olive oil." A consumer may wonder what the perfect blend is (the package lists canola and olive oils as ingredients, but says nothing about the proportions of each), but that question will arise only upon close reading of the labels.

Moreover, while mandatory information is required it is also often helpful to the manufacturer, since it doubles as litigation insurance.

Should a consumer complain about being fooled by PurOliva's packaging, the company is protected by that very ingredient list that is mandated by government agencies. Mandatory labels in the end are the insurance policy for the larger, louder, more colourful voluntary labels that are commonly placed on the front of the package.

Selling Health

The growing evidence that the industrial food system is associated with climbing rates of obesity and diet-related disease prompts many consumers to seek out healthier alternatives. Long-term effects of additive-laden processed foods are becoming impossible to hide among the increasingly unhealthy populations of the industrial world. Consumer demand for better food and growing pressures from health practitioners and government agencies have compelled manufacturers to convince their consumers that they can respond to those concerns. Food labels are now commonly communicating misleading messages of health, such as the previously described labels of Kraft Singles processed cheese and Nature Valley granola bars. That the messages are effective marketing strategies is made possible by the cunning work of manufacturers as well as by the fragmented understandings of food and nutrition.

Scientific studies have pointed to specific ingredients as being "bad" or "good" for human health, making nutritional makeup the sole determining factor in whether foods are bad or good. When avoiding particular nutrients and choosing others is so often equated with health, the door to misleading marketing is wide open. If a consumer's main concern is getting enough calcium, overlooking all the other nutritional facts is easy. This fragmented understanding of nutrition also fails to take freshness, sustainability, and nutrient interactions into consideration. Michael Pollan (2007, 2008) describes this understanding as **nutritionism**.[3] Although the term was coined only in 2002 by Gyorgy Scrinis (Pollan 2008:27), the trend of nutritionism

started in the early 1980s with scientific codification of dietary components, which has over the years transformed food into "nutrients." Pollan writes: "Drink coffee with your steak, and your body won't be able to fully absorb the iron in the meat. The trace of limestone in the corn tortilla unlocks essential amino acids in the corn that would otherwise remain unavailable" (Pollan 2007:7). Nutritionism in its cultural context is merely another form of **scientific reductionism**, the attempt to reduce complex interactions to isolated simple relations.

The reductionism is often justified as simplification, a way to make complex scientific information more accessible to the general public. A recent McGill University study on usability of nutritional labelling suggests that this simplification may be desirable—a Yale University–developed labelling system, NuVal, scores foods' nutritional value as a single number on a scale of 0 to 100 and was found to be the easiest, most accessible way for consumers to identify healthy foods (Helfer and Schultz 2014). However, according to the NuVal website's FAQ page, the score is based on assessment of the traditional nutrition label information. In other words, it is a bit of information that further reduces food to fuel and removes the need for consumers to be informed about their food and its complex life. Emily Yates-Doerr (2012) describes nutritional labelling as black-boxing of nourishment. Drawing on Bruno Latour's work, she explains that black boxes are often used in technical drawings in place of complex machinery that the users of those drawings don't need to understand, as the user should only be concerned with input and output of that "black box." As she eloquently writes:

> Nutritional black boxes give an appearance of stability to the otherwise processual experiences of nourishment. . . . Nutritional black boxes also make formerly separate objects—take the classically incommensurate apple and orange—appear in like terms. We no longer consider: How do they taste? We instead ask: How many vitamins

do they have? We presume that the sum of the parts will equal the whole, and we consequently count the nutrients in apples and oranges to know their value . . . we lose sight of the relationships formed in eating, which can never be accurately fixed and measured. *Nourishment will never simply be nutrients.* (pp. 308–9, emphasis added)

As Canadian communication scholar Charlene Elliott explains, this is part of a larger cultural trend where health and nutrition are medicalized and moralized (2014). Labels serve to cement the sanctity of individual health as something mechanical and based on rational choice—and thus removed from pleasure or social context to emphasize the "working body," a body that can perform as a working citizen and not burden the public health-care system. This disassociates health from *feeling* good and treats potentially pleasurable eating experiences as risk behaviours (Elliott 2014).

Such cultural reliance on scientific reductionism (treating food as nutrients) results not only from reductionist nutritional science but also from a particular advertising discourse that has for decades attempted to sell health through reducing the human body to a machine. "The term 'body maintenance' indicates the popularity of the machine metaphor for the body," wrote Mike Featherstone in his 1982 discussion of body image and commercialism (p. 24), arguing that the phenomenon was a direct product of consumer culture and its aggressive discourse of advertising. Whereas industrial food is largely responsible for increased levels of sugars, fats, sodium, and chemical preservatives in North American diets (as they are all used in large quantities to improve taste, appearance, and/or shelf life of food), once the awareness of the health effects of processed foods arose, the same manufacturers started cashing in on consumers' apprehensions. Health claims of all sorts are made for marketing purposes, although they frequently highlight a product's levels of one or two nutrients and in effect only obscure other

ingredients. These claims also obscure the production and processing aspects of food, and, in their selection of information to be emphasized, they imply that any other information is unnecessary. Meanwhile, reductionist claims are also the mainstay of the weight-loss industry whose worth is estimated to be in the tens of billions of dollars (BBC 2003). Ironically, most of those profits go to the pockets of the very food manufacturing giants associated with the highly processed and additive-laden foods that cause weight problems in the first place. The Jenny Craig weight-loss brand, for example, is owned by Nestlé, and Slimfast is a part of the Unilever empire (Patel 2007).

One of the more troubling examples of how the reductionist approach has been exploited by the food industry is evident in the now obsolete Health Check approval program. Run by the Heart and Stroke Foundation of Canada (HSFC), the program promoted heart-healthy foods by giving products a stamp of approval. In addition to about 15,000 products in Canadian stores, HSFC also approved menu items in restaurants. HSFC evaluated the foods based on Canada's Food Guide, but it measured only certain individual nutrients—sodium and fat—and it did not even evaluate added sugar content. A 2008 CBC exposé claimed that many nutritionists and dieticians questioned the nutritional value of some Health Check–approved foods, and that many non-approved foods had much better nutritional values. By singling out only a handful of nutrients, HSFC effectively allowed food manufacturers to promote their products as healthy when in fact those products had reduced levels only of certain nutrients. Moreover, the stamp came with an annual licensing fee of $1,225 to $3,625 per product and was promoted by the HSFC as a business- and brand-building strategy (Health Check 2010). The label that appeared to be a shortcut to healthy eating was, in reality, both a marketing tool and a stamp of approval for the depersonalized industrial food system. After much criticism, the program was discontinued in 2014.

Responsibility

Labels provide information, however selective, but by doing so, they also individualize responsibility for eating habits. Once the information has been conveyed to the consumer, responsibility has been transferred with it, which helps circumvent demands for better policy options. Research on the social determinants of health indicates that the most important determinant of an individual's poor health is poverty (Mikkonnen and Raphael 2010). Food insecurity and poor nutrition are both associated with lower socio-economic status (Tarasuk 2001). Healthy foods are more expensive per calorie (Drewnowski and Darmon 2005), and choosing them requires at least some knowledge of nutrition, thus linking healthy food choices to social factors such as education and income levels. Even the most effective health promotion materials do this. A recent study in the United States indicates that using Physical Activity Calorie Equivalent Labeling—menu labels that display food energy in physical activity calorie equivalents—"may influence parents' decisions on what fast-food items to order for their children and encourage them to get their children to exercise" (Viera and Antonelli 2015:1). However, this type of labelling still does nothing to challenge our food environments and the preponderance of unhealthy foods in convenient, inexpensive locations; it simply provides an additional tool for individual responsibility. Individual responsibility is one of the basic tenets of the neo-liberal order. It is a mechanism that shifts the onus from those who profit in the market (in this case the food industry) to those who "choose" to participate in that market as rational actors (in this case eaters). The notion of consumer choice and the consequent implied responsibility alleviate the burden of social responsibility from the profiting industry, as well as from the governments that fail to hold that industry accountable.

Food labels communicate with the individual consumer, not society. As such, they suggest that healthy diets are determined at the individual level. Most critics of industrial food see reform and modification of politics and policy as the most effective changes (see Koç and Dahlberg 1999), calling for economic policy reform (Qualman 2007) and a wide range of public-health policy improvements that would include everything from municipal planning to education programs (see Nestle and Jacobson 2000). The industry, however, has resisted such change (Nestle 2002), repeatedly invoking the free-market principles of consumer demand and individual choice as the justifications for their problematic practices. Labels, in their service to the industry, indicate that eliminating unhealthy food items need not happen at the processing or regulatory level but should be left to the workings of individual choice. Making health an individual responsibility lets both the industry and public policy makers off the hook (Nestle 2009). This individualization of diet choices downloads the responsibility from the industry, which continues to profit, to the consumer, who is faced with limited and at times confusing information.

One of the most heated debates in contemporary food studies (as well as in policy making) centres around the issues of responsibility and choice. The popularity of Michael Pollan's work, the Slow Food movement (Petrini and Waters 2007), and alternative food options cause ripples in the food system and also highlight the importance of being an informed consumer and making the right purchasing choices. But this shift has incited a reaction from critics such as Julie Guthman, who advocates political and policy reform, and sees the shift to "informed consumer" as a "highly privileged and apolitical idea" (2007a:78), and declares "I am fed up with the apolitical conclusions, self-satisfied biographies of food choices, and general disregard for the more complex arguments that scholars of food bring to these topics" (2007b:264).

The road to a better food system is probably somewhere in the middle and includes individual choice, which once organized—as the effectiveness of historical mass boycotts tells us—can turn itself into a formidable political force. But choice is difficult in a complex, problematic food system, and it can be effective only when combined with appropriate policy changes.

Labels, however, shift all the responsibility to the consumer; moreover, they imply that the industry is quite capable of communicating with the consumer, and that policy change is not needed. The inadequacy of this implication is evident in a recent labelling initiative. Much has been made of the recent New York City law requiring fast-food chains to label their items with calorie counts, but the move does not affect the ingredients nor the way the items are prepared. Instead, the new label suggests to the consumer that if eating cheap chain food makes them overweight, it is their own fault. Additionally, a survey of low-income minority communities in New York City found that most consumers paid no attention to the labels and that even those who read them still did not change their purchasing habits (Elbel et al. 2009).

In the perverse reach of industrial food the focus on individual responsibility also encompasses the responsibility for others. The above-described case of Kraft Singles is a great example because, in addition to associating the product with healthy eating, it plays into parental responsibility with the slogan "good food to grow up on." Even the choices that are not nutrition related, such as choosing fair-trade products, imply that the individual consumer bears the responsibility for the ills of the industrial food system. Hence some critiques of ethical consumer choices have addressed the marketing power of guilt and the role of products as status symbols (Guthman 2003, 2007a). Whatever the case, food labelling clearly does little to change the food system itself, and by providing the industry with the veil of honesty it actually reinforces the status quo.

Alternative Food Choices— The Organic Example

As fragmented as it may be, consumer resistance to the industrial food system runs deep in the industrialized world. Consumers who can afford to choose alternatives are redefining themselves as food citizens and are making choices that chip away at the system. From organic and vegetarian purchases to the Slow Food movement and fair-trade products, consumers choose not to support the kind of production that characterizes the global industrial food system (Allen 2008; DuPuis and Gillon 2009). By reclaiming the power to make decisions about food, citizens are shaking a metaphorical fist at industrial food and its ideological foundations. In doing so they create new spaces for production, exchange, and consumption of food upon which other social relationships can be built (Blay-Palmer 2007), and they open new understandings of food and food economy.

Some alternatives, such as community gardens and community-supported agriculture, take approaches that place food more or less outside of the dominant economy. However, much of the resistance has been unable to step outside of consumer culture and the free-market economic framework. In the spirit of individual choice and responsibility, many of the alternatives demonstrate the "voting with your dollar" concept, promoting improvements to certain aspects of the food economy but leaving the underlying economic underpinnings intact. As such, many of the alternative food choices have failed to substantially alter the foodscape and instead have lent themselves to the very system they once sought to oppose.

Organic foods may be the most salient example of this co-opted resistance. For several decades organic foods in North America represented a full-fledged alternative, a product of chemical-free, small-scale, diverse farming, which relied on social relationships for marketing and manifested the "back-to-the-land" resistance to the dominant ideologies and economic system. Organic foods for many years meant shrinking the gap between the consumers and the sources of their food. But as the popularity of organic foods grew, instead of presenting a greater challenge to the industrial food economy they became a new marketing opportunity for large industrial players. The greater demand in fact allowed for greater distancing, and, set in the landscape of consumer culture, organic foods quickly fell into the trap of certification, standardization, and labelling shortcuts. Labels replaced interpersonal trust and helped to reduce organics from more sustainable alternatives to merely chemical-free foods within the industrial food system. With labels to mediate trust, large food industry players launched their own organic lines (such as Loblaws' President's Choice Organics) and bought up successful independent organic labels (for example, Coca-Cola's purchase of Honest Tea line of bottled organic teas). Critics have been challenging this trend both in scholarly writings (Freyer and Bingen 2015) and in activism (Corporate Watch, n.d.), but with little success. With most organic brands now owned by industry giants (Howard 2008) and sold through chains like Loblaws and Walmart, organics are now largely a part of the very system they once opposed.

Now mostly produced and distributed on a large scale, organics have become industrial food, albeit grown without pesticides, chemical fertilizers, and artificial hormones. Labelling regulation has helped this process by providing communicative shortcuts through standardized certification. Buying organic in Canada now means that the consumer needs to look for only one logo—Canada Organic—a standardization move ensuring that organic foods can be produced and sold within the industrial system and that the consumers need not know where or how their organic food was grown. For instance, a package of organic soy milk available at a Canadian dollar store bears the Canada Organic logo, but also states that the product was "prepared and packaged in Canada" giving no indication of where in Canada it was prepared and by whom, and, more important, no indication of the source of the organic ingredients. The label effectively reduces "organic" to "chemical-free," rendering all other aspects of the organic philosophy irrelevant. By making it easier for consumers to identify organic products, the logo in essence restates that the

distancing is fine and need not be revisited. As David Conner writes of organic labels:

> The information on the label is restricted to how the food was produced, and at best is a proxy for the on farm environmental impacts of production. It provides no information on how the producer treats his or her labor force, how many miles the food has traveled, how the farm contributes to the community and local economy, etc. . . . It does nothing to address the "corporatization" and consolidation of the food system. (2004:31)

In removing all the other, once-important, characteristics of organic foods, organic standardization and the labels that represent it imply that the consumers' demand for organics is only about removing the potentially harmful chemicals from their diets. The emphasis on individual health trumps environmental and social well-being and contributes to further fragmentation of food information. The connection between socio-economic status and health—whether real or perceived—and premium prices on organics have also turned organic food into a symbol of social status (Guthman 2003), making it desirable for more than just its nutritional value.

The environmental benefits of eliminating chemicals may still be significant on an industrial organic farm, and thus help promote the foods as "greener" options. But industrial farms, characterized by intensive and specialized production, are not good for ecosystems even if elimination of chemicals makes them more acceptable than their chemical-using counterparts. As well, processing and distribution in the industrial model cause problems associated with packaging and transportation, which organic products still require.

Most of all, national organic labels do nothing to shrink the distance between the consumers and the source of their food. To those who have the luxury of choosing organics, the labels offer an opportunity for self-congratulatory purchases marked by a stamp that tells little and obscures much. They also allow for responsible decision making with respect to individual health and strengthen the relationship between the industry and the consumer. Indeed, they open doors to industrial organics that may be chemical-free but are far from being socially or environmentally sustainable.

Meanwhile, the small, diverse organic farms that nurtured organic agriculture over the years have now become secondary to industrial organics. Having practised comprehensively sustainable farming that made organics popular in the first place, those producers now have to play by the rules of the industrial food system—the very system they once resisted. By reducing organics to a label, the industrial food system has managed to co-opt a sustainable alternative.

Conclusion

Food labelling has had its bright moments, and many attempts have been made to make labelling more honest, transparent, and informative. Government agencies and consumer groups alike have occasionally tried to hold the food industry more accountable, and many of the labelling guidelines have been designed in response to consumer demands. But even when successful, such attempts seem to only promote the idea that the system is working like a well-oiled machine. In September 2010, *Globe and Mail* reported that the US Food and Drug Administration (FDA) issued a warning to Dr Pepper Snapple Group and Unilever, asking the companies to stop making "unsubstantiated nutritional claims about their green tea-flavoured beverages," part of their respective Canada Dry and Lipton product lines. The companies are expected to remove the labels that claim the beverages contain antioxidants, and failing to do so may result in a court appearance. Their misleading labelling already helped launch the products onto the market, yet they are expected only to stop making such claims, without being subjected to any fines or other penalties unless they ignore the FDA's warning.

Similarly, the makers of Ben & Jerry's ice cream recently succumbed to pressure from the Center for Science in the Public Interest to stop using the "all natural" labels on their products that contain alkalized and partially hydrogenated ingredients (Fulton 2010). But the move ultimately benefited the company by creating a media blitz and allowing them to brag about the quality of their products while reiterating the vagueness of the "all natural" label.

These instances not only reinforce the impression that the food system is under control, but also remind us that it is only the big players in the system that matter. Effectiveness of labelling regulation is measured by industry's compliance; small producers hardly ever make the news. Additionally, the big players wield a great deal of influence—partly through lobbying (Nestle 2002), but also partly through their ability to shape voluntary labelling. In Canada, for example, large grocery chains refuse to carry products labelled "non-GMO." The argument is that such labels imply that products free from genetically modified organisms (GMOs) are somehow superior, thereby threatening the sales of products that cannot make such claims. With the decision to shun "non-GMO"-labelled products, the grocery chains effectively declared the label nonsensical, and, perhaps more importantly, re-established the hierarchy of power in the system.

While making minor corrections to the foodscape, labels still operate within the confines of the industrial system. They serve the industry much more than they control it. Their ultimate message is that the food system as a whole cannot be changed and neither can the workings of the global economy, with all its negative environmental and social consequences. The best we can hope for, labels seem to say, is to get selected information and have faith that we can make the right choices within the existing system. The more we rely on labels, the more we accommodate the problematic industrial food system and the less likely we are to act as agents of real change. A truly reimagined food system would not need an ever-increasing number of labels, because certifications, standards, and labels are the front line of the industrial food system. Labels are not needed for food grown in community gardens, preserves purchased from a friend, or bread bought from a neighbour's bakery. Ensuring the availability of food that is economically fair, socially responsible, and environmentally sound will require us to become active agents in the system—both as individuals and as communities. A sustainable food system entails informed and responsible choices made within a context of comprehensive well-being. Labels, as communicative shortcuts across numerous interventions, are but reminders that such a context does not exist. They provide a bandage for all that is wrong with the industrial food system, but they cannot fix its fundamental problems. If they did, labels would render themselves obsolete.

Discussion Questions

1. What are the connections between food labelling and advertising?

2. Can food labels be useful in countering problems associated with food and social determinants of health?

3. Can alternative food choices be useful in countering problems associated with food and social determinants of health?

4. How do labels facilitate "distancing" in the food system?

Further Reading

1. Drewnowski, Adam, and Nicole Darmon. 2005. "The Economics of Obesity: Dietary Energy Density and Energy Cost." *American Journal of Clinical Nutrition* 82(1):265S–73S.
   This study looks at the cost of nutrient-dense foods in comparison to low-nutrient calorie-dense foods and argues that the problem of obesity is highly correlated to poverty, and that this correlation is growing as price disparity between healthy and unhealthy foods grows.

2. Elliott, Charlene D. 2014. "Communication and Health: An Interrogation." *Canadian Journal of Communication* 39(2):9–21.
   Elliot provides an excellent account of the role of communication tools, including labelling, in the cultural framing of health, nutrition, and individual responsibility.

3. Guthman, Julie. 2007. "Commentary on Teaching Food: Why I Am Fed Up with Michael Pollan et al." *Agriculture and Human Values* 24:261–4.
   This is one of Guthman's several pieces to offer a scathing critique of the self-congratulatory approach to alternative food choices, and writings that present those choices as the individualized and often apolitical and class-biased solutions to the problems of the industrialized food system.

4. Yates-Doerr, Emily. 2012. "The Opacity of Reduction: Nutritional Black-Boxing and the Meanings of Nourishment." *Food, Culture and Society: An International Journal of Multidisciplinary Research* 15(2):293–313.
   Yates-Doerr vividly explains how the reductionism of nutrition labels can be confusing despite "its pretense of simplicity" and argues that nourishment is more complex for more people than mere nutrient information based on fixed rules.

Video Suggestion

1. **Freedhoff, Yoni. 2012. *What's a Food Industry to Do?* www.weightymatters.ca/. 13 min.**
   This video provides a concise and insightful look into packaging labels such as "no sugar added" and takes the food industry to task for the health claims made on a range of processed foods.

Notes

1. In Ontario, at least 30 per cent of the wine has to be from Ontario to be labelled "cellared in Canada." In British Columbia, however, a "cellared in Canada" wine can be made with 100 per cent imported wine.

2. The nutritional comparison is based on the manufacturer-provided nutritional information on the packaging for both products.

3. Pollan did not coin the term (and he freely acknowledges that fact), but he greatly popularized it.

References

Allen, Patricia. 2008. "Mining for Justice in the Food System: Perceptions, Practices, and Possibilities." *Agriculture and Human Values* 25:157–61.

Altieri, Miguel A., and Clara I. Nicholls. 2005. *Agroecology and the Search for the Truly Sustainable Agriculture.* Mexico: United Nations Environment Programme.

BBC. 2003. "The Diet Business: Banking on Failure." 5 February. Accessed 27 February 2015. http://news.bbc.co.uk/1/hi/business/2725943.stm.

Blay-Palmer, Alison. 2007. "Relational Local Food Networks: The Farmers' Market @ Queen's." Pp. 111–17 in *Interdisciplinary Perspectives in Food Studies*, ed. Mustafa Koç, Rod MacRae, and Kelly Bronson. Toronto: McGraw-Hill Ryerson.

Canadian Food Inspection Agency. 2008. *Guidelines Defining Product of Canada and Made in Canada on Food Labels and Advertising.* Accessed 15 September 2014. http://www.inspection.gc.ca/english/fssa/labeti/inform/prodcane.shtml.

———. 2014. "Food Labelling Modernization Engagement Summary Report on Key Issues—June 2014." Accessed 12 February 2015. http://www.inspection.gc.ca/food/labelling/labelling-modernization-initiative/eng/1370111174659/1370111346666.

Caswell, Julie A. 1998. "How Labeling of Safety and Process Attributes Affects Markets for Food." *Agricultural and Resource Economics Review* 27(2):151–8.

CBC. 2007. "Marketplace: Product of Canada, eh?." Video. 27 October.

———. 2008. "Marketplace: Does HealthCheck Logo Hype Health or Sell Food?." Video. 23 January.

Cook, Guy, and Kieran O'Halloran. 1999. "Labels Literacy: Factors Affecting the Understanding and Assessment of Baby Food Labels." Pp. 145–56 in *Language and Literacies: Selected Papers from the Annual Meeting of the British Association for Applied Linguistics*, ed. Teresa O'Brian. Clevedon, UK: Short Run Press.

Conner, David S. 2004. "Expressing Values in Agricultural Markets: An Economic Policy Perspective." *Agriculture and Human Values* 21(1):27–35.

Corporate Watch. (n.d.). "Corporate Control of Organic." Accessed 24 November 2015. https://corporatewatch.org/content/corporate-organics-corporate-control-organic

Deaton, B.J., and John P. Hoehn. 2005. "The Social Construction of Production Externalities in Contemporary Agriculture: Process versus Product Standards as the Basis for Defining 'Organic.'" *Agriculture and Human Values* 22(1):31–8.

DeLind, Laura B. 2002. "Transforming Organic Agriculture into Industrial Organic Products: Reconsidering National Organic Standards." *Human Organization* 59(2):198–208.

Drewnowski, Adam, and Darmon, Nicole. 2005. "The Economics of Obesity: Dietary Energy Density and Energy Cost." *American Journal of Clinical Nutrition* 82(1):265S–273S.

DuPuis, E. Melanie, and Sean Gillon. 2009. "Alternative Modes of Governance: Organic as Civic Engagement." *Agriculture and Human Values* 26:43–56.

Elbel, Brian, Rogan Kersh, Victoria L. Brescoll, and L. Beth Dixon. 2009. "Calorie Labeling and Food Choices: A First Look at the Effects on Low-Income People in New York City." *Health Affairs* 28(6): w1110–21. doi: 10.1377/hlthaff.28.6.w1110

Elliott, Charlene D. 2014. "Communication and Health: An Interrogation." *Canadian Journal of Communication* 39(2):9–21.

Featherstone, Mike. 1982. "The Body in Consumer Culture." *Theory, Culture and Society* 1(2):18–33.

Freyer, Bernhard, and Jim Bingen, eds. 2015. *Re-thinking Organic Food and Farming in a Changing World.* Boston: Kluwer and Springer.

Fulton, April. 2010. "Ben & Jerry's Takes 'All Natural' Claims off Ice Cream Labels." National Public Radio, 27 September. Accessed 27 September 2014. http://www.npr.org/blogs/health/2010/09/27/130158014/ben-jerry-s-takes-all-natural-claims-off-ice-cream-labels?sc=fb&cc=fp.

Globe and Mail. 2010. "FDA Slams Lipton, Canada Dry for Nutritional Claims." *Globe and Mail* online, 7 September.

Guthman, Julie. 2003. "Fast Food/Organic Food: Reflective Tastes and the Making of 'Yuppie Chow.'" *Social and Cultural Geography* 4(1):45–58.

———. 2007a. "Can't Stomach It: How Michael Pollan et al. Made Me Want to Eat Cheetos." *Gastronomica* 7(2):75–9.

———. 2007b. "Commentary on Teaching Food: Why I Am Fed Up with Michael Pollan et al." *Agriculture and Human Values* 24:261–4.

Health Check. 2010. "Food Manufacturers: Help your Customers Make Healthy Food Choices." Accessed 27 November 2014. http://www.healthcheck.org/page/licensee-overview-0.

Helfer, Peter and Thomas R. Shultz. 2014. "The Effects of Nutrition Labeling on Consumer Food Choice: A Psychological Experiment and Computational Model." *Annals of the New York Academy of Sciences* (Special Issue: "Paths of Convergence for Agriculture, Health, and Wealth") 1331:174–85.

Hobbs, Jill E. 2002. "Consumer Demand for Traceability." Paper presented at the International Agricultural Trade Research Consortium Annual Meeting, December. Accessed 13 January 2015. http://ageconsearch.umn.edu/bitstream/14614/1/wp03-01.pdf.

Howard, P. 2008. "Who Owns What in the Organic Food Industry." Accessed 23 December 2014. http://www.certifiedorganic.bc.ca/rcbtoa/services/corporate-ownership.html.

Kenner, Robert, dir. 2008. *Food, Inc.* Video. Los Angeles: Participant Media.

Kent, George. 2005. *Freedom from Want: The Human Right to Adequate Food*. Washington, DC: Georgetown University Press.

Kneen, Brewster. 1995. *From Land to Mouth: Understanding the Food System*. 2nd edn. Toronto: NC Press.

Koç, Mustafa, and Kenneth A. Dahlberg. 1999. "The Restructuring of Food Systems: Trends, Research, and Policy Issues." *Agriculture and Human Values* 16:109–16.

Lang, Tim, and Michael Heasman. 2003. *Food Wars: The Global Battle for Mouths, Minds and Markets*. London: Earthscan/James & James.

Mikkonnen, Juha, and Dennis Raphael. 2010. *Social Determinants of Health: The Canadian Facts*. Toronto: York University School of Health Policy and Management.

Nestle, Marion. 2002. *Food Politics: How the Food Industry Influences Nutrition and Health*. Berkeley: University of California Press.

———. 2009. "Food Politics: Personal Responsibility vs. Social Responsibility." Lecture at the University of Toronto, 21 January 2009.

Nestle, Marion, and Michael F. Jacobson. 2000. "Halting the Obesity Epidemic: A Public Health Policy Approach." *Public Health Reports* 115:12–24.

Patel, Raj. 2007. *Stuffed and Starved: Markets, Power and the Hidden Battle for the World's Food System*. Toronto: HarperCollins.

Perelman, M. 2003. *The Perverse Economy: The Impact of Markets on People and the Environment*. New York: Palgrave Macmillan.

Petrini, Carlo, and Alice Waters. 2007. *Slow Food Nation: Why Our Food Should Be Good, Clean, and Fair*. New York: Rizzoli Ex Libris.

Pilcher, Jeffrey M. 2005. "Industrial *Tortillas* and Folkloric Pepsi: The Nutritional Consequences of Hybrid Cuisines in Mexico." Pp. 235–50 in *The Cultural Politics of Food and Eating*, ed. James L. Watson and Melissa L. Caldwell. Malden, MA: Blackwell Publishing.

Pollan, Michael. 2006. *The Omnivore's Dilemma: A Natural History of Four Meals*. New York: Penguin.

———. 2007. "Unhappy Meals." *New York Times*, 28 January. Accessed 26 August 2010. http://www.nytimes.com/2007/01/28/magazine/28nutritionism.t.html?_r=0.

———. 2008. *In Defense of Food: An Eater's Manifesto*. New York: Penguin.

Qualman, Darrin. 2007. "The Farm Crisis & Corporate Profits." Pp. 95–110 in *Interdisciplinary Perspectives in Food Studies*, ed. Mustafa Koç, Rod MacRae, and Kelly Bronson. Toronto: McGraw-Hill Ryerson.

Rinella, Steven. 2005. *The Scavenger's Guide to Haute Cuisine*. New York: Miramax Books.

Roosen, Jutta, Jayson L. Lusk, and John A. Fox. 2003. "Consumer Demand for and Attitudes toward Alternative Beef Labeling Strategies in France, Germany, and the UK." *Agribusiness* 19(1):77–90.

Schlosser, Eric. 2001. *Fast Food Nation: The Dark Side of the All-American Dream*. New York: Houghton Mifflin.

Shiva, Vandana. 1999. *Stolen Harvest: The Hijacking of the Global Food Supply*. Cambridge, MA: South End Press.

Tansey, Geoff, and Tasmin Rajotte. 2008. *The Future Control of Food: A Guide to International Negotiations and Rules on Intellectual Property, Biodiversity and Food Security*. London: Earthscan.

Tarasuk, Valerie. 2001. "Discussion Paper on Household and Individual Food Insecurity." Ottawa: Health Canada. Accessed 9 September 2010. http://www.hc-sc.gc.ca/fn-an/alt_formats/hpfb-dgpsa/pdf/nutrition/food_sec_entire-sec_aliments_entier-eng.pdf.

USDA Economic Research Service. 2008. "Use of Nutrition Labels Declining, Especially among Young Adults." *USDA Amber Waves*. Accessed 28 February 2015. http://www.ers.usda.gov/amber-waves.aspx.

Viera, Anthony J., and Ray Antonelli. 2015. "Potential Effect of Physical Activity Calorie Equivalent Labeling on Parent Fast Food Decisions." *Pediatrics* 135(2):e376–e382.

Winson, Anthony. 1993. *The Intimate Commodity: Food and the Development of the Agro-Industrial Complex in Canada*. Toronto: University of Toronto Press.

Yates-Doerr, Emily. 2012. "The Opacity of Reduction: Nutritional Black-Boxing and the Meanings of Nourishment." *Food, Culture and Society: An International Journal of Multidisciplinary Research* 15(2):293–313.

17 Questioning the Assumptions of Genetically Modified Crops in Canada

E. Ann Clark

Learning Objectives

Through this chapter, you can

1. Understand the role of government in the evolution of GM crops in Canada
2. Become familiar with the central dogma of GM and with the evidence that disputes it
3. Become aware of the broader implications of GM in control of the global food supply
4. Compare the expectations and the outcomes of the Canadian Biotechnology Strategy

Introduction

> The knowns of biotechnology are minute; the unknowns are vast.
> — Ingeborg Boyens (1999)

This is not a story about genetic modification (GM). What follows is an analysis of the 35-year-old decision to tie the success of GM—the most contentious branch of biotechnology[1]—to Canada's national interest (Abergel and Barrett 2002). In effect, the current domination of Canadian field crop agriculture by GM was predetermined as a matter of government policy. By 2013, Canada hosted 10.8 million hectares or 6 per cent of global GM land (James 2013), with approximately 80 per cent of maize, 65 per cent of soy (Statistics Canada 2014), and almost all canola and sugar beet land in Canada occupied by GM crops. Globally, GM consists almost entirely of industrial crops grown for livestock feed or for processing into oil, fibre, sugar, and ethanol—not for direct human consumption.

Canada's zeal in promoting GM crops is matched by few other nations; the United States, Brazil, Argentina, India, and Canada now account for almost 90 per cent of all GM land (James 2013).

Starting in the early 1980s, biotechnology was one of three promising but unproven technologies charged with the task of propelling Canada out of a protracted recession (Abergel and Barrett 2002). Canada deemed biotechnology to be not just a technology—like robotic milking—but rather, the springboard to boost national economic competitiveness. Acknowledging this far-reaching intention is critical to unwrapping both the expansion of GM and government behaviour toward GM in subsequent decades.

Canada promoted the commercial success of biotechnology through a wide range of domestic as well as international initiatives, including "tax incentives for research . . . subsidies for research and development, trade policy, regulatory frameworks and standards, and intellectual property rights . . . [including structural changes to] universities, research centres, government departments, and educational and training institutions" (Abergel and Barrett 2002). The intentional mustering of public resources behind private sector biotechnology was by no means limited to Canada (Wright 1994).

Domestically, the decision that biotechnology was in the national interest was reached without public consultation (Abergel and Barrett 2002), instead, "favouring [citizen] engagement as an important aspect of legitimizing top-down decisions taken largely between the state and industry" (Howlett and Migone 2010). Domestic consumption of GM products was sustained by Parliament rejecting a succession of private member's bills calling for mandatory labelling (CBC 2013).

To ensure global markets, Canada became one of several grain-exporting countries to aggressively champion GM agriculture abroad. Canada had signed the 1992 Rio Convention on Biological Diversity, but it is notably absent from the list of 168 signatories to the 2000 Cartagena Protocol on Biosafety (CPB), which operationalized the Rio Convention (CBD 2014).

Why? A member of the Canadian delegation, Michelle Swenarchuk, reported that:

> developing countries . . . were concerned about the rapid proliferation and aggressive marketing of genetically modified food and seeds. . . . Northern exporting countries, including Canada, sought a weak protocol, and had actually caused the collapse of negotiations in Cartagena in 1999, by refusing to agree to include LMOs[2] shipped for food. (2000)

Does Canada's willingness to defend the marketability of GM crops by forcing people to buy products they do not want reflect changes in how Canada sees the world and how the world views Canada?

From this background, this chapter explores some of the assumptions that appear to have anchored 35 years of unstinting government support for GM crops in Canada. The chapter is structured in the form of questions, with each section concluded by a synthetic subsection—*Why does this matter?*—to make a cohesive narrative.

Terminology is defined, because ambiguous terminology can discourage public engagement. Expected benefits, risks, and the design of the regulatory process are then related to the early euphoria about GM. Evidence challenging the fundamental premises of GM is examined. The claimed contributions of GM and conventional plant breeding to Canadian agriculture are then compared. Gene patenting is viewed through the real-world lens of farmers and farm communities. The final section compares approved GM crops with what was claimed at the outset, challenging the premise that GM would revolutionize agriculture.

What Is GM?

The most contentious subset of biotechnology is genetic modification. The term GM, which is used synonymously with recombinant DNA technology, genetic engineering (GE), and transgenesis, will be understood to mean the forcible insertion or alteration of genetic information in a host organism in ways that would not occur naturally. GM can include insertion of new traits, such as for herbicide resistance. GM can also be used to silence natural traits, such as the enzymes that cause browning in the Arctic apple (Mellon 2014).

GM excludes **mutagenesis**, which carries additional risks, conventional plant breeding defined as crossing between related plants, and marker assisted selection (Fagan et al. 2014:20–55). GM can apply to crops, animals, and microbes, but this chapter will focus on crops.

A transferred gene is termed a **transgene**. Reading and controlling expression of a transgene typically requires genetic information from several different organisms, all of which are combined into a gene cassette for insertion. However, as transgenes are not used alone in commercial applications, the term *transgene* will be understood to be synonymous with the gene cassette carrying the transgene.

Why Does This Matter?

Canada lumps mutagenized and GM crops, as well as other food innovations, into the uniquely Canadian category of novel foods (Health Canada 2014a). Failure to clearly define terms obscures the differences in risks associated with GM, mutagenesis, tissue culture, more recent interventions such as dsRNA-based GM (Heinemann et al. 2013; Mellon 2014), and even synthetic genes (Holdrege 2014). The risks posed by different methods of inducing genetic change need to be clearly understood in order to devise appropriate risk assessment protocols.

Why GM Crops?

GM was envisioned as a revolutionary technology enabling unimaginable advances in agriculture—the focus of the present chapter—as well as medicine (Hopkins et al. 2007).

Quotes from Boyens (1999) capture the optimism that surrounded the emergent GM sector:

> The advent of recombinant DNA technology is comparable to the discovery of quantum physics. (Richard Godown, Biotechnology Industry Organization [1984])

> [Agricultural biotechnology will] rank on the Richter scale alongside major transforming technologies such as the steam engine, the transistor, and the computer. (Sano Shimoda, President BioScience Securities [1998])

This world view was prominent during the drafting of the National Biotechnology Strategy in 1983, which morphed into the **Canadian Biotechnology Strategy** in 1998 (Health Canada 2005). Lotter (2009) described the confidence that desired genes would be precisely identified, snipped out, and inserted into new hosts, avoiding the lengthy process of conventional plant breeding. Breeders would no longer be limited by the native genetic entitlement of crops.

As with any unproven technology, GM crops were pitched to government decision makers based on assumptions for expected benefits, potential risks, and hence on the design of regulatory protocols. Approval of GM crops in Canada starting 20 years ago featured first-generation claims based on increasing yield, reducing biocide dependence, and enhancing income. Agro-chemicals morphed into life sciences, claiming that GM crops benefited not just farmers but also society and the environment.

More recently, Gartland et al. (2013) envisioned a rainbow of second- and third-generation GM products, with red (medical/pharmaceutical), white (industrial feedstocks), and green (agriculture/forestry) portfolios. Human vaccines grown in plants, novel antibiotics, anti-malarial compounds, bioplastics, and vitamin-A enriched golden rice were viewed as "bringing benefits for all, through increased food production, supporting climate change adaptation and the low carbon economy, or novel diagnostics" (p. S6).

The potential for unique risks from GM crops was largely dismissed. "Regulators have generally taken the position that GM derivatives are so similar to the conventional varieties . . . that the two can be considered 'substantially equivalent'" (RSC 2001:177). Canada positioned **substantial equivalence**, an undefined concept which inexplicably relies on nutritional composition to determine equivalence, as the key portal for GM approval. "In practice, the designation of a candidate GM crop variety as 'substantially equivalent' to other, non-GM, varieties essentially pre-empts any requirement in Canada to assess further the new variety for unanticipated characteristics" (p. 180). The critical review of GM regulation in Canada conducted by RSC (2001) yielded 53 recommendations. However, as documented five years later by Andrée (2006), little substantive change has been made.

Perhaps in response to rigorous criticism, the term *substantial equivalence* has now been excised, but the pivotal assumption of substantial equivalence remains embedded in Canadian GM protocols.

Why Does This Matter?

As will be elaborated below, 20 years in commerce have failed to substantiate either the early optimism of quantum gains or the casual dismissal of unique GM risks. Globally, almost all GM land is sown to crops bearing just two traits: herbicide resistance (HR) to control weeds, and *Bt* (*Bacillus thuringiensis*) to combat insect pests, despite early and ongoing GM promises.

Government has declined to publicly acknowledge the underperformance of GM crops over the past 20 years, and indeed, continues to dismiss potential risks (Health Canada 2012). The similarly disappointing Human Genome Project may explain why Gisler et al. (2011) hypothesized that "strong social interactions between enthusiastic supporters weave a network of reinforcing feedbacks that lead to widespread endorsement and extraordinary commitment . . . beyond what would be rationalized by a standard cost-benefit analysis in the presence of extraordinary uncertainties and risks" (p. 412). Perhaps the curiously muted view of Canadian government and academia could be interpreted as groupthink, where a cohesive group makes seemingly indefensible decisions by failing to consider alternatives, suppressing dissent, and discrediting the arguments of others.

It has been argued that GM will yet deliver on its many promises, given time. However, applications awaiting approval in both Europe and the United States (data not available for Canada) profile the continuing global dominance of HR and *Bt*. The only pending exceptions are modified flower colour in carnation and altered composition traits in maize and soy in Europe (GMO Compass 2014), and in the United States, a bruising-resistant potato and a freezing-tolerant eucalyptus (USDA/APHIS, n.d.).

The 35-year redirection of public resources toward the commercial success of a proprietary technology has also detracted from Canada's capacity to develop public-good alternatives, such as organic farming or management-intensive grazing. Full-cost accounting—to taxpayers—must reflect not simply returns on public investment in GM but also the costs of failing to create resilient and robust public-good alternatives.

Hyperbole, omission, and suppression are characteristic of an emergent technology. When government is independent of industry, scrutiny in the public interest would be expected to cull unsubstantiated claims. When the interests of government and industry intertwine, however, questions arise about conflicts between the public good and private gain (Moore 2002).

Is GM Based on a Valid Premise?

Commercial GM rests upon the premise that a gene coding for a desired trait—and only the desired trait—can be extracted from one organism and inserted into the genome of another organism, to transfer and achieve stable expression of the desired trait.

However, fundamental flaws in the central dogma of GM quickly became evident. The precarious footing of GM was nowhere better demonstrated than through the anomalous findings of the Human Genome Project (HGP). The HGP revealed that instead of each gene coding for a specific protein (or trait), "genes appear to operate in a complex network, and interact and overlap with one another and with other components in ways not yet fully understood" (quoted by Lotter 2009).

Evidence challenging the central dogma of GM has arisen from several sources:

- *The transgene itself.* Schubert (2008) traced several examples, including golden rice, where the intended intervention of a transgene disregards the remarkable complexity of plant metabolism, inadvertently triggering unexpected and harmful outcomes.

- *The processes of transformation and transgenesis.* Both of the primary methods for inserting genes—*Agrobacterium* mediation, where a disabled pathogen infects plant cells with a transgene, and particle bombardment, which blasts cells with metal particles bearing the transgene—are actually mutagenic (Wilson et al. 2006). Further complicating what was supposed to be a tidy process, tissue culture—which is routinely used to convert those cells into which genes have been successfully inserted into plants—is also unambiguously mutagenic (Wilson et al. 2006).

Thus, each regenerated transformed cell (*transformant*) comes from a unique **insertion event**. Most transformants are clearly dysfunctional and die or are discarded. Those transformants retained for analysis and commercialization are termed *Events*. An Event is not synonymous with a transgene.

- *Randomness.* Contrary to early—and still oft-repeated—claims, forcible insertion of a transgene into a new host genome is not precise but random. Transgenes can insert on any chromosome, and potentially at multiple locations, in a single cell (Fagan et al. 2014). Location influences expression not just of the transgene but of other unrelated genes (Wilson et al. 2006).
- *Position effects and copy number.* Events with the same transgene can differ in trait expression, depending on where the transgene actually inserts into the host genome, as well as on the number of copies that insert. For example, the same *Bt* transgene was commercialized in maize from at least three different insertion Events—as *Bt*176, *Bt*11, and MON810. However, concentration of the resulting *Bt* endotoxin differed by two orders of magnitude among the three Events (Sears et al. 2001).

- *Unintended effects.* As explained by Wilson et al. (2006), each insertion Event has the potential to alter a wide range of wholly unpredictable traits (Roessner et al. 2001; Schubert 2008; Bortolotto et al. 2014; Fagan et al. 2014). Tagashira et al. (2005) compared metabolic profiles from five insertion Events with the same transgene for sweetness in cucumber. Transgenic cucumbers differed significantly from the parental plant in 38 of 47 metabolites, including amino acids, organic acids, sugars, alcohols, and other compounds. Significant differences ranged from 9 to 23 among the five insertion Events. Clearly, the *process* of GM has altered the potential risk portfolio in ways that are unrelated to the GM *product* and which could not have been screened against.

The agronomic impact of undetected gene expression in an approved GM Event is now apparent. In a commercialized soy line, Bortolotto et al. (2014) found that insertion of a *Bt* transgene active against one class of pests had inadvertently favoured proliferation of another class of pests. They concluded that this effect was "less likely to directly result from the toxin presence but indirectly from unintended changes . . . caused by the insertion of the transgene" (p. 728).

- **Stacking.** Shi et al. (2011) reported that interaction among stacked transgenes *(see p. 262)* can further alter both transgene expression and the expression of unrelated genes.

Why Does This Matter?

The fundamental premise of GM has been invalidated, which should—at a minimum—have obliged changes to risk assessment protocols to safeguard the public interest. Transgene insertion is random, inaccurate, and disruptive. Gene expression is not absolute but contextual. One cannot just slice and splice a transgene into a new genetic background and expect to transfer that trait and no others.

The literal impossibility of devising a laboratory protocol to identify and screen against unknown harms has been unambiguously demonstrated. Yet, use of animal trials to detect hidden gene expression, as discussed by Pusztai (2002) and refined by Séralini et al. (2011), is not mandatory and is seldom apparent in Canadian decisions (Health Canada 2014a).

GM proponents have long insisted that GM should be assessed solely on risks, if any, posed by the intended *product* and not on the *process* by which it was achieved. This view has dominated GM regulation in Canada and the United States, although not in Europe. Evidence cited above challenges the merit of product-based risk assessment regimes.

What Has GM Actually Done?

At issue is the contribution of GM versus conventional plant breeding to agriculture. Over a 20-year lifespan, has GM materially improved the performance of agriculture beyond what has been achieved by conventional breeding?

Conventional breeding over thousands of generations by farmers and professional plant breeders has selected for desirable traits among the tens of thousands of genes in each modern crop. In contrast, a GM variety is just a conventionally bred variety into which a single proprietary transgene[3] has been inserted through GM or by crossing with a variety that had previously been fitted with a transgene.

It bears repeating that of the tens of thousands of genes in a GM variety, *all but the single transgene result from conventional plant breeding*. However, the presence of that single transgene confers the GM designation to the entire variety, obscuring the overwhelming and ongoing role of conventional breeding in offering every other feature of the so-called GM variety.

Claims of GM contributions to agriculture are many and creative (Brookes and Barfoot 2013; James 2013). However, estimates of yield, biocide use, and profitability benefits to farmers in the United States and elsewhere (data not available for Canada) are inconsistent, controversial, and era dependent (Gurian-Sherman 2009; Benbrook 2012; Brookes and Barfoot 2013; Fernandez-Cornejo et al. 2014).

Creative claims aside, over the past 20 years, GM has offered essentially two commercial traits—HR and *Bt*. Therefore, valid claims of GM performance must necessarily derive just from these two GM traits. All other claims of performance of GM varieties must necessarily be attributed to conventional breeding.

Yield

Yield features prominently in GM claims, as indeed it must to validate the position that GM is essential to feeding the world. However, high yield in a GM variety fitted with HR, for example, results from conventional breeding for yield—not from GM for HR. HR addresses one and only one thing—weeds. HR can "increase" yield—or more accurately reduce yield loss—only when yield is actually limited by weeds. Any weed-control method could justifiably make this same claim. The claim that HR offers *more* is plausible if premised on a cropping system that has created intractable weeds—weeds that are uncontrollable by other methods. A two-year canola trial over five western Canadian locations found that HR outyielded conventional weed control practices in just 6 of 30 contrasts, all occurring at sites and in years of particularly problematic weeds (Harker et al. 2000).

Government acting in the public interest might have viewed the widespread occurrence of intractable weeds as suggestive of a dysfunctional cropping system. Instead, regulators accepted weed intractability as a justification for HR, first for glyphosate-based HR and then, to cope with glyphosate-resistant weed biotypes, for stacking of 2,4-D- and dicamba-based HR.

The same logic applies to claims of higher yield from the *Bt* trait. By itself, *Bt* can increase yield when the one and only thing affected by *Bt*—specific insect pests—is yield limiting. Yield can be decimated by some pests targeted by *Bt*, such as European corn borer (ECB). However, incidence of ECB, and hence risk of catastrophic yield loss, is sporadic and unpredictable at the time of sowing. The costly *Bt* trait is valuable when pest levels happen to be high, but when they are low, offers little or no benefit (Cox et al. 2009; Jemison and Regberg-Horton 2010).

Biocide Use

Biocides include both the herbicides used with HR crops and the insecticides expected to be replaced by *Bt* crops. Long experience with biocides demonstrates conclusively that resistance in target organisms makes *time since introduction* a key element in assessing benefit. Therefore, claims of reducing biocide use with GM are also era dependent.

Glyphosate, the active ingredient in Monsanto's Roundup line of herbicides, is a broad-spectrum herbicide widely used not simply for HR but for everything from preparing a seedbed to desiccating canola prior to harvest. Glyphosate accounted for 59 and 42 per cent of all herbicide active ingredient applied to GM and non-GM crop types, respectively, in Ontario in 2008 (adapted from McGee et al. 2010). Landbase was similar (OMAFRA 2014), but 10 times as much glyphosate was applied per hectare of GM as of non-GM crops.

Employing commercial HR implicitly requires herbicide use, and glyphosate-based HR has dominated global GM from the outset. Global overuse of glyphosate in both GM and non-GM applications has produced hundreds of glyphosate-resistant biotypes drawn from 32 weed species (weedscience.org, n.d.). Surveys in 2013 reported that glyphosate-resistant weed biotypes affect an estimated 25 million hectares in the United States, with biotypes from one or more of kochia, marestail, and giant ragweed resistant to glyphosate on 0.45 million hectares in Canada (Fraser 2013). Farmers' difficulty in accessing seed for varieties *not* fitted with the glyphosate HR trait encourages overreliance on glyphosate.

In the United States, mandatory practices (Monsanto 2014:32) have delayed resistance in corn borer in maize and in bollworm in cotton (Huang et al. 2011). In contrast, field-evolved resistance to these and other *Bt* transgenes has been reported elsewhere, as in cotton in India (Dhurua and Gujar 2011), Australia (Downes and Mahon 2012), and China (Li et al. 2007; Wan et al. 2012), and in maize in South Africa (Van den Berg et al. 2013), Puerto Rico (Storer et al. 2012), Brazil (Farias et al. 2014), and the United States (Gassmann 2012). Failure of GM-based corn rootworm control has reportedly manifested as a run on insecticide in the United States (Berry 2013).

No Canadian data appear to be available to assess the claim that GM reduces biocide dependence. For the United States, Benbrook (2012) reported that GM did indeed reduce biocide use through 2001, but in the United States and elsewhere, the trend was reversed by spread of HR weed biotypes, inclusion of additional herbicides to compensate for resistance, breakdown of some *Bt* traits, and stimulation of secondary pest outbreaks (Hagenbucher et al. 2013). Herbicide use on soybeans more than doubled between 1996 and 2012, from 28 to 58 million kilograms, with glyphosate increasing from 15 to 83 per cent of the total (USDA/NASS 2014).

In the aggregate, over the first 16 years of GM in the United States, cumulative biocide use *increased* by 183 million kilograms—amounting to a 7 per cent increase attributable to GM (Benbrook 2012). The aggregate figure is the net of a 239 million kilogram *increase* in herbicide use with HR and a 56 million kilogram *decrease* in insecticide use with *Bt*. This calculation does not include the *Bt* insecticide self-generated by *Bt* crops, nor the systemic biocide pre-treatments on crop seed (Benbrook 2012; Seidler 2014).

Profit

Although farmers were the intended beneficiaries of first-generation GM, little evidence exists in the refereed literature or government databases on Canadian farmer experience with GM. A 2003 survey of 370 Prairie farmers found that the greatest cited benefit among GM users was operational. HR widened the window during which a herbicide can be sprayed, thus enabling farming of a larger landbase (Mauro and McLachlan 2008). Among 10 farmer-ranked benefits, increased yield was sixth and increased revenue ranked last. Thus, the primary farmer-perceived advantages of GM were convenience and the ability to farm a larger hectarage—not yield or income. Without discounting the importance of these practical advantages, this survey does not support the claims pitched to government 20 years ago.

Why Does This Matter?

Public entitlement to the accumulated benefits of thousands of years of conventional breeding is now controlled by the proprietors of a few patented genes. Inserting a single proprietary transgene into a conventionally bred variety means that access to that variety—and all that it offers in terms of yield and other desired traits—is restricted to farmers willing to pay for the transgene,[4] whether needed or not. As discussed below, the traceability of that single transgene also contributes to the shift in control over the food system from the farm community to the purveyors of seed and chemicals.

Is GM seed worth it for farmers? As of 2014, the USDA/NASS (2014) reported that for maize, soy, and cotton, respectively, GM seed costs 49, 46, and 100 per cent more than non-GM seed in the United States (data not available for Canada). For US farmers, between 2001 and 2014, maize, soy, and cotton seed price increased 65, 40, and 142 per cent faster, respectively, for GM than for non-GM seed. Can these dramatic price differences be justified by the presence of a single transgene?

So what has GM contributed over the past 20 years? The expansion of GM crops across the Canadian landscape has been rapid and extensive. However, interpretation of this trend needs to acknowledge the control afforded to a few

corporations by massive consolidation in the seed trade (Howard 2009; 2013). Roughly 85 per cent of the hundreds of maize hybrids on offer across Canada are now GM or mutagenized (CSTA 2014). Roseboro (2013) cited evidence from around the world that farmer access to seed of non-GM varieties is diminishing or gone. While benefits to farmers, society, and the environment remain unclear, GM has facilitated control (see below) over the seed trade, and hence, over the food supply.

Estimated contributions of GM to agricultural performance remain controversial and era dependent. Yield, stress tolerance, reliability, and nutritional value continue to improve through conventional breeding, but reports of GM contributions are inconsistent. For both HR and Bt, early claims of higher yield and also of reduced biocide dependence are challenged by resistance and secondary pest proliferation. Complex communities respond to selection pressure—whether from agro-chemicals or from Bt.

How Did a Patented Gene Unmake Agriculture?

Field crop agriculture has traditionally consisted of farmers growing crops from saved seed. Genes moved uncontrollably among fields through pollen and seed movement. The encroachment of owned varieties, which largely displaced saved seed in the developed world (Kloppenburg 2005), was not affected by gene uncontainability. Varietal pollen blowing over fencelines incurred no legal liability, because what was owned was the particular set of carefully selected desirable genes that made up a given variety. Crossing among varieties diluted desired characteristics, reduced the value of the resultant seed, and encouraged farmers to buy fresh seed annually.

The arrival of patented genes fundamentally changed the structure of agriculture, relationships among neighbouring farmers, and control over the food supply. Proprietary transgenes move, just like all genes. But unlike varieties, transgenes can be tracked into farmers fields, enabling litigation, threats of litigation, and ultimately, tight control over crop genetics.

Because of the *Monsanto v. Schmeiser* decision of the Supreme Court of Canada (2004), ownership of a single transgene now confers ownership over the entire, conventionally bred genetics of a GM variety—including the inadvertently contaminated, homegrown line of a seed-saving farmer. The Schmeisers, over 70 years old, were lifelong seed-savers and had bred their own farm-adapted line of canola. Yet according to the Supreme Court decision, the unintended presence[5] of Monsanto's proprietary transgene—in canola harvested from the Schmeisers' own fields and then replanted on their own land without invoking the utility of the transgene[6]—not only infringed Monsanto's patent but also sacrificed the genetic improvements of a lifetime. Replanting their own—contaminated—seed was disallowed:

> The majority in Monsanto stressed that it is the gene and cell that are patentable, not the plant per se. However, the distinction is specious, a point recognised in the dissenting opinion. . . . The patented gene is part of every cell of the host plant, and therefore, the infusion of the gene confers, in substance, the right to control use (to exclude or include) on the patent-holder. (Ziff 2005)

For a clear and thorough background and analysis of the practical implications of the Supreme Court decision, see Ziff (2005) and Abergel (2012).

Genes have always moved, but gene ownership has made gene movement systematically deleterious to farmers and to society at large. A single contamination event, as from a neighbouring farmer, contaminates the harvested crop with one or more proprietary transgenes—compromising identity-preserved (IP) status for organic and other growers (Mittelstaedt 2009; FAWW and OF 2014; Foster 2014; Polansek 2014). Genetic contamination also delivers contaminated seed to the soil seedbank, where it can remain dormant

for up to several years. Germination in subsequent years poses permanent liability—legally if the seed is saved for planting, economically if the crop is IP as organic or for a restrictive market (Foster 2014; *Sustainable Pulse* 2014), and agronomically, if the trait is HR (Arnason 2015).

Why Does This Matter?

Intellectual property rights now trump farmer property rights. Farmers signing Monsanto's Technology/Stewardship Agreement (Monsanto 2014:32) are subject to a breathtaking array of intrusive provisions, including providing "copies of any records, receipts, or other documents that could be relevant . . . Acreage History . . . Farm and Tract Detail. . . . Listing and corresponding aerial photographs . . . [and] documentation, and dealer/retailer invoices for seed and chemical transactions." They are also obliged to "identify and to allow Monsanto and its representatives access to land . . . bins, wagons, or seed storage containers . . . for purposes of . . . taking samples of crops, crop residue or seeds." Such contractual provisions obscure the image of farmers as independent decision makers.

The uncontainability of transgenes ensures risk of contamination every year. Seed dormancy, which is non-negligible in crops such as canola and alfalfa, prolongs risk over years. GM arguably weakens farming communities by encouraging reporting on neighbours for perceived violations (Monsanto 2014:5). The catastrophic implications of unavoidable contamination have produced lawsuits among neighbours (*Sustainable Pulse* 2014), inadvertently compromised IP contracts, and cancelled expected premiums on crop prices. The very fabric of rural communities unravels as neighbour relations deteriorate.

In the absence of liability protection against unavoidable contamination, farmers are defenceless against encroachment and domination by the GM sector. Government disinclination to legislate protection for farmer interests would be unfathomable, without foreknowledge of the Canadian Biotechnology Strategy.

What Is the Commercial Success of Canadian Contributions to GM Events Approved in Canada?

A total of 94 GM crop submissions have been made and approved in Canada (Health Canada 2014a) since 1994. Of these, 32 were for HR, and 20 were for *Bt*. Stacked traits, which now account for 27 per cent of the 175 million hectares of global GM land (James 2013), accounted for another 18 submissions. Of the remaining submissions, 12 were for quality traits, such as oil quality, amino acid composition, and ethanol utility; 9 were for other traits, such as a wine yeast; and 3 were for virus resistance.

Approved Events may be commercialized or withdrawn based on agronomic, marketing, or other issues. For example, Events for potato, tomato, and flax (box 17.1) were withdrawn. Commercial success of virus-resistant papaya and ML01 yeast has been limited by consumer rejection. "The extent of actual use of ML01-yeast by US-American vintners is unknown. Many . . . have joined a declaration saying that they are not using GM organisms in their wine" (GMO Compass 2009).

Reflecting global trends, 75 per cent of the 94 GM crop submissions approved by Health Canada between 1994 and 2014 were for HR, *Bt*, or stacked traits. Of the remaining submissions, Enogen maize for ethanol, AC Glengarry soy for oil quality, ML01 wine yeast, and virus-resistant squash and papaya appear to have been successfully commercialized.

Canadian Contributions?

How well has the Canadian Biotechnology Strategy contributed to genetic improvement of crops in Canada? Twenty years of support for Canadian research and development has generated a total of four GM crop submissions approved in Canada (Health Canada 2014a):

- CDC Triffid, a sulfonylurea-resistant flax (box 17.1), in 1998 by Dr. Alan McHughen
- AC Glengarry, a low-linolenic soy, in 2000, by Agriculture and Agri-Food Canada
- Canola-quality *Brassica juncea* lines PC97-03, PC98-44, and PC98-045, in 2001, by the Canola Council of Canada (PC97-03 was withdrawn in April 2001)
- ML01, a wine yeast, in 2006, by Dr. Hennie Van Vuuren at UBC

Box 17.1 Whatever Happened to That GM Flax?

CDC Triffid is a GM HR flax engineered for resistance to sulfonylurea herbicide by Alan McHughen at Saskatchewan's Crop Development Centre (CDC). Triffid was never commercialized. In fact, it was immediately deregistered and withdrawn from the market in 2001 at the insistence of Prairie farmers, owing to fears of market rejection.

CDC Triffid reappeared in 2009 as a contaminant of Canadian flax exported to, and rejected by, 34 countries including many in Western Europe as well as Japan and Brazil. The source of the contamination remains unknown, but "Dr. McHughen did prompt controversy by giving away packets of the seeds free of charge for what he calls 'educational purposes.' A condition of accepting his Triffids was to agree not to grow them, but he concedes some farmers might have thrown the seeds into their hoppers and planted them anyway. 'I can't rule out that possibility,' he said" (Mittelstaedt 2009).

As of 2014, farmers were still trying to flush the risk of Triffid from their storage bins and seeders, to regain formerly lucrative export markets (Cross 2013) (figure 17.1).

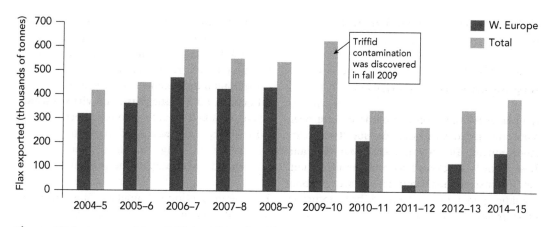

Figure 17.1 Impact of CDC Triffid on Canadian Flax Exports, 2004–5 to 2013–14

Source: Adapted from Canadian Grains Commission (2014)

Of these four, successful commercialization contributing to the Canadian economy appears to have been achieved by just two Canadian-origin submissions: AC Glengarry and ML01 wine yeast, dating from about 10 to 15 years ago. Almost all GM Events approved in Canada resulted from research conducted elsewhere, with ownership vested almost entirely in offshore corporations.

Why Does This Matter?

What came to be known as the Canadian Biotechnology Strategy (CBS) vested Canadian hopes for economic revitalization in three technologies—of which biotechnology, including GM, was one (Health Canada 2005). After 35 years, realized social benefits to Canadians from GM crops approved in Canada remain elusive.

For the four Canadian-origin GM products that evolved from the overtly nurturing framework of the CBS, outcomes have been muted and decidedly mixed. Given the "**lemon effect**" (Furtan et al. 2003) of GM contamination in decimating the flax export market (figure 17.1), and export markets in general (MacArthur 2014; Polansek 2014), the GM social balance sheet needs to reflect negative as well as positive impacts.

Conclusion

Has GM contributed materially to Canadian agriculture? It might have been assumed that the decision to intentionally link Canada's economic welfare with the commercial success of GM would have encouraged monitoring of the intended outcomes. However, credible evidence of expected farmer benefits in terms of yield, biocide use reduction, and farmer income is unclear. With just two traits on offer in Canada and elsewhere, it is, at a minimum, arguable whether either HR or Bt has offered benefits that could not have been achieved through conventional breeding or improved cropping system design.

After a scant 20 years in commerce, the early promise of even these two traits is failing. Trait stacking to cope with mounting resistance is a short-term expedient to prolong commercial viability while repositioning farmers on the pesticide treadmill.

While GM crop improvement has essentially stalled on HR and Bt, conventional plant breeding continues to offer new advances in everything from drought tolerance to bio-fortified crops. Yet, as reported for the United States, public investment in conventional plant breeding and varietal development has declined precipitously with the ascendency of GM (Kloppenburg 2005; NOC 2011).

The CBS-driven reconfiguration of Canadian agricultural research infrastructure in both government and academic labs has doubtless improved understanding of both the basic science and methods needed to advance the proprietary GM sector. However, it is unclear whether the benefits—if any—of GM crops are commensurate with the costs borne by society and the environment. The downstream costs **externalized** by the CBS go well beyond the direct outlay of taxpayer funds over 35 years of research subsidies and tax incentives. A brief sampling could include:

- rural communities frayed by distrust among neighbours (Schiffman 2013)
- control over the food supply further relinquished to a few corporate entities (ETCGroup 2008; Howard 2013)
- increased exposure to biocides in air, water, and food, and their potential health effects (Johal and Huber 2009; Paganelli et al. 2010; Domingo 2011; Shehata et al. 2013; Battaglin et al. 2014; Bøhn et al. 2014; Krüger et al. 2014; Swanson et al. 2014); that have aroused a disturbing level of disinterest from government

- lost opportunities for urgently needed research in the public interest, such as devising farming systems that are ecologically sustainable, resilient in the face of changing climate, and capable of recycling nutrients effectively between farms and cities (MacRae et al. 2009)
- missing generations of graduate students, whose training in public-good research should have evolved the scientists Canada will need to craft solutions that go beyond GM
- the perception of Canada as a global bully, forcing trade in products that are not needed or wanted

Despite 35 years of unwavering government support, GM has proven more difficult to operationalize and commercialize than originally anticipated. The analogy of what to do when you find you are riding a dead horse ("Dead Horse Strategies," n.d.) is apt. It is time to get beyond buying a bigger whip, killing all the other horses so this one will look the same, calling the horse a joint venture and letting others ride it, and declaring that the horse is better, faster, and cheaper, because it is dead. It is time to get a new horse.

Discussion Questions

1. Would GM dominate Canadian agriculture without a history of overt government support? Individual gene patenting? Consolidation in the seed trade?

2. What evidence suggests fundamental flaws in the central dogma of GM?

3. If GM had never been invented, would Canadian farmers and farm communities, consumers, and the environment be better off, worse off, or the same as today?

4. Has the Canadian Biotechnology Strategy been a good investment for Canadian taxpayers?

Further Reading

1. Fagan, John, Michael Antoniou, and Claire Robinson. 2014. *GMO Myths and Truths. An Evidence-Based Examination of the Claims Made for the Safety and Efficacy of Genetically Modified Crops and Foods*, 2nd edn, version 1.0.
http://earthopensource.org/wordpress/downloads/GMO-Myths-and-Truths-edition2.pdf.
A thorough overview of a wide variety of issues bearing on GM agriculture and medicine.

2. Fernandez-Cornejo, Jorge, Seth Wechsler, Mike Livingston, and Lorraine Mitchell. 2014. "Genetically Engineered Crops in the United States." ERR-162 USDA/ERS. http://www.ers.usda.gov/media/1282246/err162.pdf.
   Statistical analysis of trends in GM adoption in the United States, from an economic perspective.

3. James, Clive. 2013. "Global Status of Commercialized Biotech/GM Crops: 2013." ISAAA Brief No. 46. Ithaca, NY: ISAAA. http://www.isaaa.org/resources/publications/briefs/46/executivesummary/.
   Perspective of a pro-GM lobby group.

4. Royal Society of Canada. 2001. *Elements of Precaution: Recommendations for the Regulation of Food Biotechnology in Canada.* Ottawa. https://rsc-src.ca/sites/default/files/pdf/GMreportEN.pdf.
   The single most authoritative critique of Canadian GM regulation, by the scientific elite of Canada, at the request of the Canadian government.

Video Suggestions

1. Robin, Marie-Monique. 2008. *The World According to Monsanto.* https://www.nfb.ca/film/world_according_to_monsanto. 109 min.
   Drawn from a three-year investigation, the filmmaker takes an holistic view of issues raised by the global prominence of Monsanto. Interviews with many key players, including farmers, policy makers, and researchers, bring a human dimension to this complex story. A compelling, gripping, and credible analysis.

2. Verhaag, Bertram. 2011. *Scientists Under Attack: Genetic Engineering in the Magnetic Field of Money.* https://vimeo.com/136415800. 59 min.
   Viewers will be chilled by the real-life experiences of scientists who dared to ask meaningful questions about possible risks of GM crops. Industry-driven strategies to suppress, discredit, and destroy academic and government opposition are exposed.

Notes

1. Most definitions of biotechnology acknowledge the novelty of contemporary genetic manipulation. However, according to Health Canada (2008), "Biotechnology has been used by humans for thousands of years . . . to make cheese, ferment wine and beer and make bread by using micro-organisms. . . . Over time, we have also domesticated and selectively bred some animals and plants to meet human needs."

2. LMO stands for "living modified organism," a synonym for GMO.

3. One or a few; multiple HR and *Bt* transgenes may be incorporated in a single variety.

4. For Monsanto products, farmers must also sign a Technology Use Agreement (TUA)—now referred to as a Technology/Stewardship Agreement; see specifically the Terms & Conditions (Monsanto 2014:32).

5. Allegations of theft of patented seed were withdrawn prior to the start of the first *Schmeiser* trial. The Supreme Court finding of patent infringement explicitly acknowledged that how the genes got into the field was irrelevant to their decision (see Ziff 2005).

6. The errant gene was for resistance to Monsanto's Roundup herbicide. The Schmeisers showed herbicide receipts demonstrating that they had used other herbicides, not Roundup, on the contaminated crop.

References

Abergel, Elisabeth. 2012. "The Paradox of Governing through the Courts: The Canadian GMO Contamination Debate." Pp. 260–75 in *Critical Perspectives in Food Studies*, ed. M. Koç, J. Sumner, and A. Winson. Don Mills, ON: Oxford University Press.

——— and Katherine Barrett. 2002. "Putting the Cart Before

the Horse: A Review of Biotechnology Policy in Canada." *Journal of Canadian Studies* 37(3):135–61.

Andrée, Peter. 2006. "An Analysis of Efforts to Improve Genetically Modified Food Regulation in Canada." *Science and Public Policy* 33(5):377–89.

Arnason, Robert. 2015. "RR Soybean Growers Opt for Non-GM Canola." Accessed 6 January 2015. http://www.producer.com/2015/01/rr-soybean-growers-opt-for-non-gm-canola/.

Battaglin, W.A., M.T. Meyer, K.M. Kuivila, and J.E. Dietze. 2014. "Glyphosate and Its Degradation Product AMPA Occur Frequently and Widely in U.S. Soils, Surface Water, Groundwater, and Precipitation." *Journal of the American Water Resources Association* 50(2):275–90.

Benbrook, Charles. 2012. "Impacts of Genetically Engineered Crops on Pesticide Use in The U.S.—The First Sixteen Years." *Environmental Sciences Europe* 24:24.

Berry, Ian. 2013. "Pesticides Make a Comeback: Many Corn Farmers Go Back to Using Chemicals as Mother Nature Outwits Genetically Modified Seeds." *Wall Street Journal*, 21 May. Accessed 24 December 2014. http://www.wsj.com/news/articles/SB10001424127887323463704578496923254944066.

Bøhn, T., M. Cuhra, T. Traavik, et al. 2014. "Compositional Differences in Soybeans on the Market: Glyphosate Accumulates in Roundup Ready GM Soybeans." *Food Chemistry* 153:207–15.

Bortolotto, O.C., G.V. Silva, A. de Freitas Bueno, et al. 2014. "Development and Reproduction of *Spodoptera eridania* (Lepidoptera:Noctuidae) and Its Egg Parasitoid *Telenomus remus* (Hymenoptera:Platygastridae) on the Genetically Modified Soybean (Bt) MON 87701 × MON 89788." *Bulletin of Entomological Research* 104(6):724–30.

Boyens, Ingeborg. 1999. *Unnatural Harvest: How Genetic Engineering Is Altering Our Food.* Toronto: Doubleday Canada.

Brookes, G., and P. Barfoot. 2013. "Key Environmental Impacts of Global Genetically Modified (GM) Crop Use 1996–2011." *GM Crops and Food: Biotechnology in Agriculture and the Food Chain* 4:109–19.

CBC. 2013. "Government Rejects Bill for Mandatory Labelling of GM Food." 22 May. Accessed 1 January 2015. http://www.cbc.ca/archives/categories/economy-business/agriculture/genetically-modified-food-a-growing-debate/government-rejects-bill-for-mandatory-labelling-of-gm-food.html.

Canadian Grains Commission. 2014. *Canadian Grain Exports* (annual). 17 October. Accessed 15 December 2014. http://www.grainsCanada.gc.ca/statistics-statistiques/cge-ecg/cgem-mecg-eng.htm.

CSTA (Canadian Seed Trade Association). 2014. Corn Hybrid Database. Accessed 6 December 2014. https://secure.best-lane.com/csta/hybrid/hybrid.php.

CBD (Convention on Biological Diversity). 2014. "Parties to the Protocol and Signature and Ratification of the Supplementary Protocol." Accessed 1 January 2015. https://bch.cbd.int/protocol/parties/.

Cox, William J., John Hanchar, and Elson Shields. 2009. "Stacked Corn Hybrids Show Inconsistent Yield and Economic Responses in New York." *Agronomy Journal* 101:1530–7.

Cross, Brian. 2013. "Flax Growers Try to Flush Triffid from System." *Western Producer*, 11 January. Accessed 8 December 2014. http://www.producer.com/2013/01/flax-growers-try-to-flush-triffid-from-system%E2%80%A9/.

"Dead Horse Strategies." n.d. Accessed 7 January 2015. http://www.dbrmfg.co.nz/Next%20Step%20Dead%20Horse%20Strategies.htm.

Dhurua, Sanyasi, and Govind T. Gujar. 2011. "Field-Evolved Resistance to Bt Toxin Cry1Ac in the Pink Bollworm, *Pectinophora gossypiella* (Saunders) (Lepidoptera: Gelechiidae), from India." *Pest Management Science* 67:898–903.

Domingo, José L. 2011. "Human Health Effects of Genetically Modified (GM) Plants: Risk and Perception." *Human and Ecological Risk Assessment* 17:535–7.

Downes, Sharon, and Rod Mahon. 2012. "Evolution, Ecology and Management of Resistance in *Helicoverpa* spp. to Bt Cotton in Australia." *Journal of Invertebrate Pathology* 110:281–6.

ETCGroup. 2008. "Who Owns Nature? Corporate Power and the Final Frontier in the Commodification of Life." Accessed 15 November 2014. http://www.etcgroup.org/content/who-owns-nature.

Fagan, John, Michael Antoniou, and Claire Robinson. 2014. *GMO Myths and Truths. An Evidence-Based Examination of the Claims Made for the Safety and Efficacy of Genetically Modified Crops and Foods.* 2nd edition, version 1.0. Accessed 15 November 2014. http://earthopensource.org/wordpress/downloads/GMO-Myths-and-Truths-edition2.pdf.

Farias, Juliano R., Renato J. Horikoshi, Antonio C. Santos, and Celso Omoto. 2014. "Geographical and Temporal Variability in Susceptibility to Cry1F Toxin from *Bacillus thuringiensis* in *Spodoptera frugiperda* (Lepidoptera: Noctuidae) Populations in Brazil." *Journal of Economic Entomology* 107(6):2182–9.

FAWW and OF (Food and Water Watch and OFarm). 2014. "Organic Farmers Pay the Price for GMO Contamination." March 2014. Accessed 21 November 2014. http://www.foodandwaterwatch.org/pressreleases/survey-organic-farmers-pay-the-price-for-gmo-contamination/.

Fernandez-Cornejo, Jorge, Seth Wechsler, Mike Livingston, and Lorraine Mitchell. 2014. "Genetically Engineered Crops in the United States." ERR-162 USDA/ERS. Accessed 4 December 2014. http://www.ers.usda.gov/media/1282246/err162.pdf.

Foster, Brendan. 2014. "GM Crops: Organic Farmer Loses Court Case over Alleged Contamination." *The Guardian*, 28 May. Accessed 7 January 2015. http://www.theguardian.com/environment/2014/may/28/gm-canola-organic-farmer-loses-court-case-over-alleged-contamination.

Fraser, Kent. 2013. "One Million Acres of Glyphosate Resistant

Weeds in Canada: Stratus Survey." Accessed 6 November 2014. http://stratusresearch.com/blog/one-million-acres-of-glyphosate-resistant-weeds-in-Canada-stratus-survey/.

Furtan, W.H., R.S. Gray, and J.J. Holzman. 2003. "The Optimal Time to License a Biotech 'Lemon.'" *Contemporary Economic Policy* 21(4):433–44.

Gartland, K.M.A., F. Bruschi, M. Dundar, et al. 2013. "Progress towards the 'Golden Age' of Biotechnology." *Current Opinion in Biotechnology* 24S:S6–S13.

Gassmann, Aaron J. 2012. "Field-Evolved Resistance to Bt Maize by Western Corn Rootworm: Predictions from the Laboratory and Effects in the Field." *Journal of Invertebrate Pathology* 110:287–93.

Gisler, Monika, Didier Sornette, and Ryan Woodard. 2011. "Innovation as a Social Bubble: The Example of the Human Genome Project." *Research Policy* 40:1412–25.

GMO Compass. 2009. "Wine." 15 January. Accessed 15 December 2014. http://www.gmo-compass.org/eng/database/food/280.wine.html.

———. 2014. "GMO Database. Genetically Modified Food and Feed: Authorization in the EU." Accessed 10 December 2014. http://www.gmo-compass.org/eng/gmo/db/.

Gurian-Sherman, Doug. 2009. "Failure to Yield: Evaluating the Performance of Genetically Engineered Crops." Union of Concerned Scientists. Accessed 3 January 2015. http://www.ucsusa.org/sites/default/files/legacy/assets/documents/food_and_agriculture/failure-to-yield.pdf.

Hagenbucher, Steffen, Felix L. Wäckers, Felix E. Wettstein, et al. 2013. "Pest Trade-Offs in Technology: Reduced Damage by Caterpillars in Bt Cotton Benefits Aphids." *Proceedings of the Royal Society B: Biological Sciences* 280. doi: 10.1098/rspb.2013.0042

Harker, K.N., R.E. Blackshaw, K.J. Kirkland, et al. 2000. "Herbicide-Tolerant Canola: Weed Control and Yield Comparisons In Western Canada." *Canadian Journal of Plant Science* 80:647–54.

Health Canada. 2005. "Canada's Biotechnology Strategy." 6 December. Accessed 12 December 2014. http://www.hc-sc.gc.ca/sr-sr/tech/biotech/role/strateg-eng.php.

———. 2008. "About Biotechnology." 5 May. http://www.hc-sc.gc.ca/sr-sr/tech/biotech/about-apropos/index-eng.php.

———. 2012. "Health Canada and Canadian Food Inspection Agency Statement on the Séralini et al. (2012) Publication on a 2-Year Rodent Feeding Study with Glyphosate Formulations and GM Maize NK603." 23 October. Accessed 25 February 2015. http://www.hc-sc.gc.ca/fn-an/gmf-agm/seralini-eng.php.

———. 2014a. "Approved Products." 15 October. Accessed 15 November 2014. http://www.hc-sc.gc.ca/fn-an/gmf-agm/appro/index-eng.php.

———. 2014b. "Regulatory Transparency and Openness." 16 December. Accessed 15 December 2014. http://www.hc-sc.gc.ca/home-accueil/rto-tor/index-eng.php#s4.

Heinemann, Jack A., Sarah Zanon Agapito-Tenfen, and Judy A. Carman. 2013. "A Comparative Evaluation of the Regulation of GM Crops or Products Containing dsRNA and Suggested Improvements to Risk Assessments." *Environment International* 55:43–55.

Holdrege, Craig. 2014. "When Engineers Take Hold of Life: Synthetic Biology." *In Context* 32. Accessed 7 December 2014. http://natureinstitute.org/pub/ic/ic32/synbio.pdf.

Hopkins, Michael M., Paul A. Martin, Paul Nightingale, et al. 2007. "The Myth of the Biotech Revolution: An Assessment of Technological, Clinical and Organisational Change." *Research Policy* 36:566–89.

Howard, Phillip H. 2009. "Visualizing Consolidation in the Global Seed Industry: 1996–2008." *Sustainability* 1:1266–87.

———. 2013. "Seed Industry Structure 1996–2013." Accessed 17 December 2014. https://www.msu.edu/~howardp/seedindustry.html.

Howlett, Michael, and Andrea Riccardo Migone. 2010. "The Canadian Biotechnology Regulatory Regime: the Role of Participation." *Technology in Society* 32:280–7.

Huang, Fangneng, David A. Andow, and Lawrent L. Buschman. 2011. "Success of the High-Dose/Refuge Resistance Management Strategy after 15 Years of Bt Crop Use in North America." *Entomologia Experimentalis et Applicata* 140:1–16.

James, Clive. 2013. "Global Status of Commercialized Biotech/GM Crops: 2013." ISAAA Brief No. 46. ISAAA: Ithaca, NY. Accessed 15 December 2014. http://www.isaaa.org/resources/publications/briefs/46/executivesummary/.

Jemison, John, and Chris Regberg-Horton. 2010. "Assessing Bt Silage Corn in Maine." *Crop Management* 9(1). doi:10.1094/CM-2010-1022-01-RS

Johal, G.S., and D.M. Huber. 2009. "Glyphosate Effects on Diseases of Plants." *European Journal of Agronomy* 31:144–52.

Kloppenburg, Jack Ralph. 2005. *First the Seed: The Political Economy of Plant Biotechnology*, 2nd edn. Madison: University of Wisconsin Press.

Krüger, Monik, Philipp Schledorn, Wieland Schrödl, et al. 2014. "Detection of Glyphosate Residues in Animals and Humans." *Journal of Environmental and Analytical Toxicology* 4:210. doi: 10.4172/2161-0525.1000210

Li, Guo-Ping, Kong-Ming Wu, Fred Gould, et al. 2007. "Increasing Tolerance to Cry1Ac Cotton from Cotton Bollworm, *Helicoverpa armigera*, Was Confirmed in Bt Cotton Farming Area of China." *Ecological Entomology* 32:366–75.

Lotter, Don. 2009. "The Genetic Engineering of Food and the Failure of Science—Part 1: The Development of a Flawed Enterprise." *International Journal of Sociology of Agriculture and Food* 16(1):31–49.

MacArthur, Mary. 2014. "Roundup Ready in Alfalfa Exports 'Catastrophic.'" *Western Producer*, 28 November. Accessed 6 December 2014. http://www.producer.com/2014/11/roundup-ready-in-alfalfa-exports-catastrophic/.

MacRae, R., R.C. Martin, M. Juhasz, and J. Langer. 2009. "Ten Percent Organic within 15 Years: Policy and Program Initiatives to Advance Organic Food and Farming in Ontario, Canada." *Renewable Agriculture and Food Systems* 24(2):120–36.

Mauro, Ian J., and Stéphane M. McLachlan. 2008. "Farmer Knowledge and Risk Analysis: Post-Release Evaluation of Herbicide-Tolerant Canola in Western Canada." *Risk Analysis* 28(2):463–76.

McGee, Bill, Hugh Berges, and Denise Beaton. 2010. "Survey of Pesticide Use in Ontario, 2008 Estimates of Pesticides Used on Field Crops, Fruit and Vegetable Crops, and Other Agricultural Crops." Accessed 1 December 2014. http://www.omafra.gov.on.ca/english/crops/facts/pesticide-use.htm.

Mellon, Margaret. 2014. "Gene-Silencing and the 'Arctic' Apple." *LiveScience*, 22 November. Accessed 12 December 2014. http://www.livescience.com/48870-genetically-engineered-arctic-apple.html?cmpid=514645.

Mittelstaedt, Martin. 2009. "Attack of the Triffids Has Flax Farmers Baffled." *Globe and Mail*, 27 October, 6. Accessed 4 December 2014. http://www.theglobeandmail.com/news/national/attack-of-the-triffids-has-flax-farmers-baffledarticle4216261/.

Monsanto. 2014. "Monsanto Technology /Stewardship Agreement." Accessed 10 December 2014. http://www.monsanto.com/sitecollectiondocuments/technology-use-guide.pdf.

Moore, Elizabeth. 2002. "The New Direction of Federal Agricultural Research in Canada: From Public Good to Private Gain?" *Journal of Canadian Studies* 37(3):112–34.

NOC (National Organic Coalition). 2011. "Seeds & Breeds: Public Plant and Animal Breeding." Accessed 8 January 2015. http://www.nationalorganiccoalition.org/seedsandbreeds.

OMAFRA. 2014. "Historical Provincial Estimates by Crop, 1981–2014 (Metric Units)." 5 December. Accessed 22 December 2014. http://www.omafra.gov.on.ca/english/stats/crops/estimate_hist_metric.htm.

Paganelli, Alejandra, Victoria Gnazzo, Helena Acosta, et al. 2010. "Glyphosate-Based Herbicides Produce Teratogenic Effects on Vertebrates by Impairing Retinoic Acid Signaling." *Chemical Research in Toxicology* 23(10):1586–95.

Polansek, Tom. 2014. "China Rejections of GMO U.S. Corn Cost Up to $2.9 bln—Group." *Reuters*, 16 April. Accessed 6 December 2014. http://www.reuters.com/article/2014/04/16/syngenta-corn-costs-idUSL2N0N82DF20140416.

Pusztai, Arpad. 2002. "Can Science Give Us the Tools for Recognizing Possible Health Risks of GM Food?" *Nutrition and Health* 16(2):73–84.

Roessner, Ute, Alexander Luedemann, Doreen Brust, et al. 2001. "Metabolic Profiling Allows Comprehensive Phenotyping of Genetically or Environmentally Modified Plant Systems." *The Plant Cell* (13):11–29.

Roseboro, K. 2013. "GE Seed Monopoly: Fewer Choices, Higher Prices." *Sound Consumer*, September. Accessed 23 December 2014. http://www.pccnaturalmarkets.com/sc/1309/ge_seed_monopoly.html.

RSC (Royal Society of Canada). 2001. "Elements of Precaution: Recommendations for the Regulation of Food Biotechnology in Canada." Ottawa. Accessed 1 November 2014. https://rsc-src.ca/sites/default/files/pdf/GMreportEN.pdf.

Schiffman, Richard. 2013. "Life in the Rural Police State of Monsanto." *TruthOut*, 19 June. Accessed 9 January 2015. http://www.truth-out.org/news/item/16985-life-in-the-rural-police-state-of-monsanto.

Schubert, David. 2008. "The Problem with Nutritionally Enhanced Plants." *Journal of Medicinal Food* 11(4):601–5.

Sears, Mark K., Richard L. Hellmich, Diane E. Stanley-Horn, et al. 2001. "Impact of Bt Corn Pollen on Monarch Butterfly Populations: A Risk Assessment." *Proceedings of the National Academy of Sciences of the United States of America* 98(21):11937–42.

Seidler, Ramon J. 2014. "Pesticide Use on Genetically Engineered Crops." White paper. Accessed 12 November 2014. http://static.ewg.org/agmag/pdfs/pesticide_use_on_genetically_engineered_crops.pdf.

Séralini, Gilles-Eric, Robin Mesnage, Emilie Clair, et al. 2011. "Genetically Modified Crops Safety Assessments: Present Limits and Possible Improvements." *Environmental Sciences Europe* 23:10.

Shehata, Awad A., Wieland Schrödl, Alaa. A. Aldin, et al. 2013. "The Effect of Glyphosate on Potential Pathogens and Beneficial Members of Poultry Microbiota In Vitro." *Current Microbiology* 66:350–8.

Shi, Guanming, Jean-Paul Chavas, and Joseph Lauer. 2011. "Commercialized Transgenic Traits, Maize Productivity and Yield Risk." *Nature Biotechnology* 31(2):111–14.

Statistics Canada. 2014. *Table 001-0072 Estimated Areas, Yield, Production of Corn for Grain and Soybeans, Using Genetically Modified Seed, Quebec and Ontario, In Metric and Imperial Units.* CANSIM (database). Last updated 4 December. Accessed 15 December 2014. http://www5.statcan.gc.ca/cansim/pick-choisir?lang=eng&p2=33&id=0010072.

Storer, Nicholas P., Mary E. Kubiszak, J. Ed King, et al. 2012. "Status of Resistance to Bt Maize in *Spodoptera frugiperda*: Lessons from Puerto Rico." *Journal of Invertebrate Pathology* 110:294–300.

Supreme Court of Canada. 2004. *Monsanto Canada Inc. v. Schmeiser*, [2004] 1 S.C.R. 902, 2004 SCC 34. Accessed 15 November 2014. http://scc-csc.lexum.com/scc-csc/scc-csc/en/item/2147/index.do.

Sustainable Pulse. 2014. "Steve Marsh GM Contamination Case Fails in Western Australian Supreme Court." 23 December. Accessed 25 December 2014. http://sustainablepulse.com/2014/05/28/steve-marsh-gm-contamination-case-fails-australian-supreme-court/#.VJnGsScc.

Swanson, Nancy L., Andre Leu, Jon Abrahamson, and Bradley Wallet. 2014. "Genetically Engineered Crops, Glyphosate and the Deterioration of Health in the United States of America." *Journal of Organic Systems* 9(2):6–37.

Swenarchuk, Michelle. 2000. "The Cartagena Protocol on Biosafety." *Canadian Environmental Law Association Intervenor* 25(1). http://www.cela.ca/article/international -trade-agreements-commentary/cartagena-protocol -biosafety.

Tagashira, N., W. Plader, M. Filipecki, et al. 2005. "The Metabolic Profiles of Transgenic Cucumber Lines Vary with Different Chromosomal Locations of the Transgene." *Cellular and Molecular Biology Letters* 10:697–710.

USDA/APHIS. n.d. "Biotechnology: Petitions for Determination of Nonregulated Status." Accessed 7 December 2014. http://www.aphis.usda.gov/biotechnology/petitions_ table_pending.shtml.

USDA/NASS. 2014. "QuickStats." Accessed 15 December 2014. http://quickstats.nass.usda.gov/data/printable/5403492A- 7F8E-3D7E-A3B1-DDADDE04E5E9

Van den Berg, Johnnie, Angelika Hilbeck, and Thomas Bøhn. 2013. "Pest Resistance to Cry1Ab Bt Maize: Field Resistance, Contributing Factors And Lessons From South Africa." *Crop Protection* 54:154–60.

Wan, Peng, Yunxin Huang, Huaiheng Wu, et al. 2012. "Increased Frequency of Pink Bollworm Resistance to Bt Toxin Cry1Ac in China." *PLoS ONE* 7(1): e29975.

weedscience.org. n.d. "Weeds Resistant to EPSP Synthase Inhibitors (G/9)." http://weedscience.org/summary/moa.aspx.

Wilson, Allison K., Jonathan R. Latham, and Ricarda A. Steinbrecher. 2006. "Transformation-Induced Mutations in Transgenic Plants: Analysis and Biosafety Implications." *Biotechnology and Genetic Engineering Reviews* 23(1):209–38.

Wright, Susan. 1994. *Molecular Politics: Developing American and British Regulatory Policy for Genetic Engineering, 1972–1982*. Chicago: University of Chicago Press.

Ziff, Bruce. 2005. "Travels with My Plant: *Monsanto v. Schmeiser* Revisited." *University of Ottawa Law and Technology* 2(2):493–509.

18 Global Food Security Governance

Key Actors, Issues, and Dynamics

Matias E. Margulis and Jessica Duncan

Learning Objectives

Through this chapter, you can

1. Understand the concept of global food security governance

2. Understand the role and functions of key institutions in global food security governance

3. Contextualize the major changes in global food security governance since the 2007–8 global food price crisis

4. Understand the key debates, issues, actors, and dynamics in global food security governance

5. Identify major future challenges for global food security governance

Introduction

This chapter introduces readers to the concept and contemporary features of **global food security governance (GFSG)**. While some form of what we would recognize as global food security governance has existed since the postwar era (after 1945), in recent decades there has been a dramatic change in the institutions and practices seeking to govern production, distribution, and access to food that travels across borders. These changes in global food security governance matter because they directly shape the macro-structures within which food systems function. Therefore, understanding the changes in global food security governance is crucial for understanding the prospects and challenges for transitioning to just and sustainable food systems.

In order to put such changes into context, and to understand their significance for the food system, we begin by defining the concepts of food security and global governance. The **Food and Agriculture Organization (FAO)** of the United Nations defines **food security** as "a situation that exists when all people, at all times, have physical, social, and economic access to sufficient, safe and nutritious food that meets their dietary needs and food preferences for an active and healthy life" (FAO 2001). The FAO's definition acknowledges the complex factors and dynamics that contribute to food insecurity at the individual or global level. This includes barriers such as physical ones (e.g. distance to food sources and/or markets faced by rural and isolated communities or the existence of food deserts in lower-income urban neighbourhoods), social barriers (e.g. cultural practices that require women and children to eat after adult males) or economic barriers (e.g. when sufficient safe and nutritious food is unaffordable).

The term *global governance* is widely used to refer to the modern practice of governing transborder problems and includes the institutions, actors, rules, norms, and power relations that shape the global order. The concept of global governance is concerned with global-scale problems such as HIV/AIDS, air pollution, climate change, and migration that are beyond the capacity of any single nation-state to manage on its own (Rosenau 1995). Such processes and resulting forces have changed the political, economic, and social landscape (core principles of the international order), leading to a redistribution of "power within the international systems away from the nation-state to new international non-state actors" (Muldoon 2004:4). However, the concept is not meant to suggest global rule but rather governance taking place across local, sub-national, national, regional, and international levels (Brühl and Rittberger 2001:2). Taken together, we can define global food security governance (GFSG) as the institutions, actors, rules, norms, and power relations that shape the practice of governing how food is produced, distributed, and accessed across borders. Although this is an expansive definition, conceptual fluidity is necessary given the complexity of the food system and the myriad of political, social, economic, and ecological dynamics that shape individuals', communities', and nations' food security.

Even in the twenty-first century, food insecurity remains a major and persistent global problem with nearly 800 million people estimated by the FAO as undernourished, and another 2 billion people (and rising) suffering from overweight and obesity. Yet it is important to understand that hunger is not a natural phenomenon but a result of historically specific forms of interplay among political, economic, and social institutions.

We observe that contemporary global food security governance shows some general characteristics. First, GFSG is normatively oriented toward progressively achieving food security at the global level. This is evident not only in the creation of the FAO in 1943 to "ensure freedom from hunger" but today in the 2015 UN **Sustainable Development Goals** (SDGs) that call to "end hunger, achieve food security and improved nutrition, and promote sustainable agriculture." Second, GFSG is not the responsibility of any single global institution but in fact is a composite of formal international organizations and other global forums. Third, GFSG is experiencing an unprecedented period of opening up rule making to non-state actors, including the private sector, global civil society, and new social movements (each with differentiated sources of power and authority). Fourth, as a result of the 2007–8 global food price crisis, politicians and policy makers increasingly recognize the potential threat to food security posed by an interdependent food system, finally framing food security as a matter of significant national, regional, and, particularly, global urgency (Mayes and Kirwan 2013).

To better understand and explore these dynamics, the rest of this chapter is organized as follows. Six contemporary case studies are presented, each organized around specific institutions that play a key role in GFSG. In these case studies, consideration is given to the various issues, actors, and dynamics that are driving changes in GFSG. In the concluding section we summarize the chapter and reflect on Canada's role in GFSG.

Case Study 1: Committee on World Food Security

The UN **Committee on World Food Security** (**CFS**) is an intergovernmental committee that aims to be the leading global platform for countries and other stakeholders to work toward strong food security policies. As such, it occupies a key position in GFSG. However, this was not always the case. When the 2007–8 global food price crisis peaked, there was a struggle for leadership with old and new actors vying for influence in GFSG. The **Group of Eight (G8)** countries, which include Canada, made a push for leadership, proposing a Global Partnership for Agriculture, Food Security and Nutrition; other actors included the UN Secretary-General and the Rome-based food agencies (such as the FAO), networks of civil society organizations, the private sector, and philanthropic foundations. The stakes were high: the winner could have a great deal of influence over who eats, and how.

Concerns were raised by some countries and civil society organizations about the G8's top-down approach and lack of consultation. There was also concern that the G8's proposed Global Partnership did not build on existing institutions but was trying to start something new. Civil society actors expressed concern that the Global Partnership would promote the models of production and development that created the very problems governments were now trying to solve: depletion of natural resources, high-input dependency, reliance on fossil fuels for production and distribution, and continued focus on external markets. Partly in response to this and to concerns raised about the Global Partnership, FAO member states backed the reform of the CFS.

The goals of the CFS reform were to become the "the foremost inclusive international and intergovernmental platform for a broad range of committed stakeholders" and to work toward "the elimination of hunger and ensuring food security and nutrition for all human beings" (CFS 2009: para. 4).

The reformed CFS includes member states, participants, and observers; a key element in the reform is the active inclusion of participants from civil society organizations and the private sector organizations. In contrast to other global initiatives related to food security, the reformed CFS committed itself to "take into consideration the views of all participants and stakeholders to the fullest extent possible in order to foster ownership and full participation" (CFS 2009: para. 18). But more than just participation, the CFS agreed to "seek to achieve a balance between inclusiveness and effectiveness" by ensuring "that the voices of all relevant stakeholders—particularly those most affected by food insecurity—are heard" (CFS 2009: para. 2). Participants in the CFS engage in negotiation on par with the states up to the point where the states reach consensus. This means that when the states agree about the wording of a policy, even if all the participants disagree, the negotiations are over. The rationale is that states are responsible for taking final decisions because they are accountable for implementing them. Participants also contribute to the day-to-day work of the CFS, including contributing to setting the agenda and proposing individuals for expert panels. For example, civil society and private sector organizations are responsible for selecting individuals to sit on the CFS Advisory Group; this is important because this body advises the executive interstate body of the CFS (known as the Bureau). In recognition of power imbalances and the diversity of civil society, the Civil Society Mechanism has four seats on the Advisory Group, and the Private Sector Mechanism and Philanthropic Foundations have only one each; in theory, this gives greater voice to civil society concerns.

So far we have established that the CFS was reformed to play a more active and central role in food security policy and governance at the global level. The CFS reform sought to ensure that participants can meaningfully engage in policy processes. But what are these processes?

Each year the CFS meets for its annual session. At these sessions member states, including Canada, and participants negotiate policy recommendations on topics of relevance to food security. These negotiations are called policy round tables. Table 18.1 illustrates the themes of the policy round tables that have taken place since the 2008 reform. The outcomes of the policy round tables are listed in the Global Strategic Framework, which works to "improve coordination and guide synchronized action by a wide range of stakeholders" (CFS 2009: para. 6.iii) by providing an overarching framework and a single reference document with practical guidance on core recommendations for food security and nutrition strategies, policies, and actions (CFS 2012: para. 7). The idea is that the Global Strategic Framework provides a "one-stop-shop" for policy makers and thus reinforces the CFS's role in global policy convergence. Although global policy convergence has been lacking and a single reference document on best practices has great potential to improve matters, we note there is little evidence that policy makers at the country level are making use of the Global Strategic Framework.

This is but one challenge facing the CFS. Indeed, in practice, the CFS faces several important challenges. First, while most governments have agreed that the CFS is the foremost international platform for discussing food security policies at the global level, many governments such as Canada support competing multilateral food security initiatives outside of the CFS (e.g. those launched by the G8) (Margulis 2015). This serves to undermine the CFS and the participatory processes it claims to uphold. Furthermore,

while the CFS tries to place food security at the centre of all its decisions, albeit with varying success, this is not the case in other settings, such as the G8, where economic priorities tend to trump food security. At G8 meetings agriculture is promoted as a driver of the economy and producer of jobs, and it is assumed that this will ultimately lead to food security.

A second challenge facing the CFS is that while it has earned international legitimacy and has secured enthusiastic support, especially from civil society actors, the committee and its outputs lack influence, recognition, and power. This may change as the CFS continues its work, but it is unlikely that it will ever be able to compete for influence with G8 initiatives, for example, where heads of state and greater financial resources are involved. A third challenge to having greater influence is that the CFS is not able to set binding targets or to enforce any policies, meaning that everything they produce are recommendations and voluntary for states to implement. Finally, the CFS has struggled to find effective monitoring strategies and therefore is also lacking the tools to gauge its own impact. That said, the CFS has many opportunities to develop progressive food

Table 18.1 CFS Policy Round Tables 2010–14

CFS Session	Policy Round Table
36 (2010)	Addressing Food Insecurity in Protracted Crises: Issues and Challenges Land Tenure and International Investment in Agriculture Managing Vulnerability and Risk to Promote Better Food Security and Nutrition
37 (2011)	How to Increase Food Security and Smallholder-Sensitive Investment in Agriculture Gender, Food Security, and Nutrition Food Price Volatility
39 (2012)	Climate Change Social Protection
40 (2013)	Investing in Smallholder Agriculture for Food Security and Nutrition Biofuels and Food Security
41 (2014)	The Role of Sustainable Fisheries and Aquaculture for Food Security and Nutrition Food Losses and Waste in the Context of Sustainable Food Systems
42 (2015)	Water for Food Security and Nutrition
43 (2016)	Sustainable Agricultural Development for Food Security and Nutrition, Including the Role of Livestock
44 (2017)	Sustainable Forestry for Food Security and Nutrition

security policy recommendations and support the global coordination and coherence of food security governance. Much of the potential of the CFS is linked to its participatory structure, and it represents a best practice in global governance (Duncan 2015). Whether this can help to improve food security on the ground, however, remains to be seen in the years to come.

Case Study 2: International Food Trade

The **World Trade Organization (WTO)** is a supranational institution that plays a major role in regulating international trade, including international agriculture trade, domestic agriculture policy, and by extension, world food security. The WTO's predecessor, the **General Agreement on Tariffs and Trade (GATT)**, which governed international trade between 1947 and 1994, had excluded agriculture trade from the progressive multilateral tariff reductions that applied to trade in industrial goods. This made the GATT less relevant to food security than the WTO. The WTO governs a set of sectoral trade agreements, three of which are highly relevant to agriculture and food—the **Agreement on Agriculture (AoA)**, **Agreement on the Application of Sanitary and Phytosanitary Measures (SPS)**, and **Agreement on Trade-Related Aspects of Intellectual Property Rights (TRIPs)**.

These three WTO agreements have been instrumental in internationalizing agriculture policy and initiating a global shift toward market-driven world agricultural trade. The AoA set a schedule for legally binding reductions and limits on tariffs and subsidies and established strict criteria that define the scope of contemporary state-supported agricultural policy interventions—such as domestic food aid, rural livelihood support, agricultural extension, and crop insurance—and the conditions under which such policies are permissible under international law. The SPS established binding international standards for food safety and criteria that specify when states may reasonably restrict agricultural trade to protect human, animal, and plant health. TRIPS required that WTO members put in place strong national intellectual property rights regimes including geographical indicators of agricultural goods (e.g. Parma ham, champagne, etc.) and plant variety protection. In sum, the WTO and its subsidiary agreements have brought agriculture trade and farm policy under a system of binding international law and constrain the state's autonomy in this policy field. These have been unprecedented events in the international governance of agriculture and food with implications for food security.

Multilateral trade negotiations under the GATT and WTO are called "rounds"; they are open-ended, multi-year interstate negotiations based on a request and offer process. They are typically named after the country or city where they were officially launched by trade ministers. Agriculture and food security have featured as key issues of inter-state disagreement in the Doha Round. The WTO Doha Round, which started in 2001, has been the most protracted set of trade negotiations. Unlike the Uruguay Round, where the United States and European Union were successful in forcing the rest of the GATT membership to accept their compromise agriculture trade deal, the current Doha Round has been characterized by a significant shift in geopolitics that has witnessed Southern assertiveness and, thus far, an effective blocking strategy against the United States by the so-called **Agriculture Group of Twenty (Ag-G20)**, a coalition of developing countries led by Brazil, India, and China (Clapp 2006). The Ag-G20, supported by the majority of the WTO's South-based membership (i.e. over 120 countries), has demanded tighter agricultural trade rules on Northern subsidies while also permitting more flexibility for developing countries to pursue food security goals. This position is galvanized by the South's long-held view that the AoA and other WTO agreements are highly unbalanced and support the economic interests of the North at the expense of Southern economic development.

Thus far during the Doha Round, Southern countries have negotiated for greater "policy space" to put in place pro-poor food security policies. Such policies include the provision of domestic food aid programs, food reserves, and other services directed at resource-poor, small-scale farmers. Food import–dependent countries (the majority of WTO members) have also demanded assurance from food exporters of continued international food and financial aid to ensure a smooth transition to higher world food prices in the future—an outcome already foreseen in the Doha Round prior to the 2007–8 global food price crisis. Concern about higher food prices are a long-simmering trade friction among food importers and exporters at the WTO. Net importers of food have argued since the beginning of the Doha Round that the North, including Canada, has failed to live up to its commitment to support these countries during times of high food prices that was agreed as part of the deal that created the WTO (see Margulis 2014).

There has been major resistance to the increasing the power of the WTO in GFSG. In 2008, over 200 NGOs, under the banner "Our World Is Not for Sale" wrote an open letter to trade ministers rejecting the WTO as a solution to the global food price crisis. NGOs such as Oxfam and the Institute for Agriculture Trade Policy (IATP) have published several reports outlining why the Doha Round is likely to offer little in the way of pro-food security outcomes, a position also advocated by the former UN Special Rapporteur on the right to food (De Schutter 2011a). There is also a deep skepticism expressed by global civil society in what appears to be an attempt by major food exporters such as Canada to appropriate the global food price crisis as an opportunity to promote trade liberalization. Thus, despite the breakdown of interstate negotiations on agricultural trade, the WTO continues to be a key site of political contests for control of GFSG.

Case Study 3: Group of Eight and Group of Twenty

The Group of Eight (G8) and the **Group of Twenty (G20)** have emerged as key players in GFSG. The G8 and G20 are informal international institutions, better described as forums where the world's advanced and emerging economies meet to discuss pressing issues related to the world economy, international security, and social issues and to coordinate international policy in these fields.[1] The histories of the G8 and the G20 are intertwined; the G20 is an expansion of the original G7/8 members of advanced economies (i.e. France, Germany, Italy, Japan, the United Kingdom, the United States, Canada, and Russia) to include emerging and middle-income countries such as Brazil, India, China, Mexico, Argentina, South Africa, South Korea, Indonesia, Saudi Arabia, and Turkey. The G8/G20 convene annual summits with a rotating presidency among members and hold high-level meetings at the head of state and ministerial level. At the summits, members issue communiqués that represent a consensus position on particular policy issues. Members will also use summits to launch new intergovernmental initiatives and financial commitments ranging from counter-terrorism to financial regulation to official development assistance.

In response to the 2007–8 global food price crisis, at the 2008 G8 Leaders Summit in Japan, the French government rallied support for the so-called **Global Partnership for Agriculture and Food Security (GPAFS)**. As discussed above, the GPAFS was interpreted by some parts of the UN system and a number of NGOs as an effort on the part of Northern states to maintain control over the food crisis agenda and to rein in the UN. Indeed, G8 states did not want the CFS to be given authority to make recommendations on new forms of global regulation or to obligate G8 members to new financial commitments. Whereas the idea of a GPAFS initially called for the involvement and consultation of a variety of actors, in practice this was not the case. The G8-led process was dominated by the United States, European Union, Japan, Canada, and Australia, and expert advice was sourced primarily from the World Bank. NGOs and the private sector have not been active in the development of the GPAFS. One notable exception is the Bill & Melinda Gates Foundation, which has emerged as an increasingly influential actor in global food security governance. However, it is unclear whether officials from the Gates Foundation are playing considerable roles, given that the G8 process is not transparent.

International NGOs and Southern producer organizations have been largely excluded from G8 processes. There is no formal consultation processes in G8 summits. However, some NGOs have been invited to make short statements to G8 officials. Many NGO actors are publicly critical of what they identify as the G8's narrow focus on agricultural investment and reluctance to regulate private investment; in turn, they have launched several global campaigns to push the G8 to prioritize the protection of the human right to food and ensure the accountability of private actors investing in impoverished agrarian communities.

Case Study 4: Global Agricultural Land Grabbing

Foreign investment by states, transnational corporations, institutional investors, and domestic elites in agricultural land (also known as the **global land grab**) after the 2007–8 global food price crisis has emerged as a prominent issue in global food security governance. Investment in agricultural land raises several concerns, ranging from the lack of prior and informed consent of local communities whose land is sold or leased, to the risks for investors active in states with weak regulatory regimes, where land deals may be revoked if the political climate changes.

Investment in land for agriculture is a sphere of activity that has elicited the creation of a new global governance framework. In 2009, the G8

agreed to "work with partner countries and international organizations to develop a joint proposal on principles and best practices for international agricultural investment" (Group of Eight 2009: art. 113[b]). The first step was the consultations for the Principles for Responsible Agricultural Investment (PRAI), which were led by the World Bank in partnership with the FAO, the UN Conference on Trade and Development (UNCTAD), and the Organisation for Economic Co-operation and Development (OECD). A first draft of the principles was presented in 2010 and later publicly endorsed by the G8 and G20. However, many developing countries and global civil society organizations refused to endorse the PRAI, citing they had been developed without sufficient consultation and participation. As a result, in late 2012 negotiations on responsible agricultural investment were moved to the CFS, to be resumed with a more central focus on food security and vulnerable groups. This process was completed in October 2014 with the endorsement of the Principles for Responsible Investment in Agriculture and Food Systems.

From the outset, the idea of responsible agriculture investment has been to establish a set of standards for private, foreign investment in agriculture that would encourage investment in that sector but also minimize negative social and ecological consequences. General objectives include standards for free, prior, and informed consent before the transfer of land, fair compensation of existing land users, and maximizing economic opportunities and protecting food security for local communities. The PRAI follow various international standards and best practices relevant to investment in agriculture (and investment more generally) but with an emphasis on transparency and sustainability. An international code of conduct for investors is seen by global policy makers as critical to maintaining the political consensus on increasing investment in developing countries' agriculture (Margulis and Porter 2013). For example, in 2010 the G8 and G20 combined pledged US$20 billion for a multi-donor agriculture and food trust fund.

More recently the G8 recently established the US$3 billion New Alliance for Food Security and Nutrition. These programs are intended to stimulate public and private investment in developing countries' agricultural sectors.

The effectiveness of responsible agricultural investment hangs on the assumption that increasing transparency and establishing criteria for best practices will lessen investment-related risks and increase the benefits of private investment in agriculture. However, there are serious questions whether a focus on transparency and governance is sufficient in this case: the range of investors and producers is far more diverse than in other sectors, such as extractive industries, and land grabbing is highly variegated with respect to the range of commodities being produced (i.e. food, feed, biofuels, and other industrial inputs), the methods of production, end use, and final market destinations. De Schutter (2011b) argues the framing of responsible investment itself is problematic as it starts from the premise that the problem is weak institutions and economic considerations; this does not take into account wider social and livelihood dynamics among rural people that are not founded on market dynamics. Locher et al. (2012) note that initiatives such as PRAI work from the premise that stable, individual property rights regimes exist in host countries; this is in fact not the case in many developing countries. Therefore, it is not clear that the emphasis on weak governance and property rights addresses the problems of social exclusion and ecological risk that frame the current debate and drive demands for agricultural land and its governance.

The politics of responsible investment in agriculture are highly contentious. The legitimacy of this element of GFSG has been under scrutiny because of the fact the initial principles were developed by international organizations with the support of the G8 instead of a universal body such as the UN. However, as noted above, civil society actors stated that the final principles fell short of what was needed to support small-scale food producers and enhance food security.

Despite lingering disagreements among states, civil society, and private actors on how best to regulate investment in agricultural land, the negotiation of international principles and the support for these processes by the G8 and CFS demonstrates how GFSG is expanding to address new and diverse challenges.

Case Study 5: Global Climate Change

Food systems are not only dependent on the environment; they are also one of the greatest drivers of environmental change (UNEP 2011). In recognition of this, the CFS held a policy round table on climate change and food security in 2012. Proponents argued that the CFS had a mandate to develop policy recommendations on fundamental issues affecting food security from a food security perspective (as opposed to an environmental change perspective). However, one prominent tension in these negotiations was the claim that the CFS did not have jurisdiction over climate change and was thus overstepping its mandate. It was argued that climate change was the responsibility of the **United Nations Framework Convention on Climate Change (UNFCCC)**. The UNFCCC is an international environmental treaty that was negotiated at the Rio Earth Summit, known officially as the UN Conference on Environment and Development, in June 1992. It is the primary actor in global climate change governance, but it does not yet directly address agriculture or food security. The objective of the UNFCCC is to "stabilize greenhouse gas concentrations in the atmosphere at a level that would prevent dangerous anthropogenic interference with the climate system" (UN 1992: Article 2). Such stabilization is fundamental for food production. Importantly, the treaty did not establish binding limits on greenhouse gas emissions for individual countries and contains no enforcement mechanisms. This makes the treaty legally non-binding. Instead, the treaty provides a framework for negotiating specific international treaties (called "protocols") that may set binding limits on greenhouse gases.

The UNFCCC has produced two international mechanisms that are highly relevant to GFSG. In 2005, it launched the **Reducing Emissions from Deforestation and Forest Degradation (REDD)** mechanism which has the objective of mitigating climate change by reducing net emissions of greenhouse gases through enhanced forest management in developing countries. The mechanism includes a safeguard against the conversion of natural forest, but developing countries have the right to include plantations of commercial tree species, agricultural tree crops, and even some non-tree species such as palms (i.e. a major food and biofuel crop) as forests. No similar mechanism exists for agriculture. As noted above, agriculture has not been formally addressed within UN climate change negotiations, but the UNFCCC secretariat did invite parties and observers to submit their views on agriculture, requesting them to focus on adaptation measures and identifying and assessing agricultural practices and technologies that enhance productivity, food security, and resilience. The views will be compiled into documents and be used to organize future workshops.

The second relevant mechanism is the **Clean Development Mechanism (CDM)**, which allows a country with an emission-reduction or emission-limitation commitment to implement an emission-reduction project in developing countries. These projects earn credits that can be counted toward meeting CO_2 reduction targets. In October 2009, large-scale biofuel plantations became eligible as CDM projects, a surprise to many given the recognition of their social and environmental costs (Borras, McMichael, and Scoones 2010; Fargione, Plevin, and Hill 2010; GRAIN 2013) and strong evidence that dominant models of biofuel production release more CO_2 than burning conventional fossil fuels due to carbon emissions from land conversion and fuel processing (Searchinger et al. 2008). Biofuel production is a key example of the increasing integration of food, fuel, and financial markets. While biofuel production had been rapidly

increasing for the first decade of the new millennium, the steepest rise in biofuel production occurred in 2007–8, in line with a sharp increase in food commodity prices (High Level Panel of Experts 2011). Although many factors contributed to the crisis, the rapid rise in demand for the production of biofuels was identified as an important factor. This further illustrates the need for GFSG arrangements that integrate food, fuel, and finance considerations to ensure that policies in one area do not exacerbate problems in another.

Overall, there is a lack of coordination on the part of international actors when it comes to addressing food security and environmental sustainability in a coherent way. One attempt has been the push for **sustainable intensification**, which seeks to achieve food security by way of increased in production while minimizing negative environmental impacts and avoiding the expansion of land used for cultivation (Garnett and Godfray 2012). The term has been forwarded as a way of addressing food security challenges without aggravating environmental crises (Benton, Hartel, and Settele 2011; Tilman, Balzer, Hill, and Befort 2011). While the idea may appear to be a "win-win" solution, many have criticized the term. Loos et al. (2014) argue that the term is misleading insofar as it fails to address the central tenets of sustainability. As such, they argue that sustainable intensification is not likely to improve food security if it fails to address issues such as food accessibility. They propose giving more consideration to issues of equitable distribution of food and individual empowerment in the intensification decision process. Struik, Kuyper, et al. (2014) note that the debate on sustainable intensification often asks the wrong questions, and they remind us that the choices that have to be made require trade-offs and often criteria that mix scientific, practical, normative, and moral considerations. Correspondingly, we need governance arrangements that are capable of addressing and managing these different aspects. Collaborative and more inclusive modes of governance, such as those exhibited by the

CFS, are needed to effectively address the impacts of a changing planet on food systems (Barling and Duncan 2015). Yet what is clear is that the challenge of addressing the complex relationship between climate change and food security is promoting (albeit slowly) the mainstreaming of sustainability as a key objective of GFSG.

Case Study 6: Global Food Sovereignty

Food sovereignty, as a concept, framework, movement, and project, emerged in response to increased globalization of food systems and the spread of corporate power into the lives of small-scale food producers, encroaching on their livelihoods and nature (Pimbert 2009). It has since provided a robust and galvanizing critique of the organization and impacts of the dominant food system and as such plays a central role in global food security governance.

Food sovereignty defends peasant livelihoods and advocates agro-ecological technologies as a matter of social justice. Food sovereignty is closely associated with **La Vía Campesina**, an international movement which brings together millions of peasants, small and medium-sized farmers (including Canadian farmers), landless people, women farmers, Indigenous people, migrants, and agricultural workers from around the world. A food sovereignty approach promotes agrarian and food rights for peasants through a highly prescriptive agenda focused on reducing global food trade and reorienting food systems around local production grounded in agro-ecological principles (Clapp 2014; Wittman, Desmarais, and Wiebe 2010). Food sovereignty, as vision, project, and movement, has been conditioned by the contours of the food regime, emerging as a project in the 1990s during a period of intensifying global agrarian crisis, rapid trade liberalization, and structural adjustment policies that saw a loss of support for domestic agricultural sectors across the global South (McMichael 2014). It has since

become a "powerful mobilizing frame for social movements, a set of legal and quasi-legal norms and practices aimed at transforming food and agriculture systems" (Edelman 2014:659).

Food sovereignty and food security are often presented as opposing concepts, with food sovereignty supporters often making reference to the limitations of food security and proposing food sovereignty as an alternative. Clapp (2014:206) argues that this oppositional framing is problematic and that the "juxtaposition of food security and food sovereignty as competing concepts is more confusing than helpful." Clapp calls on us to engage in a more constructive dialogue on how best to address pressing issues facing the global food system.

There are examples where this dialogue is taking place, in part because of the introduction of food sovereignty into food policy forums. More specifically, the food sovereignty movement has played an important role mobilizing small-scale food producers, undertaking a strong analysis of modern food systems, forwarding a coherent critique of the industrialized food system, and proposing possible solutions. Indeed, the power of food sovereignty in global food security governance can be seen in the mobilization of a vast number of diverse food producers under one clear vision. The fact that the food sovereignty movement goes beyond critique to provide solutions and also advances those solutions through food production practices further strengthens their position within global food security governance.

The relationship between food sovereignty and food security remains complex, context-dependent, and contested. While some argue that food sovereignty is a precondition to food security, others challenge the potential of food sovereignty approaches to achieve food security (Aerni 2011). However, the emergence of food sovereignty as a key force in global food security governance serves to illustrate the links between and across local and global governance arrangements. Consider, for example, that food sovereignty is increasingly recognized in more formal governing environments. At the national level, food sovereignty has been integrated into laws or constitutions of Bolivia, Ecuador, Mali, Nepal, Senegal, and Venezuela. At the 2012 Latin America and Caribbean FAO Regional Conference, governments requested that the FAO "organize a wide-ranging and dynamic debate with the participation of civil society and academia to discuss the concept of food sovereignty, whose meaning had not been agreed by FAO Member Countries or the United Nations System" (FAO 2012: para. 25). The Quebec government adopted a provincial food sovereignty law in support of local food production. Food sovereignty is playing an increasingly influential role in global food security governance, not only as a framework that helps to position alternatives to the dominant neo-liberal food systems but also to mobilize small-scale food producers to create links between local and global food security governance and to play a more active role in these governance arrangements. As such, understanding food sovereignty as a movement, as a set of practices, and as a political framework is important to understanding the dynamics of global food security governance.

Conclusion

We began this chapter by defining GFSG as the institutions, actors, rules, norms, and power relations that shape the practice of governing how food is produced, distributed, and accessed across borders. We argued that a broad definition was necessary to account for the complexity of the food system and the multiple dynamics of food security. Through the case studies we have mapped out key dynamics that not only illustrate this complexity but also show why such complexity matters. Food security is as political as it is social: governance of food security does not exist outside of complex systems of competing understandings, norms, and values. Given that hunger is the result of historic and ongoing social, political, and economic interactions from the local up to the global level, understanding global governance is fundamental not only to understanding

food security but also to supporting transition toward just and sustainable food systems.

As we noted in the introduction, contemporary GFSG has a few generalizable characteristics. First, GFSF is normatively oriented. Second, it is a composite of formal international organizations and other global forums. Third, GFSG is undergoing a period of opening up of rule and decision making. As part of this, we identified a move away from US and G8 domination toward increased engagement and influence of emerging and developing countries (e.g. Ag-20 at the WTO), as well as of civil society and the private sector (e.g. the CFS). We highlighted the increasing influence of philanthropic foundations, notably the Bill & Melinda Gates Foundation, and the growth of public–private partnerships (PPPs). Further reflection on the case studies also illustrates that within and across the institutions that make up GFSG, there is a great deal of fragmentation and a lack of clear leadership (i.e. no single organization is solely in charge of food security). Alongside fragmentation, the challenge of overlapping jurisdiction further muddles questions of responsibility. Finally, GFSG is marked by struggles for power, with each organization and actor operating within organizations seeking to shape the terms of the debate.

The world faces a huge challenge: to transition to just and sustainable food systems that ensure food security. We have argued that this is in many ways a problem of governance. Yet, we are facing an important moment in the evolution of GFSG: the path toward a just and sustainable food system is paved with opportunities and threats. As explored above, a major opportunity is that food security remains high on the political agenda, meaning that there is political interest and awareness and the potential for political will to reform GFSG. Importantly, the political interest and awareness that was sparked by the 2007–8 global food price crisis has been sustained. This interest has not only led to greater awareness of the challenges facing food security at a global level but also prompted increased integration of other concerns (e.g. climate change and trade).

Alongside these opportunities, there are also notable threats. The crisis has reinforced the productivist paradigm, for example, through calls to produce more food to "feed 9 billion by 2050" (Tomlinson 2011). Calls for sustainable intensification have been critiqued for further reinforcing this productivist approach and for failing to address ecological challenges and the rights and practices of the majority of the world's small-scale farmers and food producers. Furthermore, it diverts attention to increased production and away from issues of distribution, over-consumption, and the ongoing nutrition transition toward high-resource foods (i.e. dairy and meat). This suggests, in the short term, that struggles over GFSG are likely to be heavily shaped by efforts to mediate competing perspectives: on the one side for smaller-scale, agro-ecological approaches to food production and on the other for sustainable intensification. The case studies also demonstrate growing corporate influence within GFSG as these actors become integrated in political governance in addition to exercising market power; this suggests an increasingly industry-mediated vision of sustainability (Barling and Duncan 2015), which often contradicts and undermines efforts undertaken by civil society actors and some states.

States continue to play a key role in GFSG. On the one hand greater engagement of other actors at multiple scales and policy spaces increases the possibilities of holding states to account for their commitments. On the other hand the complexity of GFSG also permits states scope to pursue contradictory policy goals. Canada is a case in point. Following the 2007–8 global food price crisis the government of Canada made food security a key priority in its foreign policy agenda.

Indeed, Canada is among the strongest supporters of G8-led work on food security, in particular the promotion of public–private partnerships such as the New Alliance for Food Security and Nutrition and the Global Agriculture and Food Security Program, a multi-donor trust fund that promotes public and private agricultural investment in developing countries (Margulis 2015). Canadian development assistance for agriculture and food security has also increased. At the same time, the government of Canada has pursued an agenda of limiting the influence of the CFS and its multi-stakeholder process, for example, by seeking to reduce the Committee's political authority and by signalling its lack of political support for CFS-developed initiatives to institutionalize the human right to food as a key norm in GFSG. As a member of the WTO, the government of Canada continues to pursue aggressive trade liberalization of developing countries' agricultural sectors and has not shown itself to be supportive of recent efforts to protect food security, as seen in its criticism of the government of India's new national food stockholding regime. Also, it is well known that Canada during the Harper years pursued an exit from binding commitments on climate change. An understanding of the issues, actors, and dynamics of GFSG shows how the actions of a state such as Canada, which claims to be a champion of world food security because it provides development aid to agriculture and supports G8-led efforts, is in fact far more complex and potentially contradictory. This reminds us of the value of a GFSG approach that sheds light on the fluidity of rules and governance practices shaping the macrostructures within which food systems function and the challenges for transition to just and sustainable food systems.

Discussion Questions

1. What is global food security governance?

2. What are the biggest challenges facing global food security governance?

3. Should actors focus only on local food security solutions? Why do global institutions matter for local food security?

4. What are the benefits and challenges of opening up global food security governance to non-state actors such as global civil society and private sector organizations?

5. Should exclusive interstate clubs such as the G8 or more universal organizations such as the CFS take the lead in global food security governance? Why or why not?

6. How does greater knowledge of the complex linkages between climate change and food security shape the agenda of global food security governance?

7. Why do some global institutions support productivity solutions for food security and others support agro-ecological approaches? What might explain this apparent dichotomy?

8. What actions are the government of Canada taking to enhance or undermine global food security governance?

Further Reading

1. Carolan, M.S. 2013. *Reclaiming Food Security.* New York: Routledge.
   In this book, Carolan argues that food security has come to be closely associated with access to cheap calories, but that this has come at a great cost. The book reviews the evolution of the concept of food security with particular focus given to the conceptual relationship with agri-food and international policy over the last century.

2. Clapp, J. and S. Murphy. 2013. "The G20 and Food Security: A Mismatch in Global Governance?" *Global Policy* 4(2):129–38. doi: 10.1111/1758-5899.12039
   This paper argues that the G20 is not the most appropriate forum for the development of food security policy. Instead of addressing the structural economic dimensions of food security, the G20 promoted measures that supported the status quo of the current global economic framework.

3. Committee on World Food Security 2014. *The Global Strategic Framework for Food Security and Nutrition.* Rome. FAO. http://www.fao.org/cfs/cfs-home/global-strategic-framework/en/.
   The Global Strategic Framework has been designed to be a dynamic document to be regularly updated by the Committee on World Food Security Plenary. The purpose of the GSF is to improve coordination and guide synchronized action by a wide range of stakeholders in support of global, regional, and country-led actions to prevent future food crises, eliminate hunger, and ensure food security and nutrition for all human beings.

4. Duncan, J. 2015. *Global Food Security Governance: Civil Society Engagement in the Reformed Committee on World Food Security.* London: Routledge.
   In this book, the author presents the reform process of the Committee on World Food Security and the development of the Civil Society Mechanism. The author illustrated how, where, and why civil society is impacting global food security processes.

5. FAO. 2014. *The State of Food Insecurity in the World.* Rome: FAO. http://www.fao.org/3/a-i4030e.pdf.
   The State of Food Insecurity in the World (*SOFI*) is an annual publication of the UN's Food and Agriculture Organization. Each year the report focuses on a specific issue related to food security while also providing a summary of key statistics related to food security around the world. The 2014 report notes that sustained political commitment at the highest level is fundamental for hunger eradication.

6. Foresight. 2011. *The Future of Food and Farming: Final Project Report.* London: Government Office for Science. https://www.gov.

uk/government/uploads/system/uploads/attachment_data/file/288329/11-546-future-of-food-and-farming-report.pdf.
This report reviews the pressures on the global food system between 2011 and 2050. The broader Foresight report focuses on five key challenges for the future and provides a comprehensive review of the global food price crisis of 2007–8.

7. Garnett, T, and C. Godfray. 2012. *Sustainable Intensification in Agriculture: Navigating a Course through Competing Food System Priorities*. Food Climate Research Network and the Oxford Martin Programme on the Future of Food. University of Oxford. http://www.fcrn.org.uk/sites/default/files/SI_report_final_0.pdf.
This report reviews concepts and positions in the debate on sustainable intensification. The authors call for a more balanced debate on sustainability and intensification, arguing that sustainability should address environmental, economic, and social sustainability.

8. Loos, J., D. Abson, M. Chappell, et al. 2014. "Putting Meaning Back into 'Sustainable Intensification.'" *Frontiers in Ecology and the Environment* 12:356–361. http://dx.doi.org/10.1890/130157
This article looks at calls made by leading scientists for "sustainable intensification." The authors argue that the prominent definition does not in fact promote "sustainability" because it fails to take up established principles that are central to sustainability. They argue that sustainable intensification is likely to fail in improving food security due to the narrow focus on food production; sustainable solutions also need to address equitable distribution of food and individual empowerment.

9. McKeon, N. 2015. *Food Security Governance: Empowering Communities, Regulating Corporations*. London: Routledge.
This book provides a provoking review and analysis of food governance. Importantly, it sets food security within the context of this evolving global governance. The book uncovers the power dynamics that lie at the core of global food security and reify the so-called objective myths of the corporate global food system.

10. NGO/CSO Forum for Food Sovereignty. 2007. "Declaration of Nyéléni." 27 February. Nyéléni Village, Sélingué, Mali. http://www.nyeleni.org/IMG/pdf/DeclNyeleni-en.pdf.
In February 2007, at the Forum for Food Sovereignty, an estimated 500 delegates from more than 80 countries, representing a variety of organizations and social movements, adopted the Nyéléni Declaration. The Declaration lays out the parameters and principles of food sovereignty.

11. Wittman, H., A.A. Desmarais, and N. Wiebe. 2010. *Food Sovereignty: Reconnecting Food, Nature and Community*. Oakland, CA: Food First Books.
This book presents examples of how marginalized populations in the North and South resist the industrialized food system. Through case studies, the book illustrates how food sovereignty approaches can increase production of ecologically sustainable and safe food and ensure more equitable access.

Video Suggestions

1. Centre for International Governance Innovation. *Food Security*. www.youtube.com/watch?v=ZSunKHpA2xE. 2 min.
In this video, Jennifer Clapp discusses key challenges facing food security and highlights the impact of access, volatile food prices, and vulnerable populations.

2. Chicago Council on Global Affairs. *Food Security at the G8: Changing the Development Landscape*. www.youtube.com/watch?v=ytwNoE-I-Us. 73 min.
In this video, representatives of G8 members discuss the changing development priorities and international co-operation on food security.

3. **Cornell Transnational Learning.** *Robert Paarlberg—Who Makes Global Food Policy?* www.youtube.com/watch?v=lj9I4IWi_ds. **17 min.**
   Watch this video to gain more insight of the role of states in the relationship between food policy and the world food system.

4. **FAO.** *Hunger and Nutrition: Key Figures and Challenges.* www.youtube.com/watch?v=KxvIIKhI41Y. **2 min.**
   The FAO has compiled key hunger and nutrition data from 1992 to 2014. This video explains both the progress made and the nutritional challenges that remain to be tackled in the twenty-first century.

5. **FAO Market.** *CFS 40: Q & A with Kostas Stamoulis, Secretary CFS.* www.youtube.com/watch?v=Uc4j8gwXN8A. **6 min.**

Learn about the reformed Committee on World Food Security and the relationship to global food security governance.

6. **Global Justice Now.** *Not the G8/Raj Patel/Food Sovereignty.* www.youtube.com/watch?v=XyI1GyYDcyg. **17 min.**
   In this video, Raj Patel thinks about feeding the world in the twenty-first century and asks: Do we need farmers?

7. **Transnational Institute.** *What Are the Causes of the Global Food Price Crisis?* www.youtube.com/watch?v=aJK3NfT8AKA. **4 min.**
   Philip McMichael discusses factors that contributed to the global food price crisis from a historical perspective.

Note

1. For an institutional history of the G7/G8 see Hugo Dobson, *The Group of 7/8* (London: Routledge, 2007).

References

Aerni, P. 2011. "Food Sovereignty and Its Discontents." *African Technology Development Forum Journal* 8(1/2):23–40. http://www.atdforum.org/IMG/pdf_Philipp_Aerni-2.pdf.

Barling, D., and J. Duncan. 2015. "The Dynamics of the Contemporary Governance of the World's Food Supply and the Challenges of Policy Redirection." *Food Security*. doi:10.1007/s12571-015-0429-x

Benton, T., T. Hartel, and J. Settele. 2011. Food Security: A Role for Europe. *Nature* 480(7375):39. doi:10.1038/480039d

Borras, S.M.J., P. McMichael, and I. Scoones. 2010. "The Politics of Biofuels, Land and Agrarian Change: Editors' Introduction." *The Journal of Peasant Studies* 37(4):575–92. doi:10.1080/03066150.2010.512448

Brühl, T., and V. Rittberger. 2001. "From International to Global Governance: Actors, Collective Decision-Making, and the United Nations in the World of the Twenty-First Century." Pp. 1–47 in *Global Governance and the United Nations System*, ed. V. Rittberger. New York: United Nations University Press.

CFS. 2009. *Reform of the Committee on World Food Security: Final Version*. FAO. Rome. http://www.fao.org/fileadmin/templates/cfs/Docs0910/ReformDoc/CFS_2009_2_Rev_2_E_K7197.pdf.

———. 2012. *Global Strategic Framework for Food Security and Nutrition: First Version*. Rome. http://www.fao.org/docrep/meeting/026/ME498E.pdf.

Clapp, J. 2006. "WTO Agriculture Negotiations: Implications for the Global South." *Third World Quarterly* 27(4):563–77.

———. 2014. "Food Security and Food Sovereignty: Getting Past the Binary." *Dialogues in Human Geography* 4(2):206–211. doi:10.1177/2043820614537159

De Schutter, O. 2011a. "Compatibility of the WTO and the Post-Global Food Crisis Agenda: Putting Food Security First in the International Trade System." Briefing note by UN Special Rapporteur on the right to food. http://www.srfood.org/images/stories/pdf/otherdocuments/20111116_briefing_note_05_en.pdf.

———. 2011b. How Not to Think of Land-Grabbing: Three Critiques of Large-Scale Investments in Farmland. *The Journal of Peasant Studies* 38(2):249–79. doi:10.1080/03066150.2011.559008

Duncan, J. 2015. *Global Food Security Governance: Civil Society Engagement in the Reformed Committee on World Food Security*. London: Routledge.

——— and D. Barling. 2012. "Renewal through Participation in Global Food Security Governance: Implementing the

International Food Security and Nutrition Civil Society Mechanism to the Committee on World Food Security." *International Journal of the Sociology of Agriculture and Food* 19(2):143–61.

Edelman, M. 2014. "Food Sovereignty: Forgotten Genealogies and Future Regulatory Challenges." *The Journal of Peasant Studies* 41(6):959–78. doi:10.1080/03066150.2013.876998

FAO. 2001. *The State of Food Insecurity.* ROME: FAO

———. 2012. *Thirty-Second FAO Regional Conference for Latin America and the Caribbean.* Buenos Aires.

Fargione, J.E., R.J. Plevin, and J.D. Hill. 2010. "The Ecological Impact of Biofuels." *Annual Review of Ecology, Evolution, and Systematics* 41(1):351–377. doi:10.1146/annurev-ecolsys-102209-144720

Foresight. 2011. *The Future of Food and Farming: Final Project Report.* London. https://www.gov.uk/government/uploads/system/uploads/attachment_data/file/288329/11-546-future-of-food-and-farming-report.pdf.

Garnett, T., and C. Godfray. 2012. *Sustainable Intensification in Agriculture: Navigating a Course through Competing Food System Priorities: A Report on a Workshop.* Oxford. http://www.futureoffood.ox.ac.uk/sites/futureoffood.ox.ac.uk/files/SI%20report%20-%20final.pdf

GRAIN. 2013. "Land Grabbing for Biofuels Must Stop." *Against the Grain.* Accessed 2 April 2013. http://www.grain.org/article/entries/4653-land-grabbing-for-biofuels-must-stop.

Group of Eight (G8). 2009. "Responsible Leadership for a Sustainable Future." Declaration of the L'Aquila Summit, 8 July. http://www.g8italia2009.it/static/G8_Allegato/G8_Declaration_08_07_09_final,0.pdf.

High Level Panel of Experts. 2011. *Price Volatility and Food Security.* Rome. http://www.fao.org/fileadmin/user_upload/hlpe/hlpe_documents/HLPE-price-volatility-and-food-security-report-July-2011.pdf.

La Vía Campesina. 2007. "Declaration of Nyéléni: Declaration of the Forum for Food Sovereignty." *Nyéléni 2007.* Accessed 6 February 2015. http://nyeleni.org/spip.php?article290.

Locher, M., B. Steimann, and B. Raj Upreti. 2012. "Land Grabbing, Investment Principles and Plural Legal Orders of Land Use." *The Journal of Legal Pluralism and Unofficial Law* 44(65):31–63. doi: 10.1080/07329113.2012.10756681

Loos, J., D.J. Abson, M.J. Chappell, et al. 2014. "Putting Meaning Back into 'Sustainable Intensification.'" *Frontiers in Ecology and the Environment* 12(6):356–61. doi:10.1890/130157

Margulis, M.E. 2014. "Trading out of the Global Food Price Crisis? The WTO and the Geopolitics of Agro-Power." *Geopolitics* 19(2):322–50.

———. 2015. "Canada at the G8 and UN Committee on World Food Security: Forum-shifting in global food security governance." *Canadian Foreign Policy Journal* 21(2):164–78.

———, Nora McKeon, and Saturnino M. Borras Jr. 2013. "Land Grabbing and Global Governance: Critical Perspectives." *Globalizations* 10(1):1–23.

———, and Tony Porter. 2013. Governing the Global Land Grab: Multipolarity, Ideas and Complexity in Transnational Governance." *Globalizations* 10(1):65–86.

Mayes, D., and J. Kirwan. 2013. "Food Security: A Fractured Consensus." *Journal of Rural Studies* 39:1–6. doi:10.1016/j.jrurstud.2012.12.001

McMichael, P. 2014. "Historicizing Food Sovereignty." *The Journal of Peasant Studies* 41(6):933–57. doi:10.1080/03066150.2013.876999

Muldoon, J.P. 2004. *The Architecture of Global Governance: An Introduction to the Study of International Organizations.* Oxford: Westview Press.

Pimbert, M. 2009. *Towards Food Sovereignty: Reclaiming Autonomous Food Systems.* London: International Institute for Environment and Development.

Rosenau, J.N. 1995. "Governance in the Twenty-First Century." *Global Governance* 1(1):13–43.

Searchinger, T., R. Heimlich, R.A. Houghton, et al. 2008. "Use of U.S. Croplands for Biofuels Increases Greenhouse Gases through Emissions from land-Use Change." *Science* 319(5867):1238–40. doi:10.1126/science.1151861

Struik, P., T. Kuyper, L. Brussaard, and C. Leeuwis. 2014. "Deconstructing and Unpacking Scientific Controversies in Intensification and Sustainability: Why the Tensions in Concepts and Values?" *Current Opinion in Environmental Sustainability* 8:80–88. doi:10.1016/j.cosust.2014.10.002

Tilman, D., C. Balzer, J. Hill, and B.L. Befort. 2011. "Global Food Demand and the Sustainable Intensification of Agriculture." *Proceedings of the National Academy of Sciences of the United States of America* 108(50):20260–4. doi:10.1073/pnas.1116437108

Tomlinson, I. 2011. "Doubling Food Production to Feed the 9 Billion: A Critical Perspective on a Key Discourse of Food Security in the UK." *Journal of Rural Studies* 29:81–90. http://www.campaignforrealfarming.org/wp-content/uploads/2011/11/tomlinson...pdf

United Nations. 1992. "Framework Convention on Climate Change." *International Legal Materials* 31: 849–73. http://unfccc.int/files/essential_background/background_publications_htmlpdf/application/pdf/conveng.pdf

UNEP. 2011. *Food and Ecological Security: Identifying Synergy and Trade-Offs.* Nairobi, Ken.: UNEP. http://www.unep.org/ecosystemmanagement/Portals/7/Documents/unep_policy_series/Food and Ecological solutions JS.pdf

Wittman, H., A.A. Desmarais, and N. Wiebe. 2010. *Food Sovereignty: Reconnecting Food, Nature and Community.* Oakland, CA: Food First Books.

19 Municipal Governance and Urban Food Systems

Wendy Mendes

Learning Objectives

Through this chapter, you can

1. Understand and define what constitutes a food system

2. Distinguish what makes a food system urban

3. Identify who makes decisions about urban food systems, and why this matters in the context of broader food system goals

4. Explain the ways that food has returned to the agendas of municipal governments, urban planners, and interested citizen groups

5. Understand how new forms of municipal governance are expressed through urban food system policies and programs

Introduction

Every day in cities around the world, millions of hungry mouths depend on food that has often travelled thousands of kilometres to reach supermarket shelves. Yet many of us remain unaware of how this happens. Until recently, few of us questioned the conditions under which food is grown, processed, and transported in and out of our cities, let alone the far-reaching social, economic, and environmental impacts on our communities and our planet. As Carolyn Steel reminds us:

> When you think that every day for a city the size of London, enough food for thirty million meals must be produced, imported, sold, cooked, eaten and disposed of again, and that something similar must happen every day for every city on earth, it is

remarkable that those of us living in cities get to eat at all. (2008:ix)

The "gargantuan effort" required to feed cities has played a central part in the rise and fall of urban civilizations from the time of the ancient Romans to the present day (ibid.). Over the course of the twentieth century, global changes placed unprecedented pressure on cities and their **food systems**, including intensive rural-to-urban migration, loss of farmland, the rise of technologies such as intensive mechanized farming and refrigeration allowing for long-distance food transportation (Mougeot 2006; Pothukuchi and Kaufman 1999, 2000; Mendes 2007, 2008; Morgan 2009). These shifts, along with the effects of climate change, environmental degradation, and public-health crises, have drawn our focus back to food and food systems as issues of major importance to cities.

Today, food is reappearing on the agendas of a growing number of municipal governments and emerging as a pressing concern for the many urban dwellers who are changing the food system by flocking to community gardens, engaging in urban farming, shopping at farmers' markets, planting urban orchards, educating themselves about the sources of their food, participating in community kitchens and community food events, and serving on **food policy councils**. A food system includes all the activities and processes by which people produce, obtain, consume, and dispose of their food. It also includes the inputs and outputs that make the system run. But what exactly makes a food system urban? Who makes decisions about **urban food systems**, and why does "urban" matter in the context of broader food system goals? This chapter examines these questions by tracing some of the ways that food has returned to the agendas of municipal governments, urban planners, and interested citizen groups. We then explore how new forms of municipal governance are expressed through urban food system policies and programs.

Feeding Twenty-First-Century Cities

After decades of neglect, municipal governments in cities worldwide are increasingly developing **food policy** commitments (Koç, MacRae, Mougeot, and Welsh 1999; Mendes 2007, 2008; Mendes, Balmer, Kaethler, and Rhoads 2008; Morgan 2009; Reynolds 2009; Sonnino 2009; Morgan and Sonnino 2010; Mansfield and Mendes 2013; Roberts 2014; Cohen and Ilieva 2015). Canadian cities such as Vancouver, Victoria, Toronto, and Ottawa, and American cities such as Seattle; Philadelphia; Madison, Wisconsin; Baltimore; New York; San Francisco; and Portland, Oregon, have significant food policy commitments as part of their formal mandates. Cities in the global South

take an equally active interest in food systems; many of these have emerged as global leaders and innovators in municipal food policy. For instance, Belo Horizonte, Brazil, has been implementing policies based on the principle of food security as a right of citizenship since 1993. Its programs span a wide range of initiatives including urban agriculture, subsidized food sales, supply and regulation of food markets, food and nutrition assistance, job and income generation, and partnership with the federal Zero Hunger Strategy (Rocha 2001; Rocha and Lessa 2010). Together, all these programs are delivered at a cost of no more than 2 per cent of the city's total budget (Rocha and Lessa 2010). Rosario, Argentina, has been recognized for its food policy development with a United Nations Best Practice Award for its Urban Agriculture Programme.[1] This program arose from Argentina's 2001 economic crisis, which caused poverty levels in Rosario to reach 50 per cent (Spiaggi 2005).

Before we examine in detail the implications of the return of food to municipal agendas, it is first helpful to define some of our central concepts, beginning with food policy. A food policy is "any decision, program or project that is endorsed by a government agency, business, or organization which effects [sic] how food is produced, processed, distributed, purchased, protected and disposed" (Vancouver Food Policy Council 2015).

Food policies are an interconnected set of subsystems ranging from the household to the global level (Dahlberg 1992, 1994). Using a systems approach to discuss food policy reflects the need to holistically address problems in the ways that food is produced, processed, distributed, consumed, and recycled, instead of addressing individual problems of the food system in isolation (Garrett and Feenstra 1997). Although we might think that the most far-reaching food policy decisions are made in international or national arenas (in debates over food aid, international trade, or genetically modified organisms, for example), many observers argue that the most profound changes are in fact taking place in cities. This makes sense in light of the estimate that more than half the world's population lives in urban areas (United Nations 2014). The question then becomes: What makes food policies urban? The Food and Agriculture Organization (FAO) of the United Nations describes **urban food policy** as:

> a set of goals, objectives, strategies or programs designed to improve access of urban households to stable supplies of good quality food through efficient, hygienic, healthy and environmentally sound food supply and distribution systems. (Argenti 2000:12)

Urban food policies are those decisions and actions that fall within the jurisdiction of municipal governments, whether addressed through zoning, bylaws, or other forms of land use regulation, or through partnerships with other levels of **government**. Another common characteristic of present-day urban food policies is their association with broader goals of social, environmental, and economic sustainability in cities (Koç and Dahlberg 1999). Concretely, urban food policies that are couched in terms of sustainable food system goals might include policies that

- support opportunities to grow food in the city (e.g. community or rooftop gardens, urban farms, community orchards, urban aquaculture)
- encourage reduced distance between food production and consumption (e.g. policies supporting farmers' markets, community-supported agriculture, local food procurement policies)
- give a city's most vulnerable populations improved access to nutritious and affordable food (e.g. free or low-cost food and food recovery programs)
- ensure that neighbourhoods have grocery stores or farmers' markets within walking or cycling distance
- create infrastructure and education on food waste management (e.g. medium- and large-scale food composting, food waste diversion, community composting programs)
- nurture citizen-based groups to advise on

municipal food policy issues (e.g. food policy councils, neighbourhood food networks)
- support food celebrations that enhance social inclusion and community capacity building
- integrate food policies into comprehensive or neighbourhood plans (IDRC and UMP 2003; Mendes 2007, 2008; HB Lanarc 2009; Mansfield and Mendes 2013).

Policies alone do not automatically result in sustainable urban food systems. Policies must be "put to work" by the authority that creates them or the practitioners (and community partners) who are guided by them. One group that often works closely on the design and implementation of urban food policies is urban planners. Professional land use planning is concerned with the spatial organization of the city: how it is used, by whom, and for what purposes. Planning the ways cities are built and lived in has been done for millennia. However as a profession, **land use planning** (sometimes called "urban planning" or "town planning") is relatively new. Planners use tools including zoning; bylaws (or ordinances, as they are called in some places); building codes and other standards for housing; transportation, sanitation, water supply, and sewage systems; and public-health policies. Planners also use facilitation techniques to bring together grassroots, non-profit, and private sector stakeholders to formulate solutions to common problems.

Urban planners are far from the only professionals involved in decisions about urban food systems. Others include engineers, architects, and urban designers, all of whom can help shape our urban foodscapes, whether by building infrastructure for large-scale composting of food waste, designing buildings to enable rooftop gardening, or ensuring that cities' transportation networks and storage facilities support efficient movement and storage of enough food to supply the population.

Although food was conspicuously absent from urban planning in the latter half of the twentieth century, there are many signs that food system issues are returning to city planning in both the global North and the global South

(Pothukuchi and Kaufman 1999, 2000; Morgan 2009; FAO 1998, 2000a, 2000b). Food system planning, as it is sometimes called, is perceived in some jurisdictions as a planning subdiscipline in its own right. In food system planning, such issues either are urban planners' primary focus or are integrated into more traditional areas of planning. For example, an urban planner focusing primarily on housing might use food system planning "tools" or approaches by incorporating community garden plots into a housing development, building facilities for residents to compost their food waste, or ensuring that there are grocery stores within walking or cycling distance.

Among the signs that food system planning is becoming more common in municipal governments is the 2007 American Planning Association (APA) policy on community and regional food planning. This policy encourages APA members to help build stronger, sustainable, and self-reliant local food systems. The APA policy suggests that a city that can supply and control its food needs will have more influence over what its residents eat, will provide greater availability of fresh foods, and can protect itself against disruptions in food distribution (APA 2007). In addition, the policy points out that dollars spent on locally produced food have a greater chance of cycling back through the community, and that growing food closer to its points of sale reduces greenhouse gases released in transport (ibid.). Examples of APA policy guidelines include:

1. Develop plans, regulations and economic incentive programs to provide accessible and well-serviced sites for public markets, farmers' markets, small-scale processing facilities, and distribution centres for food produced in the region.
2. Encourage mixed-use neighbourhood design and redevelopment to include small and mid-sized grocery stores, farmers' markets, and community gardens to allow residents to grow their own food.
3. Prepare comprehensive plans and neighbourhood plans that recognize community gardens, farm/garden stands, and farmers'

markets uses that enhance overall community vitality.
4. Support development of vegetable gardens, edible landscaping, and related infrastructure on publicly owned lands, such as schoolyards, parks and greenways, and tax-foreclosed properties.
5. Provide incentives and special zoning provisions to integrate locally supported agriculture (e.g. community gardens, urban agriculture, small farms) into existing settlements and new areas of residential development.
6. Explore possibilities for recycling food wastes through composting and biofuel development (adapted from APA 2007).

At the same time, food system planning should be understood as one "ingredient" in more comprehensive policies and plans to create healthier, more resilient cities. Urban development models such as "healthy cities," "green cities," "walkable cities," and "sustainable cities" offer visions for integrating food system issues into city planning and design. For example, improving access to nutritious, locally produced food through farmers' markets can be one aspect of broader strategies for alleviating poverty and improving the health of urban populations. Promoting urban agriculture can form part of more encompassing policies that aim to "green" the city, protect urban biodiversity, and provide vibrant public gathering spaces and opportunities for recreation. Food system planning in cities can also form part of strategies to reduce CO_2 emissions by reducing dependence on long-distance food transportation. Support of economic activities such as small-scale food processing, food business incubation, and street-food vending can strengthen the local economy.

Table 19.1 provides a helpful illustration of the interactions between elements of the urban food system and areas of responsibility of local governments (land use and growth management, transportation, urban design, energy and infrastructure, buildings and housing, parks and open space, waste management, and social/economic development).

Table 19.1 The Food System: Opportunities for Integrating Food and Agriculture into Sustainable Community Planning

Agriculture & Food System Elements	Key Performance Areas of Local Government							
	Land Use & Growth Management	Transportation	Urban Design	Energy & Infrastructure	Buildings & Housing	Parks & Open Space	Waste Management	Social/Economic Development
Production	• Contain urban growth and protect agricultural land • Permit community gardens as a use in all land use designations	• Provide end-of-trip cyclist facilities (secure, weather-protected bike storage) near community gardens	• Enhance the public and private realms through food amenities, including community and private gardens, edible landscaping, green roofs, etc.	• Use production space to manage storm water • Use waste heat from infrastructure (e.g. sewer lines) and other as an energy source for greenhouses	• Insulate buildings and provide urban habitat through the use of green roofs and vertical landscaping	• Integrate edible landscaping and permit gardening as a use and recreation opportunity in parks and public open spaces • Ensure required gardening infrastructure including water hook-up and secured sheds	• Provide for composting space in gardening areas to help divert waste from the landfill	• Use all food system elements in social programming (e.g. skills development and education) and as part of a larger economic branding/marketing strategy (e.g. food precincts and related destinations)
Processing	• Permit context appropriate scales of food processing as a use in all land use designations	• Provide end-of-trip cyclist facilities (secure, weather-protected bike storage) for processing facilities • Ensure good transit access to processors	• Provide community-scale processing options (e.g. bread ovens, fruit presses) as amenities in private and public developments	• Use waste heat as an input into processing activity, and/or as an output for other processing or industrial uses	• Design community centres to accommodate community kitchens for processing activity (canning, preserving, etc)	• Provide community-scale processing options (e.g. bread ovens, fruit presses) in parks and public open spaces, where appropriate	• Support food processing waste diversion programs to reduce organic waste	

Table 19.1 (continued)

Agriculture & Food System Elements	Key Performance Areas of Local Government							
	Land Use & Growth Management	Transportation	Urban Design	Energy & Infrastructure	Buildings & Housing	Parks & Open Space	Waste Management	Social/Economic Development
Transport	• Cluster various food-related uses (e.g. processing, retail, etc) to reduce transportation pressures for goods movement, and to increase walkability	• Ensure Transportation Master Plans include a food transport component	• Design for convenient yet pedestrian-friendly food drop-off/ loading areas at the rear of buildings containing food retailers and restaurants	• Promotion of biodiesel or other alternative energy powered vehicles (including people powered) for the local transport of foods?	• Provide food drop-off and distribution areas in multi-family and possibly other buildings (e.g. Community Supported Agriculture drop-off points)	• Provide end-of-trip facilities (secure, weather-protected bike storage) near gardens in parks • Ensure good transit service to garden areas	• Support waste collection efforts that also rescue quality organic waste from retailers and restaurants (i.e. unused nearly expired food) for food emergency organizations	
Storage	• Permit food storage in all land use designations as part of food-secure/ resilient neighbourhoods	• Create multi-functional underground parking areas for cool storage (e.g. root cellars, beer cellars, etc.)	• Include food storage components in site and neighbourhood design (e.g. root cellars, beer cellars, etc.)	• Use renewable and/or waste energy to cool large food storage areas	• Provide food storage areas in units and buildings (e.g. pantries)	• Consider integrating community root cellars into parks and other public spaces	• Co-locate or incorporate waste diversion facilities/areas near/in food storage areas	
Retail, Wholesale & Marketing	• Support food retailers as important uses in complete, mixed-use neighbourhoods	• Provide end-of-trip cyclist facilities (secure, weather-protected bike storage) in food retail areas • Ensure good transit access to food retailers	• Ensure food retailers are designed to a scale and character appropriate for walkable, vibrant neighbourhoods	• Use renewable or waste heat from infrastructure as an energy source for retailers/ wholesalers	• Incorporate food retailers (e.g. grocery stores) into residential developments as part of complete, mixed-use neighbourhoods	• Co-locate food retailers and parks to support complete, vibrant communities	• Support food retailer waste diversion programs to reduce organic waste	

continued

Table 19.1 (continued)

Agriculture & Food System Elements	Key Performance Areas of Local Government							
	Land Use & Growth Management	Transportation	Urban Design	Energy & Infrastructure	Buildings & Housing	Parks & Open Space	Waste Management	Social/Economic Development
Eating & Celebration	• Support restaurants and other eating venues as important uses in complete, mixed-use neighbourhoods	• Provide end-of-trip cyclist facilities (secure, weather-protected bike storage) at eating establishments/venues • Ensure good transit access to eating establishments/venues	• Encourage sidewalk cafes and other opportunities for food celebration in the public and private realms through pedestrian-oriented design guidelines	• Use renewable or waste heat from infrastructure as an energy source for eating establishments	• Ensure community centres are designed to accommodate community kitchens for processing (canning, preserving, etc.)	• Design and integrate celebration opportunities (e.g. picnic tables for food fairs, community dinners, etc) into parks and other public open spaces	• Support restaurant waste diversion programs to reduce organic waste	
Nutrient Recycling & Waste Management	• Support composting as an important activity in all land use designations	• Utilize biodiesel and/or waste oil as a transportation fuel (e.g. green fleet)	• Design compositing facilities into the public realm (e.g. appropriate receptacles) to divert organic waste from the landfill	• Utilize waste oil (e.g. vegetable oil) in a digester for power generation	• Ensure all multi-family and other buildings in which food is consumed include organic waste separation stations and/or storage	• Use composted organic waste as a fertilizer in parks and other public areas	• Utilize bio-diesel and/or waste oil as part of garbage pick-up/delivery fleet	

Source: de la Salle and Holland (2010:44-47)

Table 19.1 demonstrates the extent to which food system planning is a matter of city and municipal authorities "doing what they already do in a better way" (Argenti 2000:3). Or, as Toronto's consultation report "Food Connections: Toward a Healthy and Sustainable Food System for Toronto" describes it:

> The goal is not to make food a priority that competes against other issues for resources but to identify opportunities where food can address and enhance local government objectives. (City of Toronto 2010:15)

In this way, rather than, "What can a city do for its food system?" the question is, "What can a more resilient food system do for a city?" (Mougeot 2006).

What Does Municipal Governance Have To Do with It?

So far we have seen how food and food systems are once again recognized as issues of great importance to the functioning of cities and the well-being of urban dwellers. We also learned what makes *urban* food policy distinct, and the role of urban planners as one profession (among others) closely involved in developing and implementing urban food policies. However, a broader question remains: Who exactly is responsible for making decisions about urban food systems? At one time we might have answered "government," but recent decades have seen important shifts in this assumption where food systems and many other issues are concerned.

While government can be understood to refer to the exercise of authority over a political jurisdiction by the "state" (whether a municipality, region, or country), **governance** broadens this understanding to refer to a more transparent and participatory process of decision making, involving not only the formal institutions of the state ("government") but equally those in **civil society**.

The shift from *government* to *governance* signals a recognition that multiple groups and interests are (or should be) meaningfully involved in identifying a community's concerns and proposing solutions to address them. There is increasing interest in practices of governance in light of critiques that government has become less transparent and less participatory, with decisions made behind closed doors. In light of this, it is not surprising that an emphasis on principles of inclusive, participatory governance is seen frequently in areas related to sustainable development where consultations, action planning, and visioning exercises are the legitimizing "stamp of approval" on any policy exercise or public debate (Dorcey and McDaniels 2001).

Issues of governance and participatory decision making are particularly important where

---

Box 19.1 Defining Civil Society

Civil society is seen as a social sphere separate from both the state and the market. The increasingly accepted understanding of the term civil society organizations (CSOs) is that of non-state, not-for-profit, voluntary organizations formed by people in that social sphere. This term is used to describe a wide range of organizations, networks, associations, groups and movements that are independent from government and that sometimes come together to advance their common interests through collective action. Traditionally, civil society includes all organizations that occupy the "social space" between the family and the state, excluding political parties and firms. Some definitions of civil society also include certain businesses, such as the media, private schools, and for-profit associations, while others exclude them.

Source: World Health Organization (2015).

urban food systems are concerned, because decisions about food systems often involve many stakeholders with varying interests. The "food movement" draws together a wide range of perspectives from citizen groups, including public-health advocates who focus on nutrition education and community-based strategies to address food insecurity; sustainable agriculture activists who express concern about food safety, the disappearance of productive land, increasing distances between producer and consumer, environmental degradation, and corporate concentration of agri-business; anti-poverty advocates who want to reduce hunger and disadvantage; and anti-globalization activists who protest the homogenization of culture, goods, and services, including food (Bouris 2005).

Such a wide range of stakeholders, combined with a common focus on social justice and a commitment to including the voices of marginalized groups, have led some observers to assert that broad and active participation in decision making is not merely a preferable approach but an *essential* aspect of addressing food systems (Barling, Lang, and Caraher 2002; Wekerle 2004; Allen 1999, 2010; Anderson 2008; Fodor 2011). As a result, urban food initiatives lead the way in innovation in municipal governance with strong citizen participation, inclusiveness, broad accountability, and cross-cutting approaches to food system issues that simultaneously benefit the economy, the environment, and public health (Wekerle 2004; Toronto Food Policy Council 2002; MacRae 1999; Welsh and MacRae 1998; Fodor 2011). While these claims are not without their detractors and criticisms, we can identify a number of examples of the principles of participatory decision making and new forms of governance being expressed through urban food system policies and programs. We will briefly review three such examples: (1) municipal **food charters** and food strategies; (2) food policy councils; and (3) neighbourhood food networks. Important to keep in mind is the extent to which these examples reflect a specific focus on the

interests and jurisdictional powers of *municipal* governments and their methods of governance.

Municipal Food Charters and Food Strategies

The United Nations International Covenant on Social, Economic and Cultural Rights includes "the fundamental right of everyone to be free from hunger" (1966). But what does this statement mean for cities, and how can such a covenant be enforced by a municipal government? In recent years a new type of "rights" document has emerged that is specific to cities and their food systems: the municipal food charter. A food charter is a municipally endorsed policy document that expresses key values and priorities for improving a city's food system. Typically, a food charter combines vision statements, principles, and broad action goals supporting a municipal government's food strategy. A number of municipal governments currently have food charters; Canadian examples include Toronto and Sudbury in Ontario; Saskatoon and Prince Albert in Saskatchewan; and Kamloops, Merritt, and Vancouver in British Columbia.

Food charters are a good example of participatory governance because they are often created through community-based processes involving a local food policy council and other citizen groups in partnership with a municipal government. In this way, a food charter embodies principles of participatory decision making: the process of creating the charter is just as important as the charter itself. For instance, the Vancouver Food Policy Council found that the process of formulating a food charter engaged individuals and organizations from all aspects of the food system in finding creative solutions to local food challenges (City of Vancouver 2007a). Before presenting the proposed food charter to Vancouver City Council for formal endorsement, the Vancouver Food Policy Council held many workshops and public forums with a wide

Box 19.2 Vancouver Food Charter

January 2007

The Vancouver Food Charter presents a vision for a food system which benefits our community and the environment. It sets out the City of Vancouver's commitment to the development of a coordinated municipal food policy, and animates our community's engagement and participation in conversations and actions related to food security in Vancouver.

Vision

The City of Vancouver is committed to a just and sustainable food system that
- contributes to the economic, ecological, and social well-being of our city and region;
- encourages personal, business and government food practices that foster local production and protect our natural and human resources;
- recognizes access to safe, sufficient, culturally appropriate and nutritious food as a basic human right for all Vancouver residents;
- reflects the dialogue between the community, government, and all sectors of the food system;
- celebrates Vancouver's multicultural food traditions.

Preamble

In a food-secure community, the growing, processing, and distribution of healthy, safe food is economically viable, socially just, environmentally sustainable and regionally based.

Some members of our community, particularly children, do not have reliable access to safe and nutritious food. In addition, much of the food we eat travels long distances from where it is grown and processed and is dependent on fossil fuels at every stage. Dependency on imports for our food increases our impact on the environment and our vulnerability to food shortages from natural disasters or economic set-backs. Overall food security is increasingly influenced by global factors that affect our community's ability to meet our food system goals.

Community food security needs the involvement of all members of our community, including citizens, consumers, businesses, and governments. When citizens are engaged in dialogue and action around food security, and governments are responsive to their communities' concerns and recommendations, sound food policy can be developed and implemented in all sectors of the food system and the community.

In 2002, the City of Vancouver adopted sustainability as a fundamental approach for all the City's operations. The goal of a just and sustainable food system plays a significant role in achieving a "Sustainable Vancouver."

Principles

Five principles guide our food system:

Community Economic Development

Locally based food systems enhance Vancouver's economy. Greater reliance on local food systems strengthens our local and regional economies, creates employment, and increases food security.

continued

Ecological Health

A whole-system approach to food protects our natural resources, reduces and redirects food waste, and contributes to the environmental stability and well-being of our local, regional, and global communities.

Social Justice

Food is a basic human right. All residents need accessible, affordable, healthy, and culturally appropriate food. Children in particular require adequate amounts of nutritious food for normal growth and learning.

Collaboration and Participation

Sustainable food systems encourage civic engagement, promote responsibility, and strengthen communities. Community food security improves when local government collaborates with community groups, businesses, and other levels of government on sound food system planning, policies and practices.

Celebration

Sharing food is a fundamental human experience. Food brings people together in celebrations of community and diversity.

To create a just and sustainable food system, we in Vancouver can:

- Be leaders in municipal and regional food-related policies and programs
- Support regional farmers and food producers
- Expand urban agriculture and food recovery opportunities
- Promote composting and the preservation of healthy soil
- Encourage humane treatment of animals raised for food
- Support sustainable agriculture and preserve farm land resources
- Improve access to healthy and affordable foods
- Increase the health of all members of our city
- Talk together and teach each other about food
- Celebrate our city's diverse food cultures

Source: City of Vancouver (2007b).

range of community groups and organizations throughout the city. The result was a food charter that reflected a food system vision and the goals of a broad cross-section of the city's residents, while providing opportunities to educate people and raise awareness about food system issues. By the time the Vancouver Food Charter was officially enacted, it reflected meaningful citizen "ownership" resulting from its wide-ranging input.

A municipal food charter can embody a range of food system goals. For example, the Vancouver Food Charter identifies five principles of a "just and sustainable food system": community economic development, ecological health, social justice, collaboration and participation, and celebration (City of Vancouver 2007b). Other food charters, such as Toronto's, identify a host of commitments including "championing the right of all residents to adequate amounts of safe, nutritious, culturally-acceptable food without the need to resort to emergency food providers," and "encouraging community gardens that increase food self-reliance, improve fitness, contribute to a cleaner environment, and enhance community development" (City of Toronto 2001).

Far from being merely a symbolic gesture, a municipal food charter can be a powerful statement used to justify and legitimize further policy development. Or, it can be a building block for more encompassing policy on specific food system issues. For instance, a food charter that identifies the goal of encouraging more community gardens (as Toronto's does) might be used to justify an urban agriculture strategy or incentives for builders to include community gardens or urban orchards in their development applications.

Independent of food charters (or combined with them) are comprehensive city-wide food strategies that bring together a range of food policy goals under one umbrella, along with a vision, goals, and targets for a city's food system. A municipal food strategy is an official plan or road map that helps city governments integrate a full spectrum of urban food system issues within a single policy framework (Mansfield and Mendes 2013). Cities including Seattle and San Francisco (US), London (UK), and Toronto and Vancouver (Canada) have municipal food strategies in place (ibid.).

While these strategies may vary in their format and approach, what they hold in common is a focus on integration and coordination of food system efforts. For instance, the London (UK) Food Strategy, launched in 2006, attempts to take "a holistic view of the food that the city produces, stores, delivers, sells, consumes and wastes" (Reynolds 2009: 417). The Toronto Food Strategy, launched in 2010, states that "many of the ingredients to produce health, environmental, economic and social benefits through food are already in place, available to be leveraged by a strategy and connected through a common vision" (Toronto Public Health 2010: 6). Similarly, Vancouver's Food Strategy commits to "integrate individual food policies into a more coordinated food systems approach, and align food system goals within broader City

plans and processes" (City of Vancouver 2013:4). Together, the emergence of municipal food strategies reveals an important evolution in the ways that cities and their residents look to food systems as a tool to improve overall quality of life, instead of treating individual food system issues in isolation.

Food Policy Councils

A food policy council (FPC) is one of the most common citizen-led vehicles for influencing urban food policies and embodying a more participatory approach to municipal governance. An FPC is an officially sanctioned voluntary body made up of stakeholders from various segments of a state/provincial or municipal food system (Borron 2003:4). MacRae describes FPCs as:

> multi-sectoral roundtables . . . where many interests are represented and many different kinds of sectoral resources can be offered to solve problems. (1999:195)

FPC membership might include representatives from various sectors and organizations, including gardeners, processors, producers, distributors, grocers, restaurateurs, environmentalists, anti-hunger activists, business people, educators, health and nutrition professionals, school administrators, and food waste disposal experts (Dahlberg 1994; Yateman 1994). One of the defining functions of an FPC is to create working collaborations between citizens, community agencies, and government officials that give voice to food-related concerns and interests. An FPC is asked to examine the operation of an urban food system and provide ideas or recommendations on improving it. While the contributions of citizen advisory committees may at times be largely symbolic, FPCs, in contrast, are often one of the more dynamic innovations in city governments across North America and beyond (Borron 2003; MacRae 1999; Dahlberg 1994; Yateman 1994; Roberts 2010, 2014). Reinforcing this view, it is often claimed that an FPC is uniquely positioned to contribute directly to policy development and municipal governance, to increase the capacity of the city to act on sustainability principles, and to:

> increase public and City understanding of the synergies flowing from the linkages of programs directed towards food security, healthy public policy, and social, economic and environmental sustainability. (Toronto Food Policy Council 2002:9)

This unique positioning of FPCs stems from a number of elements including strong citizen participation, broad accountability, and active working committees. Perhaps more suggestively, however, FPCs also claim distinctive characteristics such as the ability to lobby and advocate for food issues, and a cross-cutting approach to food system issues (ibid.). As the Toronto FPC describes it:

> [Food policy councils are] an exciting experiment in working through an emerging 21st century set of relationships between politicians, government staff and engaged citizens. Perhaps [they] anticipate what some have called the reinvention of government. (ibid.:17)

While the goals of advocacy and direct citizen involvement might be expected from the groups outside of local government, what makes an FPC so compelling is that it claims to represent a reconfigured approach to food issues drawing from the expertise of both governmental and non-governmental actors. Some food system scholars theorize FPCs as exemplary "networked movements" (Wekerle 2004; MacRae 1999; Welsh and MacRae 1998). As such, the ways that an FPC informs programs and policy and participates in other networked activities from positions in civil society and in partnership with the local state is the subject of growing interest to scholars and practitioners (Wekerle 2004).

Food system scholar Mark Winne estimates that over 100 jurisdictions in the United States and Canada have established food policy groups to provide a systematic focus on food system issues (Mendes and Nasr 2011). While food policy councils continue to develop in many regions, an equally interesting trend is emerging at an even smaller scale in cities: the neighbourhood.

Neighbourhood Food Networks

As many scholars and policy makers observe, food system initiatives often originate from the local communities they serve. In many cases, it is individuals, community groups, or local non-profit organizations that spearhead food policy efforts "in their own backyard." We see this place-based tendency in a host of food system initiatives ranging from urban agriculture and farmers' markets to community kitchens and emergency food distribution (Wekerle 2004; Clancy 2004; Welsh and MacRae 1998; Levkoe, Saul, and Scharf 2010). Often in defence against what are perceived to be the homogenizing effects of globalization and the breakdown of a sense of community, neighbourhood food initiatives typically emphasize inclusiveness, equity, empowerment, community action, local decision making, and defining a sense of place. The localization of food system issues is thought to provide "deep social benefits" to communities as a whole (Norberg-Hodge, Merrifield, and Gorelick 2002:79). As one food system scholar notes, "the ideas that 'place matters' and '[local] scale matters' have been argued to be crucial to the community food security approach" (Allen 1999:119).

For many years, projects such as community kitchens, neighbourhood food celebrations, and community gardens have been initiated and led by local communities. In some cities, the sheer number of projects in some neighbourhoods, combined with high community capacity and funding support from public, private, and non-profit sources, has led to the "scaling up" of individual projects into formal neighbourhood-based networks where different projects, and the groups responsible for them, are connected. The rationale for creating larger networks is often that food system strategies and solutions must move beyond single organizations or groups of residents. This approach has the double benefit of taking a more encompassing systems approach to food issues while building social networks and community capacity.

An example can be found in Vancouver, British Columbia, where at least 12 neighbourhood food networks (NFNs) operate in different areas of the city. These include the Grandview Woodland Food Connection, Renfrew Collingwood Food Security Institute, Downtown Eastside Right to Food Network, Trout Lake Cedar Cottage Food Security Network, Westside Food Security Collaborative, and many others. NFNs tend to share some characteristics in their composition and broad mandates. They are typically made up of coalitions of individual residents, community

leaders, workers from health and other social agencies, municipal staff, and representatives from faith-based organizations, with a goal of identifying and addressing food system priorities in their respective communities. At the same time, NFNs may have distinctive methods for and approaches to tackling issues in their neighbourhoods depending on local conditions and the needs and abilities of residents. A number of studies of Vancouver's current and emerging neighbourhood food networks have been undertaken (Fodor 2011; Carr and Fodor 2012). These studies examine the success and challenges of the neighbourhood food network movement, as well as looking ahead to the future of NFNs.

In Vancouver, NFNs are moving beyond the boundaries of their respective neighbourhoods by creating a "network of neighbourhood food networks" that not only connects the existing NFNs with each other to share knowledge and ideas, but

---

Box 19.3 Vancouver Neighbourhood Food Networks (VNFNs)

Across Vancouver, networks of committed people are focusing on food justice and resilience at the neighbourhood level. Creation of these Neighbourhood Food Networks (NFNs) represent the will of community members, organizations, and agencies to collaborate on community-based food initiatives and programs. VNFNs provide a space for NFN representatives from across the city to collaborate, share best practices and advocate for food justice with a unified voice.

NFN Areas of Focus include:

- **Growing Food Locally:** Community and school gardens connect people around the rich experience of growing food and foster environmental stewardship.
- **Celebrations and Events:** Celebrating food helps meet physical, spiritual, social, and emotional needs, while increasing social connection and community awareness around food security.
- **Food for All:** Accessing food includes drop-in meals, bulk buying clubs, mobile produce markets, emergency food access, and more. We acknowledge and work to break down barriers that prevent people from accessing nutrient-rich, affordable, and personally acceptable food.
- **Education and Engagement:** NFNs share knowledge and resources around every level of our food systems. Education and engagement takes the form of workshops, community kitchens, lectures and films, advocacy, and research.

Source: Vancouver Neighbourhood Food Networks (2015).

equally help guide the development of new NFNs in parts of the city where they do not yet exist. The NFNs and their work to create a network of food networks are being supported by a range of organizations including the municipal government, the Vancouver Heath Authority, the Vancouver Food Policy Council, and other partners. In this sense, NFNs offer a compelling illustration of a more participatory form of municipal governance that combines grassroots citizen-led initiatives, city-wide citizen advisory groups (food policy councils), municipal planning departments, and health or social agencies. Together, this blend shows how addressing food system issues at different scales within the city itself can inspire a new way of approaching not only food but also a host of emerging concerns for which we will require complex and agile solutions as we progress into the most urbanized century in history.

Conclusion

This chapter examined the ways in which food and food systems are once again being recognized as issues of great importance to the functioning of cities and the well-being of urban dwellers. We learned what makes *urban* food policy distinct and about the role of urban planners as one profession (among others) closely involved in developing and implementing urban food policies. As well, we examined shifts in municipal governance toward more participatory and inclusive methods for improving the resilience of the urban food systems upon which so many of us rely.

Discussion Questions

1. What is a food system?

2. What makes a food system urban?

3. Who makes decisions about urban food systems, and why does this matter in the context of broader food system goals?

4. What are some indications that food is returning to the agendas of municipal governments, urban planners, and interested citizen groups?

5. What are the links between participatory governance and food system planning in cities?

Further Reading

1. Born, B., and M. Purcell. 2006. "Avoiding the Local Trap: Scale and Food Systems in Planning Research." *Journal of Planning Education and Research* 26:195–207.
   A reading that advances food system planning analyses by challenging the tendency to assume that "local" is necessarily preferable.

2. Mendes, W. 2008. "Implementing Social and Environmental Policies in Cities: The Case of Food Policy in Vancouver, Canada." *International Journal of Urban and Regional Research* 32(4):942–67. An article that analyzes the challenges of *implementing* food system agendas within local governments using the case of Vancouver, Canada.

Food Systems and Urban Planning

3. Pothukuchi, K., and J. Kaufman. 1999. "Placing the Food System on the Urban Agenda: The Role of Municipal Institutions in Food Systems Planning." *Agriculture and Human Values* 16(2):213–24.

4. Pothukuchi, K., and J. Kaufman. 2000. "The Food System: A Stranger to the Planning Field." *Journal of the American Planning Association* 66(2):112–24.

Two foundational readings that were among the first to identify and analyze the absence of food system issues from urban agendas and examine the opportunities and challenges posed by the "return" of food to urban planning.

Municipal Food Strategies

5. City of Seattle. 2012. "Seattle Food Action Plan." Seattle, WA. Accessed 25 February 2015. http://www.seattle.gov/Documents/Departments/OSE/Seattle_Food_Action_Plan_10-24-12.pdf.

6. City of San Francisco. 2009. "Healthy and Sustainable Food Directive." San Francisco, CA.

7. London Development Agency. 2006. *Healthy and Sustainable Food for London: The Mayor's Food Strategy.* Accessed 25 February 2015. https://www.london.gov.uk/sites/default/files/FoodStrategySummary2006.pdf.

8. London Development Agency. 2007. *Healthy and Sustainable Food for London: The Mayor's Food Strategy.* Accessed 25 February 2015. https://www.london.gov.uk/sites/default/files/London%20Food%20Strategy%20Implementation%20Plan%202007.pdf.

9. City of Vancouver. 2013. *What Feeds Us: Vancouver Food Strategy.* Accessed 25 February 2015. http://vancouver.ca/files/cov/vancouver-food-strategy-final.PDF.

Urban Agriculture in the Global South

10. Mougeot, L. 2006. *Growing Better Cities: Urban Agriculture for Sustainable Development.* Ottawa: International Development Research Centre.

11. Redwood, M. 2009. *Agriculture in Urban Planning: Generating Livelihoods and Food Security.* Ottawa: International Development Research Centre.

Two books that focus on one specific dimension of food system planning, urban agriculture, within the context of the developing world (or "global South").

Municipal Food Policy in North American Cities

12. Hatfield, M. 2012. *City Food Policy and Programs: Lessons Harvested from an Emerging Field.* Accessed 6 November 2015. https://www.portlandoregon.gov/bps/article/416389.

13. MacRae, R., and K. Donahue. 2013. *Municipal Food Policy Entrepreneurs: A Preliminary Analysis of How Canadian Cities and Regional Districts are Involved in Food System Change.* Accessed 6 November 2015. http://foodsecure-Canada.org/sites/default/files/municipalfood-policyreport_may13_0.pdf.

Two studies that scan municipal food policies in North American cities.

Video Suggestions

1. *What Feeds Us.* www.youtube.comwatch?v=QGjKPcBz9YM. 5 min.
Food policy and food system planning in Vancouver, Canada.

2. CMAP GO TO 2040. *Planning for a Sustainable Local Food System.* www.youtube.com/watch?v=fbTxNkVdM38. 5 min.
The importance of local food as it travels from the farm to the table.

3. Foodtank. "26 Films Every Food Activist Must Watch." http://foodtank.com/news/2013/09/twenty-six-films-every-food-activist-must-watch.
Twenty-six films, some short and some long, about the food system.

4. NET Nebraska and Harvest Public Media. *Tossed Out: Food Waste in America.* http://harvestpublicmedia.org/content/tossed-out. 29 min.
Program on the pressures on our landfills posed by food waste.

5. PBS. *Food Forward Pilot: Urban Farming.* www
   .pbs.org/food/features/food-forward-pilot-urban
   -farming/. 30 min.

Episode on urban farming from the Public Broadcasting Service series *Food Forward: Urban Agriculture across America.*

Note

1. Urban agriculture refers to the practice of growing plants and raising animals in and around cities. A more comprehensive definition describes urban agriculture as "[a]n industry located within (intra-urban) or on the fringe (peri-urban) of a town, a city, or a metropolis, which grows or raises, processes, and distributes a diversity of food and non-food products. It (re)uses on a daily basis human and natural resources, products, and services largely found in and around that urban area and, in turn, supplies on a daily basis human and material resources, products, and services largely to that urban area" (Mougeot 2006:82). Throughout history, urban agricultural practices have been an integral part of city life. Over the course of the twentieth century, as "urban" and "rural" land uses became more separated, urban agriculture became a less-accepted activity that in some cases was deemed illegal. Recent decades have seen a strong revival of urban agriculture, with food growing in cities once again becoming a widespread and legitimate activity. Factors explaining the renewed interest in urban agriculture include rapid urbanization, food shortages, "peak oil," economic crises, and large-scale impacts of climate change. The "return" to urban agriculture has also been linked to a recognition that it can act as a catalyst for community capacity building, promoting health and nutrition, increasing social inclusion, and creating vibrant public gathering places.

References

Allen, P. 1999. "Reweaving the Food Security Safety Net: Mediating Entitlement and Entrepreneurship." *Agriculture and Human Values* 16:117–29.

———. 2010. "Realizing Justice in Local Food Systems." *Cambridge Journal of Regions, Economy and Society* 3:295–308.

Anderson, M.D. 2008. "Rights-Based Food Systems and the Goals of Food Systems Reform." *Agriculture and Human Values* 25:593–608.

Argenti, O. 2000. *Food for the Cities: Food Supply and Distribution Policies to Reduce Urban Food Insecurity. A Briefing Guide for Mayors, City Executives and Planners in Developing Countries and Countries in Transition.* Rome: Food and Agriculture Organization of the United Nations, Food into Cities Collection, DT/430–0E.

American Planning Association (APA). 2007. *Policy Guide on Community and Regional Food Planning.* Accessed 16 February 2015. https://www.planning.org/policy/guides/pdf/foodplanning.pdf.

Atkins, P., and I. Bowler. 2001. *Food in Society: Economy, Culture, Geography.* London: Arnold.

Barling, D., T. Lang, and M. Caraher. 2002. "Joined-Up Food Policy? The Trials of Governance, Public Policy and the Food System." *Social Policy & Administration* 36(6):556–74.

Borron, S.M. 2003. "Food Policy Councils: Practice and Possibility." Unpublished report. Eugene, OR: Congressional Hunger Center.

Bouris, K. 2005. "Examining the Barriers and Opportunities to Local Food System Planning in the Georgia Basin: Of Planners, Politics and the Public." Unpublished masters' thesis. University of British Columbia, School of Community and Regional Planning.

Carr, P., and Z. Fodor. 2012. *Sustainability on the Table: A Way Forward for Vancouver's Neighbourhood Food Networks.* Accessed 25 February 2015. http://www.smartfund.ca/docs/sustainability.pdf.

City of San Francisco. 2009. "Healthy and Sustainable Food Directive." San Francisco, CA.

City of Seattle. 2012. "Seattle Food Action Plan." Seattle, WA. Accessed 25 February 2015. http://www.seattle.gov/Documents/Departments/OSE/Seattle_Food_Action_Plan_10-24-12.pdf.

City of Toronto. 2010. "Food Connections: Toward a Healthy and Sustainable Food System for Toronto." Unpublished report.

———. 2001. *Toronto Food Charter.* Accessed 25 February 2015. http://foodsecureCanada.org/sites/default/files/TorontoFoodCharter.pdf.

City of Vancouver. 2013. *What Feeds Us: Vancouver Food Strategy.* Accessed 25 February 2015. http://vancouver.ca/files/cov/vancouver-food-strategy-final.PDF.

———. 2007a. *Vancouver Food Charter: Backgrounder.* Accessed 25 February 2015. http://vancouver.ca/files/cov/Van_Food_Charter_Bgrnd.pdf.

———. 2007b. *Vancouver Food Charter.* Accessed 25 February 2015. http://vancouver.ca/files/cov/Van_Food_Charter.pdf.

Clancy, K. 2004. "Potential Contributions of Planning to Community Food Systems." *Journal of Planning Education and Research* 23(4):435–8.

Cohen, N., and R. Ilieva. 2015. "Transitioning the Food System: A Strategic Practice Management Approach for Cities." *Environmental Innovation Societal Transitions.* http://dx.doi.org/10.1016/j.eist.2015.01.003

Dahlberg, K. 1992. "Report and Recommendations on the Knoxville, Tennessee Food System." Unpublished report.

———. 1994. "Food Policy Councils: The Experience of Five Cities and One County." Paper presented at the Joint Meeting of the Agriculture, Food and Human Values Society and the Society for the Study of Food and Society, Tucson, AZ, 9–12 June.

de la Salle, J., and M. Holland, eds. 2010. *Agricultural Urbanism: Handbook for Building Sustainable Food and Agriculture Systems for 21st Century Cities.* Winnipeg, MB: Green Frigate Books.

Dorcey, A.H.J., and T. McDaniels. 2001. "Great Expectations, Mixed Results: Trends in Citizen Involvement in Canadian Environmental Governance." Pp. 247–302 in *Governing the Environment: Persistent Challenges, Uncertain Innovations,* ed. E.A. Parson. Toronto: University of Toronto Press.

Fodor, Z. 2011. "People Systems in Support of Food Systems: The Neighbourhood Food Justice Network Movement in Vancouver, British Columbia." Unpublished final project. University of British Columbia, School of Community and Regional Planning.

Food and Agriculture Organization of the United Nations (FAO). 2015. "Urban and Peri-urban Agriculture in Latin America and the Caribbean: Quito." Accessed 25 February 2015. http://www.fao.org/ag/agp/greenercities/en/GGCLAC/quito.html.

———.1998. "Feeding the Cities." In *The State of Food and Agriculture.* Food into Cities Collection DT/399–8E. Rome: FAO.

———. 2000a. *Agriculture towards 2015–30.* Technical interim report.

———. 2000b. "Seminar Addresses Feeding Asia's Cities." *FAO News Highlights,* 30 November.

Garrett, S., and G. Feenstra. 1997. *Growing a Community Food System.* Community Ventures series. Puyallup, WA: Washington State University Cooperative Extension, Puyallup Research & Extension Center.

HB Lanarc. 2009. "Food & Agriculture Brief." Unpublished document.

International Development Research Centre & Urban Management Program for Latin America and the Caribbean (IDRC and UMP). 2003. *Policy Briefs: Guidelines for Municipal Policymaking on Urban Agriculture.* Accessed 25 February 2015. https://idl-bnc.idrc.ca/dspace/handle/10625/32512.

Koç, M., and K. Dahlberg. 1999. "The Restructuring of Food Systems: Trends, Research, and Policy Issues." *Agriculture and Human Values* 16:109–16.

———, R. MacRae, L.J.A. Mougeot, and J. Welsh. 1999. "Introduction: Food Security as a Global Concern." Pp. 1–7 in *For Hunger-Proof Cities: Sustainable Urban Food Systems,* ed. M. Koç, R. MacRae, L.J.A. Mougeot, and J. Welsh. Ottawa: International Development Research Centre.

Levkoe, C., N. Saul, and K. Scharf. 2010. *In Every Community A Place for Food: The Role of the Community Food Centre in Building a Local, Sustainable, and Just Food System.* http://metcalffoundation.com/wp-content/uploads/2011/05/in-every-community.pdf.

London Development Agency. 2006. *Healthy and Sustainable Food for London: The Mayor's Food Strategy.* Accessed 25 February 2015. https://www.london.gov.uk/sites/default/files/the_mayors_food_strategy_2006.pdf.

———. 2007. *Healthy and Sustainable Food for London: The Mayor's Food Strategy.* Accessed 25 February 2015. https://www.london.gov.uk/sites/default/files/London%20Food%20Strategy%20Implementation%20Plan%202007.pdf.

MacRae, R. 1999. "Policy Failure in the Canadian Food System." Pp. 182–94 in *For Hunger-Proof Cities: Sustainable Urban Food Systems,* ed. M. Koç, R. MacRae, L.J.A. Mougeot, and J. Welsh. Ottawa: International Development Research Centre.

Mansfield, B. and W. Mendes. 2013. Municipal Food Strategies and Integrated Approaches to Urban Agriculture: Exploring Three Cases from the Global North. *International Planning Studies* 18(1):37–60.

———. 2007. "Negotiating a Place for 'Sustainability' Policies in Municipal Planning and Governance: The Role of Scalar Discourses and Practices." *Space & Polity* 11(1):95–119.

———. 2008. "Implementing Social and Environmental Policies in Cities: The Case of Food Policy in Vancouver, Canada." *International Journal of Urban and Regional Research* 32(4):942–67.

———, K. Balmer, T. Kaethler, and A. Rhoads. 2008. "The Role of Urban Agriculture in Enhancing Green Communities: Experiences from Portland, Oregon and Vancouver, British Columbia." *Journal of the American Planning Association* 74(4):435–49.

Mendes, W., and J. Nasr with T. Beatley et al. 2011. "Preparing Future Food System Planning Professionals and Scholars: Reflections on Teaching Experiences." *Journal of Agriculture, Food Systems, and Community Development* 2(1):15–52.

Morgan, K. 2009. "Feeding the City: The Challenge of Urban Food Planning." *International Planning Studies* 14(4):429–36.

——— and R. Sonnino. 2010. "The Urban Foodscape: World Cities and the New Food Equation." *Cambridge Journal of Regions, Economy and Society* 5 (3): 209–24.

Mougeot, L. 2006. *Growing Better Cities: Urban Agriculture for Sustainable Development.* Ottawa: IDRC.

Norberg-Hodge, H., T. Merrifield, and S. Gorelick. 2002. *Bringing the Food Economy Home: Local Alternatives to Global Agribusiness.* London: Zed Books.

Pothukuchi, K., and J. Kaufman. 1999. "Placing the Food System on the Urban Agenda: The Role of Municipal Institutions in Food Systems Planning." *Agriculture and Human Values* 16(2):213–24.

——— and ———. 2000. "The Food System: A Stranger to the Planning Field." *Journal of the American Planning Association* 66(2):112–24.

Reynolds, B. 2009. "Feeding a World City: The London Food Strategy." *International Planning Studies* 14(4):417–24.

Roberts, W. 2010. "Food Policy Encounters of a Third Kind: How the Toronto Food Policy Council Socializes for Sustainability." Pp. 173–200 in *Imagining Sustainable Food Systems: Theory and Practice*, ed. A. Blay-Palmer. Surrey, UK: Ashgate Press.

———. 2014. *Food for City Building: A Field Guide for Planners, Actionists & Entrepreneurs*. Kindle Edition: Hypenotic Inc.

Rocha, C. 2001. "Urban Food Security Policy: The Case of Belo Horizonte, Brazil." *Journal for the Study of Food and Society* 5(1):36–47.

——— and I. Lessa. 2010. "Urban Governance for Food Security: The Alternative Food System in Belo Horizonte, Brazil." *International Planning Studies* 14(4):389–400.

Sonnino, R. 2009. "Feeding the City: Towards a New Research and Planning Agenda." *International Planning Studies* 14(4):425–35.

Spiaggi, E. 2005. "Urban Agriculture and Local Sustainable Development in Rosario, Argentina: Integration of Economic, Social, Technical and Environmental Variables." Pp. 187–202 in *Agropolis. The Social, Political and Environmental Dimensions of Urban Agriculture*, ed. L.J.A. Mougeot. Ottawa: International Development Research Centre.

Steel, C. 2008. *Hungry City: How Food Shapes Our Lives*. London: Random House.

Toronto Food Policy Council. 2002. "Introducing the Toronto Food Policy Council: Who We Are, What We Do, and How We Do It." Unpublished report.

Toronto Public Health. 2010. *Cultivating Food Connections: Toward a Healthy and Sustainable Food System for Toronto*. Accessed 17 February 2016. http://www1.toronto.ca/city_of_toronto/toronto_public_health/health_communications/files/pdf/food_connections_report.pdf.

United Nations. 1966. International Covenant on Social, Economic and Cultural Rights. Accessed 25 February 2015. http://www.ohchr.org/EN/ProfessionalInterest/Pages/CESCR.aspx.

———. 2014. "World Urbanization Prospects." Accessed 25 February 2015. http://esa.un.org/unpd/wup/Highlights/WUP2014-Highlights.pdf.

Vancouver Food Policy Council. 2015. "What Is Food Policy?" Accessed 25 February 2015. http://www.vancouverfoodpolicycouncil.ca/what-is-food-policy/.

Vancouver Neighbourhood Food Networks. 2015. "About VNFN." Accessed 25 February 2015. http://vancouverfoodnetworks.com/.

Wekerle, G.R. 2004. "Food Justice Movements: Policy, Planning, and Networks." *Journal of Planning Education and Research* 23(4):378–86.

Welsh, J., and R. MacRae. 1998. "Food Citizenship and Community Food Security: Lessons from Toronto, Canada." *Special issue of Canadian Journal of Development Studies* 19:237–55.

World Health Organization. 2015. *Civil Society*. Accessed 25 February 2015. http://www.who.int/trade/glossary/story006/en/.

Yateman, H. 1994. *Food Policy Councils in North America: Observations and Insights*. Final Report: World Health Organization's Travelling Fellowship.

Part V

Food for the Future

A critical perspective in food studies not only critiques present practices but also offers alternatives that point toward a more sustainable future. These alternatives can range from new ways of thinking about food and food systems to grassroots activities in rural and urban communities.

The chapters in this final part look ahead to a food system that is environmentally sound, socially just, and economically fair. Chapter 20 centres on the importance of policy for a more sustainable food system. Arguing that food policy has not been designed and implemented to reflect the fact that food is a biological requirement for life, MacRae puts forward a set of principles, values, and goals that would be consistent with a coherent, joined-up food policy. The chapter also provides a broad but comprehensive accounting of the policy instruments, structures, and governance models that need changing to achieve such a transformation.

In chapter 21, Sumner asks two questions: What should replace the global corporate food system, which is increasingly viewed as unsustainable? How will we know if the replacement is more sustainable? Sumner then outlines the theoretical parameters of a sustainable food system, anchoring it in the civil commons—co-operative human constructions that protect and/or enable universal access to life-goods. Above all, she concludes, a sustainable food system would ensure that everyone ate nutritious food of their choice, within the ecological limits of the planet.

Chapter 22 investigates how to actualize sustainable food systems. The well-researched problems associated with the global industrial food system have given rise to visions of more sustainable food systems, but significant barriers stand in the way of their realization. McInnes and Mount explore the theories behind the visions by examining how actors within the food system navigate in and around the food system they are trying to change; the targets, priorities, and practices they employ; and how these strategies account for the implications of scale.

In chapter 23, Levkoe adopts a pan-Canadian perspective to investigate alternative food initiatives and food movements, with a focus on collaborative food networks. He examines the ways these networks might have a greater impact in achieving their vision for a more socially just and ecologically sustainable food system in order to uncover new possibilities for future research as well as to connect more broadly with food movements on a global scale.

In the final chapter of this part and of the book, chapter 24, Desmarais proposes a radical framework for alternative food systems based on the concept of food sovereignty developed by La Vía Campesina, considered by many to be the world's most politically significant transnational agrarian movement. Food sovereignty focuses on the right of peoples and governments to determine their own agriculture systems, food markets, environments, and modes of production. Food sovereignty not only negates the current global food system, based on the rights of transnational food corporations as enshrined in trade agreements and the rules of the World Trade Organization, but also opens up spaces to imagine and build an agriculture that can feed the world and cool the planet.

20 Food Policy for the Twenty-First Century[1]

Rod MacRae

Learning Objectives

Through this chapter, you can

1. Discover how policy has previously determined, and could determine in the future, food system functions and activities

2. Understand how current food policy is deficient

3. Examine the range of policy changes required to create a sustainable and health-promoting food system

Introduction

Without food, air, and water, most organisms, including humans, cannot survive. As other chapters have described, the health of hundreds of millions is compromised by the way the dominant food system operates. The recovery thresholds of many environments on which humans depend have already been surpassed (e.g. in many fisheries), and other environments are significantly compromised, particularly those with unproductive soils associated with salinization and degradation, agriculturally contaminated water courses and bodies, and agriculturally altered habitats that lead to species decline. Individual and social identities and cultures are also intimately connected to food (see chapters 4 and 9 in this volume). Food policy must now be designed and implemented to reflect fully the essential reality of our dependence on food.

Policy is the set of rules, spoken or unspoken, that determines how things are run. In this chapter, I focus on government policy, because, if

properly designed and implemented, it can influence the policies of everyone else operating in the food system (see chapters 1 and 2 in this volume). In the industrial world, private firms are the key "expressions" of food system thinking, but they are unlikely to modify their approaches unless forced to by other actors. Government policy change is potentially one of these influencing forces.

During the twentieth century, the dominant thinking about markets framed our rules about food (see chapters 1 and 8 in this volume). Food was largely something to be bought and sold in the marketplace rather than a biological and cultural necessity (to appreciate its cultural importance, imagine a social event without food). Although many people still had gardens, and some still hunted and fished, the days of providing almost everything for ourselves were largely gone. Government farm policy primarily supported the buying and selling of food, especially in international markets. Farm overproduction served the interests of food firms because it helped to keep prices paid to farmers and processors low. And the food system was actually designed to encourage people to over-consume to generate profits for the same food companies benefiting from low farm prices. This consumption and the diseases it produced appeared to be economically positive because they drove up health-care costs and made our economic accounts, especially the gross national product (GNP), look better. In the twenty-first century, all this must change.

A Brief Historical Review of Canadian Food Policy

Similar to most industrial countries, Canada has never had a coherent and integrated national food policy. Agricultural production has been the primary driver of food-related policy since Canada's founding. In the nineteenth century, agricultural policy was mostly about Canada's obligations to Britain and efforts to establish national boundaries, particularly by attracting new farmers to the Prairies (Skogstad 1987). The Constitution Act, 1867 codified fragmentation by dividing responsibilities for food between the federal and provincial governments in ways that have since frequently generated conflict. Agricultural historian Vernon Fowke stated in the 1940s, "government assistance has been typically extended to agriculture because of what agriculture was expected to do for other dominant economic interests in return for assistance, rather than for what such assistance might do for agriculture" (Fowke 1946:272). The political influence of the grain and livestock sectors on eating patterns and nutrition recommendations originates in this period, a time when governments began providing significant supports (Fowke 1946).

The relationship between food and health in particular received some attention from policy makers as far back as the first part of the twentieth century. Early efforts to regulate food focused on sanitation and prevention of adulteration (MacDougall 1990)—vital work, but not reflecting the importance of nourishment

to health. There is little indication, for example, that the pioneering work of some UK medical doctors (McCarrison 1943; Picton 1946), examining the relationship between food production systems, food quality, and health, had any impact on Canadian policy makers. Food also received some favourable attention from health professionals after vitamins were discovered in the 1920s, but even then, certain food industries had significant influence on the kinds of eating patterns advocated by health professionals (Ostry 2006).

Canadian food policy remains, however, rooted in a traditional food safety and fraud prevention framework. Hedley (2006) links this approach to the thinking of political philosopher John Stuart Mill:

> governments ought to confine themselves to affording protection against force and fraud: that these two things apart, people should be free agents, able to take care of themselves and that so long as a person practices no violence or deception to the injury of others in person or property, legislatures and governments are in no way called upon to concern themselves about him. (Mill 1965:800)

This thinking, modified by Keynesian economic analyses on the food production side, remains firmly in place on the food consumption side (Hedley 2006), meaning that governments have usually been very reluctant to intervene in food consumption. One exception occurred during the Second World War, when Canadian governments strongly shaped the food marketplace, recognizing that the price system could not properly allocate food and related resources. The federal government used a wide range of instruments to encourage the supply of certain goods, set prices, and ration consumption (Britnell and Fowke 1962; Moseby 2014). This represents the only time food demand and supply were closely coordinated. Unfortunately, the coordinating structures and regulations were quickly dismantled post-1945.

As industrial approaches to agriculture took hold in North America and Europe after the Second World War and the number of diversified farms declined, farmers increasingly organized around the dominant crops and animals they produced. Divisions along commodity lines were created and solidified. Farm organizations evolved to dominate farm-level input into the policy apparatus (Forbes 1985; Skogstad 1987). Consequently, there were and remain few voices speaking to the need for systems approaches to policy development, and even fewer people in policy circles to hear the message.

There was, though, a brief period in which food policy and the language of food systems were considered. The federal government in the late 1970s was influenced by a number of factors: Norway's work on food policy development (Norwegian Ministry of Agriculture 1975); the Nutrition Canada National Survey of 1970–1972 (Sabry 1975); the Lalonde Report on health promotion (Lalonde 1974); and the *Report of the Committee on Diet and Cardiovascular Disease* (Health Canada 1976). Financial problems for farmers and dramatic food price increases also applied pressure.[2] The federal government's food strategy was consequently developed in 1977–8. Led by Agriculture Canada and Consumer and Corporate Affairs, there was a Deputy Ministers' Committee on Food Policy and an Interdepartmental Steering Group on Food Policy.

But their work was confined to seven major policy areas: income stabilization and support; trade policy and safeguards; research, information, and education; marketing and food aid; the processing, distribution, and retailing sectors; consumer concerns; and price stability, nutrition, and food safety. And their philosophy did not significantly depart from earlier approaches to agricultural policy. For example: "Government policies must continue to develop and expand Canada's production and export strengths to ensure the adequacy of safe and nutritious food supplies for the domestic and export markets at reasonable prices which are responsive to competitive forces over time" (Interdepartmental Steering Group on Food Policy 1978).

To their credit, policy makers were concerned that national nutritional priorities should not be overridden by the economics of agriculture. They asked that Nutrition Impact Statements be prepared for policy initiatives related to food.[3] Yet, overall, they believed that efficient operation of the marketplace was the best way to meet policy objectives.

Aside from the limitations and contradictions inherent in this emerging policy and the struggles of interdepartmental collaboration, what really halted this initiative was Agriculture Canada's unwillingness to support it. The department's reluctance was rooted in the changes such an approach would impose on its traditional clients—the food production, processing, and distribution sectors. The ministry was unwilling to entertain the possibility that it had broader responsibilities.

Agriculture Canada did, some years later, adopt a nutrition policy statement in support of Health Canada's work on nutrition, but again one that reflected the primacy of production over nourishment of the population: "In order to support the Canadian agri-food industry, Agriculture Canada has a major responsibility with respect to nutrient composition and nutritional value of agri-food products" (Agriculture Canada 1989).

Canada's Action Plan for Food Security (CAPFS), adopted on 16 October 1998, was another, ultimately aborted, attempt at developing a national food policy. It was Canada's response to the World Food Summit of 1996, at which Canada's then agriculture minister, Ralph Goodale, was considered a star player. While it identified targets to achieve food security nationally and globally, using a multi-sectoral approach involving all levels of government, civil society organizations, and the private sector, it was a stillbirth, quickly forgotten with little public reaction to its implementation failures. CAPFS recognized that food security implied "access to adequate food and sufficient food supplies and that poverty reduction, social justice and sustainable food systems are essential conditions"

(Agriculture and Agri-Food Canada 1998:24). But, it was riddled with tensions and contradictions about social, economic, and environmental priorities, imbued as it was with Canada's long-standing commitment to a productionist agricultural approach (Koç and Bas 2012).

Separate from CAPFS, in 2002, the federal, provincial, and territorial governments agreed to a new agricultural policy framework with five "pillars": business risk management, environmental protection, food safety, innovation, and rural renewal. Although an important attempt to make agricultural policy making more coherent, it failed to address the full range of issues that should make up a national food policy, being particularly weak on health, social, and cultural matters beyond those related to food safety. Renewed every five years or so since 2003,[4] the framework reflects an awareness that significant environmental issues need to be addressed, especially in the face of threats to Canada's international reputation on agri-environmental performance, but the impact of programs implemented to date has only been modest.[5] Moreover, new programs, including investments in ethanol biofuels and genetic engineering, may actually cause more detrimental environmental and economic impacts over the long term. However, to governments' credit, the agreement exists and created many new structures and lines of communication. It provides a potential—though partial—template for a national food policy.

Midway through the first decade of the twenty-first century, Agriculture and Agri-Food Canada (AAFC), Health Canada, and the Public Health Agency of Canada (PHAC) resumed discussions of a national food policy framework, but little information is publicly available on their motivation or progress. A 2005 draft document (*National Food Policy Framework: Overview* 2005) indicates that a central theme was policy coordination: the need to create a system-wide approach to link, through collaboration and multidisciplinary thinking and implementation, the domains of agriculture, fisheries, health protection and promotion, and food inspection.

However, the supply side of the food story, including food safety matters, appears to have remained the focus (Hedley 2006), and the policy scope remains somewhat narrow, only modestly expanded from earlier food policy iterations. The commentary on the role of consumers focuses mostly on fraud prevention, building consumer confidence, and individual (rather than structural) commitments to healthy living—the historical approaches to consumer-related interventions. Interestingly, the draft refers to CAPFS and its implementation. In fact, virtually all aspects of social development are proposed for implementation through CAPFS. On the surface, this appeared to be a way to revitalize CAPFS, but little has transpired since 2005.

Health Canada's involvement in food policy continues to be limited, its role confined to improving the nutritional quality of the food supply, defined primarily through providing dietary guidelines, monitoring nutrition labelling, and meeting the Food and Drugs Act regulations, many of which define what a food is (e.g. ice cream must contain a minimum specified level of dairy fat), rather than its role in a healthy diet or how its nutritional value might be optimized. The healthy-eating guidelines are not mandatory in any sense and they have been only minimally integrated into other policy arenas. Most Canadians have little idea how to implement them in their meals.

Equally problematic, no traditional or current common arrangement links the institutions that share responsibility for regulating consumer choice in food, food products, and production processes. Such issues would need to be managed by at least four federal cabinet committees: social affairs, economic affairs, foreign affairs and defence, and national security. As well, few issues rest within one order of government. While federal–provincial meetings of ministers are common in Canada, they tend to be restricted to similar mandates: health, agriculture, or environment. Joint meetings of health and agriculture ministers, for example, are rare or non-existent. As a result, there are exceedingly limited opportunities for joint action across ministerial mandates and orders of government to deal with the breadth of the food–health–environmental linkages (Hedley 2006:24).

Three federal opposition parties have presented significant food policy electoral platforms since 2010, with the New Democratic (Atamanenko 2010) and Liberal (Ignatieff 2010) parties holding consultations. The Canadian Federation of Agriculture developed a vision of a food strategy, and the People's Food Policy Project of Food Secure Canada, building on hearings from the late 1970s, conducted a community-based process to develop a comprehensive national food policy (People's Food Policy Project 2011; see also chapter 22). The Canadian Agri-Food Policy Institute (CAPI 2011) produced a food strategy report as did the Conference Board of Canada (Bloom 2014). While encouraging, these are all partial initiatives, lacking in scope or depth, or both. The 2015 federal election that brought the Liberals back to power represents another opportunity for a national food policy as the new minister of Agriculture and Agri-Food was instructed in his mandate letter to create one.

Policy for the Twenty-First Century

The Challenges of Food Policy Change

According to MacRae (2011), food policy development is a complex issue for policy makers, because

- the intersections between policy systems are historically divided intellectually, constitutionally, and departmentally
- governments lack institutional places from which to work, and the instruments of multi-departmental policy making are immature; there is no "department of food"
- supporting new approaches means addressing existing and entrenched policy frameworks and traditions

- the **externalized costs** of the conventional food, health, economic, and social systems must be addressed, and these costs are only partially understood and quantified
- food must be understood as more than a marketable commodity, which creates problems for certain departments
- it challenges many of the central tenets of current agricultural and economic development, and a curative (rather than preventative) health-care system

Consequently, there are numerous obstacles to be overcome in changing food policy.

Overcoming the Current Paradigm and Goals

Ideally, the food system would be rooted in a new ecological and health-oriented paradigm that is consistent with profound ideas of sustainability (see chapter 21 as well as the discussion below). With increasingly complex problems has come the realization that traditional Canadian government policy goals, institutional arrangements, and instruments are insufficient to meet this paradigm. Earlier eras of state regulation revolved around a productivist paradigm that worked well when the state had significant capacity and the issue was targeted (Howlett 2005). But in the era of bilateral and multilateral trade arrangements and international institutions based on **neo-liberalism**, many traditional policy and regulatory tools have been replaced to support these new policy orientations. More dramatically, in response to their trade commitments, some states appear to have given up some of their capacity to determine national priorities (see chapters 1 and 2 in this volume). Governments are searching for new and effective regulatory instruments without unduly straining what limited human and financial resources they are prepared to devote to solutions (Gunningham 2005). Food and agricultural policy themes are acutely affected by this regulatory situation, by the complexities of the changes required, by larger shifts in the loci of the national state's decision making, and by the new prominence of health concerns about food.

Ideally, the goals of the food system would be joined up (Barling, Lang, and Caraher 2002), that is, be coherent, connected, transparent, and comprehensive. A joined-up policy unites activities across all pertinent domains, scales, actors, and jurisdictions, employing a wide range of tools and governance structures to deliver these goals. In contrast, the current approach is to provide "an ample supply of safe, high quality food at reasonable prices for all Canadians,"[6] often referred to as Canada's "cheap food policy."

The Obstacles of Current Governance Structures

Ideally, there would be a set of coordinated governance structures, rooted in the new paradigm and goals, which would facilitate actions across the multiple actors and jurisdictions of the food system. But the current governance structures are enormous, dispersed, and varied. "For food safety alone, it is estimated that there are 90 statutes and 37 agencies across the country whose mandate, in some way, encompasses food" (*National Food Policy Framework* 2005:8).[7] Beyond the main legislation are numerous regulations, regulatory directives, and protocols; three layers of government carrying out different or overlapping functions in a more or less coordinated fashion;[8] and several agencies involved within each layer (although certain ones tend to be central, e.g. the Canadian Food Inspection Agency [CFIA] federally). Numerous functions are carried out: for example, training and education, pre-market consultations, product approvals and licensing, labelling and advertising, monitoring, inspection, post-market monitoring, recalls, enforcement, policy making, and import controls.[9] These functions target multiple operations within the food chain, such as farms, processing plants, warehouses, retail stores, restaurants, and import businesses and their foreign facilities, as well as a full range of food and packaged products.[10]

The other significant problem associated with governance structures is the limited role of Parliament. Most recent significant federal government decisions in agriculture have not been publicly debated. Instead, the recent tendency is to use existing legislation as a foundation from which the appropriate line department and central agencies take action (usually AAFC or CFIA, the Privy Council Office [PCO] and the Prime Minister's Office [PMO]). Orders-in-council and the departmental Estimates (part of the budget process) are used to create any additional necessary authorities.[11] Two recent high-profile examples, the Agricultural Policy Framework (APF) and genetically modified organism (GMO) regulation, were largely products of the bureaucracy, with some broad oversight from the central agencies and cabinet. Limited parliamentary discussion of the APF has occurred on "hot-button" issues (such as farm financial safety nets), usually at the committee level. Similarly, Parliament's participation in GMO regulation has been the result of private member's bills on mandatory GMO labelling of foods. Although public consultations often take place in association with these largely bureaucratic initiatives, they are rarely designed to facilitate a national consensus. Rather, the pattern is to generate numerous ideas from which government officials can choose their preferred approach. This process has produced frustration among stakeholders, who increasingly display much cynicism and annoyance in consultations, further limiting useful discussion.

The Absence of Good Feedback Mechanisms

Ideally, a national food policy would have robust feedback mechanisms sending signals to the main actors about how the food system is functioning and which interventions are working (and which are not). "Feedback allows the system to regulate itself by providing information about the outcome of different actions back to the source of the actions" (Malhi et al. 2009:469).

Canada's policy system is generally weak on feedback mechanisms. Much economic and social data is collected, but environmental, health promotion, and cultural information is limited. Equally important are the failures in sharing useful information. A significant amount of environmental data is private, held by farmers, farm organizations, or private data collection agencies. Public agencies do not have access, for reasons of price or fear of legal action if the private data reveal poor performance. Given the absence of collaborative mechanisms related to jurisdictional divisions (see above), information and analysis do not move readily across public agencies. Although the situation has improved recently, public agencies are seldom well connected to the organizations with an interest in food policy, treating many of them with suspicion. Although new forms of regulatory pluralism are emerging (MacRae and Abergel 2012), governments and food system actors are not yet particularly skilled at, or committed to, their implementation.

The Limited Set of Subsystem Elements

Ideally, the policy system would be deeply knowledgeable about food system function and have numerous instruments at its disposal to solve problems. But, at all levels, a limited range of policy tools and instruments are currently used, based on a lack of knowledge or resources, or paradigmatic opposition. Human resources are limited at all levels of the system, which means that policy actors are in short supply or not properly resourced and equipped. There is a significant lack of capacity to deal with complexity.

The Key Elements of Food Policy Development for the Twenty-First Century

Table 20.1 summarizes the elements that need changing to create better food policy in the twenty-first century. Unfortunately, we are

unlikely to see dramatic changes in governance and Parliament's role in the short to medium term (MacRae and Abergel 2012) to facilitate better food policy development. Therefore, change agents must alter existing mechanisms and elements. A major restructuring of governing units would be desirable, along the lines proposed by MacRae and the Toronto Food Policy Council (TFPC) (1999), but this will be feasible only after implementation of some of the changes proposed here.

Ideally, changes would be inspired and dynamically influenced by a major paradigmatic shift in how we understand the role of the food system in society. Lang and Heasman (2004) have referred to this as the "ecologically integrated paradigm," which places a premium on health promotion. The following proposals are all based on gradual policy changes consistent with such a paradigmatic shift.

Goals (and Policy Statements)

Ideally, a comprehensive food policy would create a food system that reflected the biological and social realities of food (see table 20.2, adapted from MacRae 1999, 2011; MacRae and TFPC 1999).

Key Principles on Which to Build Food Policy Frameworks

Twenty-first-century food policy requires adherence to a different set of principles than those that currently dominate the food system:

1. *Integrated responsibilities and activities.* Systems reflect the interconnectedness of activities in agriculture, food, health, culture, and social and economic development. Professionals have expertise across these domains and work collaboratively with others.
2. *An emphasis on macropolicy.* The policy-making process starts with global questions and options, and then, as appropriate, develops more specific policy tools and interventions consistent with the macropolicy.

Table 20.1 Key Policy Elements Requiring Changes

Policy statements	These are usually high-level statements, delivered or approved by members of governing parties.
Legislation	In recent Canadian tradition, legislation is broad and enabling and is revised infrequently, but change requires new legislation and modification of existing acts.
Regulatory changes	Senior bureaucracies create regulations that interpret legislation and guide its application. For a list of legislation and regulations pertinent to food policy change in Canada, see Annexes 8 and 9 of CAPI (2009).
Regulatory protocols and directives	Since regulations themselves are also relatively vague, agencies must create detailed regulatory protocols and directives to guide day-to-day activities and decision making. These are not always public.
Other instrument choices and changes	Governments often use a range of other instruments, including programs, educational mechanisms, and taxes or tax incentives to support their policy statements, legislation, and/or regulations.
Structural changes	The loci of decision making often significantly affect how changes are made (Hill 1994).

Source: Adapted from MacRae (2011).

Policy making is about identifying what is societally desirable.

3. *Transdisciplinary policy development.*
   - Because food is a multi-dimensional endeavour, policy units must include professionals with a diverse range of training, only one of which is economics. In this system, economics and science are tools to help society achieve identified goals.
   - Policy makers are well linked to the diverse groups affected by problems.
   - A more diverse group of people is involved in policy work, and community development principles are employed.

4. *Food systems policy.* Policy makers apply systems thinking to the analysis of problems and design of solutions. The framework of Malhi et al. (2009) is useful in this regard, as it includes the paradigm of the system, its goals, the system structures (including governance), the feedback mechanisms that help inform system activities and performance, and the subsystem elements (in a policy sense, this includes the actors and the policy tools). To be effective, all these layers are interconnected.

5. *Demand–supply coordination.* The presumption has been that the food marketplace efficiently allocates resources with minimal state intervention to ensure equitable and efficient distribution. However, as many chapters in this volume describe, this is not actually happening. Demand and supply must be coordinated beyond market functions. (adapted from MacRae 1999, 2011; MacRae and the TFPC 1999)

Structures, Feedback Loops, and Subsector Elements

Describing the structures, feedback loops, and subsector elements to implement all the required changes is beyond the scope of this chapter (see MacRae 2011; MacRae and Winfield, in review), so table 20.2 sets out in broad terms which portfolios need to be changed, organized according to the goals for the food system based on the new paradigm. Most nations in the industrialized world have to address similar kinds of issues to create their own national food policies. Some of the portfolios described do not currently exist, as they cross existing lines of responsibility or

Table 20.2   Goals of the Food System and Key Portfolios Requiring Changes

Goal	Portfolios to be Changed to Meet the Goal
1. Everyone has the resources to obtain the quality and quantity of food they need to be healthy and the knowledge to optimize nutritional health.	• Labour force and economic development strategies in and beyond the food system • Income support and security architecture, policies, and programs (social assistance) • Community growing spaces • Fisheries management • Aboriginal hunting and fishing rights and access to traditional foods, Aboriginal housing, food mail programs, Aboriginal economic development and housing (on-reserve and off-reserve), pollution reduction, food production in Aboriginal communities • Equitable access to the food distribution system, retail stores, and alternative projects • Consumer food information systems • Breastfeeding promotion
2. Food production, processing, and consumption are suited to the environmental, economic, technological, and cultural needs, potentials, and limits of the distinct regions of Canada. Food supply and quality are dependable. They are not threatened by social, political, economic, and environmental changes.	• Regional optimal consumption planning • Agricultural planning • Fisheries planning
3. The food system provides an essential public service, and is linked to other public services such as health care and education. Ownership of food system resources is widely and often publicly held.	• Health promotion planning • Integrating food into educational processes • Reducing corporate concentration and broadening ownership of food system assets
4. Food is safe both for people who produce, work with, and eat it, and for the environment.	• Food safety • Food quality
5. Resources (energy, water, soil, genetic resources, forests, fish, wildlife) are used efficiently with no ecological waste.	• Sustainable food and aquaculture production, processing, and consumption • Agricultural land protection • Energy efficiency in the food system • Protecting genetic resources • Municipal organic waste and sewage sludge management
6. The resources of the food system are distributed in a way that ensures that those who provide the most essential tasks have a decent income. In particular, people in rural communities have enough work and income to maintain or improve their lifestyle and to care for the rural environment.	• Farm market income • Business risk management programs • Support to small and medium-sized enterprise processing in rural communities • Temporary foreign worker programs • Wage improvements for farm, restaurant, and food-service workers
7. Everyone who wants to be involved in determining how the food system works has a chance to participate.	• Food system governance • Food citizenship
8. Opportunities are available for creative and fulfilling work.	• Intergenerational farm transfer and new farmer programs • Rural development
9. Food creates positive personal and cultural identity, and social interaction.	• Work–life balance • Food and culture • Food and body image
10. Our food system functions in a way that allows other countries to develop food systems with similar purposes and values, and we prioritize trade with those countries.	• Trade agreements (both bilateral and multilateral) • Food export mandates, supports, and programs • Food aid policy

include unaddressed policy arenas. Most portfolios would require alterations to legislation, regulation, and programs at all three levels of government.

Conclusion

Clearly, complex and multi-faceted changes are required, based on a **joined-up food policy** approach (Barling, Lang, and Caraher 2002). Canada faces challenges similar to those in other jurisdictions in the industrial world, making this a long-term agenda. Despite the imperative for change, the forces favouring the status quo are powerful, as many chapters of this volume describe. Multiple jurisdictions, enormous complexity, hundreds of thousands of actors, and global forces all mean that minimizing state functions and letting market forces run free is not the best course of action for developing a food system.

Completely rewriting the Constitution Act, 1867 to better align food system function with appropriate jurisdictions and to limit jurisdictional disputes is not a viable option in the near term. As well, because food and agriculture files do not usually generate parliamentary debate unless they represent a "hot-button" issue, it is unlikely that a complex, multi-dimensional, and multi-departmental food policy issue would undergo substantive parliamentary discussion.[12] Such policy is unlikely to be a PMO priority, and

cabinet participation in policy making has been eroded, so that agriculture or health ministers are not likely to bring forward significant food and agriculture legislation without PMO approval (Savoie 1999). This has effectively removed many traditional advocacy levers for civil society organizations. Potential shifts, however, in approaches to regulatory pluralism and government present short-term opportunities to widen the set of actors in policy development (MacRae and Abergel 2012). But with more significant structural change possible only in the longer term (MacRae and TFPC 1999), many changes proposed here will rely on existing architecture.

Financing food policy change will also be challenging. Given current budget contractions in most industrial countries, one of the first steps is to generate savings from first-order changes to pay for second-order ones. Three areas are strategically promising here: shifting production and export subsidies to operations that generate multiple benefits (ecological, social, and financial), often referred to as **multifunctionality**; supporting the farm transition to low-input systems that reduce demands on government-funded financial safety nets; and investments in health promotion programs that reduce demands on acute care and government budgets in countries with state-funded health insurance, such as Canada. Setting up mechanisms to identify and capture the savings will be part of this challenge.

Discussion Questions

1. What explains the failure of most Western countries to have sustainable and health-promoting food systems?

2. Which level of government is most responsible for creating food policy?

3. What roles can non-governmental organizations play in creating and implementing a joined-up food policy?

4. Which goals will be most challenging to implement?

Further Reading

1. Baker, L., P. Campsie, and K. Rabinowicz. 2010. *Menu 2020: Ten Good Food Ideas for Ontario.* Toronto: Metcalf Foundation. http://metcalf-foundation.com/wp-content/uploads/2011/05/menu-2020.pdf.
   Reviews 10 key initiatives for creating a more sustainable and health-promoting food system for Ontario that enhance the economic viability of small to medium-sized farms.

2. Epp, S. 2009. *Provincial Approaches to Food Security: A Scan of Food Security Related Policies in Canada.* Winnipeg: Manitoba Food Charter. http://foodsecureCanada.org/sites/bitsandbytes.ca/files/provincial%20policy%20scan.pdf.
   A scan of policies and initiatives to create food security at the provincial and municipal levels.

3. Hutchison, L., ed. 2006. "What Are We Eating?: Towards a Canadian Food Policy." Named issue of *Canadian Issues* (Winter).
   Selected papers from a conference on food policy development entitled "What's to Eat in Canada?" held in Montreal and sponsored by the McGill Institute for the Studies of Canada.

4. Lang, T., D. Barling, and M. Caraher. 2009. *Food Policy: Integrating Health, Environment and Society.* Oxford: Oxford University Press.
   This book provides a concise, accessible, and comprehensive review of issues surrounding the production, distribution, and consumption of food, largely from the UK perspective of the authors. They share their thinking on the multiple layers and levels of public and private action required to improve food policy.

5. Rideout, K., G. Riches, A. Ostry, D. Buckingham, and R. MacRae. 2007. "Bringing Home the Right to Food in Canada: Challenges and Possibilities for Achieving Food Security." *Public Health Nutrition* 10:566–73.
   Using a right-to-food framework, this paper explores Canada's failure to implement the right to food, despite its international commitments and the need to advance food security to solve multiple food-related problems.

6. Story, Mary, Michael Hamm, and David Wallinga, eds. 2009. "Food Systems and Public Health: Linkages to Achieve Healthier Diets and Healthier Communities." *Journal of Hunger and Environmental Nutrition* Special Issue 4(3/4).
   A special issue of the journal with a range of papers from a conference on linking food policy and health promotion.

Notes

1. Portions of this chapter are reproduced with the permission of Canada's International Development Research Centre (www.idrc.ca).
2. These problems were revealed in particular by the Food Prices Review Board, which functioned in the mid-1970s.
3. Only one ever was.
4. The name has been changed to Growing Forward (I and II).
5. In truth, very few Canadian agri-environmental programs have been properly evaluated.
6. According to Hedley (2006), this or similar wording can be found in AAFC policy statements dating back to the 1960s.
7. The main relevant federal ones are: Food and Drugs Act, Canadian Food Inspection Agency Act (Bill C-60), Canadian Agricultural Products Act, Feeds Act, Fish Inspection Act, Seeds Act, Consumer Packaging and Labelling Act, Plant Protection Act, Plant Breeders' Rights Act, Health of Animals Act, Meat Inspection Act, Hazardous Products Act, and the Pest Control Products Act. The provinces and territories also have food safety legislation that covers food products that are not

registered in the federal system and provides for oversight of food-related facilities that are not generally involved in interprovincial trade (e.g. slaughtering plants not involved in interprovincial or international trade) or that serve local markets (e.g. restaurants, food retail stores). However, increasingly the provinces are amending their slaughtering rules to conform with federal ones, even for provincial plants that do not sell meat across borders.

8. A new federal–provincial–territorial framework for working on food safety was put in place in 1996, and new programs have been introduced since the Agricultural Policy Framework was adopted in 2003.

9. For an overview, see the CFIA website, www.inspection.gc.ca.

10. For a summary overview of responsibilities, commodities covered, and pertinent pieces of legislation see Exhibit 25.1 of the *2000 Report of the Auditor General of Canada* (www.oag-bvg.gc.ca/internet/English/att_0025xe01_e_10976.html).

11. This is not unique to agriculture (see Savoie 1999), but appears to play a significant role in agricultural governance.

12. Note that more limited and highly politically charged issues, such as the fate of the Canadian Wheat Board, are still occasionally part of parliamentary debate.

References

Agriculture and Agri-Food Canada (AAFC). 1998. *Canada's Action Plan for Food Security.* Ottawa: Agriculture and Agri-Food Canada. www.agr.gc.ca/misb/fsec-seca/pdf/action_e.pdf.

Agriculture Canada. 1989. "Nutrition Policy Statement." *Rapport* (Newsletter of the National Institute of Nutrition) 4(1):7.

Atamanenko, A. 2010. *Food for Thought: Towards a National Food Strategy.* Ottawa: New Democratic Party of Canada.

Barling, D., T. Lang, and M. Caraher. 2002. "Joined-Up Food Policy? The Trials of Governance, Public Policy and the Food System." *Social Policy & Administration* 36(6):556–74.

Bloom, M. 2014. *From Opportunity to Achievement: Canadian Food Strategy.* Conference Board of Canada. Ottawa.

Britnell, G.E., and V.C. Fowke. 1962. *Canadian Agriculture in War and Peace: 1935–1950.* Stanford, CA: Stanford University Press.

Canadian Agri-Food Policy Institute (CAPI). 2009. *Regulatory Reform in Canada's Agri-Food System.* Ottawa: CAPI. www.capi-icpa.ca/pdfs/CAPI_Regulatory%20Framework%20_March%204%202009_.pdf.

———. 2011. *Canada's Agri-Food Destination: A New Strategic Approach.* Ottawa.

Forbes, J.D. 1985. *Institutions and Influence Groups in Canadian Farm and Food Policy.* Monographs on Canadian Public Administration #6, Institute of Public Administration #10. Toronto: Institute of Public Administration of Canada.

Fowke, V.C. 1946. *Canadian Agricultural Policy.* Toronto: University of Toronto Press.

Gunningham, N. 2005. "Reconfiguring Environmental Regulation." Pp. 333–52 in *Designing Government: From Instruments to Governance,* ed. P. Eliadis, M.M. Hill, and M. Howlett. Montreal: McGill-Queen's University Press.

Health Canada. 1976. *Report of the Committee on Diet and Cardiovascular Disease.* Ottawa.

Hedley, D.D. 2006. "Why Is There No Canadian Food Policy in Place?" *Canadian Issues* (Winter):20–7.

Hill, M. 1994. "The Choice of Mode for Regulation: A Case Study of the Federal Pesticide Registration Review, 1988–1992." PhD dissertation. Ottawa: Carleton University.

Howlett, M. 2005. "What Is a Policy Instrument? Policy Tools, Policy Mixes and Policy Styles." Pp. 31–50 in *Designing Government: From Instruments to Governance,* ed. P. Eliadis, M.M. Hill, and M. Howlett. Montreal: McGill-Queen's University Press.

Ignatieff, M. 2010. *Rural Canada Matters: Highlights of the Liberal Plan for Canada's First National Food Policy.* Ottawa: Liberal Party of Canada.

Interdepartmental Steering Group on Food Policy. 1978. *Recent Developments in Food Strategy.* 13 December. Ottawa: Government of Canada.

Koç, M., and J. Bas. 2012. "Canada's Action Plan on Food Security: The Interactions between Civil Society and the State to Advance Food Security in Canada." Pp. 173–203 in *Health and Sustainability in the Canadian Food System: Advocacy and Opportunity for Civil Society,* ed. R. MacRae and E. Abergel. Vancouver: UBC Press.

Lalonde, M. 1974. *A New Perspective on the Health of Canadians.* Ottawa: Ministry of Supply and Services Canada.

Lang, T., and M. Heasman. 2004. *Food Wars: The Global Battle for Mouths, Minds and Markets.* London: Earthscan.

MacDougall, H. 1990. *Activists and Advocates: Toronto's Health Department 1883–1983.* Toronto: Dundurn Press.

MacRae, R.J. 1999. "This Thing Called Food: Policy Failure in the Canadian Food and Agriculture System." Pp. 182–94 in *For Hunger-Proof Cities: Sustainable Urban Food Systems,* ed. M. Koç, R.J. MacRae, L. Meugeot, and J. Welsh. Ottawa: International Development Research Centre and the Ryerson Centre for Studies in Food Security.

———. 2011. "A Joined-Up Food Policy for Canada." *Journal of Hunger and Environmental Nutrition* 6:424–57.

——— and the Toronto Food Policy Council (TFPC). 1999. "Not Just What, But How: Creating Agricultural Sustainability and Food Security by Changing Canada's Agricultural Policy Making Process." *Agriculture and Human Values* 16:187–201.

——— and E. Abergel, eds. 2012. *Health and Sustainability in the Canadian Food System: Advocacy and Opportunity for Civil Society*. Vancouver: UBC Press.

——— and M. Winfield. In review. "A Little Regulatory Pluralism with Your Counter-Hegemonic Advocacy? Blending Analytical Frames to Construct Joined-Up Food Policy in Canada." *Canadian Food Studies*.

Malhi, L., O. Karanfil, T. Merth, et al. 2009. "Places to Intervene to Make Complex Food Systems More Healthy, Green, Fair, and Affordable." *Journal of Hunger and Environmental Nutrition* 4:466–76.

McCarrison, R. 1943. *Nutrition and Natural Health*. London: Faber and Faber.

Mill, John Stuart. 1965. *Principles of Political Economy with Some of Their Applications to Social Philosophy: The Collected Works of John Stuart Mill*, VIII. Toronto: University of Toronto Press.

Moseby, I. 2014. *Food Will Win the War*. Vancouver: UBC Press.

National Food Policy Framework: Overview. 2005. Draft—Work in Progress, 21 November 2005. (The document appears to be directed to a federal–provincial–territorial committee.)

Norwegian Ministry of Agriculture. 1975. *On Norwegian Nutrition and Food Policy*. Report #32 to the Storting. Oslo: Norwegian Ministry of Agriculture.

Ostry, A. 2006. *Nutrition Policy in Canada, 1870–1939*. Vancouver: UBC Press.

People's Food Policy Project. 2011. *Setting the Table: A People's Food Policy for Canada*. Ottawa.

Picton, L.J. 1946. *Thoughts on Feeding*. London: Faber and Faber.

Sabry, Z.I. 1975. "The Cost of Malnutrition in Canada." *Canadian Journal of Public Health* 66:291–3.

Savoie, D.J. 1999. *Government from the Centre: The Concentration of Power in Canadian Politics*. Toronto: University of Toronto Press.

Skogstad, G. 1987. *The Politics of Agricultural Policy-Making in Canada*. Toronto: University of Toronto Press.

21 Conceptualizing Sustainable Food Systems

Jennifer Sumner

Learning Objectives

Through this chapter, you can

1. Understand the power of the global corporate food system
2. Become familiar with ideas about sustainability and sustainable food systems
3. Become aware of some emerging aspects of sustainable food systems

Introduction

The idea of **sustainable food systems** is gaining strength as people begin to realize the vast short-comings of our current food system. Conferences are devoted to the topic, policy makers are considering the term, and activists are organizing around the concept. Putting sustainable food systems into place, however, depends on a prior comprehension of **sustainability** itself. Without this basic understanding, we cannot assess whether changes in a particular food system make it more or less sustainable.

This chapter begins with an exploration of the term **food system**, followed by a brief description of the **global corporate food system**, which offers up such critical contradictions as scarcity and overabundance, obesity and malnutrition, and pseudo foods and organic foods. It then puts forward a new meaning for sustainability based on the concept of the **civil commons**—co-operative human constructions that protect and/or enable universal access to life-goods. After an overview of sustainable food systems, the chapter proposes a definition of such a system, briefly outlines its parameters, and provides

some examples of transitions toward sustainable food systems. From the perspective of food for the future, this conceptualization represents an intervention in the food system at the paradigm level (see Malhi et al. 2009).

Food Systems

Food systems have existed for as long as humans have been organizing their food. In earlier times, food systems ranged from simple (such as hunting and gathering) to elaborate (such as the extensive food system that supported the Roman Empire). While simple food systems still exist in a few pockets around the world, most modern food systems are generally complex and multi-layered.

According to Kaufman (2004), a food system encompasses a chain of activities that begins with the production of food and moves on to include the processing, distribution, wholesaling, retailing, and consumption of food and, eventually, the disposal of food waste. While this definition covers the main components of a food system, it does not convey the idea of a dynamic, interconnected system. Rather, it stresses a linear configuration, thus converting natural cycles into one-way flows of waste.

In contrast, Hay (2000) defines a system as a group of elements organized such that each element is in some way interdependent (either directly or indirectly) with every other element. We can combine aspects of these two explanations to define a food system as *an interdependent web of activities that include the production, processing, distribution, consumption, and disposal of food.* This interdependent web can be very local, as in the self-provisioning of small, isolated groups, or huge, as in the global corporate food system. Regardless of scale, food systems are dynamic entities built by people to satisfy their needs and desires. In this way, food systems are relational—they embody relations among humans and between humans and the environment. And since food has always been about power and money (Friedmann 1993), these relations are seldom positive. Nowhere is this more evident than in the global corporate food system.

The Global Corporate Food System

Following the definition of a food system, the global corporate food system can be understood as an interdependent web of corporate-controlled activities at the global scale that include the production, processing, distribution, consumption, and disposal of food. Several authors in this volume have critically analyzed the global corporate food system (see, for example, chapters 2, 13, and 18). In his book *Stuffed and Starved*, Patel (2007) describes the global corporate food system as a battlefield, maintaining that it is impossible to think about such a food system without looking at the power of a few corporations controlling it. For example, Goodall (2005) claims that 10 multinational corporations control over half the world's food supply, and in the United States, 95 per cent of the food Americans eat is a corporate product (McMichael 2000).

This growing control has long been facilitated by government policy (see chapter 20 in this volume). According to Patel (2007:108), "food system corporations lobby, threaten, plead and demand political favour," thus promoting the consolidation of control of the food system. In this way, "although the food system is largely in the hands of the private sector, the markets in which they operate are allowed, and shaped by, societies and governments" (Patel 2007:111).

Patel's observation helps us to understand that such markets do not take place naturally but are socially constructed. The social construction of markets is evident in Karl Polanyi's seminal work, *The Great Transformation*, in which he defines a market as "a meeting place for the purpose of barter or buying and selling" (2001:59) and describes how early markets emerged from trade and were *embedded within social relations.* Over time, various forms of trade developed and introduced enormous changes, but the economic system was still "submerged in general social relations" with these embedded markets merely "accessories of economic life" (Polanyi 2001:70–1).

Polanyi argued that disembedded markets (that is, markets that were no longer embedded in social relations) emerged with the development of a market economy during the Industrial Revolution. According to Polanyi (2001:71), "a market economy is an economic system controlled, regulated and directed by market prices; order in the production and distribution of goods is entrusted to this self-regulating mechanism." Uniquely derived from the principle of gain, such a self-regulating market requires the deliberate commodification of labour, land, and money, as well as the division of society into separate economic and political spheres. In effect, a market economy involves subordinating social institutions to the market mechanism. Throughout his book, Polanyi argues forcefully that the "market economy if left to evolve according to its own laws would create great and permanent evils" (2001:136).

The "great and permanent evils" of a deliberately unregulated market economy are clearly evident in today's global corporate food system. Rosset sums up these evils when he asks:

Why must we put up with a global food system that ruins rural economies worldwide, drives family and peasant farmers off the land in droves, and into slums, ghettos and international migrant streams? . . . That imposes a kind of agriculture that destroys the soil, contaminates ground water, eliminates trees from rural areas, creates pests that are resistant to pesticides, and puts the future productivity of agriculture in doubt? . . . Food that is laden with sugar, salt, fat, starch, carcinogenic colours and preservatives, pesticide residues and genetically modified organisms, and that may well be driving global epidemics of obesity for some (and hunger for others), heart disease, diabetes and cancer? A food system that bloats the coffers of unaccountable corporations, corrupts governments and kills farmers and consumers while wrecking the environment? (2006, quoted in Albritton 2009:200)

While these debilitating effects are becoming increasingly apparent, cracks were beginning to form in the fortress of the global corporate food system as far back as the early 1990s:

Those with common sense are becoming aware of the fragility of a food system that creates so much distance, both socially and geographically, between an unprecedentedly urban world of consumers and a global farm, linked by the perpetual motion of an oil-fueled transportation network and a shaky international monetary framework. (Friedmann 1993:213–14)

As these cracks have widened, spaces have opened up for constructing more sustainable alternatives—alternatives that are re-embedded within, and serve, society. Such alternatives begin with the meaning of sustainability itself.

Sustainability

Over a quarter of a century ago, Hill (1984:1) lamented that "there is something seriously wrong with a society that requires one to argue for sustainability." And yet, since *sustainability* was coined in 1972, it has been a subject of controversy (Sumner 2005). The watershed in the sustainability debates was undoubtedly the report of the World Commission on Environment and Development (WCED 1987), commonly known as the Brundtland Report. Published as *Our Common Future*, the report defined sustainable development as meeting the needs of the present without compromising the ability of future generations to meet their own. Even though the report brought sustainability to international attention and made it a household word, the vagueness of its definition ensured that no drastic changes were needed in the ways people treated the environment or each other. Non-renewable resource extraction and human exploitation could proceed without interruption.

Over the next two decades, people began to grapple with the meaning of *sustainability*. The original research and thinking on the subject derived primarily from worries over the destruction of natural systems and their regenerative capacity, along with a concern for the loss of Indigenous and traditional culture (Dahlberg 1993). This concern, however, gradually spread to other areas to the extent that meanings of *sustainability* now fill a spectrum of understanding from the maintenance of profitable investments on Wall Street through the Dow Jones Sustainability Index to the deep ecology of the inherent rights of nature (Sumner 2005). All in all, *sustainability* can be a confusing term that few can explain. On the one hand, many people have warm, fuzzy feelings about what it means, and they project those feelings onto the term. On the other hand, some criticize the term as too vague, overly compromised, or undefinable, and reject it altogether. And yet, as Johnston (2010:176) explains, both individuals and groups use it as a "shorthand reference to a set of future-oriented practices and values enacted in a social context, a pathway out of a complexly related set of social, political, economic and ecological problems." In addition, unlike other terms such as *equity* or *justice*, *sustainability* foregrounds the environment—the ultimate bottom line—while bringing its considerable depth and breadth of comprehension to the social and economic aspects of life. Without a clear definition of term, however, it is difficult to know whether a food system is actually becoming more or less sustainable. In addition, the aim of sustainable food systems is a more sustainable society, one that is socially responsible, economically fair, and environmentally viable. On what basis can we work toward such a society?

One way to understand sustainability is through the idea of the civil commons. According to McMurtry (1999), this term describes a long-standing way of interacting with people and the environment. The civil commons is "any co-operative human construction that protects and/or enables the universal access to life goods" (McMurtry 1999:1). This means that the civil commons is based on co-operation, not competition. It does not occur naturally, but is constructed by people, and thus centres on human agency. It protects through rules and regulations, and it enables through opening up possibilities and opportunities. The civil commons involves universal access, not access only for those who can afford it. And it provides life-goods such as clean air, unadulterated food, potable water, education, and health care, not destructive goods like junk food, violent entertainment, and weapons. Examples of the civil commons are all around us: public education, the Canadian health-care system, old-age pensions, libraries, the Charter of Rights and Freedoms, parks, and the Montreal Protocol on Substances That Deplete the Ozone Layer. In essence, the civil commons is:

> *society's organized and community-funded capacity of universally accessible resources to provide for the life preservation and growth of society's members and their environmental life-host.* The civil commons is, in other words, what people ensure together as a society to protect and further life, as distinct from money aggregates. (McMurtry 1998:24)

The civil commons can occur at multiple scales, from the local and regional to the national and global. Whatever the scale, the civil commons always has boundaries and regulations—it is not an open-access resource, which invites free-riding and depletion. For example, the Canadian health-care system is only available to citizens of Canada. While this might appear exclusionary, it provides a strong argument for institutionalizing this form of the civil commons in all countries.

One of the great and permanent evils of a market economy has been the ongoing enclosure of all kinds of commons, from the privatizing of common lands during the Industrial Revolution to the deliberate defunding of today's civil commons formations such as universal health care and school lunch programs. In a settler society such as Canada, we need to also remember the long history of the enclosure of Indigenous commons, including land seizures, and Indigenous civil commons formations, including the potlatch. Resistance to all forms of enclosure can be found around the world, laying the groundwork for a more sustainable world.

From this basic understanding of the civil commons, we can define *sustainability* as "the outcome of structures and processes that build the civil commons" (Sumner 2005). The structures can be either formal or informal, as long as they build the civil commons. Formal structures can include governments, non-governmental organizations such as Greenpeace, associations such as the Canadian Civil Liberties Association, co-operatives such as Organic Meadow, non-profit organizations such as FoodShare, and corporations such as Newman's Own. Informal structures cover traditions and customs such as co-operation, sharing, and neighbourliness. The processes include developmental activities such as teaching, learning, researching, writing, collaborating, and decision making, as long as they build the civil commons. If oriented toward the civil commons, these structures and processes can work dynamically together and build co-operative human constructions that protect and/or enable universal access to life-goods, including food.

Sustainable Food Systems

As the mother concept of sustainability evolved, it inevitably spread as it was combined with other words. Shearman (1990) argues that using *sustainability* as a modifier in compound terms such as *sustainable development* changes the way we come to understand the second half of those terms. In this way, *sustainable* is used not only as an adjective, but also as a contradiction. For Shearman, *sustainability* as a modifier implies that the status quo is inconsistent with the facts. If not, then terms like *sustainable development* would be redundant, because development would already be sustainable. The same logic applies to sustainable food systems.

The concept of sustainability was first applied to food systems in a prescient article by Stuart Hill (1984), "Redesigning the Food System for Sustainability." He proposed that:

> It is obvious that our food producing systems must be operated in a sustainable way, for to do otherwise would be to practice delayed genocide on our descendants. (Hill 1984:1)

Hill (1984) then describes some characteristics of a sustainable food system and outlines the goals of any food system: nourishment for everyone, fulfillment, justice, flexibility, evolution, and sustainability.

In spite of this promising beginning, it took many years for academics to adopt the idea. Some authors mentioned sustainable food systems in passing (Power 1999; Friedmann 2007), but did not define them. Others have dealt with the concept head-on. For example, Feenstra (2002) proposes that sustainable food systems be characterized as more environmentally sound, more economically viable for a larger percentage of community members, and more socially, culturally, and spiritually healthful. She writes that:

> They tend to be more decentralized, and invite the democratic participation of community residents in their food systems. They encourage more direct and authentic connections between all parties in the food system, particularly between farmers and those who enjoy the fruits of their labor—consumers or eaters. They attempt to recognize, respect, and more adequately compensate the laborers we often take for granted—farmworkers, food service workers, and laborers in food processing facilities, for example. And they tend to be place-based, drawing on the unique attributes of a particular bioregion and its population to define and support themselves. (Feenstra 2002:100)

Many of Feenstra's characteristics of a sustainable food system resonate with the civil commons: democratic participation, two-way communication, livable wages, food sovereignty, and especially her primary goal of a community food system—"improved access by all community members to an adequate, nutritious diet" (Feenstra 2002:100). In this way, we can understand the vital role of the civil commons in sustainable food systems. If we connect sustainability with building the civil commons, we can apply the meaning of *sustainability* to the definition of a food system formulated above: "Sustainable food systems involve an interdependent web of activities generated by structures and processes that build the civil commons with respect to the production, processing, distribution, consumption, and disposal of food." In other words, to qualify as sustainable, the activities within food systems would have to contribute to co-operative human constructs that protect and/or enable universal access to the life-good of food.

This definition not only incorporates Shearman's (1990) argument that using *sustainability* as a modifier implies that the status quo is inconsistent with the facts—that is, food systems are not automatically sustainable. It also takes his argument one step further. A new understanding of sustainability as building the civil commons means that in compound terms, the adjective *sustainable* not only implies a contradiction, but also indicates a way out of the problem. The idea of the civil commons that underpins the meaning of sustainability allows fresh insights to emerge about sustainable food systems.

Right away it becomes clear that a food system dominated by transnational corporations would preclude sustainability by definition. The fiduciary responsibility of corporations to maximize private shareholder return fundamentally conflicts with and even violates the public interest of ensuring that all citizens are fed. This incompatibility is emphasized by Michele Simon (2006), a public-health attorney, who argues that "under our current economic system it's not a corporation's job to protect public health." Since a corporation's purview does not include public health, she observes:

> Like water (and unlike most other commodities such as toys or electronics), food is indispensable and a basic human right. Why have we turned its production over to private interests? Shouldn't at least some aspects of society remain off-limits to corporate control? (Simon 2006:318)

In other words, sustainable food systems would not only be based in the civil commons, but also anchored within the public domain. This stance reflects the experience of participants in the People's Food Policy Project, many of whom suggested that:

> food should be a public good, that a just system would make healthy food accessible, affordable and universal by bringing more of it into the public sphere, for example, through universal baby-bonus-style healthy-food dollars, school programs, community gardening and non-profit community markets. . . . It was agreed that citizens should control a system that serves the needs of eaters first and protects producers who serve the consumers. (Webb 2011:28)

In addition to being based in the civil commons and anchored within the public domain,

sustainable food systems would also follow natural cycles and close loops as tightly as possible, so that positive synergies could be achieved. Overall, sustainable food systems would be governed by civil commons regulation geared toward ensuring that everyone is fed, within the ecological limits of the planet.

Components of Sustainable Food Systems

As in all food systems, sustainable food systems would include a number of components in their interdependent web of activities. Kaufman's (2004) components of a food system listed at the beginning of this chapter provide some initial thoughts about the parameters of sustainable food systems: production, processing, distribution, consumption, and disposal.

Production

In sustainable food systems, farmers would be valued and supported. People who did not own land but wanted to farm would be given access to land and mentored in the production process. A current example can be found in Cuba, where people have the right to use land as long as they grow food and are given seeds, tools, and other extension services by the government. In Canada, FarmStart is a not-for-profit organization that encourages young and new farmers to take up farming. Its mission is to facilitate, support, and encourage a new generation of farmers drawn from three different demographic groups: young people from non-farm backgrounds, second-career farmers, and new Canadians (FarmStart 2015). One of the programs it offers is Start-Up Farms, which works with new farmers to:

> provide critical support including access to land, infrastructure, and equipment as well as technical training, business planning skills development, and mentorship during the first 6 years of their enterprise start-up. (FarmStart 2015)

In sustainable food systems, producers would join civil commons organizations, such as co-operatives or collectives, to support each other and sell the food they have grown or raised on their farms. A current example can be found in Venezuela, where farmers' co-operatives control production, with the government providing assistance for managing co-operatives and for establishing processing plants, so that farmers are no longer victim to prices set by processors and distributors (Broughton 2011). In Canada, examples include the Local Organic Food Co-ops Network, a group of over 70 co-operatives based in Ontario; the Falls Brook Centre, a training and sustainable community development organization in New Brunswick; and Farmer Direct, a co-op of 70 certified organic farms in Saskatchewan, which is the first business in North America to receive domestic fair-trade certification.

Producers in sustainable food systems would be certified for a range of sustainability parameters (for example, organic production, animal welfare, living wages for farm workers) and fairly compensated for their work. Food that needs to be imported into the system, such as coffee, tea, and out-of-season fruits and vegetables, would be sourced from a worldwide network of organic fair-trade co-operatives, non-profits, or other social-economy organizations in other countries. Any surplus produced in the system would be exported through these same networks.

Processing

In sustainable food systems, processors would be organized into producers' or workers' co-operatives, non-profits, and other social-economy organizations that specialize in canning, drying, curing, freezing, preserving, slaughtering, etc. The processing would be small or medium scale at the local or regional level, to provide employment where the food grows and minimize food miles. Current examples include the Haida Gwaii Local Food Processing Co-op, which aims to create local employment and ensure that wild food resources are harvested sustainably with local benefits (Agriculture and Agri-Food Canada 2009).

Distribution

In sustainable food systems, a web of primary, secondary, and tertiary civil commons–oriented distribution hubs would be set up in order to receive food from farmers and send it to other distribution centres or consumer outlets. A current example is the Ontario Natural Food Co-op (ONFC), which distributes natural, organic, and local food to member co-ops throughout eastern Canada. Backed by a vision of living in a sustainable world from seed to plate, its mission is to "proactively bring to market natural, organic and local foods and products within a co-operative network" (ONFC 2015).

Retailing would look different in sustainable food systems. Currently, food retailers dedicate an average of 31 per cent of their shelf space to pseudo foods—laden with salt, sugar, and oil—because these items generate high profit margins (Winson 2004). In sustainable food systems, such "edible food-like substances" (Pollan 2008:1) would be taxed like cigarettes, hidden from public view, and carry health warnings. In a sustainable food system, retail options would include a combination of civil commons–oriented structures, such as farmers' markets, neighbourhood shops, consumer and worker co-ops, "100-mile" stores, and mobile outlets. Current examples include the Moss Street Market in Victoria and Fiesta Farms in Toronto; workers' co-ops like Planet Bean in Guelph, Ontario, and Just Us! Coffee Roasters Co-op in Nova Scotia; and the 100 Mile Store in Creemore, Ontario. As far as possible, retail options would be located within communities and neighbourhoods, and on public transportation routes, to facilitate physical access.

Consumption

In sustainable food systems, consumption would include the acquisition of basic, low-cost, healthy foodstuffs. This "cheap food policy" would not depend on the exploitation of the environment or those who work in the food system, but would be subsidized by the state through taxation on junk food and a realignment of agriculture and food policies and subsidies. A current example is the city of Belo Horizonte, Brazil, which declared food to be a human right and developed dozens of innovations to ensure that everyone could exercise that right—including offering farmers choice public spaces from which to sell to urban consumers, setting up low-priced food markets on city property, and opening People's Restaurants that serve meals for the equivalent of less than 50 cents (Lappé 2009). In addition, Belo Horizonte has subsidized farmers' markets in low-income areas, ensured that free meals made from unsold produce are available to participants in neighbourhood clubs serving low-income residents, developed special food packages for pregnant women—all featuring safe and nutritious food in dignified and convenient settings—and set up a department of supply and services to deal directly with making healthy food readily accessible to everyone (Roberts 2011). The example of Belo Horizonte is being taken up in a number of other places. For instance, in Toronto, FoodShare has set up Good Food Markets to sell subsidized fresh local fruits and vegetables in low-income neighbourhoods (Classens, McMurtry, and Sumner 2015). Also in Toronto, The Stop offers an array of services and initiatives, including community gardens and kitchens, after-school cooking and gardening programs, a farmers' market, community advocacy training, a nutrition and support program for new and expectant mothers, and a sustainable food systems education centre (Saul 2011).

Disposal

In sustainable food systems, food would move as short a distance as possible from its place of origin, providing the opportunity for full-circle recycling, thus healing the "metabolic rift" set up by the global corporate food system. Each household and business would either compost all its food waste for its own use or contribute it to neighbourhood composting programs for community gardens or local farms. A current example is the growth of municipal composting programs in Canada.

Implementing Sustainable Food Systems

The components outlined above open up spaces for the transition to sustainable food systems by providing working examples that we can learn from and emulate. As the examples show, sustainable food systems are compatible with a variety of economic realities: they would not eliminate family farms, private enterprise, transnational corporations, or global trade. But they would assume a growing primacy, turning the focus from promoting trade for increased profits to providing nourishing food for everyone, within the ecological limits of the planet.

The implementation of sustainable food systems would involve both top-down and bottom-up approaches at multiple scales. This is in keeping with Hinrichs's (2014:153) contention that transitions to sustainability encompass "vertical and horizontal linkages and processes, including the diverse and evolving drivers and barriers that shape possibilities for food systems change."

The top-down approaches would introduce various forms of civil commons legislation and initiatives at the municipal, provincial, national, and international scales. At the municipal level, the work of Belo Horizonte, Brazil, and the Toronto Food Policy Council offers templates for implementation. At the provincial level, the creation of the Greenbelt around Toronto prevents farmland from being paved over and thus permanently lost to other uses, including agriculture. This establishes a civil commons resource that we can collectively manage into the future. At the national level, the development of a national food policy would complement existing civil commons programs of care such as our national health-care system. And at the international scale, organizations like the Fairtrade Labelling Organizations International and the International Federation of Organic Agriculture Movements provide guidelines for moving international trade toward sustainability parameters.

The bottom-up approaches would entail grassroots projects and initiatives at both the local and the global scales. At the local level, for example, Thompson et al. (2011) describe how the Nisichawayasihk First Nation's Country Food Program in northern Manitoba is providing Nelson House First Nation residents with healthy foods, while building community and creating jobs that honour Aboriginal values. Based on "Cree principles of caring and promoting traditional and healthy ways of life," the hunted and gathered food is distributed for free to as many as 1,500 of the community's 2,500 residents, with priority given to elders, the sick, and low-income, single-parent families (Thompson et al. 2011:13). And in Nova Scotia, Beaton (2011) explains how fishers in the Bay of Fundy have teamed up with the province's oldest environmental organization—the Ecology Action Centre—to launch Atlantic Canada's first **community-supported fishery** called Off the Hook. Modelled on community-supported agriculture, Off the Hook "hopes to showcase a sustainable fishing enterprise that nurtures the connections between communities, economies and the environment" (Beaton 2011:14). At the international level, social movements focused on food act locally and network globally. The food sovereignty, organic, slow food, and fair-trade movements all set the tone for a global food system based on such values as the human right to food, local control, environmentalism, protection of heritage species, cooperation, and fair trade.

While examples abound, however, Deumling et al. (2003) remind us that making them a reality depends on overcoming special interests, providing recognition and financial support, and restructuring the current incentive system that subsidizes and encourages unsustainable behaviour. But making them a reality is worth the effort because:

> The beauty of a sustainable food system is its ability to generate benefits in numerous areas: health, biodiversity, ecological restoration, energy savings, aesthetic values, and economic justice. None of these benefits

alone may outweigh the apparent short-term gains of the current destructive system. But the sum of these benefits will make society far better off and help to avoid the trap of increasing production at the expense of people and the planet. (Deumling et al. 2003:9)

In this way, sustainable food systems can create benefits far beyond the field of food itself. Moreover, the implementation of sustainable food systems "provides an opportunity to generate the operating manual for a sustainable world, while uniting the basic need and pleasure of food with ecological and social responsibility" (Deumling et al. 2003).

Conclusion

As fossil fuels are depleted, food prices fluctuate, the climate destabilizes, and hunger continues to grow, the idea of sustainable food systems becomes more attractive—part of the social safety net of a civilized society. In the best of all possible worlds, sustainable food systems would form one aspect of a larger collective system of public care that provides a variety of life-goods, including health care, energy, transportation, daycare, education, shelter, and water. As Dahlberg (1993) reminds us, sustainable food systems need to be understood both as part of many larger systems and as made up of many smaller systems. And while individualized, charitable responses to the provision of life-goods can have some small, positive effects, only an organized, holistic, systemic public response can address the range and scale of issues we will face in an uncertain future. In other words, we need "a more sustainable, life-giving food system for all" (Feenstra 2002:105).

Currently, our food system is in the hands of the private sector, whose values and practices are geared not for sustainability, but for "profit-maximization, growth and accumulation" (Wallis 2010:35). Contrary to corporate rhetoric, such a system is organized not to feed the world, but to fatten the bank accounts of shareholders and top-level management. In our current system, "basic human needs are not met" (Allen 2008:157). Indeed, food is almost incidental to this system—it just happens to be the chosen vehicle for private enrichment. For this reason, our current food system is not remotely capable of protecting us all against hunger, especially in an era of looming economic, social, and environmental uncertainties.

In the shadow of real hunger now and more crises to come, systems based on the civil commons, anchored in the public domain and focused on the environment have the equity, resilience, power, and reach to address problems in a humane fashion. To avoid the kind of social breakdown that occurred in the aftermath of the flooding of New Orleans, for example, we need solid civil commons infrastructure ready to act for the public good, not the private profit opportunities of "disaster capitalism" (Klein 2007). Sustainable food systems would be part of this infrastructure, built into our modes of thinking, parameters of practice, and ways of life.

Discussion Questions

1. How has the global corporate food system become so powerful?

2. Define the civil commons and describe its role in sustainability.

3. What are sustainable food systems and why are they necessary?

4. Why are pseudo foods not part of sustainable food systems?

5. How is it possible to have more than 1 billion hungry people and more than 1 billion obese people in the world at the same time?

Further Reading

1. American Planning Association. 2007. *Policy Guide on Community and Regional Food Planning.* www.planning.org/policy/guides/adopted/food.htm.
   A practical handbook for considering the issues associated with planning sustainable food systems.

2. Friedmann, Harriet. 1993. "After Midas's Feast: Alternative Food Regimes for the Future." Pp. 213–33 in *Food for the Future: Conditions and Contradictions of Sustainability,* ed. Patricia Allen. New York: John Wiley and Sons.
   A seminal work that uses the myth of King Midas to illustrate how history decisively changed when the magical powers of money became deeply rooted in the real relations among people. Describes both sustainable and unsustainable alternatives to the present food economy.

3. Hill, Stuart. 1984. "Redesigning the Food System for Sustainability." Ecological Agriculture Projects, McGill University. http://eap.mcgill.ca/publications/eap23.htm.
   A classic paper that asks serious questions about food and sustainability.

4. McMichael, Phillip. 2000. "The Power of Food." *Agriculture and Human Values* 17:21–33.
   A timeless article on the power of food to both dominate and liberate people, while examining the role of development in making this happen.

Video Suggestions

1. Dodge, David, and Duncan Kinney. 2014. *Harvest Power: Energy and Compost from Rotten Food.* www.greenenergyfutures.ca/episode/67 -harvest-power-energy-and-compost-rotten- food. 5 min.
2. Kenner, Robert. 2008. *Food Inc.* www.takepart .com/foodinc. 93 min.
3. Ontario Food Terminal Board. 2014. *The Role of the Ontario Food Terminal.* www.youtube.com/ watch?v=pAFo0TZlvd0. 3 min.
4. TED.com. 2013. *Ron Finley: A Guerrilla Gardener in South Central LA.* www.ted.com/talks/ron_fin-ley_a_guerilla_gardener_in_south_central_la .html. 11 min.

References

Agriculture and Agri-Food Canada. 2009. "Government of Canada Invests in Local Wild Mushroom Industry." http://www.marketwired.com/press-release/government -of-Canada-invests-in-local-wild-mushroom-industry -943479.htm.

Albritton, Robert. 2009. *Let Them Eat Junk: How Capitalism Creates Hunger and Obesity.* Winnipeg, MB: Arbeiter Ring Publishing.

Allen, Patricia. 2008. "Mining for Justice in the Food System: Perceptions, Practices and Possibilities." *Agriculture and Human Values* 25:157–61.

Beaton, Sadie. 2011. "Angling for Change." *Alternatives Journal* 37(2):14.

Broughton, Alan. 2011. "Venezuela's Chocolate Solution." *Alternatives Journal* 37(2):20.

Classens, Michael, McMurtry J.J. McMurtry, and Jennifer Sumner. 2015. "Doing Markets Differently: The Case of FoodShare Toronto's Good Food Markets." Pp. 215–35 in *Social Purpose Enterprises: Case Studies for Social Change.* ed. Jack Quarter, Sherida Ryan, and Andrea Chan. Toronto: University of Toronto Press.

Dahlberg, Kenneth A. 1993. "Regenerative Food Systems: Broadening the Scope and Agenda of Sustainability." Pp. 75–102 in *Food for the Future: Conditions and Contradictions of Sustainability*, ed. Patricia Allen. New York: John Wiley and Sons.

Deumling, Diana, Mathis Wackernagel, and Chad Monfreda. 2003. "Eating Up the Earth: How Sustainable Food Systems Shrink Our Ecological Footprint." Agricultural Footprint Brief, Redefining Progress. www.RedefiningProgress.org.

FarmStart. 2015. Start-Up Farms. www.farmstart.ca/programs/ start-up-farms/.

Feenstra, Gail. 2002. "Creating Space for Sustainable Food Systems: Lessons from the Field." *Agriculture and Human Values* 19:99–106.

Friedmann, Harriet. 1993. "After Midas's Feast: Alternative Food Regimes for the Future." Pp. 213–33 in *Food for the Future: Conditions and Contradictions of Sustainability*, ed. Patricia Allen. New York: John Wiley and Sons.

———. 2007. "Scaling Up: Bringing Public Institutions and Food Service Corporations into the Project for a Local, Sustainable Food System in Ontario." *Agriculture and Human Values* 24:389–98.

Goodall, Jane. 2005. *Harvest for Hope: A Guide to Mindful Eating.* New York: Warner Books.

Hay, Alan. 2000. "System." Pp. 818–19 in *The Dictionary of Human Geography*, 4th edn, ed. R.J. Johnston, Derek Gregory, Geraldine Pratt, and Michael Watts. Malden, MA: Blackwell.

Hill, Stuart. 1984. "Redesigning the Food System for Sustainability." Ecological Agriculture Projects, McGill University. Accessed 27 August 2010. http://eap.mcgill.ca/ publications/eap23.htm.

Hinrichs, C. Clare. 2014. "Transitions to Sustainability: A Change in Thinking about Food Systems Change?" *Agriculture and Human Values* 31:143–55.

Johnston, Lucas. 2010. "The Religious Dimensions of Sustainability: Institutional Religions, Civil Society, and International Politics since the Turn of the Twentieth Century." *Religion Compass* 4:176–89.

Kaufman, Jerome L. 2004. "Introduction." *Journal of Planning Education and Research* 23(4):335–40.

Klein, Naomi. 2007. *The Shock Doctrine: The Rise of Disaster Capitalism.* Toronto: Alfred A. Knopf.

Lappé, Francis Moore. 2009. "A Visit to Belo Horizonte: The City that Ended Hunger." www.counterpunch.org/ lappe03182009.html.

Malhi, Luvdeep, Özge Karanfil, Tommy Merth, et al. 2009. "Places to Intervene to Make Complex Food Systems More Healthy, Green, Fair, and Affordable." *Journal of Hunger and Environmental Nutrition* 4:466–76.

McMichael, Phillip. 2000. "The Power of Food." *Agriculture and Human Values* 17:21–33.

McMurtry, John. 1998. *Unequal Freedoms: The Global Market as an Ethical System.* Toronto: Garamond.

———. 1999. "The Lifeground, the Civil Commons and Global Development." Paper presented at the annual meeting of the Canadian Association for Studies in International Development, Congress of the Social Sciences and Humanities, Sherbrooke, QC, 7 June.

ONFC (Ontario Natural Food Co-op) 2015. "Mission, Vision, and Values." www.onfc.ca/mission-vision-values.

Patel, Raj. 2007. *Stuffed and Starved: Markets, Power and the Hidden Battle for the World's Food System.* Toronto: HarperCollins.

Polanyi, K. 2001. *The Great Transformation: The Political and Economic Origins of Our Time.* Boston: Beacon Press.

Pollan, Michael. 2008. *In Defence of Food.* New York: Penguin Press.

Power, Elaine M. 1999. "Combining Social Justice and Sustainability for Food Security." Pp. 30–7 in *For Hunger-Proof Cities: Sustainable Urban Food Systems,* ed. Mustafa Koç, Rod MacRae, Luc J.A. Mougeot, and Jennifer Welsh. Ottawa: International Development Research Centre.

Roberts, Wayne. 2011. "Taking It All In." *Alternatives Journal* 37(2):8–10.

Saul, Nick. 2011. "No Stopping the Stop." *Alternatives Journal* 37(2):11.

Shearman, Richard. 1990. "The Meaning and Ethics of Sustainability." *Environmental Management* 14(1):1–8.

Simon, Michele. 2006. *Appetite for Profit: How the Food Industry Undermines Our Health and How to Fight Back.* New York: Nation Books.

Sumner, Jennifer. 2005. *Sustainability and the Civil Commons: Rural Communities in the Age of Globalization.* Toronto: University of Toronto Press.

———. "From Land to Table: Rural Planning and Development for Sustainable Food Systems." Pp. 179–224 in *Rural Planning and Development in Canada,* ed. David Douglas. Toronto: Nelson Education.

Thompson, Shirley, Asfia Gulrukh, and Aruna Murthy. 2011. "Back to Traditional Aboriginal Food." *Alternatives Journal* 37(2):13.

Wallis, Victor. 2010. "Beyond 'Green Capitalism.'" *Monthly Review* 61(9):32–48.

WCED (World Commission on Environment and Development). 1987. *Our Common Future.* New York: Oxford University Press.

Webb, Margaret. 2011. "Fire in Their Bellies." *Alternatives Journal* 37(2):27–8.

Winson, Anthony. 2004. "Bringing Political Economy into the Debate on the Obesity Epidemic." *Agriculture and Human Values* 21:299–312.

Ziegler, Jean. 2004. "The Right to Food." Report of the Special Rapporteur of the United Nations Commission on Human Rights, submitted to the General Assembly, New York.

22 Actualizing Sustainable Food Systems

Ashley McInnes and Phil Mount

Learning Objectives

Through this chapter, you can

1. Explore theories behind strategies to develop a sustainable food system
2. Examine how actors navigate within and around the food system that they are trying to change
3. Consider the implications of alternative food strategies that grow in scale
4. Understand how discourse that supports the industrial food system impacts perceptions of possibilities for food system change

Introduction

Food systems conversations in the twenty-first century are becoming increasingly complex, as producers, consumers, rural and urban communities, academics, and policy makers embrace the potential of food to address a set of interconnected issues—from nutrition and health to livelihoods and regional development (Blouin, Lemay, Ashraf, and Imai 2009). Since regional food systems are built both as alternative to and yet also within existing policy, regulatory, and legislative structures, these conversations and possibilities are framed by a global industrial food system built on liberalization of trade (Clapp 2009), corporate concentration of ownership (Rosset 2008), neo-liberal discourse (Holt-Giménez and Altieri 2013) and resource depletion (Weis 2010). These structures—and the discourse that supports them—play an important role in guiding how we think about food systems change (Marsden 2013). While the potential benefits of ecologically regenerative, socially just, community-based food systems are well rehearsed in the literature, an equally compelling body of research has identified theoretical and practical barriers, minefields that stand in the way of that potential. The pervasive reach of food systems—that makes food such a powerful vehicle for enacting strategies for sustainability—also makes these strategies susceptible to the influence of interdependent systems operating at scales from local to global, including ecological, climatic, financial, regulatory, trade, and **governance** systems (Bernstein 2014). This chapter explores significant theories behind strategies to develop sustainable food systems by examining how food system actors navigate within and around the food system that they are trying to change; the targets, priorities, and practices that they employ; and how these strategies account for the implications of scale.

Theorizing Food Systems Change

Precisely which strategies can best develop a sustainable food system has been the source of much debate in the food systems literature, and food scholars have applied a number of frameworks for understanding strategies used to create systemic change (e.g. Hinrichs 2014; Holt-Giménez and Shattuck 2011). In this chapter, these strategies are organized on a spectrum from minor adjustments to amend the current food system, to gradual shifts that facilitate transition, to fundamental changes that transform, or to a hybrid that will demonstrate alternative values—through successes at the community level—and the possibilities for fundamental change to the broader food system (see table 22.1). This section outlines the theories behind these four strategies, and identifies the ways in which each strategy supports working within or in opposition to the current food system.

Strategy 1—Amend: The Sustainable Intensification Debate

Proponents of "amend" strategies seek small changes to the current food system that could have large impacts by producing more food—and improving food security—while reducing negative environmental consequences. Working within existing food system structures, "amend" strategies are largely focused on technological innovations and transferring productionist

Table 22.1 Strategies for Food Systems Change

	Amend (Within)	Transition (Around)	Transform (In opposition)	Demonstrate (Within the cracks)
Priorities	Producing more food with lower environmental and social impact	Creating, replicating, and networking of alternative structures	Dismantling of corporate monopolies and enhancement of food sovereignty	Nurturing the values necessary for sustainable systems
Possibilities	Small modifications; a "greening" of the industrial food system and more food in areas where hunger is prevalent; very little (if any) structural change is possible	Slow transition toward a better food system through provision of alternatives	Radical and fundamental transformation of the economic, political, and food systems; structural change at all levels (community to international)	Demonstration of feasibility of alternatives through community-based action that changes values and governance
Focus	Technology: Green and efficient production methods	People: Locally adapted production methods; reconnection of producers and consumers	Regulations, power, and control (resource distribution [land, water, seed], equitable food distribution, community autonomy)	Shared social understanding of what is possible and viable, and what should be valued
Means	Technology improvements (higher yield, greener) and transfer to regions with low yields; strategies for implementing technology into sustainable food production systems	Providing alternatives to the conventional food system; producer and consumer awareness of alternative options; scaling out existing alternatives	Demands for political changes to national and international regulatory structures (e.g. trade, labour, patents, land access)	Community-based action that changes values: takes advantage of devolution, regionally uneven development

technologies to low-producing regions. Scholars who advocate **sustainable intensification** as a means to improve the food system largely fall into this camp of strategies (Garnett et al. 2013). The spread of Green Revolution technologies—including high-yielding seed varieties, machinery, synthetic pesticides, and fertilizers—has increased global food production, but the technologies have not reached all regions, and have also caused a number of environmental impacts (see Weis, chapter 9 in this volume; Pretty 2008). Scholars in this camp are concerned with reducing such impacts while meeting the needs of the rising global population, which is expected to reach 9 billion by 2050 and is increasingly consuming high-calorie and resource-intensive foods—e.g. processed foods, meat, and dairy foods—while a larger number of people are going hungry around the globe. Primary food system concerns include the need to reduce world hunger, meet rising food demand, and do so under increasing environmental stress due to climate change and declining land, water, and energy resources (Godfray et al. 2010).

Suggesting that global food production will need to rise by 70 per cent, scholars who advocate sustainable intensification emphasize technological innovations that must be implemented in highly productive regions and transferred to under-producing regions (Godfray et al. 2010). Given increasing competition for land and other resources and the ecological costs of clearing new land for food production, emphasis is placed on intensifying production on existing farmland while making better use of resources, inputs, and technologies (Garnett et al. 2013).

Some are careful to acknowledge that technological enhancement only leads to sustainable intensification when it reduces or eliminates ecological harm, and must be implemented in concert with enhanced use of ecological goods and services, collective action and human capital (Pretty 2008). However, for others the push to increase production takes priority over the means by which this is accomplished. Some have suggested that production could be raised by as much as 58 per cent by closing **yield gaps**—the difference between actual and potential yield in a particular location, given existing agricultural technology and practice (Foley et al. 2011). Yield gaps of over 50 per cent currently exist in much of Africa, Latin America, and Eastern Europe, and closing yield gaps could improve food security without cultivating additional land (Foley et al. 2011). Important innovations here include yield-enhancing technology combined with agricultural practices and technologies that reduce the environmental impacts of conventional food production. Technological strategies for developing a sustainable food system are commonly supported in international policy circles including the World Bank and the Food and Agriculture Organization of the United Nations (Holt-Giménez and Shattuck 2011).

But is there a need to raise global food production? Currently over 2,800 dietary calories per person per day are produced (FAO 2013), which is more than 600 calories above average caloric requirement. Yet almost 1.5 billion adults are overweight or obese (Popkin, Adair, and Ng 2012) while over 800 million people are undernourished (FAO 2013). In light of this inequity, increasing food production may not be sufficient to reduce hunger (Misselhorn et al. 2012). Critics of sustainable intensification argue that it focuses too closely on technological fixes that did not work during the Green Revolution and do not address the structural barriers created by trade liberalization, corporate concentration, and inequitable distribution of resources, thereby doing little to support a sustainable food system (Holt-Giménez 2013). Strategies that emphasize technological solutions have been criticized for ignoring inequitable distribution and the power relations involved in social systems (Lawhon and Murphy 2011). For instance, who owns the proposed technological innovations, and who will benefit by their implementation?

These criticisms indicate practical barriers to implementing sustainable intensification; strategies that do not directly engage those most affected by their implementation may not effectively address the needs of those that the strategies seek to support. As a result, proponents of "transition," "transform," and "demonstrate" strategies reject the focus on technology and argue that people-centred strategies are more likely to help those most affected by crises in the food system—and create sustainable food systems (Holt-Giménez 2014).

Strategy 2—Transition: Providing Alternatives to the Industrial Food System

"Transition" strategies, also termed "alternative" (Allen, FitzSimmons, Goodman, and Warner 2003) or "progressive" (Holt-Giménez and Shattuck 2011), emphasize solutions that are profoundly different from the industrial food system without directly challenging that system. Working around the industrial food system, rather than explicitly opposing it, transition strategies are primarily implemented at the community level. The means for implementing transition strategies include practical or "on-the-ground" initiatives that target local priorities by allowing individuals to opt out of the industrial food system without directly challenging that system. Transition strategies occur primarily through initiatives to shorten supply chains and reconnect producers and consumers.

Transition strategies are guided by the assumptions that creating alternative food markets and relationships, and eating differently, can change the food system (Goodman, DuPuis, and Goodman 2014). Watts, Ilbery, and Maye (2005) differentiate weak alternative market-based initiatives, which are based on product characteristics (e.g. organic) and may be susceptible to corporate co-optation and thus do little to transform the food system (see Knezevic, chapter 16 in this volume), and strong alternatives, which are based on networks (e.g. farmers' markets; consumer–farmer relations) and may be important in creating a sustainable food system (Watts et al. 2005). Similarly, Fridell (2009)

differentiates co-operative fair-trade businesses such as Planet Bean in Guelph, Ontario, and corporate social-responsibility fair-trade agendas such as that implemented by Starbucks. Through Planet Bean, coffee producers are directly linked with café workers, who can build relationships with consumers (Fridell 2009). While Planet Bean maintains a commitment to consumer education, equitable North–South trade relations, and promoting structural change, Starbucks completes the minimum action needed to reduce public criticism and capture profits in the fair-trade niche market (Fridell 2009). Starbucks's weak commitment to fair trade is demonstrated by its efforts to manipulate consumer perceptions, questionable labour practices in the global North (e.g. use of exploitative prison labour and fighting unionization efforts), and development of an alternative private supplier program with stronger environmental standards but weaker social justice standards (e.g. linking coffee bean prices to market fluctuations) than the Fair Trade certification used by Planet Bean (Fridell 2009). While lowering standards can increase corporate involvement in labelling initiatives and has resulted in a greater proportion of production under these standards, this may do little to change the food system as a whole (Friedmann 2005).

Another key premise of transition strategies is that the replication—or "scaling out"—and networking of locally based initiatives acts to create simultaneously both templates for locally based action and the collaboration necessary for a "movement of movements" (Blay-Palmer et al. 2013). Critics have identified two barriers to the effectiveness of this approach: the seemingly incompatible priorities of many of these initiatives, including viable farm incomes and food access (Allen et al. 2003; Mount 2012), and the ineffectiveness of fragmented and local-scale initiatives that address symptoms rather than the structural, state, and global causes of their problems (Holt-Giménez and Shattuck 2011).

A third theoretical barrier—for practical initiatives based in markets—is the "trickle-down" assumption that the shopping habits of elite consumers create demand for healthier, greener food items, eventually making these items more affordable for all (Friedmann 2005). In the neo-liberal context, rising consumer demand for organic/quality food items may result in a combination of lower state-enforced standards and higher voluntary standards, exacerbating existing social inequalities as wealthy consumers purchase healthy, organic, high-quality food, while poor consumers are left to purchase highly processed, low-quality food (Friedmann 2005). This assumption is based in individualistic neo-liberal logic, and distracts from necessary broad, systemic changes while privileging elite consumers and corporations that profit from the niche markets (e.g. organic, fair trade) promoted in these initiatives (Fairbairn 2012; Levkoe 2011).

As such, some scholars suggest that many transition strategies represent mild reforms that will do little to create transformative change in the food system without policy support garnered through demands for fundamental systemic change (Holt-Giménez and Shattuck 2011).

Strategy 3—Transform: Opposition, Protest, and Food Sovereignty

Holt-Giménez and Shattuck (2011) describe the current food system as a set of "tragic records": "record levels of hunger for the world's poor at a time of record global harvests as well as record profits for the world's major agrifoods corporations" (p. 111). Taking a strong stance against productivism, these scholars argue that capital-intensive technology is a key *problem* in the food system, rather than a solution (Hinrichs 2014). Indeed, Holt-Giménez (2013) argues that farmers "are losing their seeds, soil, land and livelihoods as a *result* of the expansion of the large-scale, capitalist agriculture" (p. 970) that characterizes the current food system. Over the past 30 years, low food prices combined with high input costs—including farming technologies and proprietary seeds—drove peasant and family farmers away from farming in both the global North and South. However, despite this

seemingly persistent "*crisis* of low prices" (Rosset 2008:460), today, in an era of corporate control over the food system, we are experiencing a crisis of high prices in which people who may have previously grown their own food are going hungry. As such, these scholars argue that little will change without addressing the challenges that tools of the industrial food system—including proprietary technologies, free markets, privatization of resources, monopolies, and corporate power—create for small-scale agro-ecological peasant and family farmers (e.g. Holt-Giménez 2013; Rosset 2008).

For these researchers, the rising food sovereignty movement that protests against the industrial food system is necessary to develop a sustainable food system (Rosset 2008). These scholars call for initiatives that explicitly oppose the industrial food system, and support fundamental transformation by dismantling corporate monopolies and building policy that supports equitable redistribution of land, water, and seed resources (Holt-Giménez and Shattuck 2011). Transforming the food system through broad structural changes requires collective action against the neo-liberal ideology that guides the industrial food system (Guthman 2008) and social pressure to force policy changes (Rosset 2008).

Another key focus in transform strategies emphasizes agro-ecological production methods to improve farmers' livelihoods and reduce the environmental impacts of agriculture by respecting traditional farming practices and reducing dependence on costly inputs, proprietary technologies, and seeds (Fernandez et al. 2012; Rosset 2008). Agro-ecological practices improve farm resilience and reduce negative environmental impacts of agriculture by applying ecosystem principles to farming and using biodiversity and natural cycling to reduce inputs that adversely affect the environment (Koohafkan et al. 2012). A study of subsistence farmers in India found that shifting from locally adapted seeds to high-yielding varieties led to a loss of genetic diversity in crops, which reduced crop resilience to environmental stresses such as pests and extreme weather (Bisht et al. 2014). As such, some scholars argue that agro-ecology supports social and environmental values not provided by highly productive monocultures (Pant 2014).

Two important barriers stand in the way of this strategy: the scale of action required for structural change and the inertia of policy makers. Collective action and social pressure "in opposition" has proven difficult to mobilize—particularly in those societies where the discourse of neo-liberalism has fractured the "common-sense" understanding of the collective social articulation of values. So far the food movement has been more successful in achieving behavioural change (i.e. ethical consumption choices) than the political change envisioned by early activists (Goodman et al. 2014). Bernstein (2014) argues that the expectation of political change based on the tenets of food sovereignty is unreasonable, given the diversity of actors and interests—from peasants to low-income consumers—and the scale of the program necessary to implement change. The latter would involve coordinated efforts to address numerous factors that shape global food systems, including trade liberalization, financialization, austerity, concentration throughout the food chain, control of genetic material, agrofuels, and fossil fuel addiction (Bernstein 2014). As a result, some scholars argue that, while policy-oriented initiatives are important, widespread political change will not happen instantly, and therefore political pragmatism, or a willingness to negotiate, compromise, and accept incremental results is required, since "there are no clear, practical alternatives to incremental change at this time" (Hassanein 2003:84).

While wholesale policy changes may be extremely important for long-term sustainability, many of these policies may take years, if not decades, to implement (MacRae 2011). Perhaps most importantly, policy changes can only be implemented so far as policy makers accept them. If calls for policy change are perceived as unfeasible by policy makers, these calls are unlikely to be heeded. This applies not only to radical changes such as state-level redistribution or reallocation of resources, but also to smaller changes that might rattle the "lock-in mechanisms" of the existing food supply chain, including sunk investments in infrastructure, existing training/expertise, firm values and discourse, power and lobby groups that resist change, and consumer lifestyle and preferences (Geels 2011).

Strategy 4—Demonstrate: Collective Impact

Given the theoretical and practical barriers of transition and "transform" strategies, a number of scholars suggest that alternative food system structures and practices must not only help to shape social practice but also demonstrate what is possible by transforming how regional food systems are organized and governed (Lowitt et al., in press). That is, it is not enough that alternative structures are "outside" of conventional market chains or that alternative practices are "different" or innovative: that difference, that innovation must integrate and demonstrate a core set of fundamental values—including collective subjectivities (Levkoe 2011), increased equity, and democratization of control (Cadieux and Slocum 2015)—that are both central and shared strategic priorities. Many have suggested that, since food movements are fragmented in their goals and approaches to the food crisis, there may be a need for "convergence in diversity" (Constance, Friedland, Renard, and Rivera-Ferre 2014) or a common platform that respects this diversity while providing a unified alliance that both protests against the industrial food system and provides an alternative to it (Amin 2011; Mount et al. 2013). This necessitates the construction of broad-based consensus through alliances that pull together farm and food system advocates and demonstrate the full range of value that alternative practices can bring to ecosystem and community resilience, health, and well-being. Such a strategy will entail repoliticization of change strategies by bringing together those working on political or structural issues and those working "on the ground" to share knowledge and experiences, develop a shared understanding of what must be valued in a sustainable food system, and advance feasible actions and policies to build that system (Amin 2011; Holt-Giménez and Shattuck 2011).

"Demonstrate" strategies differ from transition strategies to the extent that they explicitly identify alternative values that are essential to sustainable systems. Practical initiatives create **collective impact** by filling "cracks" in the industrial food system, providing pressure from within the system to open up new spaces of possibility for structural change (Gibson-Graham and Cameron 2007). For instance, agro-ecological production practices and direct markets provide pragmatic actions and everyday practices that may be needed to supplement the broader movements for political change (e.g. Fernandez et al. 2012; Wittman 2009). The need to link political demands with agro-ecology to achieve social, economic, and environmental goals are increasingly apparent as "both NGOs and the farmers realize that simply producing more food more ecologically will not save their livelihoods from the enclosures of the corporate food regime" (Holt-Giménez and Shattuck 2011:126). In a study of farmer-based political initiatives in Brazil, only after rejecting industrial agriculture practices and adopting agro-ecological practices were farmers able to achieve economic stability (Holt-Giménez 2009). Additionally, the initiatives support policy change by combining advocacy with action through founding schools that integrate agro-ecological training with agrarian advocacy (Holt-Giménez 2009).

Of course, as with any broadly defined categorization, the limits of "demonstrate" strategies will be tested. For example, some have suggested that, in the global North—where there are far more consumers than producers—market-based initiatives may provide an opportunity to engage members of the public uncomfortable with political activism (Stevenson, Ruhf, Lezberg, and Clancy 2007). Indeed, market-based initiatives may be vital for successful political action, if policy change requires public awareness and collective action (Stevenson et al. 2007). Further, if transforming the food system "depends on entrenching alternative values ever more deeply in everyday practices" (Goodman et al. 2014:5), then one means for bringing alternative values into everyday practices is through market-based initiatives that engage a broad spectrum of community members (Stevenson et al. 2007). Therefore, the expansion of alternative markets that enhance social and environmental values, are notably distinct from capitalist markets that value only economic returns, and create community value change through everyday practice will in fact support broader structural change (Andrée, Ballamingie, and Sinclair-Waters 2014).

For many of these scholars, the discourse of the "opposition" strategy paints a totalizing view of neo-liberal political structures that precludes the potential for alternatives to transform the food system (Andrée et al. 2014; Gibson-Graham and Cameron 2007). This capitalocentric thinking ignores the ways in which community-based market initiatives are different from traditional capitalist markets, and instead sees all forms of economic activity in relation to capitalism—whether "the same as, the opposite of, a complement to, or contained within capitalism" (Gibson-Graham and Cameron 2007:23). Criticisms of market-based initiatives—that assume such initiatives unavoidably reflect capitalism and neo-liberalism-by-association—may serve to undermine the transformative potential of such alternatives since "if there is nothing untouched by capitalism, there is no place to stand from which to combat it" (Gibson-Graham and Cameron 2007:21). Focusing too closely on whether market-based initiatives represent true alternatives to the dominant market structure may undermine and weaken community support for alternatives (Gibson-Graham 2006). Rather than focusing on the ways in which current market structures inhibit change, Gibson-Graham and Cameron (2007) advocate the politics of the possible—searching for cracks or spaces of possibility and focusing instead on the ways in which such initiatives demonstrate a desire to transform the dominant economic model.

Political initiatives that work within neo-liberal structures may have greater potential for adoption (and thus transformation) than radical calls for dismantling existing policies precisely "because of the appearance of mere reformism" (Mount and Andrée 2013:588). Eaton (2013) demonstrates this model in her investigation of the 2001 coalition to ban Roundup Ready (RR) wheat in Canada, which included environmental organizations, consumer interest groups, and producer organizations. Given federal commitment to market competitiveness and export-oriented agriculture, and an insistence by RR proponents that the only appropriate method for determining the suitability of RR wheat in Canada was through the market—i.e. by introducing the product and allowing individual choice to dictate RR wheat sales—the coalition's most convincing argument to ban RR wheat was to demonstrate that RR wheat would threaten Canada's competitiveness in export markets. Working within neo-liberal logic allowed the coalition greater success than a call for dismantling corporate power.

While alternative food initiatives are constrained by neo-liberal structures, they simultaneously influence these structures (Mount and Andrée 2013). As a result of neo-liberal processes of devolution that saw a downloading of responsibilities to regional and local governments—without attendant funding—Mount and Andrée (2013) found an increasing prevalence of hybrid food initiatives made up of public–civil society organization (CSO) partnerships, where government agencies partner with non-profits in order to access alternative funding and deliver public services. Hybrid public–CSO initiatives "may produce a strong base for strategic alliances with widespread discursive appeal and legitimacy" to policy makers (Mount and Andrée 2013:588). Developing new forms of governance not only within but because of the neo-liberal context "constitutes an important point of egress for AFNs, allowing local and regional actors to

re-frame their relations in a common-sense manner, and negotiate regionally responsive policies and regulation" (Mount and Andrée 2013:588).

There is no doubt that actions in hybrid spaces are susceptible to co-optation, a possibility in any complex governance arrangement that invites both democratization and diverse priorities. Additionally, spaces neglected by the state lack state funding, making any initiatives inhabiting these spaces precarious. Finally, by addressing the negative outcomes of neo-liberalization without specifically highlighting and challenging root causes, these actions face the charge that they are simply dressing wounds while providing implicit support for neo-liberal policies. Yet where such acts demonstrate the possibility of alternative value constructions that respond to local needs, they demonstrate the potential of strategies that operate within the cracks of neo-liberalism.

Visualizing Sustainable Food Systems: Implications of Scale

As scholars and food systems practitioners theorize *how* to develop sustainable food systems, they must also consider *what*, precisely a sustainable food system entails—in terms not only of values but also of the infrastructure and policy that supports those values. Given the increasing market share of organic and fair-trade alternatives, combined with characteristics such as product certification and global supply chains that make such alternatives compatible with the conventional food system, these two initiatives may most effectively support the development of a sustainable food system. Yet while both organic and fair-trade initiatives have improved aspects of the conventional food system in terms of environmental and social standards, respectively, they have also suffered from consumer skepticism and criticism over relaxed standards and the conventionalization of production and marketing practices (Guthman 2004; Lockie and Halpin 2005; Smith and Marsden 2004). Conventionalization occurs when an alternative niche falls prey to increased competition, intensification of production, concentration of markets, falling premiums, and a loss of producer control (for discussion, see Mount and Smithers 2014). The spectre of conventionalization limits what change strategies are possible, since sustainable food systems must be based on long-term viability for producers; structures that reproduce conventional outcomes—that is, food chains based on diminishing returns and lack of producer control—will only serve to discourage producers who are looking to alternative systems for alternative outcomes (Mount and Smithers 2014).

Such criticisms imply that local food systems may be better suited to support sustainable food systems. Yet one of the challenges of developing sustainable food systems stems from the fact that many of the factors that influence these systems—including trade, investment, regulations, and governance—operate across multiple scales, from local to global. These factors are primarily designed to facilitate global conventional food systems, yet they often raise barriers that interfere with the operations of alternative and local food systems. Most often these barriers come in the form of subsidies that lower the prices of conventional products and regulations designed to ensure that food produced and processed in large-scale industrial facilities meet food safety or international trade standards—regulations that are entirely inappropriate to the scale and practices of regional food systems (Blay-Palmer, Landman, Knezevic, and Hayhurst 2013; Mount et al. 2013).

In North America, despite the growth over the last decade of direct sales and alternative initiatives, most local food markets remain under-supplied (Boecker and Micheels 2015; Low et al. 2015). One persistent critique suggests that, without an increase in scale that involves more people, more food, and a larger proportion of economic activity, they will not have a significant impact on the broader food system (Goodman 2004; Mount 2012; Stevenson and

Pirog 2008). While education and demonstration are critical components of the modern, increasingly urban sustainable food system, in order to provide a platform for sustainable food system development and regional self-reliance (Clancy and Ruhf 2010), these alternatives must include and incorporate increased production for localized markets in peri-urban and rural regions. Of course, while increasing in scale, these alternatives must not only avoid reproducing the issues of the systems that they are replacing, they must also be seen to actively address those issues. Practically, this means that alternative systems must avoid potential pitfalls—including conventionalization and conflicts in managing supply—while developing alternative infrastructure and methods of governance, in order to increase in scale while producing sustainable outcomes.

While much of the early Canadian growth in alternatives has resulted from *scaling out*—that is, reproducing successful, small initiatives in multiple communities—for many the question remains whether these initiatives can *scale up* without losing important values and legitimacy. While small-scale alternatives could increase efficiencies through increased scales of operation, the challenge comes in doing so without sacrificing qualities that are essential to the success of small-scale initiatives, including transparency, accountability, trust, reassurance, and authenticity (Mount 2012; Rogers and Fraszczak 2014). In this regard, the lessons of the conventionalization of the organic sector serve as a cautionary tale for many alternatives. Increased scale without appropriate attention to methods that ensure viable farm incomes and enhance the connections between producers and consumers will create the conditions for the reproduction of conventional outcomes (Mount and Smithers 2014).

One significant barrier to scaling up is the fact that the aggregation, processing, distribution, and marketing infrastructure that would support local or regional-scale systems either has disappeared or is ill-equipped to meet the requirements of modern, alternative markets. While appropriate physical infrastructure receives much attention and funding in this regard (Mount 2012), without matching social infrastructure these changes will not demonstrate a viable alternative or build the support required to challenge the status quo. This social infrastructure must build alternative ways of valuing and interacting within a governance structure that fits together the complex human interests, priorities, and relationships—and their food chain—in ways that make sense. Sustainable food systems require a fine balance between elements that may appear incompatible on a spreadsheet, including producer viability, ecological enhancement, and broader social accessibility to fresh, nutritious food. Infrastructure to reproduce these systems will almost certainly require new organizational and governance structures—including co-operative and not-for-profit elements that encourage regional collaboration (Lamine 2015; Pirog, Harper, Gerencer, et al. 2014; Sumner, McMurtry, and Renglich 2014), allow for the negotiation of diverse priorities (Mount 2012), and enable the development of shared markets and values-based food supply chains (Clancy and Ruhf 2010; Renglich 2015).

However, it is early days for these efforts to scale up. Attempts to fit new alternatives into existing food distribution and marketing structures have run up against the rationales and practices that drive those structures (Bloom and Hinrichs 2010). Many communities and regions are investing in or otherwise encouraging new infrastructure—including both market-driven and co-op food hubs—as a means of offering maximum return to producers while maintaining transparency and connections throughout the food chain (Cantrell and Heuer 2014), and delivering regional economic multiplier effects (Schmit, Jablonski, and Kay 2013). It remains to be seen which models can balance the seemingly incompatible over the long term—that is, whether market-based models can balance profit with increased community food access

and ecological benefits, or alternative models can deliver producer viability along with social justice and fresh, nutritious food.

Whether scaling up or scaling out, pressures of managing and maintaining supply are inevitable (Mount, in press)—as success will attract more producers looking for high rates of return, and with increased supply, market pressures will push prices down. At the same time, larger numbers of "players" will inevitably increase the number of differing priorities to be reconciled, leading to more complex, messier governance structures. This is a critically important concern for those advocating the "collective impact" theory of food systems change. As various alternative political and practical initiatives converge, there is a need to consider which sorts of policies and governance structures support collaboration. Movements are not built on assumptions of shared values and goals, derived from umbrella concepts—such as "peasant," "food sovereignty" or "ethical consumer" (see Bernstein 2014)—but on willingness and ability to appreciate and accommodate diverse priorities, extract commonalities, and work toward mutually beneficial food systems. Collaboration is essential to produce tangible, identifiable regional examples that will demonstrate alternative value conceptions, challenge accepted wisdom, and therefore serve more effectively to garner support in the context of productivist and neo-liberal discourse that supports and entrenches the conventional agri-food system.

The defining features of neo-liberalism include privatization of what is public and marketization of everything else; deregulation to reduce state interference in the free market and reregulation to provide state interference that facilitates privatization and marketization; running public services as if they were businesses; and encouraging civil society to provide public services that do not lend themselves to bottom-line business assessments (see Castree 2008). The latter is particularly relevant to the reform, transition, and demonstrate strategies which, by ameliorating the worst of the social and environmental effects of the current system without addressing root causes, could be accused of creating the conditions for its reproduction.

Neo-liberalization relies fundamentally on a discourse which delivers the tenets of neo-liberalism with the ring of common sense. Eaton (2013) suggests that neo-liberalism in practice not only aims to adjust political economic policies in favour of agri-business, it also aims to influence how people understand the world, thereby influencing how people act. Neo-liberal discourse influences how people (such as farmers, social movement actors, and Canadians) perceive what is possible (Guthman 2008) and "makes certain policies and explanations seem natural . . . and others seem unfair" (Eaton 2013:xv).

While proponents of neo-liberalism extol the benefits of unfettered capitalism, "the very idea that the state *can* be taken out of the market is not based on the actual history of capitalism [which] reveals that capitalist social and political relations have always required a strong state to create and reproduce them" (Fridell 2013:13). These mutually reinforced bonds shape the food system: corporate influence led to neo-liberal restructuring in the Canadian food system during the 1980s (Qualman 2011), and continues to this day—for example, in multinational free-trade agreements (Fridell 2013). Trade agreements are market rules constructed by the state, and the state is a key player in ensuring the rules are followed (Fridell 2013). While proponents of capitalism may oppose state interference through social and environmental regulations, they rely on an authoritative state, both to enter into and to uphold trade agreements and capitalist market structures.

Some strategies, including those based on sustainable intensification, may place too much power in neo-liberalism and capitalism as monoliths that enforce a food system that cannot be changed—only amended. Yet strategies that advocate transformation of the food system through political demands may leave no place to stand from which to combat neo-liberalism. Other strategies find space to work around neo-liberal structures and create pockets of alternatives within the industrial food system, viewing these pockets as cracks within neo-liberalism that could be expanded to change the food system as a whole; cracks that demonstrate the possibilities for a more sustainable food system built on social equity, environmental justice, and economies that support communities.

Conclusion

While scholars have advocated a variety of strategies for developing sustainable food systems, the highest transformative potential may result from a strategy that supplements a broader movement for political change with pragmatic everyday practice (Marsden and Franklin 2013). Strategies that are capital intensive, technology based, and focused on increasing production may exacerbate key problems in food system sustainability, as such solutions do not drastically differ from those offered by the Green Revolution, which did little to alleviate widespread hunger, loss of peasant and family farmers, and environmental degradation (Holt-Giménez 2013). Some scholars instead see solutions in strategies that centre on people, whether through the provision of alternatives, demands for radical reform that supports producers and consumers, or a demonstration of collective values. Solutions based in political change are logistically complex, while solutions based in practice may suffer from parochialism. To build a sustainable food system may require a strategy that infuses solutions based in practice with the capacity to demonstrate the need for, and feasibility of, political change.

Advocates and practitioners must converge to facilitate transformative change since neither demands for radical change nor community-based initiatives will change the food system alone (Transnational Institute 2012). There is some evidence for growing convergence in Canada, as research has shown that many food organizations operate simultaneously within public, private, and community spheres, and that core priorities and projects change over time as new challenges and opportunities arise (Mount and Andrée 2013). Hybridity and fluidity within organizations indicate the difficulty in attempting to classify alternative food organizations as utilizing one of transition, transform, or demonstrate strategies. In turn, the difficulty of classifying food-movement practices highlights the challenges inherent in creating distinct strategies in theory, based on food-movement practices and approaches that often overlap or complement one another, even within one organization. These theoretical barriers provide an optimistic vision of the potential for the food movement to change the food system, as the overlap demonstrates possibilities for movement-building through alliances between diverse organizations. Additionally, the overlap demonstrates possible spaces and mechanisms for collaboration—between organizations, between those with diverse priorities, between political and pragmatic strategies—that will be essential in developing a sustainable food system.

Although there is a clear need for political change to facilitate development of a sustainable food system, initiatives that create alternatives within the current food system may be an important first step toward this change, particularly considering the current popularity of these initiatives (Marsden and Franklin 2013). Production-oriented and certain forms of market-based activities (i.e. network-based markets) provide an opportunity to engage in pragmatic, on-the-ground activities simultaneously with broader initiatives for political change (Goodman et al. 2014; Wittman 2009). Systemic change demands community engagement; initiatives that aim to engage consumers may be necessary to ensure that policy outcomes are supported by the public (Hinrichs 2014). That is, the prevalence of alternative markets may provide the means for creating a change in what people view as possible.

Yet as alternative markets increase in scale—by either scaling up or scaling out—we must consider carefully the qualities and values needed in a sustainable food system, and whether (and which) trade-offs must be made to maintain adequate food supplies. Infrastructure required to reproduce this system includes new organizational and governance structures—including co-operative and not-for-profit elements of the true food value chain. Balancing essential scale production in peri-urban and rural regions may be needed in the modern, increasingly urban sustainable food system, and education and demonstration are critical components of food system change strategies. Changing public perceptions of the way things are, the way they ought to be, and the possibilities for getting there may help destabilize the monolith of neo-liberalism and allow niche alternative markets to expand their reach, ultimately leading to the development of a sustainable food system.

Discussion Questions

1. What are some ways that individuals can support broad change in the food system?

2. What problems remain unsolved if we rely on technology to improve our food systems?

3. Would the value that adheres to "local food" be lost at a greater scale?

4. How does "neo-liberalization" influence what we think is possible as we aim to create a more sustainable food system?

Further Reading

1. Garnett, T., M.C. Appleby, A. Balmford, et al. 2013. "Sustainable Intensification in Agriculture: Premises and Policies." *Science* 341:33–4. doi: 10.1126/science.1234485

   This article defines *sustainable intensification* and explores the potential for this strategy to improve food security in the context of climate change and a growing global population. The authors outline four key premises that must underlie sustainable intensification: increasing food production, containing the increased production on existing farmland, improving environmental sustainability, and emphasizing context-dependent agricultural techniques.

2. Gibson-Graham, J.K., and J. Cameron. 2007. "Community Enterprises: Imagining and Enacting Alternatives to Capitalism." *Social Alternatives* 26(1):20–5.

   Gibson-Graham and Cameron consider how community enterprises (i.e. enterprises that combine economic goals with community benefit goals) provide an alternative to capitalism. The authors deconstruct common criticisms of these alternatives, including their lack of economic competitiveness; reinforcement of the hollowed-out, neo-liberal state by taking on state responsibilities; powerful capitalist structures that cannot be overcome; and their individualistic nature. Arguing that such criticisms serve to undermine these enterprises as alternatives, and separating capitalism from market activity, the authors provide a platform from which to stand to combat capitalism. They consider ways in which scholars and activists might support community enterprises, through both action research and purposeful consideration of alternatives to instigate a material and discursive shift toward a just economic system.

3. Hinrichs, C. 2014. "Transitions to Sustainability: A Change in Thinking about Food Systems Change?" *Agriculture and Human Values.* doi: 10.1007/s10460-014-9479-5

   Providing an overview of the concept "sustainability transitions" within the context of food systems, Hinrichs reviews two key analytical perspectives on sustainability transitions: the "multi-level perspective" (MLP) and the "social practices approach" (SPA). She outlines how these two perspectives can inform, and be informed by, food systems research, arguing that the MLP provides a framework to theorize drivers of sustainable food systems transitions, while the SPA emphasizes the importance of community engagement. She concludes that outcomes based solely on policy changes are unpredictable, and manager-driven transitions are unlikely to be successful without community support. As such, successful transitions must begin with dialogue that engages everyone.

4. Holt-Giménez, E., and A. Shattuck. 2011. "Food Crises, Food Regimes and Food Movements: Rumblings of Reform or Tides of Transformation?" *Journal of Peasant Studies* 38(1):109–44. doi: 10.1080/03066150.2010.538578

   This article provides an analytical framework outlining approaches to the food crisis, with approaches conceptualized as "Neoliberal" or "Reformist" (enacted through the corporate food regime) and "Progressive" or "Radical" (enacted through the food movement) characterized by their approach to create change, definition of a sustainable food system, key institutions, key documents, and discourse. The authors argue that transforming the food system depends on actors within the food movement, rather than those within the food regime, and that the transformative potential of the food movement depends on its political nature.

Video Suggestions

1. Fraser, E. 2014. *Empowering Small-Scale Farmers in the Developing World Part I.* https://feeding ninebillion.com/video/reducing-food-insecurity -developing-world. 6 min.

Examines the role of science and technology in reducing food insecurity.

2. **Gibson, K. 2013.** *Take Back the Economy: Distinguished Speaker Lecture for the Centre for Co-operative and Community-Based Economy.* **www.youtube.com/watch?v=NvHB5BsLv24. 52 min.**

Explains the "politics of the possible" in interpreting economic structures and advocates reclaiming the economy to better serve all people.

3. **Transnational Institute. 2012.** *Eric Holt-Giménez: What Challenges Do Food and Farming Movements Face Going Forward?* **www.youtube.com/watch?v=F5M7WW9yZls. 3 min.**

Discusses bringing together advocates and practitioners to reform food systems.

References

Allen, P., M. FitzSimmons, M. Goodman, and K. Warner. 2003. "Shifting Plates in the Agrifood Landscape: The Tectonics of Alternative Agrifood Initiatives in California." *Journal of Rural Studies* 19:61–75.

Amin, S. 2011. "Preface: Food Sovereignty: A Struggle for Convergence in Diversity." Pp. xi–xviii in *Food Movements Unite!*, ed. E. Holt-Giménez. Oakland, CA: Food First Books.

Andrée, P., P. Ballamingie, and B. Sinclair-Waters. 2014. "Neoliberalism and the Making of Food Politics in Eastern Ontario." *Local Environment*. doi: 10.1080/13549839.2014.908277

Bernstein, H. 2014. "Food Sovereignty via the 'Peasant Way': A Sceptical View." *Journal of Peasant Studies* 41(6):1031–63. doi: 10.1080/03066150.2013.852082

Bisht, I.S., S.R. Pandravada, J.C. Rana, et al. 2014. "Subsistence Farming, Agrobiodiversity, and Sustainable Agriculture: A Case Study." *Agroecology and Sustainable Food Systems* 38(8):890–912. doi: 10.1080/21683565.2014.901273

Blay-Palmer, A. 2011. "Sustainable Communities, an Introduction." *Local Environment* 16(8):747–52. doi: 10.1080/13549839.2011.613235

———, K. Landman, I. Knezevic, and R. Hayhurst. 2013. "Constructing Resilient, Transformative Communities through Sustainable 'Food Hubs.'" *Local Environment* 18(5):521–8. doi: 10.1080/13549839.2013.797156

Bloom, J.D., and C.C. Hinrichs. 2010. "Moving Local Food through Conventional Food System Infrastructure: Value Chain Framework Comparisons and Insights." *Renewable Agriculture and Food Systems* 26(1):13–23. doi: 10.1017/s1742170510000384

Blouin, C., J.-F. Lemay, K. Ashraf, and J. Imai. 2009. *Local Food Systems and Public Policy: A Review of the Literature.* Ottawa: Équiterre and the Centre for Trade Policy and Law, Carleton University.

Boecker, A., and E. Micheels. 2015. "Status of Farm Direct Marketing." *FARE Share* (May):3–4.

Cadieux, K.V., and R. Slocum. 2015. "What Does It Mean to Do Food Justice?" *Journal of Political Ecology* 22:1–26.

Cantrell, P., and B. Heuer. 2014. "Food Hubs: Solving Local." The Wallace Center at Winrock International. http://ngfn.org/solvinglocal.

Castree, N. 2008. "Neoliberalising Nature: The Logics of Deregulation and Reregulation." *Environment and Planning A* 40:131–52.

Clancy, K., and K. Ruhf. 2010. "Is Local Enough? Some Arguments for Regional Food Systems." *Choices* 25(1). http://www.choicesmagazine.org/magazine/article.php?article=114.

Clapp, J. 2009. "Food Price Volatility and Vulnerability in the Global South: Considering the Global Economic Context." *Third World Quarterly* 30(6):1183–96. doi: 10.1080/01436590903037481

Constance, D.H., W.H. Friedland, M.-C. Renard, and M.G. Rivera-Ferre. 2014. "The Discourse on Alternative Agrifood Movements." Pp. 3–46 in *Alternative Agrifood Movements: Patterns of Convergence and Divergence*, Vol. 21 in *Research in Rural Sociology and Development*, ed. D.H. Constance, M. Renard, and M.G. Rivera-Ferre. Bingley, UK: Emerald Group.

Eaton, E. 2013. *Growing Resistance: Canadian Farmers and the Politics of Genetically Modified Wheat.* Winnipeg: University of Manitoba Press.

Fairbairn, M. 2012. "Framing Transformation: The Counter-Hegemonic Potential of Food Sovereignty in the US Context." *Agriculture and Human Values* 29 217–30.

FAO. 2013. *FAO Statistical Yearbook 2013: World Food and Agriculture.* Rome.

Fernandez, M., K. Goodall, M. Olson, and E. Mendez. 2012. "Agroecology and Alternative Agrifood Movements in the United States: Towards a Sustainable Agrifood System." *Journal of Sustainable Agriculture.* doi: 10.1080/10440046.2012.735633

Foley, J.A., N. Ramankutty, K.A. Brauman, et al. 2011. "Solutions for a Cultivated Planet." *Nature* 478(7369):337–42. doi: 10.1038/nature10452

Fridell, G. 2009. "The Co-operative and the Corporation: Competing Visions of the Future of Fair Trade." *Journal of Business Ethics* 86(S1):81–95. doi: 10.1007/s10551-008-9759-3

———. 2013. *Alternative Trade: Legacies for the Future.* Halifax: Fernwood.

Friedmann, H. 2005. "From Colonialism to Green Capitalism: Social Movements and the Emergence of Food

Regimes." Pp. 229–64 in *New Directions in the Sociology of Global Development*, Vol. 11 in *Research in Rural Sociology and Development*, ed. F.H. Buttel and P. McMichael. Oxford: Elsevier.

Garnett, T., M.C. Appleby, A. Balmford, et al. 2013. "Sustainable Intensification in Agriculture: Premises and Policies." *Science* 341:33–34. doi: 10.1126/science.1234485

Geels, F.W. 2011. "The Multi-Level Perspective on Sustainability Transitions: Responses to Seven Criticisms." *Environmental Innovation and Societal Transitions* 1(1):24–40. doi: 10.1016/j.eist.2011.02.002

Gibson-Graham, J.K. 2006. *A Postcapitalist Politics*. Minneapolis: University of Minnesota Press.

—— and J. Cameron. 2007. "Community Enterprises: Imagining and Enacting Alternatives to Capitalism." *Social Alternatives* 26(1):20–25.

Godfray, H., J. Beddington, I. Crute, et al. 2010. "Food Security: The Challenge of Feeding 9 Billion People." *Science* 327(5967):812–18. doi: 10.1126/science.1185383

Goodman, D. 2004. "Rural Europe Redux? Reflections on Alternative Agro-Food Networks and Paradigm Change." *Sociologia Ruralis* 44(1):3–16.

——, E.M. DuPuis, and M. Goodman. 2014. *Alternative Food Networks: Knowledge, Practice, and Politics*. London: Routledge.

Guthman, J. 2004. "The Trouble with 'Organic Lite' in California: A Rejoinder to the 'Conventionalisation' Debate." *Sociologia Ruralis* 44(3):301–16.

——. 2008. "Thinking inside the Neoliberal Box: The Micro-Politics of Agro-food Philanthropy." *Geoforum* 39(3):1241–53. doi: 10.1016/j.geoforum.2006.09.001

Hassanein, N. 2003. Practicing Food Democracy: A Pragmatic Politics of Transformation. *Journal of Rural Studies* 19(1):77–86. doi: 10.1016/s0743-0167(02)00041-4

Hinrichs, C. 2014. "Transitions to Sustainability: a Change in Thinking about Food Systems Change?" *Agriculture and Human Values*. doi: 10.1007/s10460-014-9479-5

Holt-Giménez, E. 2009. "From Food Crisis to Food Sovereignty: The Challenge of Social Movements." *Monthly Review* 61(3):142–56.

——. 2013. "*One Billion Hungry: Can We Feed the World?* by Gordon Conway." *Agroecology and Sustainable Food Systems* 37(8):968–71. doi: 10.1080/21683565.2013.809398

——. 2014. "Feeding Nine Billion: Five Steps to the Wrong Solution." *Huffington Post*, 25 April. Accessed 1 May 2014. http://www.huffingtonpost.com/eric-holt-gimenez/feeding-nine-billion-five_b_5208388.html.

—— and M.A. Altieri. 2013. "Agroecology, Food Sovereignty and the New Green Revolution." *Journal of Sustainable Agriculture*. doi: 10.1080/10440046.2012.716388

—— and A. Shattuck. 2011. Food Crises, Food Regimes and Food Movements: Rumblings of Reform or Tides of Transformation? *Journal of Peasant Studies* 38(1):109–44. doi: 10.1080/03066150.2010.538578

Koohafkan, P., M.A. Altieri, and E. Holt-Giménez. 2012.

"Green Agriculture: Foundations for Biodiverse, Resilient and Productive Agricultural Systems." *International Journal of Agricultural Sustainability* 10(1). doi: 10.1080/14735903.2011.610206

Lamine, C. 2015. "Sustainability and Resilience in Agrifood Systems: Reconnecting Agriculture, Food and the Environment." *Sociologia Ruralis* 55(1):41–61. doi: 10.1111/soru.12061

Lawhon, M., and J.T. Murphy. 2011. "Socio-technical Regimes and Sustainability Transitions: Insights from Political Ecology." *Progress in Human Geography* 36(3):354–78.

Levkoe, C.Z. 2011. "Towards a Transformative Food Politics." *Local Environment* 16(7):687–705. doi: 10.1080/13549839.2011.592182

Lockie, S., and D. Halpin. 2005. "The 'Conventionalisation' Thesis Reconsidered: Structural and Ideological Transformation of Australian Organic Agriculture." *Sociologia Ruralis* 45(4):284–307.

Low, S.A., A. Adalja, E. Beaulieu, et al. 2015. *Trends in U.S. Local and Regional Food Systems: A Report to Congress*. Economic Research Service, United States Department of Agriculture. http://www.ers.usda.gov/publications/apo-administrative-publication-number/apo-068.aspx.

Lowitt, K., P. Mount, and A. Khan. In press. "Governing Challenges for local Food Systems: Emerging Lessons from Agriculture and Fisheries." In *Conversations in Food Studies*, ed. C. Anderson, J. Brady, and C.Z. Levkoe. Winnipeg, MB: University of Manitoba Press.

MacRae, R. 2011. "A Joined-Up Food Policy for Canada." *Journal of Hunger & Environmental Nutrition* 6(4):424–57.

Marsden, T. 2013. "From Post-Productionism to Reflexive Governance: Contested Transitions in Securing More Sustainable Food Futures." *Journal of Rural Studies*. doi: 10.1016/j.jrurstud.2011.10.001

—— and A. Franklin. 2013. "Replacing Neoliberalism: Theoretical Implications of the Rise of Local Food Movements." *Local Environment* 18(5):636–641. doi: 10.1080/13549839.2013.797157

Misselhorn, A., P. Aggarwal, P. Ericksen, et al. 2012. "A Vision for Attaining Food Security." *Current Opinion in Environmental Sustainability* 4(1):7–17. doi: 10.1016/j.cosust.2012.01.008

Mount, P. 2012. "Growing Local Food: Scale and Local Food Systems Governance." *Agriculture and Human Values* 29(1):107–21. doi: 10.1007/s10460-011-9331-0

——. In press. "Supply Management as Food Sovereignty." In *Nourishing Communities*, ed. A. Blay-Palmer, I. Knezevic, C.Z. Levkoe, P. Mount, and E. Nelson. Toronto: University of Toronto Press.

—— and P. Andrée. 2013. "Visualising Community-Based Food Projects in Ontario." *Local Environment* 18(5):578–91. doi: 10.1080/13549839.2013.788491

——, S. Hazen, S. Holmes, et al. 2013. "Barriers to the Local Food Movement: Ontario's Community Food Projects and the Capacity for Convergence." *Local Environment* 18(5). doi: 10.1080/13549839.2013.788492

—— and J. Smithers. 2014. "The Conventionalization of Local Food: Farm Reflections on Local, Alternative Beef Marketing Groups." *Journal of Agriculture, Food Systems, and Community Development* 4(3)101–19. doi: 10.5304/jafscd.2014.043.002

NFU. 2012. *Farmers, the Food Chain and Agriculture Policies in Canada in Relation to the Right to Food*. Submission of the National Farmers Union of Canada to the UN Special Rapporteur on the Right to Food.

Pant, L.P. 2014. "Critical Systems of Learning and Innovation Competence for Addressing Complexity in Transformations to Agricultural Sustainability." *Agroecology and Sustainable Food Systems* 38(3):336–65. doi: 10.1080/21683565.2013.833157

Pirog, R., A. Harper, M. Gerencer, et al. 2014. "The Michigan Food Hub Network: A Case Study in Building Effective Networks for Food Systems Change." MSU Center for Regional Food Systems.

Popkin, B.M., L.S. Adair, and S.W. Ng. 2012. "Global Nutrition Transition and the Pandemic of Obesity in Developing Countries." *Nutrition Reviews* 70(1):3–21. doi: 10.1111/j.1753-4887.2011.00456.x

Pretty, J. 2008. "Agricultural Sustainability: Concepts, Principles and Evidence." *Philosophical Transactions of the Royal Society B: Biological Sciences* 363(1491):447–65. doi: 10.1098/rstb.2007.2163

Qualman, D. 2011. "Advancing Agriculture by Destroying Farms? The State of Agriculture in Canada." Pp. 20–42 in *Food Sovereignty in Canada*, ed. H. Wittman, A.A. Desmarais, and N. Wiebe. Halifax, NS: Fernwood.

Renglich, H. 2015. "The New Wave of Food Co-ops." *Briarpatch Magazine* (May/June). http://briarpatchmagazine.com/articles/view/the-new-wave-of-food-co-ops.

Rogers, J., and M. Fraszczak. 2014. "'Like the Stem Connecting the Cherry to the Tree': The Uncomfortable Place of Intermediaries in a Local Organic Food Chain." *Sociologia Ruralis* 54(3):321–40. doi: 10.1111/soru.12041

Rosset, P. 2008. "Food Sovereignty and the Contemporary Food Crisis." *Development* 51(4):460–3. doi: 10.1057/dev.2008.48

Schmit, T.M., B.B.R. Jablonski, and D. Kay. 2013. *Assessing the Economic Impacts of Regional Food Hubs: The Case of Regional Access*. Cornell University. http://dx.doi.org/10.9752/MS145.09-2013

Smith, E., and T. Marsden. 2004. "Exploring the 'Limits To Growth' in UK Organics: Beyond the Statistical Image." *Journal of Rural Studies* 20(3):345–57. doi: 10.1016/s0743-0167(03)00044-5

Stevenson, G.W., and R. Pirog. 2008. "Values-Based Supply Chains: Strategies for Agrifood Enterprises-of-the-Middle." Pp. 119–43 in *Food and the Mid-Level Farm: Renewing an Agriculture of the Middle*, ed. T.A. Lyson, G.W. Stevenson, and R. Welsh. Cambridge, MA: MIT Press.

——, K. Ruhf, S. Lezberg, and K. Clancy. 2007. "Warrior, Builder, and Weaver Work: Strategies for Changing the Food System." Pp. 33–62 in *Remaking the North American Food System: Strategies for Sustainability*, ed. C.C. Hinrichs and T.A. Lyson. Lincoln: University of Nebraska Press.

Sumner, J., J.J. McMurtry, and H. Renglich. 2014. "Leveraging the Local: Cooperative Food Systems and the Local Organic Food Co-ops Network in Ontario, Canada." *Journal of Agriculture, Food Systems, and Community Development* 4(3)47–60. doi: 10.5304/jafscd.2014.043.004

Transnational Institute. 2012. "Eric Holt-Giménez: What Challenges do Food and Farming Movements Face Going Forward?" https://www.youtube.com/watch?v=F5M7WW9yZIs.

Watts, D.C.H., B. Ilbery, and D. Maye. 2005. "Making Reconnections in Agro-food Geography: Alternative Systems of Food Provision." *Progress in Human Geography* 29(1):22–40.

Weis, T. 2010. "The Accelerating Biophysical Contradictions of Industrial Capitalist Agriculture." *Journal of Agrarian Change* 10(3):315–41.

Wittman, H. 2009. "Reworking the Metabolic Rift: La Vía Campesina, Agrarian Citizenship, and Food Sovereignty." *Journal of Peasant Studies* 36(4):805–26. doi: 10.1080/03066150903353991

——, A.A. Desmarais, and N. Wiebe, eds. 2010. *Food Sovereignty: Reconnecting Food, Nature and Community*. Oakland, CA: Food First.

23 Alternative Food Initiatives, Food Movements, and Collaborative Networks
A Pan-Canadian Perspective[1]

Charles Z. Levkoe

Learning Objectives

Through this chapter you can

1. Understand the contributions of alternative food initiatives rooted in place and identify their broader potential through establishing relationships across sectors, scales, and places

2. Appreciate the benefits and challenges of building connections between individuals, groups, and organizations through collaborative food networks

3. Reflect on food movements' resistance to the dominant food system and simultaneous efforts to build viable solutions in the here and now

4. Challenge the discourse and practice of food movements and collaborative networks to better address multiple challenges within the dominant food system

Introduction

Around the world, individuals and groups are increasingly coming together to voice their oppositions to the social and ecological implications of the dominant food system. This has led to a proliferation of social action through **alternative food initiatives (AFIs)** that aim to challenge the system's logistics and build viable solutions. While there has been much documentation and analysis of individual AFIs, there have been far fewer studies identifying their increasing collaboration through networks and the value of working across sectors, scales, and places. Hailed as part of the new social movements (NSMs), these **collaborative food networks** have been identified as a movement of movements, with a great potential to counter the ill effects of global capitalism (Morgan 2009; Holt-Giménez and Shattuck 2011; Constance et al. 2014).

While collaborative food networks have achieved many successes, they also face formidable challenges. As they have grown in popularity, strength, and reach, there have been increasing attempts to co-opt them into the neo-liberal logic as powerful corporations search for ways to capture profits and suppress their more radical objectives and goals. Understanding these networks in greater depth through examining their histories and structures are a vital part of shaping their futures. In this chapter, I explore the establishment of collaborative food networks in Canada and how they function. I also examine the ways that they might have a greater impact in achieving their vision for a more socially just and ecologically sustainable food system. A critical analysis of these network forms and functions offers new possibilities for future research as well as for making broader connections with food movements on a global scale.

Alternative Food Initiatives

AFIs have proliferated in both number and scope in response to the numerous social, environmental, and economic challenges within the dominant food system. AFIs can be broadly described as the multiplicity of self-governed, food-related initiatives that originate primarily from within civil society but also include actors from the public and private sectors (Levkoe 2014). In general, AFIs develop in certain places in response to specific challenges faced by communities. Their work covers a wide range of activities, from educating about and growing food to developing formal policy and infrastructure. For example, AFIs include attempts to reconnect farmers and consumers to higher-quality food (e.g. through community shared agriculture projects, farmers' markets, and multi-stakeholder co-operatives), preserve agricultural lands (e.g. through land reserves, farmland preservation, and agro-ecological training), revive and protect cultural and healthy-food practices (e.g. through school food reforms, slow food, and campaigns against genetically modified foods), increase accessibility to healthy food for urban residents (e.g. through food hubs, community cooking, and urban agriculture) and to develop new processes and mechanisms that enable the participation of all people in democratic decision making around the food system (e.g. through food policy councils and round tables). While AFIs are quite diverse in their objectives, they tend to converge around a shared critique of the corporate-led industrial food system, with a broad goal to develop an alternative political food narrative and viable solutions.

AFIs have adopted a range of concepts in an attempt to articulate their objectives and goals.

These are often described as **collective action frames**, a strategy of capturing theoretical and action-oriented sets of shared beliefs and meanings that inspire and legitimate the activities and campaigns of a **social movement** (Snow and Benford 1988). For AFIs, framing has been used to render events meaningful and guide action by articulating a problem, identifying causes, suggesting solutions, and issuing calls to action. Frames are used to construct meaning and to mobilize individuals, relate to broader issues, and connect with public sentiments. There is not space in this chapter to address these different frames in any great detail, but it is important to note that each has its own history and context. Below I describe a few brief examples to illustrate this point.[2]

Since the early twentieth century in Canada, activists have used a wide range of concepts to express their perspectives. But it was not until the early 1970s that these different perspectives began to coalesce into a broader and more inclusive collective action frame. At that time, global institutions had adopted **food security** as a dominant frame for discussing the priorities, objectives, and challenges of the dominant food system. While many AFIs adopted the food security frame and mobilized around its underlying ideals of access, it was also heavily critiqued for ignoring issues of power and social control within food systems (Mooney and Hunt 2009). Central to these critiques was the idea that governments were using food security as an uncritical approach that identified the core problem of the dominant food system as scarcity (e.g. hunger) while proposing technical solutions to feed increasing populations. Further, critics observed that powerful governments and corporations were using the concept of food security to encourage a neo-liberal, free-trade agenda and to pursue a global, industrialized model for agriculture (Patel 2009).

These critiques from scholars and activists were an important contribution to developing more integrative and counter-hegemonic collective action frames. For example, in the mid-1990s, many Canadian AFIs adopted **community**

food security (CFS). Introduced by AFIs in the United States, CFS was a concept that brought together ideas of ecological and social justice as well as issues surrounding community self-reliance and the quality and culturally appropriate nature of food (Gottlieb and Fisher 1996). While CFS gained popularity primarily in North America, **food sovereignty** evolved through collaborative dialogue between global peasant and farmer organizations to challenge political and economic power in the food system (Wittman et al. 2010). The global peasant movement La Vía Campesina first introduced food sovereignty at the World Food Summit in 1996. Differing from CFS, food sovereignty evolved as a critical reaction to the experiences of peasant farmers around the world affected by shifts in national and international agricultural policy toward a neo-liberal market-driven agenda in the 1980s and 1990s. As a collective action frame, food sovereignty focuses on the rights of those who produce and consume food to reclaim control of the food system from corporate interests and global financial institutions. Over the past decade, the concept of food sovereignty has become more prominent in a wide range of academic literatures and among AFIs in Canada (Wittman et al. 2011). It has radicalized many grassroots initiatives and contributed to the evolving conversation about ways to establish a more socially just and ecologically sustainable food system.

Embracing a food systems perspective, CFS and food sovereignty have evolved as collective action frames in response to the experiences of individuals and groups working to change the food system. Further, they have provided a platform for collaboration in resistance to the dominant food system and for building viable alternatives in the here and now.

Social Movements and Collaborative Networks

AFIs are increasingly working as part of collaborative networks that cross sectors, scales, and places. Collectively, these networks can be conceptualized as diverse food movements, or as a movement of movements. NSM theory provides a theoretical framework to help understand these forms of mobilization and network structures. In the broadest sense, social movements can be described as groups of individuals or organizations that form outside the state or political party system in an attempt to promote or prevent social change. While there is no consensus on an exact definition, della Porta and Diani's (2006) review of the scholarly literature suggest that social movements are part of a "distinct social process, consisting of mechanisms through which actors engaged in collective action: are involved in conflictual relations with clearly identified opponents; are linked by dense informal networks; [and] share collective identity" (p. 20). NSM theories developed in the 1980s in response to earlier perspectives that were criticized for lacking analysis of the relationships between social and political structures, for taking the grievances of actors for granted, and for not adequately considering the role of human agency (Staggenborg 2011). NSMs typically consist of an informal, loosely organized network of supporters rather than formal members. The theories attempt to explain the diverse movement culture that arose in post-industrial economies in the global North (since the mid-1960s), and movements promoting broad goals like protecting the environment and focusing on identity-based politics such as promoting equal rights for women and ethnic and sexual minorities.

From these theories, we can study the roles that networks play in collective action and organizing processes. Instead of viewing people as acting independently, a network perspective views actors as part of social webs of interaction and attempts to understand the patterns among the relationships. Today, there is consensus among scholars that networks are central to social mobilization and that much can be learned about social movement activity by studying network relations (Diani and Bison 2004). Social movements are engaged in a distinct type of networking that does more than enhance social connectedness. For example, networks can increase the success of movements by encouraging alliance building, facilitate the diffusion of ideas and practices, contribute to a more sustained level of activity, and establish a more desirable, legitimate, and democratic form of political organization. Further, social movement networks are seen as locations where ideas, identities, and frames are shared and exchanged, contributing to the development of a broader discourse and practice beyond a particular place. Within networking spaces, "activists embody particular experiences that have been formed and nurtured within the particular places they originate and have an opportunity to share their experiences, learn from others and undertake collective action" (Levkoe 2015:175). In sum, social movement networks are central to developing solidarity across sectors, scales, and places and for engaging in social and/or political action.

Collaborative Food Networks in Canada

Regarding the relationships between AFIs, studies have shown that there are increasing connections being made through robust networks and that sustained mobilization may be constitutive of an NSM (Levkoe 2014). In Canada, while there is a long history of sector-specific mobilization there have been substantial efforts to bring together diverse AFIs across cultures and geographies to develop more socially just and ecologically sustainable food systems (Koç et al. 2008). Prior to the 1970s, most food-related initiatives were focused on specific sectors and interests such as fishing, farming, health, poverty, labour, Indigenous peoples, and the environment. Collaborative actions around the food system were complicated, due in part to Canada's large geographic size, different languages spoken, and a lack of communication technologies. Further, navigating the political system has been challenging due to the fragmentation of food-related

jurisdiction (MacRae 2011). In Canada, each level of government responsibility weighs into decision making about how food is produced, processed, distributed, accessed, consumed, and disposed of, as well as the impacts of all these factors on our health and the environment.

The following are a series of key moments that have contributed to the development of collaborative food networks in Canada. In recounting these narratives, I focus on the larger-scale networks as collective efforts to facilitate and maintain network building with a broad food system focus.[3]

The People's Food Commission[4]

The People's Food Commission (PFC) ran from 1977–80 as the first large-scale mobilization that used a comprehensive lens to address the challenges and possible solutions within Canada's food system. The initiative developed in response to the impacts of neo-liberal restructuring, including rising inflation and unemployment rates, increasing housing prices, and declining working conditions in food and farming sectors (PFC 1980). The PFC brought together thousands of people from communities across the country to make deputations based on personal and professional experiences. The information collected was synthesized into a report entitled *The Land of Milk and Money*. The report concluded that "behind the rise and fall of food prices, there were a handful of corporations who controlled and profited from the food system" (PFC 1980:81). Beyond isolated concerns, the PFC identified structural challenges and the negative impacts on small-scale farmers and fishers, along with increasing impoverishment in cities.

While the PFC generated significant energy and interest, a lack of resources limited its ability to move forward. Further, there was little political will to address the final recommendations. However, the PFC's ideas continued to permeate mobilizations across Canada in the decades that followed. Further, the critical and contextualized perspectives put forth by the PFC about corporate control, the difficulty of food producers in earning a living, and the impact of poverty on food security remain critical issues among today's collaborative food networks.

Provincial Network Organizations

By the late 1990s, there was a multitude of individuals, communities, and non-profit organizations with diverse interests and goals working on food system issues in Canada. During this time period, changes in communication technologies radically shifted the ways that social movements were organizing. For example, the accessibility and popularity of the Internet and other communication technologies made it much faster and easier for groups to connect across vast geographies (Juris 2008). At the local and regional levels, there were already many diverse coalitions initiated by small businesses (e.g. small-scale and artisanal processors and co-operatives), family farmers, regional health authorities, and food policy councils, to name only a few.

Illustrative of these connections are the emergence of provincial network organizations (PNOs) across Canada with an explicit mandate to support the work of AFIs and to foster and sustain collaboration. The first PNO was established in Newfoundland in 1998 followed shortly by the British Columbia Food Systems Network (est. 1999), Growing Food Security in Alberta (est. 2003), Food Matters Manitoba (est. 2006), Food Secure Saskatchewan (est. 2006), Sustain Ontario: The Alliance for Healthy Food and Farming (est. 2008), the Prince Edward Island Food Security Network (est. 2008), and the New Brunswick Food Security Action Network (est. 2010). In 2010, a regional network was also established in Canada's North. The provincial level is significant for organizing around food issues because under Canadian federalism, the provinces are co-sovereign jurisdictions with legislative control over a number of areas relevant to the food system including health care, agriculture, education, municipal institutions, and property and civil rights.

A study of provincial networks by Levkoe and Wakefield (2014) revealed that while the food networks are highly connected, they are extremely decentralized, and the participating AFIs hold a wide diversity of approaches and objectives. This research focused on four Canadian provinces and indicated that within the networks, different types of work are done, diverse types of relationships are established, contact occurs between multiple sectors, and work is focused at multiple scales. In spite of these differences, AFIs unanimously indicated that they were part of a food movement. Levkoe and Wakefield conclude that while AFIs might have diverse goals and little ideological coherence, working together through collaborative networks offers a platform for collective impact and opens new opportunities for political transformation.

Acting as a bridge within the networks and focusing on the provincial level, the PNOs are uniquely positioned and have a wider reach and broader perspective than locally based actors. Levkoe (2015) writes that their work "focuses on movement building through the development of infrastructure to coordinate and scale-up the interaction and exchange between distant allies embedded in place" (p. 177). PNOs are actively creating a platform for individuals and groups to come together to share information and strategies in resistance to the dominant food system. Providing an opportunity for AFIs to think and act beyond their locally based experiences, provincial networks have been critical components in laying the groundwork for broader network building and actions in the recent decades.

Pan-Canadian Food Networks

With the inauguration of the first World Food Summit in Rome in 1996 and the popular embrace of CFS and food sovereignty as collective action frames, Canadian food activists recognized a need for more comprehensive and collaborative action. In 2001, a group of academics, practitioners, non-profit organizations, and policy makers gathered in Toronto for a conference at Ryerson

University. Toward the conclusion of the meeting, a resolution was passed that supported the formation of a pan-Canadian food security network (Koç and MacRae 2001).

In 2004, the first National Food Assembly was held in Winnipeg, with the goal of bringing together AFIs and collaborative food networks to overcome the divisions between the growing food movements across the country. At a second National Assembly in Waterloo, Ontario, the following year, participants agreed to form an alliance of organizations and individuals working together to advance food security and food sovereignty. Taking the name Food Secure Canada/Réseau pour une alimentation durable (FSC/RAD), the participants agreed to three interlocking commitments:

1. *Zero hunger.* All people at all times must be able to acquire, in a dignified manner, an adequate supply of culturally and personally acceptable food.
2. *A sustainable food system.* The production and consumption of food in Canada (harvesting, processing, distributing, including fishing and other wild food harvest) must maintain and enhance the quality of land, air and water for future generations, and provide for adequate livelihoods of people working in it.
3. *Healthy and safe food.* Safe and nourishing foods that are free of pathogens and industrial chemicals must be available. No novel food (genetically modified organisms— GMOs) may enter food system without independent testing and monitoring. (Food Secure Canada, n.d.)

FSC/RAD formally incorporated as a non-profit organization in 2006 and adopted an inclusive and democratic approach. According to Cathleen Kneen (2011), the organization's chair from 2008 through 2012, the vision was to:

create a coherent food movement in Canada that could strengthen local projects and support a national food policy for a just and sustainable food system. The idea was to bring together all the very different perspectives working on food issues, insisting that ending hunger, supporting population health through healthy and safe food and ensuring the environmental (and economic) sustainability of the food system are necessarily interlinked. (p. 80)

Parallel to the establishment of FSC/RAD, another national organization emerged with an interest in food systems scholarship. Following a failed grant application to establish a national food system research partnership in 2005, a group of community representatives and academics (many of the same individuals that established FSC/RAD) agreed on the need for a network to promote critical, interdisciplinary scholarship in the broad areas of food production, distribution, and consumption. They decided to establish an association that would bring together academics and community and public sector researchers and be committed to generating new food-related knowledge in response to social needs. Taking the name the Canadian Association for Food Studies/l'Association canadienne des études sur l'alimentation (CAFS/ACÉA), founding president Mustafa Koç wrote about the need for systemic perspectives in food research that supported existing network activities:

Food is a process not a product. Looking at food as a process implies careful scrutiny of interlinkages and interconnections among these practices, processes, and structures. This awareness, in return implies the need for interdisciplinary collaboration so that we can benefit from different methodological and analytical strengths of diverse academic disciplines. (2006:1)

CAFS/ACÉA was conceived as a sister organization to FSC/RAD, to enable researchers and practitioners to meet regularly and share their work with each other and the broader public. Since its inauguration, CAFS/ACÉA has held annual assemblies that have brought together a range of scholars as well as representatives from AFIs and the collaborative food networks to engage in dialogue on issues surrounding the broad goals of improving the food system. The development of both FSC/RAD and CAFS/ACÉA as pan-Canadian food networks was the culmination of a long history of mobilization around food issues.

The People's Food Policy Project

Building on the momentum of the previous decades, in 2008, a group of FSC/RAD and CAFS/ACÉA members proposed to renew the goals and processes of the PFC to create a grassroots, comprehensive national food policy. Named the People's Food Policy (PFP), the project is an example of how the collaborative food networks were able to mobilize individuals and AFIs at the local level and to make connections at other scales. The PFP's vision was to develop Canada's first and only citizen-led food policy rooted in the concept of food sovereignty and the work of existing food movements. Describing the project, Cathleen Kneen (in Holt-Giménez et al. 2010) wrote:

> This project builds on the local organizing that is already going on in the multiplicity of food self-reliance projects in both rural and urban areas, and its method is to overcome the "individual" by starting with the personal. People are encouraged to examine the barriers to the food security projects they are engaged in, and to tease out the policies that support or have erected those barriers. (p. 234)

Over the course of two years, PFP animators and volunteers facilitated hundreds of kitchen-table talks, meetings, and events around the country. Writing teams gathered the recommendations and prepared several draft versions that were circulated publicly for comment and feedback and reviewed at FSC/RAD's 2010 National Assembly.

In April 2011, the PFP was launched on Parliament Hill in Ottawa. The PFP consists of 10 discussion papers, which include whole-of-government policy recommendations and guidelines for how the proposed changes could be put into action. In the end, the PFP project engaged over 3,500 individuals and organizations to propose a radical and democratic vision for an ecologically sustainable and just food system that would provide enough healthy, acceptable, and accessible food for all (PFP 2011). The PFP was developed as a living document (i.e. open for further revision and expansion) and was adopted by FSC/RAD as a set of guidelines for the organization's future work. Since its publication, the PFP has attracted interest from within Canada and around the globe, resonating with others attempting to develop their own national food policy processes. It also laid the groundwork for the 2012 visit by Olivier de Schutter, the UN Special Rapporteur on the Right to Food, who recognized the high level of organization among Canada's collaborative food networks.

Challenges for Collaborative Food Networks

While there have been significant successes that have resulted from AFIs mobilizing, networks alone are not a solution to the problems created by the dominant food system. While most of the networks purport to be resisting the **negative externalities** of the corporate-led industrial food system, concerns have been raised about their approaches and practices. Critical scholars and practitioners have suggested that some AFIs have adopted a selective interpretation of the problems within the food system and that their activities, therefore, have been limited in both scale and scope. If these limitations are not addressed, some fear that food-movement efforts could be easily co-opted by the dominant food system and simply reproduce existing structures of inequality and ecological degradation. Identifying the prominent criticisms of collaborative food networks is not to demean their work but to promote further reflection on their current theoretical positions and practices.

Not Adequately Addressing Social Justice

Some critics have suggested that AFIs and collaborative food networks have not adequately translated issues of social justice into practice on a programmatic level. These critics have argued that instead of addressing the structural problems that lead to social inequality (e.g. poverty, racism, gender discrimination, colonialism, etc.), AFIs predominantly speak to dominant cultural groups and cater to those that can afford the time and money to participate (Allen 1999, 2008). In Canada, many AFIs have neither adequately addressed issues of race, class, and gender and the challenges faced by workers across the food chain and Indigenous peoples, nor found ways to bridge the gap in communications between francophone and anglophone food networks. Without social justice at their core, solutions risk creating a two-tiered food system in which entrepreneurial initiatives provide expensive niche-food alternatives for those who can afford them and cheap, unhealthy food for everyone else.

Despite Canada's diversity, many collaborative food networks have been dominated by white, middle-class actors (Slocum 2006). In some cases, people from historically marginalized groups have felt excluded from food movement activity altogether. Patricia Allen (2014), a prominent food justice scholar, has recognized that while there has been an increased focus on issues of race and class, most AFIs have remained silent on the question of gender. Throughout history, women have taken responsibility for the majority of food work, but have had disproportionately lower levels of power and resources. Paradoxically, while women are often the most active in AFIs, there have been very few efforts focused on lessening gender discrimination in the food system. In addition, food network activity may even reproduce gender inequalities as women continue to take responsibility for food provisioning, including the extra time and effort required for shopping at a farmers' market or purchasing a community shared agriculture box (Som Castellano 2015).

There has also been criticism of the limited engagement with the problems faced by workers across the food system. For example, while many AFIs focus on farmer livelihoods, the people who plant seeds, harvest crops, and prepare, package, and deliver foods are not typically "farmers" in the traditional sense of the term. In general, these workers tend to be poorly paid and often work in unacceptable conditions (Gray 2014). This is true of most workers across the food system that struggle with low wages, lack of benefits, and dangerous working conditions (Sachs et al. 2014). Joanne Lo (2014), director of the US Food Chain Workers Alliance, argues that limited involvement of the millions of food workers in AFIs is a lost opportunity for food movements' potential to influence governments, corporations, and public opinion.

Another concern is the limited engagement of collaborative food networks with Indigenous peoples and the impacts of settler colonialism. In considering food systems, it is impossible to talk about agriculture, fisheries, or forest and freshwater foods without considering the unresolved land claims, broken treaties, and damaged relationships between settler and Indigenous communities. Since the arrival of European settlers to North America, Indigenous peoples have been violently displaced from their lands and forced to assimilate. Indigenous traditions around food have been treated with contempt by settler governments and viewed as detrimental to linear models of progress and development. The perpetuation of colonial structures has resulted in a loss of access to traditional territories and cultures for Indigenous communities. In all, many communities face high rates of poverty, poor health, lack of education, and limited access to public services. However, through ongoing resistance efforts, Indigenous peoples have been involved in the protection of traditional food systems including cultivation, fishing, hunting, gathering, and trading.

For Indigenous peoples, the collective right of self-determination is inextricably linked to the right to food and food sovereignty. Secwepemc scholar and activist Dawn Morrison (2011) writes:

> Consisting of a multitude of natural communities, Indigenous food systems include all land, soil, water, air, plants and animals, as well as indigenous knowledge, wisdom and values. These food systems are maintained for our active participation and cultural harvesting strategies and practices in the fields, forests and waterways, which represent the most intimate way in which we interact with our environment. (p. 98)

For many Indigenous communities, the idea of food sovereignty goes well beyond democratic control of the food system and speaks to the deep integration of food into cultures, languages, and histories (Desmarais and Wittman 2014; Grey and Patel 2014). This approach was adopted by FSC/RAD and built on established descriptions of food sovereignty. According to the People's Food Policy:

> Indigenous food sovereignty understands food as sacred and part of a web of relationships with the natural world that sustains culture and community. Food, water, soil, and air are not viewed as "resources" but as sources of life itself. (PFP 2011:9)

Further, Morrison (2011) writes, "Supporting Indigenous food sovereignty requires a deep and cross-cultural understanding of the ways in which Indigenous knowledge, values, wisdom and practices can inform food-related action and policy reform" (p. 98). With this goal in mind, there have been some significant efforts to establish meaningful relationships between settler and Indigenous communities in Canada. For example, in 2006, the Working Group on Indigenous Food Sovereignty (WGIFS) was established through the British Columbia Food Systems Network to ensure that Indigenous perspectives were part of provincial discussions. The leadership and administration of both organizations eventually supported the establishment of the Indigenous Food Systems Network, a pan-Canadian organization committed to facilitating a better understanding of the relationship between Indigenous land and food systems. These networks played a major role in bringing the voices of the Indigenous communities to participate in FSC/RAD and the PFP.

While there may be opportunities to bring Indigenous communities into existing collaborative food networks, deeper engagement might also encourage settler food movements to fundamentally alter dominant (i.e. white, middle-class, non-Indigenous) perceptions of food activism as they learn from Indigenous food sovereignty efforts (e.g. see Bradley and Herrera 2015).

Similar to these divisions, there has also been a gap in communication and collaboration between francophone and anglophone food networks in Canada. Both CAFS/ACÉA and FSC/RAD have traditionally been dominated by anglophone members. In these environments, francophone participants tend to operate primarily in English due to expressed concerns of being isolated if they function in French. While some individuals have established cross-cultural connections, much of the food system research and activism has occurred in silos. Both communities have rich histories of engagement in food system politics yet there remain distinctions between policy focuses and geographic approaches. English- and French-speaking Canadians also have different cultural and historic traditions, and although there are many commonalities, stereotypes and preconceptions have served to increase divisions. While the challenges go far deeper than language differences, offering translation for meetings and for articles and documents would be a productive first step. There have been recent efforts to bridge the gap and build stronger connections across provincial borders and between communities. For example, partnerships between youth

3. It needs to be acknowledged that there have been many other local, regional, and provincial networks that predate and/or exist parallel to the networks discussed here.

4. The narratives in this section were constructed based on my own research, some of which has been published elsewhere (e.g. see Levkoe 2014; Schiff and Levkoe 2014; and Levkoe 2015).

References

Allen, P. 1999. "Reweaving the Food Security Safety Net: Mediating Entitlement and Entrepreneurship." *Agriculture and Human Values* 16(2):117–29.

———. 2008. "Mining for Justice in the Food System: Perceptions, Practices, and Possibilities." *Agriculture and Human Values* 25(2):157–61.

———. 2014. "Divergence and Convergence in Alternative Agrifood Movements: Seeking a Path Forward." Pp. 49–68 in *Alternative Agrifood Movements: Patterns of Convergence and Divergence*, Vol. 21 in *Research in Rural Sociology and Development*, ed. D.H. Constance, M. Renard, and M.G. Rivera-Ferre. Bingley, UK: Emerald Group.

Born, B., and M. Purcell. 2006. "Avoiding the Local Trap: Scale and Food Systems in Planning Research." *Journal of Planning Education and Research* 26(2):195–207.

Bradley, K., and H. Herrera. 2015. "Decolonizing Food Justice: Naming, Resisting, and Researching Colonizing Forces in the Movement." *Antipode*. doi: 10.1111/anti.12165

Constance, D.H., W.H. Friedland, M.-C. Renard, and M.G. Rivera-Ferre. 2014. "The Discourse on Alternative Agrifood Movements." Pp. 3–46 in *Alternative Agrifood Movements: Patterns of Convergence and Divergence*, Vol. 21 in *Research in Rural Sociology and Development*, ed. D.H. Constance, M. Renard, and M.G. Rivera-Ferre. Bingley, UK: Emerald Group.

della Porta, D., and D. Diani. 2006. *Social Movements: An Introduction*. Oxford: Blackwell.

Desmarais, A.A., and H. Wittman. 2014. "Farmers, Foodies and First Nations: Getting to Food Sovereignty in Canada." *The Journal of Peasant Studies* 41(6):1–21.

Diani, M., and I. Bison. 2004. "Organizations, Coalitions and Movements." *Theory and Society* 33(3/4):281–309.

DuPuis, E.M., and D. Goodman. 2005. "Should We Go 'Home' to Eat? Toward a Reflexive Politics of Localism." *Journal of Rural Studies* 21(3):359–71.

Feenstra, G. 2002. "Creating Space for Sustainable Food Systems: Lessons from the Field." *Agriculture and Human Values* 19(2):99–106.

Friedmann, H., and A. McNair 2008. "Whose Rules Rule? Contested Projects to Certify 'Local Production for Distant Consumers.'" *Journal of Agrarian Change* 8(2):408–34.

Food Secure Canada. n.d. "What We Do." http://food-secureCanada.org/who-we-are/what-we-do.

Goodman, D., E.M. DuPuis, and M. Goodman. 2012. *Alternative Food Networks: Knowledge Practice and Politics*. New York: Routledge

Gottlieb, R., and A. Fisher. 1996. "Community Food Security and Environmental Justice: Searching for a Common Discourse." *Agriculture and Human Values* 3(3):23–32.

Gray, M. 2014. *Labour and the Locavore: The Making of a Comprehensive Food Ethic*. Berkeley: University of California Press.

Grey, S., and R. Patel. 2014. "Food Sovereignty as Decolonization: Some Contributions from Indigenous Movements to Food System and Development Politics." *Agriculture and Human Values* 32(3):431–44.

Guthman, J. 2004. *Agrarian Dreams*. Berkeley: University of California Press.

———. 2007. "The Polanyian Way? Voluntary Food Labels as Neoliberal Governance." *Antipode* 39(3):456–76.

Hamm, M., and A. Bellows. 2003. "Community Food Security and Nutrition Educators." *Journal of Nutrition Education and Behavior* 35(1):37–43.

Hinrichs, C. 2003. "The Practice and Politics of Food System Localization." *Journal of Rural Studies* 19(1):33–45.

Holloway, J. 2010. *Crack Capitalism*. New York: Pluto Press.

Holt-Giménez, E. (guest editor), R. Bunch, V.J. Irán, et al. 2010. "Linking Farmers' Movements for Advocacy and Practice." *Journal of Peasant Studies* 37(1):203–36.

———, and A. Shattuck. 2011. "Food Crisis, Food Regimes and Food Movements: Rumblings of Reform or Tides of Transformation?" *Journal of Peasant Studies* 38(1):109–44.

Johnston, J. 2008. "The Citizen-Consumer Hybrid: Ideological Tensions and the Case of Whole Foods Market." *Theory and Society* 37(3):229–70.

Juris, J.S. 2008. *Networking Futures: The Movements Against Corporate Globalization*. Durham: Duke University Press.

Kneen, C. 2011. "Food Secure Canada: Where Agriculture, Environment, Health, Food and Justice Intersect." Pp. 80–96 in *Food Sovereignty in Canada: Creating Just and Sustainable Food Systems*, ed. H. Wittman, A. Desmarais, and N. Wiebe. Halifax, NS: Fernwood.

Koç, M. 2006. "An Exciting New Organization." *The Canadian Association for Food Studies Newsletter* 1(1):1. http://cafs.landfood.ubc.ca/en/wp-content/uploads/CAFS-newsletter-1.pdf.

——— and R. MacRae. 2001. *Working Together: Civil Society Working for Food Security in Canada*. Toronto: Media Studies Working Group.

———, R. MacRae, E. Desjardins, and W. Roberts. 2008. "Getting Civil about Food: The Interactions between Civil Society and the State to Advance Sustainable Food

Systems in Canada." *Journal of Hunger and Environmental Nutrition* 3(2/3):122–44.

Levkoe, C. 2011. "Towards a Transformative Food Politics." *Local Environment: The International Journal of Justice and Sustainability* 16(7):687–705.

———. 2014. "The Food Movement in Canada: A Social Movement Network Perspective." *Journal of Peasant Studies* 41(3):385–403.

———. 2015. "Strategies for Forging and Sustaining Social Movement Networks: A Case Study of Provincial Food Networking Organizations in Canada." *Geoforum* 58:174–83.

——— and S. Wakefield. 2014. "Understanding Contemporary Networks of Environmental and Social Change: Complex Assemblages within Canada's 'Food Movement.'" *Environmental Politics* 23(2):302–20.

Lo, J. 2014. "Social Justice for Food Workers in a Foodie World." *Journal of Critical Thought and Praxis* 3(1). http://lib.dr.iastate.edu/jctp/vol3/iss1/7/.

MacRae, R. 2011. "A Joined-Up Food Policy for Canada." *Journal of Hunger and Environmental Nutrition* 6(4):424–57.

Mooney, P., and S. Hunt. 2009. "Food Security: The Elaboration of Contested Claims to a Consensus Frame." *Rural Sociology* 74(4):469–97.

Morgan, K. 2009. "Feeding the City: The Challenge of Urban Food Planning." *International Planning Studies* 14(4):341–48.

Morrison, D. 2011. "Indigenous Food Sovereignty: A Model for Social Learning." Pp. 97–113 in *Food Sovereignty in Canada: Creating Just and Sustainable Food Systems*, ed. H. Wittman, A. Desmarais, and N. Wiebe. Halifax, NS: Fernwood.

Patel, R., guest editor. 2009. "Food Sovereignty." *Journal of Peasant Studies* 36(3):663–706.

PFC (People's Food Commission). 1980. *The Land of Milk and Money: The National Report of the People's Food Commission*. Toronto: Between the Lines.

PFP (People's Food Policy). 2011. *Resetting the Table: A People's Food Policy for Canada*. http://foodsecureCanada.org/sites/default/files/fsc-resetting2012-8half11-lowres-en.pdf.

Sachs, C., P. Allen, A.R. Terman, J. Hayden, and C. Hatcher. 2014. "Front and Back of the House: Socio-Spatial Inequalities in Food Work." *Agriculture and Human Values* 31(1):3–17.

Schiff, R., and C. Levkoe. 2014. "From Disparate Action to Collective Mobilization: Collective Action Frames and the Canadian Food Movement." Pp. 225–53 in *Occupy the Earth: Global Environmental Movements*, Vol. 15 in *Advances in Sustainability and Environmental Justice*, ed. L. Leonard and S. Buryn Kedzior. Bingley, UK: Emerald Group.

Shreck, A. 2008. "Resistance, Redistribution and Power in the Fair Trade Banana Industry." Pp. 121–44 in *The Fight over Food: Producers, Consumers and Activists Challenge the Global Food System*, ed. W. Wright and G. Middendorf. University Park: Pennsylvania State University Press.

Slocum, R. 2006. "Anti-Racist Practice and the Work of Community Food Organizations." *Antipode* 38(2):327–49.

Snow, D.A., and R.D. Benford. 1988. "Ideology, Frame Resonance, and Participant Mobilization." Pp. 197–217 in *From Structure to Action: Social Movement Participation Across Cultures*, ed. B. Klandermans, H. Kriesi, and S. Tarrow. Greenwich: JAI Press.

Som Castellano, R.L. 2015. "Alternative Food Networks and Food Provisioning as a Gendered Act." *Agriculture and Human Values* 32(3):461–74.

Staggenborg, S. 2011. *Social Movements*. Toronto: Oxford University Press.

Wittman, H., A. Desmarais, and N. Wiebe, eds. 2010. *Food Sovereignty: Reconnecting Food, Nature and Community*. Halifax, NS: Fernwood.

———, ———, and ———, eds. 2011. *Food Sovereignty in Canada: Creating Just and Sustainable Food Systems*. Halifax, NS: Fernwood.

Wright, E.O. 2010. *Envisioning Real Utopias*. New York: Verso.

Building Food Sovereignty
A Radical Framework for Socially Just and Ecologically Sustainable Food Systems

Annette Aurélie Desmarais

Learning Objectives

Through this chapter, you can

1. Appreciate the limitations of the idea and practice of food security
2. Understand the key elements of food sovereignty
3. Analyze the potential and significance of food sovereignty

Introduction

When the 2007–8 food crisis triggered food riots and hit the national headlines in many countries, the official **food security** response was "more of the same" (Claeys 2009:2); that is, an emphasis on increasing global production, productivity and liberalized trade, and pursuing another green revolution through the greater use of genetically modified organisms (GMOs) in agriculture (*The Economist* 2008a, 2008b, 2009). La Vía Campesina, on the other hand, argued that the food crisis—now linked to the economic and environmental crisis—is the result of decades of destructive policies that spurred the globalization of a **neoliberal** industrial and corporate-led model of agriculture and that "the time for **food sovereignty** has come" (La Vía Campesina 2008a:7).

La Vía Campesina is an international **peasant** movement bringing together 164 organizations based in 73 countries in the Americas, Europe, Asia, and Africa (www.viacampesina. org). Many now consider it to be the world's most politically significant "transnational agrarian movement" (Borras et al. 2008:172), mainly

because of its persistent resistance to the globalization of neo-liberal agriculture and the way in which the movement works to expand, further define, and disseminate the idea and practice of food sovereignty (Desmarais 2007; Martínez-Torres and Rosset 2010; Pérez-Vitoria 2005).

Food sovereignty is also being practised in Canada. The National Farmers Union and the Union Paysanne in Quebec, both members of La Vía Campesina, first introduced food sovereignty in Canada through their efforts to effect changes in farm legislation (Desmarais and Wittman 2014).[1] Interestingly, in a session of the government of Canada's Standing Committee on Agriculture and Agri-Food Canada,[2] after having heard the testimony of seven witnesses well versed with the issues facing those living in rural Canada, André Bellavance, a member of Parliament from Quebec, commented:

It has to be said, there is a crisis in agriculture. . . . I have the feeling that we are at a crossroads. There's a political choice to be made. What kind of agriculture do we want? Do we still want family farming? Do we believe in it? And if that is what we want, then we need to take the necessary steps to ensure that this type of agriculture lasts. [Or,] do we prefer an industrial agriculture? (quoted in Standing Committee on Agriculture and Agri-Food 2007)

These are precisely the questions that many Canadians, along with millions of people around the world, are posing: Do citizens want a globalized model of agriculture that is increasingly dominated by corporate interests? Or, do we want food systems based on food sovereignty, a framework that, among other things, keeps people on the land and able to make their livelihoods from farming, and provides nutritious and safe food? These questions reflect two visions of agriculture and food and point to very real political struggles over two competing—and in many ways diametrically opposed—models of social and economic development.

While others in this book have critiqued the Canadian food system (see, for example, chapters 7, 12, and 20), this chapter explores the roots, meanings, challenges, and potential of food sovereignty as a path to socially just and ecologically sustainable food systems.

Going beyond Sustainability and Food Security—Food Sovereignty

Food sovereignty did not surface in a vacuum. A brief examination of the political, social, and economic context in which it emerged sheds light on the specific content of the food sovereignty alternative.

Concepts, however revolutionary, are often misinterpreted, misused, and usurped by those in positions of power. Consider, for example, the concept of *sustainable agriculture*. Originally embracing a conscious move away from capital-intensive, high-input,

monoculture agriculture, the idea and practice of sustainable agriculture reflected a profound respect for ecology; it focused on local production for local consumption and required environmentally friendly practices such as, among others, integrated pest management, organic or low-input and small-scale agricultural production, and polyculture. However, over a relatively short time the term acquired new meaning as international institutions— the World Bank, the International Fund for Agricultural Development, the United Nations Commission on Sustainable Development, and the Global Forum on Agricultural Research, and others—and national governments integrated environmental concerns into their policies and programs as a result of the report of the World Commission on Environment and Development (1987) called *Our Common Future*, commonly known as the Brundtland Commission Report.

In effect, the "greening" of the rural development discourse occurred within a wholehearted embrace of a free-market ideology. Nowhere is this more evident than in the Brundtland Commission Report's definition of *sustainable development*:

The concept of sustainable development does imply limits—not absolute limits but limitations imposed by the present state of technology and social organization on environmental resources and by the ability of the biosphere to absorb the effects of human activities. But technology and social organization can be both managed and improved to make way for a new era of economic growth. (World Commission on Environment and Development 1987:16)

It was the report's call for worldwide economic growth that governments and major players in international development readily embraced, thus ensuring that *sustainable development* quickly became synonymous with *economic growth*, or better yet, *sustained economic growth*.[3] Subsequently, power-holders re-envisioned "sustainability" in the practice of sustainable agriculture as the successful integration of food and agriculture into a global marketplace.[4]

Tied to this were important shifts in the meaning and practice of *food security*. The World Food Conference of 1974, using the language of food security, sought to resolve the growing world food crisis through state involvement at the national and international levels to, among other things, establish the conditions for adequate production of food and reasonable prices. Thus, the international community understood that state intervention in the market was an important element of global food security (Fairbairn 2010:22–3). However, this state-centric approach to food security was later displaced by a more market-oriented neoliberal framework. By the early 1990s, food was considered a commodity, and food security was reconceptualized as "household food security" with a focus on the individual's purchasing power, a decreased role for national governments, increased power for transnational corporations and international institutions, and the prioritization of market liberalization over social concerns (Fairbairn 2010).

Governments restructured their economies through increased trade liberalization, privatization, deregulation, and public sector reform, effectively altering rural landscapes everywhere. In agriculture, this shift meant increasing production for export at the expense of production for domestic consumption, dismantling state-supported mechanisms that had helped to ensure the survival of peasant families and small farmers, and substantially decreasing government budgets for agricultural research and extension services, while introducing legislation to enable the concentration of agricultural resources and markets into the hands of fewer and larger landowners and agri-business corporations.[5] Perhaps most importantly, with the signing of the Uruguay Round of the GATT in 1994 that created the **World Trade Organization (WTO)**, all agricultural policies now had to comply with regional trade and WTO agreements.

The WTO's **Agreement on Agriculture** reflected the belief that food security could best be reached by increasing agricultural trade accompanied by expanding the power of the WTO in global governance over food, genetic resources, natural resources, and agricultural markets. This fit well with the WTO's view of food security that increasingly emphasized ensuring access to an "adequate supply of imported food" (Stevens et al. 2000:3). In the speech to the World Food Summit: Five Years Later held in Rome in June 2002, Miguel Rodríguez Mendoza, deputy director general of the WTO, put it like this:

> History has shown that food security does not equal self-sufficiency of a country. It has more to do with international trade in food products that makes them available at competitive prices and sets the right incentives for those countries where they can be produced most efficiently. Food shortages have to do with poverty rather than with being a net food importer. Food security nowadays lies not only in the local production of food, but in a country's ability to finance imports of food through exports of other goods. (Rodríguez Mendoza 2002:1)

Currently, the United Nations Food and Agriculture Organization (FAO) defines *food security* as "a situation that exists when all people, at all times, have physical, social and economic access to sufficient, safe and nutritious food that meets their dietary needs and food preferences for an active and healthy life" (FAO 2003:28). As laudable as this goal of food security might be, Raj Patel (2010:187) argues that because "neo-liberal triumphalism" reigned in political decision making, the problem is that the international community was no longer prepared to specify what domestic and international political arrangements were necessary to create the conditions for food security to actually be realized. Instead, in Patel's words:

> the terms on which food is, or isn't, made available by the international community

have been taken away from institutions [such as the United Nations Food and Agriculture Organization] that might be oriented by concerns of food security and given to the market, which is guided by an altogether different calculus. (2010:188)

The concept of food sovereignty emerged as **peasants** and small-scale farmers struggled to survive in this harsher political and economic environment that effectively threatened their very modes of existence. As peasants and farmers were being driven off the land, rural impoverishment was on the rise, and environmental degradation worsened, organizations of peasants from the global South and small- to medium-scale farmers in the North gathered together to form La Vía Campesina to work together and develop an alternative model of agriculture.

La Vía Campesina discussed food sovereignty at its Second International Conference held in April 1996, in Tlaxcala, Mexico. Peasant and farm leaders who gathered there argued that "food security" did little to change the existing inequitable structures and policies that were destroying livelihoods and environments in the countryside in both North and South. Instead, La Vía Campesina (1996a:21) defined a different approach: food sovereignty—a framework "directly linked to democracy and justice" that exposes the power dimensions in ongoing agriculture debates and puts control of productive resources (land, water, seeds, and natural resources) in the hands of those who produce food. As Nettie Wiebe, former North American leader of La Vía Campesina, recalls:

> Food sovereignty . . . was our way of differentiating our agenda from that liberalized agenda and it was also a way to introduce a much more complex set of ideas about what it really meant to be food secure which included political power ideas about who controls resources, who has access to resources and who gets to control their own production and their own consumption. (quoted in Long 2005:25 and cited in Desmarais 2007.)

What Is Food Sovereignty?

In a nutshell, food sovereignty "is the right of peoples and nations to control their own food and agricultural systems, including their own markets, production modes, food cultures, and environments" (Wittman et al. 2010:2). Food sovereignty is a framework that keeps small-scale producers on the land and enables them to make a living from growing food. As such, it is a radical alternative to corporate-led, neo-liberal, industrial agriculture. Indeed, food sovereignty effectively "turns the global food system upside down" (GRAIN 2005).

Going beyond the concept of food security, food sovereignty stresses that it is not enough to ensure that a sufficient amount of food is produced nationally and made accessible to everyone. Equally significant are the issues of *what* food is produced, *who* grows the food, *where and how* it is produced, and at *what scale*. Most importantly, food sovereignty includes farmers' and peasants' "right to produce our own food in our own territory" and "the right of consumers to be able to decide what they consume and how and by whom it is produced" (La Vía Campesina 2003:1). Food sovereignty places those who produce and consume food at the centre of decision making and in doing so it addresses head-on issues of power and power dynamics. It is important to note that food sovereignty does not negate the need to ensure food security; instead, it stresses that real food security cannot be achieved without food sovereignty.[6]

The Tlaxcala Conference defined the basic principles of food sovereignty that were then integrated into La Vía Campesina's position (1996b) and presented to delegates to the NGO Forum on Food Security and the World Food Summit held in Rome in November of 1996. Because this position reflects the essence of food sovereignty and formed the basis of subsequent international documents, it is worth examining it closely (see box 24.1).

In a world increasingly dominated by the ideals of liberalized trade governed by

Box 24.1 La Vía Campesina Position at the World Food Summit

The Right to Produce and Access to Land

Food Sovereignty—A Future without Hunger

We, the Vía Campesina, a growing movement of farm workers, peasant, farm and indigenous peoples' organizations . . . know that food security cannot be achieved without taking full account of those who produce food. Any discussion that ignores our contribution will fail to eradicate poverty and hunger.

Food is a basic human right. This right can only be realized in a system where food sovereignty is guaranteed. Food sovereignty is the right of each nation to maintain and develop its own capacity to produce its basic foods respecting cultural and productive diversity. We have the right to produce our own food in our own territory. Food sovereignty is a precondition to genuine food security.

We, the Vía Campesina, reject the economic and political conditions which destroy our livelihoods, our communities, our cultures and our natural environment. The liberalization of trade and its economic policies of structural adjustment have globalized poverty and hunger in the world and are destroying local productive capacities and rural societies. This corporate agenda takes no account of food security for people. It is an inequitable system that treats both nature and people as a means to an end with the sole aim of generating profits for a few. Peasants and small farmers are denied access to and control over land, water, seeds and natural resources. Our response to the increasingly hostile environment is to collectively challenge these conditions and develop alternatives.

We are determined to create rural economies that are based on respect for ourselves and the earth, on food sovereignty, and fair trade. Women play a central role in household and community food sovereignty. Hence they have an inherent right to resources for food production, land, credit, capital, technology, education and social services, and equal opportunity to develop and employ their skills. We are convinced that the global problem of food insecurity can and must be resolved. Food sovereignty can only be achieved through solidarity and the political will to implement alternatives.

Long-term food security depends on those who produce food and care for the natural environment. As the stewards of food producing resources we hold the following principles as the necessary foundation for achieving food security.

Food—A Basic Human Right

Food is a basic human right. Everyone must have access to safe, nutritious and culturally appropriate food in sufficient quantity and quality to sustain a healthy life with full human dignity. . . .

Agrarian Reform

[Food sovereignty] demands genuine agrarian reform which gives landless and farming people—especially women—ownership and control of the land they work and returns territories to Indigenous peoples. . . . Peasant families, especially women, must have access to productive land, credit, technology, markets and extension services. Governments must

continued

establish and support decentralized rural credit systems that prioritize the production of food for domestic consumption to ensure food sovereignty. . . . To encourage young people to remain in rural communities as productive citizens, the work of producing food and caring for the land has to be sufficiently valued both economically and socially. Governments must make long-term investments of public resources in the development of socially and ecologically appropriate rural infrastructure.

Protecting Natural Resources

Food sovereignty entails the sustainable care and use of natural resources especially land, water and seeds. We, who work the land, must have the right to practice sustainable management of natural resources and to preserve biological diversity. This can only be done from a sound economic basis with security of tenure, healthy soils and reduced use of agrochemicals. Long-term sustainability demands a shift away from dependence on chemical inputs, cash-crop monocultures, and intensive, industrialized production models. Balanced and diversified natural systems are required. Genetic resources are the result of millennia of evolution and belong to all of humanity. They represent the careful work and knowledge of many generations of rural and indigenous peoples. The patenting and commercialization of genetic resources by private companies must be prohibited. The World Trade Organization's Intellectual Property Rights Agreement is unacceptable. Farming communities have the right to freely use and protect the diverse genetic resources, including seeds, which have been developed by them throughout history.

Reorganizing the Food Trade

Food is first and foremost a source of nutrition and only secondarily an item of trade. National agricultural policies must prioritize production for domestic consumption and food self-sufficiency. Food imports must not displace local production nor depress prices. This means that export dumping or subsidized export must cease. Peasant farmers have the right to produce essential food staples for their countries and to control the marketing of their products. Food prices in domestic and international markets must be regulated and reflect the true cost of producing that food. This would ensure that peasant families have adequate incomes. It is unacceptable that the trade in foodstuffs continues to be based on the economic exploitation of the most vulnerable—the lowest earning producers—and the further degradation of the environment. It is equally unacceptable that trade and production decisions are increasingly dictated by the need for foreign currency to meet high debt loads. These debts place a disproportionate burden on rural peoples. . . . [T]hese debts must be forgiven.

Ending the Globalization of Hunger

Food sovereignty is undermined by multilateral institutions and by speculative capital. The growing control of multinational corporations over agricultural policies has been facilitated by the economic policies of multilateral organizations such as the WTO, World Bank and the IMF. . . . [T]he regulation and taxation of speculative capital and a strictly enforced Code of Conduct for transnational corporations [are necessary].

Social Peace—A Pre-requisite to Food Sovereignty

Everyone has the right to be free from violence. Food must not be used as a weapon. Increasing levels of poverty and marginalization in the countryside, along with the growing oppression of ethnic minorities and indigenous populations aggravate situations of injustice and hopelessness. The increasing incidence of racism in the countryside, ongoing displacement, forced urbanization and repression of peasants cannot be tolerated.

Democratic Control

Peasants and small farmers must have direct input into formulating agricultural policies at all levels. . . . The United Nations and related organizations will have to undergo a process of democratization to enable this to become a reality. Everyone has the right to honest, accurate information and open and democratic decision-making. These rights form the basis of good governance, accountability and equal participation in economic, political and social life, free from all forms of discrimination. Rural women, in particular, must be granted direct and active decision-making on food and rural issues.

Source: La Vía Campesina (1996b).

undemocratic and distant global institutions, food sovereignty is nothing less than revolutionary. Food sovereignty subordinates trade relations and transcends the fetishism for agricultural commodities as it reintegrates social, ecological, and co-operative production relations; revalues land, food, and those who work the land; and addresses questions of rights and social reproduction of agrarian cultures and ecological sustainability (McMichael 2008a, 2008b). In many ways, food sovereignty is a social justice "counter-frame to food security": it cultivates solidarity over individualism, envisions food as more than a commodity, rejects "free" markets, and demands state intervention and market regulation (Fairbairn 2010). Indeed, food sovereignty demands the "right to have rights" (Patel 2010:186) and expands our understanding of human rights to include the right to land and natural resources (Claeys 2009), peasants' rights, and even the right to food sovereignty (Claeys 2014, 2015).[7]

Food sovereignty is changing the ways we think about and relate to food, agriculture, and social relations because it politicizes the current global food system and agrarian policy (Wittman et al. 2010; McMichael 2008a; Patel 2010). As such, it is best understood as a radical democratic project that, on the one hand, exposes the power dynamics in the current global food system,

and on the other hand, cultivates new spaces for inclusive debate on food and agriculture. As Patel (2006:85) argues, it does so in ways that "the deepest relations of power come to be contested publicly." Many of these claims (reflected in table 24.1) demonstrate how food sovereignty challenges corporate-led, neo-liberal, industrial agriculture.

Building a Global Movement for Food Sovereignty

Initially, food sovereignty focused on issues of production, reflecting the interests of peasants and small-scale farmers. However, food sovereignty gained momentum as La Vía Campesina worked in alliance with other **social movements**, non-governmental organizations, and community-based organizations that were using food sovereignty in efforts to shift agriculture policy in different parts of the world (NOUMINREN 2006; International Workshop 2003). Consequently, food sovereignty evolved to include pastoralists, fishers, and urban-based movements, and to encompass a broader agenda of consumption issues and gender equality.

Since it was first introduced, food sovereignty has generated much debate and action. For example, in 2001, the Our World Is Not For Sale coalition launched the "Priority to Peoples'

Table 24.1 Key Differences between Corporate-Led, Neo-liberal, Industrial Agriculture and the Food Sovereignty Framework

Goal	Neo-liberal Model	Food Sovereignty Model
Trade	"Free" trade in most commodities and services	Food and agriculture exempted from trade agreements Food geared primarily to domestic needs; excess fairly traded in regulated markets
Production priority	Food and agro-products for export and foreign exchange	Food for local markets
Crop prices	"What the market dictates" (involves mechanisms that enforce low prices to producers)	Fair prices that cover costs of production and allow farmers and farm workers a life with dignity
Market access	Increase access to foreign markets	Access to local markets End displacement of farmers from their own markets by agri-business
Subsidies	Some subsidies still allowed in the US and Europe, yet not in the global South; subsidies directed mainly to the largest farmers	Allow subsidies that do not damage small- and medium-scale farming in other countries, e.g. grants to family farmers for direct marketing, price/income support, soil conservation, conversion to sustainable farming, research, rural education, etc.
Food	Considered primarily a commodity Increasingly involves processed food containing high levels of fat, sugar, high-fructose corn syrup, and toxic residues	Considered a human right Should be healthy, nutritious, affordable, culturally appropriate, and as much as possible be locally produced under socially just conditions
Food production and provisioning	An option for the economically "efficient"	A right of peasants and small-scale family farmers, pastoralists, artisanal fishers, forest dwellers, Indigenous peoples, agricultural and fisheries workers, and migrants involved in food provision
Hunger	Caused by high prices and therefore the result of insufficient supply, production, and productivity	A problem of access and maldistribution caused by poverty and inequality
Food security	Achieved by importing food from where it is cheapest	Greatest when food production is in the hands of the hungry or when food is produced locally
Access to land	Via the market	Via systemic and state-supported agrarian reform and long-term tenure security
Seeds	A patentable commodity	A common heritage of humanity, held in trust by rural communities and cultures "No patents on life"
Rural credit and investment	From private banks and corporations	From the public sector Designed to support small- and medium-scale family agriculture
Corporate monopolies	Rarely an issue	A systemic and pathological feature of an industrialized international food system
Overproduction	No such thing, by definition	Drives prices down and pushes farmers into poverty Supply management to resolve overproduction

Table 24.1 *(continued)*

Goal	Neo-liberal Model	Food Sovereignty Model
Small- and medium-scale farmers	Anachronisms The inefficient will disappear	Guardians of culture and crop germplasm Stewards of productive resources Repositories of knowledge Building block of broad-based, inclusive economic development
Gender	Policies and programs to integrate food and agriculture into the global marketplace with little consideration of the gender division of labour and women's unpaid labour Little consideration of how the policies affect women and men differently	Aims to transform existing unequal gender relations Recognizes and respects the key roles women play in the production, gathering, distribution, preparation, and cultural dimensions of food and agriculture Demands equality and the end of all forms of violence against women
Urban consumers vs. agricultural workers	Since labour is considered a major cost in production, workers paid low wages to keep prices down for consumers	Workers need living wages
Research	Focuses on science and innovation Depends largely on new technology to fix problems caused by previously introducing new technology into the environment	Led and driven by peasants/farmers and communities
Policy development	Developed by mostly urban "experts" and may involve multi-stakeholder consultations regarding an already-defined policy agenda	Led and driven by peasants/farmers working in alliance with urban-based movements Participatory Starts from lived realities of farming families

Source: Adapted from Rosset (2003:2) and Patel (2006:84).

Food Sovereignty" statement that specified concrete mechanisms and structures to ensure food sovereignty.[8] The concept was further elaborated at two international civil society events: the World Forum on Food Sovereignty held in Cuba ("Final Declaration" 2001) and the 2002 NGO/CSO Forum on Food Sovereignty in Rome, held in conjunction with the World Food Summit: Five Years Later. Meanwhile, some universities held workshops and conferences to better understand the theoretical dimensions and practical implementation of food sovereignty. NGOs produced glossy campaign posters featuring food sovereignty, and coalitions like the

European Platform for Food Sovereignty and the People's Caravan for Food Sovereignty in Asia were formed.

This flurry of grassroots activity and pressure for an alternative vision of agriculture prompted responses from various levels of government and international bodies. Mayors in some parts of Europe endorsed a commitment to local production for local consumption, a key element of food sovereignty. The Green Party in some European countries held meetings to examine how it might help redefine European agricultural policy. And, between 1999 and 2009, food sovereignty was included in the national legislation promulgated by the governments of Venezuela, Mali, Bolivia, Ecuador, Nepal, and Senegal.

Food sovereignty was also brought to the attention of official international bodies. For example, both Special Rapporteurs on the **Right to Food**, Jean Ziegler (Ziegler 2003, 2004) followed by Olivier de Schutter (2015), were instrumental in advancing food sovereignty in human rights circles and international deliberations on agriculture. The International Assessment of Agricultural Knowledge, Science and Technology for Development (IAASTD 2009) recognized the potential of food sovereignty to help move us away from the "business as usual" approach.[9] And, since 2003, the International NGO/CSO Planning Committee for Food Sovereignty (IPC)—bringing together representatives of Indigenous peoples, fishers, farmers/peasants, youth, women, and NGOs from all regions of the world—became the principal civil society interlocutor with the FAO for work on food sovereignty.

To ensure that the concept of food sovereignty did not get distorted in the same way sustainable development did, and to strengthen the food sovereignty movement, the IPC worked with other groups, including La Vía Campesina, to organize the International Forum on Food Sovereignty, held in February 2007 in Nyéléni, Mali—an event that represents an important turning point for food sovereignty. The Nyéléni Forum brought together 500 representatives of peasants, farmers, farm workers, fishers, pastoralists, Indigenous peoples, rural women, and non-governmental development organizations from 80 countries to debate and further define food sovereignty. Participants reached consensus on some basic principles of food sovereignty (see box 24.2), opened the space for consumer associations and urban-based community organizations, and vowed to return to their respective countries to build food sovereignty networks and coalitions.

In effect, the Nyéléni Forum consolidated food sovereignty beyond its rural roots to embrace a wide range of social actors and consolidate a global food sovereignty movement. As Paul Nicholson, former member of

the International Coordination Commission of La Vía Campesina, recalls:

> Food sovereignty was not designed . . . only for farmers, but for people—that is why we call it peoples' food sovereignty. We see the need for a bottom up process to define alternative practices—an international space or platform for food sovereignty. We're talking about identifying allies, developing alliances with many movements of fisher folk, women, environmentalists and consumer associations, finding cohesion, gaining legitimacy, being aware of co-optation processes, the need to strengthen the urban-rural dialogue, to generate alternative technical models. And above all there is the issue of solidarity. (quoted in Wittman et al. 2010:7)

Since Nyéléni, the momentum for food sovereignty continues to grow as national and regional coalitions are emerging or existing ones are adopting the food sovereignty framework. In the global North, for example, social movements are consolidating a European Movement for Food Sovereignty to move European agricultural policy away from WTO rules by "re-localizing agricultural production, supporting small producers and facilitating access to land for new farmers and collectives, while challenging the dominance of industry and private interests in the production, transformation and distribution of food for European citizens" (European Coordination Vía Campesina 2010). In the United States in 2010 citizens launched the US Food Sovereignty Alliance that promises to be a key social actor in transforming the food system in that country.[10] In Canada, as a follow-up to the Nyéléni Forum, representatives of non-governmental organizations—the National Farmers Union, Food Secure Canada, and others—established the People's Food Policy Project in 2008 to engage Canadians from across the country in debates about what kind of national food and agriculture policy they want. The participatory consultation process led to the successful launch in April 2011 of *Resetting the Table: A People's Food Policy for Canada*—a Canadian food policy firmly grounded on food sovereignty principles (Kneen 2011).[11] And communities in different provinces are working to improve and strengthen instruments of food sovereignty such as orderly marketing and supply management, while others are growing community gardens, strengthening the ties between farmers and urban consumers through community shared agriculture, practising urban

---

Box 24.2 Nyéléni 2007 Principles of Food Sovereignty

Food Sovereignty

1. **Focuses on Food for People:** Food sovereignty puts people . . . at the centre of food, agriculture, livestock and fisheries policies, ensuring sufficient, healthy and culturally appropriate food for all individuals, peoples and communities; and rejects the proposition that food is just another commodity or component for international agri-business.

2. **Values Food Providers:** Food sovereignty values and supports the contributions, and respects the rights, of women and men, peasants and small-scale family farmers, pastoralists, artisanal fisherfolk, forest dwellers, indigenous peoples and agricultural fisheries workers, including migrants, who cultivate, grow, harvest and process food; and rejects those policies, actions and programmes that undervalue them, threaten their livelihoods and eliminate them.

3. **Localizes Food Systems:** Food sovereignty brings food providers and consumers closer together; puts providers and consumers at the centre of decision-making on food issues; protects food providers from the dumping of food and food aid in local markets; protects consumers from poor quality and unhealthy food, inappropriate food aid and food tainted with genetically modified organisms; and resists governance structures, agreements and practices that depend on and promote unsustainable and inequitable international trade and give power to remote and unaccountable corporations.

4. **Puts Control Locally:** Food sovereignty places control over territory, land, grazing, water, seeds, livestock and fish populations on local food providers and respects their rights. They can use and share them in socially and environmentally sustainable ways which conserve diversity; . . . and [food sovereignty] rejects the privatization of natural resources through laws, commercial contracts and intellectual property rights regimes.

5. **Builds Knowledge and Skills:** Food sovereignty builds on the skills and local knowledge of food providers and their local organizations who conserve, develop and manage localized food production and harvesting systems, developing appropriate research systems to support this and passing on this wisdom to future generations; and rejects technologies that undermine, threaten or contaminate these skills and knowledge.

6. **Works with Nature:** Food sovereignty uses the contributions of nature in diverse, low-external-input agro-ecological production and harvesting methods that maximize the contribution of ecosystems and improve resilience and adaptation, especially in the face of climate change; it seeks to heal the planet so that the planet may heal us; and, rejects methods that harm beneficial ecosystem functions, that depend on energy-intensive monocultures and livestock factories, destructive fishing practices and other industrialized production methods, which damage the environment and contribute to global warming.

Source: Nyéléni (2007).

agriculture, and supporting farmers' markets building indigenous food sovereignty (Wittman et al. 2011, Desmarais and Wittman 2014)

In the global South, from the pampas, highlands, and islands of the Americas and the drylands and river basins of Africa to the streets, lowlands, and fertile valleys of Asia, urban-based social movements, peasant organizations, rural women, and farm workers are actively engaged in building food sovereignty (Wittman et al. 2010). Arriving later to the table are academics whose contributions are significant as they raise thorny questions, expose dilemmas, and engage in debate, thus helping to expand and deepen the theory, experiences, and knowledge of food sovereignty.[12]

These are all promising developments that demonstrate an alternative agriculture is in the works. Food sovereignty goes beyond food and agriculture and creates the opportunities and possibilities to fundamentally alter social relations, cultures, and politics—indeed, it prompts us to question the very basis of modern societies (Handy and Fehr 2010). Food sovereignty is ultimately about a different way of being, a different way of relating to nature, a different way of relating with one another—what Hannah Wittman (2010) calls a new **agrarian citizenship**.[13] For example, La Vía Campesina's assertion (2008c:2) that "food sovereignty means stopping violence against women" speaks to the enormity of change required. As the Declaration of Maputo (La Vía Campesina 2008b:4) went on to say: "If we do not eradicate violence towards women within our movement, we will not advance in our struggles, and if we do not create new gender relations, we will not be able to build a new society."

Conclusion—The Challenges to Food Sovereignty

The challenges to food sovereignty are significant. Given the space limitations, I discuss only some of the most obvious ones. The first is the sheer extent and complexity of change required. After all, we are talking about a fundamental transformation of societies—one that involves the redistribution of all kinds of resources, including power. For example, in talking about only one aspect of food sovereignty, land reform, Borras and Franco (2010:107) point out that "it is difficult to imagine how any initiative towards food sovereignty can take off when the community pushing for such an alternative vision has no effective control over land resources, and those who have the control (the elite—state and non-state) have visions of development fundamentally opposed to food sovereignty." These powerful forces—including the political and economic elite, international institutions, transnational corporations, and national governments—who structured and are benefiting from neo-liberal agriculture are precisely what food sovereignty is up against, making the struggles intense, long, and in many cases life-threatening.

Rafael Alegría Moncada, a Honduran peasant leader and coordinator of La Vía Campesina, in speaking about the ongoing political upheaval in his country says that food sovereignty is not possible unless and until real democracy is established (Alegría 2011). As the Nyéléni Forum (Nyéléni 2007:5) stated "in order to be able to apply policies that allow autonomy in food production it is necessary to have political conditions that exercise autonomy in all the territorial spaces, countries, regions, cities and rural communities. Food sovereignty is only possible if it takes place at the same time as the political sovereignty of peoples." But this struggle for public engagement and widespread democracy and autonomy is often extremely dangerous. La Vía Campesina's (2006) annual reports on human rights abuses in the countryside showed how some powerful interests respond to those who advance food sovereignty.[14] Rafael Alegría knows this only too well. He has been imprisoned and has received death threats because of his role in demanding democracy and changes to legislation that would bring about a genuine agrarian reform (Marentes 2009).

When the necessary political conditions are created and food sovereignty succeeds in carving democratic spaces for debate on food and agriculture, a second challenge emerges. As Patel (2007:91) puts it, since "no 'peoples' have a single and unifying perspective on food policy" food sovereignty in effect "calls for new political spaces to be filled with argument." This brings us to the very real and messy business of building consensus. What mechanisms and processes can those advocating food sovereignty introduce to reconcile class interests and balance power dynamics to ensure that all voices are heard and acted upon? There is no easy answer to this question. The power of food sovereignty lies in its demand that such spaces for arguments be created in the first place, thus enabling people to get on with building community. Ultimately, as history tells us, community opposition can be the strongest form of resistance to the forces of global capitalism (Chatterjee 1993).

A third challenge to food sovereignty is the threat of usurpation by powerful interests who can reshape its meaning and thus dilute it of revolutionary potential. Remember that one of the reasons La Vía Campesina helped organize the Nyéléni Forum was precisely that it sought to preserve and cultivate the authenticity of the framework. Fairbairn (2010) argues that there may be less opportunity for usurpation, because food sovereignty evolved from the marginalized and oppressed, and it seeks to overturn the whole food regime within which it was created while attempting to create an entirely different one. Nevertheless, the global food sovereignty movement needs to be vigilant to ensure that food sovereignty is not misappropriated and drained of its transformatory potential.

In conclusion, there is much potential in the food sovereignty framework. It creates opportunities for a major overhaul of the existing environmentally unsustainable and socially unjust global food system, and in the process it can facilitate revolutionary social and political change. Meanwhile, the difficulties in establishing the necessary political conditions for food sovereignty to flourish should not be underestimated. The barriers to food sovereignty are everywhere, powerful, and often violent. But there are also significant cracks in the foundation of the corporate-led, neo-liberal, industrial model of agriculture that nature itself is revealing on a daily basis. Food sovereignty allows us to imagine and build alternatives that can, in the words of La Vía Campesina (2010:1) "feed the world and cool the planet"—both are absolutely necessary.

Discussion Questions

1. What are some of the major limitations of the idea and practice of food security?

2. Is a radical alternative like food sovereignty necessary? Why?

3. What are the key elements of food sovereignty, and how do these compare with the existing food system?

4. What are some of the key limitations and challenges in implementing food sovereignty?

Further Reading

1. Desmarais, Annette Aurélie. 2007. *La Vía Campesina: Globalization and the Power of Peasants*. Halifax, NS, and London: Fernwood and Pluto Books.

This book explores the social and political significance of La Vía Campesina by analyzing the main issues, strategies, and collective actions of the social movement and highlighting its efforts to build alternatives to the powerful forces of neo-liberal economic globalization.

2. Trauger, Amy, ed. 2015. *Food Sovereignty in International Context: Discourse, Politics and Practices of Place* Routledge Studies on Food, Society and the Environment. Oxford and New York: Routledge.

An interesting collection of chapters that critically explores the discourse, politics, and practice of food sovereignty in various countries including Canada, Ecuador, Italy, Switzerland, the United Kingdom, and the United States.

3. Wittman, Hannah, Annette Aurélie Desmarais, and Nettie Wiebe, eds. 2010. *Food Sovereignty: Reconnecting Food, Nature and Community.* Halifax, NS; Oakland, CA; and London: Fernwood; Food First Books; and Pambazuka Press.

This contribution critically engages debates concerning food sovereignty while exploring new research directions. The collection examines the historical rise of the industrial agricultural system, outlines the environmental and social consequences of this system, and gives voice to the peasant movements that are working on making food sovereignty a reality.

4. Wittman, Hannah, Annette Aurélie Desmarais, and Nettie Wiebe. 2011. *Food Sovereignty in Canada.* Halifax, NS: Fernwood.

This book explores how communities in various parts of Canada are actively engaged in implementing food sovereignty. By analyzing Indigenous food sovereignty, experiences with orderly marketing, community gardens, the political engagement of nutritionists, forays into urban agriculture, and links between the rural and urban, the book demonstrates that the urgent work of building food sovereignty in Canada is well under way.

Notes

1. *Farm Women and Canadian Agricultural Policy* (Roppel, Desmarais, and Martz 2006) was one of the first in-depth studies to propose food sovereignty to Canadian policy makers. Later in this chapter I explain how other social actors in Canada are using food sovereignty.

2. The Standing Committee on Agriculture and Agri-Food held meetings to investigate the extent of the farm crisis and views on the "Next Generation" Agricultural Policy Framework. The committee's final report, entitled "Fact-Finding Mission on Canada's New Agriculture and Agri-food Policy" is available at www2.parl.gc.ca/HousePublications/Publication.aspx? DocId=3066010&Language=E&Mode=1&Parl=39&Ses=1&File=18#part3.

3. The UN Declarations of the World Conferences on Environment and Development held in 1992 in Rio de Janeiro and Johannesburg specify the importance of economic growth for sustainable development. The World Bank's *World Development Reports* consistently present the view that sustained economic growth is critical for sustainable development. In 2006 the World Bank created the Commission on Growth and Development to look at issues and policies designed to ensure sustained economic growth for development.

4. This view is reflected in a number of international publications and national government policies. See, for example, the International Fund for Agricultural Development's *Rural Poverty Report 2001: The Challenge of Ending Rural Poverty*, the World Bank's *World Development Report 2008: Agriculture for Development*, Agriculture Canada's "Growing Together: A Vision for Canada's Agri-Food Industry" (1989) and Agriculture and Agri-Food Canada's national policy documents called the Agricultural Policy Framework (2003) and Growing Forward Policy Framework (2008).

5. See, for example, the FAO (2000) study of changes in 14 developing countries following the implementation of the WTO's Agreement on Agriculture. UNCTAD's (2006) study of the agricultural input industry provides evidence of the extent of corporate concentration in that sector.

6. For an excellent discussion of the convergences and divergences of food security and food sovereignty, vp, see *Dialogues in Human Geography* 4, no. 2 (2014) and especially the article by Jennifer Clapp (2014).

7. La Vía Campesina (2004) petitioned the United Nations Human Rights Commission for a declaration of peasant rights. The declaration is now being discussed by the Open-Ended Intergovernmental Working Group (OEIWG) on a UN Declaration on the Rights of Peasants and Other People Working in Rural Areas (UN Human Rights Council 2013). See the Draft Declaration (UN General Assembly 2013), and Edelman (2014) and Claeys (2014, 2015) for more analysis.

8. The statement was signed by numerous social movements and non-governmental organizations and released just prior to the Fourth Ministerial Meeting of the WTO held in Doha, Qatar. (Desmarais 2007).

9. See especially the Latin America and Caribbean (LAC) Report of the IAASTD, available at www.agassessment-watch.org.

10. See www.usfoodsovereigntyalliance.org. For an analysis of movements working for food sovereignty in the United States, see Brent, Schiavoni, and Alonso-Fradejas (2015).

11. See http://peoplesfoodpolicy.ca/ for information on the People's Food Policy Project. Wittman et al. (2011) and Desmarais and Wittman (2014) explore various food sovereignty initiatives in Canada.

12. See for example, among others, Trauger (2015), special issues of *Journal of Peasant Studies* (41, no. 6 [2014]) and *Third World Quarterly* (36, no. 3 [2015]) and *Globalizations* (12, no. 4 [2015]).

13. Agrarian citizenship "encompasses the political and material rights and practices of rural dwellers (Wittman 2009b), and is a form of citizenship based not solely on issues of rural political representation, but also on a relationship with the socio-ecological metabolism between society and nature. This notion of citizenship recognizes nature's role in the continuing political, economic, and cultural evolution of agrarian society. . . ." (Wittman 2009a).

14. See many documents on human rights violations available at www.viacampesina.org.

References

Agriculture and Agri-Food Canada. 2003. "Agriculture Policy Framework." www4.agr.gc.ca/AAFC-AAC/display afficher.do?id=1183127394087&lang=eng.

———. 2008. "Growing Forward Policy Framework." www4.agr.gc.ca/AAFC-AAC/display-afficher.do?id=1238606407452&lang=eng.

Agriculture Canada. 1989. "Growing Together: A Vision for Canada's Agri-Food Industry." www.archive.org/details/growingtogetherv00cana.

Alegría Moncada, Rafael. 2011. Interview conducted by author. Tegucigalpa, Honduras, 11 February.

Borras, Saturnino M. Jr., Marc Edelman, and Cristóbal Kay. 2008. "Transnational Agrarian Movements: Origins and Politics, Campaigns and Impact." *Journal of Agrarian Change* 8(2/3):1–36.

———, and Jennifer Franco. 2010. "Food Sovereignty and Redistributive Land Policies: Exploring Linkages, Identifying Challenges." Pp. 106–19 in *Food Sovereignty*, Wittman, et al.

Brent, Zoe W., Christina M. Schiavoni, and Alberto Alonso-Fradejas. 2015. "Contextualising Food Sovereignty: The Politics of Convergence among Movements in the USA." *Third World Quarterly* 36(3):618–35.

Chatterjee, Partha. 1993. *The Nation and Its Fragments: Colonial and Postcolonial Histories*. Princeton, NJ: Princeton University Press.

Claeys, Priscilla. 2009. "The Right to Food and Food Sovereignty: Complementary or Contradictory Discourses on the Global Food Crisis?" Paper presented at the Conference on the World Food Crisis, Zacatecas, Mexico, 13–15 August.

———. 2014. "Food Sovereignty and the Recognition of New Rights for Peasants at the UN: A Critical Overview of La Vía Campesina's Rights Claims over the last 20 Years." *Globalizations* doi: 10.1080/14747731.2014.957929

———. 2015. *Human Rights and the Food Sovereignty Movement: Reclaiming Control*. Routledge Studies in Food, Society and Environment. Oxford and New York: Routledge.

Clapp, J. 2014. "Food Security and Food Sovereignty: Getting Past the Binary." *Dialogues in Human Geography* 4(2):206–11.

De Schutter, Olivier. 2015. "Food Democracy South and North: From Food Sovereignty to Transition Initiatives." Open Democracy. https://www.opendemocracy.net/olivier-de-schutter/food-democracy-south-and-north-from-food-sovereignty-to-transition-initiatives.

Desmarais, Annette Aurelie, 2007. *La Vía Campesina: Globalization and The Power of Peasants*. Halifax, NS: Fernwood Publishing.

———, and Hannah Wittman. 2014. "Farmers, Foodies

and First Nations: Getting to Food Sovereignty in Canada." *Journal of Peasant Studies* 41(6):1153–73. doi: 10.1080/03066150.2013.876623

Edelman, Marc. 2014. "Dispatch from Geneva: A Treaty on Transnational Corporations? A Declaration on Peasants' Rights?" http://www.focaalblog.com/2014/07/17/dispatch-from-geneva-a-treaty-on-transnational-corporations-a-declaration-on-peasants-rights/#sthash.c13MKgXe.dpuf.

European Coordination Vía Campesina. 2010. "Call to Nyéléni Europe Forum and Camp." *Common Ground* 8 (September). www.eurovia.org/spip.php?article359&lang=fr.

Fairbairn, Madeleine. 2010. "Framing Resistance: International Food Regimes and the Roots of Food Sovereignty." Pp. 15–32 in *Food Sovereignty*, ed. Wittman, et al.

FAO. 2000. "Agriculture, Trade and Food Security: Issues and Options in the WTO Negotiations from the Perspective of Developing Countries." Vol. II, Country Case Studies, Commodities and Trade Division of the FAO: Rome. Accessed 14 January 2003. www.fao.org/DOCREP/033/x8731e/x8931e01a.htm.

———. 2003. "Trade Reforms and Food Security: Conceptualising the Linkages." Rome: Commodity Policy and Projections Service, Commodities and Trade Division.

"Final Declaration of the World Forum on Food Sovereignty." 2001. Havana, Cuba, 7 September. ukabc.org/havanadeclaration.pdf.

Globalizations. 2015. "Food Sovereignty: Concept, Practice and Social Movements." Special issue, 12(4).

GRAIN. 2005. "Food Sovereignty: Turning the Global Food System Upside Down." *Seedling.* (April). www.grain.org/seedling/?id=329.

Handy, Jim, and Carla Fehr. 2010. "'Drawing Forth the Force that Slumbered in Peasants' Arms': the Economist, High Agriculture and Selling Capitalism." Pp. 45–61 in *Food Sovereignty*, ed Wittman, et al.

IAASTD. 2009. *Agriculture at a Crossroads: Global Report.* Washington, DC: Island Press.

International Fund for Agricultural Development. 2001. *Rural Poverty Report 2001: The Challenge of Ending Rural Poverty.* Oxford: Oxford University Press.

International Workshop on the Review of the Agreement on Agriculture. 2003. "Towards Food Sovereignty: Constructing an Alternative to the World Trade Organization's Agreement on Agriculture." Geneva, February.

Journal of Peasant Studies. 2014. "Critical Perspectives on Food Sovereignty." Special issue, 41(6).

Kneen, Cathleen. 2011. "Food Secure Canada: Where Agriculture, Environment, Health, Food and Justice Intersect." *Food Sovereignty in Canada*, ed Wittman, et al.

La Vía Campesina. 1996a. *Proceedings of the II International Conference of the Vía Campesina.* Tlaxcala, Mexico, 18–21 April. Brussels: NCOS Publications.

———. 1996b. "The Right to Produce and Access to Land."

Position of the Vía Campesina on Food Sovereignty presented at the World Food Summit. Rome, 13–17 November.

———. 2003. "What Is Food Sovereignty?" Jakarta: Operational Secretariat of Vía Campesina.

———. 2004. "Vía Campesina in Geneva at Session of the Human Rights Commission of the UN." Geneva, 4 April.

———. 2006. *Violations of Peasants' Human Rights: A Report on Cases and Patterns of Violence.* Jakarta. www.viacampesina.org/main_en/images/sotries/annual-report-HR-2006.pdf.

———. 2008a. "An Answer to the Global Food Crisis: Peasants and Small Farmers Can Feed the World!" Jakarta, 1 May. viacampesina.org.

———. 2008b. "Declaration of Maputo: V International Conference of La Vía Campesina." Maputo, Mozambique, 19–22 October.

———. 2008c. "Declaration of the III Women's Assembly of La Vía Campesina." Maputo, Mozambique, 22–3 October.

———. 2009. "Massiva protesta en defensa de la verdadera democracia en Honduras." Press release. http://via-campesina.org/sp/index.php?option=com_content&view=article&id=762:massiva-protesta-en-defensa-de-la-democracia-en-honduras&catid=15:noticias-de-las-regiones&Itemid=29.

———. 2010. "The People Create Thousands of Solutions to Confront Climate Change!" 1 September. www.viacampesina.org/en/index.php?option=com_content&view=article&id=941:the-people-create-thousands-of-solutions-to-confront-climate-change&catid=48:-climate-change-and-agrofuels&Itemid=75.

Long, Clara. 2005. "Food Sovereignty and the Vía Campesina: The Evolution of a Counter-Hegemonic Discourse." Unpublished MSc dissertation. Department of Geography and Environment, London School of Economics and Political Science.

Marentes, Carlos. 2009. "Broaden and Maintain the International Solidarity to Stop the Repression against the Honduran People." http://viacampesina.org/en/index.php/news-from-the-regions-mainmenu-29/750-broaden-and-maintain-the-international-solidarity-to-stop-the-repression-against-the-honduran-people.

Martínez-Torres, Maria Elena, and Peter Rosset. 2010. "La Vía Campesina: The Birth and Evolution of a Transnational Social Movement." *Journal of Peasant Studies* 37(1):149–76.

McMichael, Philip. 2008a. "Food Sovereignty, Social Reproduction and the Agrarian Question." Pp. 288–312 in *Peasants and Globalization: Political Economy, Rural Transformation and the Agrarian Question*, ed. A.H. Adram-Lodhi and Cristóbal Kay. Routledge ISS Studies in Rural Livelihoods Series. New York: Routledge.

———. 2008b. "Peasants Make Their Own History, But Not Just as They Please . . ." *Journal of Agrarian Change* 8(2–3):205–28.

NGO/CSO Forum for Food Sovereignty. 2002. "Food Sovereignty: A Right for All." Political Statement of the NGO/CSO Forum for Food Sovereignty. Rome, 13 June. 222.croceviaterra.it/FORUM/DOCUMENTI520DEL%20FORUM/political%20 statement.pdf.

NOUMINREN. 2006. "Draft Declaration of Food Sovereignty for the Japanese Farmers and Consumers." Position paper presented at Nyéléni 2007 by the Japanese National Coalition of Workers, Farmers and Consumers for Safe Food and Health. Selingué, Mali, 23–7 February.

Nyéléni. 2007. Proceedings of the Forum for Food Sovereignty. Selingué, Mali, 23–7 February. www.nyeleni.org.

Patel, Rajeev. 2005. "Global Fascism, Revolutionary Humanism and the Ethics of Food Sovereignty." *Development* 48(2):79–83.

———. 2006. "International Agrarian Restructuring and the Practical Ethics of Peasant Movement Solidarity." *Journal of Asian and African Studies* 41:71–93.

———. 2007. "Transgressing Rights: La Vía Campesina's Call for Food Sovereignty." *Feminist Economics* 13(1):87–116.

———. 2010. "What Does Food Sovereignty Look Like?" In Wittman et al., *Food Sovereignty*, 186–96.

People's Food Sovereignty Network. 2001. "Peoples' Food Sovereignty Statement." Accessed 5 July 2007. www.peoplesfoodsovereignty.org.

Pérez-Vitoria, Silvia. 2005. *Le retour des paysans*. Paris: Actes Sud.

Rodríguez Mendoza, Miguel. 2002. "Trade Liberalisation and Food Security." Speech of the Deputy Director General of the WTO to the World Food Summit. Rome, 11 June. www.wto.org/English/news_e/news02_e/speech_rodriguez_mendoza_11june02_e.htm.

Roppel, Carla, Annette Aurélie Desmarais, and Diane Martz. 2006. *Farm Women and Canadian Agricultural Policy*. Ottawa: Status of Women Canada. foodstudies.ca/Documents/Farm_Women_and_the_APF.pdf.

Rosset, Peter. 2003. "Food Sovereignty: Global Rallying Cry of Farmer Movements." Institute for Food and Development Policy. *Backgrounder* 9(4). www.foodfirst.org/node/47.

Standing Committee on Agriculture and Agri-Food. 2007. 39th Parliament, 1st Session, Draft transcript of evidence. 22 February. www.parl.gc.ca/HousePublications/Publication.aspx?DocId=2737536&Language=E&Mode=1&Parl=39&Ses=1.

Stevens, Christopher, Romilly Greehill, Jane Kennan, and Steven Devereux. 2000. *The WTO Agreement on Agriculture and Food Security*. Economic Series No. 42, Commonwealth Secretariat, London.

The Economist. 2008a. "The Silent Tsunami: The Food Crisis and How to Solve It." 387(8576):13.

———. 2008b. "The New Face of Hunger." 387(8576):32–4.

———. 2009. "Whatever Happened to the Food Crisis?: World Food Prices." 392(8638):57.

Third World Quarterly. 2015. "Food Sovereignty: Convergence and Contradictions, Condition and Challenges." Special issue, 36(3).

Trauger, Amy. 2015. *Food Sovereignty in International Context: Discourse, Politics and Practices of Place*. Routledge Studies on Food, Society and the Environment. Oxford and New York: Routledge.

UNCTAD. 2006. "Tracking the Trend towards Market Concentration: The Case of the Agricultural Input Industry." Report prepared by the United Nations Conference on Trade and Development. www.unctad.org/en/docs/ditccom200516_en.pdf.

UN Human Rights Council. 2013. "First Session of the Open-Ended Intergovernmental Working Group on a United Nations Declaration on the Rights of Peasants and Other People Working in Rural Areas." http://www.ohchr.org/EN/HRBodies/HRC/RuralAreas/Pages/FirstSession.aspx.

UN General Assembly. 2013. "Declaration on the Rights of Peasants and Other People Working in Rural Areas." Human Rights Council, First Session, 9 July. http://daccess-dds-ny.un.org/doc/UNDOC/GEN/G13/149/01/PDF/G1314901.pdf?OpenElement.

Wittman, Hannah. 2009a. "Reworking the Metabolic Rift: La Vía Campesina, Agrarian Citizenship and Food Sovereignty." *Journal of Peasant Studies* 36(4):805–26.

———. 2009b. "Agrarian Citizenship: Land, Life and Power in Brazil." *Journal of Rural Studies* 25:120–30.

———. 2010. "Reconnecting Agriculture and the Environment: Food Sovereignty and the Agrarian Basis of Ecological Citizenship." *Food Sovereignty*, ed Wittman, et al.

———, Annette Aurélie Desmarais, and Nettie Wiebe, eds. 2010. *Food Sovereignty: Reconnecting Food, Nature and Community*. Halifax, NS; Oakland, CA; and London: Fernwood, Food First Books, and Pambazuka Press.

———, ———, and ———, eds. 2011. *Food Sovereignty in Canada*. Halifax, NS: Fernwood.

World Bank. 2007. *World Development Report 2007: Agriculture for Development*. Washington, DC: World Bank.

———. 2008. *World Development Report 2008: Agriculture for Development*. Washington, DC: World Bank.

World Commission on Environment and Development. 1987. *Our Common Future*. Oxford: Oxford University Press. www.un-documents.net/ocf-ov.htm.

Ziegler, Jean. 2003. "Report by the Special Rapporteur on the Right to Food: Mission to Brazil." United Nations Commission on Human Rights, 59th session. 3 January.

———. 2004. "Report Submitted by the Special Rapporteur on the Right to Food." United Nations Commission on Human Rights, 60th session. 9 February.

Glossary

agrarian citizenship A concept that links agricultural practice to environmental **sustainability** and social justice, thus defining new ways of being and interacting with nature and one another.

Agreement on Agriculture (AoA) An international, legally binding trade agreement that regulates domestic and international agriculture and **food policies**.

Agreement on the Application of Sanitary and Phytosanitary Measures (SPS) An international, legally binding agreement that regulates when states may restrict trade on the grounds of the safety of human and animal health.

Agreement on Trade-Related Aspects of Intellectual Property Rights (TRIPs) An international, legally binding agreement that requires states to implement domestic intellectual property rights regimes, including for agriculture and food-related products, practices, and technology.

Agriculture Group of Twenty (Ag-G20) A bargaining coalition of 23 developing countries at the World Trade Organization. The group is led by Brazil, India, and China; other members include Argentina, Bolivia, Chile, Cuba, Ecuador, Egypt, Guatemala, Indonesia, Mexico, Nigeria, Pakistan, Paraguay, Peru, Philippines, South Africa, Tanzania, Thailand, Uruguay, Venezuela, and Zimbabwe.

agrofuel Any agricultural crop converted into ethanol or biodiesel, generally to be used as an energy source to run automobiles and trucks. So far, most of it comes from sugar or corn crops. Depending on how one counts the energy inputs, there is debate over whether there is any energy gain at all in existing agrofuel production or any reduction in greenhouse gas emissions.

alternative food initiative The multiplicity of self-governed, food-related initiatives that aim to challenge the logic of the dominant **food system** and build viable solutions.

alternative food networks Groups of interrelated people and organizations that aim to bring structural and institutional changes to the existing mainstream practices in the **food system**.

alternative hedonism Coined by philosopher Kate Soper, the term refers to the idea that alternative forms of consumption are not only motivated by altruistic concerns and a desire for "a better world"—they can also be motivated by the self-interested pleasures of consuming differently. For example, eating a meal prepared with local foods appeals to an ethical concern for how food is produced, but also to the pleasures of conviviality and of taking the time to prepare and enjoy a homemade meal.

animal welfare The physical and psychological well-being of an animal. Poor welfare can refer to the compromised physical and/or psychological state of an animal.

aquaculture The cultivation of aquatic plants and animals. Specifically with regard to fish and seafood, aquaculture refers to a range of practices including the centuries-old carp farming in small ponds across China, the conversion of rice fields into shrimp farms across south and southeast Asia, the highly controlled marine fish farms for salmon in Canada, and the marine pens in the Mediterranean where juvenile bluefin tuna captured in the wild are held and fattened for export to the Japanese market.

biodiversity The range of plant and animal species in a given area and their complex interactions.

biodynamic agriculture A form of organic agriculture developed by Rudolf Steiner that emphasizes healthy food, healthy soil, and healthy farms.

biomedical positivism/positivist science A paradigm that views health as understandable through the application of medical sciences, which are used to create knowledge via the scientific method.

biophysical overrides The range of ways that the biological and physical problems created or exacerbated by the industrialization of agriculture are managed in order to ensure continuing productivity.

Canadian Biotechnology Strategy A multi-faceted plan beginning in the late 1970s that evolved from an industry and academic task force charged with facilitating **genetic modification** in Canada.

Canadian Community Health Survey (CCHS) A cross-sectional survey administered by Statistics Canada that collects health-related information from about 60,000 Canadians per year. The sample is designed to be representative of the 10 provinces and 3 territories, but omits individuals not at a fixed address, living on First Nation reserves, in institutions, in the Canadian Armed forces, or in some remote areas of the country.

Canadian Wheat Board A marketing agency that exported western Canadian wheat and barley for farmers, pooling prices and returning all **profits** from sales, minus marketing costs, to farmers.

capitalism An economy is capitalist to the extent that it is dominated by privately owned and controlled autonomous units that hire wage workers and seek to maximize **profits** by producing commodities for sale in the market.

certification Approval that a product and its production process meet certain criteria, whether environmental or social, such as organic standards or labour standards. The certifying body may be a government agency but is increasingly a third-party non-governmental agency, and the certification serves as a marketing incentive for producers.

charitable food assistance Food that is delivered to those in need via a charitable model rather than as part of a state-sponsored entitlement program. In Canada, charitable food assistance programs tend to be voluntary, extra-governmental, and community based. Food banks are the most common form of charitable food assistance in Canada, but charitable meal and snack programs are also found across the country.

circuits of capital/turnover time Capital typically passes through a circuit. For example, the money needed to buy material **means of production** and to hire workers is combined in a production process out of which comes a new commodity that **capitalists** then hope to sell for more money than their costs (i.e. for a **profit**). This movement from original money to invest to final profit is one turnover of the circuit. Other things being equal, the faster the turnover of capital, the greater the profit.

civil commons Any co-operative human construction that protects and/or enables universal access to life goods.

civil society The social sphere of collective action focused on shared interests, purposes, and values. Although considered distinct from the state and the market, the boundaries between these spheres can be fluid.

class relations Classes come into existence when one or more groups take all of the economic surplus above subsistence for themselves.

class/stratification Social groups divided into subsets based on their place in the process of economic production, as in masters and slaves, lords and peasants, or **capitalists** and workers. *Stratification* is a looser term that refers to any differences among people that give rise to a hierarchy of distinct strata. Common differences in stratification are birth, wealth, race, religion, ethnicity, or caste.

Clean Development Mechanism (CDM) An international scheme that allows a country with an emission-reduction target or emission-limitation commitment to implement an emission-reduction project in developing countries.

climate change adaptation The mix of planning, **policy**, technological, and infrastructural responses for coping with unfolding and projected climate changes.

climate change mitigation The need to reduce greenhouse gas emissions (carbon dioxide, methane, and nitrous oxide) and enhance sequestration capacity. Some argue that massive-scale geo-engineering (technological interventions) must be part of this discussion; others insist that this could entail untold risks.

Code of Conduct for Responsible Fisheries A non-mandatory "framework for national and international efforts to ensure sustainable exploitation of aquatic living resources in harmony with the environment" (Preface to Code) developed by the FAO and adopted in 1995. It outlines principles and standards to be observed by all parties in the fishery, including states, researchers, and those involved in the production and trade of fish.

Codes of Practice (COP) A set of national recommendations and requirements created by the National Farm Animal Care Council (NFACC) intended to guide producers on minimum standards of care for farm animals.

collaborative food networks Social structures consisting of interrelated individuals, groups, and organizations with an aim to scale up and scale out the work of **alternative food initiatives** and a goal to build a more socially just and ecologically sustainable **food system**.

collective action frames A set of concepts and theoretical perspectives that translate grievances and solutions into broader claims and invite collective action.

collective impact The accumulated value of multiple actors and initiatives that align efforts to pursue a shared agenda, develop alternatives to the current **food system**—without necessarily expressly opposing the system—and thereby create the conditions for social change through their expansion (in both number and scale).

colonization The historical and continued undermining of **Indigenous peoples'** beliefs, values, and traditions in favour of non-Indigenous beliefs, values, and traditions.

co-management a process of management in which government shares power with resource users or with producers and communities dependent on natural resource extraction, with each given specific rights and responsibilities relating to information and decision making.

Committee on World Food Security (CFS) An intergovernmental committee that aims to be the leading global platform for countries and other stakeholders on **food security** policies.

commodity chains (or systems) All stages of the specific production, distribution, and consumption of commodities such as wheat, beef, tomatoes, and fish.

commodity fetishism The tendency, in a **capitalist** economy, for the range of social and biophysical relations involved in the production of commodities (including unmeasured or undervalued costs) to be hidden and largely incomprehensible.

common property resources Natural resources that a community or society owns and manages collectively including water bodies, pastures, fisheries, forests, and clean air.

communities of food practice Networks of individuals and organizations—public, private, and non-profit—engaged in creating a regional, networked, inclusive agrifood economy.

community food security An approach that focuses on how to ensure food access and availability at the community level, using local and place-based solutions and policies.

community-supported agriculture An innovation that came of age in the 1990s, in which customers buy a farmer's crops in advance of the season and are paid in produce throughout the season.

community-supported fishery Programs modelled after the increasingly popular **community-supported agriculture** programs, offering members a regular share of fresh, sustainably harvested seafood for a pre-paid membership fee. Consumers get fresh, locally harvested fish and seafood, marine ecosystems are allowed to recover from overfishing, and fishing communities continue to thrive.

connotation versus denotation Words can both denote and connote meaning. *White*, for example denotes a particular colour, but is often seen to connote innocence or goodness. Similarly, food can connote meaning, in the way that turkey, for example, denotes a type of fowl but also connotes or suggests a celebratory meal in contemporary North America. In this way, food has an inherent "narrativity," such that a meal can tell a nuanced story in the language of food.

consumer culture A feature of late-industrial **capitalist** societies where consumerism reigns dominant, particularly over issues of production, in the public imagination. While other cultures also give symbolic weight to material objects, consumer culture is characterized by the extensive scale of capitalist commodification and the intrusion of consumer imperatives into multiple areas of everyday life.

consumerism The **ideological** dimension of consumer culture; the focus on commodity acquisition as a central feature of social life. *Consumerism* is distinct from the term *consumption*, which refers straightforwardly to the process of using up goods and services, and need not have an ideological dimension.

Convention on the Law of the Sea The United Nations Convention on the Law of the Sea (UNCLOS) is a treaty that established the 200-mile **exclusive economic zone**. It also sets out states' rights and responsibilities for use of the oceans and their resources, including transportation and seabed resources as well as high-seas fisheries. It was adopted in 1982 and came into effect in 1994.

co-opting The tendency (of the industrial model) to assimilate any resistance and commercialize this resistance for **profit**.

corporate concentration A situation where very few firms control most of the business in any given sector of the economy. It is often expressed by a four-firm concentration ratio, which expresses the percentage of business in any given sector controlled by the four leading firms. In many sub-sectors of the Canadian food industry, corporate concentration is very high.

cost–price squeeze The small or negative margins farmers realize when the costs of producing food—inputs, labour, and required capital investment—are larger than the income generated from the sale of that food.

critical dietetics An initiative that emerged from the collective unease many **dietetic** educators and practitioners were experiencing regarding the narrow approach to understanding the meanings ascribed to food and health. Critical dietetic scholars discuss how new ways of thinking and asking questions may help to expose our assumptions and familiar ways of practice in the dietetic profession.

critical race theory An analytical framework that examines the intersections of race and power and considers ways in which racialized people are marginalized.

critical social theory A sociological theory that attends to the ways in which power shapes **identities**, relationships, and social structures.

culinary versus cultural historian There is a key distinction between the culinary historian and the cultural historian. The culinary historian identifies key moments of change in food history— for example, the invention of a recipe or a food production technique. The cultural or social historian interested in food studies, by contrast, looks at the meanings and practices associated with food as indicators of cultural and social change more broadly—food being only one possible lens of approach.

demand–supply coordination A situation that occurs when demand for food is optimized for population health, and food supply is planned and coordinated to meet that optimal demand.

depeasantization The disappearance of peasant livelihoods as market economies spread in the countryside, often resulting in rural to urban migration.

descriptive practice *See* **prescriptive practice**.

dietetics A registered health profession in Canada that seeks to treat disease and maintain the health of individuals and populations through nutrition intervention.

differential profit A concept that captures the reality that some commodities in a **capitalist** economy, including **pseudo foods**, attract higher profits than average.

discourse Communication (written or spoken) and the meaning that surrounds it, which is often implicit and often **ideological**; ways of understanding an issue that circulate through a society and are enacted through everyday practices.

distancing The separation between consumers and the sources of their food typical of the industrial **food system.**

"eatertainment" The ways in which food and entertainment experiences have become conflated in contemporary consumer culture, such as in food programs on television.

eco-labelling A way of harnessing consumer choice to achieve sustainable production. It works as a marketing incentive by promoting consumer demand for fish caught or raised in environmentally and/or socially sustainable ways, and rewards producers for using responsible fisheries practices. The labels or certificates may be awarded by independent bodies such as the Marine Stewardship Council (MSC), or large supermarket chains, such as French chain Carrefour, which has its own *pêche responsable* label.

economies of scale Cost advantages, such as increased output per worker in order to reduce the relative cost of labour in production. In the context of **intensive livestock operations**, the advantages of producing at a scale where the cost per "unit" of output (each animal) is considerably lower than less intensive, smaller-scale production.

ecosystem approach An approach to fisheries management that moves away from the modelling of individual stocks to recognizing the interdependence of marine flora and fauna, as well as their sensitivity to multiple factors, from destructive fishing gear to land-based pollution.

ecosystem services A term that is generally associated with attempts to quantify and attach monetary values to the role that ecosystems play in human economies, and is something that can be approached at different scales up to the global level (e.g. rain forests in the carbon cycle).

emancipatory A stance that supports all people to live in fair societies in a manner that is congruent with their affirmative sense of self and that challenges structures and discourses that oppress and privilege.

embodiment A term that describes how our experiences of living in our physical bodies are conditioned by social structures, such as gender, racialization, sexuality, age, etc. In other words, embodiment describes how social structures and culture "get under our skin" and are experienced and lived by each of us.

ethical foodscape A food environment where a range of actors is involved in ethical eating (e.g. food corporations, **social movement** organizations, ethical food networks, individual consumers).

ethnicity The affiliation of a group of people who share a common national, cultural, or racial heritage.

eutrophication A process in which excess nutrients deposited into freshwater ecosystems and oceans around coastal riverheads produce algae blooms that deplete oxygen and can devastate aquatic life.

exclusive economic zone (EEZ) A zone of 200 miles from its coast over which a state has sovereignty, codified in the UN **Convention on the Law of the Sea** (UNCLOS), which came into effect in 1982.

exploitation The difference between the value that a working class produces and the value that it receives as wage or salary in a **capitalist** society. Marx claims that all forms of capitalist **profit** ultimately come from this difference.

extensive aquaculture A type of aquaculture where seed is usually the only form of intervention, the stock is allowed to grow on its own using natural food sources and conditions, and the stocking density tends to be lower than in **intensive aquaculture**, to which it is contrasted.

externalities Social, environmental, or economic costs or benefits that are not reflected in the market prices of products.

externalized cost A cost that is forced on those who are not a party to a transaction. For example, the costs of **GM** cropping are borne not simply by the farmer-grower but by neighbouring farmers, consumers, the broader society, and the environment.

family farm A farming operation in which the labour, management, and ownership investment is primarily supplied by family members, resulting in smaller-scale farming units.

fat phobia The systematic oppression of fat people that manifests on a one-on-one basis in various ways, including employment and education discrimination, and a lack of accessible public spaces.

fat studies A new interdisciplinary field of scholarship that critiques implicit and explicit negative stereotypes, assumptions, and stigma associated with fatness and fat bodies.

feminism A body of theory and a political movement concerned with understanding and changing the systematic marginalization of all women, but especially those who are further marginalized by racism, class, sexual orientation, (dis)ability, age, and other axes of inequities.

feminist analyses The practice of examining an issue or topic with the express purpose of emphasizing the related systems of power that result in inequity, particularly with respect to gender but also considering intersections with other axes of oppression (such as racism, classism, ableism, heterosexism, etc.).

Fish Stocks Agreement "The United Nations Agreement for the Implementation of the Provisions of UNCLOS relating to the Conservation and Management of Straddling Fish Stocks and Highly Migratory Fish Stocks." Using the precautionary principle and the best current scientific findings, it guides states in conserving and managing fish stocks both within their exclusive economic zones and in co-operation with other countries. It was adopted in 1995 and came into force in 2001.

fishing down the marine food web A phenomenon observable in recent decades as fishing intensity has increased: as larger fish higher up in the marine food chain are depleted, a greater proportion of the catch consists of smaller fish of lower weight and density. Excessive fishing of these smaller fish may in turn take away the food sources of the larger fish and prevent their regeneration, as well as affecting a protein food source for human populations who eat the smaller fish.

food Any substance that nourishes us and provides genuine sustenance. Many edible products in the supermarket do not meet this definition, and in fact detract from health and well-being.

Food and Agriculture Organization (FAO) An agency of the United Nations that leads international efforts to defeat hunger. It serves developed and developing countries and acts as a forum where states can negotiate agreements and debate **policy**.

food charters Public endorsements that identify guiding principles, values, and goals for the operation of the food system in a given locality such as a municipality or a province.

food choices versus foodways Food choices indicate decisions made by an individual about food sourcing, selection, and preparation. Foodways, by contrast, more broadly refers to the system through which food is sourced, prepared, served, and consumed. Foodways are inevitably dynamic, changing with each shift in food choice and the entrance and exit of each actor in the system.

food citizenship The sense of belonging and participating in the **food system** through food-system localization, based on values focused on the community and environmental **sustainability**.

food culture Studies of food culture focus on the *meanings* of food, and can be observed in specific institutions (e.g. cooking schools), within groups of people (e.g. Cajun food culture), and as part of everyday life interactions (e.g. the culture of fad diets).

food deserts Areas in which nutritious and affordable food is not readily accessible to residents; these neighbourhoods are often home to racialized, low-income communities.

food environments Those institutional spheres where food is displayed for sale and/or consumed; **foodscapes**.

food insecurity The inverse of **food security**, meaning that there is inadequate quantity or quality of healthy food available when needed.

food justice An alternative food discourse that emphasizes transformation of the food system and the elimination of disparities and inequalities around class, gender, race, and ethnicity in production of, exchange of, and access to food.

food labels Mandatory or voluntary messages on food packaging that serve as a communicative tool between manufacturers and consumers.

food literacy The competence, skills, and knowledge required to understand the movement of food from field to table and how this process affects humans, other forms of life, and the environment.

food miles The distance that food travels from "land to mouth" or "field to fork." The increasing recognition of the oil and carbon emissions embedded in food miles has had an important role in local food movements.

food policy The guiding principles and sets of rules that direct the actions of public or private actors involved in various aspects of food provisioning.

food policy councils Groups of citizens, politicians, and businesspeople who meet to develop municipal food policies to overcome such food-related problems as hunger, food deserts, and food insecurity.

food production A range of activities involved in the growing, harvesting, manufacture, production, and distribution of food and encompasses the processing, selling, packaging, and delivery of food locally, nationally, and internationally.

food regimes An approach to **food systems** that is global and historical. Food regime analysis combines the "bottom-up" approach of commodity studies with the "top-down" approach of **world-systems theory** and focuses on cycles of stability and transition, both lasting several decades.

food security A condition that exists when all people at all times have physical, social, and economic access to food that is safe and consumed in sufficient quantity and quality to meet their dietary needs and food preferences, and is supported by an environment of adequate sanitation and health services and care, allowing for a healthy and active life.

food sovereignty A political framework developed by **La Vía Campesina** that focuses on the right of peoples and governments to determine their own agriculture systems, food markets, environments, and modes of production. Food sovereignty is a radical alternative to corporate-led, **neo-liberal**, industrial agriculture.

food system All of the activities and processes involved in the ways that people produce, obtain, consume, and dispose of their food, including the inputs and outputs required to make the system run.

food system governance The systems and institutions by which the **food system** is directed.

foodscape A concept that refers to the physical reality of food and **food production** and also may facilitate analysis of the ways we socially construct the **food system**.

foodways The cultural, social, and economic practices associated with food that invite us to think about the way food intersects with history, culture, and tradition.

foodwork The efforts involved in **food production**, procurement, preparation, service, and clean-up. It may be paid (as employment) or unpaid in the household.

gender Socially prescribed understandings of appropriate ways of being a man or woman within society.

gendered division of labour The way in which paid and unpaid work roles have been allocated to men and women based on prevailing notions of masculinity and femininity.

gendered history An historical account that pays particular attention to the ways in which **gender** impacts people and places, as well as social, cultural, economic, and political systems.

General Agreement on Tariffs and Trade (GATT) An international agreement that governed international trade between 1947 and 1994.

genetic enhancement The yield gains made by crossing varieties *within* the same species. This was instrumental to the rising productivity gains in the second half of the twentieth century.

genetic modification (GM) The technological combination of genetic traits *between* different species that could not cross in nature (which is why this process is also described as genetic engineering).

genetically modified seeds Seeds that are engineered to express desired traits by inserting genes from unrelated species into them.

genre (from the French for "kind") A category of texts that share common characteristics. These categories tend to be relatively flexible and are redefined over time, but they serve as useful guides for writers and readers as a way to understand a particular text in relation to others.

global corporate food system An interdependent web of corporate-controlled activities at the global scale that include the production, processing, distribution, wholesaling, retailing, consumption, and disposal of food.

global food security governance (GFSG) The institutions, actors, rules, norms, and power relations that shape the practice of governing how food is produced, distributed, and accessed across borders.

global land grab The rush of foreign investment, purchases, and/or leases by states, transnational corporations, institutional investors, and domestic elites in agricultural land, primarily in developing countries.

global North See **global South**.

Global Partnership for Agriculture and Food Security (GPAFS) A failed governance initiative proposed by advanced industrialized countries to position the G8 as a leading intergovernmental body for world food security.

global South An arbitrary division of the world to show the contrasts between industrialized, developed countries mostly in the northern hemisphere with the mostly agrarian, underdeveloped countries south of the equator.

governance The principles, processes, decisions, and social interactions—including policies, norms, and discourses—that shape and administer socio-political space within and outside of the state, from the local (e.g. food hub) to the global (e.g. the global **food system**).

government The exercise of authority over a political jurisdiction by the state (whether it is a municipality, region, or country).

Group of Eight (G8) A club of the world's advanced industrialized countries that meets annually to coordinate international economic **policy**, including agriculture. Members include Australia, Canada, Germany, Italy, Japan, Russia, the United Kingdom, and the United States.

Group of Twenty (G20) A club of the world's advanced industrialized and emerging countries that meets annually to coordinate international economic **policy**, including agriculture. Members include Argentina, Australia, Brazil, Canada, China, France, Germany, India, Indonesia, Italy, Japan, South Korea, Mexico, Russia, Saudi Arabia, South Africa, Turkey, the United Kingdom, the United States, and the European Union.

guaranteed annual income (GAI) A **policy** intervention that guarantees a minimum income (also known as basic income), which carries the potential to reduce **food insecurity** in low-income households.

habitus A concept used by the sociologist Pierre Bourdieu to refer to the idea of "embodied history" or to a "way of being" that predisposes each individual to certain practices and perceptions.

healthy eating Foods and ways of eating that are defined as enhancing well-being, particularly physical health.

Holocene The short period (in a geological time scale) of relative climatic stability in which agriculture and human civilization arose, roughly the past 10,000 years. Scientists are now suggesting that, with climate change, we may be moving out of the Holocene and into the Anthropocene, an epoch marked by the influence of humans on the earth.

household food insecurity Inadequate or insecure access to food due to financial constraints.

Household Food Security Survey Module (HFSSM) A research instrument developed and used to monitor household **food security** in the United States, and included in the Canadian Community Health Survey (CCHS) since 2004.

human appropriation of the net primary product (of photosynthesis) (HANPP) A concept developed by biologists as a way of conceptualizing the scale of human impact on the biosphere, quantified in terms of the control of annual biomass production.

iconic Refers to something that is very popular and comes to represent a particular place or time. In the case of particular foods or dishes, these can be understood as "iconic" when they come to represent a particular location, region, or in rare cases, a country.

identity A person's perception of self; "who I am." It is simultaneously social and individual.

ideology A system of beliefs, values, and ideas that shape how individuals and groups interact with and view the world.

illegal, unregulated, and unreported fishing (IUU) Illegal fishing is that which contravenes the laws of a coastal state or the regulations of a regional high-seas fisheries management organization (RFMO). Unregulated fishing takes place outside the jurisdiction of a state or an RFMO, whether by vessels without nationality or in unregulated areas. Unreported fishing is that which has not been properly disclosed to the body that governs the fishery.

imperialism The spread of the **capitalist** economy on a global scale through export of capital and **colonization** of various parts of the world by industrialized countries for their raw materials and labour.

Indigenous food sovereignty A restorative framework for nurturing our relationships with one another and the culturally important plants, animals, and waterways that provide us with food.

Indigenous peoples of Canada People who hold an ancestral and ongoing connection to a particular geographic area within Canada. This includes diverse First Nations, Inuit, and Métis collectives.

industrial food system A **food system** characterized by mass production of standardized food items, driven by motives of **profit** and efficiency often at the cost of human health and environmental and social justice.

industrial grain–oilseed–livestock complex A term that describes how agricultural systems across much of the temperate world are dominated by a small number of grain and oilseed **monocultures** and a small number of livestock species reared in high-density factory farms and feedlots, with large volumes of grains and oilseeds cycled through livestock.

insertion event The forcible insertion of transgene(s) into single cells, using such processes as (1) *Agrobacterium*-mediation, where a disabled pathogen infects plant cells with a transgene, and (2) particle bombardment, where a gene gun bombards cells with metal particles bearing the transgene. With both processes, treated cells are then screened to identify successful transformants, which are then grown out to form entire transgenic organisms.

institutional racism Discriminatory policies and practices of organizations and institutions that treat certain groups unequally because of their colour, culture, or ethnic origin.

intensive aquaculture Aquaculture carried out in controlled growing conditions. In contrast to **extensive aquaculture**, it involves external seeding of the stock, intervention in the growing process, such as with supplemental feeding, disease control and water aeration, and a higher stocking density.

intensive livestock operations (ILOs) Large-scale production facilities where animals are confined and raised with industrial management techniques to maximize the largest amount of sellable product for the lowest possible cost. Also known as *factory farms* or *concentrated animal feeding operations* (CAFOs).

intercropping The cultivation of two or more crops in close proximity in order to achieve complementary biological interactions (e.g. reducing the impacts of pests) and enhance the efficiency of resource use (which entails using crops that do not compete with each other for physical space, nutrients, water, or light), with the goal of increasing the volume of what can be produced on a given land area.

interdisciplinary Integrating two or more disciplines into a single interdiscipline.

intersectionality The idea that various forms of oppression, based on **gender**, race, class, ability, sexuality, and so on, have an impact on how the others are experienced. For example, the way that black women, Asian women, and white women experience gender-based oppression is specific and informed by the particular ways that race and gender interact.

joined-up food policy Integration and coordination of policies across all the domains, departments, and jurisdictional levels that affect or are affected by **food policy**.

land grabbing Appropriation by force of land or territory that belonged to other peoples. It also refers to large-scale land acquisitions in the form of leasing or purchasing by wealthy countries, funds, or individuals, especially in developing countries following the rise in agricultural commodity prices in 2008.

land use planning The process of deciding how land is used or "developed" in urban, peri-urban, and rural areas.

lemon effect Because it is impossible to separate **GM** from non-GM grain, rejection of GM by importing nations means that GM contamination ruins the market for non-GM as well as GM growers.

likelihood The hypothetical estimation that specific statistical methods will demonstrate a higher or lower probability of something among certain groups compared to a reference group.

mass advertising and product differentiation A phenomenon of the recent industrial era, pioneered by such food processing behemoths as Kellogg's and Coca-Cola. Its purpose is to create an enduring resonance in the minds of the consuming public that certain products are superior and more desirable than competing commodities and thus worthy of the higher price they typically attract. Successful product differentiation via mass advertising results in an enduring brand.

material deprivation The inability of individuals or households to afford those goods, services, and activities that are typical in a society.

maximum sustainable yield (MSY) The largest average catch or yield that can continuously be taken from a fishery stock under existing environmental conditions without impairing its ability to reproduce itself and generate the same level of catch in subsequent years.

means of production All non-human resources utilized during the production process, such as land, factories, machineries, and agricultural implements.

monoculture The biological simplification of a farm or landscape to focus on the production of a single crop, which also typically entails a reduction in genetic diversity within that given crop type.

multidisciplinary Remaining loyal to particular disciplinary methodologies and assumptions while participating in a collaborative research strategy.

multifunctionality The recognition that agriculture is a multi-output activity that produces commodities as well as other outputs, such as ecosystem services.

mutagenesis Inducing random genetic mutations, typically through exposure to radiation or chemicals, followed by screening to identify valued progeny.

negative externalities The unintended social and environmental costs that result from a course of action and affect communities that did not choose to incur those costs.

neo-liberalism A political **ideology** that focuses on free markets and economic growth, with **policies** that emphasize deregulation, privatization, state reform (downsizing), and the creation of an outward-oriented (export) economy.

nutricentric person An individual who eats according to the logic of **nutritionism**.

nutritionism The relatively recent, predominantly Western (i.e. non-Indigenous) conceptualization of food that reduces the value and benefits of food to its nutrient profile, thereby distancing eaters from the places and contexts in which their food is produced. This comes at the expense of understanding food in relation to the rest of the body and the environment in which it is produced.

organic agriculture A form of agriculture that uses more traditional techniques such as crop rotation, green manure, compost, and biological pest control instead of industrial agro-chemicals.

peak oil The increasingly recognized term describing the fact that human economies are at, near, or have just passed the halfway point in the consumption of all global oil reserves. It poses enormous challenges for all sectors of modern industrial economies, none more so than agriculture.

peasants Rural inhabitants who make their living from the land, employ their own and family labour in production, produce for subsistence and the market, and are not driven primarily by market considerations in determining the use and/or sale of the land.

permaculture A form of agriculture that aims to simulate or utilize the patterns and features observed in natural ecosystems.

pesticide treadmill The cycle of dependence in which **monocultures** exacerbate pest problems, more or new pesticides are needed as natural predators and controls are eliminated, pest and disease resistance develops over time, and localized ecological knowledge and the ability to use non-chemical responses are lost.

policy The set of rules, spoken or unspoken, that determines how things are run.

political ecology A growing field of research on human–environment relations, environmental change, and development, combining attention to political economy, environmental science, and human ecology. There is no one methodological blueprint, however, and research in the field is located in a range of disciplines, such as geography, sociology, anthropology, political science, and environmental studies.

positivism A theory that considers knowledge to be based on natural phenomena that can be verified by the empirical sciences.

postmodernism/poststructuralism Closely associated perspectives that are critical of modernist frameworks and Enlightenment thinking, and question the modernist emphases on discovering "truth" through objectivity, progress, and scientific approaches and on studying culture through structures.

praxis The process by which theory is put into action and learning from embodiment and action is theorized.

precautionary principle The position that environmental **policy** and regulations should be heavily influenced by a recognition of the negative possibilities and worst-case scenarios associated with a given decision. This entails a large burden of proof that a given decision will have a benign impact in the long term.

prescriptive versus descriptive practice Always present is the danger of confusing prescriptive and descriptive practice—what people are being told or *advised* to do, that is, with what they *actually* do. Advertisements are a good example of prescriptive practice, while photographs of every food item consumed by an individual during the day might be an excellent record of descriptive practice, especially if taken by an unbiased photographer.

prevalence The proportion (or percentage) of the population with a given condition at a point in time. For example, the prevalence of **food insecurity** is a measure of the burden of food insecurity in a population such as in Canada or a given province.

profit The difference between a capitalist's costs and the selling price of their commodity. The prime mover of **capitalism** is the effort to maximize profit.

pseudo foods Nutrient-poor edible products that are typically high in fat, sugar, and salt; other than the excess calories they contain, they are notably low in nutrients such as proteins, minerals, and vitamins essential for health. A more inclusive category than "junk foods," it also refers to a variety of nutrient-poor edible products not traditionally thought of as "junk foods" and found in supermarkets and elsewhere among juice, dairy, and breakfast-food products, for example.

public sphere and private sphere Two halves of a socially constructed dichotomy. The public sphere encompasses the spaces and activities that occur outside of the home and is more highly valued than the private sphere, which is associated with the spaces and activities that occur within the boundaries of the home and family life.

queer theory A critical field that explores the fluidity of **genders**, sexes, and sexualities, and theorizes "queerness" as a way of conceptualizing non-normative **identity** expressions and practices.

Reducing Emissions from Deforestation and Forest Degradation (REDD) An international program with the objective of mitigating climate change by reducing net emissions of greenhouse gases through enhanced forest management in developing countries.

reflexivity The practice of reflecting on one's knowledge, experiences, and position in the world as a means of informing future actions and attitudes.

Regional Fisheries Management Organizations International groups that regulate or advise on fishing within an area of interest to its member states. Their roles vary, depending on whether they focus on a specific geographical area and all the fish stocks found within it or on an individual migratory species such as tuna, which travels through vast areas of the seas.

relations of production Relations people enter into during the production process; usually refers to **class relations** in Marxist terminology.

right to food The International Covenant on the Economic, Social and Cultural Rights (ICESCR) recognizes "the right of everyone to an adequate standard of living for himself and his family, including adequate food, clothing and housing, and to the continuous improvement of living conditions. The States Parties will take appropriate steps to ensure the realization of this right. . . ." The right to food is also recognized in the Declaration on Human Rights, the Convention on the Rights of the Child, the Convention on the Elimination of All Forms of Discrimination against Women (CEDAW), and the Optional Protocol to CEDAW.

salinization A condition caused by dissolved salt in water being left behind from evapotranspiration (i.e. as water evaporates from the land or transpires from plants), and building up in soils over time. Beyond a certain point, salinization can have very negative impacts on moisture uptake and crop yield, and land rehabilitation is very difficult and costly.

scientific reductionism A school of thought that proposes that complex phenomena can be understood through science by being broken down into simple processes/interactions, which can be studied individually. While necessary for much of scientific study, reductionism runs the risk of oversimplifying phenomena.

small-scale fisheries Fishing operations that, in contrast to more industrial offshore or mid-shore fishing, are run mainly as household enterprises and embody a culture and way of life. Seasonal fish are caught close to the operators' communities using relatively small craft, and are usually processed nearby.

social movement A group of people with common interests and purposes who work together and engage in collective action in efforts to promote or prevent social change. As a key component of civil society, it represents a collective, organized, and sustained challenge to the status quo.

soil mining A way of describing soil degradation, when the biological and physical materials of soils are depleted at a greater rate than they are returned, in which soil is effectively transformed from a potentially renewable resource to a diminishing one.

spatial colonization The process whereby food corporations secure the *physical visibility and availability* of the product within a particular **food environment**. This process highlights the power of food processors to place product *in the most visible and effective selling spaces* in a food environment. Processors and retailers have aggressively promoted the spatial colonization of **pseudo foods** because of their high rates of return on investment (see **differential profit**).

stacking Creating an organism with two or more **transgenic** traits, bearing, for example, transgenes coding for resistance to both glyphosate and 2,4-D herbicides.

standard industry practice In the context of **intensive livestock operations**, procedures and/or approaches to animal food production that are considered conventional by producers and industry leaders.

story versus history The term *story* indicates a narrative developed intentionally by an individual or community, whereas the term *history* might otherwise imply an unmediated record of a sequence of events.

stratification *See* **class/stratification**.

structural adjustment programs Rigid fiscal **policies** imposed on debtor nations in the **global South** by international financial institutions such as the World Bank and the International Monetary Fund, often requiring severe cuts to social programs.

substantial equivalence An undefined term that is the key decision threshold in **genetic modification** regulation in Canada. GM is considered substantially equivalent to non-GM by comparing levels of selected nutrients and anti-nutrients. Once deemed substantially equivalent, no special testing is required. Unmeasured parameters, such as hidden effects of unintended gene expression, are not acknowledged.

supply management Legislated limits on the amount of production in the poultry, egg, and dairy sectors to match domestic requirements while ensuring costs of production are met by the established pricing.

sustainability The ability to meet present needs without compromising the ability of future generations to meet their own needs; it aims to keep balance between social, economic, and environmental priorities in society; it also refers to the outcome of structures and processes that build the **civil commons**.

Sustainable Development Goals (SDGs) A set of UN-sponsored international commitments adopted in 2015 to promote economic and social development in a sustainable manner.

sustainable food system An interdependent web of activities generated by the interactions of structures and processes that build the **civil commons** with respect to the production, processing, distribution, retailing, consumption, and disposal of food.

sustainable intensification A productivist approach to agriculture that simultaneously increases **food production** and reduces environmental impacts, primarily through technologies and more efficient use of inputs to improve yields on existing farmland. Most commonly supported by international **policy** circles, this approach often overlooks the knowledge, expertise, needs, and visions for sustainability of those most keenly aware (through direct experience) of challenges in the **food system** (e.g. producers, fishers, consumer groups, marginalized communities).

temporary migrant farm labour The shortage of farm workers in some countries results in the temporary migration of farm workers. Unlike permanent immigrants who have rights to settle, temporary farm workers have to go back at the end of their contract. This makes them vulnerable to poor living and working conditions.

the body A term used in sociological and cultural studies to conceptualize the social, cultural, and symbolic aspects of the material body, including the construction of **identity**.

total allowable catch (TAC) A catch limit set for a particular fishery, generally for a year or a fishing season, calculated as a proportion of the **maximum sustainable yield** for that species.

transdisciplinary Integrating and uniting conceptual, theoretical, methodological, and translational perspectives from various disciplines, as well as outside the academy.

transdisciplinary scholarship A holistic approach to academic research and writing in which individuals strive to work across disciplinary boundaries and to create knowledge that is not bound or owned by any discipline(s) in particular.

transgene A gene or genetic material that is transferred through the processes of **genetic modification** from one organism to another, typically unrelated, organism; once present, transgenes may then be transferred naturally by conventional plant breeding into new hosts.

turnover time *See* **circuits of capital**.

United Nations Convention on the Law of the Sea (UNCLOS) *See* **Convention on the Law of the Sea**.

United Nations Framework Convention on Climate Change (UNFCCC) An international environmental treaty that was negotiated at the Earth Summit in 1992, known officially as the UN Conference on Environment and Development.

urban food policy Food system decisions and actions that fall within the jurisdiction of urban municipal governments, through zoning, bylaws, or other forms of land use regulation, or through partnerships with other levels of government.

urban food system A **food system** specific to the urban setting in which it is located, but also nested within regional, provincial/state, national, and international food systems.

La Vía Campesina An international movement that coordinates peasant organizations of small and middle-scale producers, agricultural workers, rural women, and Indigenous communities in Asia, Africa, America, and Europe. It claims to represent an estimated 200 million peasant families globally and is widely considered to be an important transnational **social movement**.

world-systems theory A global and historical approach to **capitalism**, which dates its origins to the creation of a world market through colonial expansion roughly 500 years ago. Key to the theory is its recognition that for the first time in history the market became bigger than any national territory, that the system of national states arose at about the same time, and that the power hierarchy among states shapes the market and is shaped by it.

World Trade Organization (WTO) A supranational institution and set of international trade agreements that play a major role in regulating international trade, including international agriculture trade, domestic agriculture **policy**, and, by extension, world **food security**.

yield gaps The difference between actual yield and potential yield in a given location if best existing agricultural technology and practices were used.

Index

Note: Page numbers in bold refer to key terms; page numbers in italics refer to illustrations.